American Public Policy

American Public Policy
Promise and Performance

Ninth Edition

B. Guy Peters
Maurice Falk Professor of American Government
University of Pittsburgh

Los Angeles | London | New Delhi
Singapore | Washington DC

Los Angeles | London | New Delhi
Singapore | Washington DC

FOR INFORMATION:

CQ Press
An Imprint of SAGE Publications, Inc.
2455 Teller Road
Thousand Oaks, California 91320
E-mail: order@sagepub.com

SAGE Publications Ltd.
1 Oliver's Yard
55 City Road
London, EC1Y 1SP
United Kingdom

SAGE Publications India Pvt. Ltd.
B 1/I 1 Mohan Cooperative Industrial Area
Mathura Road, New Delhi 110 044
India

SAGE Publications Asia-Pacific Pte. Ltd.
3 Church Street
#10-04 Samsung Hub
Singapore 049483

Printed in the United States of America

Library of Congress Cataloging-in-Publication Data

Peters, B. Guy.
American public policy: promise and performance / B. Guy Peters.—9th ed.

p. cm.
Includes bibliographical references and index.

ISBN 978-1-4522-1871-7 (pbk.)

1. United States—Politics and government. 2. Political planning—United States. 3. Policy sciences. I. Title.

JK271.P43 2013
320.60973—dc23   2012020438

This book is printed on acid-free paper.

Acquisitions Editor: Charisse Kiino
Production Editor: Laura Stewart
Copy Editor: Patrice Sutton
Typesetter: C&M Digitals (P) Ltd.
Proofreader: Talia Greenberg
Indexer: Teddy Diggs
Cover Designer: Edgar Abarca
Marketing Manager: Jonathan Mason

12 13 14 15 16 10 9 8 7 6 5 4 3 2 1

Contents

PART ONE
The Nature of Public Policy

PART TWO
The Making of Public Policy

PART THREE
Substantive Policy Issues

**PART FOUR
Analyzing Public Policy**

Tables and Figures

Preface

Public policy is the fundamental reason that scholars and citizens should be concerned about government, whether in the United States or in any other country. As much as we may find voting and elections entertaining or find interest in the ways lobbyists cajole public officials, in the end, the outcome of the political process is a set of policies that affect the lives of citizens, often in profound ways. As Harold Lasswell argued more than seventy years ago, politics is about "who gets what." The policy choices of the United States are particularly important, given that the economic and military power of this single country establishes parameters within which many other political systems make their own policy choices.

At times, public policies change rather rapidly and dramatically, and at times, they persist for long periods with only incremental changes. Most voters expected rapid change after the election of President Barack Obama in 2008, but the complex political process in Washington slowed that change. Likewise, the policy process itself may appear stable, yet it also undergoes slight changes in response to changing political ideas and the changing relative power of institutions and individuals. Therefore, relatively frequent updates concerning both process and substance are required to capture the contemporary nature of the U.S. government and the dynamics of this extremely complex system for governing and making policy.

The characteristics of continuity and change have been very evident since the last edition of this book. Despite strong efforts by political leaders, some policies, such as Social Security, have been changed hardly at all, whereas others, such as health care, are in the process of almost monumental change. The policy process in Washington is on the surface unchanged, but sharp ideological divisions between the two major parties have made it more difficult and more contentious.

This book is an attempt to provide a rather comprehensive view of policy and policymaking in the United States. Part 1 explains the nature of public policy and includes a new chapter, "Explaining Policy Choices," that outlines several alternative approaches to understanding the policymaking process and evaluating its outcomes. Part 2 describes the structure of the policymaking system and the process through which ideas and demands are converted into policy. While the "stages" model used in this analysis is generic, there are a number of important peculiarities in U.S. government that must be examined if we are to understand how the system succeeds—and why it fails—in making choices. If nothing else, the multiple divisions caused by the separation of powers, federalism, and a decentralized bureaucracy tend to make the process more difficult than in other countries.

Part 3 examines a number of important policy areas in the United States. These are discussed primarily at the federal level, although state and local governments have a significant impact on each of these areas as well. A detailed analysis of the role of each level of government would require a much larger book.

The final section, Part 4, provides an introduction to two forms of policy analysis. One depends on economic assumptions and is an attempt to make government more efficient and cost-effective. The other focuses on the normative element of public policy, an element of analysis often ignored when people think about policy. Rather than asking questions of efficiency, normative analysis is concerned with equity and justice. Neither of these modes of analysis can provide a complete answer to the difficult question of what is good policy, but in combination, they may begin to help readers develop an answer.

Although I have attempted to be as comprehensive as possible, some aspects of policy must be left out in the interest of space. Perhaps most significant, this is a book about federal policy and the federal level of government, although in the United States state and local governments are also significant actors. I have had to make choices about which policies to include and which to exclude from more detailed discussions. This is done in part because of my own interests but largely because of the impact of those policies on citizens.

I would like to acknowledge the academics whose reviews helped make this new edition possible: Susan Opp, Colorado State University; Paul Pope, University of Texas at Brownsville; Saundra K. Schneider, Michigan State University; and David Webber, University of Missouri. I also thank Dwain Smith for revising the ancillary materials, which include a test bank of exam questions and lecture slides for instructors as well as a student website (located at www.cqpress.com/cs/peters) that features chapter summaries, review questions, practice quizzes, and annotated web links.

This is the ninth edition of *American Public Policy* and is the fourth to be published by CQ Press. It has been a pleasure to work with Charisse Kiino, Patrice Sutton, Nancy Loh, and all the other editors and staff at CQ Press. They have been professional, patient, and supportive in preparing this edition and in helping to prepare the enhanced teaching aids for instructors. This edition should continue the movement toward making the book even more student— and professor—friendly than the previous ones.

B. Guy Peters
Pittsburgh, Pa.
June 2012

PART ONE

The Nature of Public Policy

CHAPTER 1

What Is Public Policy?

GOVERNMENT IN THE UNITED STATES has grown from a small, simple "night watchman state" providing defense, police protection, tax collection, and some education into an immense network of organizations and institutions affecting the daily lives of all citizens in countless ways. The United States is not a welfare state in the sense that most European states are, but there is now an extensive array of social and health programs that serve an increasing proportion of the population. The size and complexity of modern government make it necessary to understand what public policies are, how those policies are made and changed, and how to evaluate the effectiveness and morality of policies.

Government in the United States is large. Today, its revenues account for one dollar in three of total national production. Despite the widespread political rhetoric, this money is rarely wasted; most of it returns to citizens through a variety of cash benefit programs or in the form of public services. Likewise, one working person in six is employed by government—mostly in local governments. But the range of activities of modern government in the United States is not confined to such simple measures as spending money or hiring workers. Governments also influence the economy and society through many less obvious instruments such as regulation, insurance, and loan guarantees.

Government in the United States today also is complex and is becoming more complex every day. The institutions of government are becoming more complicated and numerous. More than 89,500 separate governments now exist in the United States, many of which provide a single service and undergo little or no public oversight through elections.[1] Much public business is now conducted through public corporations and quasi-autonomous public bodies. There are also a number of increasingly complex relationships between the public and private sectors, as the private and not-for-profit sectors are becoming heavily involved in delivering public services.[2] The subject matter of government policy is more complex and technical than it was even a few years ago. Governments must make decisions about the risks of nuclear energy, the reliability of technologically sophisticated weapons systems, and the management of a huge and remarkably convoluted economic system. Attempting to influence socioeconomic problems—poverty, homelessness, deficiencies in education—may be even more difficult than addressing problems arising in the physical and scientific worlds, given the absence of a proven method of solving social problems.[3] Even when the subject matter of policy is less complex, increasing requirements for participation and accountability make managing a public program a difficult undertaking, often more difficult than managing in the private sector.

This book is intended to help the reader understand the fundamental processes and content of public policy that underlie the size and complexity of American government. It is meant to increase knowledge about how public policies are made, what the policies of the United States are in certain areas, and what standards should be applied in evaluating those policies. I begin with a discussion of the policy process in the United States—concentrating on the federal level—and the impact of the structures and procedures of that government on the content of policies. I then discuss the means that those in government and citizens alike can use to evaluate the effects of public policies and the methods that will enable them to decide what they want, and can expect, to receive from government.

Defining Public Policy

Samuel Johnson once commented that patriotism is the last refuge of fools and scoundrels. To some degree, public policy has become just such a refuge for some academic disciplines. As public policy studies are now popular, everything government does is labeled *policy*. I adopt a somewhat more restrictive definition of *public policy*.

Stated most simply, *public policy* is the sum of government activities, whether pursued directly or through agents, as those activities have an influence on the lives of citizens. Operating within that definition, we can distinguish three separate levels of policy, defined by the degree to which they make real differences in the lives of citizens. At the first level, we have policy *choices*—decisions made by politicians, civil servants, or others granted authority that are directed toward using public power to affect the lives of citizens. Congress members, presidents, governors, administrators, and pressure groups, among others, make such policy choices. What emerges from all those choices is a policy that can be put into action. At the second level, we can speak of policy *outputs*—policy choices being put into action. Here, the government is actually doing things: spending money, hiring people, or promulgating regulations that are designed to affect the economy and society. Outputs may be virtually synonymous with the term *program* as it is commonly used in government circles.[4]

Finally, at the third level, we have policy *impacts*—the effects that policy choices and policy outputs have on citizens, such as making them wealthier or healthier or the air they breathe less polluted. These impacts may be influenced in part by other factors in the society—economic productivity, education, and the like—but they also reflect to some degree the success or failure of public policy choices and outputs. These policy impacts also may reflect the interaction of a number of different programs. Successful alleviation of poverty, for example, may depend upon a number of social programs, education, economic programs, and the tax system. If any of these does not perform well, it may be impossible for government, and the society that it represents, to reach its desired goals.

Several aspects of public policy require some explanation. First, although we are focusing on the central government in Washington, we must always remember that the United States is a federal system in which a large number of subnational governments also make decisions. Even when they attempt to cooperate, the levels of government often experience conflicts over policy. For example, attempts by the George W. Bush administration to enforce national standards for education through the No Child Left Behind program encountered opposition from the states and eventually also from Congress, each with its own ideas about what those standards should be and how they should be enforced. Even within the federal government, the actions of one agency may conflict with those of another. The U.S. Department of Agriculture, for example, still subsidizes the growing of tobacco, while the U.S. Office of the Surgeon General encourages citizens not to smoke.

Second, not all government policies are implemented by government employees. Many are actually implemented by private organizations or by individual citizens, and the involvement of the private sector in implementation continues to increase.[5] We must understand this if we are to avoid an excessively narrow definition of public policy as concerning only those programs directly administered by a public agency. A number of agricultural, social, and health policies involve the use of private agencies operating with the sanction of, and in the name of, government. Even the cabin attendant on an airplane making an announcement to buckle seat belts and not to smoke is implementing a public policy. As government has begun to use an increasing number of alternative mechanisms, such as contracts, for implementation, private sector providers are becoming increasingly important in delivering public policy.

Even if a government implements a program directly, it may not act through its own employees. The federal government in particular depends on state and local governments to implement a large number of its programs, including major social programs such as Medicaid, the "workfare" reforms to the welfare system, and a good portion of environmental policy. The degree of control that the federal government can exercise in those instances may be as small as, or even smaller than, when programs are delivered through private sector agents, who often depend on government for contracts and loans and therefore may be very compliant with demands from Washington.

Third, and most important, we are concentrating on the effects of government choices on the lives of individuals within the society. The word *policy* is commonly used in a number of ways. In one usage, it denotes a stated intent of government, as expressed in a piece of legislation or a presidential speech. Unfortunately, any numbers of steps are required to turn a piece of legislation into an operating program, and all too frequently, significant changes in the intended effects of the program result from difficulties in translating ideas and intentions into actions. In this analysis, we will place greater emphasis on the effects of policies than on the intentions of the individuals who formulated them. We must also have some degree of concern for the legislative process, which produces the good intentions that may or may not come to fruition.

Our definition recognizes the complexity and the interorganizational nature of public policy. Few policy choices are decided and executed by a single organization or even a single level of government. Instead, policies, in terms of their effects on the public, emerge from a large number of programs, legislative intentions, and organizational interactions that affect the daily lives of citizens. For example, environmental issues now are handled not only by the Environmental Protection Agency but also by the Department of the Interior, the Department of Agriculture, the Department of Health and Human Services, and even the Department of Defense.[6] This conception of policy also points to the frequent failure of governments to coordinate programs, with the consequence that programs cancel one another out or produce a costly duplication of effort.[7] The question about government that Harold Lasswell posed many years ago, "Who gets what?" is still central for understanding public policy.

The Instruments of Public Policy

Governments have a number of instruments through which they can influence society and the economy and produce changes in the lives of citizens. For example, government can choose to provide education by directly supplying that service, by providing vouchers that parents can use to pay for their children's education, or by subsidizing privately managed charter schools (see chapter 13). The choice of which instrument to employ for any particular situation may depend on the probable effectiveness of the instrument, its political palatability, the experiences of the policy designers, and national or organizational tradition. Furthermore, some policy instruments may be effective in some circumstances but not in others. Unfortunately, governments do not yet have sufficient knowledge about the effects of their "tools," or the relationship of particular tools to particular policy outcomes, to be able to make effective matches.[8] It appears that most choices are now made out of habit and familiarity, not out of certain knowledge of effectiveness.

Law

Law is a unique resource of government. It is not available to private actors, who have access to the other instruments of policy discussed here.[9] Governments have the right to make authoritative decrees and to back up those decrees with the legitimate power of the state. In most instances, simply issuing a law is sufficient to produce compliance, but monitoring and enforcement are still crucial to the effectiveness of the instrument. Citizens may obey speeding laws most of the time, but the prospect of a police officer with a radar set makes compliance more probable. Citizens daily obey many laws without thinking about them, but police, tax collectors, and agencies monitoring environmental damage, occupational safety, and product safety (to name only a few) are also busy attempting to ensure compliance through their enforcement activities.

We should make several other points about the use of law as an instrument of public policy. First, laws are used as the means of producing the most important outputs of government: rights. Such laws are usually of a fundamental or constitutional nature and are central in defining the position of citizens in society. In the United States, the fundamental rights of citizens are defined in the Constitution and its amendments, but rights also have been extended in a variety of other legislation. This extension has been most significant for the rights of nonwhites and women, as reflected in the passage of the Voting Rights Act of 1965, the Equal Employment Opportunity Act of 1972, and the Civil Rights Act of 1991. The Americans with Disabilities Act (1990) extended a variety of rights to people with various forms of disability, with the courts tending to expand the applicability of that law to groups, such as AIDS sufferers,[10] for whom it was perhaps not intended by the framers of the legislation. Law is now being used by some groups to attempt to extend rights to homosexuals, and other groups also use law to attempt to limit those rights (see chapter 16).

Second, the United States uses laws to regulate economic and social conditions to a greater extent than most countries do. The United States is frequently cited as having a small public sector in comparison with other industrialized countries because of lower levels of taxing and spending. If, however, the effects of regulations are included, government in the United States approaches being as pervasive as it is in Europe.[11] The costs of government's interventions in the United States tend to appear in the price of products, however, as much as in citizens' tax bills.[12] This indirect effect of intervention tends to be less visible to the average citizen than a tax and therefore is more palatable in a society that tends to be skeptical about government.

Third, law can be used to create burdens as well as benefits. This is certainly true for tax laws and is also true, for example, of legislation that mandates the recycling of metal, glass, and plastic. Often, a law that creates benefits for one group of citizens is perceived by others to be creating a burden; environmental laws satisfy conservationists but often impose costs on businesses. Any action of government requires some legal peg on which to hang, but the ability of a simple piece of paper to create both rights and obligations is one of the essential features of American public policy.

Services

Governments also provide a number of services directly to citizens, ranging from defense to education to recreation. In numbers of people employed, education is by far the largest directly provided public service, employing more than nine million people. The Department of Defense employs just under another three million people, military and civilian. Government tends to provide services when there is a need to ensure that the service is provided in a certain way (education) or where the authority of the state (policing) is involved. Furthermore, services tend to be delivered directly to parts of the population that are less capable of making autonomous decisions on their own, such as children and the mentally impaired.

The direct provision of public services raises several questions, especially as continuing pressures exist for government to control expenditures and to "privatize."[13] An obvious question is whether the direct provision of services is the most efficient means of ensuring that a service is delivered to citizens. Could that service be contracted out instead? A number of public services have been contracted out to private corporations, including traditional government services, such as firefighting, tax collection, and operating prisons.[14] Contracting out removes the problem of personnel management from government, a problem magnified by the tenure rights and pension costs of public employees under merit systems. Also, government tends to build a capacity to meet maximum demand for services such as fire protection and emergency medical care, resulting in underutilization of expensive personnel and equipment. This tendency to create too much capacity can be corrected in part by contracting out.

Another interesting development in the direct provision of services is the use of quasi-governmental organizations to provide services.[15] There are some services that government does not want to undertake entirely but that require public involvement for financial or other reasons. The best example is Amtrak, a means of providing public subsidies for passenger train service in the face of declining rail service in the United States. Government may also choose quasi-governmental organizations for programs that require a great deal of coordination with private sector providers of the same service, or when the service is in essence a marketable one. At an even greater degree of separation, governments also use not-for-profit organizations to provide public services. The George W. Bush administration pressed for wider use of such organizations, especially faith-based organizations. President Barack Obama continued the emphasis, working to mobilize not-for-profit organizations early in his administration.

Money

Governments also provide citizens, organizations, and other governments with money. Approximately 65 percent of all money collected in taxes by the federal government is returned to the economy as transfer payments to citizens. Transfers to citizens range from Social Security and unemployment benefits to payments to farmers to support commodity prices. Interest on the public debt is also a form of transfer payment, one that now absorbs nearly 8 percent of total federal spending. Another 10 percent of tax receipts is transferred to other levels of government to support their activities.

The use of money transfers to attempt to promote certain behaviors is in many ways an inefficient means for reaching policy goals. The money paid out in Social Security benefits, for example, is intended to provide the basics of life for the recipients, but nothing prevents those recipients from using it to buy food for their pets rather than for themselves. The claims about how "welfare" payments are used and abused are legion, if often inaccurate. Thus, although the direct provision of services is costly and requires hiring personnel and erecting buildings, many transfer programs, though less expensive, are much less certain of reaching the individuals and achieving the goals for which they were intended.

Money dispersed to other levels of government can be restricted or unrestricted. Of the over $500 billion given to state and local governments in 2010, most were distributed as categorical grants, with an increasing proportion being given as block grants. Categorical grants channel resources more directly to the problems identified by the federal government as needing attention, but they also tend to centralize decision making about public policy in Washington.[16] Categorical grants also tend to encourage state and local spending through matching requirements and to create clienteles that governments may not be able to eliminate after the federal support has been exhausted. Although this pattern of funding was largely associated with social and economic programs, the Clinton administration's program for funding the hiring of additional police created expectations among citizens that local governments will have to fulfill in the future, and Homeland Security funding has created the same effect after the Bush administration.

The federal government has less control over the impact of block grants than over the effects of categorical grants.[17] Block grants allow greater latitude for state and local governments to determine their own priorities, but most still have some strings attached. Also, giving block grants to the states tends to concentrate power in state governments rather than allowing local (especially city) governments to bargain with Washington directly. Given that state governments are, on average, more conservative than local governments—especially large city governments that need federal grant money the most—block grants have been a useful tool for Republican administrations to control public spending.[18]

Taxes

The government giveth and the government taketh away. But the way in which it chooses to take away may be important in changing the distribution of burdens and benefits in society. In the United States, we are familiar with tax "loopholes," or, more properly, *tax expenditures*.[19] The latter term is derived from the theory that granting tax relief for an activity is the same as subsidizing that activity directly through an expenditure program.[20] For example, in 2010, the federal government did not collect roughly $79 billion in income tax payments because of mortgage interest deductions and another $16 billion because state and local property taxes were deductible. This is in many ways exactly the same as government subsidizing private housing in the same amounts, a sum far greater than the amount spent on public housing by all levels of government. The use of the tax system as a policy instrument as well as for revenue collection is perhaps even less certain in its effects than transfer payments, for the system is essentially providing incentives rather than mandating activities. Citizens have a strong incentive to buy a house, but there is no program to build houses directly. These instruments are, however, very cheap to administer, given that citizens make all the decisions and then file their own tax returns.

Taxes may also be used more directly to implement policy decisions. For example, there are proposals to substitute taxes on pollution for direct prohibitions and regulation of emissions. The logic is that such an action would establish a "market" in pollution; those firms willing to pay the price of polluting would be able to pollute, while those less willing (or, more important, less able) because of inefficient production means would have to alter their modes of production or go out of business. The use of market mechanisms is assumed to direct resources toward their most productive use, whereas regulations at times may inhibit production and economic growth. Critics argue that what is being created is a "market in death," when the only real solution to the problem is the prohibition or severe restriction of pollution.

Tax incentives are a subset of all incentives available to government to encourage or discourage activities. The argument for their use, as was well expressed by Charles Schultze, is that private interests (e.g., avarice) can be used for public purposes.[21] If a system of incentives can be structured effectively, then demands on the public sector can be satisfied in a more efficient and inexpensive manner than through direct regulation. Clearly, this form of policy instrument is applicable to a rather narrow range of policies, mostly those now handled through command and control regulation, but even in that limited range, the savings in costs of government and in the costs imposed on society may be significant. The use of such incentives, as opposed to command and control regulation, also conforms to traditional American ideas about limited government and the supremacy of individual choice.[22]

Other Economic Instruments

Government has a number of other economic weapons at its disposal.[23] Governments supply credit for activities such as a farmer's purchase of land and supplies.[24] When it does not directly lend money, the government may guarantee loans, thus making credit available (e.g., for student loans or Federal Housing Administration [FHA] mortgages) where it might otherwise be denied. Governments can also insure certain activities and property. For example, federal flood insurance made possible the development of some lands along the coasts of the United States, thereby creating both wealth and environmental degradation. Almost all money in banks and thrift institutions is now protected by one of several insurance corporations within the federal government. Thus, in the economic downturn of 2008 and 2009, individual bank accounts were protected.

Although these instruments may be important to their beneficiaries and may influence the spending of large sums of money, they do not appear as large expenditures in most government accounting schemes. Thus, as with regulations and their costs, the true size of government in the United States may be understated if one looks simply at expenditure and employment figures. In addition, the ability of these programs to operate "off budget" makes them not only less visible to voters but also more difficult for political leaders and citizens to control. Only when there are major problems, as in the bursting of the housing bubble and the credit crisis in 2008, do government insurance, guarantee schemes, and federal "bailouts" make the news.

Suasion

When all other instruments of policy fail, governments can use moral suasion to attempt to influence society. Government as a whole or particular political officials are often in a good position to use such suasion because they can speak in the name of the public interest and make those who oppose them appear unpatriotic and self-ish. As Theodore Roosevelt said, the presidency is a "bully pulpit." Suasion, how-ever, is often the velvet glove disguising the mailed fist, for governments have formal and informal means of ensuring that their wishes are fulfilled. So when John F. Kennedy "jawboned" steel industry officials to roll back a price increase, the patri-otism of the steel officials was equaled by their fear of lost government contracts and Internal Revenue Service investigations of their corporate and personal accounts.

Suasion is an effective instrument as long as the people regard the govern-ment as a legitimate expression of their interests. There is evidence that the faith and trust of American citizens in government has been declining (see Table 1.1) in response to the excesses of Vietnam, Watergate, budget deficits, the inade-quate response to Hurricane Katrina, and so forth. Congress members in par-ticular are regarded very poorly by the public. As governments lose some of their legitimacy, their ability to use suasion naturally declines, pushing them toward more direct tools of intervention; that could lead to increases in government employment and taxation and perhaps to an accelerated downward spiral of

TABLE 1.1   Public Perception of Honesty and Ethics in Various Professions
(percentages of "Very high" and "High" responses combined)

	1976	1981	1985	1990	1992	1995	2005	2008	2011
Pharmacists	n.a.	59	65	62	66	66	67	70	73
Clergy	n.a.	63	67	57	54	56	54	56	52
Medical doctors	56	51	50	52	52	54	65	64	70
College teachers	49	45	53	51	50	52	n.a.	n.a.	n.a.
Engineers	49	48	53	50	48	53	n.a.	n.a.	n.a.
Police	n.a.	44	47	49	42	41	61	56	54
Journalists	33	32	31	30	27	23	28	25	26
Bankers	n.a.	39	38	32	27	27	41	23	25
Lawyers	25	25	27	22	18	16	18	18	19
Business executives	20	19	23	25	18	16	16	12	18
Local officeholders	n.a.	14	18	21	15	21	n.a.	20	n.a.
Real estate agents	n.a.	14	15	16	14	15	20	17	20
Labor union leaders	12	14	13	15	14	14	16	16	18
U.S. senators	19	20	23	24	13	12	16	n.a.	n.a.
State officeholders	n.a.	12	15	17	11	15	n.a.	12	n.a.
Members of Congress	14	15	20	20	11	10	14	12	7
Car salesmen	n.a.	6	5	6	5	5	8	7	7

Sources: Gallup Poll Monthly, November 1995, 31; Gallup Poll, January 18, 2005; Gallup Poll, November 7, 2008; Gallup Poll, June 23, 2011.

Note: n.a. = not available.

government authority. In 2012, the public views Congress members as only slightly more favorably than car salesmen, who anchored the bottom of the scale. On the other hand, police had achieved a major increase in respect, in part because of their heroism after 9/11. One exception to the trend of declining trust in government may be in times of war, as President George H. W. Bush showed during the Persian Gulf crisis. The second President Bush also used suasion and manipulated powerful national symbols in the "war on terror," although his ability to do so declined as his term ended.

The Effects of Tools

Governments have a number of instruments with which they attempt to influence the economy and society by distributing what burdens and benefits they have at their disposal. The most fundamental benefits governments have to confer are rights. These are largely legal and participatory, but with the growth of large entitlement programs that distribute cash benefits to citizens, rights may now be said to include those programs as well.

Governments also distribute goods and services. They do so directly by giving money to people who fall into certain categories (e.g., the unemployed) or by directly providing public services, such as education. They also do so less directly by structuring incentives for individuals to behave in certain ways and to make one economic decision rather than another. Governments also distribute goods and services through private organizations and through other governments, in attempts to reach their policy goals. A huge amount of money flows through the public sector, where it is shuffled around and given to different people.[25] The net effect is not as great as might be expected from the number of large expenditure and revenue programs in operation in the United States, but that effect is to make the distribution of income and wealth somewhat more equal than would be the case through the market alone.[26]

Finally, governments distribute burdens as well as benefits. They do this through taxation and through programs such as conscription for military service.[27] Like expenditures, taxes are distributed broadly across the population, with state and local taxes tending to be collected from an especially broad spectrum. Even the poorest citizens have to pay sales taxes on many things they purchase, and they must pay Social Security taxes as soon as they begin to work. In other words, everyone in society benefits from the activities of government, but everyone also pays for them.

The Environment of Public Policy

Several characteristics of the political and socioeconomic environment in the United States influence the nature of policies adopted and the effects of those policies on citizens. Policy is not constructed in a vacuum; it is the result of the interaction of all the background factors with the desires and decisions of those who make policies. Neither individual decision makers nor the nature of "the system" appear capable alone of explaining policy outcomes. Instead, policy emerges from the interaction of a large number of forces, many of which are beyond the control of decision makers.

Conservatism

American politics is relatively conservative in policy terms. The social and economic services usually associated with the mixed-economy welfare state are generally less developed in the United States than in Europe, and to some extent they have declined since the 1990s. In general, that is the result of the continuing American belief in limited government. As Anthony King has said, "The State plays a more limited role in America than elsewhere because Americans, more than other people, want it to play a limited role."[28] The Republican domination of electoral politics for much of the past three decades emphasizes the underlying conservatism of Americans. The election of Barack Obama, however, also shows that there are limits to that conservatism and that the American public has some underlying commitment to social values. That said, the rise of the Tea Party movement and the appeal of some libertarian candidates in the Republican primaries of 2012 indicate how intense the conservative ideology is for some elements within the population.

Several points should be brought out that counter the description of American government as a welfare state laggard. First, the government of the United States regulates and controls the economy in ways not common in Europe, and in some areas such as consumer product safety, it appears to be ahead of many European governments. If the effects of regulation are tabulated along with more direct public interventions into the economy, the U.S. government appears more similar to those of other industrialized countries. We also tend to forget about the activities of state and local governments, which frequently provide gas, electricity, water, and even banking services to their citizens.

It is easy to underestimate the extent of the changes in public expenditures and the public role in the economy that followed World War II. Let us take 1948 as the starting point. Even in that relatively peaceful year, defense expenditures were 29 percent of total public expenditures and 36 percent of federal expenditures. At the height of the Cold War, in 1957, defense expenditures were 62 percent of federal expenditures and 37 percent of total public expenditures. In contrast, in 2006, defense expenditures were 7 percent of total expenditures and 15 percent of federal expenditures. Spending on social services—including education, health, social welfare, and housing—increased from 7 percent of total spending in 1948 to over 64 percent in 2003. Even for the federal government, social spending now accounts for more than 50 percent of total expenditures. American government and its policies may be conservative, but they are less so than commonly believed, and less so in the early twenty-first century than in the 1950s.

It is also easy to overestimate the conservatism of the American public because Americans are often very ambivalent about government.[29] Lloyd A. Free and Hadley Cantril described Americans as "ideological conservatives" and "operational liberals"[30] because they tend to respond negatively to the idea of a large and active government but positively to individual public programs (e.g., Social Security, police protection, and education). For example, a majority of voters leaving the polls in California after voting in favor of Proposition 13, to cut taxes severely in that state, were in favor of reducing public expenditures for only one program—social welfare. For most programs the researchers mentioned, larger percentages of respondents wanted to increase expenditures than wanted to reduce them.[31] Likewise, citizens express great skepticism about government in polls, but in the 2008 elections, the voters approved most propositions on state and local ballots to raise revenues for specific purposes, as well as voting for a liberal president and Congress. Even in the tide of conservative victories in the 2010 election, a number of ballot initiatives proposing new taxing and spending were successful.

The huge federal deficit is to some degree a function of this set of mismatched ideas about government; politicians can win votes both by advocating reducing taxes and by advocating spending for almost any program. For example, surveys show that the majority of Americans believe that they pay too many taxes and that the federal government wastes almost half of all the tax money it collects.[32] On the other hand, there are generally majorities in favor of a variety of social programs, especially those for the more "deserving poor"—the elderly, unemployed workers whose companies have closed, divorced and widowed mothers, and the like. Furthermore, although Americans dislike the idea of socialized medicine, they also dislike the inequality in health in the United States (see chapter 11).

Participation

Another attitudinal characteristic that influences public policy in the United States is the citizen's desire to participate directly in government. A natural part of democratic politics, public participation has a long history in the United States. The cry "No taxation without representation" was essentially a demand to participate. More recently, populist demands for participation and the right of "the little man" to shape policy have been powerful political forces. In a large and decentralized political system that deals with complex issues, however, effective participation may be difficult to achieve. Although the 2008 elections saw an increase in voter turnout, especially among young people and minorities, the low rate of participation in most elections appears to indicate that citizens do not consider the voting process a particularly effective means of influencing government. Furthermore, many experts believe that citizens are not sufficiently informed to make decisions about such complex technical issues as nuclear power. Still, citizens argue that they should and must have a role in those decisions.

Government has increasingly fostered participation. The laws authorizing "community action" in 1964 were the first to mandate "maximum feasible participation" of the affected communities in urban renewal decisions. Similar language was written into a number of other social and urban programs. The regulatory process also imposes requirements for notification and participation that, in addition to their positive effects, have slowed the process considerably. Government also has been allowing more direct participation in agency rule-making, with affected interests allowed to negotiate among themselves the rules that will govern a policy area.

The desire for effective participation has to some degree colored popular impressions of government. Citizens tend to demand local control of policy and to fear the "federal bulldozer." Although objective evidence may be to the contrary, citizens tend to regard the federal government as less benevolent and less efficient than local governments. The desire to participate and to exercise local control then produces a tendency toward decentralized decision making and a consequent absence of national integration. In many policy areas, such decentralization is benign or actually beneficial. In others, it may produce inequities and inefficiencies. But ideological and cultural desires for local control may override practical arguments.

Ideas about participation in the United States also have at times had a strong strand of populism, meaning the belief that large institutions—whether in government, business, or even labor—are inimical to the interests of the people. The antigovernment, antitax rhetoric that President George W. Bush used so effectively is one example of that populist style in American politics. That style of populism can be contrasted with a rather different approach by President Obama, who appealed to the American people with an all-inclusive message of unification that defies partisanship. The populist ideas have reasserted themselves in 2010 and after in both the Tea Party and the Occupy movements. The institutions of government have begun to respond to demands for effective participation, and *empowerment* has become one of the more commonly used words in government circles.[33] Balancing popular demands for greater direct democracy with the requirements of governing an immense landmass with over 300 million citizens will continue to be a challenge for American democracy.

Elections determine who controls Congress and the presidency, and therefore set the parameters for policy choices in American government. A volunteer for Rep. Marcy Kaptur, D-OH, hands out campaign literature on January 29, 2012.

Pragmatism

The reference to ideological desires seemingly contradicts another cultural characteristic of American policymaking, pragmatism—the belief that one should do whatever works rather than follow a basic ideological or philosophical system. For most of our collective history, American political parties have tended to be centrist and nonideological; perhaps the surest way to lose an election in the United States has been to discuss philosophies of government. Ronald Reagan questioned that characteristic of American politics to some degree, interjecting an ideology of government that was partly continued by George H. W. Bush. Bill Clinton's self-description as a "new Democrat" represented a return to greater pragmatism. George W. Bush claimed to be a "compassionate conservative" in his first election campaign, but his style, and especially that of members of Congress, transformed American politics into something of a battle of ideologies.

The years following the election of Barack Obama as President have, however, been marked by partisan and ideological debate. A long history of compromise was transformed into one of opposition and gridlock. The clearest manifestations of this were in battles over the debt ceiling and over the administration's policies to combat the recession. While Congress, the president, and other political elites continue to wrangle and make partisan pronouncements, the American public has expressed its dismay and disgust with the inability of the political system to make effective decisions to address the problems of the nation.[34]

One standard definition of what will work in government is "that which is already working," and so policies tend to change slowly and incrementally.[35] The fundamentally centrist pattern of U.S. political parties has tended to produce agreement on most basic policies, and each successive president tends to jiggle and poke policy but not attempt significant change. A crisis such as the Great Depression or a natural political leader such as Reagan may introduce some radical changes, but stability and gradual evolution are the most acceptable patterns of policymaking. Indeed, American government is different after Reagan but not as different as he had hoped or intended.[36] Nor was George W. Bush able to change very much of the system, and even during the Great Recession, Barack Obama was generally incapable of bringing about the type of grand change that he proposed during his campaign. The battle over reform of Social Security typifies this persistence of policies (see chapter 12). There has been concern about the financial soundness of this crucial program for years, but no agreement has coalesced on the direction or degree of change. The pragmatism of the policy process in the United States was clearly manifested in the defeat in 2005 of attempts at radical change in the Social Security program.[37]

As mentioned above, the pragmatism of American politics has been declining. Several issues over which there appears to be little room for compromise have split the American public. The obvious example is the abortion issue, which intruded into the debate over national health care reform during the Clinton administration, with some members of Congress refusing to support any bill that paid for abortions and others opposing any bill that did not.[38] Other issues with a moral, religious, or ethnic basis also have taken more prominent places in the political debate, leaving fewer possibilities for compromise or pragmatic resolution of disputes. The religious right has become especially important in the internal politics of the Republican Party, as groups such as the Christian Coalition and the Family Research Council have taken over at local and even state levels and attempted to shape the party's national policies.[39]

The seeming decline in pragmatism in American politics is not just a function of religion. The political parties themselves have become more ideological.[40] Congressional politics has become more sharply divided along party lines, and compromise has become much more difficult to achieve. Even when the country was facing potential financial disaster, President Obama's stimulus plan received no Republican votes in the House of Representatives and only three in the Senate.[41] The votes on subsequent economic issues such as raising the debt ceiling were partisan based. Citizens say that they do not like the wrangling among parties, but the parties seem more committed to their own views of politics than in the past.

Wealth

Another feature of the environment of American public policy is the country's great wealth. Although it is no longer the richest country in the world in per capita terms, the United States is the largest single economy in the world by a large margin. This wealth permits the U.S. government great latitude for action so that even the massive deficits experienced in the 1980s and 1990s (and now recurring in the twenty-first century) have not required government to alter its folkways. The federal government can continue funding a huge variety of programs and policy initiatives, even while trying to control the size of the budget (see chapter 7).

That great wealth is threatened by two factors, however. First, the U.S. economy is increasingly dependent on the rest of the world. That is apparent in financial and monetary policy, as the United States has become the world's largest debtor, but it is true especially in dependence on raw materials from abroad. We are familiar with the nation's dependence on foreign oil, but the economy is also heavily dependent on other countries for a range of commodities necessary to maintain its high standard of living. The American economy historically has been relatively self-sufficient, but increasing globalization in recent decades has emphasized its relationship to the world economy.[42]

Wealth in the United States is also threatened by the relatively slow rate of capital investment and savings. The savings rate for the average American family was 2.7 percent in 2011, indicating that relatively little capital is available for investment. The average American worker is still very productive but has lost some ground to workers in other countries. Also, many U.S. factories are outmoded, so competition on the world market is difficult. These factors, combined with relatively high wages, mean that many manufacturing jobs have gone overseas and more are likely to do so. The U.S. government has had to borrow abroad to fund its deficits, and the country has chronic balance of payments problems because exports trail imports. Such international trade problems are not often direct domestic concerns of American politicians, although the Democrats have attempted to make them more of a concern in recent presidential campaigns.

In addition to the changing distribution of wealth in the United States relative to the remainder of the world, the internal distribution of wealth has been changing and changing rapidly. Although there was substantial economic growth in the first decade of the twenty-first century, most of economic growth went to the most affluent segments of society, while the real earnings of most citizens were stagnant or even declining. The economic (and political) strength of the United States has been built on a large middle class, a group that is now under threat. They are in part under threat because of the international trade issues and falling wages used as a means of competing with overseas manufacturers.

Diversity

The diversity of the American society and economy provides a great deal of richness and strength to the country, as well as real policy problems. One of the most obvious diversities is the uneven distribution of income and wealth. Even with the significant social expenditures mentioned earlier, approximately forty-six million people (1 in 6) in the United States live below the poverty line (see chapter 12). The persistence of poverty in the midst of plenty remains perhaps the most fundamental policy problem for the United States, if for no other reason than that it affects so many other policy areas, including health care, housing, education, crime, and race relations. Moreover, there is growing concentration of income and wealth in the very affluent stratum at the top of society that may undermine confidence in the economic and social justice of the political system.

Diversity of racial and linguistic backgrounds is another significant factor affecting policy in the United States. The underlying problems of social inequality and racism persist despite many attempts to correct them. The "two Americas" had never been so visible as they were in New Orleans after Hurricane Katrina.[43] The concentration of minority group members in urban areas, the continuing influx of immigrants, and the unyielding economic distress of some cities combine to exacerbate the underlying problems. Again, this diversity affects a variety of policy areas, especially education. Race in particular pervades policymaking and politics in the United States, and that fundamental fact conditions our understanding of education, poverty, and human rights.[44] These issues of diversity have now become more apparent politically in the debate over immigration policy.

The social and economic characteristics of the country taken as a whole are also diverse. The United States is both urban and rural, both industrial and agricultural, both young and old. It is a highly educated society with several million illiterates; it is a rich country with millions of people living in poverty. In at least one state, California, there already is no majority ethnic group, and in a few generations that may be true for the country as a whole. American policymakers cannot concentrate on a single economic class or social group but must provide something for everyone if the interests of the society as a whole are to be served. But serving that whole range of social interests forces government to spend for other purposes the resources that could be applied to rectifying the worst inequalities of income and opportunity.

World Leadership

The United States is an economic, political, and military world leader. Since the collapse of the Soviet Union, it is the only remaining superpower. If America sneezes, the world still catches cold because the sheer size of the American economy is so important in influencing world economic conditions, as the 2008 financial crisis demonstrated. Despite the upheaval in global political alignments, the world still expects military and diplomatic leadership for the West to come from the United States. For example, the heavy involvement of the American military in Iraq and Afghanistan may have made world response to humanitarian crises in Darfur and other parts of Africa less feasible.

The U.S. position as world leader imposes burdens on American policymakers. Although the Cold War had ended, the role of peacekeeper required a good deal of U.S. military might even before the war on terror escalated military spending. Burdens also arise from the need to provide diplomatic and political leadership. The U.S. dollar, despite some battering and significant competition, is still a major reserve currency in the world economy, and that status imposes additional economic demands on the country. The role of world leader is an exhilarating one, but it is also one filled with considerable responsibility and economic cost. Indeed, the globalization of the economic system is making many Americans rethink the desirability of major international involvement. American acceptance of such a role may also be waning as the costs (human and material) of involvement in Iraq and Afghanistan and a greater sense of insecurity at home have turned more attention inward rather than outward to the world.

The policies that emerge from all these influences are filtered through a large and extremely complex political system. The characteristics of that government and the effects of those institutional characteristics on policies are the subject of the next chapter. Policy choices must be made, and thousands are made each day in government; the sum of those choices, rather than any one, decides who gets what as a result of public policies. In the United States, more than in most countries, there are a number of independent decision makers whose choices must be factored into the final determination of policy.

Summary

American public policy is the result of complex interactions among a number of complex institutions. It also involves a wide range of ideas and values about what the goals of policy should be and what are the best means of reaching them. In addition to the interactions that occur within the public sector are the interactions with an equally complex society and economy. Indeed, society is playing an increasingly important role in policymaking and implementation, with reforms in the public sector placing increasing emphasis on the capacity of the private sector to implement, if not make, public policy.

Making policy requires reaching some form of social and political consensus among all these forces. There does not have to be full agreement on all the values and all the points of policy, but enough common ground must be found to pass and implement legislation. Building those coalitions can extend beyond reaching ideological agreement to include bargaining and horse trading, which assign a central role to individual policy entrepreneurs and brokers. There is so much potential for blockage and delay in the American political system that some driving force may be needed to make it function.

CHAPTER 2

The Structure of Policymaking in American Government

THE STRUCTURES THROUGH WHICH public policy is formulated, legitimated, and implemented in the United States are extremely complex. It could be argued that American government has a number of structures but no real organization, for the fundamental characteristic of the structures is the absence of effective coordination and control. The absence of central control is largely intentional. The framers of the Constitution were concerned about the potential for tyranny of a powerful central executive; they also feared the control of the central government over the constituent states. The system of government the framers designed divides power among the three branches of the central government and further between the central government and state and local governments. As the system of government has evolved, it has become divided even further, as individual policy domains have been able to gain substantial autonomy from central coordination. To understand American policymaking, therefore, we must understand the extent of the fragmentation that exists in this political system and the (relatively few) mechanisms devised to control that fragmentation and enhance coordination.

The fragmentation of American government presents some advantages. First, having a number of decision makers involved in every decision should reduce errors, as all must agree before a proposal can become law or be implemented as an operating program; there will be full deliberation. The existence of multiple decision makers should also permit greater innovation both in the federal government and in state and local governments. And as the framers intended, diffused policymaking power reduces the capacity of central government to run roughshod over the rights of citizens or the interests of socioeconomic groups. For citizens, the numerous points of access to policymaking permit losers at one level of government, or in one institution, to become winners at another point in the process.

Americans also pay a price for this lack of policy coherence and coordination. It is sometimes difficult to accomplish *anything,* and elected politicians with policy ideas find themselves thwarted by the large number of decision points in the policymaking system. The policymaking situation in the United States in the 1980s and 1990s was described as *gridlock,* in which the different institutions blocked one another from developing and enforcing policies.[1] The crisis provoked by the attacks of September 11, 2001, eliminated that gridlock for a short period, but it soon returned, even in some aspects of national security. For example, the USA PATRIOT Act could not be renewed in late 2005 because of sharp partisan differences over domestic wiretapping. That partisan gridlock became even more of a barrier to policymaking after the 2010 election, with a Republican-controlled House of Representatives facing a Democratic Senate and president.

The division of government into many separate policy fiefdoms also means that programs may cancel one another out. For example, progressive (if decreasingly so) federal taxes and regressive state and local taxes combine to produce a tax system in which most people pay about the same proportion of their income as tax. The surgeon general's antismoking policies and the Department of Agriculture's tobacco subsidies attempt to please both pro- and antitobacco interests. The apparent inability or unwillingness of policymakers to choose among options means that policies will be incoherent, and the process continues seemingly without any closure. It also means that because potential conflicts are resolved by offering every interest in society some support from the public sector, taxes and expenditures are higher than they might otherwise be.

I have already mentioned the divisions that exist in American government. I now look at the more important dimensions of that division and the ways in which they act and interact to effect policy decisions and real policy outcomes for citizens. *Divided government* and *gridlock* have become standard descriptions of American government, and their impact, as well as that of federalism, must be considered in analyzing the way in which policy emerges from the political system. But we should be careful to understand the extent to which gridlock really exists as more than simply a convenient description of institutional conflict. We need to question the extent to which gridlock will be reduced or eliminated when, as after the 2008 elections, the presidency and Congress are controlled by the same party.

Federalism

The most fundamental division in American government traditionally has been *federalism,* or the constitutional allocation of governmental powers between the federal and state governments. This formal, constitutional allocation at once reserves all powers not specifically granted to the federal government to the states (Ninth and Tenth Amendments) and establishes the supremacy of federal law when there are conflicts with state and local law (Article 6). Innumerable court cases and, at least in part, one civil war have resulted from this somewhat ambiguous division of powers among levels of government.

By the first years of the twenty-first century, American federalism had changed significantly from the federalism described in the Constitution. The original constitutional division of power assumed that certain functions of government would be performed entirely by the central government, and other functions would be carried out by state or local governments. In this "layer cake" federalism, or separated powers model, the majority of public activities were to be performed by subnational governments, leaving a limited number of functions such as national defense and minting money as the responsibility of the federal government.[2]

As the activities of government at all levels expanded, the watertight separation of functions broke down, and federal, state, and local governments became involved in many of the same activities. The layer cake then was transformed into a marble cake, with the several layers of government still distinct but no longer horizontally separated from one another. This form of federalism still involved intergovernmental contacts through central political officials. The principal actors were governors and mayors, and intergovernmental relations remained on the level of high politics, with the representatives of subnational governments acting almost as ambassadors from sovereign governments and as suppliants for federal aid. Furthermore, in this form of federalism, the state government retained its role as intermediary between the federal government and local governments.

Federalism evolved further from a horizontal division of activities into a set of vertical divisions. Whereas functions were once neatly compartmentalized by level of government, the major feature of "picket fence" federalism is the development of policy subsystems defined by policy rather than level of government.[3] Thus, far-reaching decisions about health policy are made by specialized networks involving actors from all levels of government and from the private sector. Those networks, however, may be relatively isolated from other subsystems making decisions about highways, education, or whatever. The principal actors in these subsystems frequently are not political leaders but administrators and substantive policy experts. Local health departments work with state health departments and with the Department of Health and Human Services (HHS) in Washington in making health policy, and these experts are not dependent on the intervention of political leaders to make the process function. This form of federalism is as much administrative as it is political, and it is driven by expertise as much as by political power.

In many ways, it makes little sense to discuss federalism in its original meaning; it has been argued that contemporary federalism is as much facade as picket fence. A term such as *intergovernmental relations* more accurately describes the complex, crazy quilt of overlapping authority and interdependence among levels of government than does a more formal, constitutional term such as *federalism.*[4] In addition to being more oriented toward administrative issues than high politics, contemporary intergovernmental relations are more functionally specific and lack the coherence that might result if higher political officials were obliged to be involved in the principal decisions. Thus, as with much of the rest of American politics, intergovernmental relations often are without the mechanisms that could generate effective policy control and coordination.

Despite the complexity, overlap, and incoherence that exist in intergovernmental relations, one can still argue that centralization of control in the federal system has increased.[5] The degree of dependence of state and local governments on federal financial support for their services has varied over the past several decades. The Reagan administration reduced federal support for state and local activities, especially social services, but the level of federal support has been creeping back up (see Table 2.1). Along with financing has come increased federal control over local government activities. In some cases, that control is absolute, as when the federal government mandates equal access to education for those with disabilities or establishes water quality standards for sewage treatment facilities. In other instances, the controls on state and local governments are conditional, based on the acceptance of a grant: If a government accepts the money, it must accept the controls accompanying that money.

In general, the number and importance of mandates on state and local governments and the conditions attached to grants have been increasing. For example, the Department of Health and Human Services threatened to cut off funding for immunization and other public health programs in states that did not implement restrictions on procedures performed by doctors and dentists

TABLE 2.1   Changing Levels of Federal Grants-in-Aid to State and Local Governments

	1970	*1980*	*1985*	*1990*	*1995*	*2000*	*2007*
Total amount ($ millions)	24,065	91,385	105,852	135,325	224,991	284,659	443,797
Percentage of state and local expenditures	29.1	39.9	29.6	25.2	31.5	31.3	31.9

Source: Historical Tables, *Budget of the United States Government* (Washington, DC: Office of Management and Budget, 2008).

with AIDS. Even the existence of many federal grant programs may be indicative of subtle control from the center, inasmuch as they direct the attention, and especially the money, of local governments in directions they might not otherwise have chosen.

In addition to controls exercised through the grant process, the federal government has increased its controls over subnational governments through intergovernmental regulation and mandating. Regulations require the subnational government to perform a function such as wastewater treatment, whether or not there is federal money available to subsidize the activity. These regulations are certainly intrusive and can be expensive for state and local governments. Even when the mandates are not expensive and are probably effective, such as the requirement that states raise the minimum drinking age to twenty-one or lose 5 percent of their federal highway money, they can still be perceived as "federal blackmail" of the states.[6]

One part of the "Contract with America" promoted by the incoming Republican majority in Congress in 1994 was to end unfunded federal mandates, and the assault on mandates was the first section of the "contract" enacted into law. In particular, the Unfunded Mandates Reform Act of 1995 requires the Congressional Budget Office to estimate the mandated costs of legislation reported out of committee in Congress. This provision by no means outlaws federal mandates, but it does require that members of Congress at least know what they are doing to the states and localities if they pass particular legislation. That measure did not in any way affect existing mandates, nor will the federal government have to pay the bill for those. Conservatives believe that in practice the legislation has been largely toothless,[7] while liberals believe that environmental and consumer standards are in danger of being undermined. The shift from mandates to the suggestions to control drunk driving that were part of the 1998 highways bill indicates something of a shift in attitudes about mandates—there is still some attempt to impose federal priorities but mostly through suasion rather than direct command. That said, the No Child Left Behind program of President George W. Bush imposed potentially huge costs on the states and localities (for testing and for supporting students in "failing schools") with little funding attached.

One factor complicating intergovernmental relations has been the proliferation of local governments in the United States. As fiscal constraints on local governments have caused problems for mayors and county commissioners, new local governments have been created to circumvent those restrictions. States frequently restrict the level of taxation or bonded indebtedness of local governments, but when a local government reaches its legal limit, it may simply create a special authority to undertake some functions that the general-purpose local authority formerly carried out. For example, as Chicago faced severe fiscal problems in 2005, it sold its Skyway toll road to a private contractor; it leased Midway Airport to combat the financial crisis of 2008.

An average of almost five hundred local governments is created every year, primarily special districts to provide services such as transportation, water, sewerage, fire protection, and other traditional local government services.[8] The new special-purpose governments multiply the problems of coordination and may frustrate citizens who want to control tax levels but find that every time they limit the power of one government, a new one is created with more fiscal powers. They also present problems of democratic accountability. The leaders of special-purpose governments often are not elected, and the public can influence their actions only indirectly through the general-purpose local governments (cities and counties) that appoint the boards of the special-purpose authorities.[9]

The economic circumstances of the late 1980s and early 1990s—rapidly mounting federal deficits and healthy state treasuries—tended to push power back toward the states.[10] The recession of the early 1990s ended public surpluses in almost all states and turned eyes in state capitals back toward Washington and the incoming Democratic administration. The Clinton administration, however, proved to be as decentralizing as most previous Republican administrations and perhaps even more so. For example, the welfare reform passed in 1996 was a major decentralization of power to the states, and the general pattern of policy change was to increase the powers of states and localities vis-à-vis Washington. Like President Clinton, President George W. Bush also had been a governor and brought a decentralizing agenda with him to the White House, but the September 11 attacks tended to move power back toward Washington more clearly than at any time since the 1960s. The Bush administration was, in fact, one of the most centralizing in recent American history and involved the federal government in local education, law enforcement, and health issues in ways that previous administrations had not thought appropriate. Some of the attempts at central control, such as using federal drug statutes to prevent Oregon from implementing its own "death with dignity" law, went too far even for a Supreme Court that seemed to accept greater centralization in issues such as gun control in the District of Columbia.[11]

Despite those earlier trends, the American federal system still centralizes power more than was planned when the federal system was formed. The grant system has been purchasing a more centralized form of government, although the shift in power appears to have come less from power hunger on the part of federal bureaucrats and politicians than from the needs to standardize many public services and to promote greater equality for minorities. Furthermore, even if federal programs are intended to be managed with no strings attached, there is a natural tendency, especially in Congress, to demand the right to monitor the expenditure of public funds to ensure that the money is used to attain the desired goals. In an era in which the accountability of government is an increasingly important issue, monitoring is likely to increase in intensity, even when Republican members of Congress stress the need to limit federal power.

The Obama administration has also tended to centralize, although without a few comments on the sort of federalism that it would find most congenial; in large part, this centralization has been the result of the fiscal crisis beginning in 2008 and the poor condition of state and local finances. For example, the Stimulus Package of 2009 provided billions of dollars to state and local governments to support infrastructure programs and some service delivery in areas such as education. Likewise, the passage of the health reform acts places the federal government in a much more central position in health care.

Separation of Powers

The second division of American government exists within the federal government itself and, incidentally, within most state and local governments as well. The Constitution distributes the powers of the federal government among three branches, each capable of applying checks and balances to the other two. In addition to providing employment for constitutional lawyers, this division of power has a substantial impact on public policies. In particular, the number of "veto points" in the federal government alone makes initiating any policy difficult and preventing change relatively easy.[12] It also means, as I mentioned when discussing the incoherence of American public policy, that the major task in making public policy is forming a coalition across a number of institutions and levels of government. Without "legislating together" in such a coalition, either nothing will happen, or the intentions of a policymaker will be modified substantially in the policy process.[13]

The president, Congress, and the courts are constitutionally designated institutions that must agree to a policy before it can be fully legitimated. The bureaucracy, although it is only alluded to in the Constitution, is now also a force in the policy process with which elected politicians must contend. Despite its conservative and obstructionist image, the bureaucracy is frequently the institution most active in promoting policy change, as a result of government workers' close connections with the individuals and interests to which they provide services, as well as their own ideas about public policy.[14] The bureaucracy is also given latitude to elaborate congressional legislation, as well as to adjudicate the application of laws within each policy area.[15]

The bureaucracy—or, more properly, the individual agencies of which it is composed—has interests that can be served through legislation.[16] The desired legislation may only expand the budget of an agency, but it usually has a broader public policy purpose as well. Administrative agencies can, if they wish, also impede policy change or perhaps even block it entirely. Almost every elected or appointed politician has experienced delaying tactics by nominal subordinates who disagree with a policy choice and want to wait until the next election or cabinet change to see if someone with more compatible policy priorities will come into office. The permanence of the bureaucrats, along with their command of technical details and of the procedural machinery, provides bureaucratic agencies much more power over public policies than one would assume from reading formal descriptions of government institutions. It has become increasingly evident that agencies may drive the congressional agenda almost as much as Congress shapes the agenda of the agencies.[17]

The institutional separation in American government has led to a number of critiques based on the concept of divided government.[18] Those critiques argue that American government is incapable of being the decisive governance system required in the twenty-first century and that some means must be found of generating coherent decisions. This has been an issue especially when the presidency and Congress have been controlled by different political parties, as they were during the later part of George W. Bush's presidency, or the second half of President Obama's administration. In both cases, there were also divisions within their own parties that made policymaking difficult. Despite the impacts of divided government, David Mayhew, Charles O. Jones, and other scholars have argued that the system can govern effectively because it is capable of making decisions and even of rapid policy innovation.[19]

Whether the policymaking system is efficient or not, one principal result of the necessity to form coalitions across a number of institutions is the tendency to produce small, incremental changes rather than major revamping of policies.[20] This might be described as policymaking by the lowest common denominator. The need to involve and placate all institutions within the federal government—including the many component groups of individuals within each—and perhaps state and local governments as well means that only rarely can there be more than minor changes in the established commitments to clients and producer groups if the policy change is to be successful.[21] The resulting pattern of incremental change has been both praised and damned. It has been praised for providing stability and limiting the errors that might result from more significant shifts in policy. If only small policy changes are made and those changes do not stray far from previously established paths, then it is unlikely that major mistakes will be made.

The jiggling and poking of policies characteristic of incremental change is perfectly acceptable if the basic patterns of policy are acceptable, but in some areas such as health care and mass transportation, a majority of Americans have said (at least in polls) that they would like some significant changes from the status quo.[22] The existing system of policymaking appears to produce major desired changes only with great difficulty; the increasing partisanship in Congress has made change even more difficult. In addition, the reversibility of small policy changes, assumed to be an advantage of incrementalism, is often overstated.[23] Once a program is implemented, a return to the conditions that existed before the policy choice is often difficult. Clients, employees, and organizations are created by any policy choice, and they usually will exert powerful pressures for the continuation of the program.

The division of American government by the constitutional separation of powers doctrine creates a major institutional confrontation at the center of the federal government. Conflicts between the president and Congress over such matters as war powers, executive privilege, and the budget also test and redefine the relative powers of institutions. These conflicts became more apparent in 2005 with revelations of the use of presidential authority to wiretap Americans' phones without a judicial warrant, as well as other uses of the fight against terrorism to justify increased presidential action. Is the modern presidency inherently imperial, or is it still subject to control by Congress and the courts? Does too much checking by each institution of the others generate gridlock and indecision? Likewise, can the unelected Supreme Court have as legitimate a rule-making role in the political system as the elected Congress and president? Do the regulations made by the public bureaucracy really have the same standing in law as the legislation passed by Congress or decrees coming from the court system? These questions posed by the separation of powers doctrine influence substantive policy as well as relationships among the institutions.

Subgovernments

A third division within American government cuts across institutional lines within the federal government and links it directly to the picket fence of federalism. The results of this division have been described variously as "iron triangles," "cozy little triangles," "whirlpools," and "subgovernments."[24] The underlying phenomenon that these terms describe is that the federal government rarely acts as a unified institution making integrated policy choices but tends instead to endorse the decisions made by portions of the government. Each functional policy area tends to be governed as if it existed in splendid isolation from the remainder of government, and frequently, the powers and legitimacy of government are used to advance individual or group interests in society, rather than a broader public interest.[25]

Three principal actors are involved in the iron triangles still so relevant for explaining policymaking in the United States. The first is the interest group, which wants something from government, usually a favorable policy decision, and must attempt to influence the institutions that can act in its favor.

Fortunately for the interest group, it usually need not influence all of Congress or the entire executive branch but only the relatively small portion concerned with its particular policy area. For example, farmers who want continued or increased crop supports need not influence the entire Department of Agriculture but only those within the Agricultural Stabilization and Commodity Service who are directly concerned with their crop. Likewise, in Congress, they need only influence the Commodities Subcommittee of the House Agriculture Committee; the Senate Subcommittee on Agricultural Production and Stabilization of Prices; and the Rural Development, Agriculture, and Related Agencies Subcommittees of the appropriations committees in the Senate and House. In addition to the usual tools of information and campaign funds, interest groups have an important weapon at their disposal: votes. They represent organizations of interested individuals and can influence, if not deliver, votes for a representative or senator. Interest groups also have research staffs, technical information, and other support services that, although their outputs must be regarded with some skepticism, may be valuable resources for members of Congress or administrative agencies seeking to influence the policy process.

The second component of these triangular relationships is the congressional committee or subcommittee. These bodies are designated to review suggestions for legislation in a policy area and to make recommendations to the whole Senate or House of Representatives. An appropriations subcommittee's task is to review expenditure recommendations from the president, then to make its own recommendations on the appropriate level of expenditures to the entire committee and to the whole chamber. Several factors combine to give these subcommittees substantial power over legislation. First, subcommittee members develop expertise over time, and they are often regarded as more competent to make decisions concerning a policy than the whole committee or the whole house.[26] Norms have also been developed that support subcommittee decisions for less rational, and more political, reasons.[27] If the entire committee or the entire house were to scrutinize any one subcommittee's decisions, it would have to scrutinize all such decisions, and then each subcommittee would lose its powers. These powers are important to individual Congress members because each wants to develop his or her own power base in a subcommittee or perhaps even the entire committee.[28] The time limitations imposed by the huge volume of policy decisions that Congress makes each year also mean that accepting a subcommittee's decision may be a rational means of reducing the workload of each individual legislator.

Congressional subcommittees are not unbiased; they tend to favor the very interests they are intended to oversee and control. The reason is largely that the Congress members serving on a subcommittee tend to represent constituencies whose interests are affected by the policy in question. As one analyst argued, "A concerted effort is made to ensure that the membership of the subcommittee is supportive of the goals of the subgovernment."[29] For example, in 2012, the members of the Energy and Mineral Resources Subcommittee of the House Resources Committee included representatives from the energy-producing states of Texas (2), California, Louisiana (2), West Virginia, Alaska, Pennsylvania, Ohio, and Oklahoma and from the mining states of Arizona, Colorado, and Nevada; there were representatives from Maryland and New Jersey. This pattern is not confined to natural resources. The Housing and Community Development Subcommittee of the House Banking, Finance, and Urban Affairs Committee has representatives from all the major urban areas of the United States.

These patterns of committee and subcommittee membership are hardly random; they enhance the ability of Congress members to deliver certain kinds of benefits to constituents, as well as the members' familiarity with the substantive issues of concern to their constituents. Subcommittee members also develop patterns of interaction with the administrative agencies over which they exercise oversight. Individual members of Congress and agency officials may discuss policy with one another and meet informally. As both parties in these interactions tend to remain in Washington for long periods, the same Congress members and officials may interact for many years. The trust, respect, or simple familiarity this interaction produces further cements the relationships between committee members and agency personnel, and it also tends to insulate each individual policy area from meddling by outside interests.

Obviously, the third component of the iron triangle is the administrative agency, which, like the pressure group, wants to promote its interests through the policymaking process. The principal interests of an agency are its survival and its budget. The agency need not be, as is often assumed, determined to expand its budget—it may wish merely to retain its fair share of the budget pie as it expands or contracts.[30] Agencies are not entirely self-interested; they also have policy ideas that they wish to see translated into operating programs, and they need the action of the congressional committee or subcommittee for that to happen. They also need the support of organized interests in the process.

Each actor in an iron triangle needs the other two to reach its goal, and the style that develops is symbiotic. The pressure group needs the agency to deliver services to its members and to provide a friendly point of access to government. The agency needs the pressure group to mobilize political support for its programs among the affected clientele. Letters from constituents to influential representatives and senators must be mobilized to argue that the agency is doing a good job and could do an even better job if given more money or a certain policy change. The pressure group needs the congressional committee again as a point of access and as an internal advocate in Congress. And the committee needs the pressure group to mobilize votes for its members and to explain to group members how and why they are doing a good job in Congress. The pressure group can also be a valuable source of policy ideas and research for busy politicians. Finally, the committee members need the agency as an instrument for producing services to their constituents and for developing new policy initiatives. The agency has the research and policy analytic capacity that Congress members often lack, so committees can profit from their association with the agencies. And the agency obviously needs the committee to legitimate its policy initiatives and provide it with funds.

All the actors involved in a triangle have similar interests. In many ways, they all represent the same individuals, variously playing the roles of voter, client, and organization member. Much of the domestic policy of the United States can be explained by the existence of functionally specific policy subsystems and by the absence of effective central coordination. This system of policymaking has been likened to feudalism, with the policies being determined not by any central authority but by aggressive subordinates—the bureaucratic agencies and their associated groups and committees.[31] Both the norms of policymaking and the time constraints of political leaders tend to make central coordination and policy choice difficult. The president and his staff (especially the Office of Management and Budget) are in the best organizational position to exercise such control, but the president must serve political interests, just as Congress must, and he faces an even more extreme time constraint. Thus, decisions are rarely reversed once they have been made within the iron triangle, except in a crisis. For example, following the 2001 terrorist attacks, there was pronounced movement toward greater presidential control over a range of organizations and less separation among the policy subsystems. That change was most pronounced in the area of homeland defense, but to some degree, all organizations in government have become less particularistic.

One effect of the subdivision of government into a number of functionally specific subgovernments is the incoherence in public policy already mentioned. Virtually all societal interests are served through their own agencies, and there is little attempt to make overall policy choices for the nation. These functional subgovernments at the federal level are linked with functional subsystems in intergovernmental relations—the picket fences described earlier. The result of this segmentation of decision making is that local governments and citizens alike may frequently receive contradictory directives from government and may become confused and cynical about the apparent inability of their government to make up its mind.

A second effect of the division of American government into a number of subgovernments is the involvement of a large number of official actors in any one policy area. The proliferation of actors is in part recognition of the numerous interactions within the public sector and between the public and private sectors, in the formulation and implementation of any public policy. For an issue area such as health care, the range of organizations involved cannot be confined to those labeled *health* but must expand to include consideration of the social welfare, nutritional, housing, educational, and environmental policies that may have important implications for citizens' health.[32] But the involvement of an increasing number of public organizations in each issue area also reflects the lack of central coordination, which allows agencies to gain approval from friendly congressional committees for expansion of their range of programs and activities.

From time to time, a president will attempt to streamline and rationalize the delivery of services in the executive branch, and in the process, he generally encounters resistance from agencies and their associated interest groups. For example, when creating the cabinet-level Department of Education, President Jimmy Carter sought to move the educational programs of the (then) Veterans Administration (VA) into the new department.[33] In this attempt, he locked horns with one of the best organized and most powerful iron triangles in Washington— the Veterans Administration, veterans organizations, and their associated congressional committees. The president lost. Subsequently, the veterans lobby was sufficiently powerful to have the VA elevated to a cabinet-level department. Presidents do not always lose: President Clinton was able to downsize or eliminate several organizations during implementation of his National Performance Review, including several that had substantial political clienteles.[34] George W. Bush also was successful in a massive reorganization to create the Department of Homeland Security, but that reform has not produced most of the results desired. It appears that there has been substantial internal conflict over policy and reduced effectiveness in some areas.[35] The administration of George W. Bush attempted to use performance management techniques to improve control over agencies, with at best limited success.[36]

As easy as it is to become enamored of the idea of iron triangles in American government—they do help explain many of the apparent inconsistencies in policy when viewed broadly—there is some evidence that the iron in the triangles is becoming rusty.[37] More groups are now involved in making decisions, and it is more difficult to exclude interested parties, leading Charles O. Jones to describe the current pattern as "big sloppy hexagons" rather than "cozy little triangles."[38] For example, debates over health care reform include not just representatives of the medical professions, the hospitals, and health insurers but also a range of other interests such as small business, organized religion, and organized labor. A simple Internet search on most any policy issue will reveal a wide range of groups expressing their views and attempting to influence public—and congressional—opinion.[39]

The concepts of *issue networks* and *policy communities* involving large numbers of interested parties, each with substantial expertise in the policy area, now appear more descriptive of policymaking in the United States as well as other

AP Photo/Jacquelyn Martin

The economic crisis beginning in 2008 led to major policy interventions by the federal government attempting to stimulate the economy. These initiatives included support for public infrastructure, such as this project to replace a sidewalk ramp in Silver Spring, Maryland, and required the involvement of both the President and Congress to be enacted.

industrialized democracies.[40] These structures of interest groups surrounding an issue are less unified about policy than were the iron triangles, and they may contain competing ideas and types of interests to be served through public policy—the tobacco subsystem may even be invaded by health care advocates. There has been some rusting of the iron in the triangles, but the indeterminacy and lack of coherence of networks make them less valuable in the day-to-day work of governing. As important as the network idea has been for explaining changes in federal policymaking, it does not detract from the basic idea that policymaking is very much an activity that occurs within subsystems.

American government, although originally conceptualized as divided horizontally into levels, is now better understood as divided vertically into a number of expert and functional policy subsystems. These virtually feudal subsystems divide the authority of government and attempt to appropriate the mantle of the public interest for their own more private interests. Few of the actors making policy, if any, have any interest in altering these stable and effective means of governing. The system is effective politically because it results in the satisfaction of most interests in society. It also links particular politicians and agencies with the satisfaction of those interests, thereby ensuring their continued political success.

The basic patterns of decision making in American politics are *logrolling* and the *pork barrel,* through which, instead of clashing over the allocation of resources, actors minimize conflict by giving one another what they want. For example, instead of contending over which river and harbor improvements will be authorized in any year, Congress has tended to approve virtually all proposals, so that all members can claim to have produced something for the folks back home. Or Congress members from farming areas may trade positive votes on urban development legislation for support of farm legislation by inner-city Congress members. This pattern helps incumbents to be reelected, but it costs taxpayers a great deal more than would a more selective system.

Although logrolling tends to spread benefits widely, being directly involved in the decision-making subsystem tends to produce more benefits for Congress members and their constituents. That could be seen easily in the distribution of funds from the 2005 SAFE Transportation Equity Act. This act provided a good deal of highway spending for all the American states but tended to favor the states and congressional districts represented on the transportation committees in both houses of Congress (see Table 2.2). The most famous example of this pork barrel spending was a bridge to a sparsely populated island in Alaska, which became a symbol of federal waste and congressional excess. Also, the adding of "earmarks," or special spending provisions for constituencies, to bills has come under increased scrutiny following the 2006 investigations of lobbying.[41] The Republican primary battles of 2011–2012 had all the candidates opposed to wasteful earmarking (which seemed to be earmarks to states other than their own).[42]

Logrolling and pork barrel policymaking are very effective as long as there is sufficient wealth and economic growth to pay for subsidizing large numbers of public programs.[43] Nevertheless, this pattern of policymaking was one (but by no means the sole) reason for the federal government's massive deficits in the 1980s and early 1990s, which have returned in recent years, and it appears that it can no longer be sustained comfortably. Various attempts at budget reform have endeavored to make pork barrel politics more difficult to pursue. In particular, the PAYGO system in Congress, by requiring consideration of alternative uses of money or an alternative source of revenue, made it more

TABLE 2.2   Per Capita Appropriations in Highway Bill of 2005, by Representation on Congressional Transportation Committees

No representatives	One representative	Multiple representatives
$31.78	$43.56	$48.36

difficult, at least for a while, for Congress to spend (see chapter 7). Given the divisions within American government, however, it is difficult for the policymaking system as a whole to make the choices among competing goals and competing segments of society that would be necessary to stop the flow of red ink from Washington.

Public and Private

The final qualitative dimension of American government that is important in understanding how contemporary policy is made is the increasing confusion of public and private interests and organizations. These two sets of actors and actions have now become so intermingled that it is difficult to ascertain where the boundary between the two sectors lies. The leakage across the boundary between the public and private sectors, as artificial as that boundary may be, has been occurring in both directions. Activities that once were almost entirely private now have greater public sector involvement, although frequently through quasi-public organizations that mask the real involvement of government. Functions that are nominally public have significantly greater private sector involvement. The growth of institutions for formal representation of interest groups and for implementation of policy by interest groups has given those groups perhaps an even more powerful position in policymaking than that described in the discussion of iron triangles. Instead of vying for access, interest groups are accorded access formally and can exert a legitimate claim to their position in government.

The other major component of change in the relationship between public and private has been the privatization of public activities.[44] The United States traditionally has had an antigovernment ethos; that set of values was articulated strongly, and the positive role of the federal government was minimized, during the 1980s.[45] At the state and local levels, a large number of functions—hospitals, garbage collection, janitorial services, and even prisons—have been contracted out or sold off as a way to reduce the costs of government.[46] In the administration of George W. Bush, the most evident privatization trend was the opening of federal land to private mining and forestry.

The blending of public and private is reflected to some degree in employment.[47] Table 2.3 shows public employment in twelve policy areas, as well as the changes that occurred from 1970 to 2000. By 1980, for example, only education comprised more than 80 percent public employees, and that percentage was dropping. Even two presumed public monopolies—defense and police protection—had significant levels of private employment. The two policy areas differ, however, in the form of private employment. Defense employment in the private sector is in the production of goods and services that the armed forces use, whereas in policing, a number of private police officers actually provide the service.

TABLE 2.3   Percentages of Public Employment in Selected Policy Areas, 1980–2005

Policy area	1980	1990	2000	2005
Education	85	83	82	80
Postal service[a]	73	70	62	63
Highways[b]	68	62	61	58
Tax administration[c]	57	55	40	37
Police[d]	60	56	55	56
Defense[e]	59	62	63	64
Social services[f]	35	32	23	22
Transportation	31	34	31	32
Health	30	37	33	34
Gas/electricity/water	27	24	17	13
Banking[g]	I	I	I	I
Telecommunications	I	I	I	I

Sources: Bureau of the Census, *Census of Governments,* quinquennial; Department of Defense, *Defense Manpower Statistics,* annual; Employment and Training Administration, *Annual Report.*

a. Private sector counterparts are employees of private services, couriers, etc.

b. Private sector counterparts are employed by highway construction contracting firms.

c. Private sector counterparts are tax accountants and staffs, H&R Block employees, etc., some only seasonal.

d. Private sector counterparts are security guards, private police, etc.

e. Private sector counterparts are employed by military suppliers.

f. Private sector counterparts are employed in social work and philanthropy, many only part-time.

g. In 2009 proportion will have increased because of bailout of banks.

The development of mechanisms for direct involvement of interest groups in public decision making is frequently referred to as *corporatism* or *neocorporatism.*[48] The terms refer to the representation in politics of members of the political community not as residents of a geographical area but as members of functionally defined interests in the society—labor, management, farmers, students, the elderly, and so forth. Associated with this concept of representation is the extensive use of interest groups both as instruments of input to the policy process and as means of implementing public policies. The United States is a less corporatist political system than most industrialized democracies but still has corporatist elements. Most urban programs mandate the participation of community residents and other interested parties in decision making. Crop allotment programs of the U.S. Department of Agriculture have used local farmers' organizations for monitoring and implementation for some time, and fishing quotas are negotiated with local fishery management councils.[49] County medical societies have been used as professional service review organizations for Medicare and Medicaid, checking on the quality and cost of services, and medical and legal associations license practitioners on behalf of government. In addition, as of the early twenty-first century, there were approximately 6,500 advisory bodies in the federal government, many containing substantial interest group representation.[50]

A number of other organizations also implement public policy. For example, when cabin attendants in an airplane require passengers to fasten their seat belts, they are implementing Federal Aviation Administration policies. Universities are required to help implement federal drug policies (by requiring statements of nonuse by new employees) and federal immigration policies (by requiring certification of citizenship or immigration status). Manufacturers of numerous products must implement federal safety and environmental standards (e.g., installing seat belts and pollution-control devices in automobiles), or they cannot sell their products legally.

The increasing use of quasi-public organizations, changes in the direction of a limited corporatist approach to governance in the United States, and privatization (largely through contracting) raises several questions concerning responsibility and accountability in government. These changes involve the use of public money and, more important, the name of the public by groups and for groups that may not be entirely public. In an era when citizens appear to be attempting to exercise greater control over their governments, the development of these forms of policymaking "at the margins of the state" may be an understandable response to financial constraints but may exacerbate underlying problems of public loss of trust and confidence in government.

The Size and Shape of the Public Sector

We have looked at some qualitative aspects of the contemporary public sector in the United States. What we have yet to do is examine the size of that public sector and the distribution of funds and personnel among the various purposes of government. As was pointed out, drawing clear distinctions between public and private sectors in the mixed-economy welfare state is difficult, and growing more difficult, but we will concentrate on the expenditures and personnel that are clearly governmental. As these figures include only those expenditures and employees that are clearly public, they inevitably understate the size and importance of government in the United States. The understatement is perhaps greater for the United States than would be the case for other countries because of government's attempts to hide the extent of its involvement in the private sector.

Table 2.4 contains information about the changing size of the public sector in the United States since the post–World War II era and the changing distribution of expenditures and employment.[51] Most obvious in this table is that the public sector in the United States has indeed grown, with expenditures increasing from less than one-quarter to more than one-third gross national product. Likewise, public employment has increased from 11 percent of total employment to over 15 percent. The relative size of the public sector, however, has decreased from the mid-1970s, especially in terms of the percentage of employment. Although the number of public employees increased by over four million from 1994 to 2009, government's share of total employment declined slightly, despite the increasing employment at the state and local levels. There was a slight

TABLE 2.4   Growth of Public Employment and Expenditures, 1950–2009

Year	Civilian public employment (in thousands)			Public expenditures (in thousands)		
	Federal	*State and local*	*Total*	*Federal*[a]	*State and local*	*Total*
1950	2,117	4,285	6,402	$44,800	$25,534	$70,334
1960	2,421	6,387	8,808	97,280	54,008	151,288
1970	2,880	10,147	13,028	208,190	124,795	332,985
1980	2,876	13,315	16,191	576,700	432,328	1,009,028
1990	3,105	14,976	18,081	1,243,125	976,311	2,219,436
2000	2,799	17,506	20,305	1,689,300	1,720,899	3,420,200
2006	2,695	19,327	22,022	2,635,200	1,898,200	4,533,400
2009	2.824	19,809	22,632			

Year	As percentage of total employment			As percentage of GNP		
1950	3.6	7.3	10.9	15.7	8.9	24.6
1960	3.7	9.7	13.4	19.2	10.7	29.9
1970	3.7	12.9	16.6	21.2	12.7	33.9
1975	3.4	14.2	17.6	22.5	14.4	36.9
1980	2.9	13.1	16.0	20.0	16.4	36.4
1990	2.6	12.5	15.1	23.2	18.2	41.4
2000	2.1	12.8	14.9	16.7	24.1	40.8
2006	2.0	13.4	15.4	17.0	23.7	40.7
2009	2.0	13.6	15.6			

Source: U.S. Census Bureau, *Statistical Abstract of the United States* (Washington, DC: GPO, annual).

a. Does not include federal monies passed through grant programs to states and localities for final expenditure at state and local levels.

increase at the end of this period, due in part to declining private employment in the recession. Government in the United States is large, but it does not appear to be the ever-increasing Leviathan that its critics portray it to be.[52]

It is also evident that growth levels of public expenditures are more than twice as large, relative to the rest of the economy, as public employment figures. Public expenditures as a share of gross national product have continued to increase slightly. The differences relative to the private sector and the differences in the patterns of change are largely the results of transfer programs, such as Social Security, which involve the expenditure of large amounts of money but require relatively few administrators. In addition, purchases of goods and services from the private sector (for example, the Department of Defense's purchases of weapons from private firms) involve the expenditure of large amounts of money (over $260 billion in 2006) but generate little or no employment in the public sector. In 1988, however, those purchases created approximately 2.1 million jobs in the private sector, a figure similar to the number of people then in the armed forces.[53] From these data it appears that some portions of "big government" in the United States are more controllable than others, even during the eight-year term of a popular president determined to reduce the size of the public sector.

The distribution of expenditures and employment among levels of government also has been changing. In 1950, the federal government spent 64 percent of all public money and employed 33 percent of all public employees. By 2006, the federal government spent approximately 60 percent of all public money but employed only 12 percent of all civilian public employees.[54] The remarkable shift in employment relative to a rather stable distribution of expenditures is again in part a function of the large federal transfer programs, such as Social Security. It also reflects the expansion of federal grants to state and local governments and the ability of the federal government to borrow money to meet expenditure needs, in contrast to the requirement that state and local governments balance their budgets.

In addition, the programs that state and local governments provide— education, social services, police and fire protection—are labor intensive. The major labor-intensive federal program, defense, had declining civilian and uniformed employment even before the apparent end of the Cold War in the late 1980s. These data appear to conflict somewhat with the popular characterization of the federal government as increasingly important, or intrusive, in American economic and social life. Although it is a large institution, employing over four million people when the armed forces are included, its level of employment actually had been declining, absolutely as well as relatively, and the major growth of government employment was occurring at the state and local levels. The increased emphasis on security, at home and abroad, in response to the terrorist attacks of 2001 is shifting more employment to the federal government, both in the military and in homeland security, but the major action in public employment is at the state and local levels.

Another factor in the federal government's declining share of employment is the shift from defense programs toward social programs. In 1952, national defense accounted for 46 percent of all public expenditures and for 49 percent of all public employment. By 2009, defense had been reduced to 9 percent of all spending and less than 3 percent of public employment. By contrast, a panoply of welfare state services (health, education, and social services) accounted for 20 percent of public expenditures in 1952 and 24 percent of public employment. By 2009, these services accounted for 64 percent of spending and 57 percent of all public employment. Within the welfare state services, education has been the biggest gainer in employment, with more than seven million more employees in 2009 than in 1952. Social Security programs alone increased their spending by well over $400 billion during that time period. The United States is often described as a "welfare state laggard," but the evidence is that although it is still behind most European nations in the range of social services, a marked increase has been occurring in the social component of American public expenditures and employment.

It was argued that the landslide victories of the Republican Party in the presidential elections from 1980 to 1988, and even the narrow victories in 2000 and 2004, were a repudiation of that pattern of change and that they should have produced little increase, or actual decreases, in public spending for social programs. There was a slight relative decrease in social spending from 1980 to 1992—in part a function of increasing expenditures for other purposes, such as interest on the public debt—but sustained decreases remain difficult to obtain. Most social programs are entitlement programs, and once a citizen has been made a recipient of benefits, or has made the insurance contributions to Social Security, future governments find it difficult to remove those benefits. This is especially true of programs for the retired elderly, as they cannot be expected to return to active employment to make up losses in benefits, and unfortunately for budget cutters, public expenditures are increasingly directed toward the elderly. For example, in 2009, approximately 53 percent of the federal budget went to programs (Social Security, Medicare, housing programs, and so forth) for the elderly. As the American population continues to grow older, spending for this social group will increase. What is true in particular for the elderly is true in general for all entitlement programs, and reducing the size of the government's social budget will be difficult indeed.

We have been concentrating attention on public employment and public expenditures as measures of the size of government, but we should remember that government influences the economy and society through a number of other mechanisms as well. For example, the federal government sponsors a much larger housing program through the tax system—through the tax deductibility of mortgage interest and property taxes—than it does through the Department of Housing and Urban Development (see Table 10.3, chapter 10). Government also provides a major educational program of guaranteed and subsidized student loans that shows up only indirectly in figures on public spending.

In the United States, because of the generally antistatist views of many citizens, regulation has been the major form of government intervention in the economy, rather than the more direct mechanisms used in other countries. The regulatory impact of government on the economy can be counted in the billions of dollars—one estimate was more than $21,000 per household in 2000.[55] Reliance on such indirect methods of influence was heightened by the conservative Congresses over the past fifteen years, although the George W. Bush administration eliminated a number of environmental and health regulations. The conservatives in Congress were, however, successful in creating requirements for government to report the estimated costs of its regulations.[56] As governments continue to find less intrusive ways of making and implementing policy—using loans rather than expenditures, for example—assessing the size, shape, and impact of government in the United States based solely on public spending figures and public employment becomes less and less accurate.

The first decade of the twenty-first century has been one of extremely dramatic change in the role of the public sector in the United States. The economic crisis created by the failures of a number of banks has produced the largest expansion of federal power, and spending, since Franklin Roosevelt's New Deal. The federal government has assumed effective ownership of a number of banks and has embarked on massive public spending in an attempt to revive the economy. This large-scale spending may undermine attempts to promote a national health program and to enhance the performance of the educational program.

Summary

American government in the new century is large, complex, and to some degree unorganized. Each individual section of government, be it a local government or an agency of the federal government, tends to know clearly what it wants, but the system as a whole lacks overall coordination, coherence, and control. Priority setting is not one of the strongest features of American government. An elected official coming to office with a commitment to give direction to the system of government will be disappointed in the extent of his or her ability to produce desired results, by the barriers to policy success, and by the relatively few ways in which the probability of success can be increased. These difficulties, however, may be compensated for by the flexibility and multiple opportunities for citizen inputs characteristic of American government.

Despite the problems of coordination and control and the tradition of popular distrust of government, contemporary American government is active. It spends huge amounts of money and employs millions of people to perform a bewildering variety of tasks. These activities are not confined to a single level of government; all three levels of government are involved in making policy, taxing, spending, and delivering services. This activity is the reason why the study of public policy is so important. It is a means of understanding what goes on in the United States and why government does the things it does. The emphasis in the next portion of this book is on the processes through which policy is made. All governments must follow many of the same procedures when they make policy: identify issues, formulate policy responses to problems, evaluate results, and change programs that are not producing the desired results. American governments do all these things, but they do them in a distinctive way and produce distinctive results.

CHAPTER 3

Explaining Policy Choices

MOST OF THIS BOOK describes the stages of the policy process and individual policy areas. In each of the descriptive components of the book, there are implied ways of explaining how decisions are made and why policies are adopted in the way that they are. The *stages model* of policy, for example, assumes that the process of making policy plays a significant part in determining the outcome. This simple explanation has a great deal of validity, given that at each stage of the process certain types of solutions will have a better chance than others of being successful. At the implementation stage, for example (see chapter 6), policies that require fewer independent decisions and that have more robust instruments available are more likely to be successful than more complex policies.

Although the stages model is a useful heuristic, it is but one of several explanations of how decisions can, and should, be made when making policy. Some of these models are based on economic reasoning and make strong assumptions about optimal policies. Optimality may not be achieved in the "real world" of making policy, but the optimal models are a useful standard against which to compare the results of actual policy processes. The majority of the models I will discuss, however, will be political models that attempt to explain how political forces and political institutions shape choices.

Power and Public Policy

Power is fundamental to all models of policymaking, including the stages model. Many scholars would argue that the simplest way to understand policymaking or any other form of political activity is to understand who has the power to make things happen. So if we want to understand why a law is adopted in a particular manner in Congress or is implemented in a particular way within the bureaucracy, we need to identify who has the power and therefore can make other actors comply with their wishes. Although power is to some extent a function of formal positions in government—the presidency, for example—it also may be a function of the characteristics of the individuals themselves or a product of other resources, such as money, that enable them to be effective in politics.

Whatever the basis of the power, those who have it are able to overcome the opposition of others.[1] Power can be manifested in a number of ways in the policymaking process. The most obvious is when one actor is capable of getting what it wants in fights over legislation or regulations. In the United States, for example, it is often assumed that corporate interests have that capacity.[2] At other times, the exercise of power may be simply the power to prevent action or indeed to prevent some issues from ever being considered.[3] However power is manifested, it is a factor that always must be considered when examining the choices made by governments.

The policymaking process, especially in a complex setting such as U.S. government, involves countervailing power, with all the actors involved having some resources that they can bring to bear. Even individuals and groups outside the mainstream of political life can bring some resources, including moral claims, to bear on the final decision. Therefore, simply saying that policymaking is about the exercise of power is not sufficient, and we must attempt to understand how this fundamental resource for actors in governing is used.

The Policy Process—The Stages Model

The study of public policy in political science has several important but somewhat disparate dimensions. The largest single body of research has been on the policy process.[4] This approach to policy is inherently political, arguing that the policy choices that governments make are primarily a function of the political process through which they are made and the institutions in which they are made. Most process models attempt to explain policy choices by understanding the actors who are involved at each stage, as well as understanding linkages among the stages. These models are, however, far more useful for describing the process than they are as means of explaining outcomes. We will deal with the stages model of policy in some detail in chapters 4–8, and I will not detail the assumptions of each of its aspects. That said, it is important to consider the way in which adopting a stages model of this type shapes thinking about policy in the United States and also some of the analytic issues raised by this approach.

The conventional process model of policymaking begins with agenda setting or problem definition; then it proceeds through a series of steps such as program design, legitimating, budgeting, and evaluation but typically does not make any strong assumptions about the political mechanisms that are used to manage that movement (see Figure 3.1). Although some elements within the general model,

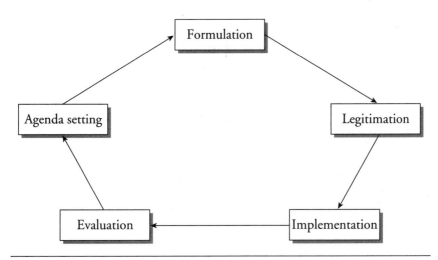

FIGURE 3.1   The Stages Model

such as agenda setting,[5] rely on policy entrepreneurs to provide agency within the process, the general models tend to be largely devoid of that animation. Especially in a political system with as many institutional "veto points" and "veto players" as that of the United States, we need to understand better how the process can be made to work and who drives the action of policymaking forward.[6]

The conventional stages model, as useful as it is, also tends to assume that the stages discussed come in the order laid out in the model and that the process is taking place anew, with relatively little concern for the past. In reality, however, both of those implicit assumptions tend to be incorrect. First, the order may be less linear in practice than it appears in the model. For example, the process of implementation often involves policy formulation because the administrative decisions needed to make programs work in essence transform the policy. Likewise, important policy issues often arise when other programs are being budgeted and it becomes clear that for a program to work other programs will need to be changed or perhaps given additional resources.

It is also important to remember that most policymaking is actually revising and—we hope—improving existing policies.[7] Some policy issues—for example, the budget—return to the agenda automatically, whereas others may remain dormant for some time. In both cases, however, policymaking involves working with existing programs. In some ways, this is an easier process for the political institutions, given that the basic parameters of public intervention have been determined and the involvement of the public sector has been legitimated. On the other hand, however, existing programs have clients and employees, and those groups may resist changes. Thus, the political coalition process may involve more overt conflicts than the relatively infrequent cases in which the public sector chooses to intervene for the first time.

That point raises the importance of conflict in understanding the policy process. The stages model as usually used in political science does not reflect the degree of conflict that may exist in these crucial political processes; rather, the process appears to move along smoothly to its conclusion. At each stage, and as programs and policies move from one stage to the next, there will be conflicts. Furthermore, each stage of the process may involve different sets of actors with different concerns about the programs. For example, as a program moves from formulation and legitimation on to the process of implementation, the state governments are likely to become involved, given that in the United States most federal programs require some state-level implementation. This may transform conflicts about policy substance into ones of funding for the state governments.

In summary, the stages model is a very useful heuristic device for mapping the route that policies take from being just a good idea to being a functioning program, but it provides little explanation for the choices that are made. Many of the stages of the process, such as agenda setting and implementation, have well-developed theoretical explanations for choices, but the links among the stages, and the overall model itself, lack such capacity for explanation. Other approaches in political science may be able to provide more compelling explanations for policy choices.

Institutional Models of Policy

The stages model is based to some extent on the institutions that are involved in making policy; it tends to assume that certain institutions are associated with certain stages. For example, legislatures are generally crucial for legitimating policy choices and also for budgeting, and the bureaucracy is generally responsible for implementing policy. In addition to those specific institutional linkages, we should also consider a more general institutional model for making policy decisions. Institutions do matter, but we need to specify how they exert their influence.[8]

As the new institutionalism has become a major approach to contemporary political science, the role of institutions has become more clearly conceptualized.[9] Although there are several contending approaches to the role of institutions, they accept the general idea that institutions are crucial for understanding why the public sector functions as it does. New institutionalism emphasizes the normative elements of institutions and the "logic of appropriateness" that provides a guide for action to their members. From this perspective, individuals learn to behave in certain ways in organizations because of organizational values rather than because of the utilitarian consequences of the policies selected. For example, being a member of the U.S. Senate is learned, and members tend to become effective only after they have mastered the formal and informal rules of that institution.

Another way of thinking about the role of a logic of appropriateness is that organizational cultures shape the policies that the organization advocates and implements. The individuals who work in many agencies and departments have their own views of what constitutes good government and good policy and will attempt to have government implement those policies. Political leaders at times find it difficult to overcome these internal logics, for example, when more conservative administrations attempt to change the policy directions of the Environmental Protection Agency or when more liberal administrations confront the Department of Defense.[10]

Whereas such normative institutionalism assumes that policy choices are motivated by an internal logic of appropriateness, historical institutionalism emphasizes the importance of path dependency and the persistence of policy decisions once they are made. Whether simply because it is difficult to change ongoing programs or because of the positive reinforcement that programs receive, once they are initiated, they tend to be "path dependent"—in other words, they tend to follow the status quo—unless there is some sufficient external shock that can disrupt the stability and create a new equilibrium in the policy.[11]

The historical institutionalist perspective is very useful for describing what happens in the policy process, but it is less useful for explaining how choices are made and, more important, why change might occur. Persistence and inertia are rather standard stereotypes of the policy process and often do describe what is happening. We also need, however, means of understanding and explaining policy choices that move away from the status quo, that enable governments to reform and, one hopes, improve policy. Historical institutionalism has begun to think about these ideas of change,[12] but the underlying nature of the approach is to emphasize persistence and the continuity of policy.

Rational choice models of institutions assume that institutions are sets of incentives and rules that shape the rational actions of the individuals who operate within government.[13] These models address some classic problems in political science and policymaking, including the "tragedy of the commons," in which rational individual action leads to the exhaustion of common resources. Furthermore, institutions can help to create equilibrium in situations—legislatures, for example—in which cyclical majorities may make reaching a decision difficult.[14] Perhaps most important for policymaking, rational choice models of institutions have examined the difficulties that institutional design may pose for making decisions.[15] So, for example, the U.S. government, with its multiple institutions, presents special problems for decision making that may not be encountered in less complex systems of governing.

Finally, discursive models of institutions are founded primarily on the ideas and discourses that guide the institution.[16] In this perspective, similar to the normative institutionalism, the institution is shaped by the discussions that members use to persuade one another and to persuade the outside world about the actions undertaken by the institution. The discursive model, however, is not as stable as the normative approach, and the present configuration within the institution reflects a short-term equilibrium that will be altered through continuing debate and discussion.

Advocacy-Coalition Framework

One important addition to process models of policy that contains the conflict missing in the stages model is Sabatier and Jenkins-Smith's advocacy-coalition framework (ACF).[17] This model is concerned explicitly with policy change and argues that policy change comes about through the clash of ideas, as manifested in an existing policy coalition and a potential replacement. In any policy subsystem, there are core beliefs, and those beliefs are supported by coalitions of actors—experts, interest groups, political parties. When these core beliefs are challenged, the conflicts can be worked out through bargaining, often generating a new synthesis about policy that will in turn be institutionalized and set the stage for the next round of policy change.

The advocacy-coalition framework was developed specifically to deal with issues in which there is substantial disagreement about values or feasibility—for example, the clash between environmentalists and industry. This disagreement is taking place in a policy subsystem that is at least partially insulated from the remainder of the political system. If a policy does not have those "wicked" characteristics, then perhaps it can proceed nicely through the path described by the stages model. Many policy proposals, however, involve major disagreements about both ends and means and therefore require some means of resolving the conflict.[18] The ACF is primarily about change and the need to move from one policy equilibrium to another, and to do so when there are some basic disagreements about the best policy.

Most policy subsystems, such as those described in the ACF, tend to be rather stable until they are confronted by some external shock or by an opportunity for learning from other successful cases. When such a disturbance occurs, different sets of perceptions and ideas are activated, and conflicts emerge over the reactions to the shocks and the need to create some new equilibrium. In the development of the new equilibrium, the contending parties are assumed to maintain their core beliefs, but at the same time, they can bargain over issues and options that do not directly threaten those core beliefs. So, for example, an environmentalist would not be expected to yield on his or her commitment to ecological values but might negotiate over acceptable levels of pollution or over the use of particular pieces of land, possibly achieving operational coalitions with industry representatives.

The advocacy-coalition framework model also provides a means of understanding how change may occur within the seemingly stable, path-dependent models of historical institutionalism. The ACF is a means of introducing conflict into those models and understanding the dynamics of policy change in the context of apparent stability.[19] This model emphasizes that a great deal of the change that occurs in policy is a function of clashes of ideas, as well as clashes of economic interests, as would be at the center of rational choice theories. In this perspective, sometimes the best ideas win, rather than the most powerful.

Policy Causes Politics

Another strand of theorizing about policy in political science has to some extent reversed the logic of the stages model and argues that policy produces politics.[20] This model involves the assumption that four fundamental types of policy—distributive, regulatory, redistributive, and constituent—tend to be associated with certain types of political action. For example, redistributive policies such as Social Security are assumed to be associated with a type of politics in which political elites (often the president and his advisers in the private sector) create a policy and appeal to class divisions to build support for it. Salisbury and Heinz used a similar set of policy variables but related them more to the types of demands being placed on the policymaking system and the degree of the system's fragmentation.[21]

The model developed by Theodore Lowi has motivated a great deal of empirical research as well as a number of theoretical critiques.[22] Perhaps its most fundamental contribution, however, has been to make political scientists think about policies in more analytic categories. There is always the tendency to think about policies in terms of the names one finds on government buildings— agriculture, defense, and housing, for example. That manner of thinking is useful, but only up to a point, and it may mask some of the internal variations in individual policy areas.

A slightly different version of the "policy causes politics" approach is the argument made by Gary Freeman and others that differences across political systems are not as great as differences across policy areas. That is, the technical and political foundations of a policy area such as health may be more similar across countries than are those foundations for disparate policy areas within a single system. As policy ideas spread across national boundaries, the common aspects of policy may become more similar. Pressures from globalization and from Europeanization have tended to homogenize policy across national boundaries, further reinforcing Freeman's argument.[23]

Policy Styles

To be able to understand public policy, it is important to consider the policy choices made by any one country (or subnational unit) and compare them with the choices made by other countries. That comparison could be done on a policy-by-policy basis, as described for the welfare state below, or we could typify a policymaking style for the political system in question. In this case, rather than politics being assumed to cause policy, policy is being used to characterize the political systems and as the lens through which to compare them.

Jeremy Richardson did the first major analysis of policy styles in western Europe, arguing that the policy styles in those countries could be characterized by two variables:[24] One was an active-reactive dimension, assessing the extent to which a country attempted to anticipate policy problems. The other dimension was the extent to which the political system operated by reaching consensus decisions versus the dominant political group—generally a party in control of government—being able to impose its view. So, for example, the need of the United States to create a consensus among multiple institutions and its general aversion to government planning would place it in one cell, while the United Kingdom might share the tendency to reactive solutions to problems but would have a stronger government, able to impose decisions.

Richardson's model is not the only approach to understanding policy styles. Frans van Waarden, for example, has been concerned with identifying the dimensions of policy styles that can be used to assess the capacity of political systems to make and implement policies effectively. His dimensions include such factors as links with society and legalism, which shape the politics of public policy. Interestingly, in this analysis, the presumably weak government of the United States appears to have the capacity to be much stronger than it is usually thought to be. The reactive policy style of the United States, therefore, may be a function more of its political culture and the long-standing laissez-faire tradition than of institutional factors within government itself.

For policymaking in a single country, such as the United States, the utility of the policy styles approach is to understand some of the implications of the manner in which policies are made and implemented in that country and what the options might be. For example, the reactive policymaking style of the United States has meant that the country does not anticipate major problems and therefore may have difficulty responding to problems such as floods, hurricanes, and declining infrastructure, as evidenced by Hurricane Katrina in New Orleans in 2005 and the collapse of Minneapolis's I-35W bridge in 2007. On the other hand,

© Joe Raedle/Pool/Corbis

President Barack Obama visits the tornado-ravaged community of Joplin, Missouri, on May 29, 2011. A natural disaster such as a tornado always provokes some sort of policy response. The severity and immediacy of a crisis will cause governments to act quickly and decisively.

as Frans van Waarden points out, the capacity to mobilize after recognizing problems helps to ameliorate conditions once the disasters occur.[25] The major question, then, is the extent to which citizens are willing to bear the costs and dangers of the reactive style.

Furthermore, there may be greater differences across policy areas in a single country than there are across countries.[26] For example, the United States may be very reactive in a policy area such as health care, except when policy windows open as one did for Medicare and Medicaid in the 1960s (see chapter 11), and as another did after the election of Barack Obama in 2008. But American government may be very active in foreign policy and some areas of education. The internal dynamics of these policy areas may be very different, with government having greater latitude for action without influence from interest groups in foreign policy than in most areas of domestic policy.[27]

Policy Instruments

Implementation studies have been concerned with the ability to transform stated policies into effective action. The ability to make that difficult translation from law to action involves a number of components; an important one is the choice of one or more policy instruments.[28] The basic idea of policy instruments is that the public sector can achieve its goals using a variety of different types of programs—subsidies, regulation, vouchers, and so forth—and each of these will have different substantive and political characteristics that will influence the likelihood of success.

While it is common to think of these instruments in more or less technical terms, it is crucial to remember that they do have a strong political dimension. For example, as the politics of governing has changed to cast suspicion on direct public sector interventions, many of the conventional "command and control" instruments of the public sector, such as regulation, have been exchanged for softer instruments, such as recommendations and nonbinding agreements.[29] The choice of policy instruments may also reflect the need to build coalitions to have legislation adopted. For example, much of the federal support for university students in the United States has been provided through private bank loans guaranteed by government. Although it might be more efficient to have the loans managed through the universities, it was important to create a political ally in the banking industry.

The study of policy instruments leads to a number of other, even more difficult issues about public policy and the possibilities of effective public sector intervention. The most fundamental of these is that the choice of instruments raises the possibilities of policy design. Do policy analysts, whether in political science or not, have the ability to design better policies than those designed through political mechanisms? To do so requires some understanding of the causes of policy problems and the relationship of those problems to the instruments available to address them, and some normative basis to evaluate the outcomes of the policy intervention.[30] The design issue also raises the question of whether the simple functional categories we generally use for policy are sufficient to capture the complexity of the challenges of attempting to match instruments to policy problems.[31]

Bounded Rationality, Multiple Streams, and Incrementalism

Economic models of policymaking stress the rationality of human action when humans act politically or use rational, economic criteria to assess the quality of decisions (see below). In the former case, rational choice models of politics argue that the best way to understand how politicians,[32] bureaucrats,[33] and interest groups,[34] among others, act when making policy is to consider those individuals as rational utility maximizers. People operate within the context of formal, legal institutions, but advocates of rational choice argue that we can best understand their behavior by beginning with those basic motivations.

Scholars have advanced any number of critiques of the rationalist model of policymaking. While still adopting some of the basic orientation toward rationality, scholars using the bounded rationality approach point to the extreme difficulty of making fully rational decisions and argue that rationality can best be seen as bounded by organizational, political, and cultural parameters that constrain the choices that an individual will have to make. This school of policymaking is based on the work of Herbert Simon and has continued through other literature that has emphasized the difficulties in depending on models that assume entirely rational decision making.

The garbage can model of organizational decision making is one of the important contributions of the bounded rationality approach.[35] The basic idea of the garbage can is that the multiple constraints on policy prevent real-world implementation of the rational model of policies to pursue goals. Rather, in the garbage can, streams of opportunities converge almost at random, so it is difficult to predict what policies will be adopted. For example, John Kingdon has discussed agenda setting in policy as the opening of windows of opportunity that present the opportunities to use solutions.[36] The confluence of those streams may mean that solutions pursue goals, rather than the usual assumption that programs are formulated to solve problems. This is often a function of the organizational nature of politics. Bureaucratic organizations have commitments to instruments and other "solutions" and hence may want to find ways of using their instruments. This behavior may be especially evident when the organization is threatened by termination or by other organizations competing for their turf.

The garbage can model has been generalized to the multiple streams approach to policymaking.[37] The logic of this approach is that three streams of factors—problems, politics, and policy characteristics—converge in more or less accidental manners. The substantive discussions of policy in chapters 9–16 point to a number of instances in which policy choices have been made through such a convergence. For example, the crumbling infrastructure in the United States might have continued to crumble if the economic crisis of 2009 had not provided an opportunity for funding public works to get people back to work.[38] This process is not entirely accidental, however; policy entrepreneurs play a crucial role in bringing together the various streams and in using, if not creating, windows of opportunity. Thus, although elements in the streams may emerge somewhat randomly, there is a need for some political or administrative actor to bring the streams together and produce effective action.

The logic of bounded rationality that rejects comprehensive rationality when considering policymaking appears also in the incrementalist approach to policy. *Incrementalism* has two distinct elements, but both support the basic logic that making comprehensively rational policy decisions is impossible and perhaps even unwise.[39] The empirical approach to incrementalism has examined repetitive policymaking—especially on the budget. Those studies have found that the volume and complexity of decisions lead decision makers to fall back on simple incremental rules of thumb rather than attempt to make perfect allocations of funds. The assumption is that by making a series of small adjustments over time, appropriate allocation of funds will be achieved.

The normative argument for incrementalism is that in the long run better decisions are made by "successive limited comparisons" of a policy choice to the status quo and by gradually adapting policies through trial and error and learning.[40] The argument is that this allows retreats if poor initial choices are made and prevents costly investments in poorly designed programs. On the other hand, incrementalism can be seen as excessively conservative, retaining existing policies for longer than might be justified and preventing significant reforms.

The Private Sector, Iron Triangles, and Networks

The liberal, pluralist tradition of politics in the United States has provided the private sector a rather ambiguous position in policymaking. To some extent, the involvement of interest groups and other private actors in policy is illegitimate. The groups that gain access to policy often have a great deal of influence, and their actions are often hidden from public view. The increasing openness of the private sector to the media and other forms of scrutiny has made the involvement of those groups more obvious to the public and has often made policymaking appear even less "in the public interest" than it is meant to be.

Even in the absence of apparent corrupt practices, the interaction of the public and private sectors in the United States has been described as "iron triangles," in which there is a symbiotic relationship among interest groups, congressional committees and subcommittees, and administrative agencies.[41] The interest groups need access to Congress and to the administrative agencies who serve their members. The agencies need support (on their budgets and other legislation) from Congress, and they use interest group support to obtain it. Congress members want to be reelected and need effective programs that serve their constituencies, as well as support (including financial support) from interest groups. These three sets of actors have worked together effectively and are able to prevent interference in their cozy relationships.

The continuous expansion of interactions between citizens and government has to some extent eroded the exclusivity of the iron triangles and has produced important changes in the ways that private sector actors become involved in the public sector. In particular, networks of public actors have been formed around numerous policy areas that include a range of private sector actors who have some involvement with the policy. For example, the health summit that President Obama called early in his term involved a number of federal and state officials but was mostly populated by a range of medical professionals and insurance and other corporate executives. The conventional iron triangle description of American politics has been supplanted by an understanding of the complex networks that now surround many policy areas.[42] A growing body of literature on network theory points to the role of social actors in governing.[43]

Optimal Decision Making

The models of policymaking presented thus far are politically driven, their motivations coming from the need to reconcile competing interests and political pressures. The outcomes of those processes are often very disappointing to the participants, but they do reflect the manner in which institutions function and their ability to begin with a contradictory set of values and interests and produce an outcome. Furthermore, these political models often can be illuminated by comparative analysis, using other cases to understand better how policies are made and how they may be improved.

Another approach to policy is to attempt to develop more abstract models of optimal policy processes and optimal policies. Whereas political models are driven by process, most economic models are driven by attempts to define optimal policy outcomes and to design institutional arrangements that may be capable of producing those desirable outcomes. While these optimal models may not be achievable in the real world of politics, they can function as a useful standard against which to compare "real" policy processes and policy outcomes. In addition, if the utilitarian assumptions are converted into measurements, the models can be used to advise policymakers about the best choices.

The starting point for economic analysis of policy is the justification for public sector intervention into the economy and society. If one believes that the market can produce optimal economic outcomes, then any interventions into that market must be justified by some form of market failure.[44] Public goods are one of the classic cases in which markets do not work effectively. Markets cannot efficiently produce goods such as national defense or public parks that, once created, are difficult to prevent all citizens' enjoying.[45] Therefore, these goods (and services) may have to be delivered through the public sector and financed through taxation. Markets may also fail because of externalities, meaning that the total social costs—for example, pollution—of some activities are not included in the market price of a product. And markets may also fail because the participants do not have adequate information and therefore cannot make optimal decisions. This is the (economist) justification for regulations that force producers to provide consumers information about risks of the products.

Economic models of policy also look at the capacity to change from one policy position to another, especially to find so-called Pareto optimal moves that make at least one person better off without harming anyone else. The problem is that few such opportunities present themselves in the real world of public policy, and most policy choices involve making choices that may benefit some people but at the same time make others worse off.[46] Similarly, optimal budget making in the public sector is supposed to be an allocation in which the marginal utility of a dollar spent for each and every activity covered by the budget is equal.

In addition to these more abstract economic models of policy, more applied approaches such as cost-benefit analysis (see chapter 17) apply the same utilitarian logic for thinking about public policy. In other words, the best policy is one that maximizes total utility, with that utility being considered in economic terms. Even attributes such as environmental quality are reduced to monetary values, so that the costs and benefits can be compared easily. Unlike Pareto optimal moves, however, this version of welfare economics accepts that decisions will have negative consequences for some people and assesses the balance between the positive and negative contributions to total social utility.

Constructivist Models

I have argued above that one of the problems with the normative economic models of policymaking is that they do not have as close a connection with the complexities of reality as do the political science models. Constructivist, or argumentative, models of policy, on the other hand, argue that the reality of policy-making must be constructed through social and political processes. The existence and nature of some policy problems may be obvious—public pensions, perhaps—but most must be created and defined. Some policy problems—the environment or spousal abuse—may be excluded from the agenda of government until a policy entrepreneur or a confluence of events brings attention to them.

The logic of constructivism has been linked to the general problem of policy design.[47] That is, not only are policy problems constructed politically but so too are the overall patterns of the public sector's response to a problem once constructed. Just as ideas can be used to understand policy problems, they can also be linked to the solution of those problems, and solutions must also be constructed. The ideas used may be general orientations toward politics and governing—for example, limited government—or they may be more specific ideas about particular policies, such as Keynesian approaches to economics.

Drug policy has been one of the best examples of the constructivist logic in policy in the United States. Although few people would disagree that there is a real policy problem there, the question is what type of problem it is. The definition of the problem will influence the political forces that are brought to bear on it.[48] In the case of drugs, the policy has been constructed primarily as an issue of criminal justice, and therefore, law enforcement organizations have become central in implementation.[49] If, however, drugs had been considered more of a health issue or a social issue, then a very different set of organizations and different policy instruments would have been central to the solutions that government would have pursued.

The constructivist position in policy analysis has a close relationship to the agenda setting literature. If issues are to be placed on the agenda of the public sector, then they must be defined in a way that makes them acceptable to important political forces and that can be used to mobilize support. The constructivist position, therefore, is not a passive one but often depends upon active political intervention by entrepreneurs—organizations as well as individuals—to define the policy and make it function as intended. The constructivist position is also closely connected to the advocacy-coalition framework model, given that there may be several alternative conceptions of a policy and that different entrepreneurs will contend to have their own views dominate.

Deliberative policy analysis represents one variant of the general constructivist approach to policy. The logic of deliberative analysis is that better policies can be chosen through interactions of the affected actors, and even the interactions of ordinary concerned citizens, than through the imposition of more technocratic solutions by experts.[50] The logic is that there are a number of interests and points of view in society, and the policy process should not privilege one view or one set of actors. In the American context, the New England town meeting, with open discussions of policy, is used as a model of such deliberations, although organizing such discussions for larger political units and more complex issues is at best problematic.

The majority of thinking about public policy has been in a strongly objective model, attempting to measure policies as dependent variables and then finding the factors that explain those policy choices. Likewise, economic and utilitarian values tend to undergird much of this analysis, assuming that policies are best understood in terms of improving the economic well-being of those affected by them. One strand of reasoning in political science, however, argues that policy is best understood in more linguistic terms. The assumption of deliberative models is that the discourse surrounding a policy and conflicts among alternative discourses defines the ways in which policy choices are made.[51] Of course, utilitarian values is one discourse, but only one among many possible sets of values that can guide policy choices.

Discourse and deliberative models are often best applied in areas such as science policy and some aspects of environmental policy, where there are often widely diverging understandings of the nature of the policy. Herbert Gottweiss, for example, has examined the deliberative aspects of research on human biology, and there have been a number of analyses of environmental policy that apply the deliberative approach.[52] These studies have demonstrated the range of values that may be involved in complex policy issues, as well as something of the ways in which those almost inherent conflicts may be resolved.

Summary

Policymaking is an extremely complex process, involving a wide range of actors and ideas. This chapter has been my attempt to provide some alternative approaches for understanding that process and evaluating the outcomes. Many of these themes are echoed in other parts of this book. For example, when discussing the agenda-setting process (see chapter 4), we can see the importance of framing issues and hence can see how constructivist approaches to policy can be used. Likewise, the discussion of the evaluation of policy (see chapter 8) is closely related to the normative economic models discussed in this chapter. It is important, therefore, not to separate policy analysis from the understanding of substantive policy dynamics.

It is also important not to separate conflict and political action from thinking about policy. Too often the search for optimal outcomes by policy analysts ignores the political debates and the deeply entrenched conflicts that define policymaking. Ultimately public policy is, as Harold Lasswell argued, concerned with "who gets what," and making those choices will provoke intense political activity.[53] The institutions and processes of policymaking help to channel the demands of groups into effective action and enable government to make decisions in the face of those competing demands.

Finally, these alternative conceptions of the policy process represent some of the richness of the discipline of political science, but they also represent some of the possible confusion. This is especially a problem if a student is seeking a single "right answer" and finds it frustrating that there may not be one. The availability of these multiple approaches does allow the student, or the policy analyst, to triangulate and to see what light each of several different approaches may shed on the policy process being researched. For example, institutions may matter, but the exercise of overt political power may matter as well. The use of these multiple lenses[54] provides a richer view of the reality and, while providing no simple answer, helps us to understand how policy is made and what its effects may be.

The Making of Public Policy

PART TWO
The Making of
Public Policy

CHAPTER 4

Agenda Setting and Public Policy

Two parts of the policymaking process that occur rather early in the sequence of decisions leading to the actual delivery of services to citizens are crucial to the success of the entire process—*agenda setting* and *policy formulation.* They are important because they establish the parameters within which any additional consideration of policies will occur. Agenda setting is crucial because if an issue cannot be placed on the agenda, it cannot be considered, and nothing can possibly happen in government. Policy formulation then begins to narrow and structure consideration of the problems on the agenda and to prepare a plan of action to rectify them. These two stages are also linked because it is often necessary to have a solution before an issue can be accepted on the agenda. Moreover, how a problem is defined as it is brought to the agenda determines the kinds of solutions that will be developed to solve it.

Agenda Setting

Before government can make a policy choice, a particular problem in the society must have been deemed amenable to public action and worthy of the attention of policymakers. Government gives no consideration at all to many real problems, largely because the relevant political actors are not convinced that government has any role in attempting to solve them. On the other hand, once accepted as a part of the general, systemic agenda, problems tend to remain for long periods, although some of them do come on and off the active policy agenda.

One of the best examples of a problem being accepted as part of the agenda after a long period of exclusion is the problem of poverty in the United States. Throughout most of the nation's history, poverty was perceived not as a public problem but as merely the result of the (proper) operation of the free market. The publication in 1963 of Michael Harrington's *The Other America* and the growing mobilization of poor people brought the problem of poverty to the agenda and indirectly resulted in the launching of a wide-ranging effort to eradicate it.[1] Once placed on the agenda, poverty has remained an important public issue, although different administrations have given different amounts of attention to it. For example, the effects of the economic crisis since 2008 highlighted growing inequality in the United States and the return to higher levels of poverty (see chapter 9).

Another obvious case of external events contributing to setting the policy agenda is that the perceived poor quality of American elementary and secondary education, especially in science and technology, did not become an issue at the federal level until the Soviet Union launched *Sputnik I.* It has again become an issue as American children's test scores continue to be poor compared with those of children in many other countries in the world, especially those in Asia. Once cast as a national defense issue, education is now debated more in terms of economic competitiveness (see chapter 13). The attacks of September 11, 2001, and the Hurricane Katrina disaster in 2005 brought into focus the question of America's preparedness for disasters, as well as the general capacity of government at all levels to work effectively. In these cases, a dramatic public event awakened the populace to an existing social problem that needed to be addressed.[2]

The best example of an issue being removed from the policy agenda remains the repeal of Prohibition, by which the federal government said that preventing the production and distribution of alcoholic beverages was no longer its concern. Despite the end of Prohibition, all levels of government have nonetheless retained some regulatory and taxing authority over the production and consumption of alcohol, and of course governments have prohibition programs for a number of other drugs as well. The movement to privatize some public services (usually at the local level) also has removed some issues from direct concern in the public sector, although again a regulatory role usually continues.

What can cause an issue to be placed on the policy agenda? The most basic cause is a perception that something is wrong and that the problem can be ameliorated through public action. This answer in turn produces another question: What causes the change in perceptions of problems and issues? Why, for example, did Harrington's book have such far-reaching influence on the public, when earlier books about social deprivation, such as James Agee's *Let Us Now Praise Famous Men,* had relatively little impact?[3] Did the timing of the "discovery" of poverty in the United States result from the election of a young, seemingly liberal president (John Kennedy), who was succeeded by an activist president (Lyndon Johnson) with considerable sway over Congress? When do problems cease to be invisible and become perceived as real problems for public consideration?

Issues also appear to pass through an "issue attention cycle," in which they are the objects of great public concern for a short period and generate some

Although high gasoline prices depend upon many factors beyond the control of government, they do irritate citizens. That irritation, in turn, will produce government actions. The president and Congress cannot afford to ignore issues that affect so many people.

response from government.[4] The initial enthusiasm for the issue is generally followed by more sober realism about the costs of policy options available and the difficulties of making effective policy. This realism is followed in turn by a period of declining interest, as the public seizes on a new issue. The histories of environmental policy, drug enforcement, and, to some degree, the women's movement illustrate this cycle very well. Also, after some honeymoon period, the political forces opposed to involvement in these policy areas have the opportunity to mobilize and to slow further initiatives.

Just as individual issues go through an issue attention cycle, the entire political system may also experience cycles of differential activity. One set of scholars has described this pattern as "routine punctuated by orgies."[5] A less colorful description, developed by Frank Baumgartner and Bryan D. Jones, is "punctuated equilibria."[6] Some time periods—because of energetic political leaders or large-scale mobilization of the public, or for a host of other possible reasons—are characterized by greater policy activism than others. Those periods of activism are followed by periods in which the programs adopted during the activist period are rationalized, consolidated, or perhaps terminated.[7]

In this chapter, I discuss how to understand, and how to manipulate, the public agenda. How can a social problem be converted into an issue and brought into a public institution for formal consideration? In the role of policy analyst, one must understand not only the theoretical issues concerning agenda setting but also the points of leverage within the political system. Much of what happens in the policymaking system is difficult or impossible to control: the ages and health of the participants, their friendships, constitutional structures of institutions and their interactions, and external events, to name but a few of the relevant variables. Some scholars have argued that agendas do not change unless there is an almost random confluence of events favoring the new policy initiative.[8] Such random factors may be important in explaining overall policy outcomes, but they are not the only pertinent factors to consider when one confronts the task of bringing about desired policy changes. Despite all the imponderables in a policymaking system, there is still room for initiative and for altering the political behavior of important actors.

It is also important to remember that social problems do not come to government fully conceptualized, with labels already attached. Policy problems need to have names if government is to deal with them, and labeling or framing is itself a political process.[9] For example, how do we conceptualize the problem of illegal drugs in the United States? Is it a problem of law enforcement, as it is commonly treated, or is it a public health problem, or a problem of education, or a reflection of poverty, despair, and social disorder?[10] Perhaps drug use indicates something more about the society in which it occurs than it does about the individual consumers usually branded as criminals. There are a number of possible answers to such definitional questions, but the fundamental point is that the manner in which the problem is conceptualized and defined determines the remedies likely to be proposed, the organizations that will be given responsibility for the problem, and the final outcomes of the public intervention into it.

Kinds of Agendas

Until now, we have been discussing "the agenda" in the singular and with the definite article. There are, however, different agendas for the various institutions of government, as well as a more general agenda for the political system as a whole. The existence of these agendas also is to some degree an abstraction. Most agendas do not exist in any concrete form; they exist only in a collective judgment about the nature of public problems or as fragments of written evidence, such as legislation introduced, the State of the Union message of the president, or a notice of intent to issue regulations appearing in the *Federal Register.* On the other hand, cases appealed—and especially cases accepted for appeal—do constitute a clear agenda for the Supreme Court.

Roger Cobb and Charles Elder, who produced some of the principal writing on agendas in American government, distinguished between the systemic and institutional agendas. The systemic agenda consists of "all issues that are commonly perceived by members of the political community as meriting public attention and as involving matters within the legitimate jurisdiction of existing governmental authority."[11] This is the broadest agenda of government and includes all issues that might be subject to action or that are already being acted on by government. It is a definition, however, that implies a consensus on the systemic agenda that may not exist. Some individuals may consider a problem—abortion, for example—as part of the agenda of the political system (whether to outlaw abortion or to provide public funding for it), while others regard the issue as entirely one of personal choice. The southern states' reluctance for years to include civil rights as part of their agendas indicated a disagreement over what fell within the "jurisdiction of existing governmental authority." Setting the systemic agenda is usually not consensual, as it is a crucial political and policy decision. If a problem can be excluded from consideration, then those individuals and organizations that benefit from the status quo are assured of victory.[12] It is only when a problem is placed on the agenda and made available for active discussion that the forces of change have some opportunity for success.

The second type of agenda that Cobb and Elder discuss is the institutional agenda: "that set of items explicitly up for active and serious consideration of authoritative decision-makers."[13] An institutional agenda is composed of the issues on which the individuals in power within a particular institution actually are considering taking action. These issues may constitute a subset of all the problems they will discuss, as the complete set will include "pseudoissues" discussed to placate clientele groups but without any serious intention to make policy.[14] Actors within institutions run a risk, however, when they permit discussion of pseudoissues: Once they appear on the docket, something may actually be done about them.

A number of institutional agendas exist—as many as there are institutions—and there is little reason to assume any agreement among institutions as to which problems are the most appropriate for consideration. As with conflicts over placing issues on the systemic agenda, interinstitutional conflicts will arise in moving problems from one institutional agenda to another. The agendas of bureaucratic agencies are the narrowest, and a great deal of the political activity of those agencies is directed at placing their issues onto the agendas of other institutions. As an institution broadens in scope, the range of its agenda concerns also broadens, and those interested in any particular issue will have to fight to have it placed on a legislative or executive agenda. This is especially true of the conversion of *new problems* into active issues. Some older and more familiar issues will generally find a ready place on institutional agendas. Some older issues are *cyclical issues*: A new budget must be adopted each year, for example, and many other public programs are designed to include periodic reviews. There is a quadrennial defense review for national security policy.[15] Other, older agenda items may be *recurrent issues,* indicating primarily the failure of previous policy choices to produce the intended or desired impact on society. Even recurrent issues may not be returned easily to institutional agendas when existing programs are perceived to be "good enough," or when no new solutions are readily available. Indeed, the beneficiaries of a program may work hard to keep it off an active agenda, lest new legislation upset the existing policy.[16]

Jack Walker classes problems coming on the agenda in four groups.[17] Walker defines issues that are dealt with time and time again as either "periodically recurring" or "sporadically recurring" issues (similar to our cyclical and recurrent issues). He also examines the role of crises in placing issues on the agenda, as well as the difficulties of having new or "chosen" problems selected for inclusion on agendas. Within each institution, those interested in an issue must use their political power and skills to gain access to the agenda. The failure to be included on any one institutional agenda may be the end of an issue, at least for the time being.

Finally, we should note that these recurring issues also constitute an opportunity to open other issues that might otherwise not be so easy to address. For example, the return of the need to authorize increases in the public debt in 2011 gave conservatives in Congress an opportunity to force reductions in spending on social policy and domestic discretionary spending.[18]

Who Sets Agendas?

Establishing an agenda for society, or even for one institution, is a manifestly political activity, and control of the agenda gives substantial control over the ultimate policy choices. Therefore, to understand how agendas are determined requires some understanding of the manner in which political power is exercised in the United States. The idea of a punctuated equilibrium may be a good description of the process of change, but it does not explain how the punctuations come about. The most important answer to that question is that political power is used to alter the agenda.[19] As might be imagined, there are a number of different conceptualizations of just how power is exercised. To enable us to understand the dynamics of agenda setting better, I will discuss three important theoretical approaches to the exercise of political power and the formation of policy agendas: *pluralist, elitist,* and *state-centric.*

Pluralist Approaches

The dominant, though far from undisputed, approach to policymaking in the United States is pluralism.[20] Stated briefly, the pluralist approach assumes that policymaking in government is divided into a number of separate arenas and that the interests and individuals who have power in one arena do not necessarily have power in others. The American Medical Association, for example, may have a great deal of influence over health care legislation but little influence over education or defense policy. Furthermore, interests that are victorious at one time or in one arena will not necessarily win at another time or place. The pluralist approach to policymaking assumes that there is something of a marketplace in policies, with a number of interests competing for power and influence, even within a single arena. The competitors are conceived as interest groups competing for access to institutions for decision making and for the attention of central actors in the hope of producing their desired outcomes. The groups are assumed, much as in the market model of the economy, to be relatively equal in power, so that on any one issue any interest might be victorious. Finally, the actors involved in the political process generally agree on the rules of the game, especially the rule that elections are the principal means of determining policy. The principal function of government is to serve as an umpire in this struggle among competing group interests and to enforce the victories through public law.

The pluralist approach to agenda setting would lead the observer to expect a relatively open marketplace of ideas for new policies. Any or all interested groups, as a whole or within a particular public institution, should have the opportunity to influence the agenda. These interest groups may not win every time, but neither will they systematically be excluded from decisions, and the agendas will be amenable to adding new items as sufficient political mobilization occurs. This style of agenda setting may be particularly appropriate for the United States, given the multiple institutions and multiple points of access in the structure of the system.[21] Even if an issue is blocked politically, the courts can enable otherwise-disadvantaged groups to bring it into the policy process, as happened with civil rights and with some aspects of sexual harassment.

Elitist Approaches

The elitist approach to American policymaking seeks to contradict the dominant pluralist approach. It assumes the existence of a power elite that dominates public decision making and whose interests are served in the policymaking process. In the elitist analysis, the same interests in society consistently win, and they are primarily those of business, the upper and middle classes, and whites.[22] Analysts from an elitist perspective have pointed out that to produce the kind of equality assumed in the pluralist model would require relatively equal levels of organization by all interests in society. They then point out that relatively few interests of working- and lower-class individuals are effectively organized; compared to many of its European counterparts, American labor is not particularly well organized or powerful. Although all individuals in a democracy certainly have the right to organize, elitist theorists point to the relative lack of resources (e.g., time, money, organizational ability, and communication skills) among members of the lower economic classes.[23] Thus, political organization for many poorer people, if it exists at all, may imply only token participation, and their voices will be drowned in the sea of middle-class voices described by E. E. Schattschneider.[24] The claims of elitism have been reinforced in 2011 and 2012 by increasing awareness of the economic and political power of the richest 1 percent of the American population.[25]

The implications of the elitist approach are rather obvious. If agenda formulation is crucial to the process of policymaking, then the ability of elites to keep certain issues off the agenda is crucial to their power. Adherents of this approach believe that the agenda in most democratic countries represents not the competitive struggle of relatively equal groups, as argued by the pluralist model, but the systematic use of elite power to decide which issues the political system will or will not consider. Jürgen Habermas, for example, argues that the elite uses its power systematically to exclude issues that would threaten its interests and that those "suppressed issues" represent a major threat to democracy.[26] If too many significant issues are kept off the agenda, the legitimacy of the political system can be threatened, along with its survival in the most extreme cases.

Peter Bachrach and Morton Baratz's concept of "nondecisions" is important here. Bachrach and Baratz define a *nondecision* as a decision that results in the suppression or thwarting of a latent or manifest challenge to the values or interests of the decision maker. More explicitly, nondecision making is a means by which demands for change in the existing allocation of benefits and privileges in the community can be suffocated before they are even voiced, or kept covert, or killed off before they gain access to the relevant decision-making arena—or failing all else, maimed or destroyed in the decision-implementing stage of the policy process.[27] A decision not to alter the status quo is a decision, whether it is made overtly through the policymaking process or is the result of the application of power to prevent the issue from ever being discussed.

These issues may not remain suppressed forever, even in the face of powerful economic and political elites. For example, large-scale discontent with the banking industry and business in general has placed on the agenda a number of issues that might have been unthinkable previously. These responses to economic crises have included placing caps on the salaries and bonuses of individuals in the private sector.

State-Centric Approaches

Both the pluralist and elitist approaches to policymaking and agenda setting assume that the major source of policy ideas is in the environment of the policymakers—primarily interest groups or other powerful interests in the society. It is, however, quite possible that the political system itself is responsible for its own agenda.[28] In a state-centric analysis, the environment is not filled with pressure groups but with "pressured groups" activated by government. As governments become more interested in managing the media and in influencing public opinion, the state-centric view may be more viable.[29]

The state-centered concept of agenda setting conforms quite well to the "iron triangle" conception of American government but would place the bureaucratic agency or the congressional committee, not the pressure group, in the center of the policy process.[30] This approach does emphasize the role of specialized elites within government but, unlike elitist theory, does not assume that the elites are pursuing policies for their own personal gain. Certainly, their organizations may obtain larger budgets and greater prestige from the addition of new programs, but the individual administrators have little or no opportunity to appropriate any of that budgetary increase.

In addition, the state-centric approach places the major locus of competition over agenda setting within government itself, rather than in the constellation of interests in society. Agencies must compete for legislative time and for budgets; committees must compete for attention for their particular legislative concerns; and individual Congress members must compete for consideration of their own bills and their own constituency concerns. These actors within government are more relevant in pushing agenda items than are interests in the society. This competition may be not only about getting an issue on the agenda but also about framing it in a particular manner that will advantage one agency or another.

One interesting question arises about agenda setting in the state-centric approach: What are the relative powers of bureaucratic and legislative actors in setting the agenda? An early study by the Advisory Commission on Intergovernmental Relations argued that the source of the continued expansion of the federal government was within Congress.[31] The authors of that study argued that Congress members, acting out of a desire to be reelected or from a sincere interest in solving certain policy problems, have been the major source of new items on the federal agenda. The behavior of Congress in the early twenty-first century would seem to support that contention, given the number of programs initiated by Congress, even when the legislative branch presumably was dominated by conservatives from 2000 to 2006.[32] Other analyses have placed the source of most new policy ideas in the bureaucracy as much as, or more than, in Congress.[33] Also, the nature of American government requires that the president and Congress work together to set agendas and make policy, and presidents may have as much to do with the expansion of the public sector as does Congress.[34] Because the chain of events leading to new policies is complex, it may be difficult to determine exactly where ideas originated, but there is (at least in this model) no shortage of policy advocates.[35]

The agenda resulting from a state-centric process might be more conservative than one resulting from a pluralist process but less conservative than one from the elitist model. Government actors may be constrained in the amount of change they can advocate on their own initiative; they may have to wait for a time when their ideas will be acceptable to the general public. Members of Congress can adopt a crusading stance, but that is a choice usually denied to the typical bureaucratic agency. Except in rare instances—efforts by the surgeon general and the Food and Drug Administration to reduce cigarette smoking, perhaps—a government-sponsored agency may be ahead of public opinion but only slightly so.

When we consider a state-centric approach in the United States, we must also remember that state and local governments are often far ahead of the federal government in addressing issues. Historically, that was the case for issues such as Social Security and environmental regulation, and it is true at present for a number of more inclusive programs of health care. At least a dozen states have investigated implementing broader programs to address the health care needs of their citizens. For example, in 2006, Massachusetts enacted a health care reform law that mandated health insurance for all its residents and provided subsidies for those who could not afford to purchase it. State innovations like this one helped pave the way for the emergence of health care reform as a major point on President Obama's agenda (see chapter 11).[36]

Which approach to policymaking and agenda formation is most descriptive of the process in the United States? The answer is probably all of them, for the proponents of each can muster a great deal of evidence for their position. More important, one approach rather than another might better describe policymaking for particular kinds of problems and issues. For example, we would expect policies that are very much the concern of government itself (e.g., civil service laws or perhaps even foreign affairs) to be more heavily influenced by state-centric policymaking than other kinds of issues. Certain kinds of problems that directly affect powerful economic interests would be best understood through elite analysis. Energy policy and its relationship to the major oil companies might fit into that category. Finally, policy areas with a great deal of interest group activity and relatively high levels of group involvement by both clients and producers—education is a good example—might be best understood through the pluralist approach. Unfortunately, these categorizations are largely speculative, for political scientists have only begun to produce the kind of detailed analysis required to track issues as they move on and off agendas.[37]

From Problem to Issue: How to Get Problems on the Agenda

Problems do not move themselves on and off agendas. Nevertheless, a number of their characteristics can affect their chances of becoming a part of an active, systemic, or institutional agenda. We should remember, however, that most problems do not come with these characteristics clearly visible to most citizens or even to most political actors. Agendas must be constructed and the issues defined by a social and political process in a manner that will make them most amenable to political action.[38] Furthermore, it usually requires an active policy entrepreneur to do the political packaging that can make an issue appear on an agenda.[39]

The Effects of the Problem

The first aspect of a problem that can influence its placement on an agenda is whom it affects and to what extent. We can think about the extremity, concentration, range, and visibility of problems as influencing their placement on agendas. The more extreme the effects of a problem, the more likely it is to be placed on an agenda. An outbreak of a disease causing mild discomfort, for example, is unlikely to produce public action, but the possibility of an epidemic, life-threatening disease, such as AIDS, usually provokes some kind of public action. This is especially true for a disease such as avian flu, which unlike AIDS, tends not to have any stigma associated with it and which may be especially deadly for the elderly and the very young.[40] Although less extreme, the rapidly increasing prices for gasoline in 2008 produced a number of reactions from the public sector.

Even if a problem is not life threatening, a concentration of victims in one area may produce public action. The unemployment of an additional 50,000 workers, while certainly deplorable, might not cause major public intervention if the workers were scattered around the country, but it might well do so if the workers were concentrated in one geographical area. Most industries in the United States are concentrated geographically (automobiles in Michigan, aerospace in California and Washington, oil in Texas and Louisiana), and that makes it easier for advocates of assistance to any troubled industry to get the help they want from government. Even conservatives, who tend to oppose government intervention in the economy, usually appear happy to assist failing industries when it is clear that there will be major regional effects.

The range of persons affected by a problem may also influence the placement of an issue on an agenda. In general, the more people affected or potentially affected by a problem, the greater is the probability that it will be placed on the agenda. There are limits, however. A problem may be so general that no single individual believes that he or she has anything to gain by organizing political action to address it. An issue that has broad but only minor effects therefore may have less chance of being placed on the agenda than a problem that affects fewer people but affects them more severely.

The intensity of effects, and therefore of the policy preferences of citizens, is a major problem for those who take the pluralist approach to agenda setting.[41] Many real or potential interests in society are not effectively organized because few individuals believe that they have enough to gain from establishing or joining an organization. For example, although every citizen is a consumer, few effective consumer organizations have been established, whereas producer groups are numerous and are effective politically. The specificity and intensity of producer interests, as contrasted to the diffuseness of consumer interests, creates a serious imbalance in the pattern of interest group organization that favors producers. An analogous situation would be the relative ineffectiveness of taxpayers' organizations compared with organizations of clientele groups, such as defense industries and farmers, that are interested in greater federal spending. The organizational imbalance against consumers and taxpayers has been mitigated somewhat since the 1980s but still exists. The apparent increase in the power of lobbyists over the past decade contributes to the continuing imbalance in favor of producer interests.[42]

Finally, the visibility of a problem may affect its placement on an agenda as an active issue. This might be called "mountain climber syndrome." Society appears willing to spend almost any amount of money to rescue a single stranded mountain climber but will not spend the same amount of money to save many more lives by, for example, controlling automobile accidents or vaccinating children. Statistical lives are not nearly so visible and comprehensible as an identifiable individual stuck on the side of a mountain. Similarly, the risks of nuclear power plants have been highly dramatized in the media, while less visibly an average of 150 men die each year in mining accidents, and many others die from black lung disease contracted in coal mines. The existing environmental effects of burning coal, although certainly recognized and important, appear to pale in the public mind when compared to the possible effects of a nuclear accident. The Fukushima accident in Japan may have only reinforced this calculus of risk in the popular mind.

Analogous and Spillover Agenda Setting

Another important aspect of a problem that can affect its being placed on an agenda is the presence of an analogy to other public programs. The more a new issue can be made to look like an old issue, the more likely it is to be placed on the agenda. This is especially true in the United States because of the traditional reluctance of American government to expand the public sector, at least by conscious choice. For example, the federal government's intervention into medical care financing for individuals with Medicare and Medicaid was dangerously close to the then-feared "socialized medicine."[43] It was made more palatable, at least in the case of Medicare, by making the program appear similar to Social Security, which was already highly legitimate. The administration of George W. Bush continued this pattern by making a program to support drug costs for the elderly a part of Medicare and using many existing private insurers, such as Blue Cross, to administer the plans.[44] If a new agenda item can be made to appear as only an incremental departure from existing policies, rather than an entirely new venture, its chances of being accepted are much improved.

Also, the existence of one government program may produce the need for additional programs. This spillover effect is important in bringing new programs onto the agenda and in explaining the expansion of the public sector. Even the best policy analysts in the world cannot anticipate the consequences of all the policy choices the government makes. Thus, the adoption of one program may soon lead to the adoption of other programs directed at "solving" the problems created by the first program.[45] For example, the federal government's interstate highway program was designed to improve transportation and to serve domestic defense purposes. One effect of building superhighways, however, has been to make it easier for people to live in the suburbs and work in the city. Consequently, the roads assisted in the flight to the suburbs of those who could afford to move. This, in turn, contributed to the decline of central cities, which created a need for the federal government to pour billions of dollars into urban renewal, Urban Development Action Grants, and a host of other programs for the cities. Although the inner cities would probably have declined somewhat without the federal highway program, the program certainly accelerated the process.

Policies in modern societies are now tightly interconnected, and they may have so many secondary and tertiary effects on other programs that any new policy intervention is likely to have results that spread like ripples in a clear lake. To some degree, the analyst should anticipate those effects and design programs to avoid negative interaction effects, but he or she can never be perfectly successful in doing so. Tax policies in particular tend to spawn unanticipated responses, as individuals and corporations seek creative ways of legally avoiding paying taxes and the Internal Revenue Service tries to close unanticipated loopholes.[46] As a consequence, "policy is its own cause," and one policy choice may beget others.[47]

Relationship to Symbols

The more closely a problem can be linked to important national symbols, the greater is its probability of being placed on the agenda. Mundane programs may thus be wrapped up in rhetoric about freedom, justice, and traditional American values. Conversely, a problem will not be placed on the agenda if it is associated primarily with negative values. There are, of course, some exceptions: Although the gay community is not a positive symbol for many Americans, the AIDS issue was placed on the agenda with relative alacrity, even before its spread among other sectors of the population.[48]

There are several interesting examples of the use of positive symbols to market programs and issues that might not otherwise have been accepted on the agenda. Although American government has generally been rather slow to adopt social programs, those associated with children and their families have been more favorably regarded. Therefore, if someone wants to initiate a social welfare program, it is well to associate it with children, or, possibly with the elderly. It is perhaps no accident that the basic welfare program in the United States was long known as Aid to Families with Dependent Children. The reforms of the AFDC program used first "families" (Temporary Assistance to Needy Families, or TANF) and then "opportunity" (Personal Responsibility and Work Opportunity Reconciliation Act)—perhaps equally powerful symbols—to justify change. The 1994 crime bill contained a variety of social programs (the famous "midnight basketball" provisions) that might not even have made it to a vote if they were not attached to the symbolic issue of crime control.

Symbol manipulation is an extremely important skill for policy analysts. For example, creation of the label "death tax" for the inheritance tax had no small effect on the attempts at repeal in 2001. The symbolism helped to obscure the extremely regressive nature of the change in tax policy.[49] In addition to being rational calculators of the costs and benefits of programs, analysts must be capable of relating programs and program goals to other programs, of elucidating the importance of the problem, and of justifying the program to actors who may be less committed to it and its goals. Placing a problem on the agenda of government means convincing powerful individuals that they should make the effort necessary to rectify it. The use of symbols may facilitate that process when the problem itself is not likely to gain wide public attention.

The Absence of Private Means

In general, governments avoid accepting new responsibilities, especially in the United States, with its laissez-faire tradition, and especially in a climate of budgetary scarcity (even when a balanced budget has been attained). The market, rather than collective action, has become the standard against which to compare good policy.[50] There are, however, problems in society that cannot be solved by private market activities alone. Two classic examples are social problems that involve either public goods or externalities.

Public goods are goods or services that, once produced, are consumed by a relatively large number of individuals and whose consumption is difficult or impossible to control—they are not "excludable." This means that it is difficult or impossible for any individual or firm to produce public goods, for they cannot be effectively priced and sold.[51] If national defense were produced by paid mercenaries, rather than by government, individual citizens would have little or no incentive to pay the group of fighters because citizens would be protected whether they paid or not. Indeed, citizens would have every incentive to be "free riders"—to enjoy the benefits of the service without paying the cost. Government has a remedy for such a situation: It can force citizens to pay for the service through its power of taxation.

Externalities are said to exist when the activities of one economic unit affect the well-being of another and no compensation is paid for benefits or costs created externally.[52] Pollution is a classic case: It is a by-product of the production process, but its social costs are excluded from the selling price of the products the manufacturer makes. Thus, social costs and production costs diverge, and government may have to impose regulations to prevent the private firm from imposing the costs of pollution—such as damage to health, property, and amenities—on the public. Alternatively, government may develop some means of pricing the effects of pollution and imposing those costs on the polluter.[53]

All externalities need not be negative. Some activities create public benefits that are not included in the revenues of those producing them. If a dam is built to generate hydroelectric power, the recreational, flood control, and economic development benefits cannot be included as part of the revenues of a private utility, although government can include those benefits in its calculations when considering undertaking such a project with public money (see chapter 17). Thus, some projects that appear infeasible for the private sector may be feasible for government, even on strict economic criteria.

Public goods and externalities are two useful categories for consideration, but they do not exhaust the kinds of social and economic problems that have a peculiarly public nature.[54] Of course, issues of rights and the application of law are considered peculiarly public. In addition, programs that involve a great deal of risk may require the socialization of that risk through the public sector. For example, lending to college students who have little credit record is backed by government as a means of making banks more willing to take the risk. These loans illustrate the general principle that the inability of other institutions in society to produce effective and equitable solutions may be sufficient to place an issue on the public agenda.

The Availability of Technology

Finally, a problem generally will not be placed on the public agenda unless there is a technology believed to be able to solve it. For most of the history of the industrialized nations, people assumed that economic fluctuations were, like the weather, acts of God. Then, the Keynesian revolution in economics produced what seemed to be the answer to those fluctuations, and governments soon placed economic management in a central position on their agendas. In the United States, this new technology was reflected in the Employment Act of 1946, pledging the U.S. government to maintain full employment. The promise of fine-tuning the economy through Keynesian means, which appeared possible in the 1960s, has since become increasingly elusive. The issue of economic management, however, remains central to the public agenda, with politicians being evaluated very much on the economy's performance (see chapter 9). Subsequent governments have provided new technologies (e.g., *supply-side economics* during the Reagan years), but they have not been able to evade responsibility for the economy. Much of the debate in the primary campaign in 2012 has assumed, however, that the best technology for government to support for economic growth is to do little or nothing.

Another way of considering the role of technology in agenda setting is the "garbage can model" of decision making, in which solutions find problems, rather than vice versa.[55] A problem may be excluded from the agenda simply because of the lack of an instrument to do the job, and the example of economic management points to the dangers of the lack of an available instrument. If government announces that it is attempting to solve a problem and then fails miserably, public confidence in the effectiveness of government will be shaken. Government must then take the blame for failures along with the credit for successes. The garbage can model also illustrates the relationship between agenda setting and policy formulation because an issue is not accepted as a part of the agenda unless it is known that a policy has been formulated, or is ready on the shelf, to solve the problem. Solutions may beg for new problems, like a child with a hammer finding things that need hammering, and organizations that have a particular technology will attempt to use that technology to advance their own position in the political process.[56]

As with all portions of the policymaking process, agenda setting is an intensely political activity. Indeed, it may well be the most political aspect of policymaking because it involves bringing to the public consciousness an acceptance of a vague social problem as something government can, and should, attempt to solve. It may be quite easy for powerful actors who wish to do so to exclude unfamiliar issues from the agenda, making active political mobilization of the less powerful necessary for success. Rational policy analysis may play only a small role in setting the agenda for discussion; such analysis will be useful primarily after it is agreed that there is a problem and that the problem is public in nature. In agenda setting, the policy analyst is less a technician and more a politician, understanding the policymaking process and seeking to influence that process toward a desired end.[57] That involves the manipulation of symbols and the definition of often vague social problems. Nevertheless, agenda setting should not be dismissed as simply political maneuvering; it is the crucial first step on the road to resolving any identified problem.

Policy Formulation

After the political system has accepted a problem as part of the agenda for policymaking, the logical question is what should be done about it. We call this stage of the process *policy formulation,* meaning the development of the mechanisms for solving the public problem. At this point, a policy analyst can begin to apply analytic techniques to attempt to justify one policy choice as superior to others. Economics and decision theory are both useful in assessing the risks of particular outcomes or in predicting likely social costs and benefits of various alternatives. Rational choice, however, need not be dominant; the habits, traditions, and standard operating procedures of government may prevail over rational activity in making the policy choice. But even such seemingly irrational sets of choice factors may be, in their way, quite rational: The actors involved have experience with the "formula" to be used, are comfortable with it, and consequently can begin to make it work much more readily than they could a newer instrument in which they may have no confidence, even if that instrument is technically superior.

The Clinton administration's formulation of its health care reform proposal demonstrates some of the pitfalls of rationalistic and expert policy formulation. Although the proposal may have been excellent technically, it simply did not correspond to the familiar political and administrative patterns of the United States. Likewise, the attempts of George W. Bush to privatize Social Security may have made sense to (some) economists but did not to citizens who were committed to the existing program. In a more general sense, the rationalistic appearance of the Obama administration's response to the economic crisis has been politically damaging to the administration.

The federal government has followed several basic formulas in attempting to solve public problems. In economic affairs, for example, the United States has relied on regulation more than on government ownership of business, which has been more common in Europe. In social policy, the standard formulas have been social insurance and the use of cash transfer programs rather than direct delivery of services. The major exception to the latter formula has been the reliance on education as a means of rectifying social and economic inequality. And finally, there has existed a formula of involving the private sector as much as possible in public sector activity through grants, contracts, and use of federal money as leverage for raising money from private sources and from state and local governments.

We should not be too quick to criticize the federal government for its lack of innovation in dealing with public problems. Most governments do not use all the tools available to them.[58] Also, there is very little theory to guide government policymakers trying to decide what tools they should use.[59] In particular, there is very little theory or practical advice that links the nature of public problems with the most appropriate ways of solving them. As a consequence, a great deal of policy formulation is done by inertia, by analogy, or by intuition.

Who Formulates Policy?

Policy formulation is a difficult game because any number of people can and do play; there are few rules. At one time or another, almost every kind of policy actor will be involved in formulating policy proposals, although several kinds of actors are especially important. Policy formulation is also very much a political activity but not always a partisan activity. Political parties and candidates, in fact, are not as good at promulgating solutions to problems as they are at identifying problems and presenting lofty ambitions for society to solve them. Expertise begins to play a large role here because the success or failure of a policy instrument will depend to some degree on its technical characteristics, as well as on its political acceptability.

The public bureaucracy.   The public bureaucracy is the institution most involved in taking the lofty aspirations of political leaders and translating them into concrete proposals. Whether one accepts the state-centric model of agenda setting or not, one must realize that government bureaucracies are central to policy formulation. Even if programs are formally introduced by Congress members or the president, it is quite possible that their original formulation and justification came from a friendly bureau.

Bureaucracies presumably are the masters of routine and procedure. The commitment to procedures is at once their strength and their weakness. They know how to use procedures and how to develop programs and procedures to reach desired goals. Yet an agency that knows how to do these things too well may develop an excessively narrow vision of how to formulate answers for a particular set of problems. As noted earlier, certain formulas have been developed at the governmental level for responding to problems, and much the same is true of individual organizations that have standard operating procedures and thick rule books. Many of the administrative reforms undertaken during the 1990s sought to jog bureaucracies from those established routines, but old habits are difficult to break, and organizations often reverted to their old ways of doing business after the pressure of the reformers had been removed. Of course, some commitment to established programs and approaches may not be all bad, as it may complicate the task of reformers who want to embark on untried programs.[60]

Certainly, familiarity with an established mechanism can explain some of the conservatism of organizations in the choice of instruments to achieve their ends, and faith in the efficacy of the instrument also helps explain reliance on a limited range of policy tools. One important component of the restrictiveness of choice, however, appears to be self-protection. That is, neither administrators nor their agencies can go very wrong by selecting a solution that is only an incremental departure from an existing program. This is true for two reasons: (1) such a choice will not have as high a probability of failure as a more innovative program, and (2) an incremental choice will almost certainly keep the program in the hands of the existing agency. Hence, reliance on bureaucracy to formulate solutions may be a guarantee of stability, but it is unlikely to produce many successful policy innovations.

Also, agencies will usually choose to do *something* when given the opportunity or the challenge to do so. Making policy choices is their business, and it is certainly in their organizational self-interest to respond to a problem. The agency personnel know that if they do not respond, some other agency soon will, and their agency will lose an opportunity to increase its budget, personnel, and clout. Agencies do not always act in the self-aggrandizing manner ascribed to them,[61] but when confronted directly with a problem already declared to need solving, they will usually respond with a solution—one that involves their own participation.

There is one final consideration about bureaucratic responses to policy problems: An agency often represents a concentration of a certain type of expertise. Increasingly, this expertise is professional, and a growing percentage of the employees of the federal government have professional qualifications.[62] In addition to helping an agency formulate better solutions to policy problems, expertise narrows the vision of the agency and the range of solutions that may be considered. Professional training tends to be narrowing rather than broadening, and it tends to teach that the profession possesses *the* solution to a range of problems. Thus, with a concentration of professionals of a certain type, an agency will tend to produce only incremental departures from existing policies. For example, although both the Federal Trade Commission and the Antitrust Division of the Department of Justice are concerned with eliminating monopolistic practices in the economy, the concentration of economists in the former and lawyers in the latter may generate different priorities.[63]

The occupation of public manager itself is becoming more professionalized, so the major reference group for public managers will be other public managers, a factor that may further narrow the range of bureaucratic responses to policy problems. Much of the drive of the new public management,[64] however, has been to empower public managers to make more of their own decisions and to be more significant forces in implementing, if perhaps not making, public policy. Thus, senior bureaucrats may be expected to employ their professional expertise and that of their colleagues to develop new programs and strategies in addition to simply making programs perform well.

Think tanks and shadow cabinets.   Other sources of policy formulation are the think tanks that pervade Washington and state capitals around the country.[65] These are organizations of professional analysts and policy formulators who usually work on contract for a client in government, often an agency in the bureaucracy. We would expect much greater creativity and innovation from these organizations than from the public bureaucracy, but other problems arise in the types of policy options they propose. First, an agency may be able virtually to guarantee the kind of answer it will receive by choosing a certain think tank. Some organizations are more conservative and will usually formulate solutions relying more on incentives and the private sector, whereas other consultants may recommend more direct government intervention. Their reports are likely to have substantial impact, not only because they have been labeled as expert but also because they have been paid for and therefore should be used.

Another problem that arises is more a problem for the consultants in think tanks than for the agencies, but it certainly affects the quality of the policies they recommend. If the think tank is to get additional business from an agency, the consultants believe—perhaps rightly—that they have to tell the agency what it wants to hear. In other words, a consulting firm that says that the favorite approach of an agency is entirely wrong and needs to be completely revamped may be both technically correct and politically bankrupt. A problem of ethical judgment hence arises for the consulting firm, as it might for individual analysts working for an organization: What are the boundaries of loyalty to truth and loyalty to the organization?

Three particular think tanks have been of special importance in U.S. policy formulation. Traditionally, the two dominant organizations were the Brookings Institution and the American Enterprise Institute (AEI). During the Republican Nixon, Ford, and Reagan administrations, the Brookings Institution was often described as "the Democratic party in exile." The Clinton administration tapped a number of Brookings staff members for appointments, and Barack Obama followed a similar strategy, appointing former Brookings fellows Susan E. Rice as ambassador to the United Nations and Peter Orszag as director of the Office of Management and Budget. On the other side of the fence, the AEI has been the home of moderate Republican officials, although relatively few were tapped by the more conservative George W. Bush administration. Both of these think tanks support wide-reaching publication programs to attempt to influence elite public opinion, in addition to their direct involvement in government.

The third major think tank is the Heritage Foundation, which came to prominence during the Reagan years as an advocate of a number of neoconservative policy positions, especially privatization and deregulation.[66] It was less prominent in the George H. W. Bush administration than it had been during the Reagan years, but it was extremely prominent during the administration of George W. Bush, with its proposals central to policy formulation in some fields. The number of think tanks on the political right has been increasing, funded largely by industry and wealthy individuals. Prominent among them are the Cato Institute, Citizens for Tax Justice, and the National Center for Policy Analysis. There also has been some resurgence of think tanks on the political left, such as the Center for Budget Priorities. Perhaps most important, these developments demonstrate the continuing polarization of political ideas in the United States.

Universities also serve as think tanks for government, especially the growing number of public policy schools and programs across the country that, in addition to training future practitioners of the art of government, provide a place where scholars and former practitioners can formulate new solutions to problems. Robert Reich, for example, developed some of the ideas he later attempted to implement as secretary of labor while at the Kennedy School of Government at Harvard.[67] In addition to the policy programs, specialized institutes, such as the Institute for Research on Poverty, at the University of Wisconsin, and the Joint Center on Urban Studies, at Harvard and MIT, develop policy ideas in their specific policy areas.

It is sometimes difficult to determine where think tanks end and interest groups and lobbying organizations begin. The term *think tank* has a more positive connotation than does *interest group,* so lobbying groups have gone to some lengths to appear as if they were doing objective public policy research. If we go to the Internet and begin to look at the range of opinions that appear on any issue, we can find a number of "institutes," "centers," or "foundations" that are attempting to influence opinion; a careful analysis will reveal that these are really subsidiaries of interest groups.[68]

Interest groups.   Another important source of policy formulation is interest groups, which must not only identify problems and apply pressure to have them placed on the agenda but also supply possible remedies. Those cures will almost certainly serve the interests of their group members, but that is only to be expected. It is the task of the authoritative decision makers to take those ideas about policy choices with as many grains of salt as necessary to develop workable plans for solving the problem. Given the continued existence of iron triangle relationships in many policy areas, a close connection is likely to exist between the policy formulation ideas of an agency and those of the pressure group. The policy choices that established pressure groups advocate will again be rather conservative and incremental; such groups rarely produce sweeping changes from the status quo in which they and their associated agency have a decided interest.

The public interest groups, such as Common Cause, the Center for the Public Interest, and a variety of consumer and taxpayer organizations, contradict the traditional model of policy formulation by interest groups. Perhaps the major task of these organizations is to break the stranglehold that the iron triangles have on policy and attempt to broaden the range of interests represented in the policymaking process. These groups are oriented toward reform. Some of the issues they have taken up are substantive, such as the strengthening of safety requirements for a variety of products sold in the marketplace. Other issues are procedural, such as campaign reform and opening the regulatory process to greater public input. In general, however, no matter what issue they decide to interest themselves in, these groups advocate sweeping reforms as opposed to incremental changes, and they are important in providing balance to the policy process, as well as providing a strong voice for reform and change.

Members of Congress.   Finally, although we have previously tended to denigrate the role of politicians in formulating policy, a number of Congress members do involve themselves in serious formulation activities instead of just accepting advice from friendly sources in the bureaucracy.[69] Like the public interest groups, these senators and representatives are generally interested in reform, for if they were primarily interested only in incremental change, there would be little need for their involvement. Some are also interested in using formulation and advocacy as means of furthering their careers, adopting roles as national policymakers as opposed to the more common pattern of emphasizing constituency service.

Congress as an institution in the early twenty-first century is better equipped to formulate policy than it has ever been, even considering the policy challenges it faces. There has been a continuing growth in the size of congressional staffs, both the personal staffs of representatives and senators and the staffs of committees and subcommittees.[70] For example, in 1965 Congress employed just over 9,000 people; by 2000, the number had increased to over 31,000, and the number continues to increase slowly. These employees are on the public payroll at least in part to assist members of Congress in doing the research and drafting necessary for active policy formulation, and they are important in rectifying what some consider a serious imbalance between the power of Congress and that of the executive branch. For example, the Congressional Budget Office now shadows the Office of Management and Budget, providing an independent source of advice on budgeting and a range of other issues. The contemporary deadlock within Congress has tended to lessen the opportunities for congressional legislative action, but some policy entrepreneurs do remain.[71]

How to Formulate Policy

The task of formulating policy involves substantial sensitivity to the nuances of policy (and politics) and a potential for the creative application of the tools of policy analysis. In fact, many of the problems that the government faces require substantial creativity because little is known about the problem areas. Nevertheless, governments may have to react to a problem whether or not they are sure of the best, or even a good, course of action. In many instances, the routine responses of a government agency to its environment will be sufficient to meet the problems that arise, but if the routine response is unsuccessful, the agency will have to search for a more innovative response and perhaps involve more actors in policy formulation. In other words, a routine or incremental response may be sufficient for most policy problems, but if it is not, the policymaking system must look for something else. Making policy choices that depart radically from incremental responses requires methods of identifying and choosing among alternatives.

Two major barriers may block government's ability to understand the problems it confronts. One is the lack of some basic facts about the policy questions at hand. The most obvious example is defense policy, in which governments often lack information about the capabilities and intentions of the opposing side. Indeed, since the end of the Cold War, it has become difficult even to identify the potential enemies, much less anticipate their actions. Similarly, in assessing risks from various toxic substances or nuclear power plants, there may not be sufficient empirical evidence to determine the probabilities of undesirable events occurring or their probable consequences.[72] Even more difficult for government is that frequently there are no agreed-on indicators of the nature of social conditions, and even widely accepted indicators for economic variables, such as gross national product and unemployment rates, are somewhat suspect.[73]

Perhaps more important, government decision makers often lack adequate information about the underlying processes that have created the problems they are attempting to solve. For example, to address the poverty problem, one should understand how poverty comes about and how it is perpetuated. But despite the masses of data and information that have been generated, there is no accepted model of causation for poverty. This lack of a causal model may be contrasted with decisions about epidemic diseases made by public health agencies using well-developed and accepted theories about how diseases occur and spread. Clearly, different decision-making procedures should be used to attempt to solve different kinds of problems.

Figure 4.1 demonstrates possible combinations of knowledge of causation and basic facts about policy problems. The simplest type of policymaking involves *routine* policy, such as Social Security. Making policy in such areas, with adequate information and an accepted theory of causation, primarily requires

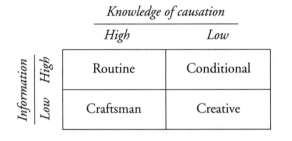

FIGURE 4.1   Kinds of Policy Formulation

routine adjustment of existing policies, and for the most part the changes made will be incremental.[74] This relative simplicity would be complicated if fundamental theories about creating a desirable retirement situation or the mechanism for financing such a system were seriously altered (see chapter 12).

Creative policy formulation lies at the other extreme of information and knowledge held by decision makers. In this instance, they have neither an adequate information base nor an adequate theory of causation. Research and development operations, such as those in the National Institutes of Health or in numerous agencies within the Department of Defense, provide important examples of policy formulation of this type.[75] Another example may be the formulation of policies for personal social services, such as counseling. In these instances, a great deal of creativity and care must be exercised in matching the particular needs of the individual with the needs of the agency for efficient management and accountability. Such policies require building in reversibility of policy choices, so that creative formulations that prove unworkable can be corrected.

In some situations, there may be sufficient information but an inadequate understanding of the underlying processes of causation. These policymaking situations require the formulation of *conditional* policies, in which changes in certain indicators trigger a policy response of some sort, even if only the reconsideration of the existing policy. It is possible that government can know that certain policies will produce desired results, even if the underlying processes are not fully understood. Following the general loss of faith in Keynesian theories of economic management, it may be that macroeconomic policy is made in this manner. There are several accepted indicators of the state of the economy—unemployment, inflation, and economic growth rates, for example—and changes in these indicators may trigger relatively standard reactions, even if the policymakers cannot always specify, or agree on, their underlying logic.[76] It is also generally advantageous to build a certain amount of automaticity into the policy response, or at least to provide some insulation against political delay or interference. In economic management, for example, countries with relatively independent central banks have been more successful than those with more politicized central banks, although most central banks have become more politicized after the beginning of the economic downturn in 2008.[77]

Finally, in some policy areas, governments may have a model of causation for the problem but lack sufficient information to be confident in any policy response they may formulate. Defense policies may fit this category of *craftsman* policies, for governments appear to understand quite well how to respond to threats and how to go to war, although they frequently have only limited, and possibly distorted, information about the capabilities and intentions of their adversaries. Formulating policies of this type depends on developing a number of contingencies and potential forms of response, as well as identifying means of assessing the risks of possible occurrences. The complex policy deliberations of the U.S. government concerning the possible nuclear capabilities of North Korea and Iraq illustrate the "craftsman" nature of defense and foreign policy. In other words, formulating such policies involves building a probabilistic basis for response, rather than relying on the certainty that might be taken for granted in other policy areas. The eventual discovery that Iraq did not possess weapons of mass destruction, as the Bush administration believed, demonstrates the potential risks of this approach to policy formulation.

These four categories of policymaking are important, but how a policy is defined is a political issue, and the clever policy formulator will attempt to define problems and issues so that they will fit into one category or another. For example, if a problem lies within an agency's range of action, it will attempt to keep it there by defining it as routine. Any agency or interest group that wants to shift the definition—whether to improve the policy or to increase its budget—will attempt to define it as requiring more of a craftsman or creative solution.

Aids for Policy Formulation

Given the difficulties of formulating effective policy responses to many problems, it is fortunate that some techniques have been developed to assist in the task. In general, these techniques serve to clarify the consequences of certain courses of action and to provide a summary measure of the probable effects of a policy along a single scale of measurement, usually money, so that different policy alternatives can be more effectively compared with one another. I discuss two of these techniques only briefly here, reserving a more detailed exposition and discussion of cost-benefit analysis for chapter 17. It is important, however, to understand at this point in the discussion something about the considerations that one might take into account when selecting a policy alternative.

Cost-benefit analysis.   The most frequently applied tool for policy analysis is cost-benefit analysis. The utilitarian assumptions and methodology underlying this technique reduce all the costs and benefits of proposed government programs to a quantitative, economic dimension and then compare available alternative policies using that standard. In this mode of policy analysis, economic considerations are almost always paramount. As the methodology has been developed, attempts have been made to place economic values on factors that might be primarily noneconomic, but the principal means of evaluating programs remain utilitarian.[78]

Cost-benefit analysis is in some ways deceptively simple. The total benefits created by a project are enumerated, including those that would be regarded as externalities in the private market (amenity values, recreation, and the like). The costs of the program are also enumerated, again including social costs (e.g., pollution or inequalities). Long-term costs and benefits are also taken into account, although they may be discounted or adjusted because they will occur in the future. Projects whose total benefits exceed their total costs are deemed acceptable; then choices can be made among the acceptable projects. The general rule is to adopt the project with the greatest net total benefit for society (total benefits minus total costs) and then all others that fit within the total available budget.

Later, I will discuss some of the more technical problems of cost-benefit analysis. It is important here to talk about some of the ethical underpinnings of the technique, as they have a pronounced effect on the formulation of policy alternatives. The fundamental ethical difficulties arise from the assumptions that all values are reducible to monetary terms and that economic criteria are the most important ones for government when making policy. There may well be some values, such as civil liberties, human life, or the environment, that many citizens would not want reduced to dollars and cents.[79] Even if such a reduction were possible, it is questionable whether the primary goal of government should be maximizing economic welfare in the society.

Decision analysis.   Cost-benefit analysis assumes that certain events will occur: A dam will be built; it will produce X kilowatts of electricity; Y people from a nearby city will spend Z hours boating and waterskiing on the newly created lake; farmers will save Q dollars in flood protection and irrigation but lose N acres of land for farming. Decision analysis, in contrast, is geared toward making policy choices under conditions of less certainty.[80] It assumes that in many instances government, having inadequate information, is making probabilistic choices about what to do—that, in fact, government may be almost playing a game, with nature or other human beings as the opponent. As pointed out, governments often do not have a very good conception of the policy instruments they choose, and that lack of knowledge, combined with inadequate knowledge about patterns of causation within the policy area, can be a recipe for disaster. However, if we have some idea about the probabilities of certain outcomes (even without a model of causation), there is a better chance of making better decisions.

Take, for example, a situation in which a hurricane appears to be bearing down on a major coastal city. On the one hand, the mayor of that city can order an evacuation and cause a great deal of lost production as well as a predictable number of deaths during the rush to escape the city. On the other hand, if he or she does not order the evacuation and the hurricane actually does strike the city, then a far larger loss of life will occur. Of course, the hurricane is only forecast to be heading in the general direction of the city, and it may yet veer off. What should the mayor do? How should he or she assess the risks and the possible outcomes of the decision?[81]

This decision-making problem can be organized as a "decision tree," in which the mayor is essentially playing a game against nature (see Figure 4.2). The mayor has two possible policy choices: evacuate or not evacuate. We can assign probabilities to the two potential occurrences in nature—hit or miss the city—based on the best information available from the weather bureau, and we have estimates of the losses that would occur as a result of each outcome. In this analysis, we assume that if the hurricane strikes, the loss of property will be approximately the same whether or not the city is evacuated. As the problem is set up, the mayor makes the smallest possible error by choosing to evacuate the city. By doing that, the mayor may cause an expected unnecessary loss of $7 million ($10 million multiplied by the probability of the event of $.70$) if the hurricane does not hit, but there would be an expected unnecessary loss of $30 million if the evacuation was not ordered and the hurricane did actually strike. Such a simple decision will be easy to make if there is sufficient information available.

Decision	Probability	Nature	Expected loss
Evacuate	–0.3 ———	Hurricane hits	$0
	–0.7 ———	Hurricane misses (Loss = $10 million)	$7 million
Not evacuate	–0.3 ———	Hurricane hits (Loss = $100 million)	$30 million
	–0.7 ———	Hurricane misses	$0

FIGURE 4.2   A Decision Tree on Evacuation

In more complex situations, when many facts need to be considered simultaneously, the decision-making process becomes more difficult, especially when one faces a human opponent rather than nature. Even then, the technique, like cost-benefit analysis, is only an aid to decision making and policy formulation. Decisions still must be made by individuals, who will consider ethical, economic, and political factors before making a judgment about what should be done. And as the results of policy formulation will be felt in the future, the exercise of judgment is especially important. When an issue is newly placed on the agenda, the first formulation of a solution will to some degree structure subsequent attempts at solution. It therefore will have an enduring legacy that must be considered very carefully.

Policy Design

All the aids that government can bring to bear when formulating policy still do not generate an underlying approach to policy design. That is, no technical means of addressing public problems relate the characteristics of those problems to the instruments that might be used to solve them or to the values that would be used to evaluate a policy's success.[82] Without such a comprehensive approach to design, much policy formulation in government is accomplished by intuition or inertia or by analogy with existing programs. The inertial pattern produces frequent mistakes and often much wasted time and effort. Thus, one of the many tasks of policy analysis is to develop a comprehensive approach to the problems of formulating effective policies—it requires not only some idea of what "good" policies are but also some strategies for developing processes that can produce desirable policies.

In the United States, any such comprehensive approach to policy design is likely to be resisted. In the first place, the generally antistatist values of U.S. politics make a planned, rationalistic approach unacceptable to many politicians and citizens. Second, as was pointed out earlier, for institutional as well as ideological reasons, American politics tends toward incremental solutions to problems rather than imposition of comprehensive frameworks or use of design concepts for policymaking.[83] Attempting to impose a design on a policy area may threaten the interests of agencies and committees that believe that they "own" the problem and that they have been responsible for the development of the existing policy over time. Third, there is as yet inadequate agreement on the nature of many of the most important policy problems that the U.S. government now faces, and even less on the nature of the solutions. Important policy problems such as poverty, crime, poor education, and the like still lack clear definitions of causes or solutions. These important political realities should not, however, prevent policy analysts from attempting to understand social problems in a less haphazard fashion than is sometimes encountered in government or from advocating innovative program designs for solving them.

Summary

In this chapter, I have taken the policymaking process through its first stages: considering problems and then developing some mechanisms for solving them. Both activities—and indeed the entire activity of policymaking—are political exercises, but they also involve the application of techniques and tools for analysis. The tools for agenda setting are largely political, requiring the "selling" of agenda items to authorized decision makers, who may believe that they already have enough to do. Agenda setting also requires a detailed knowledge of the issue in question so that it can be related, first, to the known preferences of decision makers, and second, to existing policies and programs. Agenda setting is in some ways the art of doing something new so that it appears old.

The techniques that can be applied to policy formulation are more sophisticated technically, but they also require sensitive political hands that can use them effectively. To a great extent, the use of old solutions for new problems applies in formulation as well as in agenda setting. For both agenda setting and policy formulation, incremental solutions are favored in the United States. This incrementalism produces a great deal of stability in the policy process, but it makes rapid response to major changes in the economy and society difficult.

The solutions that emerge from these first stages of the policy process, then, are designed to be readily accepted by legislators and administrators who must authorize and legitimate the policies selected. A more comprehensive approach to design might well produce better solutions to problems, but it would face the barrier of political feasibility. The task of the analyst and advocate, then, becomes stretching the boundaries of feasibility to produce better public policies.

CHAPTER 5

Legitimating Policy Choices

ONCE IT HAS BEEN DECIDED that a certain program is required, or is feasible, as a response to a policy problem, that choice must be defended as a legitimate one for government to make. No matter what course of action is decided on, it is almost certain that some citizens will believe themselves disadvantaged by the choice. At a minimum, any public program or project will cost money, and citizens who pay taxes and receive (or perceive) no direct benefits from it will frequently consider themselves to be harmed by the policy choice. Because policy choices inevitably benefit some citizens and not others, a great deal of attention must be given in a democratic government to the process by which decisions are made. It is by means of the official process of government that substantive policy decisions are legitimated; that is, the process attaches the legitimate authority of the state to the policy that is chosen.

Legitimacy is a fundamental concept in the discipline of political science, and it is important in understanding policymaking. Legitimacy is conventionally defined as a belief on the part of citizens that the current government represents a proper form of government and a willingness on their part to accept the government's decrees as legal and authoritative.[1] The vast majority of Americans regard the government of the United States as the appropriate set of institutions to govern the country. And most Americans consequently accept the actions of the government as authoritative (as having the force of law), as long as they are carried out in accordance with the processes established in the Constitution or by procedures derived from them. It is understood that all policies adopted must be within the powers granted to the federal government by the Constitution. The boundaries of the policies considered constitutional have expanded during the history of the United States, but the limits current at the time establish the boundaries of legitimate action. So, for example, the federal government in 2010 can become involved in economic policy areas that it could not have in 1910, although perhaps fewer than in the late 1960s or early 1970s.

Several things should be understood about legitimacy as it affects contemporary policymaking in the United States. First, legitimacy is largely a psychological property. Legitimacy depends on the majority's acceptance of the appropriateness of a government. A government may come to power by all the prescribed processes, but if the population does not willingly accept that government or the rules by which it gained power, then in practice it has no legitimacy. For example, many constitutions (including those of France and Britain) give government the right to suspend civil liberties and declare martial law, but citizens accustomed to greater freedom may find it difficult to accept decrees such as that,[2] unless a crisis such as the attacks of September 11, 2001, intervenes to expand the range of acceptable action. Changes in a government may cause some citizens to question the legitimacy of a new government's actions.

Legitimacy has substantive as well as procedural elements. It matters not only how issues are decided but also what is decided. The government of the United States might decide to nationalize all oil companies operating in the country. (It will not do this, but just imagine so for a moment.) The decision could be reached with all appropriate deliberation as prescribed by the Constitution, but it would still not be acceptable to the majority of citizens. A more realistic example is provided by the wars in Vietnam and then in Iraq, which were conducted according to the procedures of the Constitution but nevertheless rejected as illegitimate by a significant proportion of the population. As a consequence of the Vietnam War, Congress passed the War Powers Act, which changed the procedures by which the United States could become involved in any future foreign conflicts.[3] The substantive question of legitimacy therefore produced a procedural response, although the debate in 2002 and 2003 over the ability of President George W. Bush to attack Iraq demonstrated that the procedures are themselves far from clear. At a less dramatic level, the attempts on the part of Congress to increase its own pay during 1989 and 1990 were procedurally correct but raised such an outcry from the public that they could not be implemented; the American public clearly regarded the action as illegitimate. Congress has since changed the way its pay is determined, so increases automatically follow increases in the cost of living unless Congress acts to stop the increase, but even that automatic procedure has created questions with some voters.[4]

The limits of government activity became major political questions during the congressional elections of 2010, and those issues persisted into the 2012 presidential election. The rise of the Tea Party movement, opposed to most forms of government intervention into society, has placed the question of the limits of government more in the center of American politics.[5] While seeming radical after the expansion of American government since World War II, this movement is yet another manifestation of the populist tradition in American politics that rejects large institutions in social and political life and promotes ideas of individualism.

Legitimacy is both a variable and a constant—it differs among individuals and across time. Some citizens of the United States may not accept the legitimacy of the current government. For example, some African American activists rejected the legitimacy of the U.S. government and called for the formation of a separate African American nation within the country. On the other side, white supremacists and some religious sects have organized settlements in parts of the West that reject the authority of all the constituted governments, and they even have engaged in armed conflict with federal agents. Citizens also appear more willing to accept the actions of state and local governments than those of the federal government.

A general decline in confidence in American institutions has been occurring, and it has been especially pronounced for government institutions other than the military (see Table 5.1).[6] There was some upturn in confidence in the 1980s, but that has decayed, and Americans now have less confidence in government than they have had in the past. In particular, Congress now is one of the least-respected institutions in the United States. The various scandals during the second Clinton administration reduced citizens' confidence in the presidency. The first years of the George W. Bush administration seemed to restore legitimacy to the office, despite the extreme confusion of the 2000 election,[7] but scandals of another sort in 2005 and 2006 and failures in economic management reduced the president's approval ratings to the lowest point ever.[8]

The economic crisis beginning in 2008 has posed a major challenge to the legitimacy of American government. Although public confidence in government is to some extent an emotional attachment to the symbols of the system, another major part of legitimacy derives from the effectiveness of government.[9] Somewhat

TABLE 5.1   Confidence in American Institutions, 1983–2008 (combined percentages saying "Great deal" or "Quite a lot")

	2008	2006	2004	2002	1998	1996	1993	1990	1988	1985	1983
Military	71	73	75	71	64	66	68	68	58	61	53
Organized religion	48	52	53	53	59	57	53	56	59	66	62
Supreme Court	32	40	46	41	42	45	44	47	56	56	42
Presidency	26	33	52	50	22	39	43	n.a.	n.a.	n.a.	n.a.
Public schools	33	37	41	n.a.	37	38	39	45	49	48	39
Newspapers	24	30	30	16	31	32	31	39	36	35	38
Organized labor	20	24	24	11	26	25	26	27	26	28	26
Big business	20	18	24	16	22	24	22	25	25	31	28
Congress	12	19	30	22	28	20	22	24	35	39	28

Sources: Various Gallup Polls, CNN/Gallup Polls, and Harris Polls.

Note: n.a. = not available.

paradoxically, although most Americans say they do not want government heavily involved in the economy, when the economy has difficulties, government is blamed for its inaction. The latest economic crisis is no different and is perhaps even more destructive of legitimacy because it has undermined the housing market, which many people counted on as their major investment.[10]

In societies that are deeply divided ethnically or politically, the rejection of the sitting government by one side or another is a constant fact of life. Even a government that is widely accepted may lose legitimacy or strain its legitimate status through unpopular activities and leaders. The Vietnam War and the Watergate scandal illustrate the low point to which the legitimacy of even a widely accepted political regime may fall. Nevertheless, the American government was able to survive those problems, as well as such subsequent problems as the Iran-Contra controversy, several scandals during the Clinton administration, and failures in responding to Hurricane Katrina, and continue to govern with legitimate authority.

Because of the variability of legitimacy, a fully legitimated government may gradually lose its legitimate status over time. A series of blatantly unpopular or illegal actions may reduce the authority of a government, making it open to challenge, whether of a revolutionary or more peaceable nature. Or a government may lose legitimacy through incompetence rather than unpopular activities, as has been demonstrated in the handling of both Iraq and the economic problems beginning in 2008. Citizens in most countries have a reservoir of respect for government, and governments can add to or subtract from that stock of authority. As a result, governments are engaged in a continuing process of legitimation for themselves and their successors.

Finally, government must somehow legitimate each individual policy choice. No matter how technically correct a policy choice may be, it is of little practical value if it cannot be justified to the public. For example, the decision to correct the formula for indexing Social Security pension benefits, once it was discovered that the increases it produced were unjustifiably large, was absolutely correct. But it created a huge political controversy and a sense of betrayal among some elderly citizens (see chapter 12). Policy analysts, in their pursuit of elegant solutions and innovative policies, frequently forget this mundane point, and that forgetfulness can present a real barrier to their success.[11] To design a policy that can be legitimated, a policy analyst must understand the political process. That process will define the set of feasible policy alternatives in a more restrictive fashion than does the economic and social world—that is, more programs could work than could be adopted within the political values of the American system. Thus, the task of the policy analyst is to be able to "sell" his or her decisions to the individuals who are crucial to their being legitimated. That does not mean that the analyst must advocate only policies that fit existing definitions of

Characteristics of decisions

		Majoritarian	Nonmajoritarian
Range of actors	*Mass*	Referendums	—
	Elite	Congress	Courts; Administrative regulations

FIGURE 5.1   Modes of Legitimation

feasibility, but it does mean that the analyst must have a strategy for expanding that definition if a highly innovative program is to be proposed.[12]

In general, legitimation may be performed through the legislative process, through the administrative process designed for the issuing of regulations (secondary legislation), through the courts, or through mechanisms of direct democracy. As shown in Figure 5.1, these modes of legitimation can be seen as combining characteristics of decisions—majoritarian and nonmajoritarian—and the range of actors involved.[13] The nonmajoritarian mass cell is empty in the figure, but it might be filled by revolutionary or extremely powerful interest group activities. Indeed, the ongoing political controversy over abortion policy may fall into this cell, given that there is apparently no popular majority for the policies being pushed by an intense and active minority, although that minority has been successful in some states (see chapter 16). We will discuss each type of legitimation and its implications for the policy choices that might be feasible as a result of each process.

Legislative Legitimation

In the United States, we traditionally have equated lawmaking with Congress, the principal legislative body at the federal level, or with similar bodies in the states. That notion is now excessively naive, for the workload and the technical content of many subjects on which decisions have to be made have overwhelmed Congress. The loss of capacity to legislate effectively has occurred despite the growth of legislative staffs and the increased availability of policy advice for legislators. Governments are simply too large and involved in too many issues to permit a large legislative institution, such as Congress, with all its intricate procedures, to make the full range of decisions required to keep the society functioning (from a public policy perspective). This problem was highlighted when it seemed that no members of Congress had read the 1,000-page economic stimulus bill that they voted on in 2009.

Of course, Congress remains the crucial source for primary legislation. That is, although administrative bodies are responsible for writing regulations in large numbers, Congress must supply the basic legislative frameworks within which the other bodies operate. Congress tends to pass legislation written in relatively broad language, allowing administrators latitude for interpretation. Thus, despite various attempts to reassert the authority of Congress in opposing the "imperial presidency," it is best to think about the legitimating role of Congress as the authorizing of relatively diffuse statements of goals and structures. Those broad statements are then made operational by the executive branch, which fills in the details by writing regulations and by the implementation process.

Congress also retains its supervisory powers—oversight—so that if the executive branch strays too far when writing regulations, Congress can reassert its intentions in constructing the legislation.[14] Until 1983, Congress had virtually unlimited power to pass "legislative vetoes," which required agencies issuing certain types of regulations to submit them to Congress for approval. Although the Supreme Court declared that the legislative veto is excessive meddling by one branch of government in the affairs of another and so is not constitutional,[15] Congress has nevertheless continued to use similar instruments in other policy areas.[16] If nothing else, Congress can always amend a law to clarify its intentions—or, if it must, even repeal the previous legislation.

Congress places great emphasis on procedural legitimation and has established elaborate procedures for processing legislation.[17] In fact, its institutions and procedures have become so well developed that it is difficult for legislation to be passed. Typically, a bill must be passed by a subcommittee, by a full committee, and by floor action in each house. And because one house is unlikely to pass a bill in exactly the same form as the other, conference committees are often necessary to reconcile the two versions. More arcane procedural mechanisms, such as filibusters, amendments, and recommitals, can slow down or kill legislation at a number of points if it fails to attract the necessary majority at the proper time. Or to put it the other way around, all that the opponents of a bill have to do is to muster a majority at one crucial point to prevent its passage.[18] Evidence from lobbying investigations in 2005 and 2006 also indicated the extent to which less formal rules permit Congress members to add money earmarked to benefit their constituents to legislation.[19]

Legislative procedures are important as mechanisms to prevent unnecessary or poorly formulated legislation from becoming law, but they can also frustrate good and needed legislation. The ability of the opposition to postpone or block civil rights legislation during the 1950s and 1960s demonstrated clearly the capacity of legislative procedures to thwart the apparent majority will of Congress. More recently, the continuing inability to produce a national health insurance bill, or to pass a strong bill to control tobacco, indicates the difficulties of passing legislation even when a significant portion of the population favors some change from the status quo.[20] Also, the threat of throwing the United States into default on its obligations in the debate on the debt ceiling was insufficient to prevent the use of an array of procedural devices.[21] A committed and well-supported minority is thus able to use legislative procedures to achieve its own ends.

Legitimation through the legislative process is majoritarian. It depends on building either simple or special majorities at each crucial point in the process. The task of the policy analyst or the legislative leader is to construct such majorities. In addition to appealing for support on the basis of the actual qualities of the proposed legislation, the analyst can form the needed majorities in several other ways. One method, which has been referred to as *partisan analysis*,[22] involves convincing members of Congress that the piece of legislation that the analyst wants is something that they want as well. The trick here is to design the legislation in such a way that it will appeal to a sufficient number of interests to create a winning coalition. For example, the National Defense Education Act of 1958, which still funds some international programs, was passed by a coalition of Congress members interested in education and in defense. The title of the bill indicates that it was intended to serve those two purposes and affect those two areas. It brought together liberals favoring a stronger federal role in education and conservatives favoring a stronger defense posture. More recently, some Democrats supported changes in Medicaid and Medicare that the George W. Bush administration favored as a strategy to prevent passage of more conservative legislation.

Another strategy for forming coalitions that is similar to partisan analysis is *logrolling*,[23] in which coalitions are formed not around a single piece of legislation but across a set of legislative initiatives. In the simplest example, Representative A favors bill A but is indifferent to bill B. Representative B, on the other hand, favors bill B but is indifferent to bill A. The logical thing for these two members to do is to trade their votes on the two pieces of legislation, with A voting for bill B and B voting for bill A. Several bills may be involved in vote trading over time. In some ways, logrolling is a rational activity because it allows the passage of legislation that some members of Congress—and presumably their constituencies—favor intensely but that might not otherwise be able to gain a majority. But logrolling also has the effect of bringing about the approval of a great deal more legislation than would otherwise be passed, thus boosting public expenditures and taxation. It enables relatively narrow interests in the nation to develop coalitions for their legislation that may not be justifiable in terms of the broader public interest.

As well as being a majoritarian body, Congress has universalistic norms that promote the spreading of government expenditures very broadly.[24] This is commonly referred to as *pork barrel legislation,* or as the parochial imperative, in

American politics. Pork barrel legislation often concerns capital expenditures, of which the classic examples are river and harbor improvements. Obtaining such capital projects for their home districts has become a measure of Congress members' success; some argue that "bringing home the bacon," instead of policymaking on broad national issues, has become the dominant activity of Congress.[25] The tendency in designing legislation of this kind is to spread benefits as broadly as possible geographically and to create a majority by benefiting virtually anyone who wants a piece of the "pork." As with logrolling, this pattern of decision making tends to increase the costs of government. Douglas Arnold pointed out that pork barrel legislation costs very little when compared with national defense or Social Security,[26] but it stands as an example of the way in which government misuses money by funding projects with relatively minor social benefit in order to ensure the reelection of incumbent members of Congress. Spending on pork barrel projects has increased, in part through earmarked expenditures.[27] The political importance of this style of decision making may outstrip the actual amount of money spent, as it has become a symbol of waste and abuse in government and was a target of reform for Barack Obama as he took office.

This description of legitimation through the legislative process does not paint the most favorable picture of Congress. Actually, a good deal of congressional decision making is based on the merits of legislation. To the extent that partisan analysis, logrolling, and pork barrel legislation characterize the actions of Congress, however, the legislative process has certain effects on the kinds of rules that can be legitimated. It can be argued that the process almost inevitably produces broad and rather diffuse legislation. The necessity of building a coalition requires that one take care not to offend potential members and that the proposed legislation produce benefits for individual legislators and their districts. As a consequence, a bill must be designed to be amenable to partisan analysis and must not be so clearly worded as to reduce the number of possible coalition members. This strategy of obfuscation allows administrators to make politically charged decisions on difficult issues by deflecting criticism from individual members of Congress.

Both logrolling and pork barrel legislation are related to the expansion of government beyond the bounds that could be set if there were no possibility of vote trading. The possibility of trading votes and building coalitions across pieces of legislation fuels a tendency to adopt public projects that are marginal in terms of social productivity. It is obvious that the world of policymaking is not perfectly rational, but these patterns of institutional decision making seem to exacerbate the irrational character of much of politics, producing programs that benefit the few at the expense of the many.[28] Logrolling and the pork barrel also make reducing the size of unneeded programs difficult. For example, the only effective way for Congress to accomplish the closing of redundant military bases in the early 1990s was to specify in advance that an independent commission would recommend closings, which would then be voted on as a group. Otherwise, logrolling might have prevented the closing of any bases at all. This self-denying restraint appeared to break down in 1998, when Congress demanded more influence in retaining bases that the Department of Defense itself wanted to close.[29] This process continued through summer 2005, when several apparently redundant bases escaped closure after coalitions to retain them were formed across partisan and geographical lines.[30] The proposed decline in defense spending after 2012 will again likely produce another round of debates over the geographical distribution of the losses.

These difficulties in congressional decision making suggest more general points concerning social decision making. In its simplest terms, the problem is, How can a set of conflicting social preferences best be expressed in a single decision? Congress faces this problem when it attempts to combine the preferences of its members and their constituents in a single decision whether or not to adopt a piece of legislation; the same general problem arises in clubs, committees, and college faculty meetings.

One underlying problem facing decision makers in legislatures and elsewhere is the varying intensity of preferences of the participants. We encountered this problem when discussing the logic of logrolling—in a majoritarian system, it may be possible to construct a majority composed of individuals who are not much interested in a proposal or do not feel intensely about it. This decision-making problem is in part a function of each legislator's having only one vote, whereas individuals in the market setting have more than one dollar and can apply their resources differentially depending on their preferences and the intensity of those preferences. Logrolling is one means of attempting to overcome the intensity problem, but it can be successful only in a limited set of circumstances with a certain distribution of preferences.

In majoritarian institutions with one vote per member, it is difficult to reflect accurately the preferences of the participants in a manner that creates their greatest net satisfaction. Generating such an optimal decision is made more difficult if in a number of successive decisions (e.g., voting on amendments), the order in which options are eliminated affects the final preferences.[31] In examining choices of this type, the economist Kenneth Arrow argued that it is impossible to devise a social-choice mechanism that satisfies the logical conditions for rationality.[32] The only way in which such decisions can be arrived at, in Arrow's framework, is to impose them, which he rejects on philosophical grounds. But the imposition of administrative regulations as another means of legitimating decisions has some characteristics of imposed solutions, although the procedures for adopting regulations have been sanctioned legally.

Once Congress has enacted legislation, it has played its major role in legitimating policy, but its involvement in the policy process is not over. We have already pointed out that the administrative agencies perform a major role in translating legislation into specific regulations. Congress then exercises some degree of oversight over the actions of the agencies.[33] The committees that initially approved the legislation monitor the way in which the agencies implement it and can act legislatively to correct anything the agencies may do incorrectly. Congress may not even have to do anything directly—often it can rely on its implicit authority over legislation and budgets to gain compliance from the agencies.

Oversight is in essence a second round of legitimation by Congress, which passes the initial legislation and then looks over the shoulders of the implementers to ensure that its intentions are followed. This oversight activity can be only so effective, however, because of the scarcity of time and the need of congressional actors to proceed with the next round of legislation. Furthermore, even the well-staffed U.S. Congress may lack the necessary expertise to judge the numerous, complex, and technical regulations that the administrative agencies issue and their even more numerous administrative decisions. This means that oversight tends to be more "fire alarm" (reaction to crises) than "police patrol" (routine scanning of the relevant environment).[34]

The divided government in the United States after the 2010 elections had led to a growth of oversight activities, especially over federal government responses to the economic crisis. Specific issues such as the huge financial losses of Fannie Mae (Federal National Mortgage Association) and Freddie Mac (Federal Home Loan Mortgage Corporation) provoked substantial congressional response, and policies such as the Troubled Asset Relief Program (TARP) also were targets for Congress, and especially congressional Republicans. More generally, Congress created the Congressional Oversight Panel in 2008, headed by Elizabeth Warren, to address some of these economic policy issues. These oversight opportunities, like many others, constitute both political and policymaking opportunities for Congress.

Regulations and the Administrative Process

Most rulemaking in the United States and other industrialized societies is now done through the regulatory process.[35] I use the term *regulatory process* in a broad context, to include the rulemaking activities of executive branch agencies as well as those of independent regulatory commissions.[36] Administrative or independent regulatory bodies can issue binding regulations that are subsidiary to congressional legislation—these regulations are sometimes referred to as *secondary legislation.* Issuing such regulations is definitely a legislative or legitimating activity because it makes rules for the society, but the rules must be pursuant to primary legislation that Congress has already adopted.

The volume of regulation writing in the federal government is immense, as can be judged by the size of the *Federal Register,* a daily publication containing all regulations and proposed regulations (approximately 80,000 pages per year), and by the size of the *Code of Federal Regulations* (CFR), which contains all the regulations currently in force. An example of the volume of regulatory activity is provided by the Occupational Safety and Health Administration (OSHA) in the Department of Labor. OSHA, which has been a frequent target of the critics of government regulation, issued 4,600 regulations during the first two years of its existence and continues to issue hundreds of new regulations each year. As of 2010, these amounted to over 4,700 pages of rather fine print in the CFR. Taken together, three areas of public policy—agriculture, labor, and the environment—account for rules requiring approximately 25,000 pages in the *Code of Federal Regulations.*

Although conducted through a legal process, the decision making required for adopting regulations is not majoritarian. If it were, many of the regulations adopted by OSHA and other regulatory bodies might never be approved. Decision making in the regulatory process can be more technical and less tied to politics than is decision making in Congress, although political considerations cannot be neglected entirely, especially by agencies within executive branch departments. Executive branch agencies are directly responsible to the president and consequently are under pressure to issue regulations that address the president's political priorities. Recent presidents have taken greater pains than their predecessors to know what regulations are being issued and to ensure that they match presidential priorities. President George W. Bush, for example, pushed forward a number of regulations during the last days of his administration that President Obama promptly attempted to rescind.[37] Even the regulations issued by independent regulatory agencies cannot afford to stray too far from the basic political and ideological norms of the public; if they do, the agency threatens its own survival or at least its latitude to issue further regulations.

One way in which government has attempted to keep regulatory activity in check is through *regulatory analysis,* the attempt to apply cost-benefit analysis and other forms of economic analysis to regulations before they are adopted. President Reagan, for example, required executive agencies to submit all new regulations for review by the Office of Management and Budget (OMB) and later to report their plans for regulatory activity for the subsequent year. These regulatory reviews were as much political as economic, and they resulted in critics' referring to OMB as the "regulatory KGB."[38] The Republican Congress first elected in 1994 took regulatory analysis even further by mandating, through a formal regulatory review statute (Public Law [Pub. L.] 104-208), that OMB submit to Congress an economic impact assessment of each new regulation. Although the review of regulations by the president's Office of Management and Budget has in many cases been political and ideological, it also has served a legitimation function. In the first place, the elected presidency does have greater legitimacy than does the unelected bureaucracy, especially given the generally low opinion that Americans have of the bureaucracy. It can be further argued that because the techniques used in regulatory analysis are "rational," regulations that survive it may be more likely to make a positive contribution to the well-being of society.[39] That conception of positive contribution is primarily economic, however, rather than taking into account a broader range of concerns (see chapter 17).

Even by the time of the George H. W. Bush administration, some analysts were arguing that deregulation had gone too far, spurring a number of important new regulations, including significant new air pollution standards. The Clinton administration adopted a more activist position in environmental and economic regulation, but it attempted to include more public involvement and public disclosure in the writing of regulations, even though some of the tools of regulatory analysis remained in place.[40]

The George W. Bush administration placed a moratorium on regulation and in 2007 issued an executive order that greatly centralized regulatory power in the executive branch. Barack Obama promptly revoked that executive order and called on the OMB director to assist him in crafting a new plan for regulatory review. Although this came rather late in his administration, President Obama has undertaken some significant attempts at reforming regulation and making a number of administrative processes substantially easier for citizens and businesses.[41]

Public Access to the Regulatory Process

The process of making regulations is open to the public's influence, as well as that of the president and OMB. The Administrative Procedures Act and several other laws affecting the issuing of regulations require that agencies accept advice and ideas from interested citizens as the process goes forward and that time be given at each stage for affected interests in the society to respond to agency initiatives.[42] For some segments of the economy, in fact, the regulatory process may be more democratic than decision making in Congress. The regulatory process permits affected interests to have direct access to decision makers. In deliberations in Congress, affected interests may be excluded from effective involvement, especially if they represent an interest not widely considered "legitimate" by Congress members. Furthermore, regulatory outcomes may be "in the public interest" to a greater extent than those Congress devises, given that special interest influences are funneled through an administrative process and frequently made subject to judicial review.[43]

Access to the regulation-writing process does not, of course, mean that the ideas of the affected interests or of public interest groups will dominate the decisions finally made. Simply granting access does not protect the interests of segments of the society that are not sufficiently well organized, or sufficiently alert, to make their presentations to the agency. Maintaining access to agency decision making is by no means cost free, so many less well-funded groups may be excluded. This has led some agencies, such as the Federal Trade Commission, to provide funding for interests that might not otherwise have the lawyers and other resources to participate effectively.[44] There are no guarantees of success, but the procedures do indicate the openness of the regulatory process to a range of ideas and opinions.

The Processes of Writing Regulations

There are two principal ways in which regulation writers collect ideas and opinions. The first, *formal rulemaking,* appears somewhat like a court proceeding, with a formal hearing, the taking of oral testimony from witnesses, and the use of counsel.[45] Formal rulemaking is a time-consuming and cumbersome process, but it is deemed necessary when the social and economic interests involved are sufficiently important. Examples of formal rulemaking are the approval of new medications by the Food and Drug Administration and the licensing of nuclear power plants by the Nuclear Regulatory Commission. The written records generated in such proceedings are important, given that these rulings are important to many elements in society and may be the subject of subsequent discussion and litigation. The procedure for licensing nuclear power plants and the degree of public participation have slowed approval of these facilities and may be a barrier to building new ones (see chapter 14).

The second method of collecting inputs is *informal rulemaking,* which proceeds through several steps. First, the agency must publish in the *Federal Register* a notice of its intent to issue a certain regulation. A period of several months is specified, during which individuals and groups who believe themselves potentially affected by the rule can offer opinions and make suggestions about its content. After the designated time has passed, the agency may issue a draft of the regulation that it would ultimately like to be put into effect. The draft may be based on the suggestions received from affected interests, or it may be what the agency had been planning all along. Then, there is another waiting period for responses to the draft regulation, which may be made directly to the agency or submitted indirectly by having a friendly member of Congress contact the agency with proposed alterations. Then, based on these responses as well as its own beliefs, the agency issues the final regulation, which will have the force of law.

In addition to the two principal forms of rulemaking, administrative law has developed two other ways of adopting regulations. *Hybrid rulemaking* represents an attempt at compromise between the thoroughness of the formal process and the relative ease of the informal process.[46] Hybrid rulemaking came about in part because of the courts,[47] but it also was required by some acts of Congress, especially for environmental policy.[48] Although it does not entail full-scale judicial proceedings, it may require the opportunity to cross-examine witnesses, so as to create a full judicial record that can be the basis for an appeal if further judicial proceedings are demanded.

The other emerging form of rulemaking is *negotiated rulemaking*. Given the complexity of many of the policy areas into which government must now venture and the number of interests involved in each policy, it may be easier to negotiate rules than to attempt to make them administratively.[49] This process can save a great deal of future ill will among the affected interests, and it may actually create policies superior to those that might emerge from a more centrally directed process. Congress recognized the validity of this form of rulemaking by passing the Negotiated Rulemaking Act of 1990 to specify the conditions under which it can be used and the procedures required. Language about negotiated rulemaking has also been included in the authorizing legislation for several executive agencies.[50] While negotiated rulemaking is an attempt to open the process to a variety of actors and thus make it somewhat more democratic, there are also pressures to make the process more technocratic. In particular, there has been increasing interest in regulatory analysis.

The legitimate force of a regulation comes from passage of a statute by Congress and from correct procedures (as specified in the Administrative Procedures Act) in issuing the regulation. In general, issuing a regulation takes about eighteen months from beginning to end and allows for substantial representation of affected groups and individuals. Although the law makes some provision for emergency rulemaking by some agencies, attempts to short-circuit the process will probably result in a regulation's being rejected, no matter how reasonable on its face, if it is appealed through the court system.

The role assigned to affected interests in the regulatory process brings up another point about social decision making. In part as a means of justifying slavery, John C. Calhoun argued that a proper democracy would take into account not only the majority of individuals but also a majority of interests in society. His idea of "concurrent majorities" would have assigned greater importance to pressure groups than does most of American political thought and would have made the opinions of such groups more central in the process of writing regulations. The fundamental point is that a decision should reflect not a simple majority but rather a more complex agreement among a range of segments of society.

The role of interest groups in decision making about regulations is similar to the development of "neocorporatism" in western Europe.[51] The principal difference is that interest groups in the United States usually are not granted quasi-official status as representatives of an economic or social group, as they are in much of Europe. Affected U.S. interest groups are rarely brought together to negotiate a compromise decision, as they might be in many European systems.[52] The Clinton administration took such a step, however, in organizing a conference between logging interests and conservationists in the Pacific Northwest to discuss their differences over protection of the spotted owl.[53] The Bush administration involved industrial groups heavily in making decisions about energy policy, provoking challenges to the exclusivity of the process.[54] In the United States, decision making is still carried out largely within the agency itself, however, with interest groups involved primarily as sources of information. In addition to protecting the interests of their members, interest groups frequently make substantive points about proposed regulations and can help prevent agencies from making errors in their rules.

Finally, regulatory decision making is threatened by the classic problem of *agency capture,* in which agencies that regulate a single industry have tended to become advocates for their industries rather than impartial protectors of the public interest.[55] Capture results from the agencies' need to maintain political support when, especially in the case of independent regulatory commissions, the only logical source of such support is the regulated industry itself. The public is usually too amorphous a body to offer the specific support an agency requires to defend its budget, or even its very existence, before Congress. Thus, reforms intended to remove political pressures from regulatory decision making, by making the agencies independent, have succeeded only in making them independent of one source of political pressure but dependent on another. In Theodore J. Lowi's terminology, the public interest is appropriated for private gain.[56]

The capture argument is less applicable to newer regulatory agencies, which operate across a number of industries, than it is to single-industry regulatory bodies.[57] For example, both the Consumer Product Safety Commission (CPSC) and the Occupational Safety and Health Administration regulate virtually every industry in the country; their advocacy and protection of any one industry might only injure other industries. It is generally too difficult for an industry to capture these cross-cutting regulators, and they are therefore more likely to operate in the public interest—although an agency itself may be permitted to define the public interest. These organizations are not immune from political pressures, however. The George W. Bush administration quickly became embroiled in a conflict over its appointments to the CPSC when it attempted to make the organization more friendly to business in general than it had been during the Clinton years.

The economic crisis following 2008 has provoked a more aggressive form of economic regulation in the United States. In particular, the Obama administration created the Consumer Financial Protection Bureau as part of the

Mark Wilson/Getty Images

The Consumer Financial Protection Bureau (CFPB) is one response of the federal government to the financial crisis beginning in 2008. The formulation of this policy response involved the White House and Congress in a substantial policy debate. President Barack Obama shakes hands with Richard Cordray (r), whom he nominated as director of the CFPB during a press conference on July 18, 2011.

Dodd-Frank Act addressing the crisis. This bureau was designed to address some of the issues that had become apparent as the causes of the economic crisis became more apparent. This organization is given substantial powers to protect consumers against credit card and mortgage companies that were overcharging or deceiving their customers.

Regulation is a central process in the legitimation of policies, although it is one that many citizens would challenge. Many critics, both popular writers and academics, comment negatively on the making of laws by bureaucrats without the direct congressional involvement that they consider essential for legitimation.[58] These regulatory procedures are "due," however, and they have been ordained by several acts of Congress. Each regulation adopted must have a legislative peg to hang on, but unlike acts of Congress, regulations tend to make specific judgments and decisions, and by so doing, they affect individual interests more directly. Many regulations issued through this process have been criticized as impractical and unnecessary—everyone has his or her favorite silly regulation. Presidents have also been concerned about the effects of regulation on the economy and society and, in general, have sought to create more deregulation than regulation, although the recent economic crisis may alter that trend.[59] Although the regulatory process offers a possibility of greater objectivity and scientific rationality than the more politicized arena of Congress, the very attempt to apply such strict criteria for decisions is the source of many objections.

The Courts

The courts provide another nonmajoritarian means of legitimating policies. Just as the administrative process has assumed an increasing role in legitimation, the courts have become increasingly involved in issuing authoritative policy statements. Some critics have argued that public policy in the United States is dominated by the court system, and not to the benefit of the types of policies generated.[60] Along with complaints against the administrative process, there have been complaints about judge-made law as a usurpation of congressional prerogatives. Of course, the courts have been involved in legitimating actions and issuing law-like statements in the United States for some time. However, perhaps because of increasing litigation involving social issues (such as gay marriage) and the willingness of the courts to make declarations about remedies to remove violations of the Constitution from federal laws, popular awareness of the role of the courts in making rules for society has grown.

The constitutional basis for the courts to make legitimating decisions is the "supremacy clause," which says that all laws and treaties made in pursuance of the Constitution are the supreme law of the land. In *Marbury v. Madison*, Chief Justice John Marshall decided that it was incumbent on the courts to decide whether or not a law conformed to the Constitution and to declare, if it did not, that the law was void. Following from that fundamental declaration of judicial power, the courts have been able to make rules based on their interpretation of the Constitution. Particularly crucial to their role in legitimating actions is their ability to accept or reject the remedies proposed by the parties to particular disputes. If an action is declared unconstitutional, the courts frequently become involved in determining the actions needed to correct that unconstitutionality.

The most obvious examples of courts prescribing remedies to situations they find unconstitutional have been in cases involving school desegregation and prison overcrowding. In several cases—for example, *Swann v. Charlotte-Mecklenburg Board of Education*—the courts declared that boundaries between school districts constituted intent on the part of local governments to maintain or create racial segregation of the schools and that cross-district busing was the logical remedy for the problem. In other cases, the courts declared that seriously overcrowded prisons constituted cruel and unusual punishment, violating the

Eighth Amendment to the Constitution. Judges then decided that they would take over the prison systems and run them directly to correct the situation, or they would make very specific policies that state administrators were obliged to follow.[61] These decisions represent greater involvement of the courts in mandating state and local government actions than many citizens consider proper.

The role the courts have assumed in legitimating action is twofold. In its simplest sense, the courts may further legitimate the actions of other decision makers by declaring that their actions are acceptable under the Constitution. As mentioned above, American society appears to be becoming increasingly litigious, so that more and more issues are not fully decided until they have been ruled on by the courts. Litigation presents an important means of protecting individual rights in the policymaking process, but it can also greatly slow the implementation of policy. Putting an issue into the court system is sometimes a means of winning a conflict simply by delay, as with the largely successful attempts to block construction of nuclear power plants.

In a second sense, the courts take part in policy legitimation by deciding that certain conditions that exist in society, especially if they are sanctioned by government, are in contradiction of the Constitution and then offering solutions to the problems. The role of the courts in school desegregation is an example of this kind of legitimation, and it occurred not only in busing cases but also in the entire process of desegregation, beginning with *Brown v. Board of Education* (1954). The courts have acted relatively independently of other political institutions and have been active in making decisions and offering remedies that they believed were derived from sound constitutional principles. Just as administrative agencies need a legal peg to hang their rulemaking on, so too do the courts need a constitutional peg on which to hang their interventions. Such terms as *due process* and *equal protection* are sufficiently broad to permit a wide scope for judicial involvement in legitimation activity. For example, the right to privacy was derived from other basic rights in the Constitution, and that right has been used to place limits on state laws outlawing abortion, a continuing policy debate in the United States (see chapter 16).

Because the role of the courts is to judge the constitutionality of particular actions and to protect individual liberties against incursions by government or other individuals, decision making in the courts can be expected to be different from decision making through a legislative body. In many ways, the decisions that courts make are more authoritative than other legitimating decisions, both because of the courts' connection to constitutional authority and because of the absence of any ready recourse once appeals through the court system are exhausted. The courts leave less room for compromise and vote trading than does a legislative body, and they have a less clearly defined constituency, if they have any constituency at all. Finally, a court decision is narrower, speaking to the particular case in question, rather than a general principle of policy to be implemented in other specific cases. Thus, court decisions legitimate certain actions but leave future decisions somewhat ambiguous, whereas decisions taken by both legislatures and administrative agencies are attempts to develop more general principles to guide subsequent actions and decisions.

Popular Legitimation

The three methods of legitimation discussed so far share one common feature: They are all performed by elites through political institutions. A number of American states provide mechanisms for direct democracy that allow voters to legitimate policy decisions.[62] The referendum is in part a way for state legislatures to pass the buck to the people on issues that the legislators fear might be too hot for the good of their future political careers. Alternatively, in some instances, the public can use these mechanisms to bypass legislatures entirely or to prod them into action. Despite some agitation, direct democracy mechanisms have not been adopted at the federal level.

A *referendum* is a vote of the people on an issue put to them by the legislature or some other authoritative body. Approval by popular vote is required before the measure in question can become law. The majority of states in the United States employ referendums for some policy decisions—typically to pass bond issues and to change the state constitution—but some states use them to enact other legislation as well. An issue thought by the legislature to be sufficiently important, or highly charged politically, may be put to the voters for a decision. This practice certainly satisfies the tenets of democracy, but because voter turnout on referendums is low, it may lead to small numbers of relatively uninformed voters deciding issues of great importance that might be better left to more deliberative bodies. Furthermore, money for publicity campaigns is at least as important in referendums as it is in campaigns for office, so more powerful and affluent interests may be able to influence these elections significantly.

An even more extreme means of involving the public in policymaking is the *initiative,* which permits voters not only to pass on an issue put to them by government but also to place an issue on the ballot themselves. If the requisite number of signatures to a petition is obtained, an item can be placed on the ballot at the next election and will become law if approved by the voters. A number of significant policy measures—most notably the so-called Proposition 13, limiting property taxes and several important environmental laws in California— have been adopted through the initiative process. The initiative poses many of the same problems as the referendum. One difficulty is that important policy disputes, such as the use of nuclear power, become embroiled in political campaigns, so the complex issues involved become trivialized and converted into simple yes–no questions. The initiative provides an avenue for the expression of popular opinion, however, and it gives real power to the voters, who often think of themselves as absent from representative policymaking institutions.

Initiatives sometime are used to overcome legitimation activities by other actors, notably the courts. For example, in the 2008 elections, a number of popular referendums were used to overcome judicial decisions on social issues such as same-sex marriage.[63] Even then, however, the battles may not end because the courts may argue that even popular votes cannot override fundamental rights.

In addition to these established mechanisms for popular involvement, there are continuing calls for additional means of citizen involvement that would go beyond mere voting or public hearings. Such mechanisms are usually discussed under the term *deliberative democracy* or sometimes *strong democracy*.[64] The basic idea is that in a true democracy, the role of citizens would not be confined to selecting their leaders but would extend to the debate and selection of policies. This model has worked in the traditional New England town meeting, and the advocates of expanded participation would like to make it more general. The difficulty is in making it work in a country of 300 million people.

Even if it cannot work for such a large aggregation, deliberative democracy could perhaps be applied in smaller settings when making public policy. For example, there is a tradition of public hearings in the policy process at all levels of government in the United States. The typical pattern has been for citizens to make statements of their views to a decision-making body. In some areas, however, this pattern is being revised to allow citizens to discuss policy among themselves and perhaps even make the final decisions themselves. Ideas such as "citizens' juries" and "deliberative elections" are providing opportunities for increased participation by ordinary citizens.

Summary

Legitimation is at once the most difficult and the simplest component of the policymaking process. It generally involves the least complex and technical forms of policy analysis, and the number of actors is relatively limited, except in initiatives and referendums. On the other hand, the actors involved are relatively powerful and have well-defined agendas of their own. Consequently, the task of the policy analyst seeking to alter perceptions and create converts to new policies at the legitimation stage is difficult. The type of formal evidence used at other stages of the process may not carry much weight at this stage, and political factors become paramount.

The barriers that the policy analyst faces in attempting to push through his or her ideas are sometimes individual and political, as when members of Congress must be convinced through partisan analysis or vote trading to accept the analyst's concept of the desirable policy alternative. Conversely, the task may be one of altering substantial organizational constraints or mediating turf wars on a decision that would facilitate the appropriate policy response to a problem. The problem may also be a legal one, of persuading the courts to respond in the desired fashion to a set of facts and to develop the desired remedy for the perceived problem. Or, finally, the problem may be a political one in the broadest sense—that is, to persuade the voters (through the political mastery of the analyst) to accept or reject a particular definition of an .issue and its solution. This is a great range of problems for the analyst, and it demands an equally great range of skills.

No individual is likely to have all these skills, but someone must make strategic choices as to which skills are the most appropriate for a particular problem. If the problem is to get a dam built, then Congress is clearly the most appropriate arena. If the problem is a civil rights violation, the best place to begin is probably the court system. If the problem is a specialized environmental issue, then the regulatory process is the appropriate locus for intervention. Policies do not simply happen; they must be made to happen. This is especially true given the degree of inertia in American government and the number of points at which action can be blocked. It frequently occurs that the major task of the policy analyst is to define clearly the problem that must be solved. Once that is done, the solution may not be simple, but at least it is potentially analyzable, and a feasible course of action may become more apparent.

CHAPTER 6

Organizations and Implementation

WHEN PEOPLE WALK around Washington, D.C., they see a number of buildings with blue signs in front of them proclaiming that this is the home of the Department of Commerce, or the Federal Trade Commission, or any of a hundred other organizations. These buildings are the concrete (sorry for the pun) manifestation of the organizational basis of governing. Without these organizations, often collectively referred to as "the bureaucracy," very little will happen in government.

Once a piece of legislation or a regulation has been accepted as a legitimate public law, in some ways, the easiest portion of the policymaking process has already transpired; government must then put the legislation into effect. To do so requires developing organizations that will apply the principles of the legislation to specific cases, monitor the performance of the policies, and perhaps propose improvements in their content and administration. Even policies that are primarily self-administered or that rely on incentives rather than formal regulations require an organizational basis for administration, although the organizations can certainly be smaller than those needed to implement programs that depend on direct administration and supervision. For example, collecting the income tax, which is largely self-administered, requires many fewer people per dollar collected than collecting customs duties, even leaving aside the role of customs agents in controlling smuggling.

American political thinkers have generally denigrated the roles of public administrators and bureaucrats in policymaking. The traditional attitude has been that policy is made by legislatures, and that administrators merely follow the guidelines the legislation sets forth. Such an attitude fails to take into account the important role of administrative decision making, and especially the importance of decision makers at the bottom of the organization, in determining the effective policies of government.[1] The real criminal justice policy of a nation or city is to a great extent determined by the way the police enforce the laws, just as the real social welfare policy is determined by decisions made by caseworkers or even receptionists in social service agencies. We have noted that bureaucrats play an important role in interpreting legislation and making regulations to put it into effect; they also make important decisions while applying laws and regulations to individual cases.[2]

It is also customary to consider government as an undivided entity and to regard government organizations as monolithic. In fact, that is not the case at all. We have mentioned that American government is divided horizontally into a number of subgovernments and vertically into levels of government in a federal system. But within the federal bureaucracy, and even within a single cabinet-level department, there are a number of bureaus, offices, and sections, all competing for money, legislative time, and public attention. Each has its own goals, ideas, and concepts about how to address the public problems it is charged with administering. As in the making of legislation, those ideas will influence the implementation of legislation. Implementation often involves conflicts and competition, rather than neat coordination and control, and struggles over policy content persist long after Congress and the president have enacted legislation. Policies, as operating instruments, commonly emerge from those conflicts as much as they do from the initial design of legislation. Policies should not necessarily be designed to be implemented easily, but anyone interested in policy outcomes must monitor implementation as well as formulation.

Dramatis Personae

The organization of the federal government is complicated not only because of the number of organizations it comprises but also because of the number of different kinds of organizations. There is no single organizational format for accomplishing the work of government, and the various organizations exist in different relationships to elective officials and even to government authority as a whole. In addition to the three constitutionally designated institutional actors—the president, Congress, and the courts—at least eight different organizational formats exist within the federal government (see Table 6.1).[3] One of these is a catchall category for organizations that are difficult to classify within the other major types.

The absence of a basic organizational format weakens central policy coordination and thus contributes to the incoherence of the policy choices the federal government makes. Moreover, the eight forms of organizations themselves have a great deal of internal variation. As Table 6.1 shows, the organizations differ greatly in size; they can also differ greatly in their internal organization. For example, the Department of Agriculture consists of almost fifty offices and bureaus, whereas the Department of Housing and Urban Development is structured around several assistant secretaries and their staffs, with few operating agencies within the department.

TABLE 6.1   Examples of Employment in Federal Organizations

Kind of organization	Employment
Executive departments	
Department of Defense (civilian)	675,700
Department of Education	4,331
Executive Office of the President	
Office of Management and Budget	482
Council on Environmental Quality	18
Legislative organizations	
Government Accountability Office	3,172
U.S. Commission on International Religious Freedom	17
Independent executive agencies	
Social Security Administration	62,400
Appalachian Regional Commission	9
Independent regulatory commissions	
Nuclear Regulatory Commission	3,713
Commodity Futures Trading Commission	442
Foundations	
National Science Foundation	1,350
African Development Foundation	29
Public corporations	
U.S. Postal Service	757,400
Neighborhood Reinvestment Corporation (NeighborWorks)	322
Other	
Smithsonian Institution	4,833
Office of Government Ethics	76

Source: Office of Personnel Management, *Federal Civilian Workforce Statistics, 2007.*

The most familiar forms of organizations are the fifteen *executive departments,* such as the Department of Defense and the Department of Health and Human Services. Each of those is headed by a secretary who is a member of the president's cabinet and who is directly responsible to the president. The executive departments should be regarded not as uniform wholes but as collections, or "holding companies," of relatively autonomous agencies and offices.[4] Departments vary in the extent to which their constituent agencies respond to central direction. Some, such as the Department of Defense, have relatively high degrees of internal coordination; others, such as the Department of Commerce, are extremely decentralized.[5]

Although the cabinet departments are important, in some instances, an individual agency may have more political influence than does the department as a whole. One such agency is the Federal Bureau of Investigation (FBI), which is part of the Department of Justice but often can operate as if it were independent. In some instances, it is not entirely clear why an agency is located in one department rather than another—for example, why the U.S. Forest Service is located in the Department of Agriculture rather than the Department of the Interior, or why the U.S. Coast Guard is now located in the Department of Homeland Security, rather than in Treasury, Commerce, Defense, or Transportation, where it has resided at various times in its history.

Although the executive departments are linked to constituencies and provide services directly to those constituencies, the organizations within the *Executive Office of the President* exist to assist the president in carrying out his tasks of control and coordination of the executive branch as a whole.[6] The most important units within the Executive Office of the President are the Office of Management and Budget (OMB), the Council of Economic Advisers, the National Security Council (NSC), the Domestic Policy Council, and the White House Office. The first two assist the president in his role as economic manager and central figure in the budgetary process. The NSC provides advice and opinion on foreign and defense issues, independent of that provided by the Departments of State and Defense, and the Domestic Policy Council performs a similar role for domestic policy. The White House Office manages the everyday complexities of serving as president of the United States and employs a number of personal advisers for the president. The units within the Executive Office of the President now employ roughly 1,800 people—an insignificant number compared with a total federal civilian workforce of more than two million but quite large when compared with the personal offices of the chief executives of other nations.[7]

Congress has also created organizations to assist it in policymaking. The three most important *legislative organizations* are the Government Accountability Office (GAO), the Congressional Budget Office (CBO), and the Congressional Research Service. Legislatures in democratic political systems generally audit the accounts of the executive to ensure that public money is being spent legally. The Government Accountability Office (formerly named the General Accounting Office) was strictly a financial accounting body for most of its existence but in the 1970s began to expand its concerns to the cost-effectiveness of expenditures.[8] For example, in one of its reports, the GAO agreed that the Internal Revenue Service (IRS) had been acting perfectly legally in the ways it sought to detect income tax evaders but recommended changing the IRS program to one the GAO considered more efficient. Few organizations in the federal government have escaped similar advice.[9] The CBO has its major policy impact on the annual preparation of the budget; its role is discussed thoroughly in chapter 7. The Congressional Research Service, located within the Library of Congress, assists Congress in policy research and prepares background material for individual members and committees.

In addition to the executive departments responsible to the president, there are a number of *independent executive agencies.* They perform executive functions, such as implementing a public program, but they are independent of the executive departments and generally report directly to the president. The independence of these agencies can be justified in several ways. Some, such as the National Aeronautics and Space Administration (NASA), are mission agencies created outside departmental frameworks so as to have greater flexibility in completing their mission. Others, such as the Environmental Protection Agency (EPA) and the Small Business Administration, are organized independently to highlight their importance and in recognition of the political power of the interest groups supporting them. Moving the Social Security Administration out of the Department of Health and Human Services in March 1995 was recognition of the importance and size of that organization, which spends close to one-quarter of the federal budget. Other organizations such as the General Services Administration and the Office of Personnel Management provide services to a number of government departments, so locating them in any one department might create management difficulties.

The fifth form of organization is the *independent regulatory commission.* Three such organizations are the Federal Trade Commission, the Federal Energy Regulatory Commission, the Consumer Product Safety Commission, and the newly created Consumer Financial Protection Bureau. These commissions are different from independent executive agencies in that they do not perform executive functions but act independently to regulate certain sectors of the economy.[10] Once the president has appointed the members of a commission, the formulation and application of its regulations are largely beyond his control. The absence of direct political support often results, however, in the "capture" of the regulatory commissions by the interests they were intended to regulate.[11] Over time, lacking ties to the president or Congress, the independent agencies may seek the political support of the regulated interests to obtain their budgets, personnel, or legislation from the other institutions in government. The tendency toward capture is not so evident in agencies that must regulate several industries—the Federal Trade Commission or Consumer Product Safety Commission, for example.[12] Not all economic regulation is conducted through the independent commissions, and some important regulatory agencies, such as the Occupational Safety and Health Administration (OSHA) and the Food and Drug Administration (FDA), are in executive departments—OSHA in the Department of Labor and the FDA in Health and Human Services.

There are also several *foundations* within the federal government, the principal examples being the National Science Foundation, the National Endowment for the Humanities, and the National Endowment for the Arts. The foundation format is intended primarily to separate the organization from the remainder of government because of a justifiable fear of creating a national orthodoxy in the arts or in science and thereby stifling creativity. Again, the foundation's relative autonomy enables government to support the activities while being removed from the decisions. The independence of the foundations is far from complete, however, for Congress has not been reluctant to intervene in their decisions, for example, by criticizing projects supported by the National Endowment for the Arts that conservatives alleged were "pornography."[13] The NEA responded with a "general standard of decency" for projects it funds, a provision that the Supreme Court said did not violate the First Amendment.[14] The president can also attempt to influence the foundations, primarily through the appointment of directors and board members.

The government of the United States has generally avoided becoming directly involved in the economy other than through regulation, but there are a number of *public corporations* in the federal government.[15] For example, since 1970, the U.S. Postal Service has been a public corporation rather than part of an executive department, as it was before. That one public corporation employs over 750,000 people, or almost one-third of all federal civilian employees. Another public corporation, the Tennessee Valley Authority, has about 6 percent of the total electrical generating capacity of the United States. There are also some very small public corporations, such as the Overseas Private Investment Corporation, which employs less than 200 people.

A public corporation is organized much like a private corporation, with a board of directors and stock issued for capitalization. The principal difference is that the board members are all public appointees and the stock is generally held entirely by the Department of the Treasury or by another executive department. There are several reasons for choosing the corporate form of organization. One is that these organizations provide marketed goods and services to the population and hence can be better managed as commercial concerns.[16] This is also a means of keeping some government functions at arm's length, so the president and Congress are not held directly responsible for the actions of the organizations.

In addition to the wholly owned government corporations, there is a group of organizations described as "quasi-governmental," or in the "twilight zone." Examples of these are the National Railroad Passenger Corporation (Amtrak), the Corporation for Public Broadcasting, and the Federal Reserve Board. These organizations have some attributes of public organizations—most important, access to public funding—but they also have some attributes of private organizations. They are similar to public corporations except that a portion of their boards of directors is appointed by private sector organizations; the board of Amtrak is appointed in part by the member railroad corporations. Also, some of their stock may be owned by the cooperating private sector organizations. Employees of these quasi-governmental organizations generally are not classified as public employees, and they generally are not subject to other public sector regulations, such as the Freedom of Information Act.

The justification for the formation of quasi-governmental organizations such as these is again to permit government to become involved in a policy area without assuming any real or apparent direct control. The federal government subsidizes certain activities—passenger railroad service would almost certainly have vanished from the United States without Amtrak—but its intervention is not as obvious as other forms of public sector involvement in the economy. Intervention by a quasi-governmental organization also gives the public a greater role in decision making and provides greater representation of private interests such as affected corporations. And as with the Corporation for Public Broadcasting, this form of organization permits the federal government to become involved in an area from which it has traditionally been excluded.

It is important to understand just how vital these quasi-governmental organizations are to the federal government. For example, the Federal Reserve Board fits comfortably into this twilight zone, given its isolation from executive authority and its relationship to its member banks. But the Federal Reserve Board is responsible for making monetary policy for the United States and thereby has a significant—probably now the most significant—influence on the nation's economic conditions.[17] Similarly, the Corporation for Public Broadcasting is a significant complement to commercial radio and television broadcasting, although Congress often fails to support public broadcasting with anything like the funds available to commercial broadcasting.[18]

The quasi-governmental organizations in the federal government have been in the public eye during the 2008 and 2009 economic crisis more than they might have liked. Two of these organizations, the Federal National Mortgage Association (Fannie Mae) and the Federal Home Mortgage Corporation (Freddie Mac), were government-sponsored corporations that served as a secondary market for mortgages, enabling private banks to make more home loans than they might otherwise. In the process of performing this task, however, these two organizations came to hold a number of almost worthless subprime mortgages and were so threatened that the federal government had to buy, and in essence nationalize, them.[19] The economic crisis also led to the partial inclusion of several banks and insurance companies into this quasi-governmental arena of government.

Finally, there is the catchall category *other organizations,* which contains several regional commissions that coordinate economic or environmental policy in parts of the country. Various claims commissions, the Administrative Office of the United States Courts, and the Sentencing Commission operate on the fringes of the judicial process. And organizations such as the Smithsonian

Institution, the National Academy of Sciences, and the American Red Cross are mentioned in federal legislation and receive subsidies, but they are far removed from the mainstream of government action.

We should note several other points about the complexity of the structure of the federal government. One is the redundancy built into the system. First, both Congress (through the Congressional Budget Office) and the Executive Office of the President (through the Office of Management and Budget) have organizations to deal with budgeting and with many other economic aspects of government. Because of the doctrine of separation of powers, such duplication makes a great deal of sense, but the overlap still conflicts with conventional managerial thinking about eliminating duplicative organizations.

Second, we have seen that some units in the Executive Office of the President duplicate activities of the executive departments. Most notably, presidents appear to demand foreign policy advice other than that provided by the Departments of State and Defense, and they get it from the National Security Council. This demand may be justified, as the executive departments have their own existing policy commitments and ideas, which may limit their ability to respond to presidential initiatives in foreign policy. But during at least every administration since Richard Nixon's, conflicts have arisen between the two sets of institutions, and the management of foreign policy may suffer as a result. In most instances, the conflict has been perceived as one between the experienced professionals in the Department of State and committed amateurs in the National Security Council. Such conflicts were evident at the outset of the Iraq War and have persisted to some extent throughout the conflict.

In other policy areas, several federal organizations may regulate. For example, both the Federal Trade Commission and the Antitrust Division of the Department of Justice are concerned with antitrust policy and monopolies.[20] Some redundancy in this activity can be rationalized as a means of limiting error, as well as providing alternative means for accomplishing the same tasks and even alternative definitions of the issues.[21] If the redundant institutions are occupied by ambitious men and women, however, the potential for conflict, "gridlock," or excessive regulation is substantial.[22]

It is also interesting that not all central fiscal and management functions of the federal government are located in the Executive Office of the President. Several important management functions—monetary policy, personnel policy, debt management, and taxation—are controlled by agencies outside the president's office, one by an organization in the twilight zone. This diffusion of duties and responsibilities limits the president's ability to implement his policy priorities and consequently to control the federal establishment for which he is held accountable politically and to some extent legally. Reactions to the fiscal crisis in 2008 and 2009 indicate that these organizations can work together effectively when necessary, but in more normal times, they will operate quite separately.[23]

Third, we have mentioned variations in the "publicness" of organizations in, or associated with, the federal government. Some organizations are clearly public: They receive their funds from the federal budget; their employees are hired through public personnel systems; and they are subject to legislation such as the Freedom of Information Act, which attempts to differentiate public from private programs.[24] Other organizations appear tied to the private sector as much as to government: They receive some or all of their funds as fees for services or interest on loans; they have their own personnel policies; and they are only slightly more subject to normal restrictions on public organizations than is Starbucks. For a president—who will be accountable to voters and to Congress for the performance of the federal government—this presents an immense and perhaps insoluble problem. How can the president really take responsibility when so many of the organizations charged with implementing his policies are beyond effective control? This is but one of many difficulties a president encounters when attempting to put his policies into effect, and it is a bridge to our discussion of implementation.

The issue of the publicness of organizations arose in a particularly controversial form in President George W. Bush's proposal to use "faith-based organizations" to deliver a range of social services.[25] The organizations involved are primarily private, and the tradition of the separation of church and state in the United States makes their affiliation with government more suspect than would be the case with other private organizations. Many citizens expressed concern about the possibility that the organizations would proselytize recipients of their services or make religious adherence a criterion for receiving them. Some of the organizations themselves expressed doubts about closer involvement in the public sector, fearing that entanglement with government would reduce their capacity to maintain religious and programmatic freedom. All of that said, President Obama announced his own attempts to involve faith-based organizations in delivering public services.

Implementation

All the organizations we have been discussing are established to execute legislation or to monitor that execution. Once enacted, laws do not go into effect by themselves, as was assumed by those in the (presumed) tradition of Woodrow Wilson, who discussed "mere administration."[26] In fact, one of the most important things to understand about government is that it is a minor miracle that implementation is ever accomplished.[27] There are so many more ways of blocking intended actions than there are of making results materialize that all legislators should be pleased if they live to see their pet projects not only passed into law but also actually put into effect. Although this is perhaps an excessively negative characterization of implementation, it should underline the extreme difficulties of administering and implementing public programs.

A large number of factors may limit the ability of a political system to put policies into effect. Rarely will all the factors affect any single policy, but all must be considered when designing a policy and attempting to translate it into real services for citizens. Any one of the factors may be sufficient to cause the failure or suboptimal performance of a policy, and all may have to be in good order for the policy to work. In short, it is much easier to prevent a policy from working than it is to make it effective.

The Legislation

The first factor that affects the effective implementation of a policy is the nature of the legislation that establishes it. Laws vary in their specificity, clarity, and the policy areas they attempt to influence, as well as in the extent to which they bind the individuals and organizations charged with implementing them to perform in the way the writers intended. Unfortunately, both legislators and analysts sometimes overlook the importance of the legislation. Laws that are easier to implement are, everything else being equal, more difficult to pass. Their specificity may make it clear who the winners and losers are and thus complicate the task of building the political coalitions necessary for passage.

Policy Issues

Legislators frequently choose to legislate in policy areas where they lack sufficient information about the causes of problems to enable them to make good policy choices. If we refer to the four kinds of policy formulation discussed earlier (see Figure 4.1), we can estimate the likelihood of effective implementation of a policy. We anticipate that the highest probability of effective implementation will occur with both sufficient information about the policy area and adequate knowledge of the causes of the problems. In such situations, government can design legislation to solve, or at least ameliorate, the problem. On the other hand, effective implementation is not likely in policy areas where there is inadequate information and little knowledge about problem causes.

The other two possible combinations of knowledge of causation and information may differ very little in their likelihood of effective implementation, although we would expect a somewhat better probability when there is knowledge of the patterns of causation, as opposed to more basic information. If the underlying process is understood, it would appear possible to formulate policy responses based on available information, however poor the information may be. When there is inadequate information, policy responses involve a certain amount of excessive reaction, or overkill. If the underlying process is misunderstood, or is not understood at all, there is little hope of effectively implementing

President Lyndon Johnson and his wife, Lady Bird, center left, leave the home in Inez, Kentucky, of Tom Fletcher, a father of eight who told Johnson he'd been out of work for nearly two years, on April 24, 1964. The president visited the Appalachian area in eastern Kentucky to see conditions firsthand and announce his War on Poverty from the Fletcher porch.

AP Images

a policy except by pure luck. In such instances, governments often wind up treating symptoms, as they do with the problems of crime and delinquency, instead of dealing with the underlying social processes.

Perhaps the best example of a large-scale policy formulation and implementation in spite of inadequate knowledge of patterns of causation was the War on Poverty in the United States during the 1960s. There were (and are) as many theories about the causes of poverty as there were theorists, but there was little real understanding even of the basics of the economic and social dynamics producing the problem.[28] War was thus declared on an enemy that was poorly understood. Sen. Daniel P. Moynihan put it this way:

> This is the essential fact: The Government did not know what it was doing. It had a theory. Or rather a set of theories. Nothing more. The U.S. Government at this time was no more in possession of a confident knowledge as to how to prevent delinquency, cure anomie, or overcome that midmorning sense of powerlessness than it was the possessor of a dependable formula for motivating Vietnamese villagers to fight Communism.[29]

Not only was it a war, but it was also a war based on something approaching a dogma about the plan of attack—for example, using large-scale and rather expensive programs involving direct services to clients. Arguably, the programs were doomed to fail because they were based on dubious assumptions about the society and the mechanisms for approaching such problems. But the interventions, if misguided, had the political appeal and visibility that smaller-scale efforts would have lacked.

A more recent example of a policy made without adequate knowledge was the Strategic Defense Initiative and subsequent attempts to build an antimissile defense during the George W. Bush administration. These policies "forced" the development of technologies that would be at least as important for domestic as for defense purposes.[30] The Bush administration's stress on alternative power sources for automobiles is another recent example of technology forcing (see chapter 14).[31] The Obama administration's agreement with automobile manufacturers to increase the gas mileage of their products significantly will also depend upon developing new technologies.[32]

Technology forcing is an interesting if somewhat novel approach to designing public programs, but it is not one that can be recommended as a strategy for policymaking. It has been successful in some policy areas, in part because the problems being dealt with were aspects of the physical world rather than the more complex social and economic realities that governments often face.[33] The potential difficulties should not be taken to mean that governments should just keep to their well-worn paths and do what they have always done in the ways they always have. Instead, they should caution that if one expects significant results from programs based on insufficient understanding of the subject matter, those expectations are likely to be dashed.

Political Setting

Legislation is adopted through political action, and the political process may plant within legislation the seeds of its own destruction. The very compromises and negotiations necessary to pass a bill may ultimately make it virtually impossible to implement. An example is the thousand-page stimulus bill adopted in early 2009. The speed with which it was drafted and the compromises contained within it began to produce implementation problems almost as soon as it was adopted.

The effects of the political process on legislation are manifested in different ways. One is vague language: Lack of clarity may be essential to develop a coalition for passage, as every time a vague term is made specific, potential coalition members are lost. But by phrasing legislation in vague and inoffensive language, legislators risk leaving their intent unclear to those who must implement the law, thus allowing the implementers to alter the meaning of the program substantially. Phrases such as "maximum feasible participation," "equality of educational opportunity," "special needs of educationally deprived students," and that favorite vague concept "public interest" are all subject to various interpretations, many of which could betray the true intent of the legislators. Even words about which most citizens can agree may produce problems during implementation, as when the Reagan administration attempted to define ketchup as a "vegetable" under the School Lunch Program, and more recently, the tomato sauce on pizza also was considered to meet the criterion of a vegetable.[34]

In addition to coalitions formed for the passage of a single piece of legislation, other coalitions may have to be formed across several pieces of legislation—the classic approach to logrolling. To gain support for one favored measure, a coalition-building legislator may have to trade his or her support on other measures. In some instances, this may simply increase the overall volume of legislation enacted. In others, it may involve passing legislation that negates, or decreases the effects of, desired legislation. Some coalitions that must be formed are regional, so it may become virtually impossible to give one region an advantage, even one justified by economic circumstances, without making commensurate concessions to other regions, thereby nullifying the intended effect. It is also difficult to make decisions that are redistributive across economic classes—either the legislation will be watered down to be distributive (everyone gets a piece of the pie) or additional legislation will be passed to spread the benefits more broadly. A good deal of the politics of taxation exemplifies this tendency in writing legislation.[35]

Similar problems of vagueness and logrolling can occur when other institutions make rulings that must be implemented. In a number of instances, a judicial decision intended to mandate a certain action has been so vague as to be difficult or impossible to implement. One of the best examples of this lack of clarity is the famous decision in *Brown v. Board of Education,* which ordered schools to desegregate with "all deliberate speed." Two of those three words, *deliberate* and *speed,* appear somewhat contradictory, and the decision did not specify exactly what the phrase meant. Similarly, the police are prohibited from searching an individual, an automobile they stop, or a home without "probable cause," but that phrase was left largely undefined until a series of cases required the courts to be clearer. The process of writing regulations in administrative agencies, intended to clarify and specify legislation, can itself create ambiguities, which require more regulations to clarify and cause more delay in implementation.

In summary, politics is central to the formulation of legislation, but the results of the political process often are such that legislation cannot be implemented effectively. The compromises necessitated by political feasibility may result in just the reductions in clarity and purpose that make laws too diffuse to be implemented so as to have a real effect on society. The vagueness of legislation may make room for another type of politics dominated more by interest groups than by elected officials.

Interest Group Liberalism

Theodore J. Lowi's concern about government involvement in the more abstract aspects of human behavior helps illuminate some of the problems of vagueness in legislation.[36] Lowi's argument is that the United States has progressed from concerted and specific legislation, such as the Interstate Commerce Act of 1887, which established clear standards of practice for the Interstate Commerce Commission, to abstract and general standards, such as "unfair competition" in the Clayton Act of 1914. The tendency has been extended through even more general and diffuse aspects of human behavior in the social legislation enacted after the 1960s to regulate what Lowi refers to as the "environment of conduct." It is simply more difficult to show that a person has discriminated against another person on the basis of race, color, or sex than it is to show that a railroad has violated prohibitions against discriminatory freight rates.

Lowi believes that the problems arise not from the commendable intentions of these vague laws but from the difficulty of implementing them. The diffuseness of the targets specified and the difficulty of defining standards subject policies for regulating those behaviors to errors in interpretation during implementation. It also becomes more difficult to hold government accountable when it administers ambiguous legislation. The "interest group liberalism" inherent in U.S. politics, in which the public interest tends to be defined in terms of many private interests, and especially the private interests of better-organized groups, means that the implementation of a piece of legislation will generally differ greatly from the intentions of those who framed it. Implementation will be undertaken by agencies that are themselves tied to clients and to particular definitions of the public interest, and which will not want to be swayed from their position. Problems of accountability created by the deviation of policies in practice from the intentions of their framers can only alienate the clients and frustrate the legislators, and perhaps the administrators as well.

The Organizational Setting

As noted earlier, most implementation is undertaken by organizations, especially organizations in the public bureaucracy. Given the nature of public organizations, and of organizations in general, the probability that one of them will effectively implement a program is not particularly high. The reason is not moral failings on the part of the bureaucracy but simply the internal dynamics of large organizations, which often limit their ability to respond to policy changes.

To begin to understand what goes wrong when organizations attempt to implement programs, a model of "perfect" administration may be useful. Christopher Hood proposes five characteristics of perfect administration of public programs:

1. Administration would be unitary; it would be one vast army all marching to the same drummer.
2. The norms and rules of administration would be uniform throughout the organization.
3. There would be no resistance to commands.
4. There would be perfect information and communication within the organization.
5. There would be adequate time.[37]

Clearly, these conditions are often absent in organizations, and almost never are all of them present. Because governments depend on large organizations to implement their policies, difficulties inherent in large organization—public or private—arise. The difficulties need not be insurmountable, but they need to be understood and anticipated if possible, if successful implementation is to occur. Just what characteristics and difficulties in organizations lead to difficulties in implementation?

Organizational Disunity

Organizations are rarely unitary administrations—indeed, a number of points of disunity almost always exist in organizational structures. One is the disjunction between the central offices of organizations and their field staffs. Decisions may be made by politicians and administrators sitting in national capitals, but those decisions must be implemented by people in the field who may not share the values and goals of the administrators in the home office.

The disjunction of values may take several forms. A change in central values and programs may occur as a result of a change in presidents or in Congress, and the field staff may remain loyal to the older policies. For example, the Clinton administration inherited a government shaped in most areas by twelve years of Republican presidents. The George W. Bush administration, in turn, had to deal with the residual organizational values from the Clinton years.[38] After eight years of Republican dominance, the Obama administration expressed some concerns about the reliability of some public organizations. Problems with field staff over policy changes produce frustration for politicians nominally in control of policymaking and make implementation of policies that violate the norms of the existing field staff extremely difficult.

A more common disparity between the goals of field staffs and those of the home office may occur as the field staff is "captured" by clients. Field staff members are frequently close to their clients, and they may adopt their clients' perspective in their own relationships with the remainder of the organization.[39] This can happen when the clients are relatively disadvantaged and the organization is attempting either to assist them or to exercise some control over them. The identification of staff members with their clients is fostered by frequent contact, sympathy, empathy, and quite commonly genuine devotion to a perceived mission that is in contrast to the mission fostered by the central office. This pattern of conflict between central and field staffs emerged when welfare reform (see chapter 12) began to have negative impacts on recipients and social workers attempted to protect their clients.[40] Whatever the cause, this identification makes implementation of centrally determined policy difficult.

Field staffs may also find that if they are to perform their tasks effectively, they cannot follow all the directives coming to them from the center of the organization. In such instances, to obtain substantive compliance, the organization members may not comply with procedural directives. For example, in a classic study of the FBI, Peter M. Blau found that field agents frequently did not comply with directives requiring them to report the offering of a bribe by a suspect.[41] The agents had found that they could gain greater cooperation from a subject by using the threat to have the person prosecuted for offering the bribe at any time. Their performance of the task of prosecuting criminals was probably enhanced, but it was done at the expense of the directive from the central office.

Eugene Bardach and Robert A. Kagan have argued that regulatory enforcement in the United States could be improved if field staffs were granted greater latitude for independent action.[42] They believe that rigidities resulting from strict central controls actually produce less compliance with the spirit of regulations than would a more flexible approach. This interest in enhancing regulatory latitude can, however, be contrasted with the continuing (and strengthening) interest in control over bureaucracies, especially regulatory bureaucracies. Congress is concerned with efficient enforcement, but it is often more concerned with ensuring that what is being implemented corresponds with its intentions.[43] In attempting to design programs to ensure compliance, lawmakers paradoxically may limit enforcement.

Standard Operating Procedures

Organizations develop standard operating procedures (SOPs). When a prospective client walks into a social service agency, the agency follows a standard pattern of response: Certain forms must be filled out, designated personnel interview the prospective client, and specific criteria are applied to determine the person's eligibility for benefits. Likewise, if a blip appears on the radar screen of a defense installation, a certain set of procedures is followed to determine if the blip is real and, if so, whether it is friendly or hostile. If it should be hostile, further prespecified actions are taken.

Standard operating procedures are important for organizations because they reduce the amount of time spent processing each new situation and developing a response. The SOPs are the learned response of the organization to particular problems; they represent to some extent the organizational memory in action. SOPs may also be important for clients, as they are adopted at least in part to ensure equality and fairness. Without SOPs, organizations might respond more slowly to each situation, they might respond less effectively, and they would probably respond more erratically.

Although SOPs are generally beneficial for organizations, they can also constitute barriers to good implementation. This is most obvious when a new policy or a new approach to an existing policy is being considered. An organization is likely to persist in defining policies and problems in the standard manner, even when the old definition or procedure no longer helps it fulfill its mission. For example, when Medicare was added to the responsibilities of the Social Security Administration, the agency faced an entirely new set of concerns in addition to its traditional task of making payments to individuals. In particular, it assumed responsibility for limiting the costs of medical care. It chose to undertake that responsibility in much the same way that it would have attempted to manage problems arising from pensions—by examining individual claims and denying those that appeared to be unjustified. It took the Social Security Administration some time to focus attention on more fundamental and systemic problems of medical cost inflation and to develop programs such as diagnostic-related groupings (see chapter 11). The agency took some time even to cope with adding the Supplemental Security Income program, which was much closer to its original portfolio of income maintenance policies but more similar to a means-tested program than to a social insurance program.[44]

There is thus a need to design public programs and administer organizations that will consistently reassess their goals and the methods they use to reach them. In some instances—for example, correlating the number of births and the future need for schools—the response should be programmed to be almost automatic; other situations will require more thought and greater political involvement. Organizations do not like to perform such reassessments, which may threaten both the employees of the organization and its clients. One reason for creating organizations with standard operating procedures is to ensure some stability and predictability, but that stability can become a barrier to success when problems and needs change.

Standard operating procedures also tend to produce inappropriate or delayed responses to crises. The military, perhaps more than any other organization, tends to employ SOPs and to train its members to carry them out in the absence of commands to the contrary. The brief invasion of Grenada in 1983 encountered difficulties when the communication SOPs of the navy and army did not correspond, so the soldiers on the island could not communicate with the ships providing them support. Soldiers found that the best way to communicate was to use their telephone credit cards to call the Pentagon, which would then communicate with the navy. The response of the air force to the airplanes aimed at New York and Washington on 9/11 was slowed because they were conditioned to think of threats coming from across the borders of the United States, not from within. Like the military, fire and police units develop standard operating procedures, and some of those routines—and the consequent inability to recognize the novelty of new events—appear to have contributed to the huge loss of life among firefighters when the World Trade Center collapsed.

A standard means of avoiding the constraining effects of SOPs is to create a new organization to run a new program. When the Small Business Administration was created in 1953, Congress purposely did not locate it in the Department of Commerce, whose SOPs tended to favor big business. The Office of National Drug Control Policy was established within the Executive Office of the President to ensure both its priority and its independence from other organizations such as the Drug Enforcement Administration and the Customs Bureau. There are, of course, limits to the number of new organizations that can be set up, for the more that are created, the greater the chance that interorganizational barriers to implementation will replace the barriers internal to any one organization. Drug policy suffers from coordination problems among the numerous agencies—the three just mentioned, as well as the Coast Guard, the Department of Defense, the FBI, and numerous state and local authorities, among others—involved in the policy area. This lack of coordination is evident even after the creation of a national "drug czar" to provide direction to the programs.

SOPs aid in the implementation of established programs, whereas they are likely to be barriers to change and to the implementation of new ones. Procedures may be too standardized to permit effective response to nonstandard situations or nonstandard clients; they may create rigidity and inappropriate responses to novel situations. Established procedures often prompt organizations to try to classify new problems as old ones for as long as they can and to continue to use familiar responses even when the problems appear demonstrably different to an outsider.

Organizational Communication

Another barrier to effective implementation is the improper flow of information within organizations. Because government organizations depend heavily on the flow of information—just as manufacturers rely on the flow of raw materials—accurate information and the prevention of blockages of information are extremely important to their success. Unfortunately, organizations, and particularly public organizations, are subject to inaccurate and blocked communication.

In general, information in bureaucracies tends to be concentrated at the bottom of the hierarchy.[45] Field staffs are in closer contact with the organization's environment, and technical experts tend to be clustered at the bottom of organizations, with more generalist managers concentrated at the top. This pattern means that if the organization is to respond to changes in its environment and if it is to make appropriate technical decisions, then information at the bottom must be transmitted to the top, and then directions must be passed back down to the bottom for implementation. Unfortunately, the more levels through which information has to be transmitted, the greater is the probability that it will be distorted when it is finally acted on.

The distortion in communications may result from random error or from *selective distortion,* as when officials at each stage of message transmission attempt to transmit only the information that they believe their superiors wish to hear or that they think will make them look good to their superiors. The superiors, in turn, may attempt to estimate what sort of distortion their subordinates may have introduced and try to correct for it.[46] The result of the transmitting of messages through a hierarchical organization thus is frequently rampant distortion and misinformation that limit the organization's ability to make effective decisions.

Some characteristics of an organization may improve the transmission of information through its hierarchy. If organization members share a common technical or professional background, their communication with one another should be less distorted. But a common language can also prevent an organization from responding to new situations or producing innovative solutions and diminish its ability to communicate effectively with other organizations. Attempts by the organization to create internal unity through training and socialization should improve internal patterns of communication.[47] And the "flatter" the organization is—the fewer levels through which communication must go before being acted on—the less distortion is likely to occur.[48]

Another way to improve communication in organizations is to create more, and redundant, channels. President Franklin Roosevelt developed personal ties to lower-level members of federal organizations and placed his own people in organizations to be sure that he would receive direct and unvarnished reports from the operating levels of government.[49] A president or manager might also build in several channels of communication to make them function as checks on one another. Again, Roosevelt's frequent development of parallel organizations (e.g., the Works Progress Administration and the Public Works Administration) provided him with alternative channels of information about the progress of his

New Deal. In more contemporary times, the creation of several channels of advice and communication to the president about national security policy and drug policy may be a way of ensuring that the information he receives is both accurate and complete.

A particularly interesting threat to effective organizational communication is secrecy.[50] Although a certain level of secrecy is important for some government organizations, it can inhibit both communication and implementation. Secrecy frequently means that a communication cannot be shared because it has been classified; other parts of the organization or other organizations are consequently denied what they need to know. The Cuban missile crisis provides numerous examples of how the military's penchant for secrecy can prevent a rapid response to situations. Secrecy can produce inefficiency, as when FBI agents had to spend time reporting on one another when they infiltrated subversive organizations, such as the Ku Klux Klan. To make themselves more acceptable to the organizations they had infiltrated, the agents tended to be among the most vociferous members, and consequently, they became the subjects of a disproportionate share of reports by other agents. More recently, the Central Intelligence Agency's (CIA) identification of spies in its midst was slowed because parts of the organization were unwilling to share information with other parts of the public sector. Secrecy may be counterproductive even when it is justified. For example, one argument holds that the interests of military deterrence are best served by informing an adversary of the full extent of one's arsenal instead of masking its strength, since uncertainty may create a willingness to gamble on the strength of the opponent, whereas openness may prevent war.

In modern organizations, knowledge is power, and the inability of an organization to gather and process information from its environment will harm its performance. Clearly, the management of communication flows within an organization is an important component of taking raw information and putting it into action. Most organizations face huge problems in performing even this simple (or apparently simple) task and as a consequence do not implement their programs effectively. Their internal hierarchical structures, differential commitment to goals, and differences in professional language all conspire to make organizational communication more difficult than it may appear from the outside.

Time Problems

Hood points to two time problems that inhibit the ability of public organizations to respond to situations in their policy environments. One is a linear time problem, in which the responses of the organization tend to lag behind the need for the response.[51] This often happens in organizations that have learned their lessons too well and that base their responses on previous learning rather than on current conditions. The problem is similar to what occurs with standard operating procedures, but it has less to do with processing individual cases than with designing the mechanisms for putting new programs into effect. Organizations frequently implement programs to deal with a crisis that has just passed rather than with the crisis they currently face or might soon face. To some degree, the U.S. armed forces in Vietnam used the lessons they had learned, or thought they had learned, in World War II and the Korean conflict. Unfortunately for them, a highly mechanized, technologically sophisticated, and logistically dependent fighting force broke down in a tropical guerrilla war. Lessons presumably learned from the Gulf War proved to be something of a problem in the Iraq War.

Government also has at times failed to respond even to obvious social changes, such as demographic ones. The fact that newborn babies will five or six years later require places in public schools sometimes seems to amaze public officials. Governments have not prepared well for the baby boomer generation that will begin to reach retirement age around 2012 but have allowed this large population to proceed through the life cycle without making adequate plans for the burdens it will impose on the Social Security retirement system and on health care (see chapters 11 and 12).

Other time problems are cyclical, and delay in acting can contribute to their persistence and severity. This is especially important in making and implementing macroeconomic policy, in which, even if the information available to a decision maker is timely and accurate, any delay in response may exaggerate economic fluctuations. If a decision maker responds to a threatened increase in inflation by reducing money supplies or reducing spending, and if that response is delayed for a year, or even for a few months, it may only accelerate an economic slowdown that has emerged in the meantime from other causes. Thus, it is not sufficient merely to be right; an effective policy must be both correct and on time if it is to have the desired effect.

Horseshoe-Nail Problems and Public Planning

The final organizational problem in implementation arises when organizations plan their activities incompletely or inaccurately. Hood calls these "horseshoe-nail" problems because failure to provide the nail results in the loss of the horse and eventually the battle.[52] And because government organizations often must plan for implementation with limited information, problems of this kind are likely to arise in the public sector. Examples abound: passing requirements to inspect coal mines but failing to hire inspectors, as emerged after several mine disasters in Pennsylvania and West Virginia; requiring clients to fill out certain forms but neglecting to have the forms printed; forgetting to stop construction of a $160 million highway tunnel that leads nowhere once the plan to build the rest of the highway is abandoned. There are countless examples of this political and policy version of Murphy's law.[53]

To ensure effective management and implementation, planners must identify the crucial potential blockages in their organization and allow for them in their planning. With a new program or policy, such planning may be extremely difficult; the problems that will arise may be almost impossible to anticipate. Some planners use these difficulties to justify incremental or experimental approaches when introducing new policies. Instead of undertaking large projects with the possibility of equally large failures, they may substitute smaller projects whose failure or unanticipated difficulties would impose minimal costs but would help prepare the organization to implement full-scale projects. The problem, of course, is that such programs often are not permitted to grow sufficiently to reach an effective level but may remain small and "experimental."

Some programs will be effective only if they are comprehensive and implemented on a large scale. Paul Schulman's analysis of the National Aeronautics and Space Administration points out that a program such as the space program designed to reach a major goal within a limited time and with engineering as opposed to a pure research focus—must be large in scale to be effective.[54] It has been argued that the War on Poverty, instead of being the failure portrayed in the conventional wisdom, actually was never tried on a scale that might have made it effective. In contrast, the so-called "war on cancer" was implemented in the 1970s as if it were a program that required a centralized mission format, whereas in reality, it required a more decentralized structure to allow scientific research to pursue as many avenues as possible.[55] Those who design programs and organizations must be very careful to develop them to match the characteristics of the problem and the state of knowledge about the subject. Even if objectively correct, a strategy may still provoke political criticism, as the failure to launch a "war on AIDS" did in many circles.[56] The "war on terror" may be better fought by a collection of largely autonomous and decentralized, albeit coordinated, organizations than by the comprehensive and hierarchically organized program that is the presumed purpose of the Department of Homeland Security.

Interorganizational Politics

Few policies, if any, are designed and implemented by a "single lonely organization."[57] Although individual organizations have their problems, many more difficulties are encountered in the interactions among several organizations attempting to implement a policy. The problems of organizational disunity and communication become exaggerated when the people involved are not bound even by a presumed loyalty to a single organization but have competing loyalties to different organizations, not all of them interested in the effective implementation of a particular program.[58] The tendency may be exaggerated when a central element in implementation is private contractors, whose goals of profit and contract fulfillment conflict with goals of service delivery and accountability in the public sector.[59]

Jeffrey L. Pressman and Aaron Wildavsky, who popularized the concern for implementation several decades ago, speak of the problems of implementing policies through a number of organizations (or even within a single organization) as problems of "clearance points"—defined as the number of individual decision points that must be agreed to before any policy intentions can be translated into action.[60] Even if the decision makers at each clearance point are favorably disposed toward the program in question, there may still be impediments to reaching agreement on implementation. Some problems may be legal, some may be budgetary, and others may involve building coalitions with other organizations or interests in the society.

Statistically, one would expect that if each decision point is independent of the others and if the probability of any individual decision maker's agreeing to the program is 90 percent (.9), then the probability of any two agreeing is 81 percent (.9 × .9). For three points, the probability would be 73 percent (.9 × .9 × .9), and so forth. Pressman and Wildavsky determined that there were at a minimum seventy clearance points in the implementation of the Economic Development Administration's decision to become involved in public works projects in Oakland, California.[61] With this number of clearance points, the probability of all of them agreeing, given an average probability of 90 percent for each clearance, would be less than one in a thousand. Only if there were a probability greater than 99 percent at each clearance point would the odds in favor of implementation be greater than fifty-fifty. Of course, implementation is not just a problem in statistics, and the political and administrative leaders involved in the process can vastly alter the probabilities at each stage. With so many independent clearance points and limited political resources, however, a leader may well be tempted to succumb to the inertia inherent in the implementation system.

Judith Bowen has argued that the simple statistical model that Pressman and Wildavsky propose may understate the probability of successful implementation.[62] Bowen points out that if persistence is permitted and each clearance point can be assaulted a number of times, the chances for successful implementation increase significantly. She also explains that the clearance points may not be independent, as assumed, and that success at one clearance point may produce increased probability of success at subsequent ones. The clever implementer can also make strategic choices about which clearance points to try first and how to package the points so that some success can be gained even if the whole campaign is not won. Thus, although successful implementation is still not perceived to be a simple task, it is subject to manipulation, as are other stages of the policy process. The clever policy analyst can improve his or her probabilities of success by understanding how to intervene most effectively.

The administrative reforms of recent decades have tended to exacerbate the problems of implementation by including more actors in the process, especially private sector (both for-profit and not-for-profit) organizations. A common admonition now is that governments should "steer but not row"[63]—that is, governments should make policy but depend on other organizations that may be more efficient for the actual implementation. This strategy is presumed both to reduce costs (and public employment) and to boost the quality of the services delivered to citizens. Whether those goals are achieved or not, it is clear that the new style of administration builds in more clearance points and hence more opportunities for policies to go astray in the implementation process.

Vertical Implementation Structures

One problem in implementation occurs vertically within the hierarchical structures of government. I have described some problems of intergovernmental relations in the United States that are associated with the several levels of government. The impact of intergovernmental relations is especially evident with federal social and urban legislation, in which all three levels of government may be involved in putting a single piece of legislation into effect. For example, the welfare reforms of the 1990s depended on the actions of state governments, local governments, and private contractors to move poorer citizens off public assistance and into productive work, and that has produced an immense implementation problem.[64] Some of the failures to rebuild quickly in the Gulf states following Hurricane Katrina can be linked to the complexity of the implementation structures.

A vertical implementation structure gives rise to several possibilities for inadequate implementation or none. One source of such problems is simple partisan politics, when state or local governments and the federal government are controlled by different political parties and consequently have different policy priorities. Localities may for other reasons have different policy priorities than the federal government and may choose to implement programs differently than the federal government desires. Two good examples of such differences can be seen in the resistance of local governments to federally mandated scattering of public housing in middle-class neighborhoods and in the resistance of most state and local governments to federal proposals to locate nuclear waste disposal facilities in their territory. The state of Nevada, for example, fought the federal government for more than twenty years over the proposed location of a repository for nuclear waste at Yucca Mountain.

Even if local governments want to do what the federal government would have them do, they sometimes lack the resources to do it. Local governments have attempted to resist various federal mandates, such as day care quality standards, claiming they lacked the funds to meet the standards imposed.[65] States and localities sometimes have few incentives to comply with federal directives. For example, in the Elementary and Secondary Education Act of 1965 the states were to receive their grants merely for participating in the program, without having to do anything in particular to improve education.

The increasing emphasis on the use of the private sector to achieve public purposes means that implementation is increasingly being performed by private groups as well as by subnational governments. For example, tenants organizations have begun to manage public housing projects, and churches and other charitable organizations became contractors for services under the AmeriCorps volunteer program in the Clinton administration. This pattern of implementation can easily create the problems of capture described earlier. For instance, some attempts to regulate the amount of fish that can be caught in the Atlantic have been implemented by the affected parties (fishermen and processors, among others) through eight management councils, with the result that overfishing has been permitted and fish stocks have been seriously depleted.[66]

Horizontal Implementation Structures

In addition to problems incurred in achieving compliance across several levels of government, difficulties may occur in coordinating activities and organizations horizontally. That is, the success of one agency's program may require the cooperation of other organizations, or at least the effective coordination of their activities. As one simple example, the Department of Agriculture has assisted the Department of Health and Human Services in implementing the Women, Infants and Children's (WIC) nutrition program by bargaining to keep the price of infant formula lower, so that the funds provided by WIC to women can go farther.

Coordination can break down in several ways. One is through language and encoding difficulties. Individual agencies hire certain kinds of professionals and train all their employees in a certain manner. As a result, the Great Society–era Model Cities Program's housing experts decided that the problems of residents resulted from substandard housing, whereas employment experts thought that the problems arose from unemployment, and psychiatric social workers perceived them as resulting from personality problems. Each group of professionals, in other words, was oblivious to the perspectives of the other groups and consequently found it difficult to cooperate in treating the "whole client"—one of the stated objectives of the Model Cities Program. This was strongly demonstrated in the pattern of referrals among agencies. The vast majority of referrals of clients from one agency to another occurred within policy areas, rather than across policy areas.[67] Clients who visited an agency seeking health care would frequently be referred to another agency, most commonly another health care agency rather than a social welfare agency that might help them receive enough money to obtain better nutrition, which might have been as effective as medical care in improving their health.

Sometimes, the objectives of one organization conflict with those of other organizations. At a basic level, an organization may be unwilling to cooperate in the implementation of a program simply because the success of another agency may threaten its own future prospects. On a somewhat higher plane, organizations may disagree about the purposes of government or about the best way to achieve the goals on which they do agree. Or an agency may want to receive credit for providing a service that inevitably involves the cooperation of many organizations, and its insistence on receiving credit may prevent anything from happening. For example, several law enforcement agencies knew about a major drug shipment, but they allowed it to slip through their fingers because they could not agree on which of the "cooperating" agencies would make the actual arrest and receive the media attention.

Even a simple failure to think about coordination and to understand linkages among programs may prevent effective implementation. Most citizens have heard their share of horror stories about the same streets being dug up and repaired in successive weeks by different city departments and private utilities. Equally dismaying stories are told of reporting requirements issued by a variety of federal agencies that require contradictory definitions of terms or that involve excessive duplication of effort by citizens. Corruption is rarely at the root of these problems, but that neither prevents the loss of efficiency nor makes citizens any happier about the problems of management in their government.

Coordination of programs appeared to become more difficult during the 1990s, and the problems become more important every day. As the federal government began to rely more on the private sector and on state and local governments to deliver public programs, it became more difficult to provide integrated services. This remains true despite widespread pressure to make the public sector more "user friendly" and "customer oriented."[68] Effective coordination is increasingly important as the interactions among various program providers become more evident. For example, social programs are increasingly dependent on effective job training programs, and economic success is increasingly dependent on educational policy. The demands of homeland security require a number of organizations to coordinate and cooperate in ways that previously have not been considered.

From the Bottom Up?

Scholars have argued that many implementation problems are a function of their being considered from a top-down perspective.[69] That is, the person evaluating implementation looks at what happens to a law and considers that the bureaucracies have failed because they have not produced outcomes exactly like those intended by the framers of the legislation. The assumption here, rather like Hood's, is that bureaucracies should march to a single drummer and that the drummer should be Congress or the president. Anticipating such an orderly approach may be expecting too much from the U.S. government, given its complexity and the multiple and competing interests organized within the system. Indeed, the appropriate questions may be, In what policy areas can we accept slippage between goals and outcomes? and, What can be done to produce greater compliance in the most sensitive areas?[70]

An alternative to the top-down perspective is to think of implementation from the bottom up, or through "backward mapping."[71] This approach holds that the people who design public programs should think about the ease, or even the possibility, of implementation during the development stage. Programs should consider the interests of the lower echelons of the bureaucracy, their contacts with the program's clients, and indeed the values and desires of the clients themselves. With these factors in mind, policymakers should then design policies that can be readily implemented. The program may not fulfill all the original goals of the policy formulators, but it will be able to gain a higher degree of compliance than a program based on strict legal norms of compliance and autonomy of policy formulators.

The bottom-up concept of implementation and program design is appealing, for it promises rather easy victories in the complicated wars involved in making programs work. Even if those promises could be fulfilled, however—and there are reasonable doubts—there are important problems with the approach. The most important is the normative problem that political leaders and their policy advisers have the responsibility (and usually the desire) to formulate programs that meet their political goals and fulfill the promises made in political campaigns.[72] Programs that are implemented easily may not meet those goals. That is perhaps especially true when conservative administrations attempt to make changes in social programs through field staffs committed to more liberal goals or when liberals attempt to carry out expansionary economic policies through more conservative economic institutions inside and outside government. Governments may wind up doing what they can do, or what they have always done, rather than what they want to do.

In addition, the ability of agency field staffs to define what is feasible may allow them substantially greater control over policy than is desirable within a democratic political system. Their definition of *feasibility* may be excessively conservative, limiting the options that might be available with proper design. Indeed, there may be little reliable evidence about what really is feasible in implementation and what is really impossible.[73] Too-facile definitions of feasibility may undervalue the abilities and leadership of politicians and administrators alike.

The Third Generation?

After the original top-down and bottom-up implementation studies, and some attention to political factors in implementation, there might be said to be a third generation of thinking about the problem.[74] It attempts to replace these relatively simple models with more complex descriptions of the relationships that exist in the process of implementation. Much of the earlier literature on implementation tended to provide a single answer, regardless of the question. The third wave, on the other hand, tends to show answers to most questions about implementation with the accurate if somewhat unsatisfying, "It depends."

The real task for understanding implementation, then, is to identify what factors serve as contingencies for success or failure. Some of the factors are expressly political, and others are a function of the type of policy being implemented. Still others may be a function of the organizations that are used as the agents of implementation. Specifying why a program succeeds or fails involves the identification and interaction of all these factors. That is a complex research task, just as it is a complex practical task to design an implementation structure that can actually make a program function in something close to the manner intended by the people who designed it.

The study of interorganizational politics has been extended to cover more completely the organizations in the private sector.[75] These organizations add to the complexity of implementation, but they also add to the capacity of the public sector to make its programs work, and work efficiently.

Summary

American government is a massive, complex, and often confusing set of institutions. It contains numerous organizations but lacks any central organizing principle. Much of the structure of American government was developed on an ad hoc basis to address particular problems at particular times. Yet even with a more coherent structure, many of the same problems might still arise in the implementation of programs. Many problems are inherent in any government but are exacerbated by the complex and diffuse structure of government in the United States. For public policy, implementation is a vital step in the process of governing because it involves putting programs into action and producing effects for citizens. The difficulty of producing desired effects, or indeed any effects, means that policy is a much more difficult commodity to deliver to citizens than is commonly believed. The barriers to effective implementation often discourage individuals and organizations from engaging in the activities devised for their benefit. Public management then becomes a matter of threatening or cajoling organizations into complying with stated objectives or of convincing those organizations that their goals can best be accomplished through the programs that have been authorized.

CHAPTER 7

Budgeting:
Allocation and Public Policy

IMPLEMENTING PUBLIC POLICIES requires money as well as institutional structures. The budget process provides the means of allocating the available resources
among numerous competing purposes. In principle, all resources in the society
are available to government, although in the United States, a politician who
openly expressed such a position probably would not last beyond the next election. Moreover, almost all the purposes for which politicians and administrators
wish to spend public money have some merits. The question is whether those
merits are sufficient to justify using the resources in the public sector instead of
in the private sector. Finding answers to such questions requires economic and
analytical judgment, as well as political estimates of the feasibility of proposed
policies.

When President Barack Obama assumed office in 2009, he faced a number
of significant budget issues. He inherited a large deficit from the Bush administration, and the economic crisis was adding to it at an unprecedented rate.
Furthermore, during the campaign, Obama had made a number of commitments to health care, education, and the environment. He had also pledged to
attack pork barrel spending and entitlement programs. But it was not clear how
much could be saved through those means.[1] In short, President Obama had
major budget problems. The battles with Congress over the budget in the time
since his election have demonstrated not only the extent of those problems but
also the central political position of the budget.

For any president, two aspects of budgeting sometimes merge. The question
of system-level allocation between the public and private sectors is the first. How
many activities or problems justify government intervention into the economy
for the purpose of taxing and spending?[2] Could the best interest of society be
served by keeping the money in the hands of businesses or individuals for their

investment decisions, thereby allowing some potentially beneficial programs in government to go unfunded? Or do the equity, equality, and economic growth potentially produced through a public project justify officials' expending political capital to pass and collect or increase a tax? The system-level questions also include the proportion of its expenditures government should finance through taxes and fees; in other words, how large a deficit could the United States afford to run?[3]

The second aspect is how available public sector resources should be allocated among competing programs. When they devise a budget, decision makers function within resource constraints—they must base their decisions on the assumption that no more revenue will come in (or that no larger deficit will be accepted). Decision makers must therefore attempt to allocate available money for the greatest social, economic, and political benefit. Doing that is not an easy task, of course, because of differing opinions about what uses of the money would be best. Decision makers also are often constrained by commitments to fund existing entitlement programs before they can begin to allocate the rest of the funds to other worthy programs.[4] Because money can be divided almost infinitely, however, it offers a medium for resolving social conflicts that indivisible forms of public benefits, such as rights, often do not. Therefore, although there are a number of possible justifications for budgetary decisions, we must be aware that political considerations tend to dominate and that many of the most effective arguments revolve around votes and coming elections.

Characteristics of the Federal Budget

Before discussing the *budget cycle,* through which the federal budget is constructed each year, we should explain several of the budget's fundamental features. These features are in some ways not only beneficial to decision makers but also serve to constrain them and at times help create undesirable outcomes; the format of the budget is not politically neutral but directly affects the outcomes of the process. The frequent attempts to reform almost all features of the budgetary process thus encounter resistance from the interests advantaged by the status quo, so the process as well as the content of budgeting become part of the political debate.

An Executive Budget

The federal budget is an executive budget, prepared by the president and his staff, approved by Congress, and then executed by the president and the executive branch. That has not always been the case. Before 1921, the federal budget was a legislative budget, prepared almost entirely by Congress and then executed by the president. One major tenet of the government reform movement of the early twentieth century was that an executive budget was a necessity for more effective management.[5] According to that doctrine, no executive should be required to manage a budget that he or she had no part in planning or preparing.

The Budget and Accounting Act of 1921 marked a new stage in the conflict between the executive and legislative branches over their respective budgeting powers.[6] In general, budgetary power has accumulated in the executive branch and in the Executive Office of the President, in large part because of the analytical dominance of the Office of Management and Budget (OMB; it was called the Bureau of the Budget until 1971). The excesses of the Nixon administration—and to some degree those of the Johnson administration during the Vietnam War—led to the establishment of the Congressional Budget Office (CBO) in a provision of the Congressional Budget and Impoundment Control Act of 1974. The CBO gives Congress much of the analytical capability that the executive branch has. The budget committees in both houses also give Congress greater control over budgeting than before passage of the act. Congress played an active part in the 1997 budget settlement that contributed to attaining a balanced budget as early as fiscal year 1998.[7] Nevertheless, Congress remains in the position of primarily responding to budgetary initiatives from the White House, rather than initiating the budget.

The Line Item

Despite several attempts at change, the federal budget remains a *line-item* budget. That is, the final budget document allocates funds into categories—wages and salaries, supplies, travel, equipment, and so forth—for specific purposes within an agency. These traditional categories give Congress some control over the executive branch, allowing the legislature, through the Government Accountability Office (formerly the General Accounting Office), to make sure that the money is spent under legal authority. It is more difficult, however, to determine if it is being spent efficiently and effectively. The rigidities of the line-item budget may actually inhibit the effectiveness of good government managers by limiting how they can spend the money. For example, it may be that more equipment and fewer personnel could do the same job better and/or more cheaply, but managers generally are not given that option.

Input controls, such as line-item budgets, are now considered inefficient means of control over public organizations and their managers. Critics have argued that it would be better to give a manager a relatively unrestricted budget and then judge him or her on the achievement of program goals. Congress, however, tends to want to maximize its oversight over the executive instead of allowing managerial flexibility. Through the Government Performance and

Results Act of 1993, Congress attempted to overlay the fundamental line-item structure of the budget with a more performance-based system of assessment and allocation, thus using output controls to replace the input controls.[8] That system has had some success, but the older patterns of emphasizing financial control rather than performance may come to dominate even a reformed budget process.

An Annual Budget

The federal budget is primarily an annual budget. Agencies now must submit five-year forecasts for each of their expenditure plans, but they are used primarily for management purposes within OMB. The budget presented to Congress and the appropriations bills that Congress eventually adopts together constitute only a one-year expenditure plan. The absence of a more complete, multiyear budget makes planning difficult for federal managers, and it does little to alert Congress to the long-term implications of spending decisions made in any one year. A small outlay in one year may result in much larger expenditures in subsequent years, and it may create a clientele that cannot be eliminated without significant political repercussions. In other cases, a project that would have to run for several years to be truly effective may be terminated after a single year. Many state and local governments in the United States now operate with multiyear budgets, but the federal government still does not. OMB's annual advice to the agencies serves as a guide for preparing budgets and provides some information about expectations for five years, but the information for the four "out years" is speculative at best.

One of the several recommendations of the Gore commission (the National Performance Review) was to move the federal government toward a biennial budget to enable organizations to plan more effectively and deliver services more efficiently.[9] Such a reform might also allow Congress to reduce the amount of time that it must devote to the budget process, freeing it to spend more time addressing its other legislative duties. Again, however, Congress does not appear to favor this reform, largely because it might lessen congressional control over the executive branch. Neither has there been much enthusiasm for capital budgeting or better identification of the investment aspects of federal expenditures.[10]

The Budget Cycle

The annual, repetitive nature of the budget cycle is important, for agency officials might behave differently if they did not know that they have to come back year after year to obtain more money from the same OMB officials and members of Congress. In addition to the emphasis that repetition places on building trust and a reputation for dependability, it allows policy entrepreneurs multiple opportunities to build their case for new programs and changes in budget allocations. Preparing the budget is an extremely long, deliberative process, requiring a year or more to complete and allowing for a great deal of analysis and political bargaining among the many parties involved.[11]

Setting the Parameters: The President and His Friends

Most of this chapter pertains to the microlevel allocation of resources among programs, rather than the setting of broad spending and economic management policy. It is necessary, however, to begin with a brief discussion of the initial decisions concerning overall levels of spending and revenue, which will influence subsequent decisions about programs. Inevitably, changes in particular programs and in socioeconomic conditions (wars, recessions, and the like) influence the total spending levels of government, so this stage mostly involves setting targets rather than making final decisions.

The first official act of the budget cycle is the development of estimates of the total size of the federal budget to be prepared for the fiscal year, the so-called spring review. Although agencies and OMB will already have begun to discuss and prepare expenditure plans, the letter from the president through OMB (Circular A-11, usually issued in June) is an important first step in the formal process, providing a statement of overall presidential budgetary strategy and of the financial limits within which agencies should begin to prepare their budgets. In addition to setting the overall parameters, the letter presents some detail on how the parameters apply to individual agencies. Naturally, the past experience of budgeting officials in each agency gives them some further sense of how to interpret the general parameters. Defense agencies, for example, knew after the inception of the war on terror that they were not necessarily bound by the parameters, whereas planners of domestic programs with little client support and few friends on Capitol Hill could only hope to do as well as the letter had led them to believe they might.

The overall estimates for spending are prepared some sixteen months before the budget goes into effect. For example, the fiscal year 2010 budget went into effect on October 1, 2009, but the planning for that budget began in June 2007 or even earlier. For any budget, this means that the economic forecasts on which spending estimates are based may be far from the prevailing economic reality when the budget is actually executed. Any deviation from those economic forecasts is important for the outcomes of the budget. The recession of 2008–2009, for example, will mean a reduction in revenues and an increase in expenditures—people who are out of work do not pay income or Social Security taxes, and they demand unemployment insurance payments and, perhaps, welfare.

The budget is a central political event each year. The importance of the budget has been emphasized by the continuing debates over deficits and debt in the federal government. Vice President Joe Biden and President Barack Obama (center) meet with House Speaker John Boehner (left) and House Majority Leader Eric Cantor (right) in the Oval Office to discuss the debt limit and deficit reduction on July 20, 2011.

Those important economic forecasts are not entirely the product of technical considerations; they are also influenced by political and ideological considerations. For example, the Reagan administration's belief that "supply-side" economics would produce larger revenues through increased economic activity led to a serious overestimation of the amount of revenue. The choice of that approach to public finance began the large federal deficits that characterized U.S. public finance for over fifteen years (see chapter 9).[12]

The preparation of economic and expenditure estimates is the result of the interaction of three principal actors—the Council of Economic Advisers (CEA), OMB, and the Treasury—which are collectively referred to as the "troika."[13] The CEA is, as the name implies, a group of economists who advise the president. Organizationally, they are located in the Executive Office of the President. The role of the CEA is largely technical, forecasting the state of the economy and advising the president on the basis of the forecasts. Its economists also mathematically model the probable effects of budgetary choices on the economy. Of course, the economics of the CEA must be tempered with political judgment, for mathematical models and economists do not run for office—but presidents must. One former chair of the Council of Economic Advisers said that he relied on his "visceral computer" for some of the more important predictions.[14]

Despite its image as a budget-controlling organization, OMB comes as close to a representative of the expenditure community as exists within the troika. Even though the agencies whose budgets OMB supervises find it difficult to perceive OMB as a benefactor, some of its personnel may be favorably disposed toward expenditures. They see the huge volume of agency requests coming forward and are aware of a large volume of uncontrollable expenditures, such as Social Security benefits, that will have to be funded regardless of changes in economic circumstances.

The Treasury represents the financial community, and historically it has been the major advocate of a balanced budget within the troika, for it must cover any debts created by a budget deficit by issuing government bonds. The principal interest of the Treasury in troika negotiations often is to preserve the confidence of the financial community at home and abroad in the soundness of the U.S. economy and the government's management of it. Some particular (and increasing) concerns of the Treasury may regard relationships with international financial organizations, such as the International Monetary Fund, that are important for maintaining international economic confidence. The increased role of the Federal Reserve in the economic policy process and in financing the deficit has made it more of a player in the budget than it had been in the past.

The Federal Reserve has to some extent begun to play part of the role that the Treasury had typically played in the budget process. Because of the importance of monetary policy in economic policy in general and the particularly important role in the economic recovery, the Federal Reserve has moved into a more central role in the budget process. This central role for the "Fed" has helped to integrate monetary and fiscal policy (see chapter 9) but also undermines its political independence that has been important for maintaining its legitimacy.

Even at this first step in the budgetary process, a great deal of hard political and economic bargaining occurs among the participants. This bargaining will be more intense in a period of economic crisis. Each member of the troika must compete for the attention of the president as well as protect the interests of the particular professional, organizational, and political community it represents in budgeting. But the bargaining is just the beginning of a long series of political debates and bargains as agencies attempt to get the money they want and need from the budgetary process.

Agency Requests

As in so much U.S. policymaking, government agencies are central actors in the budget process.[15] Whether independent or within a cabinet-level department, the agency is responsible for the initial preparation of estimates and requests for funding and working with OMB, and, if applicable, the agency's executive department budgeting personnel. OMB provides guidance and advice about total spending levels and particular aspects of the agency's budget. The agency may have to coordinate with other agencies within the department where it is located. Accomplished through a departmental budget committee and the secretary's staff, this coordination is necessary to ensure that the agency is operating within presidential priorities and that the secretary will provide support in defending the budget to OMB and Congress.

The agency must be aggressive in seeking to expand its own expenditure base while recognizing that it is only one part of a larger organization.[16] In other words, the agency must be aggressive but reasonable, seeking more money but realizing that it operates within the constraints of what the federal government as a whole can afford. The executive department must recognize its responsibilities to the president and his program, as well as to the agencies under its umbrella. The cabinet secretary must be chief spokesperson for his or her agencies at higher governmental levels, although agencies often have more direct support from interest groups and perhaps from Congress than does the department as a whole. Thus, a cabinet secretary may not be able to go far in following the president's program if that program seriously jeopardizes ongoing programs, and their clienteles, in his or her department. This problem reflects the general fragmentation of U.S. government, which places much of the power and the operational connections between government and interest groups at the agency, rather than the department, level.

An agency may employ a number of strategies in seeking to expand its funding but is restrained by the knowledge that budgeting is an annual cycle. Any strategic choice in a single year may preclude the use of that strategy in later years and, perhaps more important, may destroy confidence that OMB and Congress have had in the agency.[17] For example, an agency may employ the "camel's nose" or "thin wedge" strategy to get modest initial funding for a program, knowing that it will have rapidly increasing expenditure requirements. Even if that strategy is successful once, however, the agency may be assured that any future requests for new spending authority will be carefully scrutinized. Agencies are well advised to pursue careful, long-term strategies and to develop trust among the political leaders who determine their budgets.

Executive Review

After the agency has decided on its requests, it passes them on to the Office of Management and Budget for review. OMB is a presidential agency, one of whose principal tasks is to amass all the agency requests and conform them to presidential policy priorities and to the overall levels of expenditure desired. That may make for a tight fit, as some spending programs are difficult or impossible to control, leaving little space for any new programs the president may consider important. Even recent conservative presidents have found it difficult to make overall spending levels conform with their view that government should tax and spend less.

After OMB receives the estimates, it passes them on to its budget examiners for review. In the rare case in which an agency has actually requested the same amount, or less, than OMB had planned to give it, there is no problem. In most cases, however, the examiners must depend on their experience with the agency in question, as well as whatever information about programs and projected expenditures they can collect, to make a judgment concerning the necessity and priority of requested spending increases.

On the basis of agency requests and the information developed by the examiners, OMB holds hearings, usually in October or November, at which each agency must defend its requests. Although OMB sometimes seems to be committed to cutting spending, several factors prevent it from wielding its axe with excessive vigor. First, it is frequently possible for an agency to execute an end run around the hearing board by appealing to the director of OMB, the president, or ultimately to its friends in Congress. Also, some budget examiners come, over time, to favor the agencies they are supposed to control, so they may become advocates of an agency's requests rather than the fiscal controllers and financial conservatives they are expected to be, a pattern similar to regulatory capture.

The results of the hearing are forwarded to the director of OMB for the "director's review," which involves the top staff of the bureau. At this stage, through additional trimming and negotiation, the staff attempts to pare the final budget down to the amount desired by the president. After each portion of the budget has passed through the director's review, it is forwarded to the president for final review and then sent on for compilation into the final budget document. This stage necessarily involves final appeals from agency and department personnel to OMB and the president, as well as last-minute adjustments to take into account changes in economic forecasts and desired changes in the total size of the budget. The presidential budget is then prepared for delivery to Congress within fifteen days after it convenes in January each year. Presidents differ in the amount of time they devote to budgeting, but the budget is perceived as a statement of the priorities of the president and his administration, even if it is really prepared largely by the public servants at OMB.

In this way, the presidential budget is made ready to be reviewed through the appropriations process in Congress, but the two branches of government will already have begun to communicate about the budget. By mid-November each year, the president must submit to Congress the "current services budget," which includes "proposed budget authority and estimated outlays that would be included in the budget for the ensuing fiscal year . . . if all programs and activities were carried on at the same level as the fiscal year in progress."[18] This is a form of volume budgeting, for it posits a constant volume of public services and then determines the price. During a period with rapidly rising inflation, such as the 1970s and early 1980s, this constant-service budget can give Congress an early warning about current expenditure commitments if they are extended. But the estimates are subject to substantial inaccuracy, either purposive or accidental, so they provide a rough estimate for planning purposes, but only that.

Congressional Action

Although the Constitution specifically grants it the powers of the purse, by the 1960s and 1970s, Congress had ceased to be dominant in budgetary decisions. Congress attempted a counterattack, largely through the Congressional Budget and Impoundment Control Act of 1974 described above, which established the budget committees in each house of Congress. These committees develop two concurrent resolutions each year outlining spending limits, much as the troika does in the executive branch. As mentioned, the act also established the Congressional Budget Office to give the budget committees a staff capacity similar to what OMB provides for the president.[19] This enhanced analytic capacity is important for Congress in understanding its budgetary activity, but the need to implement somewhat more immediate and less analytic expenditure reforms has tended to make the changes less important than they might have been.

Decisions on how to allocate total spending among agencies and programs are made by the appropriations committees in both houses.[20] These committees are extremely prestigious and powerful, and those serving on them generally are veteran members of Congress. Members tend to remain on these committees for long periods, developing not only budgetary expertise but also political ties with the agencies they supervise as well as with their own constituencies.[21] The two committees—and especially the House Appropriations Committee—do most of their work through subcommittees, which may cover one executive department, such as Defense; or a number of agencies, such as Housing and Urban Development and independent executive agencies; or a function, such as public works. Most important, the whole committee does not closely scrutinize the decisions of its subcommittees, nor does the House of Representatives as a whole frequently reverse the decisions of its appropriations committee.

Scrutiny by the whole House has increased, however, in large part because of the general opening of congressional deliberations to greater "sunshine," or public view. In addition, the politics of deficit reduction has tended to place greater restraints on committee and subcommittee autonomy. The committees must now submit appropriations levels that correspond to the total spending levels permitted under the previously enacted joint resolutions on taxing and spending. Provided that the committees can keep their appropriations within those predetermined levels, they can have substantial autonomy; once an agency's budget has been accepted by a subcommittee, that budget has, in all probability, been decided.[22]

Beginning with the presidential recommendations, each subcommittee develops an appropriations bill, or occasionally two, for a total of thirteen or fourteen bills each year. Hearings are held, and agency personnel are summoned to testify and justify the size of their desired appropriations. After those hearings, the subcommittee will "mark up" the bill—make such changes as it feels are necessary from the original proposals—and then submit it, first to the entire committee and then to the House of Representatives. In accordance with the Congressional Budget Act, appropriations committees are expected to have completed markups of all appropriations bills before submitting the first for final passage, so that members have a better idea of the overall level of expenditure that would be approved. The Senate follows a similar procedure, and differences between the two houses are resolved in a conference committee.

This procedure in Congress needs to be finished by September 15 for the budget to be ready to go into effect on October 1, but the Congressional Budget Act also requires the passage of a second concurrent resolution setting forth the budget ceilings, revenue floors, and overall fiscal policy considerations governing the passage of the appropriations bills. Because there will undoubtedly be differences in the ways in which the two houses make their appropriations figures correspond with the figures in the concurrent resolution, the *reconciliation bill*, in which both houses agree on the spending totals, must be passed by September 25.

Although the reconciliation bill appears to be a technicality, it has been used to impose great effects on the budget; for example, Congress used reconciliation bills to enact three significant tax cuts during the George W. Bush administration. The need to pass a single reconciliation bill tends to move power away from the appropriations committees and subcommittees and to centralize it in the leadership, especially in the House of Representatives.[23] After all the stages have been completed, the budget (in the form of the various appropriations bills) is then ready to go to the president for his signature and execution. Although the process has clear deadlines, they are often missed, and as this has occurred in most years since 2002, Congress frequently must pass continuing resolutions to maintain funding for programs until the appropriations bills are finally passed.[24]

Although this congressional procedure is the formal means through which the budget should be adopted, in practice it has not been effective over most of the past decade. The political process has become so contentious, and the magnitude of the budget so great, that the reconciliation process has largely broken down. Through the use of continuing resolutions and the eventual passage of appropriations acts, the federal government continues to function, but the intention of the legislation to provide a more coordinated and coherent style of budgeting has not been achieved.[25] Perhaps at the extreme, the budget for the Federal Aviation Administration has not been passed (as of February, 2012) for some sixteen months, with the agency having to rely on continuing resolutions that have prevented it from pursuing its goals of modernizing the air traffic control system.[26]

It is difficult to overstate the extent to which the budget and public finance in general in the United States has become politicized, and especially so in Congress. When President Obama introduced his budget for fiscal 2013 in February 2012, the Republican leadership said that it was basically dead on arrival. The bargaining and compromise that had characterized budgeting (and other aspects of congressional action) has been replaced by opposition and stalemate.

Budget Execution

Once Congress has appropriated money for the executive branch, the agencies must develop mechanisms for spending it. An appropriations warrant, drawn by the Treasury and countersigned by the Government Accountability Office, is sent to each agency. The agency makes plans for its expenditures for the year on the basis of the warrant and submits a plan to OMB for apportionment of the funds. The funds appropriated by Congress are usually made available to the agencies on a quarterly basis, but for some agencies, there may be great differences in the amounts for each quarter. For example, the National Park Service spends a very large proportion of its annual appropriation during the summer because of the demands on the national parks at that time. Quarterly funding provides greater control over spending and prevents an agency from spending everything early in the year and then requiring a supplemental appropriation. Such overspending may still happen, but apportionment helps to control potential profligacy.

The procedures for executing the budget are relatively simple when the executive branch actually wants to spend the money appropriated; they become more complex when the president decides he does not want to spend the appropriated funds. Prior to the Congressional Budget Act of 1974, a president had at least a customary right to impound funds—that is, to refuse to spend them.[27] Numerous impoundments during the Nixon administration—as when half the money appropriated for implementing the Federal Water Pollution Control Act Amendments of 1972 was impounded from the 1973 to 1975 budgets—forced Congress to take action to control the executive and to reassert its powers over the purse.

The Congressional Budget and Impoundment Control Act of 1974 was designed to limit the ability of the president to use impoundment as an indirect means of overruling Congress when he was not able to do so through the normal legislative process (the water pollution control legislation had been passed over a presidential veto). The 1974 act defined two kinds of impoundment. The first, *rescissions,* are cancellations of budgetary authority to spend money. If he decides that a program could reach its goals with less money, or simply that there are good reasons not to spend the money, the president must send a message to Congress requesting rescission. Congress must act positively on this request within forty-five days; if it does not, then the money is made available to the agency for obligation (see Table 7.1). Congress can also rescind money on its own by passing a resolution in both houses withdrawing the agency's authority to spend.

Deferrals, on the other hand, are requests merely to delay making the obligational authority available to the agency. In this case, the deferral is granted unless either house of Congress exercises its veto power. The comptroller general (head of the Government Accountability Office) has the power to classify specific presidential actions, and at times, the difference between a deferral and a rescission is not clear. For example, attempting to defer funds for programs scheduled to be phased out is, in practice, a rescission. These changes in the impoundment powers of the president have substantially increased congressional leverage over how much money the federal government will spend each year.

Although he used the impoundment mechanism only once during his term of office, President George W. Bush proposed an "enhanced rescission authority" as a means of creating a version of a line-item veto and controlling the budget more directly at its execution.[28] Under his proposal, the authority would have

TABLE 7.1   Rescissions Proposed and Enacted, by President

President	Number proposed	Number accepted	Amount proposed (millions)	Amount enacted (millions)
Ford	152	52	$7,935.0	$1,252.2
Carter	89	50	4,608.5	2,116.1
Reagan	602	214	43,436.6	15,656.8
Clinton	186	103	9,557.7	4,318.6
Bush	1	0	23,000.0	470.0[a]
Obama	0	0	0	0

Sources: General Accounting Office, *Frequency and Amount of Rescissions,* OGC–7–9 (Washington, DC: U.S. General Accounting Office, September 26, 1997); calculated from Office of Management and Budget, *Budget of the United States* (annual).

a. Not technically a rescission under the terms of the Impoundment Control Act, but funds were withheld.

extended to tax expenditures as well as to specific projects, and Congress would have been forced to make an up or down decision rather than simply ignoring the president's message. Such an enhancement of the rescission authority, as well as a constitutional amendment permitting a line-item veto, remains under consideration, although there has been little congressional action. The proposal for "enhanced rescission" authority resurfaced in 2010, but again with little action in Congress.[29]

Budget Control

After the executive branch spends the money Congress has appropriated, Congress must check to be sure that the money was spent legally and properly. The GAO and its head, the comptroller general, are responsible for a postexpenditure audit of federal spending. Each year, the comptroller general's report to Congress outlines deviations from congressional intent in the ways government agencies have spent their money. Requests from individual Congress members or committees may produce earlier and perhaps more detailed evaluations of agency spending or policies. Each year, the GAO provides Congress and the interested public with hundreds of evaluations of expenditures, as well as general audit reports on federal spending.

The Government Accountability Office has undergone a major transformation from a simple accounting organization into a policy-analytic organization for the legislative branch.[30] It has become concerned not only with the legality of expenditures but also with the efficiency with which the money is spent. Although GAO reports on the efficiency of agency expenditures have no legal standing, any agencies wishing to maintain good relations with Congress are well advised to take those findings into account. Congress will certainly be aware of any adverse reports when it reviews agency budgets the following year and may expect to see some changes in the way in which the agency conducts its business. The GAO recommendations also form one part of the ongoing process of congressional oversight of administration. The problem with GAO controls— whether accounting or policy analytic—is that they are largely ex post facto, meaning that the money will probably have been spent long before the conclusion is reached that it has been spent either illegally or unwisely.

Problems in the Budget Process

As we have seen, a long and complex process, taking almost eighteen months to complete, is required to perform the difficult task of allocating federal budget money among competing agencies. The process involves substantial bargaining and analysis, from which emerges a plan for spending billions of dollars. But even this complex process, complicated by numerous reforms of congressional budgeting and deficit-fighting procedures, cannot control federal spending as completely as some would desire, nor can it provide the level of fiscal management that may be necessary for a smoothly functioning economic system. Because budgeting is inherently political as well as economic, the process may never be as rational as some would like, but there are identifiable problems that cause particular difficulty.

The major problems arising in the budget process of the federal government affect the fiscal management function of budgeting, as well as the allocation of resources among agencies. It is difficult, if not impossible, for any president or any session of Congress to make binding decisions as to how much money will be spent during any one year, or even who will spend it for what purposes, and this absence of basic controls makes the entire process subject to error. Those elected to make policy and control spending frequently find themselves incapable of producing the kinds of program or budgetary changes they campaigned for, and that can result in disillusionment for both leaders and citizens.

The Deficit

It would be difficult to follow American politics as it moved toward the election of 2012 without becoming aware of the issue of the budget deficit. The existence or prospect of a deficit has been a major force driving budget reform in the United States, for deficits and public debt are very negative symbols in the country's political discourse.[31] As the substantial budget surplus of the early twenty-first century changed to a deficit, politicians again became concerned about charges of fiscal irresponsibility. Because of the ideological baggage associated with deficit and debt, it has been difficult at times to discuss them rationally. The definition of a *federal deficit* is itself something of an artifact of a number of decisions made about the nature of the public sector and its budget. We tend to discuss the federal budget in isolation from state and local government spending and revenues, but given the ability of the federal government to shift some of its financial burdens to lower levels of government, looking at only one level of government may give a false impression of the state of public finance (see Table 2.4).

A less obvious problem in calculating the federal deficit is the part that Social Security funds play in reducing it. At present, the Social Security Trust Fund is receiving substantially more (roughly $30 billion per year) in tax income than it is having to pay out to retirees, but that began to change rapidly around 2010, when large numbers of baby boomers begin to retire. In the meantime, that extra income enabled the Clinton administration to balance the budget (see Table 7.2).[32] Defining the budget as including Social Security funds helps government leaders present balanced budgets in the short term, but it creates immense long-term

TABLE 7.2   Estimated Federal Budget Balances with and without Social Security (in billions of dollars)

Year	With Social Security	Without Social Security
1997	−22	−103
1998	−10	−106
1999	10	−96
2000	8.5	−105
2001	28	−94
2002	90	−45
2003	−226	−378
2004	−256	−412
2005	−255	−427
2006	−242	−414
2007	−162	−349
2008	−267	−458
2009	−1,285	−1,413
2010	−1,216	−1,293

Source: Calculated from Office of Management and Budget, *Budget of the United States* (annual).

challenges to maintaining the soundness not only of the retirement system (see chapter 12) but also of the budget system. The federal government also controls public employee retirement funds, which it has at times manipulated to keep the deficit figure lower than it would otherwise be.[33]

Government accounting standards are being strengthened to take account of obligations such as unfunded pensions, but room remains for manipulating figures for political advantage.[34] For example, Social Security, Medicare, the federal debt, and civil service retirement obligations are all well known, but the budget has no clear mechanism for funding them.[35]

Another, related aspect of the deficit problem comes from the federal government's retaining what is called a "cash accounting system," rather than looking at the obligations being created for the future.[36] When a program is passed, it has future consequences that can be predicted, and it can be argued that government has accrued those future costs with its current decision.[37] Likewise, tax decisions have long-range revenue consequences that an annual budget may not capture.

The absence of a separate capital budget is another less obvious definitional problem. All state governments in the United States save one must, according to their state constitutions, have balanced budgets. But the states separate out their capital projects—roads, bridges, schools, and the like—into separate capital budgets, and they can borrow money, by issuing bonds, to build them. The federal budget does not separate capital from current expenditures. A good deal of federal borrowing is for projects for which borrowing is reasonable. Even good fiscal conservatives borrow money to buy a house or an automobile. With that in mind, the usual (if inaccurate) analogy between government and private household budgeting can be maintained even if government borrows extensively. If we took the spending that reasonably could be labeled *capital* out of the total budget, the federal government could be seen to have run a surplus, or at least a much smaller deficit, for a number of years. The deficits since 2002, however, have been so massive that the separation of capital spending would make little difference other than to make the nature of public spending more transparent.

This discussion of Social Security funds and capital budgeting should make it clear that many of the terms used in public policy have no single, accepted definition. Instead, *definitions*, like all other parts of the process, are constructed politically. It pays for incumbent politicians to calculate the deficit with Social Security revenues counted in, although some fiscal conservatives argue that this is actually a misuse of the funds and that the entire system should be privatized to prevent just such "abuses."

These technical issues about the budget deficit should not blind us to the increasingly politicized discussion of deficits and debt. The debate over raising the debt ceiling in 2011 demonstrated the intensity of the political commitments and also provided an opening to address other issues about public expenditure, such as entitlement commitments.[38]

Uncontrollable Expenditures

Much of the federal budget is uncontrollable in any one year (see Table 7.3). Many federal spending programs cannot be controlled systematically without making policy changes that would be politically unpalatable.[39] For example, a president or Congress can do very little to control spending for Social Security

TABLE 7.3   Changes in "Uncontrollable" Federal Expenditures (in percentages)

Type of Expenditure	1976	1980	1990	1992	1995	2000	2003	2006	2010
Controllable	63.7	46.8	40.0	38.7	34.6	33.2	31.7	29.4	30.3
Uncontrollable	36.3	53.2	60.0	61.3	65.4	66.8	68.3	70.6	69.7

Sources: Office of Management and Budget, *Special Analyses of the FY 1995 U.S. Budget* (Washington, DC: U.S. Government Printing Office, annual); subsequent years calculated from discretionary and nondiscretionary expenditure totals.

in any one year without changing the criteria for eligibility or altering the formula for indexing (adjustment of the benefits for changes in consumer prices or workers' earnings). Either policy choice would produce a major political conflict that might well make it impossible. Some minor changes, such as changing the tax treatment of Social Security benefits for beneficiaries with other income, may be entertained, but the vast majority of outlay for the program is essentially uncontrollable.

The most important uncontrollable expenditures are the large entitlement programs, such as Social Security, Medicare, and unemployment benefits.[40] They cannot be readily cut, and government cannot accurately estimate, while planning the budget, exactly how much money will be needed for them. President Obama has promised to reform these entitlements but will face very strong pressures for maintaining commitments.[41] Actual spending will depend on levels of inflation, illness, and unemployment, as well as on the number of eligible citizens who actually take advantage of the programs. Outstanding contracts and obligations also constitute a significant share of the uncontrollable portion of the budget, although these can be altered over several years, if not in a single year. The major controllable component of the federal budget is the defense budget. The end of the Cold War made defense a particularly attractive target for budget cutting, but the apparent shift from large strategic forces to tactical (personnel-intensive) forces reduced the overall savings, and the big shift toward defense spending in the George W. Bush administration increased the discretionary budget, which has persisted under President Obama.[42]

The uncontrollable elements of the budget mean that even a president committed to reducing federal expenditures and producing a balanced budget (without figuring in a short-term Social Security surplus) will find it difficult to determine where reductions will come from. Congress has begun to grapple with controlling these expenditures but finds the political forces supporting entitlements difficult to overcome.[43] Some discretionary social expenditures have been reduced over the past decade, but the bulk of federal expenditures have increased (see Table 2.4) and likely will continue to do so.

Backdoor Spending

Linked to the problem of uncontrollable expenditures is *backdoor spending*—spending decisions that are not made through the formal appropriations process. These expenditures to some degree reflect an institutional conflict within Congress between the appropriations committees and the substantive policy committees. They also reflect the difficulties of making the huge number of spending decisions that must be made each year through formal and somewhat recondite procedures. There are three principal kinds of backdoor spending.

Borrowing authority. Agencies are sometimes allowed to spend public money not appropriated by Congress if they borrow that money from the Treasury—for student loan guarantees, for instance.[44] It has been argued that these are not actually public expenditures because the money will presumably be repaid eventually. In many instances, however, federal loans have been written off, and even if the loans are repaid, the government may not know when that repayment will occur because students do not begin paying off loans until they complete their education.[45] The ability of government to control spending for purposes of economic management is seriously impaired when the authority to make spending decisions is so widely diffused.

The presence of myriad loans, loan guarantees, and other contingent obligations is becoming more evident to government, and it reduced some of the glee about the apparent end of the federal deficit during the last years of the Clinton administration.[46] There are few effective controls over loans, loan guarantees, or insurance obligations. For example, there are a dozen major federal insurance programs with authority to borrow over $60 billion,[47] and although some decision makers would like to impose firmer budget ceilings on them, finding the way to do so and preserve all their insurance coverage is difficult.

Contract authority. Agencies also may enter into contracts that bind the federal government to pay a certain amount for specified goods and services without going through the appropriations process. Then, after the contract is let, the appropriations committees are placed in the awkward position of either appropriating the money to pay the obligation or forcing the agency to renege on its debts. This kind of spending is uncontrollable in the short run, but any agency attempting to engage in such circumvention of the appropriations committees probably will face the ire of those committees when attempting to have its next annual budget approved. Congress has been developing rules that make spending of this type increasingly difficult for agencies. Still, the general shift toward implementation of public programs through third parties makes contracting a more important part of the process of governing.

Permanent appropriations. Certain public programs have authorizing legislation that requires the agencies responsible to spend money for designated purposes almost regardless of other conditions. The largest expenditure of this kind is payment of interest on the public debt; in 2010, this payment totaled over $350 billion, more than 12 percent of total federal spending that year.[48] Federal support of land grant colleges is a permanent appropriation that began during the administration of Abraham Lincoln. In the case of a permanent appropriation, the appropriations committees have relatively little discretion (other than to add to the spending) unless they choose to renege on standing commitments.

The Overhang

Money that Congress appropriates for a fiscal year need not actually be spent during that fiscal year; it must only be *obligated*. That is, the agency must contract to spend the money or otherwise make commitments about how it will be spent, and the actual outlay of funds can come some years later. In 2007, there existed a total budget authority of about $2.79 trillion (see Figure 7.1), with only $2.2 trillion appropriated during that year.[49] Thus, the "overhang" was almost one-fourth as large as the amount of money Congress appropriated during that fiscal year. The president and the executive agencies could not actually spend all that overhang in the single fiscal year—a good deal of it was in long-term contracts—but it represented a substantial amount in unspent obligations for the agencies and the government as a whole.

The overhang makes it difficult for a president to use the budget as an instrument of economic management. A principal component of economic

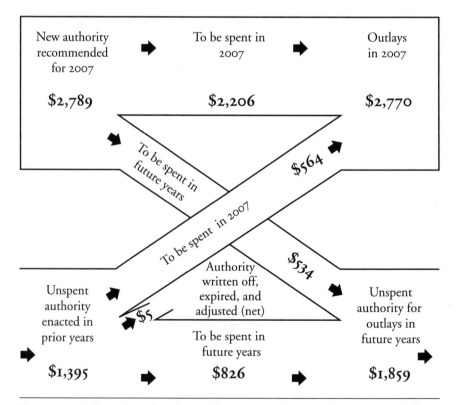

FIGURE 7.1   Relationship of Budget Authority to Outlays, Fiscal Year 2007 (in billions of dollars)

management, even in a post-Keynesian era, is the amount of public spending; because of the overhang, the president and Congress cannot always control the actual outlay of funds. The agencies may have sufficient budget authority, convertible into actual outlays, to damage presidential forecasts of spending. They might do that, not out of malice, but out of a perceived need to keep their programs operating as they think best, especially if the president were seeking to restrict the creation of new obligational authority.

Intergovernmental Budget Control

Just as a president cannot control the overhang within the federal government, he cannot control the taxing and spending decisions of thousands of state and local governments, making it impossible to exercise the kind of fiscal management he might like. In 2008, the federal government itself spent only a little over half of the total amount of money spent by governments in the United States. Although it has the capacity to stimulate state and local governments' expenditures through matching grants, encouraging reductions in their expenditures is more difficult. The federal government has even less control over revenue collection. For example, in 1963, the Kennedy administration pushed through a tax cut at the federal level, only to have nearly the entire effect negated by state and local tax increases. The Bush tax cuts of 2001 and 2003 suffered a similar fate, as states enacted a variety of spending and revenue programs in their wake.

The principles of federalism appear to reserve to state and local governments a perfect right to decide on their own levels of revenues and expenditures. However, in an era in which the public budget is important for economic management as well as for the distribution of funds among organizations, there may be a need for greater overall control. This control need not be imposed unilaterally by the federal government but could perhaps be decided by "diplomacy" among representatives of the several levels of government, as it is in Germany and to some extent in Canada.[50] The potential effects on economic performance of uncoordinated fiscal policies were to some degree demonstrated by the large state and local government surpluses of the mid-1980s, at the time that the federal government was running large deficits.[51] Depending on one's point of view, that was either a good thing (helping to reduce total public borrowing) or a bad thing (counteracting the economic stimulus of the deficit). In either case, it represented the absence of an integrated fiscal policy in the United States.

Reprogramming and Transfers

The first four problems we have identified in the federal budgetary process primarily affect the total level of spending. The next two problems, reprogramming and transfers, affect levels of spending by individual agencies and the purposes for which the agencies spend their money.

Reprogramming refers to the shifting of funds within a specific appropriations account. A congressional appropriations bill contains a number of appropriations accounts, which in turn contain a number of program elements. For example, the appropriations bill for the Department of Agriculture contains an appropriations account for crop supports, which is subdivided into separate program elements for cotton, corn, wheat, and so on. Reprogramming involves shifting obligational authority from one program element to another. Procedures for making reprogramming decisions have been thoroughly developed only in the Department of Defense. In general, there is a threshold (variable by agency) below which agencies are relatively free to reprogram funds but above which they must obtain approval from an appropriations committee or subcommittee, although not from the entire Congress. There are also requirements for reporting reprogramming decisions to the appropriations committees.[52]

Transfers are more serious actions, for they involve transferring funds from one appropriations account to another. In the Department of Agriculture bill referred to above, a transfer might involve shifting funds from crop supports to the Farmers Home Administration or to rural electrification. As with reprogramming, outside the Department of Defense, few established procedures exist for controlling the transfer of funds, other than specific prohibitions in the cases of certain functions.

Both reprogramming and transfers of funds are important in providing the executive branch with some flexibility in implementing its programs and in using public funds more effectively. These activities have been the subject of many abuses, however, and are ripe for reform and improvement. In particular, they frequently allow an agency to circumvent the judgment of the entire Congress through an appeal to the appropriations committee, or perhaps even to its chair. In the institutional battles for control over the budget, this is an area where Congress may want to be more active.

The Defense Budget

In principle, budgeting for defense should present relatively few problems. The defense budget is huge, and it involves a number of complex programs and the purchase of very expensive equipment, but so do a number of other parts of the federal budget. Two major problems, however, have become apparent during the past several years. One is the continuing problem of secrecy. Part of total defense spending is not subject to the usual controls in Congress but goes through a more limited review because of fears of revealing secrets to potential enemies. One estimate is that almost $32 billion was allocated in this manner in 2008.[53] Secrecy also may make it easier for Congress members to hide pork barrel projects.

The second problem in the defense budget is that the George W. Bush administration financed the military operations in Iraq and Afghanistan through emergency supplemental appropriations rather than through the regular defense budget. Critics argue that these expenses were not surprises, like Hurricane Katrina, but were foreseeable and should have been debated as part of the normal budget process.[54] The need to include Iraq and Afghanistan was especially evident given that supplemental and emergency appropriations do not receive the scrutiny that the regular appropriations acts do (see below). Upon taking office in 2009, Barack Obama departed from this strategy and included war funds in the overall defense budget.

Supplemental Appropriations

Agencies may also require supplemental appropriations, made outside the normal budget cycle, to cover shortfalls during the fiscal year. Agencies sometimes simply run out of money, either because of improper management or, more often, because of changes in the demand for services or poor estimates of demand for a new service. For example, during a recession, the demand for unemployment assistance will naturally increase, and supplemental funding will be required. Likewise, a year of poor weather may force additional funding for crop insurance in the Department of Agriculture. Or a new program, such as food stamps, may acquire more clients than anyone anticipated during the early years of its existence.

Supplemental appropriations are not insignificant amounts of money. In 1996, $3.52 billion was appropriated through supplementals. The figure ballooned to over $5 billion in 2002 with the impact of terrorism. Although a few supplemental actions reduced the amounts appropriated, additions to agency obligational authority ranged from $1.8 million for land acquisition for the U.S. Fish and Wildlife Service to almost $500 million for the Department of Defense for additional expenses incurred in operations in Somalia and Bosnia. There was also $225.5 million for the Soil Conservation Service, to aid recovery from disastrous floods in the Midwest. Deficit reduction strategies (discussed later in this chapter) have changed budget procedures and reduced the size of supplemental appropriations, but they are still an avenue for additional spending.

Requests for supplemental appropriations may be a useful strategy for agencies attempting to expand their funding. An agency may be able to initiate a program with minimal appropriations through the usual budgetary process, anticipating wide acceptance of its program by prospective clients, and then return to Congress for supplemental appropriations when clients materialize and demand benefits. Supplementals frequently are not scrutinized as carefully as regular appropriations, and their relative invisibility may permit friendly Congress members to hide a rapidly expanding program. Scrutiny of supplementals has increased because of the requirement that expenditure proposals be "deficit neutral," but they still are usually easier to push through Congress than regular appropriations. Obvious and frequent abuse of the supplemental appropriations process will damage the relationship between an agency and Congress, however, and that may hurt more than help the agency in the long run.

Earmarks

The deficits in the federal budget have not been lessened by the increasing use of so-called earmarked appropriations added to appropriations bills.[55] Members of Congress who want to create special benefits for individuals in their constituencies are able to do so by adding riders to bills, generally after they have already gone through the appropriations committees. Once these provisions are part of the final act, Congress members are reluctant to overturn them because they want to ensure that their own earmarks are not eliminated. There were 587 earmarks in the defense appropriations bill in 1994; there were 2,837 in 2006.[56] In all, there were more than 15,000 of these earmarks in 2006, although this had dropped to slightly less than 10,000 by 2010.[57]

Providing benefits for their constituencies is one way that incumbent Congress members are able to stay in office. But the lack of scrutiny of these expenditures eliminates an important function of Congress in maintaining fiscal responsibility. Spending money for pork barrel projects may also leave less money for general public services, even in crucial areas such as defense.[58] Some analysis indicates that pork barrel programs are used to build coalitions for broader public goals.[59] Earmarks have become more visible after several scandals and allegations of congressional corruption in providing earmarked funds to campaign contributors.[60]

President Obama has promised to reduce the use of earmarks, but the absence of a line-item veto makes this task difficult (see below).[61] Spending bills come to the president with all the earmarks attached, meaning that he must sign the entire bill or veto it. Not signing an appropriations bill will mean that many public programs will have no funding, so presidents tend to sign them. Unless some negotiations with Congress can restrain the use of earmarks, this practice is likely to continue to be a problem for budgeting.

Assessing the Outcomes: Incrementalism or What?

A standard term used to describe changes in budget allocations in the United States is *incremental*. Any number of meanings are attached to this word.[62] Broadly, *incrementalism* means that changes in an agency's budget from year to year tend to be predictable, but the word has taken on several additional, more specific interpretations. First, incremental decision making is described as a process that is not "synoptic," or not fully rational[63]—that is, incremental decision making does not involve examining sweeping alternatives to the status quo and then making a decision about the optimal use of budgetary resources. Rather, incremental decision making involves "successive limited comparisons," or the sequential examination of marginal changes from the status quo and decisions about whether to make those marginal adjustments to current policies.[64] An incremental decision-making process builds on earlier decisions, seeking means to improve the existing situation rather than altering current policies or budgetary priorities completely. In budgetary terms, this means that an agency can expect to receive in any year approximately what it received the previous year, plus a little more to adjust for inflation or expanded services.

Advocates of incremental decision making argue that it is actually more rational than the synoptic method. Because it provides an experiential base from which to work, the incremental method offers a greater opportunity to make good policy choices than does the apparently more rational synoptic method. In addition, errors made in an incremental decision-making process can be more easily reversed than can major changes made in a synoptic process. In many ways, incremental decision making is a cost-minimizing form of rationality rather than a benefit-maximizing approach. Incrementalism reduces costs, first, by limiting the range of alternatives and thereby limiting the research and calculation costs for decision makers, and second, by reducing the costs of change, particularly of error correction. Because in an incremental world few choices involve significant deviations from existing policies or appropriations, there is little need to make major adjustments either in the actual programs or in the thought patterns of decision makers about the policies. Given the limited calculating capacity of human beings—even with the aid of modern technology—and the resistance of most individuals and organizations to change, incrementalism can be argued to be a rational means for making choices.

Incrementalism also is used to describe the pattern of outcomes of the budgetary process. In particular, Otto A. Davis, M. A. H. Dempster, and Aaron Wildavsky demonstrated that there is a great deal of stability in the increase in agency appropriations from year to year.[65] The changes in budgets are not only small but also quite stable and predictable, so the best estimate of an agency's budget in one year is the previous year's budget plus a stable percentage increase. Some agencies grow more rapidly than others, but each exhibits a stable pattern of growth.

Several factors contribute to incremental budgeting in the United States. One is that such a large percentage of the budget is uncontrollable that few significant changes in appropriations can be made from year to year. Also, most empirical examinations of incremental budgeting have been made during periods of relative economic stability and high rates of economic growth. As less favorable economic conditions became more common in the United States, the incrementalism appropriate for rich and predictable budgeting systems diminished.[66] These changes in the economic climate of budgeting are to some degree reflected in the reform efforts I will describe later in the chapter.

Most important, the repetitive and sequential nature of budgeting tends to produce incremental budget outcomes. A budget must be passed each year, so minor adjustments can be made from year to year as the need arises, thus avoiding the need to attempt to correct all the problems of the policy area at once. The annual cycle prevents an agency from trying to "shoot the moon" in any one year—to expand its budget base greatly, perhaps with flimsy evidence. The sequential nature of the process requires several actors to make their own decisions one after another, and many bargains must be struck. The incremental solution not only provides a natural choice but also helps minimize the costs of bargaining among institutions. Once the precedent of a certain percentage increase for a particular agency each year has been established, it is far simpler to honor that rule than to seek a better decision for one year and then have to do the same hard bargaining and calculation in each subsequent year.

Critiques of Incrementalism

A number of criticisms have been leveled at incrementalism, both in its prescriptive capacity (decisions should be made incrementally) and in its descriptive capacity (decisions are made incrementally). The basic argument against incrementalism as a prescription for policymaking is that it is excessively conservative—the status quo is perpetuated long after better solutions are available. This is true for some program decisions as well as for spending decisions. Incrementalism may be a perfectly rational means of policymaking so long as all parties agree that a policy or program is functioning well and is well managed. But how many policies currently fall in that happy category in the United States? In addition, even the incrementalist might agree that at times (e.g., during periods of crisis) nonincremental decisions are required, but the approach provides no means of identifying when and how those nonincremental decisions should be made.[67] If one uses the incremental approach to provide a prescriptive model for governmental decision making, then one must be able to specify what a "big" change would be, when it would be appropriate, and how it might be made.

Several problems also relate to incrementalism as a description of budgetary decision making. In the first place, the majority of empirical examinations of incremental budgeting have been performed at the agency level. That is certainly justifiable, given the importance of those organizations in U.S. public policy, but it is perhaps too high a level of aggregation for examining incremental budgeting.[68] When other researchers have disaggregated agency budgets into program-level budgets, they have found a great deal of nonincremental change—although, as pointed out, it is sometimes difficult to define just what is or is not an incremental change.[69] Although public organizations may have a stable pattern of expenditure change, the managers of the organizations can drastically alter priorities among the operating programs within the agency and produce more rapid change.

In addition, when the uncontrollable elements of public expenditures are removed from the analysis, the pattern of expenditure change for the controllable portion is anything but incremental.[70] As budgets have been squeezed by inflation, by citizen resistance to taxation, by presidents committed to reducing the public sector, and by large tax cuts, budgetary increments have not been granted as usual, and at times, the base has also been cut—that is, there have been real reductions in agencies' new obligational authority compared with the preceding year. Incrementalism may therefore now be descriptive only of certain kinds of expenditures and not of the budget process as a whole. Of course, since uncontrollable expenditures accounted for approximately 70 percent of total federal expenditures in 2006, the incrementalist approach may still be a useful description.

Incrementalism may apply only to certain kinds of agencies and programs such as those whose existence has been fully accepted as a part of the realm of government activity; it may not apply to newer or more marginal programs. For example, the budgets of programs such as food stamps are always more subject to change than are programs such as veterans benefits or Social Security, although all would be broadly classified as social service expenditures. The food stamp program has been in existence for a number of years but still does not have the legitimacy that other programs have developed, as evidenced by the ease with which it has been reduced in the past several budgets. Incrementalist theory also does not explain how and when programs experience big gains or big losses in their appropriations. Even if it explains a great deal of the variance in normal times, it seems incapable of explaining the most interesting and most important aspects of budgeting—who wins and who loses.

The prescriptive appeal of incrementalism is based in part on the reversibility of small changes, but in the real world of policymaking, many changes are not reversible.[71] Once a commitment is made to a client, or a benefit is indexed, it is difficult to go back and take it away. This is especially true of programs that have a "stock" component—that is, that involve the development of a capital infrastructure or a financial base.[72] Once a program such as Social Security is introduced, individuals covered under the program take the benefits into account when making their financial plans for retirement; any reduction or elimination of benefits may therefore create a hardship.

Despite these critiques, incrementalism has certainly become the conventional description of the U.S. budget process and its results. And that presumed incrementalism has prompted a number of proposals for reform of the budget process to make it more rational and to try to reduce the tendency for programs, once authorized, not only to remain in existence forever but to receive steadily increasing appropriations. It is to those attempts at reform that we now turn our attention.

Reforming Budgeting: Large-Scale Approaches in the 1960s and 1970s

For most of contemporary history, criticisms of the U.S. budget process have focused on its incremental, "irrational," and fragmented character. More recently, however, the focus has shifted from imposing rationality toward finding somewhat simplistic means of correcting the negative results of the process, including huge federal deficits. At first, several methods sought to make the consideration of expenditure priorities more comprehensive and to facilitate government's making the best possible use of its resources. The two most important budgeting reforms of that type were program budgeting and zero-base budgeting. We discuss those two reforms briefly, for even though they were implemented several decades ago, the ideas behind them remain important. After that, we turn to the less rational but perhaps more effective reforms of the 1980s and 1990s.

Program Budgeting

Program budgeting was largely a product of Lyndon Johnson's administration, although it had been tried previously in some agencies. Whereas traditional budgeting allocates personnel costs, supplies, equipment, and so forth among organizations, program budgeting allocates resources on the basis of the activities of government and the services that government supplies to society.[73] It also places a pronounced emphasis on the analysis of programmatic expenditures and the most efficient use of scarce resources.

Underlying program budgeting—or, more specifically, the planning, programming, budgeting system (PPBS)—is a systems concept. It is assumed that the elements of government policy are closely intertwined, so a change in one type of policy affects all others. For example, if one wants to improve the health of citizens in the United States, it may be more efficient to improve nutrition and housing than to invest money in medical care. Program budgeting was always looking for interactions among policy areas and for means of producing desired effects in the most efficient manner.

There were six basic characteristics of PPBS as practiced in the federal government. First, the major goals and objectives of government were to be identified; it was necessary to specify what government was attempting to do, but this identification was to be made high in the hierarchy of government, usually by the president and Congress. Whereas traditional line-item budgeting is initiated by the agencies, the concept of program budgeting began with a specification of the central goals and priorities of government, which could be supplied only by the principal political leaders.

Second, programs were to be developed according to the specified goals. How would government attempt to attain its goals? Programs were analytically defined and might not exist as organizational entities. For example, the strategic deterrence program in the Department of Defense was spread among three services: The air force had its manned bombers and some missiles, the navy had Polaris submarines, and the army had intermediate-range ballistic missiles located in Europe. *Strategic deterrence* described a set of activities of the defense establishment, but no organization was specifically responsible for it.

Third, resources were to be allocated among programs. Although many traditional line items were used in developing the program budget, the final budget document was presented as overall costs for the achievement of certain objectives. Those costs would then be justified as efficient and effective means of reaching the desired goals. PPBS thus emphasized the costs of reaching certain objectives, whereas line-item budgeting emphasizes the costs of keeping organizations or programs in operation.

Fourth, organizations were not sacrosanct in program budgeting, and there was no assumption that each program would be housed within a single agency or that each agency would provide only a single program. As in the defense example, program budgeting attempted to expand the framework of budgeting to include all the actors who contributed to the achievement of the goals. This was a realistic attitude toward the interaction of activities and organizations in producing the final effects on the society, but it made budgeting more difficult in an environment composed of many organizations, each attempting to sustain its own interests.

Fifth, PPBS extended the time limit on expenditures found in line-item budgeting, attempting to answer questions about the medium- and long-term implications of programs. Programs that appeared efficient in the short run might actually be less desirable when their long-term implications were considered. For example, most publicly supported health care programs concentrate on curative medicine, whereas it may be more efficient in the long run to emphasize prevention.

Sixth, alternative program structures were systematically analyzed in an effort to find more effective and efficient ones. Agencies were expected to present justifications for programs—to show, in other words, that the chosen program was superior to the alternatives investigated. This aspect of program budgeting relates to our previous discussion of policy formulation, for agencies were expected to develop alternatives and to examine their relative merits, using techniques such as cost-benefit analysis.

Criticism of program budgeting.   Advocates of program budgeting pointed with pride to the enhanced rationality and analytic rigor associated with it and to the way that it could break down organizational control over budgetary outcomes. Despite these apparent advantages, PPBS was not especially successful in most of its applications. There were some technical reasons for the apparent failures, but the most severe problems in implementing program budgeting were political.

Technically, applying PPBS successfully required a great deal of time and effort, as well as an almost certain knowledge of unknown relationships of spending to program success. The systems concept inherent in the method implies that if one aspect of the system is altered, the entire system must be rethought. That may mean that program budgeting actually institutionalizes the rigidity that it was designed to eliminate. Also, it is difficult if not impossible to define programs, measure their results, and evaluate the contributions of individual agencies and activities to the achievement of those results. The difficulty of measuring the effects of government is one of the major problems in public policy analysis, and such measurement occupies a central place in program budgeting.[74]

Program budgeting also had several political disadvantages. First, as mentioned, the method forced decisions to a higher level of government.[75] Agencies disliked this centralizing tendency, as did Congress members who had invested considerable effort in developing relationships with clientele groups supporting agencies. Moreover, the assumption that organizations are not the most appropriate objects of allocation ran counter to all the folkways of American government. Finally, the need to analyze systematically alternative strategies for achieving ends forced agencies to expose their programs to possible attack, as they might develop and eliminate alternative programs that others might prefer, and the explicit nature of the process brought those alternatives up for active consideration.

In short, PPBS was a dagger pointed at the central role of the agency in policymaking, and it should not have been expected to succeed, except perhaps in organizations such as the Department of Defense. That organization had a strong leader committed to the concept of program budgeting, and it produced extremely nebulous results that could be tested only against simulations or scenario-building exercises; it also had few potent political enemies. For other agencies, with much greater political opposition and with real clients demanding real services, PPBS was doomed to failure from the beginning.

The rebirth of program budgeting.   Although it has been declared dead as a formal device for allocating resources, the ideas of program budgeting continue to appear in thinking about the budget process, and especially in thinking about reforms. The basic idea of making the most efficient allocation of money among competing resources is an extremely alluring one, and politicians and analysts will attempt to pursue that rationalistic goal even in the face of massive evidence that it may not be attainable in the rough world of politics.

The Government Performance and Results Act of 1993 (GPRA) represented the rebirth of the fundamental idea of making the allocation of funds more rational.[76] The principal concept underlying this legislation was to shift the focus in assessing organizations in the budget process away from inputs and toward outcomes and "results." Thus, each organization in the federal government has been required to develop a strategic plan and a set of operational indicators of attaining the goals specified in that plan. The degree of success or failure in attaining the goals then plays a significant role in determining the budgetary success of the organization. This process involves neither the direct linkage to expenditures nor the level of analysis inherent in program budgeting, but it does depend on some of the same assumptions.

One of the consequences of this more rationalist style of budgeting was that there was much greater emphasis on identifying what government was attempting to do and assessing how well the goals were being achieved.[77] This style of budgeting can be done without tampering with the agency basis of budgeting or developing a systems framework for policy. However, even fifteen years after the adoption of this legislation, the difficulties of measurement and implementation are only beginning to be overcome.

The administration of George W. Bush extended the idea of performance budgeting to include an assessment of the progress that organizations were making in implementing a range of goals, such as "e-government," improved financial management, and use of private contractors when possible. Called "PART" (Program Assessment Rating Tool), this addition to the GPRA process evaluates every program but provides relatively weak measures of performance.[78] It tends to emphasize the management of the programs rather than the services provided to clients, and hence, efficiency may dominate effectiveness and equity considerations.

Zero-Base Budgeting

If program budgeting required an almost superhuman analytical capability and rafts of data, the conceptual underpinnings of zero-base budgeting (ZBB) are extremely simple. Whereas traditional incremental budgeting operates from the assumption that the previous year's budget (the "base") was justified and so increments are all that need examination, ZBB holds that a more comprehensive examination of all expenditures should be conducted. That is, there should be no base, and the entire spending plan should be justified. It was assumed that weaker programs that were being extended largely through inertia would be terminated, or at least severely cut, and more meritorious programs would be fully funded.

Zero-base budgeting was carried out during Jimmy Carter's administration on the basis of *decision units*, which might be agencies but frequently were smaller components such as operating programs within an agency. Each budget manager was expected to prepare a number of "decision packages" to reflect his or her priorities for funding. These packages were to be presented in rank order, beginning with a "survival package" that represented the lowest level of funding on which the unit could continue to exist. On top of the survival package, additional decision packages were to reflect, first, the continuation of existing programs at existing levels of service and then expansions of service. Each decision package was to be justified in terms of the services it would provide at an acceptable cost.

Decision packages prepared by lower-level budget managers were passed up the organizational hierarchy to higher-level managers, who prepared consolidated decision packages ranking priorities among the several decision units that they might supervise. These rankings were then passed up and consolidated further, ending in the Office of Management and Budget. All the rankings from the lower levels were passed along with the consolidated packages, so higher levels could examine lower-level managers' preferences and their justifications. Like program budgeting, ZBB was geared toward multiyear budgeting to better understand the implications of budget choices made during any one budget cycle.

Zero-base budgeting, again like program budgeting, had several apparent advantages. Obviously, the method would eliminate incremental budgeting. The agency's base is no longer protected but must be defended—although in practice the survival level might function as a base. Also, ZBB focused on cost-effectiveness in the justifications of the rankings of decision packages and even of the survival level of funding. A chief advantage of zero-base budgeting was the involvement of managers at relatively low levels of the organization in the consideration of its priorities and goals. Also, the method considered the allocation of resources in package terms, whereas the incremental budget assumes that any additional money can be effectively used. It makes substantially greater sense to think of increments of money that can produce additional services than simply to add more money without regard for the threshold values for service provision and efficiency.

Nevertheless, there were a number of glaring difficulties with zero-base budgeting. For example, implementing it threatened the existence of some agencies. In practice, a number of factors such as powerful clientele groups and uncontrollable expenditures could negate the concern that many administrators might have had about ZBB, but it was nevertheless clear that its intent was to question the existence of each program every year.

Additionally, there was simply no means by which OMB, held to a reasonable size, or a Congress with its other commitments, could carefully consider the entire budget each year. Instead, there would be either a superficial analysis of each program under the guise of a zero-base review—probably with incremental results—or a selective review of a number of more controversial programs. Either would be an acceptable means of reducing the workload, but neither would constitute a significant departure from the incremental budget or justify the massive effort required to prepare the necessary documents.

In addition, ZBB threatened established programs by reopening political conflicts during each budget cycle. It is a virtue of traditional incremental budgeting that once a program has been agreed to, it is accepted and is not subject to significant scrutiny unless there are major changes in the environment or serious administrative problems in the agency. With zero-base budgeting, however, the existence of a program was subject to question each year, and the political fights over authorizing its existence might have to be fought again and again. Of course, this presented no problem for well-established and popular programs, but it was certainly a problem for newer and more controversial ones. ZBB also tended to combine financial decisions with program decisions, placing perhaps an excessive burden on budgetary decision makers.

From Scalpels to Axes: Budget Reform from the 1980s to the 2000s

Incrementalist budgeting patterns have been more seriously challenged by the government's continuing fiscal problems than by the analytic methodologies proposed in program budgeting and (to some extent) zero-base budgeting. Those persistent fiscal problems have spawned a number of proposed solutions,[79] some of which have been implemented, including the Gramm-Rudman-Hollings Act (technically the Balanced Budget and Emergency Deficit Control Act of 1985), the budget agreement between Congress and President George H. W. Bush in 1990, and the Balanced Budget Act of 1997. Other proposals include a balanced budget amendment to the Constitution and the partially implemented line-item veto. Most of these are simply incrementalism turned around—they share incrementalism's tendency to substitute minimization of decision-making costs for maximization of benefits from expenditures. They are for the most part "no-think solutions," just as incrementalism has been a nonanalytic means for making budgetary decisions. But whereas incrementalism has been successful and acceptable, these methods for dealing with a complex problem have been proposed just because of their simplicity. Simple policies are perhaps only rarely the best solutions for complex problems, but they are often the most acceptable in the political world.

Gramm-Rudman-Hollings

As the deficits created by the Reagan tax cuts grew during the 1980s, Congress began to look for means to stanch the budgetary hemorrhaging. This was difficult to do by traditional means because of the logrolling and pork barrel legislative styles so typical of Congress. Congress therefore adopted a method, commonly referred to as "Gramm-Rudman-Hollings," after its sponsors, that removed some of its discretion and forced spending reductions in cases where Congress and the president could not reach agreement. Initially, it aimed to reduce the federal deficit to zero within five years (by fiscal year 1991). That target was indicative of the totemic status of a balanced budget in American thinking about public finance, but it soon proved to be an unattainable and perhaps unwise target.[80]

The idea behind Gramm-Rudman-Hollings was that to meet the declining deficit target in any year, Congress and the president could cut spending, raise taxes, or use some combination of the two. If no agreement could be reached on those actions, however, automatic cuts in spending (called *sequestrations*), half taken from defense and half from domestic programs, would be imposed. Certain types of expenditures, including interest on the federal debt, Social Security, veterans benefits, and the like, were excluded, so the automatic reductions would have to come from only 30 percent of the budget. That meant that the cuts would have to be severe.

The initial scorekeeper in the process was to be the General Accounting Office, but the Supreme Court ruled that the GAO, a legislative organization, could not perform the executive act of ordering budget cuts for specific executive agencies.[81] The scorekeeper role was then reassigned to the Office of Management and Budget, despite Congress's fears that its interests might be slighted by the change. Other changes to the act followed in 1987–1988. First, the time for reducing the deficit to zero was extended to fiscal 1993. Second, most of the truly significant cuts were postponed until after the 1988 presidential and congressional elections, thereby confirming the adage that future budget cuts are always more acceptable than current ones, especially for incumbents. Congress attempted to restore deficit reduction to its original trajectory after the election but was deterred by economic and political circumstances.

The principal factor keeping the president and Congress from reaching their targets was a sluggish, then decelerating, economy. President George H. W. Bush proposed a budget that would meet the Gramm-Rudman-Hollings target of a $64 billion deficit for fiscal 1991, but as the budget process progressed during 1990, it became clear that the actual deficit would be closer to $300 billion because of the slowed economy. The sense of crisis emerging from the negotiations then produced a new program for deficit reduction, or at least deficit management. Adopted as the Budget Enforcement Act of 1990 (BEA), it provided for the following:

1. Separation of mandatory spending from discretionary spending
2. Differentiation of three types of discretionary spending: defense, international, and domestic, with separate spending targets for each
3. A "pay-as-you-go" plan for mandatory spending and revenues so that any increase in spending or reduction in revenue required a spending reduction or tax increase elsewhere, to keep the package deficit-neutral
4. Elimination of overoptimistic or unrealistic targets for deficit reduction
5. Inclusion of loan programs in the budget calculations (they had been excluded previously)
6. The Office of Management and Budget as scorekeeper[82]

Gramm-Rudman-Hollings, like other legislative attempts at fiscal control, represents a major effort at reform of the budget process to eliminate the deficit and force government to live within its revenues. It also points to the extreme difficulties of making and implementing such an agreement. Not only were unrealistic targets set and then dismissed, but also important segments of federal financial operations, such as credit (initially) and the savings and loan bailout, were ignored. Furthermore, the automatic cuts were imposed on a relatively small proportion of the budget and therefore fell very heavily in those areas.

The other effect of Gramm-Rudman-Hollings and its sequels was to add a new level of analysis to the budget process. One crucial element of budgeting introduced in the 1990s is scorekeeping in the pay-as-you-go—or PAYGO—system. Any spending bill had to be scored to determine whether it was revenue-neutral—that is, whether it provided sufficient revenues or savings from other programs to cover the costs of the new program. Legislation not meeting that fiscal neutrality criterion had to be redesigned so that it would do so. Making the determination of neutrality is by no means simple, for it often involves a number of economic assumptions and a variety of ways to do the calculations; politics enters here as well, as in the rest of the budget process.[83] In many ways, the Gramm-Rudman-Hollings and BEA enterprises helped add to the already high level of cynicism of Americans about government.[84]

In early 1993, the incoming Clinton administration used the provisions of the Budget Enforcement Act to begin to implement its own budgetary and economic strategy. The first Clinton budget proposed a very modest increase in expenditures but a much larger increase in revenues, thereby producing some reduction in the deficit, which continued for several years.[85] But by 2003, the Budget Enforcement Act was allowed to lapse. President Bush argued unsuccessfully for continuing the PAYGO principle for discretionary spending but not for tax legislation. The logic of the BEA had been reasonably successful in restraining spending, but its constraints were not impossible to elude, and the desire of the president and Congress to pursue tax reductions, combined with the need to spend heavily on the war on terror, Iraq, and growing entitlements, led to the end of the BEA.

The deficit and debt debate in 2010 and after provoked several responses to the problem. The Budget Control Act of 2011 contained several instruments for attacking the deficit. One was to attempt to address the problem by political negotiations, through the so-called Super Committee—the Joint Select Committee on Deficit Reduction. This committee was composed of equal numbers of Democrats and Republicans and was meant to reduce the deficit by $2 trillion to match the projected amount of borrowing needed. This committee, however, was not successful in reaching an agreement and disbanded with no recommendations.[86]

The second reaction of the deficit and debt problem contained in this act was to provide for automatic sequestration of funds if Congress and the president were incapable of reducing the deficit. In this plan, if the target figure is not reached, the amount needed would be automatically taken from spending, half from defense and half from domestic discretionary expenditures. This would protect major entitlement programs, such as Social Security, but unlike many budget plans, it did also threaten the defense budget (see below).

The Balanced Budget Amendment

Among the most commonly discussed solutions to the federal budget deficit has been a balanced budget amendment to the Constitution. It would require Congress to pass a balanced budget each year unless an extraordinary majority declared that an economic emergency existed sufficient to justify running a deficit.[87] Somewhat like the PAYGO budgetary process, such an amendment would force a more explicit comparison of revenues and spending, and it would further require those involved in the budget process to be responsible for the amount of money that they appropriate. The difference, of course, is that the arrangement would be constitutional and therefore permanent.

A balanced budget amendment has had substantial political appeal and has gained some support. When it was voted on in 1993, it came close to receiving enough votes in Congress to send it to the states for ratification. Like many simple solutions to complex problems, however, it has some major shortcomings. First, as already noted, the planning for a budget begins over a year before it goes into effect and more than two years before the completion of the budget year. Both the revenue and expenditure projections on which a budget is based are influenced by the condition of the economy and its projected condition during the time the budget is to be executed.[88] It is easy to get the projections wrong—over the past twenty-five years, the official figures have overestimated revenues by an average of 3.5 percent and underestimated expenditures by an average of 3.9 percent.[89] Even if Congress acted in good faith in attempting to comply with the spirit of such an amendment, it could easily miss the target of a balanced budget badly—by an average of almost 8 percent.

In addition to potential economic problems from an unplanned deficit, a deficit might appear to be a violation of the Constitution and thus further undermine already weakened public respect for Congress. A more cynical scenario would have Congress passing a budget that, although balanced on paper, it would know had little chance of being balanced when executed. In either case, there could be substantial political damage to the legitimacy of Congress and government as a whole. The difficulties already encountered in applying Gramm-Rudman-Hollings to limit spending give some idea of how a balanced budget agreement would, or would not, work.

Deficits are not necessarily a public evil. When deficits are adopted for economic reasons—not created by political unwillingness to impose the true costs of government on citizens—they can be an important tool of economic management, following the Keynesian tradition. Passing a balanced budget amendment would only remove that management tool from the federal government without any certainty of generating economic benefits sufficient to justify the loss.

The Line-Item Veto

In his 1985 budget submission, President Ronald Reagan proposed that a presidential line-item veto be adopted, especially for appropriations bills. He was not the first president to make the recommendation—Ulysses Grant had done so—nor was he the last. Similar to powers already invested in governors in forty-three states, the line-item veto would allow the president to veto a portion of a bill while permitting the rest to be put into effect.[90] Bill Clinton also advocated this instrument of presidential power, and it had been one part of the Republicans' Contract with America. Congress, seemingly against its own institutional interests, passed legislation in 1996 giving the president the line-item veto.[91]

This selective veto is seen as a weapon to deal with Congress members' tendency to add pet projects to appropriations bills, placing the president in the awkward position of having to refuse money for a large segment of the federal government as the only way to prevent the funding of one or two small, often wasteful, projects. The proliferation of these pork barrel provisions and earmarking in the early twenty-first century is making the line-item veto appear all the more desirable.[92] Some attempt to strengthen the rules against earmarking have, despite the rhetoric against earmarking, created a good deal of consternation among members of Congress.[93]

Although justified as a way to attack the problem of growing federal deficits, the veto cannot be applied to many uncontrollable programs, such as debt interest and Social Security. Using his powers of rescission, the president can achieve some of the same ends, although he needs the agreement of Congress. In 1992, President George H. W. Bush attempted to rescind $7.9 billion, but by the time Congress had finished with the proposal, it was a rescission of $8.2 billion that contained few of the cuts the president had proposed.[94] Despite continuing to press for the line-item veto, President George W. Bush used his rescission powers only once while in office. Congress would have the option of overriding a presidential line-item veto, first by a simple majority and then by a two-thirds majority if the president maintained his convictions about eliminating the expenditure.

The line-item veto might actually encourage Congress to add more pet projects onto appropriations acts, placing the onus on the president to remove them. Indeed, in his first use of the veto (before the courts intervened), President Clinton singled out some spending items that apparently were pork, concentrated in a few congressional districts.[95] The line-item veto might also give the president independent power over public spending not intended by the framers of the Constitution or desired by the public.

The first use of the line-item veto brought several lawsuits from affected parties and members of Congress. The courts ruled that it was unconstitutional because it violated the separation of powers provisions of the Constitution by conferring legislative powers on the president in enabling him to make selective decisions about what would be spent and what would not. The Constitution gives the president the veto, but over entire bills and not over the particular parts he dislikes. Although subsequent attempts to revive the line-item veto have proved futile, the debate over it is likely to continue, especially given the recent backlash against earmarks. As with the balanced budget amendment, the episode shows that there are few magic solutions for solving budget problems, but there is a continuing need for political will and courage to solve them.

The enhanced rescission authority sought by President George W. Bush and then President Obama is an attempt to have a line-item veto that would be constitutional.[96] In this proposal, the president would have forty-five days after signing a piece of spending legislation to send to Congress a statement about which parts of the spending he would rescind (not spend). Congress would then have twenty-five days to vote on this, without amendments. This would preserve the separation of powers, while still giving the president greater powers over selecting what to spend and what not to spend.

Decrementalism

The preceding discussion of the balanced budget amendment and the line-item veto is indicative of the general problem facing American government: the control of public expenditures. While *incrementalism* has become the conventional description of budgeting, many politicians are looking for means of forcing *decrementalism,* or the gradual reduction of expenditures, on government.[97] The majority of them are on the political right—as exemplified by Republicans in the House of Representatives during the Obama administration—but even some on the left are seeking to reduce spending while hoping to be able to maintain levels of public service.[98]

In addition to the rationalistic approaches to budgeting and the Gramm-Rudman-Hollings machinery, other, somewhat blunter, instruments have been employed to try to reduce federal expenditures. One was the president's Private Sector Survey on Cost Control (the Grace Commission) in the early 1980s. That survey, similar to ones that had been conducted in most state governments, brought to Washington some 2,000 volunteers from business and other private sector organizations to examine the management of the federal government. The volunteers prepared 2,478 distinct recommendations, which were projected to save the government $424 billion a year if all were implemented.[99] Other efforts at controlling the costs of government have been even cruder, including across-the-board reductions in staffing levels and budgets and moratoriums on new programs and regulations. President Reagan and his advisers attempted to reduce the pay of public employees to 94 percent of that earned by comparable employees in the private sector—the 6 percent difference theoretically made up by the greater job security and fringe benefits associated with federal employment.[100] The Clinton administration had few proposals for changing the mechanisms for budgeting, other than the familiar arguments for a line-item veto and the proposals for a biennial budget contained in the National Performance Review.[101] The George W. Bush administration offered some ideas about cash management but little in the way of fundamental change in the budget process.

As discussed above, the United States has entered an era in which decrementalism appears to be more central to budgeting. The emphasis on reducing the federal debt has placed the need to cut expenditures more in the center of political discussion, especially given the reluctance of many involved to cut taxes. Attempts at more rationalistic procedures, such as the Budget Supercommittee, have again failed, so the latest version of across-the-board cuts—the Budget Control Act of 2011—is currently the only means available to manage the political difficulties associated with budgeting.[102]

Reaction to those proposals has been almost the opposite of that to proposals such as program budgeting and zero-base budgeting. The more recent across-the-board reform exercises have been criticized as mindless and as simply attacking government without regard to the real benefits created through some agencies and the real waste created by others. Such simplistic strategies contrast with the large-scale analytic exercises that would be required to implement PPBS or ZBB. Perhaps sadly, across-the-board exercises, such as the Budget Control Act of 2011, have a much greater chance of being implemented than do the more analytic methods.

Summary

All the attempts at budget reform described here have had some impact on the way in which the federal budget is constructed. Both program budgeting and zero-base budgeting were significant rationalistic efforts at reforming the budgetary process. Although both had a great deal to commend them, neither was particularly successful in changing the behavior of budget decision makers. The less rationalistic methods, such as Gramm-Rudman-Hollings, have had a somewhat greater impact, in part because they did not attempt to change the basic format.

Why does the traditional, line-item, incremental budget persist despite the real shortcomings of both the process and the outcomes?[103] One reason is that the traditional budget gives the legislature an excellent means of controlling the executive branch. It allocates funds to identifiable organizations for identifiable purposes (personnel, equipment, etc.), not to nebulous programs or decision units. The political and administrative leaders who manage the real organizations to which the funds are allocated can then be held accountable for how they spend the money appropriated to them. Blunt instruments tacked onto the process, such as the Budget Enforcement Act, enhance the control elements of the budget process without altering it fundamentally.

More important, although the benefits promised by both PPBS and ZBB were significant, so too were the costs, in terms both of the calculations required to reach decisions and of the political turmoil created. Incremental budgeting provides ready guidelines for those who must make budget decisions, minimizing the necessity for them to engage in costly analysis and calculation. In addition, as most political interests are manifested through organizations, the absence in incremental budgeting of threats to those organizations means that political conflicts can be confined to marginal matters instead of repeated battles over the very existence of the organizations.

In short, although incremental budgeting does nothing very well, neither does it do anything very poorly. Incrementalism is a convenient means of allocating resources for public purposes. It is not an optimal means of making policy, but it is a means that works. It is also a means of making policy in which policymakers themselves have great confidence. These factors are not in themselves sufficient to explain the perpetuation of the incremental budget process in the face of so many challenges by presumably superior systems. There are always proposals for change, but there is rarely sufficient agreement on which of the possible changes to make to move the system away from the status quo. There have been some improvements, but the system remains firmly incremental.

CHAPTER 8

Evaluation and Policy Change

THE FINAL STAGE of the policy process is to assess what has occurred as a result of the selection and implementation of a public policy and, if necessary, to change the current policy. Critics of government believe that these evaluative questions are extremely easy to answer, that the activities of government are rather simple, and that inefficiencies and maladministration could be corrected easily if only government really wanted to do so. This chapter will point out, however, that producing a valid evaluation of government programs is a difficult and highly political process in itself. It is much more difficult than evaluating most activities in the private sector.[1] Furthermore, if the evaluation determines that change is necessary or desirable, making the change is perhaps even more difficult than policy initiation—the first adoption of a policy. Government organizations have a number of means to protect themselves against change, and attempts to alter existing policies and organizations are almost certain to engender conflict.

Nevertheless, we should not be too quick to assume that government organizations are always wedded to the status quo. Change is threatening to any organization, public or private, but most organizations also know their own strengths and weaknesses and want to correct the weaknesses. The difficulties that organizations encounter in producing change arise as often from the rules imposed by Congress and from the demands of the organizations' clients as they do from internal conservatism. Most organizations, public as well as private, are engaged in continuous evaluation of their own performance, and changes in their management implemented over the past several decades have made public organizations even more conscious of how well they are doing.[2] What they must find is the means to produce effective change in that performance when they detect shortcomings.

Problems in Evaluating Public Programs

Evaluation is an important requirement for programs and organizations in government. Like other organizations, they need to know how they are performing.

In its simplest form, evaluating a public program involves cataloging its goals, measuring the degree to which the goals have been achieved, and perhaps suggesting changes that might bring the organization's performance more in line with the stated purposes of the program. Although these appear to be simple things to do, it is actually very difficult to measure the performance of a public organization unambiguously.[3] Several barriers stand in the way.

Goal Specification and Goal Change

The first step in an evaluation is to identify the goals of the program, but even that seemingly simple task may be difficult, if not impossible.[4] The legislation that establishes programs or organizations should be the source of goal statements, but we have already seen (in chapter 5) that legislation is frequently written in vague language to avoid offending potential members of the coalition necessary to pass it. As a result, it may be difficult to attach readily quantifiable goals to programs or organizations. The goals specified in legislation may be impossible or even contradictory. For example, one program had as its goal to raise all students to the mean reading level (think about it); the expressed aim of one foreign aid program was to assist the nations in greatest need, provided that they were the most likely to use the money to produce significant developmental effects. When an organization is faced merely with impossible goals, it can still do something positive, but when it is faced with contradictory goals, its own internal political dynamics become more important in determining ultimate policy choices than any legislative statement of purpose. As organizations do not function alone in the world, contradictions existing across organizations—as when the federal government continues to subsidize tobacco production and simultaneously discourages tobacco consumption—make identification of the goals of government as a whole that much more difficult.

Of course, internal political dynamics are still important in organizations whose enabling legislation states clear and unambiguous goals. A statement of goals may be important in initiating a program, but once the program is in operation, its goals may be modified. The changes may be positive, as when programs adapt to changing environmental conditions to meet new societal needs. Positive goal changes have been noted most often in the private sector, as when the March of Dimes shifted its goal from serving victims of polio to helping children with birth defects, but they also occur in the public sector.[5] For example, the Bureau of Indian Affairs has been transformed from an organization that simply exercised control over Native Americans into one that now frequently serves as an advocate for their rights and interests.[6] The Army Corps of Engineers transformed its image from one of gross environmental disregard to one of environmental sensitivity and even environmental advocacy.[7] Several organizations that were moved

into the Department of Homeland Security—for example, the Coast Guard—
have had to modify their goals to meet new international challenges.

Goal transformations may also be negative. The capture of regulatory bodies
by the industries they regulate is a commonly cited example of negative goal
change.[8] The failures of economic regulation that became apparent in 2008 may
be a function of the regulators being too close to the regulated industries. More
common is "displacement of goals" among the employees of an organization who,
although they may have been recruited on the basis of public service goals, over
time become more focused on personal survival and aggrandizement.[9] Similarly,
the goals of the organization as a whole may shift toward its own maintenance
and survival. Anthony Downs describes organizations (as well as individuals
within them) as going through a life cycle, beginning as zealots or advocates of
certain social causes but over time becoming more interested in surviving and
maintaining their budgets than in serving clients.[10] In such instances, the operating goals of a program deteriorate, even if the stated goals remain the same. The
organization may not even realize that the change has occurred, but its clients
almost certainly will.

Among the managerial changes in the public sector over the past several
decades has been an attempt to develop ways to prevent goal displacement. A
common change has been to make managers more directly responsible for the
performance of their organizations, with rewards for those whose organizations
perform well and possible dismissal for the managers of poorly performing organizations.[11] At lower levels, performance pay schemes are designed to produce
similar responsibility for performance.[12] A variety of mechanisms have been
developed to make the public sector more "consumer driven" by permitting
clients and the general public to know what is going on in organizations and to
have some influence over outcomes.[13]

Even when goals are clearly expressed, they may not be practical. The Pre-
amble to the Constitution, for instance, expresses a number of goals for the U.S.
government, but few, if any, are expressed in concrete language that would
enable a researcher to verify that they are or are not being achieved. Specifying
such goals and putting them into operation would require further political
action within the organization or the imposition of the values of the researcher
to make it possible to compare performance with aspiration. For example, the
Employment Act of 1946 pledged the government of the United States to maintain "full employment." At the time the act was passed, full employment was
declared to be 4 percent unemployment. Over time, the official definition crept
upward to 4.5 percent and then to 5 percent unemployed, and some economists
have argued that 6 percent is an appropriate level. In the context of 2012, 6 percent would appear a marvelous achievement for government. Obviously, political leaders want to declare that full employment has been achieved, and to justify

the claim, they apply pressure to change the definition of full employment. In this case, an admirable goal has been modified in practice, although the basic concept has remained a part of the policy statement. This is one instance of government playing the "numbers game" to attempt to prove that goals have been reached.[14]

Most public organizations serve multiple constituencies and therefore may have different goals for those different groups. For example, the Supplemental Nutrition Assistance Program, or SNAP program (formerly Food Stamps), performs several different functions for different groups. For the less affluent members of society, it is a means of nutritional support. For farmers, it is a means of increasing demand for their products and thereby raising prices and ensuring higher sales. For the Department of Agriculture, it enables them to become more involved in urban areas, thus expanding their constituency and perhaps also their political support. In general, the goals of these groups align well, but other programs may not be so fortunate.

Finally, it should be noted that goals may be either straitjackets or opportunities for an organization. In addition to telling an organization what it should be doing, specific goal statements tell it what it is not supposed to be doing. That may serve as a powerful conservative force within the organization and limit its creativity. The specification of goals can limit the efficiency and effectiveness of government as a whole. Any one statement of goals may divide responsibilities in ways that are less meaningful for citizens and policymakers in general than different statements might, especially if an expansion of knowledge or a change in social values occurs. So, for example, locating the U.S. Forest Service in the Department of Agriculture may mean that trees are treated more as a crop than as a natural resource, as they might be if the agency were located within the Department of the Interior. Giving any one program or organization a goal may mean that other, more efficient means of delivering the same service will not be explored or that existing duplications of service will not be eliminated.

Measurement

Once goals have been identified and expressed in clear, concrete language, the next task is to devise a means to measure the extent to which they have been attained. In the public sector, measuring results or production is frequently difficult. In fact, one fundamental problem that limits the efficiency and effectiveness of government is the absence of any ready means of judging the value of what is being produced.[15]

One of the best examples of the measurement problem occurs in one of government's oldest functions: national defense. The product called "defense" is, in many ways, the failure of real or potential enemies to take certain actions.

Logically, the best defense force would never do anything, for there would be no enemy willing to risk taking offensive actions. In fact, if a defense force is called into action, it has to some degree already failed. But measuring nonevents and counterfactual occurrences is difficult, so defense is frequently the object of surrogate measures. Thus, the megatonnage of nuclear weapons available and capable of being launched in fifteen minutes and the number of plane-hours of flight time logged by the Strategic Air Command have been used as measures of defense. In a post–Cold War era, at least until the Iraq War, the indicators of an effective defense policy were even less clear, involving as much the capacity to enforce peace settlements as the ability to wage war.[16]

The illustration from defense policy helps make the point that activity measures are frequently substituted for output measures when attempting to evaluate performance in the public sector. Some scholars, as well as some politicians and analysts, despair of finding more adequate means to measure the benefits of many public sector programs. For example, I. C. R. Byatt argues that "It is not possible to measure benefits from defense by any known techniques, nor is it easy to even begin to see how one might be developed." He goes on to say that "It is quite impossible to allocate costs to the final objectives of education."[17] He might well have extended the list to include most of the functions of the public sector. That is especially true for the federal government, which delivers few identifiable services to the public, and it explains in part why the federal government is often evaluated as the least effective of the three levels of government in the United States.

Scholarly pessimism aside, the perpetuation of activity measures serves the interests of existing organizations. First, such measures can shield them from stringent evaluations on nonprocedural criteria. Perhaps more important, action becomes equated with success, and that will have the predictable effect of raising levels of funding. It may also have the less obvious effect of giving incentives to program personnel to keep their clients in a program when its benefits are no longer needed. Despite skepticism and organizational politics, governments continue to express interest in measuring what their organizations actually deliver for the public, and reforms in recent years have attempted to focus more clearly on the impacts of government.

Several factors inhibit adequate measurement of government performance. One is the time span over which the benefits of many programs are created. For example, although the short-term goal of education is to improve reading, writing, and computation, its ultimate and more important goals can be realized only in the future.[18] They cannot be measured or even identified during the time a child is attending school. Among other things, education is supposed to increase the earning potential of individuals, make society more stable, and generally improve the quality of life for the individuals who receive it. These are elusive qualities when an evaluation must be done quickly. The time problem in evaluation is illustrated by Lester Salamon's analysis of the "sleeper" effects of New Deal land reform programs in the rural South. It was widely believed while the programs were in operation that they were failures, but significant results such as those of the new landowners' involvement in the 1960s civil rights movement became apparent thirty years after the programs were terminated.[19]

The other side of the time problem is that any effects a program produces should be durable.[20] Some programs may produce effects only after they have been in existence for years, whereas others produce demonstrable results in the short term but have no significant effects in the long run. It has been argued that the latter is true of the Head Start program. Participants in the program tend to enter school with skills superior to those of non–Head Start children, but after several years, no significant differences can be discerned. It seems that without reinforcement in later years, the effects of Head Start decay.[21] The program per se, therefore, may not be unsuccessful or ineffective; it may simply not have been carried through for a sufficient amount of time.[22]

The time element in program evaluation also produces significant political difficulties. The individuals responsible for making policy decisions are often short of time, and they must produce results quickly if their programs are to be successful. Representatives in Congress have terms of only two years before facing reelection, making it necessary that any program they advocate show some "profit" before those two years have passed. The policy process thus tends to favor short-term gains, even if they are not durable, over long-term successes. Some actors in the policy process, notably the permanent public bureaucracy, can afford to take a longer perspective, but most politicians cannot. Thus, time itself is crucial in evaluation.[23] The policymaking cycle is largely determined by the political calendar, but the effects of policies have their own timetables. Part of the job of the analyst and evaluator is to attempt to make the two coincide.

The evaluation of public programs is also confounded by other factors in the environment that affect the people to whom the programs are addressed. For example, if we try to evaluate the effectiveness of a health program for a poor population, it may be difficult to isolate that program's effects from those of a nutrition program or a housing program. In fact, several programs may be related to any observed changes, so it becomes difficult to determine which is the most efficient means of affecting the health of that community. We may be able to isolate the effects of an individual program with a more controlled social experiment, but few people would want to be the subjects of such an experiment.[24] It is difficult to hold constant all the social and economic factors that might affect the success of a public program independent of any policy; health may have improved because more people are employed and can afford more

The continuing economic slowdown in the United States has forced increasing numbers of people to rely on public sector programs such as SNAP (Supplemental Nutrition Assistance Program) as well as on private food banks. Cordahlia Ammons (right) speaks to social worker Kethia Dorelus (left) to sign her son Zach Ammons up for SNAP at the Cooperative Feeding Program in Fort Lauderdale, Florida.

Joe Raedle/Getty Images

nutritious food for their families. These problems illustrate that measurement in policy analysis is not as simple as the measurement that a scientist can make of a passive molecule or an amoeba.

Measurement of the effects of a public program can also be confounded by the histories of the program and of the individuals involved.[25] Few truly new and innovative policies are initiated in industrialized countries, such as the United States, and programs that have existed in the same policy area for some years may jeopardize the success of any new ones. Clients may well become cynical when program after program promises to "solve" their problems. Likewise, administrators may become cynical and frustrated after changing the direction of their activities several times. Any number of policy areas have gone through cycles of such change and contradiction, with inevitable effects on the morale and cooperation of clients and administrators alike. The numerous attempts to solve the problems of the poor offer the best example of endless change and confusion. In addition to creating frustration over the inability of government to make up its collective mind, a new policy may not be successful after another policy has been in place. For example, if a regime of lenient treatment and rehabilitation is tried in a prison, it may be difficult for jailers to return to more punitive methods without disruption. Interestingly, the reverse may also be true.

Another problem is that the organizational basis of some evaluations excessively limits the scope of the inquiry, so that many unintended consequences of a program are not included. For example, highway engineers probably regard the Interstate Highway System as a great success. Many miles of highways were built in a relatively short period, and they have saved many lives and many millions of gallons of gasoline—assuming that Americans would have driven the same number of miles if the superhighways had not been built. The mayor of a large city or members of the Department of Energy, however, may regard the program as a colossal failure. They realize that building highways in urban areas facilitated urban sprawl and the flight of the middle class to the suburbs, which reduced the tax base of the cities and caused social and economic problems, in addition to raising the costs of urban programs, while the surrounding suburbs grew affluent. The rapid automobile transportation that the highways promised encouraged people to move to the suburbs and consequently to consume millions of gallons of gasoline each year in commuting. Furthermore, as gasoline has become more expensive and urban living more popular, the suburbs may become the new slums, with the more affluent moving back into the cities.[26] This one program and its widespread effects demonstrate that measures that any single agency uses to evaluate its programs may be too narrow to detect many unintended social or economic consequences.

If experimentation is used to try to ascertain the utility of a program, the danger that the "reactive effects of testing" will influence the results becomes an important consideration.[27] That is, if citizens are aware that a certain policy is being tried "as an experiment," they may behave differently than they would if it were declared to be a settled policy. Those who favor the policy may work especially hard to make the program effective, whereas those who do not support it may attempt to make it appear ineffective. Even those who have no definite opinions on the policy may not behave as they would if the policy were thought to be a true attempt at change instead of an experiment. For example, if a voucher plan for educational financing is being tried, neither parents nor educational providers are likely to behave as they would if a voucher plan were stated to be fully in operation. Parents may be reluctant to place their children in private schools for fear that the voucher program will be terminated, and providers are unlikely to enter the marketplace if the number of parents capable of paying for their services is likely to decrease soon.

The simple knowledge that a policy initiative is considered to be a test will alter the behavior of those involved and consequently influence the results of the experiment, or quasi-experiment. There have been some very successful experimental evaluations of programs, such as the New Jersey Income Maintenance Experiment, but most have required some strong incentives to gain the effective participation of the subjects.[28] Researchers then may have difficulty knowing whether the participants are behaving "normally" or simply responding to the unusual, and often exciting, opportunity to be a guinea pig.

In evaluation research, problems are also encountered with research designs, experimental or not, that reduce the analysts' ability to make definitive statements about the real worth of policy. The importance and expense of public programs have led to more experimental evaluations of programs before they are implemented.[29] The experiments are concentrated very heavily in the area of social policy, in part because of the controversy surrounding many of those programs, and they are expensive, though perhaps not as expensive as implementing a poorly designed program. Conversely, not using an experimental method means that a large number of mainly unmeasured social and economic factors, not the program in question, may be the cause of any observed effects on the target population.

Targets

Identifying the targets of a program may be as difficult as identifying goals.[30] It is important for the evaluator to know not only what the program is intended to do but also whom it is intended to affect. Programs that have significant effects on the population as a whole may not have the desired effects on the more specific target population. For example, the Medicare program was intended, in part, to benefit less affluent older people, although all the elderly are eligible for it. However, although the health of the elderly population in general has improved, probably at least in part as a result of Medicare, the health of the neediest elderly has not improved commensurately. And as the program has been implemented, substantial coinsurance has been required, along with substantial deductibles if the insured enters a hospital, so that it is difficult for the neediest elderly citizens to participate.

A similar problem has been developing with the Head Start program. Conceived as a component of the War on Poverty, Head Start was primarily intended to serve lower-income families and to enable their children to participate and learn effectively once they entered school. Head Start is, however, only a part-day program, whereas in most low-income families, all the adults who can do so will be working all day, and they therefore need day care for the full day. The educational qualities of Head Start are largely absent from such day care programs, but the parents must go to work. As a result, Head Start tends to be used by higher-income families, and the target population has been largely missed or, at a minimum, has been underserved.[31]

One problem in defining a target population and measuring a program's success in reaching it is that participation in many programs is voluntary and depends on individuals who are potential beneficiaries taking up the benefit. Voluntary programs directed at the poor and the less educated members of society frequently face difficulties in making their availability widely known among the people they aim to serve. Even if it is made widely known to potential beneficiaries, factors such as pride, real and perceived administrative barriers, and real difficulties in using the benefits offered may make a program less effective than intended. An extreme example may be taken from the United Kingdom's experience with its National Health Service (NHS). One ostensible purpose of the NHS was to equalize access to medical care among members of all social classes, but the evidence after more than four decades of its existence did not indicate that such equalization had taken place.[32] The disparities in health status that existed before adoption of the NHS, and that in fact existed in the early twentieth century, had not been narrowed by an almost completely free system of medical care. Noneconomic barriers such as lack of education, transportation, free time, and simple belief in the efficacy of medical care served to ensure that although there was a general improvement in health status among the British population, little or no narrowing of class differentials occurred. The less affluent simply were not availing themselves of the services offered to the extent that they might, especially given their relatively greater need for medical services. Although the evidence is less dramatic, it appears that social programs in the United States have suffered many of the same failures in equalizing access to, and especially use of, some basic social services.

A program may create a false sense of success by "creaming" a segment of the population it serves.[33] That is to say, programs with limited capacities and stringent criteria for eligibility may select clients who actually need little help instead of those with the greatest need. This can make the programs appear successful, although those being served did not need the program in the first place, while a large segment of the neediest goes unserved. This pattern has been observed, for example, in drug treatment programs that take addicts who are already motivated to rid themselves of their habits. Likewise, some of the early successes of welfare reform in the United States may reflect that clients with the greatest motivation entered training first and got jobs—but would they have done so anyway, without the program?[34] Such programs can show success when they argue for additional public funding, but their success is actually limited. It would be a mistake for policymakers to generalize from the "successes" of such programs and assume that similar programs would work if applied to a general population with lower motivation. Of course, negative results may be produced by including too many subjects, many of whom may be inappropriate, in the population selected for treatment.[35]

As with so much of policy evaluation, defining the target population is a political exercise as much as an exercise in rational analysis. As we noted when discussing legitimation, one tendency in formulating and adopting policies is to broaden the definition of the possible beneficiaries and loosen eligibility requirements for a program. Although it helps to build the political coalition necessary for approval, this political broadening frequently makes the program's target population more diffuse and consequently makes the program more difficult to evaluate. It is therefore often unfair to blame program managers for failing to serve the target population when those who constructed the legislation have provided broad and unworkable definitions of that target. With the increasing strains on the public budget, it may become more politically feasible to target programs more tightly simply to reduce program costs.

Efficiency and Effectiveness

A related problem is the search for the philosopher's stone of efficiency in government, a search that often leads up a dead-end street. Measuring efficiency requires relating the costs of efforts to results and then assessing the ratio of the two. We have noted that measuring results is difficult in many policy areas; it is often equally difficult to assign costs to particular results, even if the results are measurable. For much the same reasons, equal difficulties may arise in attempting to measure effectiveness. Surrogate measures of the intended results are frequently developed for public programs and policies, but all require the suspension of disbelief to be accepted as valid and reliable descriptions of what is occurring in the public sector.

As a consequence of these difficulties in measuring the substantive consequences of government actions, much of the assessment of performance in government depends on the evaluation of procedural efficiency. That is, what is assessed is not so much what is produced as how the agencies go about producing it. Some of this proceduralism depends on the legal requirements for personnel management, budgeting, and accounting, but attempts to assess procedural efficiency go beyond those formal requirements. The efficiency of public agencies may be assessed by determining the speed with which certain actions occur or by ensuring that every decision goes through all the appropriate, specified procedural stages. The important point here is that goals may be displaced when evaluations are made on such a basis, as the process itself, rather than the services that the process is intended to produce, becomes the measure of all things.[36] The concern with measuring efficiency through procedures may, in fact, actually reduce the efficiency of the process in producing results for citizens because of the proliferation of procedural safeguards and their associated red tape.

Values and Evaluation

The analyst who performs an evaluation requires a value system to enable him or her to assign valuations to outcomes. But value systems are by no means constant across the population or across time, and the analyst who evaluates a single program may perceive very different purposes and priorities within its policy area. Thus, there may be no simple means of determining the proper valuation and weighting of the program's outcome. That is especially true when the program has significant unintended effects (usually negative) that must be weighed against the intended ones.[37] For instance, how do we compare the lives saved because of the greater safety of the interstate highways against the social and economic problems of center cities that the highway program may have exacerbated?

One point for consideration is that the analyst brings his or her own values to the evaluation. Despite their rational and neutral stance, most analysts involved in policymaking have proceeded beyond the "baby analyst" stage to the point at which they have values they wish to see achieved through public policy.[38] And as the analyst is in a central position in evaluation, he or she may have a substantial influence over the final evaluation of outcomes. However, the analyst's values will be but one of several sets of values involved in making that final assessment. The organizations involved will have their own collective values to guide them in evaluating outcomes, or at least their own activities. The professions with which members of the organization or external service providers identify will also provide sets of well-articulated values that may affect the assessment. Frequently, these different sets of values conflict with one another or with the values of clients or of the general public. Assessing a policy is thus not a simple matter of relating a set of known facts about outcomes to a given set of values. As in all aspects of the policy process, the values themselves may be the major source of conflict and rational argumentation and policy analysis merely the ammunition.

Politics

We must always remember that evaluations of public programs are performed in a political context. There may well be a sharp difference between the interpretation that an analyst might make about the success or failure of a program and the conclusion that political officials might draw from the same data. Most evaluation schemes, for example, may be based on total benefits for the society, but political leaders may be interested only in benefits created for their constituents; if that narrow range of benefits is significant, the overall inefficiency of a program may be irrelevant. The increasing use of pork barrel legislation to fund projects in the constituencies of individual members of Congress (see chapter 2) is a clear case in point. Political leaders may also be supportive of programs that their constituents like, whether or not the programs have any real impact on the social problems that they address.

It is also important to remember that evaluations may be done not for the purpose of evaluating a program but to validate a decision that has already been made for very different reasons. Thus, evaluations are often performed on very short notice, and the evaluators may be given little time to do their work. The purpose then may be simply to produce some sort of a justification for public consumption, not to produce a genuine answer about the quality of the program. That is, in part, why institutionalized and impartial forms of evaluation, such as those by the Government Accountability Office, are so important in the public sector. Their stability and relative impartiality offer some guarantee of the quality of the assessment made. For example, the evaluations of the Missile Defense System by the Department of Defense were quite positive, whereas the GAO found that the "successes" of the program were extremely questionable.

Increasing Requirements for Evaluation

One component of the wave of managerial change that has swept government over the past several decades is a focus on the outputs of government as opposed to the inputs (budgets, personnel, etc.).[39] The conventional means of controlling organizations in the public sector is to control their budgets and their personnel allocations stringently (see chapter 6). Evaluations based on outputs, on the other hand, examine what government organizations do and the effects of their programs. This approach to evaluation is presumed to be a superior means of understanding the programs' real contribution to public welfare.

In 1993, Congress passed the Government Performance and Results Act (GPRA), the basic idea of which was to appraise government organizations on the basis of their strategic plans and on the quantitative indicators that were developed as components of those plans.[40] As noted earlier, this legislation was an attempt to make programs justify their existence on the basis of the outputs they produced and to use changes in those outputs to judge the organizations' performance. This emphasis on outputs would, of course, enhance the need for evaluation within the federal government. The danger, as with many other exercises in evaluation, was that Congress would focus attention on a few simple, quantitative indicators and fail to understand the complexities of both the evaluation process and the programs that were being evaluated.

Other initiatives in the federal government also require increased evaluation. The National Performance Review, led by Vice President Al Gore and later renamed the National Partnership for Reinventing Government, contained some of the same emphasis on outputs as the GPRA. The Bush administration also instituted the Program Assessment Rating Tool (PART) to hold public programs accountable for their results (see chapter 7).[41] Regulatory review requires the economic evaluation of all new regulatory initiatives, although that would only touch the surface of the kind of evaluation that would be required to fully understand the impact of these rules on the economy and society. The continuing debates over educational quality also appear to require an extensive effort at evaluation, although again the effort seems to be narrowing to simple standardized tests rather than a broader assessment of quality in education.[42] The George W. Bush administration's efforts to punish poorly performing schools were based on these rather simplistic measures of progress, creating the additional risk that all schools would focus on their children's ability to pass the tests rather than on learning at a more fundamental level.

Summary

Policy evaluation is a basic political process, and although it is also an analytic procedure, the central place of politics and value conflict cannot be ignored. As increasing pressures are brought to bear on the public sector to perform its role more effectively and efficiently, evaluation will probably become an even greater source of conflict. Negative evaluations of a program's effectiveness and efficiency now will be more likely to lead to the program's termination than in more affluent times. The content of an evaluation, the values that are contained in it, and even the organization performing the evaluation will all affect the final assessment. Evaluation research is now a major industry involving numerous consulting firms ("Beltway bandits"), universities, and organizations within government itself. These evaluative organizations will have their own perspectives on what is right and wrong in policy and will bring those values with them when they perform an analysis.

The latter point is demonstrated clearly by the evaluation of a Comprehensive Employment and Training Act (CETA) program performed some years ago by both the John F. Kennedy School of Government at Harvard University and the School of Public Policy at the University of California, Berkeley. The two schools stressed different values and approaches. The JFK School researchers concentrated on the costs and benefits of the program in strict economic terms, reflecting more utilitarian values. They found the program to be failing, its costs surpassing the value of the benefits created. The Berkeley researchers, in contrast, stressed the political and participatory aspects of the program.[43] They found the program to be a great success, with the participants pleased with the outcomes and more involved in society. The difficulty is, of course, that both sets of evaluators were correct.

Policy Change

After evaluation, the next stage of the policy process is policy change. Rarely are policies maintained in exactly the same form over time; instead, they are constantly evolving. Sometimes, they evolve as the direct result of an evaluation, but more often change comes in response to changes in the socioeconomic or political environment, learning on the part of the personnel administering the program, or simple elaboration of existing structures and ideas. A great deal of policymaking in industrialized countries, such as the United States, is the result of attempts at policy change, rather than of new issues coming to the public sector for the first round of resolution.[44] Most policy areas in industrialized democracies are already populated by a number of programs and policies, so what is usually required is change rather than creation of totally new policies. Policy succession, or the replacement of one policy by another, is therefore an important concept in examining the development of contemporary public policies.

When a policy or program is reconsidered or evaluated, three outcomes are possible: policy maintenance, policy termination, or policy succession.[45] *Policy maintenance* occurs rarely as a conscious choice but happens rather as a result of simple failure to make decisions. It is possible, but unlikely, that a policy will be considered seriously and then maintained in exactly the same form. In the first place, politicians make names for themselves by advocating new legislation, not by advocating the maintenance of existing programs. Less cynically, few policies or programs are so well designed initially that they require no changes after they are put into operation. The implementation of programs frequently demonstrates weaknesses in the original design that require modification. Through what might be considered almost continuous experimentation, programs can be made to match changes in society, in the economy, and in knowledge and can thus be made to work more effectively.

It is also unlikely that many public programs will be *terminated*. Once begun, programs have a life of their own—they develop organizations, which hire personnel, and they develop a clientele, who come to depend on the program for certain services. Once clients use a service, they may find it difficult ever to return to the market provision of that service or to do without. This is especially true for programs that create a "stock" of benefits, as opposed to those that are merely a flow of resources. For example, Social Security created a stock of future benefits for its clientele, so once the program was initiated, future recipients began to plan differently for their retirement; any reduction in benefits would thus create severe hardships that the participants in the program could not have anticipated. Programs such as welfare or food stamps, which involve no planning by recipients, also create hardships if they are reduced, but the planning, or stock, element is not involved, and so it may be possible to move clients back into the market system. Public programs, policies, and organizations may not be immortal, but relatively few are ever fully terminated.[46]

Dismissing the other two options leaves *policy succession* as the most probable outcome for an existing policy or program. Policy succession may take several forms:

1. *Linear.* Linear succession involves the direct replacement of one program, policy, or organization by another or a change in an existing program's location. The replacement of the Aid to Families with Dependent Children welfare program by the Personal Responsibility and Work Opportunity Reconciliation Act of 1996 was an example of a linear succession, as was replacing Food Stamps with Supplemental Nutrition Assistance Program (SNAP) in 2008.

2. *Consolidation.* Some successions involve placing several programs that have existed independently into a single program. Moving numerous protective services into the Department of Homeland Security was to some extent a consolidation.

3. *Splitting.* Some programs are split into two or more components in a succession. For example, the Atomic Energy Commission was split in 1974 into the Nuclear Regulatory Commission and the Energy Research and Development Agency, reflecting the contradictory goals of regulation and support of nuclear energy that had existed in the earlier organization.

4. *Nonlinear.* Some policy and organizational successions are complex and involve elements of other kinds of succession. The multiple changes involved in creating the Department of Energy from existing programs (including the two nuclear energy agencies mentioned above) are an example of nonlinear succession.

Although they entail much of the same process described for making policy (see chapters 4–7), policy successions are processed in a distinctive manner. First, the agenda-setting stage is not so difficult for policy succession as it is for policy initiation. The broad issue has already been accepted as a component of the agenda and therefore needs only to be returned to a particular institutional agenda. Some issues such as debt ceilings and annual reauthorizations of existing programs automatically return to an agenda every year or even more frequently. More commonly, dissatisfaction with the existing program returns an issue for further consideration, but returning an issue to the institutional agenda is easier than its initial introduction because there are organizational manifestations of the program and identified clients who are in a better position to bring about the consideration. Furthermore, once organizations exist, it is more likely that program administrators will learn from other, similar programs and find opportunities for improving the program, or that they will simply think of better solutions to problems.

The legitimation and formulation processes will also be different from those employed in policy initiation. But instead of fewer obstacles, as in agenda setting, there are likely to be more. As noted, the existence of a program produces client and producer interests that may be threatened by a proposed policy change. This is especially true if the proposed succession involves "policy consolidation" (combining several programs) or a change in the policy instrument delivering the program in a direction that will demand less direct administration. For example, using policy consolidation to combine a number of categorical grants into block grants during the Reagan administration provoked outcries from both clients (primarily big-city mayors) and producers (administrators who managed the categorical programs). And part of the conflict over the negative income tax proposed in President Nixon's Family Assistance Plan, as well as that over some of President Carter's welfare reforms, concerned changes in the instruments used to deliver benefits, as well as ideological conflicts over the level of benefits.[47]

Thus, once a policy change of whatever kind enters an institutional arena, it is quite likely to encounter severe resistance from affected interests. That may be true even if the threat to those interests is not real—the mere prospect of upsetting established patterns may be sufficient to provoke resistance. For example, the numerous discussions on "reforming" entitlements in the budget debates of 2011 and 2012 have created anxiety among people who depend upon those programs for some or all of their income.

Of course, some policy successions may be generated within an organization rather than imposed from the outside. An array of external political forces may be strong enough to produce the change, so the organization and the clientele will gladly accede and possibly even publicly cosponsor the change. Although most public bureaucrats tend to be risk avoiders, some program managers may be risk takers, willing to gamble that a proposed change will produce greater benefits for the organization, and feel no need to attempt to hang onto what they have. Some programs may have expanded too far; their personnel may wish to pare off some of the peripheral programs to target their clientele more clearly and protect the organizational "heartland."[48] The pared-off programs will not necessarily be terminated; they may only change organizational location.

Clientele groups may seek to split a program from a larger organization to develop a clearer target for their political activities. Pressures from the National Educational Association and other educational groups to break up the Department of Health, Education, and Welfare (HEW) and establish an independent Department of Education illustrate this point. It was argued that HEW did not give educational interests the direct attention they deserved and that because the educational budget had the greatest flexibility of all the budgets in HEW (the remainder being primarily entitlement programs), any budget cutting was likely to be in education.[49]

Forming a coalition for policy change requires careful attention to the commitments of individual Congress members to particular interests and to ongoing programs. As with the initial formulation and legitimation of a policy, an attempt at policy succession requires use of the mechanisms of partisan analysis, logrolling, and the pork barrel to deliver change (see chapter 5). Again, this stage of the policy process may be even more difficult than policy initiation. Although the implications of a new policy are often vague, the probable effects of a change in an existing policy are likely to be more readily identifiable. It may be easy to persuade legislators of the benefits of a new policy on the basis of limited information, but once a program has been running for some time, information will become available to legislators that makes it much more difficult to persuade them to change a program that is "good enough."

There may, however, be many clients, administrators, and legislators dissatisfied with a program as it is being implemented, and those individuals can be mobilized to advocate change. A coalition of this kind may involve individuals from both the right and left who oppose the existing policy. The coalition built around the 1996 welfare reform illustrates this type of process—it combined liberals who wanted more funds for social programs and conservatives who wanted greater work incentives for aid recipients. Trying to bring about a policy succession by organizing such a broad coalition carries the risk that termination of the policy may be the only alternative to the status quo on which the coalition can agree. Before beginning the process, therefore, it is crucial for the analyst to have in mind the particular policy succession that he or she would like to see occur. Otherwise, allowing political forces to follow their own lead may threaten the existence of the program.

Putting any policy into effect in the intended manner is problematic at best, but several features of policy succession may make it even more difficult. First, it is important to remember that organizations exist in the field as well as at headquarters.[50] People working in the field may have policy preferences as strong as those of the home office workers, and they may not be consulted about proposed changes. Yet the field workers are the ones who must put the policy change into effect and ultimately decide the real consequences of the change. If policy change does not involve significant and clear modification of the existing policies, the field staff may well be able to continue doing what they were doing before and so subvert the intention of the succession legislation. This subversion need not be intentional; it may be only the result of inertia or inadequate understanding of the intentions of headquarters or of the legislation.

In this context, it is important to remember that organizations do not exist alone in the world, nor do policies. Each organization exists within a complicated network of other organizations, all of which must cooperate if any of them is to be successful.[51] A change in the policies of one organization may reduce the ability of other organizations to fulfill their own goals. Education and job training may now be as important for economic performance, especially in the long run, as is formal economic policy. This interaction is perhaps especially evident in the field of social policy, where a variety of programs are necessary to meet the many and interrelated needs of poor families and in which changes in any one policy or program may influence the success of all the programs. Terminating food stamps, for example, would mean that welfare payments would not be sufficient for families to buy the amounts of food they used to buy. As a consequence, housing, education, and even employment programs would be adversely affected by increasing demands. The reform of welfare during the Clinton administration changed eligibility for food stamps, but it did so in the context of a general weakening of the social safety net and a greater emphasis on employment.

As government shifts its focus from directly providing services to "new governance," in which it operates through a variety of third parties and indirect mechanisms, associating particular outcomes with particular programs may become even more difficult. Generating change in this setting implies changing not only the public sector programs and their intentions but also the network that will become responsible for delivering programs.[52] Dependence on a network for service will further complicate the process of policy change, given the resilience that characterizes the behavior of both public and private organizations.

Implementing policy succession is almost certain to be disappointing. The massive political effort required to bring about policy succession is unlikely to be rewarded in the first month, or even the first year, after the change. That is likely to create disappointment in the new program and perhaps cynicism about the policy area. As a consequence, one policy succession may generate enough disruption to engender a rapid series of changes. Once a stable set of policies and organizations has been disturbed, there will no longer be a single set of entrenched interests with which to contend, so forming a new coalition for policy change or termination may be easier. Advocates of policy change must be aware that they may produce more change than they intended once the possibility of reform becomes apparent to participants in the policy area.

Since we now understand that implementing policy succession will be difficult, we should address the problem of designing policy changes for easier implementation. The ease with which change can be brought about is a function at least in part of the design of previous organizations and programs. In an era of increased skepticism concerning government and bureaucracy, policies are being designed with built-in triggers for evaluation and termination.[53] The interest in sunset laws means that any administrator joining an organization with such a provision, or any client becoming dependent on its services, has reason to question the stability of the arrangement.[54] If the declining sense of entitlement to either employment or benefits from an organization can make future policy successions more palatable to those already connected with a program, then one major hurdle to policy change will have been overcome. However, that declining sense of entitlement may be related to a declining commitment of workers to the program, which can have negative consequences for the organization that exceed the costs of change.

It is not possible to reverse history and redesign programs and organizations that are already functioning without such built-in terminators. The analyst or practitioner of policy change must therefore be prepared to intervene in existing organizations to produce the smooth transition from one set of policies to another. One obvious trigger for such change would be a change in the party in office, especially in the presidency. Before the Reagan presidency, however, the alternation of parties in office had produced little significant policy change. The Clinton administration in many ways represented a return to that earlier pattern, for "New Democrats" seemed very similar to a moderate Republican like George H. W. Bush. The initial emphasis of the George W. Bush administration seemed to be on the downsizing of programs, but the pursuit of homeland security produced greater policy change than might have been anticipated from the campaign rhetoric. The Obama administration appears likely to produce even greater transformations than have previous administrations.[55]

Rapid changes in demand and environmental conditions may also trigger attempts at policy succession, but organizations have proved remarkably effective in deflecting attempts at change and in using change for their own purposes. At present, it is fair to say that there is no readily available technology for implementing policy succession, just as there is no reliable technology for implementation in general. A common finding is that organizations are able to interpret new policy initiatives in ways that fortify their current approaches. As with the discussion of the social construction of issues on the agenda (see chapter 4), organizations also socially construct the meaning of policy and law and do so in ways that will benefit themselves.

Summary

Policies must be evaluated, and frequently policies must be changed. But neither task is as easy as some politicians, and even some academicians, make it appear. Identifying the goals of policies, determining the results of programs, and isolating the effects of policies from the effects of other social and economic forces all make evaluating public policies tricky and at times impossible. The surrogate measures that must frequently be used may be worse than no measures at all, for they emphasize activity of any sort rather than actions performed well and efficiently, placing pressure on agencies merely to spend their money rather than always to spend it wisely.

Evaluation frequently leads to policy change, and the process of producing desired changes and implementing them in a complex political environment will tax the abilities of the analyst as well as the politician. All the usual steps in policymaking must be gone through, but they must be gone through in the presence of established organizations and clients. The implications of proposed policy changes may be all too obvious to those actors, and they may therefore resist strenuously. As often as not, the entrenched forces will be successful in deflecting pressures for change. Without the application of significant and skillful political force, then, American government often is a great machine that simply proceeds onward in its established direction. Those whose interests are already being served benefit from this inertia, but those on the outside may continue to be excluded.

PART THREE

Substantive Policy Issues

CHAPTER 9

Economic Policy

IN THE DECADES FOLLOWING WORLD WAR II, it mostly appeared that the problems of managing the economy in the United States had been solved. There were some relatively minor ups and downs, but until 2008, it seemed as if the massive economic failures of the Great Depression were a thing of the past. No one should think that any longer, as the recession that began in 2008 has shaken the confidence of citizens and policymakers alike. By spring 2009, the gross domestic product (GDP) of the United States had dropped by more than 6 percent, unemployment had reached thirty-year highs, and sales and investments had both plummeted. Some of the more apocalyptic visions of another depression of the magnitude of the 1930s appeared to have been too dramatic, but the downturn was serious enough to drastically alter the American economic landscape.

Even four years later, these problems were not solved completely by any means. Although some growth was returning to the economy and the stock market had recovered much of its losses, unemployment continued to be worryingly high, and the housing market that many Americans had depended on as their major investment continued to fall in many areas of the country. For most Americans, the economy was far from an issue of the past, and for President Obama seeking reelection, it was very clearly an issue.

Background

For many years, economic cycles and fluctuations were considered natural acts of God, beyond the control of governments or human beings. That concept of the economy changed during the Great Depression of the 1930s and during the post–World War II economic boom.[1] The magnitude and duration of the depression had been such that even conservative governments were forced to pay some attention to its effects.[2] Perhaps more important, the works of John Maynard Keynes, Knut Wiksell, and other economists provided the tools to enable government to control an economy—and the intellectual justification for using them.

The confidence of governments in their ability to manage economies was exemplified in the postwar full employment acts in both the United States and the United Kingdom, which pledged that the governments of those two nations would never again permit mass unemployment to afflict their people. That confidence was bolstered during the economic miracles of the 1950s, 1960s, and early 1970s, in which most Western nations experienced rapid and consistent economic growth, very low unemployment (the United States being a notable exception), and relatively stable prices. In the early 1960s, advisers to President John Kennedy spoke of the government's ability to "fine-tune" the economy and manipulate economic outcomes for the society by pulling a few simple economic levers given to him by Keynes.[3]

Economic policy is a central concern of government—as the Clinton campaign reminded itself during the 1992 election, "It's the economy, stupid." Similarly, the success of President Obama's campaign in 2008 was to no small degree a referendum on the Bush administration's economic policies of large tax cuts and less regulation and on the recession that was already well under way at the time of the election. Making and managing economic policy is not easy, however. A government must form a more or less coherent set of policies intended to manage the economy. That overall policy is the result of many separate decisions about matters such as spending for public programs, patterns of taxation, and the interest rate charged by the central bank (the Federal Reserve System in the United States). Even if the federal government makes relatively consistent decisions in these areas, a host of other governmental actors (fifty states and over 85,000 local governments) are also making taxing and spending decisions that affect the overall economic performance of the country.

Economic policy also depends heavily on actions by individual citizens, over which governments have little or no direct control. In the Keynesian paradigm of fiscal policy, an excess of public expenditures above revenues is supposed to stimulate the economy because citizens will spend the additional money, creating more demand for goods and services.[4] But if citizens do not spend the additional money, then the intended stimulative effect will not materialize. Only when governments choose to regulate the economy directly, through instruments such as wage and price controls, can they be reasonably confident that their actions will generate the desired behaviors. Even then, policing compliance with a wage and price policy presents severe administrative difficulties of its own, and individuals and firms have shown themselves to be extremely creative in avoiding such attempts at control.

The Goals of Economic Policy

Economic policy has a number of goals, all of which are socially desirable but some of which are not always mutually compatible. Political leaders frequently must make decisions that simultaneously benefit some citizens and impose burdens on others. For example, although it is by no means as clear as it once was, there is a trade-off between inflation and unemployment.[5] To the extent that governments attempt to reduce unemployment, they may increase inflation. The results of such a decision may benefit the worker in danger of being laid off but will harm the senior citizen living on a fixed income, as well as all citizens who hold assets of fixed value (savings bonds, for example). In general, economic policy has four fundamental goals: economic growth, full employment, stable prices, and a positive balance of payments from international trade. To these four may be added the additional, intermediate policy goal of positive structural change in the economy.

Economic Growth

Economic growth has been a boon both to citizens and to governments. Although ecology-minded citizens may question the benefits of economic growth and praise smaller and less technologically complex economic systems, most U.S. citizens still want more of everything.[6] From the post–World War II period up until at least the mid-1970s, Americans became accustomed to receiving more income each year. Economic growth translated into great increases in the availability of consumer goods, making items such as television sets and automobiles, which were not widely available in 1950, almost universally obtainable. By the beginning of the twenty-first century, the list of such goods had expanded to include multiple cars for each family and large, flat-screen TVs. Economic growth produced an average standard of living that by 2008 was much higher than that of 1950, or of 1980, or even of 1990, and almost all Americans were enjoying that affluence.[7]

Economic growth was also important in the political history of the postwar era as a political solvent to ease the transition of the United States from a "warfare state" to more of a "welfare state." Economic growth was sufficiently great that virtually every segment of the society could have its own government programs without exhausting the new wealth. Public programs grew along with private affluence, so individuals did not feel particularly disadvantaged by their taxes or by government benefits granted to others.[8] Economic growth also aided the redistribution of income to the less advantaged—one calculation is that 90 percent of the post–World War II improvement in the economic status of African Americans has been the result of economic growth rather than of redistributive public programs. The best welfare program is still a good job with a good salary, a fact emphasized by the 1996 welfare reforms that stressed work rather than direct cash benefits as the best solution to poverty and inequality.

Yet during most of the postwar period, American economic growth did not compare well with that of most major U.S. trading partners. Average annual growth in per capita gross national product (GNP) for the United States from 1960 to 1980 was 2.2 percent, whereas it was 3.1 percent for Germany, 3.8 percent for Italy, and more than 6.3 percent for Japan. In addition, the U.S. growth rate was falling (although not as rapidly as growth in most other industrialized countries); average economic growth in the 1980s was less than half what it was during the 1950s and became even slower, or negative, in the early 1990s.

After the early 1990s, however, U.S. economic performance improved significantly, outstripping most of the country's trading partners. For example, from 1990 to 2000, per capita income in the United States increased by more than 8 percent in real terms, while most U.S. trading partners saw income growth of 4 percent or less. The U.S. economy was particularly productive toward the end of that period, while growth in other major economies, such as Germany and particularly Japan, slackened. These positive results led many observers to extol the virtues of the "flexible" U.S. economy, in contrast to the more regulated economies of Europe.

U.S. economic growth in the early twenty-first century was not as rapid as in the previous decade. Although it remained better than in most European countries and Japan, U.S. growth was much slower than that of industrializing countries, such as China and India. During the first years of the twenty-first century, the economic success of the 1990s gave way to a mild recession (although for anyone who became unemployed during that time, the recession was anything but mild). Toward the middle of the decade, growth picked up but remained slower than during much of the 1990s.

All of the positive economic news for the United States, and most of the rest of the world, came to an end during 2008, with problems accelerating to the point that the more pessimistic commentators raised the prospect of a depression to rival that of the 1930s. By spring 2009, the direst of the predictions looked far too apocalyptic, but economic growth clearly had become economic decline. GNP declined by 0.5 percent in the third quarter of 2008 and by more than 6 percent in the fourth quarter of 2008 and the first quarter of 2009. The engine that had been powering increasing affluence and consumption in the American economy had gone into reverse.

Even before the actual declines in growth that began in 2008, the United States was experiencing the problems of a so-called zero-sum society, meaning that the gains that one segment of society achieved were coming at the expense of some other segment.[9] For example, during the economic growth of the Reagan years, the middle and upper classes gained at the expense (relatively and in some cases absolutely) of the poor and working classes. That pattern was exacerbated by the policies of George W. Bush, highlighted by stagnating real (adjusted for price changes) income for the average American worker. The trend toward relatively low levels of increase in real wages began as early as the 1970s, but over the past decade, real wages for the average worker became stagnant or even declined. At the same time, the real earnings of the top 5 percent of income earners increased at double-digit rates, and corporate profits also increased rapidly.[10]

Whereas previous generations could expect to do better than their parents economically, the economic future for young people entering the labor market in the near future seems uncertain. Increasing benefits for the elderly through Social Security may drain the income of working-age citizens, and any new programs for the increasing number of poor may also increase the tax burden of the middle and upper classes. Continuing uncertainty about economic growth, combined with more ideological politics, may make policymaking more contentious and difficult. Even in times of economic growth and a balanced budget, vigorous conflicts arise between advocates of tax cuts and advocates of public programs. With neither rapid growth nor a balanced budget, conflicts may be more evident.

The recession that began in 2008 persisted for several years, and economic growth in the United States since 2008 dropped significantly, then began to return in 2010 and 2011. But this economic growth was even less well distributed than in the recent past, with the working-class and lower middle-class segments of the population receiving little or nothing from the growth that has been occurring. For example, median household income in the United States declined by 2.3 percent in 2010 and was 6.4 percent lower than in 2004.[11] In 2011, income inequality in the United States was higher than at any time in the previous thirty years.[12]

The level of inequality in the United States, and particularly its increase, has become very salient politically. The distinction between the "1 percent" of the most affluent of the population and the remainder of the population has become the focus of political debate and mobilization.[13] On the one hand, the Occupy movement has camped in the center of many American cities to demonstrate about the injustice.[14] On the other side of the argument, Rick Santorum, running in the Republican primaries, extolled the virtues of inequality.

Full Employment

The benefits of full employment are obvious. Most adults want to work and use their talents. The welfare state has provided a floor for those who become unemployed, so that they and their families are unlikely to starve or do without medical care. Those social benefits, however, cannot match what people can earn by working, nor can social programs replace the pride and psychological satisfaction that come from earning one's own living. These psychological advantages are perhaps especially pronounced in the United States, where the social and political culture attaches great importance to individualism and self-reliance. That culture also explains the significantly higher rates of family problems, suicides, and alcoholism among the unemployed than among the employed. Changes in social policy have now made working almost mandatory, and the relevant question is whether the economy can provide enough jobs for all the people who want and need them.

In addition to its negative effects on individuals, unemployment has some influence on government budgets. When individuals are not working, they do not contribute to Social Security or pay income tax. They cost the government money in unemployment benefits, Medicaid payments, food stamps, and other services. Thus, increasing unemployment may upset the government's best plans to produce a balanced budget or a deficit of a certain size. Even if a higher level of unemployment is accurately anticipated, revenues are still lost and more expenditures required. Other important public programs may be funded inadequately because of the need to assist the unemployed.

The good news has been that, compared with many of its major trading partners, the United States achieved relatively low rates of unemployment. Beginning during the late 1980s and early 1990s, U.S. unemployment rates began to fall lower than those in other industrialized democracies, and in the late 1990s, unemployment was the lowest in decades. Critics argued that many of the jobs being created were for "hamburger flippers"—that is, low-paid workers in the service sector; but whereas there certainly were a number of those, there also was evidence that more highly paid jobs—many also in service industries, such as finance, computers, and so forth—were being created as well. That demand receded after 2001, and job creation failed to keep pace with economic growth, but even so, U.S. unemployment remained lower than that in many other industrialized countries, such as Germany and France.

The economic crisis that began in 2008 had the predictable impact of increasing U.S. unemployment, which reached more than 9 percent nationwide by mid-2009. Growing unemployment exacerbated other economic problems, such as home foreclosures and credit card debt, to create any number of bankruptcies among people who had worked all their lives. The effects of unemployment were increased because they were often concentrated in industries, such as automobiles and construction, that had provided thousands of workers with stable and remunerative employment for decades. The structure of the U.S. economy as a whole continues to move away from manufacturing and toward a service base.[15] In the post–Cold War period, manufacturing industries, such as aerospace, have not been employing as many people as they once did. Michigan, with its reliance on the sagging auto industry, has been hit hard by economic changes, as have some southern states that had been attracting a number of industrial jobs (see Table 9.1).

Justin Sullivan/Getty Images

A "For Sale" sign is posted in front of a foreclosed home in Richmond, California. A study of government data on subprime loans by the Center for Public Integrity showed that 56 percent of the $1.38 trillion in subprime mortgages originated from fifteen lenders in California between 2005 and 2007.

What is perhaps more important than the aggregate performance of the United States on this indicator is the concentration of unemployment by race and age. Blacks and young people have by far the highest rates of unemployment; among young African Americans, the rate still approaches one-third. And although aggregate employment figures had been good, the economy was creating different types of jobs. There were over 24 million more nonfarm jobs in the United States in 2005 than in 1990, and even with the recession, there were another 1.5 million more in 2010. Between 2000 and 2010, the number of manufacturing jobs declined by more than 6 million, while the number of service-producing jobs increased by approximately the same amount. While these numbers are influenced by the recession, they do represent structural change within the economy. Of the new service jobs created, roughly half were in restaurants, hotels, and other relatively low-wage environments, whereas the other half were in a variety of more lucrative service occupations, such as financial services, computer firms, and the like.[16]

Industrial workers accustomed to earning high wages in unskilled or semi-skilled occupations have found the structural shift in the economy very

TABLE 9.1   Unemployment in the United States, 1970–2011 (in percentages)

Across time

1970	1980	1985	1990	1995	2000	2002	2004	2006	2008	2011
4.4	7.0	7.2	5.6	5.6	4.0	5.8	5.5	4.6	5.8	9.5

By state (December 2011)

High		Low	
Nevada	12.6	North Dakota	3.3
California	11.1	Nebraska	4.1
Rhode Island	10.8	South Dakota	4.1
Mississippi	10.4	New Hampshire	5.1
North Carolina	9.9	Vermont	5.1

Source: U.S. Bureau of Labor Statistics, *Bulletin of Labor Statistics,* http://www.bls.gov/opub/#bulletins.

disturbing, but they have been almost powerless to change it. Outside government and some service industries, labor unions have been losing large numbers of members, and employees know that business can simply move jobs to lower-wage economies elsewhere if wage pressure in the United States is great. The increased prevalence of low-wage jobs often makes two incomes necessary to maintain a reasonable family lifestyle, even after the economic growth of the Clinton years. In real terms, the average worker in 2010 earned less than the average worker in 2000, and the decline continues. The pinch on middle-class families that was becoming noticeable to many families now has become very apparent to most.[17]

While some economic growth had returned to the economy by 2010, the news on unemployment did not begin to improve until late 2011. Even then, the unemployment rate remained well above target figures. Furthermore, unemployment remained especially high for young people and for members of minority groups. These individuals often have not had a sufficient working record to qualify for unemployment benefits and therefore are forced to depend upon families, charity, or public relief. The human costs of unemployment tend to outweigh the economic costs as people who had worked hard all their lives lose homes when they become unemployed, and the next generation of workers cannot get the experience they will require.

Although the level of unemployment began to decline in late 2011, problems with the labor market remained. A significant number of people with jobs were underemployed, doing jobs requiring less skill and education than they possessed, and hence, paying lower wages. Furthermore, millions of potential workers were so discouraged that they had stopped looking for work and hence did not appear in the unemployment statistics.[18] And although inflation continues to be relatively low, wage rates have not begun to increase as might be expected in a full-scale economic recovery.

Stable Prices

Unlike unemployment, inflation affects all citizens through increases in the prices they pay for goods and services.[19] Higher interest rates are also a form of inflation because they increase the cost to businesses of borrowing money, a cost that they pass on to customers in higher prices. Inflation affects different portions of the community differently, however, and it may even benefit some people. On the one hand, inflation particularly hurts those living on fixed incomes, such as the elderly who live on pensions, and those (such as college professors) who are not sufficiently well organized to gain wage increases equal to increases in price levels.

On the other hand, inflation benefits individuals and institutions that owe money because the significance of a debt is reduced as inflation erodes the real value of currency. As the biggest debtor in the society, government is particularly benefited by inflation. The amount governments owe, relative to the total production of their economies, can diminish if inflation makes everything cost more and each unit of currency worth less. Governments with progressive tax structures benefit from inflation as people whose real incomes (adjusted for changes in purchasing power) have not increased see their money incomes increase. That moves them into higher tax brackets, where they pay a larger portion of their income in taxes. Government thus receives a relatively painless (politically) increase in its revenues. Many tax reforms adopted during the 1980s were aimed in part at reducing the progressivity of taxation or requiring governments to relate the thresholds of tax brackets to inflation, so that government would not receive this automatic "fiscal dividend."

Inflation is by no means an unqualified boon for governments, however. Many benefits that governments pay out are *indexed,* meaning they are automatically adjusted for changes in the price level.[20] As a consequence, much of any increase in revenues from inflation must be paid out directly as increased benefits. The things that a government must buy, most notably the labor of its employees, also increase in price during inflationary periods. Government has been more labor intensive than the private economy, so its costs increase more rapidly than do labor costs for other "industries" in the society.[21] Governments have been major beneficiaries of advances in information technology, however. More than anything else, governments process information—so computers, e-mail, and the Internet have helped boost their productivity.

TABLE 9.2   Inflation Rates of the United States and Major Trading Partners, 1990–2007 (in percentages)

Country	1990	1995	2000	2001	2002	2003	2004	2005	2006	2007
United States	5.3	2.6	3.4	2.2	1.5	1.9	2.0	1.9	2.2	1.9
Canada	4.8	2.2	2.7	2.5	2.3	2.8	1.8	1.7	1.4	1.3
Japan	3.1	0.6	−0.6	−0.7	−0.9	−0.3	0.0	−0.2	0.2	0.0
France	3.4	1.8	1.7	1.7	1.9	2.1	2.1	1.7	.9	1.2
Germany	2.7	1.8	1.9	2.0	1.4	1.1	1.7	1.2	1.1	1.3
Italy	6.5	5.2	2.5	2.8	2.5	2.7	2.2	1.9	2.1	1.8
Sweden	6.9	2.5	1.0	2.4	2.2	1.9	0.4	0.8	1.2	1.5
United Kingdom	9.4	3.4	2.9	1.8	1.6	2.9	3.0	2.6	2.4	2.8

Source: International Monetary Fund, *International Financial Statistics,* monthly.

In the years since World War II, only the German and Japanese economies have been more successful than the U.S. economy in maintaining stable prices, although other countries such as Canada and Sweden have outperformed the United States in this respect in the past few years (see Table 9.2). Several factors explain the relative durability of the U.S. economy, including relatively low unemployment. It is also argued that the Federal Reserve Board's independence from political interference has allowed it to use monetary policy to regulate the price level effectively.[22] The relative weakness of the labor movement in the United States has meant weaker upward pressures on wages than elsewhere, although the power of large corporations might also be expected to be related to increasing prices.[23]

At the beginning of the twenty-first century, inflation was no longer perceived to be the threat that it once was, although central banks, politicians, and businesses continued to risk overreacting to that threat by restricting the money supply too tightly and thus endangering both economic growth and employment. The economic recession soon ended concerns with inflation and raised the possibility of *deflation,* or a lowering of price levels.[24] Deflation can exacerbate the problems of a recession, as it has done to some extent in Japan.[25] Deflation tends to reduce demand because consumers wait for prices to fall even more, rather than helping lead the economy out of recession. Therefore, the seeming capacity to manage prices in the U.S. economy has not been realized to the extent hoped.

A Positive Balance of Payments

The economy of the United States is relatively autarkic and relatively less involved in international trade than are the economies of most other industrialized countries.[26] It is, however, still important for the United States to manage its *balance of payments* from trade—the net of the cost of imports and the income from exports. If a country spends more money abroad than it receives from abroad, it has a negative balance of payments, whereas a country that spends less overseas than it receives has a positive balance. The final figure for the balance of payments is composed of the balance of trade (payment for real goods traded) and the balance on *invisibles*, meaning services such as insurance, banking, and shipping fees.

Over the past several decades, though the United States has usually had a positive balance on invisibles, it has had a very large negative balance overall. A number of factors have contributed to the large and seemingly ever-increasing negative balance of payments. During much of the 1980s, world oil prices were low, but they began to increase in the early 1990s and increased significantly after 2005. The United States had learned little from earlier oil crises and had again become heavily dependent on foreign oil (see chapter 14), while its demand for other foreign products, such as automobiles and electronics from Asian countries, continued to increase. By the mid-1990s and again in the 2000s, the relatively strong American economy (compared with the rest of the industrialized world) meant that U.S. demand for foreign goods rose faster than foreign demand for U.S. goods. Perhaps the only benefit from the recession beginning in 2008 was that it reduced the demand for foreign goods, especially oil.

A negative balance of payments is generally detrimental to a country's economy. In the first place, a negative balance of payments indicates that the country's products are not competitive with those of other countries. The reason may be price or quality, or that a country cannot produce a particular commodity, such as oil. More important, a negative balance of payments tends to reduce the value of the country's currency in relation to those of other nations. If a country continues to trade its money for commodities overseas, the laws of supply and demand dictate that the value of the country's currency eventually will decline, as more money goes abroad than is returned. This effect has been especially difficult for the United States because so many dollars are held overseas and used in international transactions.[27] The dollar is being replaced somewhat by the euro as the principal international currency, but it remains important. Finally, as with trade in raw materials, a negative balance of payments may indicate a country's dependence on the products of other nations—especially the "addiction to oil," which introduces a potential for international blackmail. When a great deal of a country's currency is held abroad, the value of that currency is especially vulnerable to the actions of others—governments and individuals.

International flows of capital have also posed difficulties for the United States in recent years, for several reasons. First, as money has flowed into the

United States, a number of businesses and a large amount of property are now owned outside the country.[28] These capital flows are in part offset by the overseas property and industries owned by American firms and individuals. The dependency on foreign capital makes some important industries seemingly difficult to steer toward national policy goals, although firms totally owned domestically are not always amenable to national goals, either. As money began to exit in 2002, in part as a result of increased tensions in the Middle East and fears about the treatment of foreign interests in the war on terror, the American economy began to look more vulnerable to the international market. More recently, the U.S. capital market and the dollar have been supported by large purchases by China.[29]

As the world economy becomes more internationalized, large capital flows across borders have become a fact of economic life.[30] The ease with which capital now moves impedes the ability of national governments to make domestic economic policy as they might like (and also strengthens international businesses that bargain with governments over where to locate),[31] but it does not mean that countries cannot influence the behavior of businesses and individuals. For example, there appears to be more variance in both tax policy and economic regulation than might be expected if governments had wholly lost the ability to control their economies.[32] The United States has more capacity than most countries to exercise control, given the huge size of its domestic economy and its central position in the world economy.

In fact, there is a pronounced absence of a clear connection between the flow of capital and economic indicators in the United States. Despite the continuing outflow of money through a negative balance of payments, the U.S. dollar has remained relatively strong in the international currency market. Indeed, the strength of the dollar plays some role in the balance of payments difficulties: American products are more expensive abroad than products made elsewhere, even with equal levels of productivity, because the dollar is perhaps stronger than it should be, and that naturally makes those products more difficult to sell. The value of the euro has increased relative to the dollar, favoring more U.S. exports, but not enough to overcome the large U.S. purchases from abroad.

The economic recession has, however, been more effective in reducing American imports. The public no longer is as interested in buying large-screen TVs, German cars, or French champagne. The balance of payments imbalance decreased significantly in late 2008 and 2009, although the weaknesses of American banks have meant that some of the invisible earnings in international trade have not been realized. As the United States' economy, and especially the banking sector, recovered somewhat more rapidly than that of the Eurozone, some gains in the financial sector returned after 2010.[33] The continuing financial crisis in the Eurozone makes American financial institutions and products appear not only relatively safe and desirable, but also it may have more negative consequences for the American economy.[34]

Structural Change

The final goal of economic policy is structural change, or changing the industrial and regional composition of production. Some regions of a country may be less developed than others, or the composition of production may make some regions particularly vulnerable to economic fluctuations. The experiences of Michigan during slumps in automobile production and of Louisiana and Alaska during periods of declining oil prices demonstrate the dangers of relying too heavily on a single product. Sometimes, government may want to alter the structure of the entire economy—as with the efforts of developing countries to industrialize their agricultural economies. Such an effort was made in the United States in the nineteenth century, and many industrialized countries still attempt to shift the composition of their economies in the most profitable direction.

In the United States, the federal government has been relatively little involved in promoting structural change, with the exception of regional programs such as the Tennessee Valley Authority and the Appalachian Regional Commission. It has been active in supporting and protecting defense industries, which have been crucial for the development of the technology sector. If anything, the federal government has attempted to use trade policy, including quotas on imported products such as automobiles and previously steel, to slow structural change in the economy rather than accelerate it. It is politically difficult for the federal government to support one area of the country over another, and so it tends to use rather general instruments except when trying to protect industry from foreign competition that is perceived to be unfair.

State and local governments, on the other hand, have been extremely active in attempting to promote economic development and structural change, particularly through their tax systems.[35] States permit industries moving in to take tax credits for their investments and to write off a certain percentage of their profits against taxes for some years. Local governments have fewer tax breaks to distribute (property tax relief being the most important), but they can provide grants for industrial sites and other infrastructural development to make themselves more attractive to industries. Building infrastructure is an underappreciated mechanism for economic development; in the 1990s, there was a very close relationship between investment in roads and other economic infrastructure and the growth of jobs in the states.[36]

Southern states have been especially active in promoting economic development through tax incentives. Those policies, combined with a milder climate, more available energy, and low rates of unionization, have tended to reverse the former imbalance in economic growth between the North and the South.[37] The frost belt states have tended to grow more slowly than the sun belt states, although many have prospered by focusing attention on new industries and technology. Several northern states also have boosted their economies by relying on their educational and technological resources, instead of their industrial labor force,[38] a strategy that is likely to remain effective as the United States continues to lose manufacturing jobs overseas and increasingly must turn to its educational and technological capacity to compete (see chapter 13).

In addition to regional changes and competition among areas of the country, a more general aspect of change in the economy has been increasing productivity in the workforce. Compared with those of other industrialized countries, the U.S. workforce is highly productive, and investments in a variety of technologies have increased that productivity. The decline in employment in manufacturing jobs resulted in part from productivity gains, as the application of technology and better working practices made fewer and fewer workers necessary to produce the same amount of goods. Thus, although the share of employment in manufacturing has dropped by more than eleven percentage points since 1990, the share of gross domestic product that manufacturing accounts for has remained almost constant.

Although a somewhat different meaning of structural change, the level of inequality within the American economy has become a highly politicized issue. There has been a significant and continuing concentration of income and wealth in the United States, so that the United States has become the most unequal of the major industrial economies.

The Instruments of Economic Policy

Governments have a number of weapons at their disposal to try to influence the performance of the economy. Analysts often speak of a dichotomy between monetary policy and fiscal policy,[39] and those are certainly two of the more important policy options. Others include regulations and control, financial supports for business and agriculture, public ownership, incentives, and moral suasion. Most governments use a combination, although the U.S. government tends to rely most heavily on the indirect instruments of fiscal and monetary policy.

There is some debate about whether the traditional tools of national economic management will continue to be viable, given globalization. Some argue that capital is now so mobile—and trade so important—that any attempt to influence the economy, especially through monetary policy, is doomed to failure.[40] A number of international agreements and arrangements—the World Trade Organization (WTO) and the North American Free Trade Agreement (NAFTA), for instance—restrict the capacity of the government to make autonomous decisions about economic policy.[41] However, the United States played a major role in negotiating these agreements and strongly influences policymaking within them, so the organizations and their policies are not beyond its influence.

Trade policy remains politically controversial because the groups directly harmed by increased trade do not recognize some of the more general benefits being created for the U.S. economy.[42] In particular, organized labor has resisted freer trade, preferring to attempt to preserve the jobs that union workers already had rather than accept the promise of more and better jobs through trade. Government has attempted to compensate with retraining programs, but they also are seen as offering possible future benefits against real costs now.[43] Labor is far from the only opposition to free trade and globalization, as is indicated by the unusual alliances of labor activists, environmentalists, anarchists, and a host of other groups that greet every major international meeting on trade.[44] Even the George W. Bush administration, which advocated free trade in principle, found protection measures useful in handling some trade issues.[45] The potential use of protective measures also arose in the design of the 2009 stimulus package, with proposals to place tariffs or restrictions on imports.[46]

Fiscal Policy

We have discussed the importance of the budget process in allocating resources among government agencies and between the public and private sectors of the economy. Such decisions are also central to the Keynesian approach to economic management, which stresses the importance of the public budget in regulating effective demand. Simply stated, if government wants to stimulate the economy (that is, increase economic growth and reduce unemployment), it should run a budget deficit. A deficit places more money in circulation than the government has removed from circulation, thereby generating greater demand for goods and services by citizens, who have more money to spend. This additional money, as it circulates through the economy, multiplies in its effect to an extent that depends on the propensity of citizens to spend their additional income rather than save it. Likewise, if a government wants to reduce inflation in an overheated economy, it should run a budget surplus, removing more money from circulation in taxes than it puts back in through public expenditures. The budget surplus leaves citizens with less money than they had before the government's action and so should lessen total demand.

The theory of fiscal policy is rather straightforward, but the practice presents several important difficulties. Perhaps the most important is that deficits and surpluses are not politically neutral. It is a reasonable hypothesis that citizens like to receive benefits from government but do not like to pay taxes to finance those benefits. Consequently, despite American political rhetoric lauding the balanced budget, there were fifty-six budget deficits in sixty-one years from 1950 through 2011.[47] Deficits occurred regularly even during the 1950s and 1960s, when the economy performed very well. Politicians have practiced "one-eyed Keynesianism"—reading the passages Keynes wrote about running deficits but apparently not reading the passages about running surpluses in good times.[48] Although Keynes has been disavowed by many (or even most) economic policymakers, his ideas are still considered when budgets are made, and the influence of deficits (and at least in theory, surpluses) must be considered.[49] Indeed, the massive stimulus package adopted in 2009 had clear roots in Keynesian logic.[50]

Estimating the amount of revenue the government will receive or the outlays of public programs is not simple. Even the best budget planning cannot adjust precisely the level of a deficit or surplus (see Table 9.3). When the economy begins to turn downward, government revenues decline, as workers become unemployed and cease paying income and Social Security taxes, and unemployed workers and their families begin to place demands on a variety of social programs. The decline in revenue and the increase in expenditures then automatically push the budget toward a deficit, without political leaders making any conscious choices about fiscal policy. If the recession is very deep or continues for very long, government may have to act with new programs that will further increase the deficit. Unexpected events not directly related to economic conditions also contribute to the final budget balance. Some of the increased deficit during the Bush administration came from the costs of the wars in Iraq and Afghanistan and Hurricane Katrina. The initial appropriations for relief from Katrina equaled $62 billion, out of a deficit that was three times that size.

The "full employment budget" is an aid in making decisions about the size of deficit or surplus for which to aim.[51] The idea is that the budget should be in balance during periods of full employment, defined as 5 percent unemployed. During times of higher unemployment, there would be a deficit, given the fundamental Keynesian paradigm. Therefore, a budget is calculated that would be in balance at full employment; then the added costs in social expenditures and lost revenues of actual unemployment are added to determine the deficit. That deficit is deemed justifiable because it results not from the profligacy of government but from economic difficulties. A higher deficit is seen as a political decision to spend money that will not be raised as taxes but will confer advantages on incumbent politicians facing reelection. A deficit also may be accepted for ideological reasons, as was true of the extremely large deficits of the Reagan and Bush administrations, which resulted primarily from tax cuts. Likewise, when it became apparent that the U.S. budget would begin to run a surplus in the late 1990s, there were calls from the Republican right to reduce taxes immediately rather than wait to see just what the effects of the change would be.[52]

TABLE 9.3   U.S. Federal Deficit and Debt, 1965–2011 (in millions of dollars)

Year	Deficit	Debt
1965	–1,411	322,318
1970	–2,342	380,921
1975	–53,242	541,925
1980	–73,835	908,503
1985	–212,344	1,816,974
1990	–220,740	3,206,374
1995	–163,899	4,821,018
1998	69,200	5,467,300
1999	124,600	5,606,100
2000	236,400	5,629,000
2001	127,400	5,625,000
2002	–157,800	6,198,400
2003	–377,600	6,760,000
2004	–412,100	7,354,700
2005	–318,300	7,905,300
2006	–248,200	8,451,350
2007	–162,000	8,950,744
2008	–458,600	9,996,100
2009	–1,412,700	11,875,900
2010	–1,293,500	13,528,800
2011	–1,645,100	15,476,200

Source: U.S. Office of Management and Budget, *Historical Tables* (Washington, DC: OMB, annual).

The tax cut adopted in the first months of George W. Bush's administration was Keynesian economics dressed up to some degree as conservatism. Although the benefits of the tax cut went disproportionately to the more affluent, some benefits were offered to most taxpayers, putting some money in the hands of the people most likely to spend it. The tax cut was not justified in terms of Keynesian logic and effects, however, but in terms of a desire to reduce the economic power of government and to let citizens make their own decisions. The 2003 tax cut, however, was justified as an economic stimulant. That tax cut contributed to a reversal of the long-standing commitment of American politicians—especially Republicans—to the idea of a balanced budget. The federal budget went from a surplus of $127 billion in 2001 to a deficit of over $426 billion in 2005. The injection of cash into the economy helped to maintain a level of consumer spending that temporarily stimulated the faltering economy.

The stimulus package passed in early 2009 constituted a major application of deficit spending to attempt to influence the economy. Initial projections of the 2009 deficit were well over $1 trillion, an unprecedented figure. This level of deficit was justified by the drastic economic slump, but it still presents a major challenge to the political economy of the future. The debts incurred in 2009 will have to be paid off over decades, and the interest costs may prevent adoption of other needed programs. The politics of 2011 were to a great extent dominated by the debate over deficit and debt, and the debate continued into the presidential campaign of 2012.

Making fiscal policy. Most fiscal policy decisions are made through the budgetary process outlined in chapter 7. When the president and his advisers establish the limits within which individual agencies must make expenditure decisions, they do so with a particular budget deficit or surplus in mind. Given the rhetoric and conventional wisdom of U.S. politics, it appears that most presidents initiate the process with the intention of producing a balanced budget, but few, if any, have actually succeeded in doing so. President Clinton, toward the end of his administration, was a notable exception. Presidents and Congress are overwhelmed by the complexity of the calculations and by political pressures to spend but not tax. A president's intentions may also be overwhelmed by reliance on economic policies that are meant to produce rapid economic growth but cannot do that job once implemented.

Fiscal policy is primarily a presidential concern, and it is a central issue for most presidents. Only at the level of the entire budget can overall decisions about economic management be made and be somewhat shielded from special interests demanding expenditures or tax preferences. Within the executive branch, the president receives both advice and pressure—largely in the direction of spending more. The president can attempt to rise above special interests, but department heads almost certainly cannot, given the close connections of agencies and departments to the clienteles that they serve. The cabinet secretaries may pass appeals made to them by special interests on to the president and his budget director.

Of course, the president cannot make expenditure and taxation decisions alone. Congress has been increasingly important since the mid-1970s, when the creation of the Congressional Budget Office and the increasing vigor of the Joint Economic Committee and the Joint Budget Committee greatly enhanced its capacity to make fiscal policy decisions.[53] The negotiations between the Clinton administration and Congress over the fiscal year 1994 budget pointed to the enhanced importance of Congress as an economic policymaker.[54] The Clinton administration took the budget originally proposed by the outgoing Bush administration and attempted to adapt it to conform to the economic proposals made by candidate Clinton during the 1992 campaign, including an increase in taxes and some reduction in expenditures in order to reduce the size of the federal budget deficit. This initial round of negotiations was followed by a more significant one in 1997 that laid the groundwork for a more extensive shift in budget priorities and eventually for a balanced budget in 1998.[55]

As noted, the first year of the Obama administration will have the highest deficits ever recorded, but with the active involvement of the Democratic Congress and its committees. That said, only three Republicans voted for the stimulus package in either chamber of Congress, and one of them—Arlen Specter of Pennsylvania—soon became a Democrat.[56]

Despite the competition of Congress, the budget is labeled a presidential budget, and the economic success or failure it produces (or at least with which it is coincident) generally is laid at the president's doorstep politically.[57] As a consequence, even if the budget is not the dominant influence on economic performance it is sometimes made out to be, a president will want to have his ideas implemented through the budget, so as at least to be judged politically on the effects of his own policies rather than those of Congress.

Supply-side economics. With the election of President Ronald Reagan in 1980, there came something of a revolution in fiscal policy in the United States in the form of so-called supply-side economics.[58] That theory argued that instead of inadequate demand in the American economy (the standard Keynesian critique), there was a dearth of supply, especially a dearth of investment. The fundamental idea of supply-side economics was to increase the supply of both labor and capital so that economic growth would take place. The approach argued that government intervention, especially through high taxes, was the major barrier to full participation of labor and capital in the marketplace and that measures to reduce that role would in the (not very) long run produce rapid economic growth.

Some of the analysis supporting the supply-side policies had a great deal of face validity. In particular, the U.S. economy has had a dearth of savings and investment compared with the economies of other industrialized countries (see Table 9.4). Americans save almost no money, or they assume debt at about the same rate as they save, in contrast to countries such as Japan and Germany, where citizens do not spend as much of their money. The U.S. economy has become a consumer economy, driven by large retail sales and to some extent by consumer debt, rather than by savings and investment.[59]

Savings are the capital from which business can borrow for new factories and equipment, but Americans choose to spend and to borrow to spend more, rather than to save and invest.[60] This is a genuine problem in the economy. Recent experience with tax cuts is that the public simply uses tax savings to spend more. Many tools of economic policy depend on the behavior of the public to be effective, and this supply-side theory does not appear to have had much cooperation from the public. Although capital accumulation grew somewhat during the late 1990s as the soaring stock market attracted more small investors, the havoc

TABLE 9.4   Changes in Gross Capital Formation, 1980–2007

Country	1980	1988	1993	1997	2000	2004	2007
United States	17.3	15.7	14.1	15.9	17.4	14.5	11.3
Australia	25.2	25.6	21.5	22.9	22.5	21.3	20.1
Canada	23.3	21.9	17.8	18.9	19.8	20.0	20.2
France	23.8	21.9	19.3	17.0	18.5	18.8	17.9
Germany	22.6	19.6	23.0	21.4	21.6	22.1	23.4
Japan	31.7	30.0	29.2	28.1	26.0	24.3	20.2
Sweden	20.1	20.2	14.2	14.9	17.1	16.4	14.4
United Kingdom	18.7	20.5	15.7	16.7	17.6	16.9	14.7

Source: International Monetary Fund, *International Financial Statistics,* monthly.

wreaked by the recent credit and lending crisis highlighted Americans' tendency to spend what they perceived to be gains from housing values.

The major instrument for implementing supply-side economics in the Reagan years was the Economic Recovery Tax Act of 1981 (ERTA), which, over four years, reduced the average income tax of Americans by 23 percent, with most benefits going to those in higher income brackets, presumably those most likely to invest any additional after-tax income. The fundamental assumption of ERTA was that if individuals had increased incentives to work and invest they would do so, and economic growth would result. Whereas Keynesian economics argued for providing people (usually the less affluent) with increased income through government expenditures, with the expectation that they would spend the money and create demand for goods and services, the supply-side solution, in contrast, argued for providing the more affluent with greater incentives to work and invest because they could retain more of what they earned.

The Economic Recovery Tax Act produced a massive increase in the federal deficit (see Table 9.3). Although taxes were reduced significantly, federal expenditures were not reduced nearly as much. The fiscally conservative administration did not worry, however, because it believed that lower taxes would stimulate economic growth so that, over time, more revenue would come from lower tax rates; this sharp response of government revenues to tax reductions is referred to as the "Laffer curve," after the economist Arthur Laffer.[61] Even after it became clear that the effect described by the Laffer curve had not occurred, however, the Reagan administration did not raise taxes, and low taxation became a central feature of its (and the succeeding Bush administration's) economic policies and political appeals.

The deficit problem came to a head during the construction of the fiscal year 1991 federal budget. The deficit projected for that year was a great deal more than that permissible under Gramm-Rudman-Hollings rules (see chapter 7), but neither President George H. W. Bush nor Congress wanted to take responsibility for raising taxes or reducing popular benefits. After several continuing resolutions to keep government operating without a formal budget and one failed budget bill, Bush and congressional Democrats compromised by increasing some taxes and reducing a few spending programs, but the compromise measure failed to shrink the deficit significantly.

As the twenty-first century began, budget deficits appeared to be a thing of the past, a development that was expected to have a number of positive economic consequences. Less foreign capital would be required to fund the debt, and the United States might lose its status as the world's largest debtor nation. It was anticipated that less federal borrowing would help to stabilize domestic interest rates. Finally, because government debt, like private debt, must be repaid (or at a minimum, debt interest must be paid), the prospect of paying less interest (because of both a lower ratio of debt to GDP and lower interest rates) seemed likely to free some money for new programs. The largest continuing impact of the Reagan administration had been that debt interest had kept government from spending money on new social programs for years, but in 2000, it appeared that there might soon be financial latitude to undertake new initiatives.

That optimism waned significantly in 2001 and 2002. Terrorist attacks, corporate scandals, and a general slowdown in the economy combined with tax cuts and increased spending on defense and a few domestic programs to drive the budget into major deficits by fiscal year 2003. All but the most optimistic analysts then projected that such deficits would continue for the foreseeable future, barring significant changes in the economy or in fiscal policies. The economic logic of the Bush administration, however, continued to be that by cutting taxes, and especially cutting taxes for the more affluent, more demand would be created and economic growth would follow—a policy that some critics claim contributed to the economic crisis of 2008 and 2009.[62]

The rather laissez-faire attitude that Republicans held about the deficit during the Bush administration changed markedly thereafter, and in Congress, the party became dedicated to reducing the deficit and producing a balanced budget. While this approach to fiscal policy appealed to the Tea Party and other conservatives, it was the antithesis of the Keynesian approach to promoting economic growth. One of the effects of reducing public spending, for example, has been to eliminate a number of public sector jobs, and in late 2011 and 2012, the gains in private sector employment had to some extent been offset by losses in public sector employment.[63]

Monetary Policy

Whereas the basic fiscal policy paradigm stresses demand management through varying levels of revenues and expenditures, the monetary solution to economic management stresses the importance of the money supply in controlling economic fluctuations. As with more public spending, increasing the amount of money in circulation is presumed to stimulate the economy. Extra money lowers interest rates, making it easier for citizens to borrow for investments or purchases and thus encourages economic activity. Reducing the availability of money makes it more difficult to borrow and to spend, thus slowing an inflationary economy.

In the United States, the Federal Reserve and its member Federal Reserve banks are primarily responsible for monetary policy. The Federal Reserve Board and the banks are intended to be independent from the executive authority of the president, and because their budget is only appended to the federal budget, it is also largely independent of congressional control through the budget process.[64] The members of the Federal Reserve exercise their judgment as bankers rather than submitting to control by political officials who want to manipulate the money supply for political gain. The Federal Reserve, or Fed, has exercised its independence and has refused several times to accede to presidential requests. For example, the Fed would neither cooperate with the first Bush administration in its efforts to fund continuing deficits with minimal tax increases, nor with President Clinton in his efforts to keep the economic recovery moving as rapidly as possible during 1994. On the other hand, some critics argued that Fed chair Alan Greenspan was too supportive of the George W. Bush administration and its deficit financing.[65]

The independence of the Federal Reserve has been undermined by the economic crisis of 2008 and 2009. Rather than remaining above the fray and just using its traditional monetary instruments, the Fed became deeply involved in lending money to troubled firms as well as to the government. Furthermore, the Federal Reserve has become in many ways the principal economic regulator, as the independent regulatory commissions were to some extent compromised by their failure to prevent the crisis.[66]

In its more normal operations, the Federal Reserve has a variety of monetary tools at its disposal to influence the economy, the chief ones being open market operations, the discount rate and federal funds rate, and bank reserve requirements. *Open market operations* are the most commonly used mechanism of monetary policy. The Federal Reserve enters the money markets to buy or sell securities issued by the federal government. If it wishes to reduce the supply of money, the Fed attempts to sell securities, exchanging the bonds for cash that was in circulation. If it wants to expand the money supply, it purchases securities on the market, exchanging money for the bonds.

While open market operations generally involve buying government securities, "quantitative easing" used in response to the crisis beginning in 2008 has involved purchasing other types of securities.[67] Perhaps most important, the

Federal Reserve bought large volumes of mortgage backed securities to help support the housing market that was a central problem in the economic decline. This was an unconventional style of monetary policy intervention but has apparently had a significant impact on the economy.

A more powerful option available to the Federal Reserve Bank is to change the *discount rate* and the *federal funds rate*. These are the rates of interest at which member banks can borrow money from the Federal Reserve or from one another to cover shortages in their required reserves. These rates affect interest rates in the economy as a whole, as member banks have to increase the interest rates they charge their customers if they have to pay more to borrow money from the Federal Reserve. In the basic monetary paradigm, making money more difficult or more costly to borrow will slow down economic activity and, presumably, inflation. Sometimes, the Fed does not even have to change the discount rate; all its chair has to do is mention the possibility of a change, and the economy may react.

The discount rate was very stable and low from early 1997 until 2001. Fed chair Alan Greenspan warned from time to time about the dangers of inflation and excessive demand, but the rate was kept constant. As the economy began to slow during the first years of the George W. Bush administration, the discount rate was cut again and again, reaching one of the lowest levels on record in mid-2002. Beginning early in 2003, the Federal Reserve sensed some possible return to inflation and began to raise the discount rate, but once the crisis began in 2008, the rates the Federal Reserve set began to fall, reaching all-time lows in early 2009.

Finally, the Federal Reserve Board can change the *reserve requirement*. Member banks of the Federal Reserve System must keep on deposit at the Federal Reserve banks a percentage of the total amount they have out in loans, normally around 10 percent. If the Fed raises the reserve requirement from 10 percent to 12.5 percent, then for each dollar a bank had out in loans before the change, it can lend only seventy-five cents. Banks will have to deposit more money, call in some loans, or reduce the pace at which they grant new loans. Any of these measures will substantially reduce the amount of money in circulation and should slow down economic activity. Reducing the reserve requirement makes more money available for loans and should increase economic activity. Changing the reserve requirement is a drastic action that is undertaken only if the Fed sees a need to influence the economy dramatically and quickly.

The Federal Reserve has been a paragon of conservative economic policy. Its members traditionally have been bankers or business executives who have tried to please a constituency of similar composition. The Fed's tight money policies have been criticized frequently for producing economic hardship. It repeatedly lowered rates between 2001 and 2004, fostering a massive housing bubble that burst in 2008. On the other hand, Federal Reserve actions have been defended as appropriate, given the danger of inflation fueled in part by expansive fiscal policy. The most important concerns, however, are the possibilities (a) that lack of coordination of fiscal and monetary policy will cause the two to cancel each other's effect, and (b) that coordinating the two may produce an excessive amount of correction in the economy, so changes overshoot the mark and economic fluctuations are exaggerated rather than minimized.

Regulations and Control

In general, regulation has been used not for general economic management but to achieve other economic and social goals. Regulations have been associated with cleaning up the environment, making workplaces safer, or making consumer products safer. Such regulations also have an effect on overall economic growth, however, because they make it more or less profitable to engage in certain activities. Some regulatory activities, such as antitrust regulation, have a pervasive impact on the economic structure of the society and perhaps on consumer prices for a range of goods. Regulation became more central in the debate over economic policy in 2009, as inadequate regulation was seen as an important cause of the economic crisis.[68]

Antitrust regulation has been one of the most important forms of government control of the economy.[69] Beginning with the Sherman Act in 1890, Congress has sought to ensure that a few firms did not control an industry and then extract excessive profits.[70] The criminal sanctions in the Sherman Act and the vagueness of its definitions of illegal actions made enforcement difficult, however, and the Clayton Act was passed in 1914, at the same time that the Federal Trade Commission was created. This legislation gave clearer (although still far from unambiguous) definitions of actions that constituted "combinations in restraint of trade" and provided an administrative enforcement mechanism in addition to enforcement through the courts.[71] Antitrust regulation to foster competition has been important in American economic policy, but it is possible that it has outlived its utility. A major economic policy concern since the 1990s has been external *competitiveness* rather than internal *competition*. It may be that to be competitive with many foreign firms, U.S. firms will have to be larger and have larger market shares.

The antitrust prosecution of Microsoft in 1998 brought some of the issues around antitrust policy into sharper focus.[72] An extremely successful company in international as well as domestic markets, Microsoft had been able to create a virtual monopoly in some areas of software. Should the firm be punished for being successful and for making technological advances that put it in a dominant position? Would the software market be better served by more competition and more options for the consumer, even if there were to be some problems of compatibility? There were cogent arguments on both sides of the debate, and such issues may be more common in the future as technological changes and patents for them become more crucial for economic success. Microsoft ultimately escaped with little direct punishment for what were seen as anticompetitive actions, but the company was forced to alter future practices to facilitate market entry by smaller firms.

The United States has had limited experience with wage and price controls like those that have been used in Europe, but the minimum wage has been a source of political contention. The minimum wage was first adopted during Franklin Roosevelt's New Deal as a means of ensuring that workers would have something like a living wage even in hard economic times. The wage adopted at the time may have been a living wage, but because Congress must act to increase the federal minimum, its real value has fluctuated over the years (see Figure 9.1). Businesses, especially small businesses, naturally do not want to have to pay higher wages, and whenever an increase is considered, they argue to Congress that a higher minimum wage would put them out of business or force them to get rid of workers—neither of which is an option that Congress members like to entertain.[73] Some states have increased their own minimum wage independently of the federal minimum. As of 2012, Washington state's was $9.04 per hour, and several states were also near $9.00 per hour, apparently with little impact on employment. After keeping the federal minimum wage at $5.15 for a decade, the new Democratic Congress passed legislation in 2007 that increased it in three increments over two years, to $7.25 an hour by mid-2009.

The federal minimum remains lower in real terms than it was in the 1950s. Conservatives continue to argue that the minimum wage is a deterrent to hiring, especially hiring relatively inexperienced young people. When the economy was booming in the 1990s, the minimum wage was less of an issue; in many cities, the demand for labor was such that even hamburger-flipping jobs paid above minimum wage. A slowdown in economic activity has meant greater concern about the impact of this form of economic regulation. At the same time, a political movement for a "living wage" has also been gathering momentum.

The question of economic regulation through control of wages is especially relevant for implementation of the "flexible labor market" that was considered a major source of the Clinton administration's economic success.[74] The ability of workers to move quickly and easily to follow demand and the flexibility of wage rates to adjust to a "market clearing level" were crucial for high employment in the period and secondarily for high levels of growth. In the eyes of many Europeans, the relative insecurity of the American labor market and the absence of an effective social safety net make working conditions in the United States very

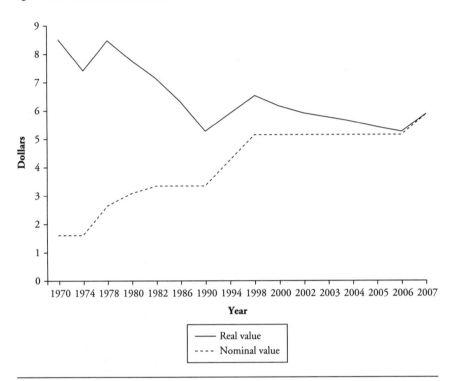

FIGURE 9.1   Value of the U.S. Minimum Wage (in dollars)
Source: Employment Policies Institute, www.epionline.org/mw_statistics_annual.cfm.

harsh, but the system has been more effective in generating jobs than the more regulated labor market structures in Europe.

By summer 2002, many Americans were searching for a more regulated economy.[75] Revelations of dishonest practices at Enron, WorldCom, and Xerox, among other firms, indicated that businesses in the United States were, with the complicity of accounting firms, engaging in rather systematic deception of both their own investors and federal regulatory authorities. In particular, the Securities and Exchange Commission, which regulates the integrity of the stock market, was proving ineffective in monitoring the activities of big businesses and the financial statements they were providing publicly. Changes such as improved accounting standards and corporate governance have increased regulation, but the need remains for increased control over business performance and standards.

Finally, the economic meltdown of 2008–2009 showed most Americans that the regulation of banks and the financial markets in the United States was inadequate. The banks had been deregulated during the 1990s and had embarked on a range of risky investment activities. They and other financial institutions began to provide so-called subprime mortgages to home buyers who did not have sufficient credit to qualify for the loans. Although they initially gave lower-income people the opportunity to achieve the American dream of owning their own home, the loans now are associated with millions of foreclosures that have caused thousands of people to lose their homes.[76]

The Dodd-Frank Act (technically the Wall Street Reform and Consumer Protection Act) represented the major congressional response to the financial crisis. This bill contained a wide range of measures designed to prevent some of the financial chaos from occurring again.[77] One of the more important provisions in the act was creating the Consumer Financial Protection Bureau to regulate institutions providing mortgages, personal loans, and student loans. In addition, there were offices established to assess the risks being undertaken by banks and other financial institutions. The act also created several organizations designed to coordinate regulation of financial markets. The failure to put these rules into effect promptly was blamed in part for the huge losses of J. P. Morgan Chase in spring 2012.

Public Support for Business

In addition to regulating the conduct of business and providing support through tax incentives, governments provide a number of more direct subsidies to industry. In the United States, the historical pattern had been that the federal government had a small role in direct subsidies to business, with the bulk of support coming from state and even local governments. The majority of the direct federal support for business and industry came as support for research and development and for the subsidization of credit. Other forms of support for industry included promotion of inland water transportation by allowing use of locks and dams on rivers at well-below-market prices, services such as free weather reports and economic information, and a variety of grants and loans for small business. Federal credit facilities are available for a host of business projects, including the facilitation of international trade through the Export-Import Bank and a variety of supports for agriculture and housing. Altogether, the federal government in 2005 supplied over $100 billion of direct and indirect support to business and industry.[78]

That indirect role for federal support changed dramatically during the recession in 2008 and 2009. Beginning with the George W. Bush administration's support for failing banks and investment houses, and continuing through the federal government's purchase of major shares in automobile manufacturers in the Obama administration, the federal government assumed an unfamiliar and largely unwelcome role in direct economic management and ownership.

Just as they compete with one another with tax incentives to attract industries to their localities, state governments can also use direct services and credits to attract industry.[79] In fact, there is some evidence that government services are more important than tax breaks in this effort. The services of state and local governments need not be extraordinary. They may only need to do things that they usually do, such as supplying transportation, water, sewers, and similar services, and do them well. Of course, some expenditures by subnational governments are extraordinary, possibly including the building of plants or more elaborate forms of infrastructure for industries that agree to situate themselves in the locality.

All these supports for business must be examined in the context of a continuing "industrial policy debate" in the United States. As the country was falling behind Japan, West Germany, and even smaller countries, such as South Korea and Taiwan, during the 1980s and thereafter in the production of basic commodities, such as steel, and finished products, such as automobiles, the question of what is wrong with American industry became a central policy issue.[80] Numerous answers to that question have been offered, including inept management, avaricious unions, and meddlesome government. Another possibility is that government does not do enough to support American industry, and what it does is poorly organized—the implication being that a more comprehensive approach to the problems of American industry and its competitiveness in the international marketplace should be adopted. Such a program might include some or all of the following elements:

1. *Direct government grants for the modernization and expansion of industry.* Despite major improvements, some of the machinery of American heavy industry is outdated in comparison with that of its competitors. Government could help by supplying grants, loans, or both. There is some assistance through the tax system but little or no direct aid.

2. *Trade policy.* U.S. government has followed free trade policies for most of the nearly seventy years since World War II, using tariffs and other restrictions on imports infrequently. It could impose tariffs and other trade barriers to help American industry get back on its feet. Voluntary arrangements exist with Japan over the import of automobiles, but some advocate broader use of those powers. The United States continues to debate the European Union over a number of trade issues—for example, subsidies to aircraft manufactures, although there are at least as many European as American complaints about unfair competition and trade policies. Even the free trade agreement with neighboring Canada and Mexico is believed by some citizens, and some politicians, potentially to undermine the American economy.[81]

The increasing importance of international trade for the American economy makes trade policy all the more important. As noted earlier, the United States continues to run big trade deficits. The relative prosperity of the late 1990s tended to exacerbate the trade deficit, as Americans found they had more money to spend and chose to spend it on foreign-made products, trips to Europe, and the like.

3. *Deregulation.* Some sections of the business community argue that the numerous safety and environmental regulations of the federal government make it difficult for U.S. industry to produce goods at a price that is competitive on the world market. In particular, businesses and unions alike are concerned with the number of jobs being lost to low-wage and low-regulation countries, such as Indonesia, Mexico, and Brazil, and they believe that less regulation would improve the competitiveness of business. In addition, the United States tends to pursue regulatory policies, such as antitrust laws, with somewhat greater vigor than is true for most of the rest of the world, also potentially inhibiting competitiveness of American industry in world markets.

4. *Research and development.* American industry has a tradition of being among the most technologically advanced in the world. Unfortunately, that has become more of a tradition than a reality. Except for a few industries such as computers, American industry appears to be falling behind many countries. Government could make a major contribution to American industry by making more funds available for research.

5. *Regional policy.* The effects of declining industry have not been spread evenly over the United States but have been concentrated in the older industrial regions, especially in the Great Lakes area. Besides dealing with the direct problems of industry, there is a need to address the human problems created by a changing industrial base in many states and localities. Such efforts may also make those localities more attractive to industries considering relocation. More recently, the decline in defense industries has made Southern California one of the more economically depressed areas of the American economy.

The interventions of the federal government into the troubled automobile industry had some elements of regional policy contained within it. In particular, this program had the effect of being a regional policy for the Midwest and especially the states of Michigan and Ohio. The big three automobile manufacturers in the United States were threatened with bankruptcy and requested $34 billion in support. As one component of the Troubled Asset Relief Program directed primarily at credit institutions, General Motors and Chrysler received loans of almost $25 billion.[82] By the beginning of 2012, these industries had recovered, were making profits, and had repaid almost all of their loans.[83]

Government has been involved in supporting industry for most of U.S. history. Many of the country's great industrial ventures, including the westward extension of the railroads, were undertaken with the direct or indirect support of government.[84] There may now be even greater need for government support for business and industry than in the past, given the declining industrial position of the United States. However, too much dependence on government to bail out losers—including the airline industry and, more recently, the big automakers— may mean that American industry ceases to be responsible for its own revitalization and will simply wait for the public sector to rescue it. That bailout may come through direct subsidies or through protectionist trade policy, or through loosening regulations on commitments such as corporate pension plans.[85] Use of trade policy for adjusting the economy is, however, increasingly constrained by international agreements, such as the North American Free Trade Agreement, and the World Trade Organization.

Public Ownership

Although it is not common in the United States, public ownership of certain kinds of industries can be important for economic management, especially influencing the location of certain industries. Even in the United States, a number of public and quasi-public corporations are involved in the economy. In 1976, there were twenty publicly wholly owned and seven partly owned corporations in the federal government. The general movement toward managerialism and privatization in government has led to increased use of the corporate form of organization, even when it appears inappropriate (the National Service Corporation, for example). Some of these industries have been privatized, but government remains more of an entrepreneur than most citizens realize.

At the state and local levels, numerous public enterprises are organized to carry out economic as well as social policy functions. Those enterprises range from publicly owned utilities, such as electricity, gas, and transportation, to functions usually associated with the private sector, such as insurance and banking. Although public enterprises ideologically are anathema in the United States, in practice, this form of organization is actually becoming more and more popular as a means of providing services while at the same time attempting to be as efficient and businesslike as possible.

Public corporations perform a variety of functions for governments. One is to provide revenue—for example, local government utilities can buy electricity at commercial rates and then distribute it at rates that yield a profit. Public corporations can be used to regulate prices and certain essential services. Although many publicly owned transportation corporations run a deficit, they maintain relatively low costs and provide greater service than would a private firm, and local governments consider those objectives important. At the federal level, corporate structures have been used for regional development in the Tennessee

Valley Authority, a largely successful attempt to transform the economy of a backward region through public action and public ownership of electric power production. Federal corporations, such as the Export-Import Bank and the Overseas Private Investment Corporation, have been active in promoting U.S. foreign trade, and the St. Lawrence Seaway and Amtrak provide transportation to promote economic growth.

One interesting variation on public ownership is the use of loan guarantees and insurance to attempt to ensure continuing employment and economic growth. A notable earlier example was the Loan Guarantee Board, which Congress created in 1979 to develop financing to keep the Chrysler Corporation in business and its workers in jobs. The federal government did not buy one share of Chrysler stock but used its economic power to keep the company alive. The federal government also spent billions of dollars to make good on its insurance commitments to depositors of failing savings and loans and banks in the early 1990s. These activities helped to preserve employment, enabled one corporation to reverse its economic fortunes, and protected the savings of millions of citizens, while helping to preserve confidence in the financial institutions of the country. It might be argued that public involvement in moribund corporations is disguised social policy and may actually slow economic growth. At least in the short term, however, it represents an important economic policy instrument.

The economic crisis beginning in 2008 initiated a new era of public ownership and direct involvement by U.S. government in the market. Directly and indirectly, the federal government now owns stakes in a number of banks, a major insurance company, and at least one automobile company.[86] The Republican opposition in Congress attempted to label this involvement "socialism," but the perceived need to do something about the recession, even something that departs from much of American history, overcame opposition. The problem, of course, becomes what role the federal government may take in management and whether its involvement in the market can serve the public interest. As noted above with the loans given to the automobile makers, the firms in which the federal government purchased stock are gradually buying back that stock.

Public Support for Labor

As well as supporting business, the public sector can also support the workforce through mechanisms such as training and education. In a more knowledge-based world economy, economic policy depends in part on the competitiveness and productivity of the labor force. The United States has done well over the past several decades in improving the productivity of its workforce. From 2000 onward, *productivity*, meaning the output per worker per hour, increased on average 2.7 percent per annum,[87] a relatively high figure compared to most other industrial democracies.

Although productivity is good for the economy as a whole, it does not necessarily mean that it is good for the individual worker, or for the labor force in general. If there is high and increasing productivity, then the economy can produce the same wealth with fewer workers. For example, the so-called jobless recovery after 2009 has been in part a product of the same number or even fewer workers being able to produce more.[88] Most of that increased productivity did not, however, go to the workers but rather tended to go into corporate profits.[89]

Another aspect of the potential for government's role in supporting the working population and the economic growth is through more aggressive training. There is some evidence that the continuing levels of unemployment after the recession is the mismatch between the requirements of jobs and the skills available among those seeking work. One estimate from the Minneapolis Federal Reserve is that one-third or more of joblessness occurring during the recession after 2008 could be eliminated if there were a better match between skills and jobs. Thus, economic success may be increasingly dependent upon education and training (see chapter 13).

Incentives

Governments can also attempt to influence economic change by providing incentives for desired behaviors. Most are tax incentives to encourage investment and economic change. The tax reforms of the 1980s eliminated many such incentives, but they still constitute a powerful economic weapon for government, and Congress has tended to return to tax incentives to support particular interests. We have already mentioned the role that state government tax incentives play in encouraging structural change in individual state economies, with some contribution to economic development in the country as a whole. The federal government also provides special incentives for selected industries and general incentives for businesses to invest, especially in research and development.

The major incentives for structural change in the U.S. economy have been the oil depletion allowance and similar allowances for other nonrenewable natural resources, permitting investors to write off against profits a portion of the investment they have made in searching for new supplies of a resource such as oil. A variety of provisions of the federal tax code serve to encourage investment in general by both corporations and individuals. The capital gains provisions of the tax laws permit profits made on investments held for over one year to be taxed at lower rates, and the Bush tax cuts also reduced taxes on dividends from investments.

Industries receive extensive tax credits for new investments and are allowed higher-than-average depreciation on investments during the first year. All these policies make it easier and more profitable for industries to invest and for economic growth to follow that investment, but none requires industry to make the investments. The administrative costs of incentive programs are comparatively small when subsidy programs are considered as the alternative, and they also are perceived as less intrusive into the market economy than the possible alternatives. But the dollar an industry saves from taxes is worth exactly the same as the dollar granted as a subsidy, and perhaps even more, since there are fewer strings attached to the dollar saved from taxes.

Moral Suasion

When all else fails, or perhaps before anything else is tried, governments can attempt to influence citizens and industries by persuasion. Persuasion works best in times of national emergency, but economic circumstances may be sufficiently dire to create the perception of an emergency.[90] Presidents, using their power as voice for the nation, are central to the use of persuasion to control economic behavior, and they can employ a variety of symbols to influence citizens. Attempting to speak for the nation as president and appealing to patriotism to get what he wanted, Lyndon Johnson exerted the power of the office when he "jawboned" industries to encourage them to restrain price increases. George H. W. Bush's purchase of a pair of socks in a shopping mall could be seen as an attempt, largely unsuccessful, to manipulate symbols to urge Americans to start buying again, and Barack Obama spent the first months of his administration attempting to buoy consumer confidence in order to combat the economic recession.

The effects of persuasion depend on the nature of the policy problem being addressed and the character of the political leader attempting to do the persuading. Industrialists are unlikely to continue to provide jobs for workers in an unprofitable factory simply because they are asked to, but citizens may well try to "buy American" to improve the balance of payments. Political leaders who are trusted and respected find it relatively easy to influence their fellow citizens, whereas those who are less popular may find more direct economic management more effective. Some economic problems—such as a budget deficit—may simply be too big to be attacked with words alone.

Summary

The management of the economy is a central concern of government. It is the area of policymaking on which governments are most frequently evaluated by their citizens. That is true not only because of the direct importance of the issue to citizens but also because of the frequent reporting of standard indicators such as the inflation rate and the level of unemployment. Even if an individual has a job and an income that keeps pace with the cost of living, he or she may believe the president is not doing a good job because of the aggregate numbers that regularly appear in the newspapers. The extent to which the performance of the economy is now laid at the feet of government, especially the president, is in marked contrast to the era before the Great Depression, when the economy was not believed to be controllable by government. The president clearly plays a crucial role in economic management because of his role as spokesperson for government, because of the importance of the presidential budget in controlling the economy, and because of the president's influence on other areas of economic policy, such as taxation.

It is important to understand, however, that the condition of the economy is not solely a presidential responsibility. Congress must approve the budget, which is the central instrument of presidential intervention in the economy. The actions of the Federal Reserve are almost totally beyond the control of the president. Furthermore, the federal structure of the United States is such that state and local governments' taxing and spending decisions have a significant impact not only on the overall stimulative or depressive effects of public expenditures but also on attempts to move industries and labor geographically. The success of national economic policies is also increasingly dependent on decisions made by other nations, by international organizations such as the International Monetary Fund, and by global markets.

Finally, citizens have a substantial impact on the state of the economy. Many presidential decisions on fiscal policy, as well as many Federal Reserve decisions about monetary policy, depend on citizens' responding in the predicted fashion. Even major aggregates, such as economic growth, depend to a great extent on the perceptions and behaviors of citizens—citizen confidence is as good an economic indicator as many more objective ones. If citizens and businesses believe that prosperity is coming, they will be willing to invest and may make their belief a self-fulfilling prophecy. Government can do everything in its power to try to influence the behavior of citizens, but ultimately, most decisions are beyond its control. Even so, the success of economic policy is a major factor in whether citizens believe that government is doing a good job.

CHAPTER 10

Tax Policy

TAX POLICY IS a fundamental component of economic policy, and it deserves some discussion in its own right. Here, we are especially concerned with the choice of revenue instruments to collect the money that the government requires to pay for its programs. In addition to raising revenues adequate to meet spending demands, taxes are used to address a number of other policy purposes. Raising the same amount of tax revenues by different means may have very different economic and political effects, and those effects should be understood when discussing tax policies.[1] For example, raising money by means of an income tax is more favorable to the poor than is raising the same amount of money through a sales tax. Different means of raising money may be more or less difficult to administer, so governments may choose ease (and certainty) of collection rather than other values, such as equity or impact on economic growth, when selecting tax policies.

Background

Table 10.1 shows the tax profile of the United States in comparison with those of other major Western countries, detailing the proportion of total tax revenue that each country derives from a number of possible revenue sources. The United States stands apart from its major trading partners in several ways. First, it relies substantially less on taxes on goods and services than the other countries. Although most states and many localities collect sales and excise taxes, there is no national sales tax comparable to the value-added tax (VAT) that almost all European countries have.[2] Fiscal pressures, especially on the Social Security system (see chapter 12), may one day make such a tax necessary, but it has been delayed longer in this country than elsewhere.

Second, the United States derives substantially more of its total tax revenue from property taxes than most other countries do. It is states and localities that

TABLE 10.1   Kinds of Tax Revenues, 2003 (percentages of total taxation)

Country	Personal income tax	Corporate income tax	Employees' social security	Employers' social security	General consumption tax	Selective commodity taxes	Property tax	Customs	Other
Australia	38.5	16.7	0.0	0.0	13.7	12.5	9.5	1.9	7.7
Belgium	31.4	7.4	9.9	19.1	15.5	7.5	3.3	0.1	4.8
Canada	34.6	10.4	6.3	8.6	15.1	9.1	10.0	0.7	5.2
Denmark	53.1	5.9	2.4	0.1	20.1	12.1	3.8	0.1	2.4
France	17.5	5.7	9.5	25.7	16.8	8.4	7.3	0.1	10.0
Germany	23.9	3.5	17.9	19.9	17.9	2.4	2.4	1.2	10.4
Italy	25.1	6.6	5.4	20.6	14.2	9.3	5.8	6.3	10.9
Japan	17.5	13.0	16.5	17.6	9.5	7.7	10.3	0.7	5.5
Sweden	31.3	5.0	5.7	22.9	18.4	7.3	3.1	0.2	7.2
Switzerland	34.3	8.5	12.0	11.8	13.4	7.0	8.3	0.6	4.3
United Kingdom	28.7	7.8	7.5	10.3	18.9	12.8	11.8	0.1	4.2
United States	35.3	8.1	11.7	13.3	8.4	6.5	12.1	0.7	3.9

Source: Organization for Economic Cooperation and Development, *Revenue Statistics of OECD Member Countries, 1965–2004* (Paris: OECD, 2006).

TABLE 10.2   Property Tax Revenue of Local Government, 1960–2008

Year	Current ($ millions)	Real ($ millions)	Percentage of total revenues
1960	15,798	17,851	47.8
1970	32,963	28,367	40.7
1980	65,607	26,594	28.2
1985	99,772	32,825	28.2
1990	149,765	38,116	26.9
1995	203,500	40,111	23.9
2000	248,500	41,653	21.7
2002	261,400	42,002	21.5
2003	286,200	43,354	22.1
2004	307,528	46,125	23.6
2005	324,639	47,561	23.8
2008	395,965	49,101	24.0

Source: U.S. Census Bureau, *Statistical Abstract of the United States* (Washington, DC: U.S. GPO, annual).

collect property taxes, which are the principal revenue source for local governments (see Table 10.2). This pattern appears to reflect an Anglo-Saxon tradition in revenue collection, for the United Kingdom, Canada, and New Zealand all use the property tax more than most other industrialized countries.[3] The local property tax is especially important for funding education (see chapter 13). Despite its historical importance, the property tax has been a declining source of revenue for local governments relative to other sources. The decline is in part political, a function of the visibility of the property tax and citizen resistance to increases. This tax is also more expensive to administer than other taxes, and local governments have sought other ways of increasing their income.[4] In particular, fees for services that local governments provide, such as garbage collection, water, and even fire protection, have become increasingly important revenue instruments.

Third, the United States relies relatively heavily on corporate taxes. Given the characterization of American politics as dominated by special interests (especially business interests), high levels of corporate taxes may require further explanation.[5] Corporations rarely bear the full burden of corporate taxation; instead, the real tax burden falls on consumers of the firms' products in the form of higher prices, on the companies' workers in lower wages, or on stockholders in the form of lower dividends. Under many economic circumstances—such as the extremely high level of corporate taxation in Japan—firms can add taxes onto the price of their products as a cost of doing business. A more political explanation

Justin Sullivan/Getty Images

Millions of Americans file their federal tax forms in mid-April each year, including Ricardo Romero, who signs his tax forms before mailing them at the post office in New York City on April 17, 2012. The personal income tax is the major source of tax revenue for the federal government, and the vast majority of citizens comply voluntarily with the tax laws.

for this practice involves the tradition of populism in many of the U.S. states that places a relatively heavier burden of taxation on corporations, and even the most conservative politicians on the national level must remember that corporations do not vote, but individual taxpayers do.[6]

Something that Table 10.1 cannot easily depict is the complexity of the tax system in the United States. Some of the complexity is a function of federalism and the number of different tax systems existing at the state and local levels (see Figure 10.1). The federal government collects approximately two-thirds of all tax revenue, but states and localities remain significant actors in taxation. There are also a number of different taxes at the federal level, so focusing solely on the personal income tax, for example, may miss some of the impact of taxation. As the tax system has evolved, even greater complexity has resulted from the many deductions, exemptions, and other special treatments ("tax expenditures" or "loopholes") that have been written into the tax laws (see Table 10.3).[7] The summary figures presented in Table 10.3 cannot capture the manner in which Congress has been able to target tax benefits to particular groups in society—for example, cattle ranchers and the owners of oil and gas leases.

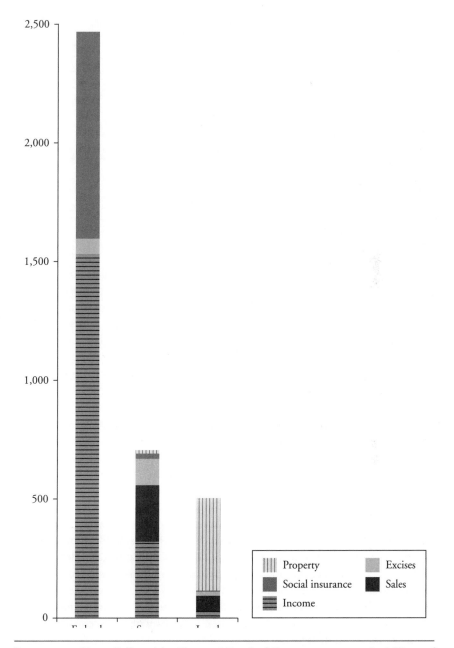

FIGURE 10.1   Taxes Collected by Type and Level of Government, 2007 (in billions of dollars)

Source: Statistical Abstract of the United States, 2009.

TABLE 10.3   Federal Spending versus Tax Expenditures for the Same Program Area, 2007 (in billions of dollars)

	Federal spending	Tax expenditures
National defense	1,176.4	3.0
Social policy	870.6	141.7
Health	257.5	137.9
Education	74.9	19.7
Housing	37.3	205.2

Source: Budget of the United States Government, Fiscal Year 2007.

Note: The Office of Management and Budget discourages adding tax expenditure figures because of different assumptions underlying the different policy areas, and therefore these numbers are only suggestive.

The tax reforms of the 1980s closed some of the more egregious loopholes in the tax system, but a number remained. Many of the remaining exclusions have good economic and social justifications (e.g., the deductibility of mortgage interest stimulates home ownership as well as the construction industry), but some loopholes (such as capital gains or oil depletion allowances) appear to benefit primarily the wealthy and the well organized. In almost every revenue bill since the major reform in 1986, some new special tax treatments have appeared, returning the tax system to the same "Christmas tree" it had been prior to reform.[8] One exception was legislation passed in 1996 that requires Congress to identify "limited tax benefits"—that is, tax breaks that go only to a relatively few individuals or firms.[9] Although this requirement has made the creation of these special benefits more public, Congress has continued to add them, in part because relatively few citizens actually monitor such special benefits. The major exceptions to that generalization are taxpayer groups, such as the National Taxpayers Union, and some more left-leaning think tanks, such as the Center for Budget and Policy Priorities.

The complexity in the tax code became an issue in the 2012 presidential campaign, with most candidates arguing in favor of simplification. At the extreme, Herman Cain wanted to have a flat 9 percent income tax, sales tax, and corporate tax with few exceptions. Less sweeping reforms advocated by other candidates also would have attempted to reduce burdens of record keeping and to enhance the perceived fairness of the system.[10] The last major overhaul of the tax system was in 1986, and the entrenched interests within the current system will make reform difficult.

The impact of tax expenditures is apparent from the data in Table 10.3, where they are compared with federal spending for the same objective. In at least one policy area, housing, the financial impact of tax expenditures is substantially greater than that of federal spending, although direct expenditures are larger for most policies. Even in two of the federal government's largest expenditure programs—Social Security and health care—tax expenditures amount to at least one-third of spending. Thus there is, as Christopher Howard has argued, a substantial "hidden welfare state" in the United States.[11]

The prevailing structure of tax expenditures also tends to create a welfare state for the middle class. As shown in Figure 10.2, with the exception of the excludability of Social Security income and the earned income tax credit, the majority of the benefits of tax expenditures accrue to people earning over $50,000 per annum, and for some provisions of the tax code, the principal beneficiaries earn over $100,000. If the benefits that go to business are added to these personal benefits for the affluent, it can be argued that the tax system produces substantial negative income redistribution (which is to some extent offset by positive redistribution through the expenditures). The apparent (and real) unfairness of many aspects of the tax system has helped to spawn tax reform in the past. A number of apparent inequities remain, however, and even more have been created in recent tax legislation. Much of the tax legislation passed in the George W. Bush administration (lower taxes on dividends, for example) conferred benefits on the more affluent.

Public Opinion and Taxation

Although they are not keen to pay taxes, Americans are not unrealistic, and most appear to realize that they have to pay a good deal of their income in taxes.[12] The major questions that arise in taxpayers' minds are whether the tax system is fair and whether they receive value for the money they pay to government. Americans also appear to want some control over how tax money is spent, and they prefer taxes that are linked to specific types of government activities—usually called "earmarked taxes"—to ones that go into the general fund.

Fairness

The public tends to have two concerns when thinking about the fairness of the tax system. One is the basic premise that everybody who benefits from government should pay at least something in taxes. Several surveys about taxes have found that the public appears to be willing to accept the basic principle of *progressivity*—that the more affluent should pay at a higher rate—so long as even the poor pay something. Indeed, there tends to be far from overwhelming public support for the idea of a *flat tax,* by which everyone pays the same tax rate, except among strong conservatives.[13]

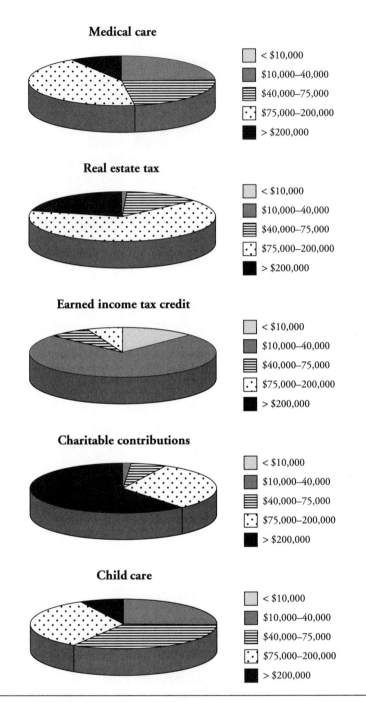

FIGURE 10.2   Distribution of Tax Expenditures by Income Level, 2007 (in percentages)
Source: Joint Committee on Taxation, *Estimates of Federal Tax Expenditures for Fiscal Years 2002–2008* (Washington, DC: U.S. Government Printing Office, October 2008).

TABLE 10.4   Opinions on Income Tax, 1963–2011 (in percentages)

"Do you consider the amount of federal income tax you pay too high, about right, or too low?"

Year	Too high	About right	Too low	No opinion
1963	52	38	1	8
1973	65	28	1	6
1985	63	32	1	4
1990	63	31	2	4
1994	56	42	—	2
1996	64	33	1	2
1998	66	31	1	2
2000	63	33	1	3
2001	65	31	1	3
2002	47	50	1	2
2003	50	46	2	2
2004	50	43	3	4
2005	61	44	2	3
2006	48	44	2	5
2007	37	55	1	7
2008	41	53	1	5
2009	46	47	1	6
2010	44	49	2	5
2011	43	50	2	5

Source: Gallup Polls, various years.

The public's other concern is whether all citizens are paying their fair share of taxes. Defining that *fair share* objectively is difficult, given the numerous conceptions of fairness,[14] but taxpayers do not appear to have any difficulty in defining fairness subjectively, as Table 10.4 shows. In the first place, it appears that although Americans tend to think that they pay too much in federal income tax, the numbers are not usually much over 50 percent. The number of citizens who think they pay too much tends to vary with economic and political circumstances. Comparison of the low numbers at the beginning of the Kennedy administration and the very high numbers during the years of the Vietnam War and Watergate suggests that these reactions may be as much measures of discontent with government as measures of actual resistance to the taxes themselves.[15] Interestingly, after years of declining confidence in government, when asked just before income taxes were due in 1997, over half of a sample of taxpayers maintained that they thought their taxes were fair, and today about half of taxpayers continue to think that the taxes they pay are generally fair.[16]

Citizens also have opinions about who else is, and should be, paying taxes. Most people see the need for some progressivity in the income tax structure; on average, they think that lower-income and middle-income people pay too much and the upper echelons of the income ladder pay too little. The large proportion who believes that middle-income people pay too much tax in part reflects the fact that most Americans think of themselves as middle class and think that they themselves pay too much federal tax. Feelings about tax unfairness were exacerbated by the George W. Bush administration's tax cuts, which went differentially to higher-income payers.[17] The administration pointed out that almost all taxpayers received some benefit from the reductions, but the differences became increasingly visible to the public.[18]

The fairness of the tax cuts passed during the Bush administration has remained an important political issue and was especially significant during the deficit debate (see chapter 7). There was implacable opposition to repealing those cuts from the Republicans in Congress, arguing that they were crucial for economic growth. At the same time, there was increasing evidence that the benefits of these tax reductions have contributed to the increasing income inequality in the United States.[19] Some very wealthy individuals, such as Warren Buffet, argued, however, that he and other wealthy people should pay more.

What does the public think of the loopholes built into the tax laws? Several surveys have produced similar findings (see Table 10.5). One is that the more commonly used deductions, such as the home mortgage deduction, are generally thought to be fair and desirable. Exemptions and deductions going to groups of people with special needs—the elderly and blind, for instance—are also considered fair. But those that are used primarily by the affluent, such as business entertainment deductions, are not considered good public policy. Again, the populism of American political culture can be seen in the beliefs that programs benefiting the average citizen and the "deserving poor" in society are good policies, but tax breaks for business and the more affluent are not.

Value for Money

Members of the public also evaluate taxes according to what they believe they receive in return—is the tax "price" for the goods and services government provides worth it, or not? Americans tend to answer that question rather differently for different levels of government. In most surveys, local governments are perceived to deliver the most for the money while the federal government delivers the least. This is perhaps to be expected, given that the federal government collects the most in tax revenue (over 60 percent in 2007) and delivers the fewest direct services to the public. Citizens see local firefighters and state workers repairing highways but see relatively few federal employees at work. When a

TABLE 10.5   Poll Respondents' Views about Fairness of Tax Deductions and Exemptions
(in percentages)

A. Perceived fairness of deductions

	Fair	Unfair	Percentage of respondents using this deduction
Charitable contributions	84	16	51
State and local taxes	76	24	32
Capital gains	51	49	12
Mortgage interest on second home	50	50	7
Fringe benefits at work	28	72	30
Business entertainment	22	78	7

B. Perceived legitimacy of deductions and exemptions

	Legitimate	Illegitimate
Elderly exemption	95	5
Blind exemption	95	5
Property tax on homeowners	93	7
Social Security income[a]	92	8
Home mortgage	92	8
Charitable contributions	71	29
Municipal bonds[b]	53	47
Capital gains	48	52

C. When two families have the same income,
do you think it is fair or unfair that one family pays less tax because they:

	Fair	Unfair	Don't know
(a) Have more dependent children	76	23	1
(b) Give more to charity	62	36	3
(c) Have more medical expenses	71	27	2
(d) Receive more income from investments	42	52	6
(e) Have a home mortgage while the other family does not	55	41	4

Sources: Sections A and B from "Tax Americana," *Public Opinion,* February/March 1986, 28; Section C, from Kaiser Foundation/Kennedy School of Government Poll, April 2003.

a. When the question about the legitimacy of deductions was asked, Social Security was totally exempt from tax; it is now 50 percent exempt.

b. Interest on municipal bonds is not taxable by the federal government.

citizen does see a federal employee, it may be an Internal Revenue Service employee or a customs agent going through his or her baggage. The federal government simply is not perceived as providing many direct services to the public.[20]

Citizens also tend to evaluate "sin taxes" positively. That is, they are likely to support taxation of alcohol, tobacco, gambling, and the like, even if they would not support other types of taxation. Voters in the state of Washington were willing to increase the price of cigarettes (most of which is tax) to $5 a pack. In one poll, almost three-quarters of the respondents said that they would accept a 5 percent increase in alcohol taxes, and almost 80 percent supported increasing alcohol taxes to pay for social programs.[21] The support for this type of taxation appears to come less from moral judgments than from a sense that people who spend money in those ways also have the money to pay taxes; the feeling is heightened when the tax is earmarked for a popular policy such as education. Furthermore, these taxes are easily avoidable, so people have only themselves to blame if they must pay them. Finally, governments tend to like these taxes because the demand for such products appears relatively inelastic—they are able to pile on high levels of tax, and the public will still buy the products.[22] There is, however, some backlash against these excise taxes among conservatives, who argue that they are simply another government limitation on individual freedom to choose one's own way of life.[23]

Both survey and behavioral evidence indicate that citizens want to have greater certainty about where their tax money is going. In surveys, citizens appear to support earmarked taxes, such as a gasoline tax to be spent on transportation needs, more than they do general taxation. If the question is simply whether respondents would vote to raise taxes, there tends to be a negative majority, but when the increase is linked to a particular expenditure—especially a popular one such as Social Security or public education—there tends to be a positive majority.

The issue of willingness to pay taxes arose very clearly in early 2001 when newly inaugurated president George W. Bush launched his efforts to push through a tax cut. At the time, a substantial budget surplus had been accumulated, and so there was a sense that sufficient money was available for spending programs, reducing the national debt, or reducing taxes. When confronted with these possibilities, citizens said they would be willing to forgo tax reductions in favor of preserving either Medicare or Social Security or both, but they favored a tax reduction over paying down the federal debt.[24] In another poll, more than 60 percent of respondents said that health, education, and Social Security were more important than a tax cut.[25] Since that time, a number of polls have demonstrated that citizens continue to want services as much as they want lower taxes.[26]

Responding in a survey that one would be willing to pay more taxes is relatively easy. A more pertinent question is whether one would actually behave that way. At the state and local levels, citizens have the opportunity to vote for or against proposals for tax increases. For some time, the approval of Proposition 13, which limited property taxes in California, made it appear that a "tax revolt" was under way and that citizens would not accept any new taxes.[27] It now appears, however, that voters have been making somewhat more sophisticated policy choices and are willing to support taxes for particular programs, while tending to oppose more general tax increases. For example, in the 2008 elections, voters approved almost two-thirds of tax referendums that linked a clear purpose to the tax, and even after several years of fiscal problems, more than half of referenda with specific expenditures attached were successful in 2010. Citizens appear to demand a clear quid pro quo in taxation.

Choices in Tax Policy

Americans obviously have made a number of choices concerning taxation that are different from the choices made in other industrialized countries, although tax reform in many countries has tended to make tax policies increasingly similar.[28] The aggregate figures presented above in Table 10.1 represent taxation decisions made by thousands of individual governments, although the federal government, as mentioned, accounts for approximately two-thirds of all taxes. What criteria might those governments be employing when they make their decisions about taxes?

Collectibility

Government must consider its ability to collect a tax and, even more important, the potential of the tax to yield enough revenue to justify the cost incurred in collecting it. The administration of taxes is expensive, and it has political costs in addition to its economic costs. One of the many criticisms of the U.S. tax system, both at the federal level and with respect to the problems resulting from multiple levels of taxation, is that its complexity makes it difficult to administer. There are very large burdens on citizens, businesses, and government itself that various alternative systems might alleviate.[29]

The two major tax "handles" for modern, industrialized governments are *income taxes* and *expenditure taxes*. By definition, almost all money in an economy is both income and expenditure, and governments can raise revenue by tapping either or both streams of economic transactions. Given that in modern economies most income is earned and most purchases are made in relatively large and identifiable organizations, governments can employ private bodies to do much of the tax collection for them. Employers typically withhold a portion of their employees' pay for income and Social Security taxes, and they are required to submit a detailed accounting of sales and profits for their own taxes. These procedures impose a cost on the private sector—one estimate is that it costs businesses over $148 billion to comply with tax laws—but they make the collection of revenue easier and less expensive for government.[30] Individual citizens also do a great deal of the work: The Internal Revenue Service has estimated that the average taxpayer requires 9.4 hours a year to keep records and to fill out and file the forms for the federal income tax. That amounts to over a billion hours of work a year for all taxpayers.[31]

The major tax handle for local governments, the property tax, is more difficult to collect. Although a house or business is a very visible piece of property, its value may be difficult to assess. Local governments have difficulty keeping their property tax rolls up to date. As a consequence, local revenues tend to lag behind inflation, and local governments must spend a good deal of time and money to assess property and collect the taxes due. Because these taxes often must be paid all at once, they are also more visible to the public. With declining property values and numerous foreclosures in 2008 and 2009, local governments found it difficult to collect the revenue they need for essential services.[32]

Fiscal Neutrality

As well as being collectible, a "good" tax is one that does not create significant distortions in the economy.[33] That is to say, the tax system should not give preference to one kind of revenue or expenditure, unless there is a very good reason to do so. If the tax system were to advantage certain types of economic activities, it could direct resources away from their most productive use and probably reduce the rate of economic growth in the society. Prior to tax reform in 1986, the tax system in the United States contained a large number of special interest provisions (loopholes). These provisions provided citizens and corporations alike with incentives to use their money in ways that might be unproductive on economic grounds (such as investing in racehorses or in loss-making businesses) but that the existing tax system rendered lucrative.

The 1986 tax reform made the tax system more fiscally neutral, but special interests continue to try to gain special tax benefits for themselves. Every year since the passage of that major tax reform has seen some special preferences creep back into the tax laws.[34] Another attempt at major change in the mid-1990s actually resulted in more preferences being added to the tax system, and Congress and the president continue to battle over others, such as a tax deduction for tuition to private elementary and secondary schools (see chapter 13). A tax reform adopted in 2001 added some general tax preferences for parents with children in higher education but not the targeted assistance sought earlier. State and local tax systems also provide a number of tax benefits that can distort economic activity, most importantly the numerous tax incentives used to attract new industry to one place or another.

The problem of fiscal neutrality was very evident as the economic crisis unfolded in 2008–2009. The numerous tax advantages given to housing by the federal tax code had led to overinvestment in housing rather than in more productive assets. The problems were, of course, exacerbated by finance opportunities that led to extremely risky investments in housing, with many mortgages given to individuals with little hope of being able to pay off the mortgage.

Buoyancy

Raising revenue is unpopular politically, so any tax that can produce additional revenue without any political activity is a valuable tax for government. A *buoyant* tax is one whose yield keeps pace with, or perhaps exceeds, the pace of economic growth and/or inflation. In principle, the progressive income tax is a buoyant tax: As individuals earn more income, they pay not only higher taxes but also higher rates of tax, so there is a fiscal dividend from the tax, with government automatically receiving a higher proportion of national income. Taxes that require reassessments or rate adjustments to keep pace with inflation, such as the property tax, are not buoyant and hence may generate political difficulties if the real value of their yield is to be maintained. This effect was evident in the "tax revolt" against the property tax in a number of states.

The fiscal dividend associated with the progressive income tax during inflationary periods led to the indexation of tax brackets. That is, as inflation increases the money income of citizens without increasing their real income, the income levels at which taxes are first charged and at which tax rates change are raised, so tax rates change at the same rate as real income. Everything else being equal, real tax income for government should therefore remain constant, without legislative action to increase rates. This kind of change was an important thrust of tax reform during the first Reagan administration. In addition, the tax reform of 1986 decreased the progressivity of the tax system by reducing the number of tax brackets from fourteen to five and then effectively to three (two rates plus a surcharge) in 1990. That basic system has remained in place since, albeit with some adjustments in the brackets—there were six brackets in 2008—and rates.

The exception to the generally declining progressivity of the federal income tax is the increasing applicability of the alternative minimum tax (AMT). A provision of 1969 legislation, the AMT was intended to ensure that affluent taxpayers did not escape paying some share of taxes because of large deductions for mortgages or charitable contributions. The tax initially affected very few taxpayers, but the number has grown rapidly, largely because the legislation did not provide for indexation. As nominal incomes increase, thousands more taxpayers have to pay the AMT, and by 2010, one in five (and nearly every married taxpayer with an income between $100,000 and $500,000) became liable for higher taxes. Unfortunately, unlike better-designed tax policies, the AMT does not do an adequate job of targeting individuals who have been abusing the tax system.[35]

Distributive Effects

Taxes can alter the income distribution within a society. Such an effect is usually thought of as benefiting the less affluent at the expense of the more affluent. However, many taxes are actually *regressive*—that is, they take a larger proportion of income from the poor than from the rich. Regressive taxes, such as sales taxes and the Social Security tax, must be justified on other grounds, such as ease of collection or their similarity to insurance premiums.

The net impact of taxes on income distribution is difficult to calculate, especially if attention is given to the effects of the government expenditures that the taxes finance. Nevertheless, there does seem to be a general finding in the United States that both the poor—especially the working poor—and the rich pay higher rates of tax than the majority of citizens do, whereas the large majority of citizens pay approximately the same tax rate.[36] This issue became central to the political agenda in 2011 when Democrats in the Senate sought to increase taxation on the wealthy to help reduce the deficit.[37] And it became even more obvious when it became apparent that Governor Mitt Romney paid a lower tax rate than average working citizens.

It is especially important that the working poor pay such a high rate of tax. They tend to consume rather than save their income, which makes almost all their income subject to sales and excise taxes. Also, all of the income of poorer workers is subject to Social Security deductions, whereas the more affluent earn substantial income above the cutoff for the Social Security tax. As of 2008, Social Security contributions cease after $102,000 of income. Anyone earning that amount or less pays 6.2 percent of his or her income as Social Security contributions, although this is currently reduced by 2 percent to help stimulate the economy. People earning $200,000, on the other hand, pay only about 3.3 percent of their total income in Social Security taxes. Finally, the working poor are simply unable to take advantage of the loopholes in the tax system that the more affluent can use, and even if they could do so, the loopholes would be worth less at their lower tax rate.

Changes in the federal tax system over the past several decades have made it less progressive. The top rate of income tax was reduced from 70 percent to

33 percent during the Reagan and George H. W. Bush administrations, and the tax burden has been shifting slightly away from income taxation and toward excise and Social Security taxes and user fees.[38] These changes have been offset in part by eliminating a number of the less defensible loopholes in the tax laws that primarily benefited the rich. The decreased progressivity of the tax system was in large part affected very consciously, through efforts like Reagan's "supply-side" strategy, to place more money in the hands of affluent investors. While the Clinton administration shifted some of the tax burden back to the more affluent and corporations, its package also imposed heavier taxes on alcohol, tobacco, and energy—taxes that tend to fall disproportionately on the less affluent. The progressivity of the tax system was reduced markedly during the administration of George W. Bush. Those with incomes over $100,000 actually paid a higher percentage of the total tax bill in 2005 than they did in 2000 (72 percent versus 67 percent), but the percentage of their income paid as income tax dropped from an average of 22.8 percent to 18.6 percent. Almost all the economic growth in that five-year period went to the more affluent, so they paid a higher total tax bill, although they were actually paying substantially lower tax rates.[39] Barack Obama's early budget resolutions signaled a move toward progressivity by increasing tax rates for those with incomes over $250,000.

Visibility

Public officials must be concerned about the political acceptability of taxes. This factor is often crucial, for low taxes are related to the historical traditions of the country, as well as to those of some states, whose populist political cultures regard the property tax as a threat to the "little man" who owns a house. The political acceptability of taxes may be a function of their visibility. Everything else being equal, the less visible a tax is, the more acceptable it will be.[40] Even though income tax is withheld from employees' checks each pay period, the citizen is still required to file a statement each year on which he or she sees the total tax account for the year. Similarly, homeowners typically receive property tax bills each year; in states and localities with high property taxes, the bills may seem huge. Both of these taxes are obvious to the taxpayer and therefore are likely to be resisted. The Social Security tax is less visible. Although it is deducted from paychecks along with the income tax, there is no annual reckoning that might bring the total tax bill to the citizen's attention, and furthermore, the employer pays half of the total Social Security bill.

The lack of a total tax bill is a very important element in a country with several levels of government, all of which levy taxes. The taxes are levied at different times and in different ways, so only the better-informed citizens are likely to know their total tax bills.[41] The United States is a low-tax country—in part because Americans want it that way—but the division among taxes and taxing units may make the total bill appear lower than it is. The "fiscal illusion" created by multiple taxing units helps to make taxes more palatable.[42] The political viability of the tax system is further enhanced because citizens tend to focus their ire on the federal government while permitting state and local taxes to creep upward.

The problem of tax visibility is one reason for considering a value-added tax (VAT) for the United States,[43] perhaps as a means of reducing the resurgent federal deficit. Unlike a sales tax, which is levied as the consumer pays for the commodity and is added on as a separate item, the VAT is levied at each stage of the production process and included in the price of the product when sold. As a result, the actual amount of the tax—and even the fact that a tax is being levied—may be largely hidden from the consumer, so there may be less political mobilization opposing it. Many fiscal conservatives are extremely wary of the VAT's invisibility, however, fearing that government could expand its activities without citizens' understanding what the real increases in their tax bill had been.

The Politics of Tax Reform

Taxation is different from most other kinds of policy in that it is essentially something that no one really wants and everyone seeks to avoid whenever possible. Former senator Russell Long of Louisiana, long a power on the Senate Finance Committee, encapsulated the nature of tax politics in this little ditty: "Don't tax you, don't tax me, tax that fellow behind the tree." The nature of tax politics is to attempt to divert the burden of taxation onto others and to build in special privileges for oneself. Because virtually no one in contemporary economic systems can avoid taxes, the next-best strategy is to ensure that everyone pays his or her fair share of the costs of government. It is partly for this reason that sales taxes are popular among all segments of society even though they are regressive.[44]

Compared with other forms of policymaking, tax policymaking has been relatively technical and legalistic.[45] The tax code is an extremely complex set of laws, made even more complex by rulings issued by the Internal Revenue Service and the tax courts concerning just what the code really means. In Congress, tax policymaking historically was the preserve of a relatively few powerful and knowledgeable Congress members and senators, such as Senator Long and former representative Wilbur Mills.[46] Changes in Congress, such as opening committee deliberations to greater "sunshine," have tended to lessen the power of the tax committees and the individuals who populate them, but finance committees still possess substantial political power.

The complexity of tax policymaking allows many special interests to have provisions they desire written into the tax code, with little notice by the general public. The special interests are represented by members of Congress whose constituencies may contain concentrations of one kind of industry or another. Adding loopholes to a tax law often is an exercise in coalition building through logrolling, as every member of Congress gets to add his or her provisions in return for support of the legislation as a whole. This process has produced a federal tax system, especially an income tax system, that many citizens perceive as highly unfair. In Harris surveys taken prior to tax reform in 1986, an average of 90 percent of respondents thought that the federal income tax was unfair, even though they thought their own taxes were about right.[47] Polls taken after the reforms were almost as negative about the tax structure, depending on how the question was asked, and the subsequent years have done little to enhance public confidence.

The Tax Reform Act of 1986

Any number of proposals for tax reform has been made in the United States, but the actual passage of a major tax reform in 1986 came as a surprise to most observers. Perhaps even more surprising was that the reform was as comprehensive as it was.[48] The tax system was simplified for the average taxpayer, a large number of the more egregious loopholes were removed, and the impact of the tax system on the less affluent was made somewhat more equitable. A year, or even a few months, prior to passage, such a change in the tax laws would have been thought impossible.

What happened to produce that major reversal of tax policymaking as usual? There is no simple answer to that question, but apparently a confluence of forces—liberal and conservative, business and labor, producers and consumers—all wanted change. President Ronald Reagan wanted to reduce the progressivity of taxes, allowing the more affluent to keep more of what they earned. Some of his conservative allies wanted to eliminate special preferences for certain industries, to produce a more equal operating environment for all industries as a means of stimulating economic growth.[49] Liberals also supported the elimination of special preferences that benefited the rich but that middle- and low-income groups could not take advantage of. Several policy entrepreneurs made heavy political investments to bring about major policy change.[50] It was a rare opportunity for advocates of various reform proposals to bring about significant change in the tax structure.[51]

Tax Reform in the 1990s

Another significant tax reform came in the later 1990s, as President Clinton and the Republican Congress finally managed to agree on some transformation of the tax code. Unlike the 1986 reform, however, these changes tended to build in more special provisions and loopholes rather than eliminate them. The final shape of the bill reflected a good deal of negotiation and logrolling between a conservative Congress and a more liberal president and represented a return to the old "Christmas tree" style of tax legislation. Although this tax bill was presented as an effort to be fairer to American families, especially those in the middle class, in reality it tended to benefit as many special interests as it disadvantaged, or more.

Perhaps the major change made in the 1997 legislation was reduction of the capital gains tax. If a citizen invests in stocks, bonds, a piece of land, or whatever—with the notable exception of houses—and later sells it at a profit, he or she has received a capital gain that is subject to tax, though at a lower rate than ordinary income. Some politicians and economists argue that this investment profit is income, and there is no justification for treating it differently from any other type of income. Indeed, given that only the more affluent in the society generally have capital gains on anything other than houses, eliminating the tax on capital gains would make the federal tax system less progressive than it is. Furthermore, a low capital gains tax, or none at all, would encourage speculation in all sorts of assets and might make the stock market and other financial markets more volatile than they already are. There are also good arguments in favor of lowering or eliminating capital gains taxation. In the first place, high capital gains taxes tend to discourage investment or, at least, do not reward investors for making good choices; investments involve risk, and having to pay full tax rates if the risk is justified does not seem fair. Moreover, capital gains are generally counted in current dollar terms and do not take into account the effects of inflation, which may make an apparently large return on an investment actually trivial.[52] Finally, an aversion to paying capital gains taxes may encourage some investors to hold onto assets after they have ceased to be as productive as would alternative uses of the same money; this is another way in which the tax system can distort the use of resources in the economy and reduce economic growth.

The combination of a soaring stock market and fears about the viability of Social Security as a source of retirement income brought about a change in the structure of investment in the United States in 1997. Many more people began to invest in the stock market, with over 40 percent of households placing some money in the market. Capital gains taxation thus became a more general issue, rather than just a concern for the wealthy, and that allowed politicians to lower the rate from 28 percent to 20 percent.[53] The 1997 legislation also repealed some credits for business investment, which may have had some long-term negative impact on economic growth in the United States. In short, tax reform was a desirable policy goal, but like almost any policy change, it was not without its critics and its negative consequences. Furthermore, it demonstrated that tax policy tends to be an area in which the conflict between conservative and progressive ideas appears very stark.

Tax Reform in the George W. Bush Administration

In 2001 and 2003, President George W. Bush won enactment of tax reforms, arguing that tax rates needed to be reduced to encourage economic growth and to put money back in the hands of ordinary citizens.[54] His proposals reflected his conservative ideology and were first made in the context of a large projected surplus in the federal budget. All taxpayers received reduced rates and an immediate refund, which was designed to provide a boost for a slowing economy. The tax "reform" of 2001 was, however, in many ways the reverse of the reforms that had preceded it, making the tax system more complex rather than simplifying it. A number of new loopholes were added, some of which benefited more-affluent citizens and corporations, and some of which—such as support for parents paying for their children's college education—were more generally available.

Another tax policy change introduced in the George W. Bush administration was the gradual reduction, and possible elimination, of the estate tax. The federal government for decades has collected a tax on estates over a certain size when their owners die. The Republican Party has been pushing for several years to have that tax eliminated, characterizing it as a "death tax" and arguing that it makes it more difficult for small-business owners to pass along a family business or farm to their children. Republicans also argue that the money in an estate has already been taxed once by the income tax, so it is unfair to tax it again. Although the vast majority of estates in the United States—98 percent, in fact—fall below the threshold at which the tax is imposed, these points have proved to be a powerful political argument.

The Democrats in Congress, on the other hand, have tended to favor retaining the estate tax, although they are generally willing, or even anxious, to raise the threshold at which the tax is first imposed—$3.5 million in 2009.[55] Supporters' justification for retaining the estate tax is the one associated with all forms of progressive taxation—the ability to pay—combined with a desire to level the playing field between generations. Indeed, part of the argument for retaining the estate tax is the classic capitalist argument that everyone should have to earn his or her own way in the world, and the tax has been supported publicly by extremely wealthy individuals, such as Bill Gates Sr.[56] Democrats have also wondered where the money would come from to fill the revenue hole left if this tax were repealed. Even though it is less than 2 percent of total federal revenue, it still amounts to roughly $70 billion a year. Repeal of the tax was defeated in

2001 and 2002, but legislation since then has lowered the rate and increased the size of the estate exempted from taxation.

Additional tax cuts were approved in 2003, under pressure from the Bush administration, which argued that they were a means of stimulating a sluggish economy and of returning more money to the people who earned it. The cuts, however, were more beneficial to the affluent and therefore did not have the stimulative effect intended. For example, a significant proportion of the total tax cut came in reduced taxes on stock dividends, an income source of little importance to the average worker. The reduction on dividend income was meant to raise the level of saving and investment in the economy, but several years after the change, the net savings rate in the United States remains stuck near zero (see chapter 9).

Tax Reform in the Obama Administration

Although President Obama promised to address some of the inequalities produced by tax reforms during the Bush administration, the economic crisis beginning in 2008 did not leave much time or financial space for any immediate fundamental reforms. That said, early in his term, Obama attacked tax loopholes for companies that were located in "tax havens"—countries with low or no taxes and strong privacy laws for companies.[57] Critics argue that this will cause companies to move away from the United States, but the proposals have also been praised as increasing fairness in the system.

Once the administration confronts more fundamental reforms, its intention appears to be to increase taxes on incomes over $250,000 per annum. The first installment of this reform was contained as a part of the stimulus package, providing citizens with a $400 tax cut for 2009. Obama also enlisted Paul Volcker, chair of the new Economic Recovery Advisory Board, to conduct a sweeping review of the tax code. The expected costs of health care reform have also produced a new discussion of a value-added tax for the United States.[58] It seems clear that this administration has addressed tax reform but also that it has a number of other important issues confronting it. Furthermore, the administration has confronted steadfast opposition from Republicans in Congress to any increases in taxes, and especially taxes on the more affluent.

Proposals for Further Fundamental Tax Reform

The tax reforms of 1986 and the less comprehensive reforms of the mid-1990s made significant changes in the tax system, but all were in the context of a progressive income tax, which is assumed as the basic source of federal revenue. That assumption, however, is being questioned in numerous proposals for reform that range from shifting the income tax to a flat rate on all income, to shifting away from the personal income tax to either integrated corporate taxation or consumption taxation. All of the proposals have some merit, but all also have political and economic costs. Perhaps the major cost of any sweeping reform of the tax system would be political: Americans may not like the existing tax system, but moving to a different system would be likely to make taxation more visible and provoke more resistance.

The flat tax.   One logical alternative to the current system is a simple, flat tax on all income, regardless of source, eliminating almost all deductions and loopholes for expenditures. The advocates of such a change argue that it would be fairer, treating all income and expenditure equally, and treating all citizens equally. The simpler, flat tax also could eliminate a good number of jobs in the Internal Revenue Service (IRS) and in the private sector tax-reporting industry, as well as reduce distress over the way in which people believe they are (mis) treated by the IRS.[59] On more technical grounds, the flat tax would be more fiscally neutral, so that decisions about how to invest could be made based on economic considerations rather than tax considerations.

As might be expected, the flat tax also has critics. First, it would almost certainly be a regressive move from the current tax structure, with the affluent having to pay less than they do now and benefiting at the expense of the larger population. The flat tax is usually discussed in the range of 17 percent of total income—a substantially lower rate than the more affluent now pay, on average, in income tax.[60] The flat tax would also eliminate the possibility of using the tax system for other public policy purposes. Despite problems with some loopholes in the tax system, tax expenditures have been a powerful tool for addressing other policy concerns, especially housing and support for charities.[61] A shift to a flat tax might also require some shifting of state tax structures, given that several states calculate their own income taxes as a percentage of the federal tax.

National consumption tax.   A more extreme solution to the problems in the federal income tax system is to move from an income tax to a consumption tax. Americans are used to general consumption taxes being levied by state and local governments in the form of sales taxes. The federal government has only used specific consumption taxes, such as those on alcohol, tobacco, and gasoline. Many other developed economies, in contrast, raise a large proportion of their revenue through a national consumption tax, usually the VAT.

The logic of a consumption tax is, first, that it places the burden on spending rather than on earning money. If one of the problems of the American economy is inadequate savings, it makes sense to tax spending money rather than saving it. Another positive aspect of the consumption tax is that it would require everyone in the society to pay some part of the tax burden. We noted earlier that Americans want to be sure that all citizens participate in funding government, and a consumption tax would certainly require that. Furthermore, the consumption tax would place the burden of record keeping on businesses, rather than the general public, thus eliminating some citizen frustrations with the tax system.

No tax is perfect, and there would certainly be some drawbacks to a consumption tax. First, to raise the same amount of money the federal government now collects, the tax rate would have to be roughly 30 percent on all purchases.[62] This is about four times higher than the highest rate of sales tax in the states and would produce a huge, if one-time-only, increase in prices.[63] Also, this alternative form of taxation would be regressive because, on average, the poor spend a much higher proportion of their income than do the more affluent. As with state and local sales taxes, a national consumption tax could be made less regressive by excluding items such as food, medicine, clothing, and the like, but then the tax rate on other goods and services would have to be even higher. Given that businesses, rather than individuals, would be liable for the consumption tax, government could not use the tax system for other purposes, such as providing the important earned income tax credit as a means of subsidizing the wages of the poor.

Some of the objections to a national consumption tax based on business transactions could be met by adopting a personal consumption tax, by which individual taxpayers would report all the money they had earned during the year and then subtract the amount they had saved. The difference would represent consumption, and it would be subject to tax.[64] This system, however, would require personal filings and would therefore require as large and intrusive an IRS as exists at present. Indeed, it might be even more difficult for the average citizen to set a correct level of tax withholding throughout the year, so that more refunds or large payments could be due at filing. It might also be difficult to determine what constitutes "savings" under this form of taxation. Are consumer durable goods savings? A house almost certainly would be, but what about a car or a washing machine?

Conservatives complain that a national consumption tax could be more easily hidden from the public than other types of taxes, given that it probably would be a part of the price of the product rather than a separate item to be paid. At a rate of 30 percent, taxpayers would notice it, but at a lower rate, to supplement the income tax, they might not. Thus, the government could use this tax to expand its revenues without the political opposition that conservatives believe could, and should, otherwise arise. Some conservatives argue that taxing consumption would be a way of punishing the more affluent for their success, rather than rewarding them for it, and therefore might be at least as great an economic disincentive as the income tax.[65] This would be especially true if differential rates of consumption tax were charged for luxury items, such as jewelry or expensive cars and boats.

Integrating corporate and personal taxation.   A more technical recommendation for changing the existing tax code is to integrate corporate and personal taxation—usually called the "comprehensive business income tax." The basic concept is that if most income earners in the United States work for some sort of organization, then those organizations, rather than the individual citizens they employ, would make the tax filings. Individual wages might be taxed, but the tax revenue could be collected at the source, leaving primarily the self-employed having to make individual filings.

Advocates give at least two reasons for such a change in the tax system. The first is to make tax administration easier. If corporations, with their computerized record keeping, could be made responsible for most tax filings, the job of collecting income taxes would be much easier. If nothing else, it would mean that "only" 24 million tax returns would be filed, compared with the current nearly 140 million.[66] Some individuals would still be responsible for filing tax forms for items such as capital gains, but the bulk of the work of record keeping and filing would be done by businesses, which have better capacities for keeping the records.

The argument for an integration of personal and corporate taxation focuses on the economic consequences of the present tax structure. Under the current system, there is some double taxation of business profits—they are taxed when the corporation earns the profits and taxed again when they are paid out to individuals as stock dividends. Double taxation is believed by many economists to tax corporate income excessively and therefore to deter investment (although it may also give firms an incentive to reinvest their profits rather than distribute them). Integration of the two forms of taxation, it is argued, would facilitate investment and savings. Some tax relief for dividends in the tax reform legislation of 2002 has reduced the level of double taxation, but it remains a viable issue.

Summary

Taxation is one public policy that most citizens would prefer not to think about but one that occupies a good deal of their time (and money). It is also the subject of a number of myths, not least of which is that the United States is a high-tax country.[67] Taxation may be anathema to most members of the public, but it is the central means for government to obtain the money it needs to survive and to provide public services. In addition to simply raising adequate revenue for survival, tax policy is also used to attain a number of policy goals. The tax expenditures through which those goals are reached are among the most controversial features of tax policy. Although in some ways an efficient means of reaching policy goals, they provide benefits to some segments of the society that may appear unfair to those who are not able to benefit from them.

Although many people are dissatisfied with the existing structure of taxation in the United States, reform remains extremely difficult. There has been one major tax reform in recent history, but its success in making the tax system simpler and fairer appears to be further diluted with each passing year. The consequences of reforming capital gains taxation in 1997 are yet to be fully understood, and given wider stock ownership, the changes seem likely to have wider impact than would have been true even a few years ago. There are few powerful political forces on the side of tax reform, but there are numerous forces attempting to use the tax system to feather their own economic and social nests. Even though most Americans are not keen on paying taxes, they would be more likely to tolerate, and comply with, a tax system that appeared fair and equitable.

CHAPTER 11

Health Care Policies

WHEN WE PICK UP our morning newspaper or watch the nightly news, we are likely to see a story about a new wonder cure for some dread disease or a person who could not get medical care because he or she did not have medical insurance. These two types of stories highlight the paradox of health care in the United States: In a country with some of the very best medical care in the world and in which huge sums are spent on medical research, approximately one person in five does not have regular access to medical care.

This paradox of medical care is a public policy problem. One great myth of American political life and public policy is that we have a primarily, or even purely, private health care system. In fact, in 2009, more than 44 percent of all health care spending in the United States was by federal government agencies of some sort, and many physicians who loudly proclaim the virtues of private medical care receive a substantial portion of their income from public medical programs, such as Medicare, Medicaid, and the State Children's Health Insurance Program (SCHIP) (see Figure 11.1).[1] On average, 81,000 patients receive treatment in Veterans Administration hospitals every day, and millions of other patients are treated in hospitals operated by state and local governments. The public sector makes a much smaller proportion of total health expenditures in the United States than it does in most other industrialized democracies, but government involvement in the provision of health care is nevertheless significant.

The extent of American government involvement in health care can be seen in part in the health care programs listed in Table 11.1. All three levels of government, including a wide variety of federal agencies, are to some degree involved in health care. Almost all the cabinet-level departments have some health care functions, as do a number of independent executive agencies. Their involvement ranges from directly providing medical care to some segments of the population (as do the Departments of Defense, Interior, and Veterans Affairs), through funding medical care for the general public, through regulating some aspects of medical care or the environmental causes of disease, to subsidizing medical research.

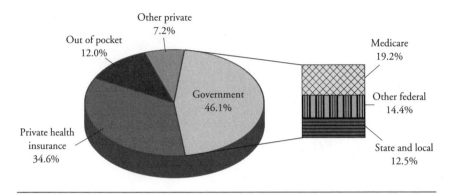

FIGURE 11.1   Sources of Payment for Health Care, 2007

Source: Centers for Medicare and Medicaid Services, *National Health Expenditure Data, 1960–2007,* www.cms.hhs.gov/NationalHealthExpendData/02_NationalHealthAccounts Historical.asp.

Without involvement of the public sector, American health care would certainly be very different and probably not as good as it is. It would not be as accessible to the poor, to children, and to the elderly, and the overall technical quality would probably not be as high as it currently is for those who nominally pay all their medical expenses privately. For one thing, the federal government is a major source of funds for medical research (over $27 billion in 2009). Without that government funding, many familiar and crucial medical advances would not have been made or would at least have been delayed.

Although the role of government in health care is larger than most American citizens believe it to be, it is still not as great as many people believe it should be. Rather than opt for more action on medical care, recent Republican administrations have reduced the federal role by cutting back federal health funding and converting categorical programs that subsidized health care at the state and local levels into block grants. Because the effectiveness of block grant programs depends much more on the priorities of state governments for implementation, there is some evidence that the states have been limiting their funding of the very expensive Medicaid program, thus reducing the quality and quantity of health care for the very poor. In 2010, well over fifty million Americans had no medical insurance, public or private, and many more had insurance that was inadequate for the risks they may face.

The problems of cost and access to care have helped produce demands for more public involvement in health care, including continuing interest in national health insurance.[2] A survey in 2007 reported that 64 percent of respondents wanted some form of universal medical care, although they disagreed on

TABLE II.I   Major Health Programs

Federal	State	Local
Department of Agriculture	State hospitals	City hospitals
Meat inspections	State mental hospitals	Sanitation
	Medicaid	Public health
	Substance abuse	
Department of Defense		
Health care for military and families		
Department of Health and Human Services		
Food and Drug Administration		
Community Health Services		
Indian Health Services		
National Institutes of Health		
Substance abuse programs		
Health education		
HMO loan funds		
U.S. Public Health Service		
Medicare		
Medicaid		
Department of the Interior		
Territorial health programs		
Department of Labor		
Occupational Safety and Health		
Department of Veterans Affairs		
VA hospitals		

the characteristics of such a program.[3] The same survey found that 75 percent of the respondents wanted fundamental changes in health care. It is one policy area in which the conservative policy ideas of past decades encounter substantial skepticism, for more than half the population has said for some time that the federal government should have a primary role in financing health care.[4] On the other hand, with typical ambivalence about government, Americans appear to want universal access to medical care without large-scale government programs.

Health care reform was a major campaign issue in 2008, and in 2009, President Obama and a scant majority of Democrats in Congress were able to pass the Affordable Care Act. This was a complex piece of legislation addressing a range of concerns in health care, but the central feature of the legislation was an individual mandate requiring that individuals who were not covered by

President Barack Obama signs the Patient Protection and Affordable Care Act on March 23, 2010. The health care act represented the first widespread involvement of the federal government in providing health insurance to the population.

employers or a public program, such as Medicaid, to purchase at least minimal coverage. This insurance would be subsidized for those with limited income who were not eligible for Medicaid. The public continues to favor health care reform in general, but the majority of citizens say they do not favor the specific legislation.

Although the major political concern has been creation of a *national* program of health insurance, the states have begun to put their own programs into place to cover the uninsured (see Table 11.2). There are marked differences, however, in levels of coverage. Some states in the Northeast have increased coverage dramatically, while in one state, Texas, almost a quarter of the population is not covered by any form of insurance. Hawaii already has a public health care system that, along with private insurance, covers almost the entire population of the state, and in 2006, Massachusetts passed legislation mandating that individuals have health insurance—the model for the federal program.[5] Maine has adopted a program to help cover the uninsured using public funds.[6] Individual states also have innovated in delivery of Medicaid services to improve coverage, although more recently the emphasis has been on lowering costs. Many states have added substantial coverage for children, funded at least in part by the federal government as a part of the welfare reforms of 1996 and SCHIP, which was enacted

TABLE 11.2   Percentage of Population Not Covered by Health Insurance, 2010

Low		High	
Hawaii	7.7	Texas	24.6
Minnesota	9.8	New Mexico	21.6
Vermont	10.0	Mississippi	21.1
Massachusetts	6.4	Nevada	21.3
Maine	9.3	Florida	20.9
	U.S. average: 15.9		

Source: U.S. Census Bureau, *Current Population Reports,* P60-226 (annual).

in 1997.[7] The major question about the public role in health care therefore appears to be the extent of federal government involvement, not whether or not the public sector should be involved.[8]

Problems in Health Care

The United States is one of the richest countries in the world, and it spends a much larger proportion of its economic resources (as a proportion of gross domestic product) on health care than does any other industrialized nation (see Table 11.3). The results of those expenditures, however, are not so impressive. In infant mortality, a commonly used indicator of the quality of medical care, the United States ranks *forty-eighth* in the world, behind most western European countries, Japan, Taiwan, and Singapore.[9] Depending on one's perspective, these figures are made better or worse if the total is disaggregated by race. For the white population in the United States, the infant mortality rate is as low as those of all but a few western European and Asian countries (3.5 per 1,000 live births in 2010). Among minorities, however, the U.S. rate is closer to those of much poorer countries (see Table 11.4). The infant mortality rate for African Americans (12.8 per 1,000 live births) is closer to rates found in the countries of the former Soviet bloc and some South American countries. Moreover, the disparity between black and white infant mortality has actually increased since 1970.

Health care of absolutely the finest quality is available in the United States, but it may be available only to a limited (and perhaps declining) portion of the population. Vast disparities in access exist among U.S. racial, economic, and geographical groups; even with Medicare, Medicaid, and other public programs, the poor, the elderly, and those living in rural areas receive less medical care and poorer care, than do white, middle-class, urban citizens.[10] Individuals in those groups report that their own health is poor, compared to that of more advantaged Americans (see Figure 11.2). Additionally, an increasing number of

TABLE 11.3   Health Expenditures as a Percentage of Gross Domestic Product, 2006

Country	Total	Public sector
United States	16.4	7.3
France	13.8	8.8
Switzerland	13.6	7.9
Germany	12.4	8.9
Austria	11.3	8.6
Canada	10.8	8.7
Sweden	10.4	8.4
Japan	9.9	7.8
Ireland	9.7	8.0
United Kingdom	9.0	8.0
Poland	7.3	5.9

Source: Organization for Economic Cooperation and Development, *Health Data 2006* (Paris: OECD, 2006).

TABLE 11.4   Infant Mortality Rates, 2009 (per 1,000 live births)

Japan	2.8	Jordan	15.0
Germany	4.0	Malaysia	15.9
Spain	4.2	Mexico	18.4
Netherlands	4.7	Syria	25.9
Canada	5.0	Bangladesh	59.0
Italy	5.5	Ethiopia	80.8
United States (white)	5.7	Zambia	101.2
Poland	6.8	Afghanistan	152.0
United States (black)	13.8	Angola	180.2

Source: CIA World Factbook 2009, www.cia.gov/library/publications/the-world-factbook/index.html.

middle-class citizens are beginning to be squeezed out of the medical care market because of rapidly increasing prices and less employer-provided health insurance. The problems that Americans confront in health care are three: access, cost, and quality.

Access to Medical Care

For any medical care system to function effectively, prospective patients must have access to it. A number of factors can deter citizens from becoming patients, and one purpose of public involvement in the medical marketplace must be to equalize access for all. Americans still differ on the extent to which they believe

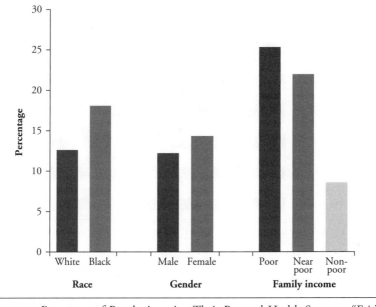

FIGURE II.2   Percentage of People Assessing Their Personal Health Status as "Fair" or "Poor," 2007

Source: U.S. Centers for Disease Control and Prevention, *Summary of Health Statistics for U.S. Adults: National Health Interview Survey, 2007.*

that equal access to medical care should be a right of citizenship ensured by the government, but most accept that all citizens require some form of protection at least against serious illnesses.[11]

The most commonly cited barrier to access to health care is economic. As most medical care in the United States is still paid for privately, those who lack sufficient income or insurance—again, there are almost fifty million Americans who do not have health insurance (see Figure II.3)—may not be able to afford it. Despite several public health care programs, medicine is still not as available to the poor as it is to the more affluent. As of 2008, approximately 30 percent of all those with incomes below the official poverty line were not eligible to receive Medicaid benefits—they were poor, but not sufficiently poor to qualify under Medicaid means tests. They are primarily the working poor, who are often employed in jobs without health care benefits and who are not eligible for Medicaid, as they would be if they were on welfare. Only 24 percent of the poor have any privately financed health insurance, and only 10 percent have any nonhospital coverage.[12] Even the elderly poor, who have Medicare because of age, must still pay for some components of their insurance, and poverty may deter some from taking full advantage of the program.

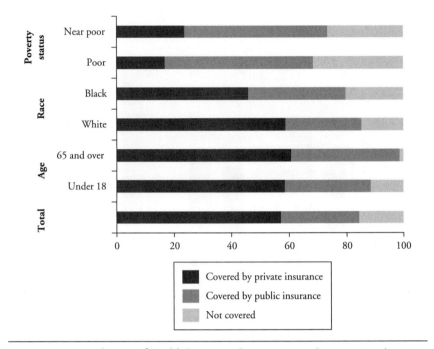

FIGURE II.3   Distribution of Health Insurance Coverage, 2007 (in percentages)

Source: Calculated from U.S. Census Bureau, *Statistical Abstract of the United States, 2007* (Washington, DC: U.S. Government Printing Office).

Note: Many citizens over age 65 have both Medicare and private "Medigap" insurance.

Members of the middle class are concerned about the rising cost of medical care and the possibility that catastrophic illness can render anyone but the very wealthy medically indigent. Most medical insurance plans have limits and may not completely cover lengthy and complicated illnesses, which can bankrupt even people who thought they were covered. Furthermore, lack of medical insurance is a problem not only for the poor. In 2008, almost two-thirds of the uninsured had incomes over $25,000 per year, and one-third had incomes over $50,000.[13] Over 80 percent of the uninsured live in families headed by people who work, usually for small firms in service industries, at least part of the year. Over half the uninsured had someone in the family who worked full time.[14] These numbers help to explain the continuing demand for reform of the U.S. health care system.

The problem of inadequate health insurance coverage is not going away; if anything, it is getting worse. From 1990 to 1995, private health insurance coverage dropped from 75 percent to 70.5 percent of the population; coverage declined further, to 68.6 percent in 2003 and then again to 67.9 percent in 2007. This decline of coverage occurred across all economic classes, hitting hardest those earning between $10,000 and $40,000 annually. In addition, workers who are covered by insurance arranged by their employers are currently required to pay, on average, more than twice as much of the total cost as they did several years ago. Even with some expansion of public coverage (largely because the population is aging and more are covered by Medicare), the total proportion of the population without insurance continues to increase.

In the contemporary U.S. medical care system, having insurance, as well as not having it, can present troubles. A worker in a job that provides health benefits may find it difficult to leave that job for one that may be better in other respects but does not offer health benefits. Thus, insurance can minimize labor mobility in the economy. In some cases, even if the new job provides insurance, that insurance will not cover preexisting conditions. If a prospective employee or a family member has been diagnosed with any serious condition that cannot be covered by the new insurance, moving between jobs may be impossible. The 1996 Kennedy-Kassebaum bill required increased portability of medical insurance, so that fewer people would lose coverage if they changed jobs.[15]

Even if economic barriers to medical care were removed, there might still be significant noneconomic barriers. Interestingly, even under the almost entirely free medical care system of the United Kingdom, differences in health status by social or economic class have not narrowed significantly.[16] Each social class is healthier on average, but disparities between the wealthy and the poor remain, indicating that there are other barriers to consuming health care, and perhaps more important, barriers to creating health, that are not removed simply by free access. Members of the poor and working classes may lose hourly wages if they go to the doctor, whereas salaried employees either do not lose pay or can take personal leave. Transportation is generally easier for the more affluent, whereas the poor rely on public transportation.

Communication is becoming perhaps the most important barrier to more equal access. More affluent and educated citizens know better how to get what they want from professional and bureaucratic organizations than do the poor, and they are more likely to be well treated by individuals and institutions than are the less well-off. A doctor is more likely to pay serious attention to the description of symptoms coming from a middle-class patient than to that from a poor patient, and the middle-class patient is more likely to demand extra diagnostic procedures and treatment. There is also some evidence that doctors do not pay adequate attention to the complaints of the elderly. Communication and bureaucratic skills are especially important in "managed care," in which numerous gatekeepers try to limit expenditures; generally, only the articulate and persistent are able to get what they want.[17] So even if all direct economic barriers were removed, there might still be serious barriers to equality in medical care, especially as the poor are generally not as healthy to begin with as the more affluent, and as a consequence may require more medical care.

These socioeconomic differences in access to health care are manifested in differential health outcomes among racial groups in the United States. Large differences appear on a number of indicators of health quality, such as chronic diseases and maternal mortality, the rate of which is more than three times higher among African Americans than for the remainder of the population.[18] The incidence of tuberculosis is also three times higher among African Americans, and deaths from diabetes-related causes occur at double the rate in the population as a whole. There is ample evidence that medical personnel do not always provide the same quality of care to members of minority groups as they do to white Americans.[19]

In addition to economic conditions and racial considerations, geography plays a significant, dual role in defining access to medical care. First, urban areas are generally better served by doctors, and especially hospitals, than rural areas. For example, in Standard Metropolitan Statistical Areas (SMSAs) in the United States, the average number of physicians per 100,000 population is 221, and the average number of hospital beds per 100,000 is 437. This contrasts with 93 physicians per 100,000 and 394 hospital beds per 100,000 in the non-SMSA regions of the country. The geographical disparities in medical services would be even more pronounced if physicians' areas of specialization and hospitals' standards and equipment were also considered. The imbalance in care does not necessarily equate with health outcomes, however. The District of Columbia has not only one of the highest ratios of physicians to population (799 per 100,000, compared to a national average of 267) but also perhaps the worst health outcomes in the country, with infant mortality more than double the national average. In 2005, the rate was 25 percent higher than in the next highest territorial unit, Mississippi.[20]

Second, there are marked regional imbalances in access to medical care. These can be related in part to urban-rural differences, but not entirely. The places in the United States best served by physicians and hospitals are the middle Atlantic states and the states of the Far West, while the worst served are the Upper Midwest and the Deep South. There are, for example, 462 doctors per 100,000 people in Massachusetts, and 415 per 100,000 in Maryland, but only 177 per 100,000 in Mississippi and 169 per 100,000 in Idaho. Although a variety of programs, public and private, have attempted to equalize the distribution, imbalances persist. The maldistribution is not as great for hospital beds, as many small communities have been able to maintain hospitals, in part to try to attract physicians and other health care workers.[21] But there is some evidence that residents of poor and rural states do not receive the same quality of medical care even when services are available.[22]

Thus, in some parts of the United States, high-quality medical care may not be available, even for someone who can afford it, without a substantial investment in travel. For any serious emergency, distance places the affected individual at even greater risk. Several pilot programs to encourage young doctors to practice in rural, "underdoctored" areas have been tried, and more are being advocated, but pronounced inequalities persist. Many rural areas have tried on their own to attract physicians, sometimes offering to finance the medical education of a young person willing to practice in their town.[23] These issues of distribution must be addressed along with economic issues if there is to be greater equality in access to health care. The federal government instituted a program for funding rural health clinics, but even those facilities appear to go to the largest settlements eligible for assistance.[24] Additional programs for capital investments in rural areas were adopted in 2006 but the inequalities have largely been unchanged.

Finally, we should note that access may not be sufficient to ensure that medical care is successful. The relatively high rate of infant mortality (especially among the minority population) is often taken as an indicator of poor access to medical care, but there is some evidence that other factors may be as important. For example, the highest rates of infant mortality (by state) tend to be less closely related to the availability of medical personnel and facilities in the state, or even to per capita income, than to the family situations into which children are born. In particular, babies born to teenage women, especially if they are single, have significantly higher mortality rates than those born to women in their twenties and thirties.[25] Smoking and alcohol abuse tend to be more prevalent among less affluent and less educated members of the society, exacerbating problems of access to medical care.

Cost

The second fundamental problem that has troubled health care consumers and policymakers is the rapidly rising cost of medical care; this is the health care "problem that won't go away."[26] Not only is it not going away, but cost has also become the driving force in health policy, especially in the private sector. The majority of Americans with health insurance now participate in some sort of "managed care plan," with cost containment as its principal objective. Critics of managed care argue that cost concerns have become too dominant and that those plans need to ensure quality as much as minimize costs.

The total cost of medical care in the United States is the result of two factors. The first is the number of medical procedures conducted. More and more procedures are performed in the United States, both because of the aging of the population and because of the new treatments that advances in medical science have made available. For example, CAT scans and MRIs, now common diagnostic techniques, cost over $1,000 per use. Controlling the number of procedures performed has become one of the key elements of managed care, which requires patients to get approval from case managers before their insurance will cover an operation or other procedure.[27] As the population of the United States ages and the array of possible procedures increases, increasing use has become more important than prices in affecting health care costs.[28]

The other factor contributing to the total cost of health care—the one that is most often discussed—is the general increase in price for all medical procedures. Table 11.5 shows changes in the prices of some components of medical care compared with the overall consumer price index (CPI) and with a composite medical care price index. It is clear from these data that medical costs as a whole have increased more rapidly than total consumer costs and that among the components of medical costs, hospital costs have increased most rapidly. Hospital costs have increased 315 percent more, over a forty-year period, than have total consumer prices, whereas total medical care costs have increased "only" 79 percent more rapidly than the CPI.

Despite a drop in 2010, there is little reason to expect the growth of health care prices to slow down.[29] Most of the savings from implementing managed

TABLE 11.5 Changes in U.S. Medical Care Costs Compared with Consumer Price Index (1982–1984 = 100)

Year	CPI	Total medical	Physicians	Hospitals	Medical commodities
1980	82.4	74.9	76.5	69.2	75.4
1985	107.6	113.5	113.3	116.1	115.2
1990	130.7	162.8	160.8	178.0	163.4
1995	152.4	220.5	208.8	257.8	204.5
2000	172.2	260.8	244.7	317.3	238.1
2001	177.1	272.8	253.6	338.3	247.6
2002	179.9	285.6	260.6	367.8	256.4
2003	184.0	297.1	267.7	394.8	262.8
2004	188.9	310.1	278.3	417.9	269.3
2005	195.3	323.2	287.5	439.9	276.0
2006	201.6	336.2	291.9	468.1	285.9
2007	207.3	351.1	303.2	498.9	290.0
2008	209.2	259.4	312.4	521.1	294.8
2009	210.8	366.4	318.9	547.1	299.9
2010	211.7	365.9	318.8	545.2	300.1

Source: Calculated from U.S. Census Bureau, *Statistical Abstract of the United States* (Washington, DC: U.S. Government Printing Office, annual).

care have already been realized, so that the underlying dynamics of medical inflation continue.[30] Because there will be more elderly citizens, requiring more health care, that increased demand will add to pressures on costs. Finally, because of the political pressures to ensure that patients in managed care have better access to a full range of treatment options, managed care may no longer be an effective barrier to medical inflation.

The importance of these cost data is that medical care is becoming more difficult for the average person to afford. Even if an individual's income keeps pace with the consumer price index, it will fall behind the increasing costs of medical care. The rapidly increasing prices mean that few people can afford to pay for a catastrophic illness requiring long-term hospitalization and extensive treatment; even the best medical insurance available will likely be exhausted by such an illness. Thus, it has become increasingly possible for even a person with a substantial income to be financially destroyed by a major illness. Another potential problem is that all the concern about the cost may undermine the quality of medical care, especially in managed care.

Health care costs are a problem for government as well as for private citizens, as almost half the total medical care bill in the United States is paid by governments. But even its large share of the medical marketplace has not enabled government to exercise any significant control over health costs, perhaps because decisions about health care spending are made not by one government but by several. And within each government are several agencies interested in health care and providing various streams of funding for it. Governments' attempts to control medical costs have therefore been diffused, and they are unable to overcome the technical and political power of health care providers, who are backed by the fears of consumers. For example, the Bush administration attempted to limit reimbursements to physicians under Medicare in 2008, but the attempt was quickly withdrawn after a large-scale political protest.[31]

To be able to control these costs, we must understand why they have been increasing so rapidly. A number of factors have been identified as causing at least part of the increase.[32] For hospitals, a rapid rise in the cost of supplies and equipment—including large capital investments, such as magnetic resonance imaging (MRI) scanners, as well as more mundane items such as dressings and surgical gloves—has been a factor. Labor costs for hospitals have been increasing rapidly, as many professional and nonprofessional employees unionize to bargain for higher wages.[33] Furthermore, good medical care is labor intensive, and although technology can make some aspects of care more efficient, patients value personal contacts with health care providers. There also may be too many hospital beds for the number of patients. Empty hospital beds imply capital costs and even some running costs that must be spread among the patients who do occupy beds. As health insurers (including government) attempt to constrain their costs by limiting hospitalizations, the hospitals find their average costs rising. The same consideration applies to overinvestment in technology. Every hospital that buys an MRI scanner, for example, must pay for it whether or not it is used very often. The United States has over 3,000 MRI systems (at several million dollars each), whereas Canada is able to get by with fewer than 100. With a population approximately eleven times as large as Canada's, the United States has approximately one hundred times as many MRI units.[34]

The complex system of funding medical care in the United States also contributes significantly to its cost. Some studies have found that 25 percent of total hospital costs are in administration—about twice the percentage that Canada pays, with its single-payer public insurance program.[35] Veterans Administration experiments with using competitive, private sector service providers found them much more expensive than similar programs managed directly by the public sector.[36] In short, the complex and decentralized finance system, rather than promoting efficiency, seems to produce extra costs.

During the 1990s, hospitals began reacting to increasing pressures from insurers (including government agencies) and also anticipating changes from national health care reform. They attempted to reduce their operating costs by reducing the number of employees, managing patient loads more effectively, and consolidating expensive services such as CAT and MRI scanning units. Managed competition programs were introduced to establish maximum payments for certain procedures and to encourage the insured to make the best use of their insurance dollars.[37] Hospital costs continue to increase, but the rate of increase has slowed. Moreover, since the best way to limit hospital costs is to keep patients out of hospitals, more surgical procedures are being done on an outpatient basis, and stays in the hospital are being shortened—at times to dangerous levels. Patients are being released "quicker and sicker."

Physician costs also have been rising, although not as rapidly as hospital costs. In addition to the general pressures of inflation in the economy as a whole, doctors' fees have been affected by increases in the cost of equipment and supplies, the rising cost of medical malpractice insurance, and the need to practice "defensive medicine" to protect against malpractice suits by ordering every possible diagnostic procedure.[38] For some specialties, such as obstetrics, the high malpractice insurance costs have been driving doctors from practice.[39] Some of the relatively high cost of physicians' services in the United States is due to the high level of specialization of American doctors.[40] Less than 5 percent of the private physicians in office-based practice in the United States are in general practice, down from 18 percent in 1980 (see Table 11.6). However, when the number of internists (who often function as general practitioners) is considered, there has been no real shift away from general practice. In addition, a higher percentage of American doctors practice in hospitals than is the

TABLE 11.6   Distribution of Physicians by Type of Practice (in percentages)

Practice	1980	1990	2000	2006
General medicine	17.6	17.0	13.1	8.3
Internal medicine	14.9	17.5	17.6	18.6
Obstetrics and gynecology	7.2	7.4	6.4	6.2
Surgery	16.0	15.2	12.9	13.0
Pediatrics	6.4	8.1	8.6	9.2
Other	38.9	34.8	41.2	44.7

Source: American Medical Association, *Physician Characteristics and Distribution in the United States* (Chicago: American Medical Association, annual).

case in many other countries, and hospital care is much more expensive than outpatient care.

Physicians have cooperated increasingly with so-called preferred provider programs, in which large insurance carriers, such as Blue Cross, negotiate lower fees for their clients and monitor the charges physicians impose. The insurers also require second opinions for expensive procedures or procedures that are often performed unnecessarily. Doctors sometimes resent interference in their clinical freedom, but these programs ensure them access to large pools of patients, all of whom by definition have insurance and who therefore present fewer problems in collecting fees than might others.[41]

Finally, the method of payment for most medical care, especially hospital care, may influence costs. Well over 90 percent of all hospital costs and approximately 80 percent of all medical expenses are paid by third-party payers, which may be private (e.g., Blue Cross) or public (Medicaid or Medicare).[42] As a result, neither doctors nor patients have an incentive to restrict consumption of medical care; it has often been perceived as "free." Individuals may, in fact, want to use all the insurance benefits they can to recover the amount they have paid as premiums over the years. This is a phenomenon known as the "tragedy of the commons," in which the rational behavior of individuals creates irrationality for society as a whole.[43] Managed care programs also provide *first-dollar coverage* (coverage beginning from the first dollar spent for treatment) for some types of care, but they now commonly impose copayments to deter consumption or at least make the consumer conscious of the costs.

The states, which have the primary responsibility for administering Medicaid, the public medical program for the poor, have been encountering large cost increases in that program. Health expenditures now account for about 10 percent of state spending. Tennessee, for example, which had a very progressive program, had to cut it extensively, and other states have had to retrench as well.[44] In addition to the usual programs for managed care and scrutiny of costs, at least one state, Oregon, has adopted a more radical plan for cost containment. The state government decided in 1989 that it wanted to be able to continue to provide care to all its citizens who could not afford private care and not lower the income level at which individuals lost eligibility. But the state also realized that it could not pay for everything for everybody.[45] It therefore decided that Medicaid in Oregon would pay only for a range of diseases—selected on the basis of cost, seriousness, and effectiveness of available treatment—that fell above a line determined by the amount of money available. So, for example, in 2007, Medicaid would pay for the 300 highest-priority disorders but not for the remainder. Also, the program would not pay for "heroic treatments" for extremely difficult cases such as babies born weighing less than 500 grams.

The Oregon policy has had its critics, who argue that this program of rationing prevents the poor from getting equal treatment and that the selection of the cutoff point for care is arbitrary.[46] It was particularly attacked by groups representing the disabled and the chronically ill. Advocates, however, maintained that the program enabled the state to continue serving all the poor and to continue providing routine and cost-effective diagnostic procedures free of charge. Although this is perhaps an extreme approach to cost containment, it does demonstrate the importance of this issue in contemporary health policy debates.

Quality

Both citizens and government must be concerned about the quality of medical care, but determining quality is difficult. Most citizens, and even doctors, cannot tell in advance how effective a treatment will be. Likewise, it is difficult to determine which doctor or hospital is likely to be most effective in providing treatment. Although almost all medical care providers are interested in providing high-quality care, it is still difficult to ensure quality services.

Citizens' obvious concern has been reflected in the increased number of malpractice suits and complaints against physicians and hospitals. Governments' concerns about quality extend from the general social responsibility for regulating the safety and effectiveness of medicines and medical devices on the market to the quality of care provided to Medicare and Medicaid patients, to a perhaps more philosophical concern with the efficacy of modern medical care as a remedy for the health problems of American citizens.[47] When a patient enters a physician's office—regardless of whether the resulting bill will be paid by Blue Cross–Blue Shield, by Medicaid, or out of pocket—he or she has the right to expect, at a minimum, competent medical care that meets current standards. Unfortunately, many patients do not receive such care, and they complain about receiving poor-quality care or medical treatment that they believe is delivered without any genuine humanity. The American Medical Association's (AMA) own statistics document a significant rate of error in diagnosis and treatment.

A more subtle problem is the way in which the quality of health care is eroded through both overtreatment and undertreatment of patients, both generally resulting from financial incentives. Overtreatment has appeared in a number of studies documenting excessive use of medical technology and drugs as a means of generating more income for physicians and hospitals. For the public sector, overtreatment means increased costs for Medicare and Medicaid patients, as well as the human costs imposed on the patients. This problem appears to be declining as fewer and fewer patients have indemnity insurance, which pays providers on a fee-for-service basis.

Rather, the current quality problem in health care is undertreatment, as managed care places pressures on providers not to provide services. Government regulators have begun to intervene to ensure that patients receive adequate care by regulating the length of hospital stay for some procedures. Because they have an economic interest in *not* providing services, health maintenance organizations and other managed care providers use screening devices—such as prohibiting doctors from informing patients about expensive treatments that might be beneficial—to prevent patients from receiving certain types of care. These "gag rules" have now been largely eliminated because of pressures from government and the medical providers,[48] and many states make insurance companies and HMOs liable if they do not provide information and needed care.[49]

The medical profession itself is supposed to be the first line of defense in maintaining the quality of medical care. State medical associations and their review boards are expected to monitor the practice of medicine and handle complaints about incompetent or unethical practitioners. Although these organizations have an interest in maintaining the integrity of patient care, they often find it difficult to discipline their fellow professionals and friends. More positively, the medical profession has taken a stand in fighting some of the excesses of the managed care industry and has sought to defend its members' clinical freedom in offering treatment.[50]

A more important philosophical question has been introduced into the discussion of the quality of care, in part by the comment of former Colorado governor Richard Lamm that "We all have the duty to die," meaning that the terminally ill perhaps should not be kept alive by heroic means when such intervention only "prolongs dying" rather than saves life.[51] Is it high-technology medicine that sustains a semblance of life that has lost most human qualities, or is it a high-technology ego trip for the physician? The physician's first commandment, *Primum non nocere* ("First, do not harm"), has traditionally been understood to require preserving life at all costs; modern technology has made that an expensive and possibly inhumane interpretation. Some patients' families have gone to court to have their loved ones removed from life support systems, but the techniques available to sustain life appear to have outpaced the ethical, legal, and policy capacity to cope with the changes.[52] In 2005, the case of Terry Schiavo in Florida raised the question of whether to maintain patients in a "persistent vegetative state" to national attention and brought the debate into the open.[53]

The ill-informed discussion of "death panels" in the Obama health care reforms did at least raise issues about the rationing of care and the quality of care.[54] The question of what care is appropriate for the very old and the terminally ill leads to the question of rationing of health care. Some countries have already imposed rather strict rationing of care—not performing organ transplants for patients over certain ages, for example.[55] This development in other systems has, in turn, produced fears that a more extensive public role in U.S. medical care will mean a greater possibility for such rationing. For consumers used to being able to purchase what they want (provided they have good insurance) in the medical marketplace, the imposition of rationing would seem on its face to be a reduction of quality.

The proposal for a "patient's bill of rights" is a more recent initiative to improve the quality of services under managed care. After much debate in Congress, a compromise bill was passed in 2001 to provide patients greater opportunities for compensation from insurers and HMOs that deny care. The compromise that made passage possible included a provision that state courts would be the locus of any lawsuits under the act and a ceiling on the amount of liability. Although useful for coping with some of the problems of managed care, this legislation depends on compensation after the fact rather than prevention to address quality in health care.

The Affordable Care Act of 2010

The Patient Protection and Affordable Care Act of 2010 is an attempt to address the problems in American health care mentioned above. The principal concern of the act is to enhance access for citizens, but there are also provisions in the legislation that may help to alleviate issues of cost and quality. This legislation was the product of rather intense political debate and has been a source of controversy ever since it was adopted. Most important, the legislation has been challenged in the courts, and these challenges reached the Supreme Court in spring 2012.[56]

The central feature of the Affordable Care Act is an individual mandate for purchasing health insurance. Individuals who are not covered by their employers, by public programs such as Medicare and Medicaid, or by purchasing their own insurance will be required to purchase at least minimal medical insurance. The task of identifying available and affordable insurance will be addressed through so-called exchanges at the state level. The policies listed in these exchanges will have to provide a range of services, and small businesses can also find policies that are available (with public subsidies) for their employees. The available policies will be regulated through both the Department of Health and Human Services and the states so that citizens have adequate information for making informed decisions.

There are also regulatory provisions in the Affordable Care Act that enhance access of the public to medical care. One of the more important of these is that individuals cannot be excluded from health insurance coverage because of preexisting conditions. This regulation therefore makes coverage available in principle to all citizens and means that insurers cannot enhance profits by excluding those individuals most likely to make claims. While this provision brings more expensive patients into the insurance market, it also means that these individuals will not be receiving their care through hospital emergency rooms and other extremely expensive delivery sites.

Accountable care organizations are supported within the Patient Protection and Affordable Care Act (PPACA) as a means of addressing problems of cost as well as access. These organizations are to some extent a return to the older idea of health maintenance organizations (HMOs) that were central to reform attempts in the 1970s. The logic of accountable care organizations (ACOs) is that a set of medical providers would agree to provide care for patients who would pay an organization a flat fee per year for all their medical care, or at least there are bundled payments for physician services and other types of medical care. This mode of provision should help to address the cost issues discussed above, given that it moves provision away from fee-for-service and thus removes incentives for excessive provision. The ACO model has been applied most clearly in pediatric care through SCHIPS, but already it is being diffused.[57]

The major effects of the PPACA on costs would be through creating more effective markets in health insurance, including requiring insurers to reveal publicly the level of overheads and profits in their operations. There have been a wide range of estimates of the net economic impact of the legislation, but the majority of such analyses argue that overall medical costs could be reduced. The PPACA had other cost control components as well, notably cost review panels for Medicare and Medicaid. The Independent Payment Advisory Board was designed to review levels of payment to physicians and to find means of controlling them. Like other measures contained within the act, these provisions have been controversial and highly politicized, with Republicans in the House of Representatives attempting to eliminate funding.[58]

Quality issues in health care are also addressed through the Affordable Care Act. The idea of the accountable care organization is to some extent one of improving quality. Not only does this plan for service delivery improve quality through reducing unnecessary services, but it further will have its services evaluated regularly through the Center for Medicare and Medicaid Services. There is also an emphasis on "evidence based medicine," and the act also funds a program for innovation in health care.[59] Finally, the PPACA also emphasizes preventive medicine and with that there should be an improvement in the overall health status of the population.

The passage of this health care legislation might have been seen as a major boon for the American public, but there has also been significant political opposition. Although the idea of the individual mandate was proposed originally by the conservative Heritage Foundation and adopted by the state of Massachusetts when Mitt Romney was governor, it has been labeled as a major invasion of individual liberties by the political right. In addition, a number of political campaigns concerning "death panels" and other presumed problems in the legislation spread concern about the impacts of the law on the quality of care. Even when some of the benefits of the law were being implemented, the public continued to question its efficacy.

Unlike opposition to health care reform in the past, however, much of the current opposition comes from segments of society who would be likely to benefit. The Tea Party and other groups opposed to the legislation have convinced many people that the legislation will undermine the quality of health care in the United States and will eliminate choice for patients.[60] Much of the opposition in 2012 at the time of the Supreme Court hearings on the constitutionality of the legislation comes from working-class and lower middle-class citizens whose access to health care would probably be improved. This again demonstrates the extent to which American politics has become highly ideological and partisan.

Public Programs in Health Care

Despite rhetoric about a free enterprise medical care system in the United States, even before the passage of the Affordable Care Act there were numerous public programs providing direct medical services to some segments of the population, offering medical care insurance for others, and supporting the health of the entire population through public health programs, regulation, and research. Many citizens question the efficacy of these programs, especially the regulatory ones, but they are evidence of the large and important role of government in medicine. I now discuss several major government programs in medical care, with some attention to the policy issues involved in each, and the possibilities of improving the quality of health care through public action.

Medicare

The government medical care program with which most citizens are familiar is Medicare, adopted as part of the Social Security Amendments of 1965. The program is essentially medical insurance for the elderly and disabled who are eligible for Social Security or Railroad Retirement benefits, and it has several components. Part A, financed principally through payroll taxation, is a hospitalization plan. As of 2011, it covers the first 60 days of hospitalization but requires the patient to pay the first $1,568. It also covers hospitalization during the 61st to 90th days but requires a copayment of $289 per day. It requires a copayment of $578 per day for up to 60 more "lifetime reserve" days (for each Medicare recipient over his or her lifetime). This portion of the plan also covers up to 100 days in a nursing care facility after release from the hospital, subject to a $144.50 copayment by the insured after the first 20 days.

Part B of Medicare is a supplementary insurance program covering doctors' fees and other outpatient services. These expenses are also subject to deductibles and to coinsurance, with the insured paying the first $140 each year, plus 20 percent of allowable costs. This portion of the Medicare program is financed by enrollees, who pay a monthly premium of $99.90.[61] Insured persons bear a rather high proportion of their medical expenses under Medicare, given that it is a publicly provided insurance program. The program is, however, certainly subsidized, and it is still a bargain for the average retired person, who might not be able to purchase comparable coverage in the private market because the elderly have, on average, significantly higher medical expenses than the population as a whole.

In 2006, Medicare put coverage for prescription drugs in effect—the so-called Part D drugs are potentially a serious financial burden for the elderly, who typically take several expensive drugs for chronic health problems. The new program appears well intentioned, but most participants and most providers (doctors and pharmacists) have found it extremely confusing and difficult to manage. The program is based on using private insurers, who market various plans to Medicare enrollees. In 2009, program participants must pay the first $295 of their annual drug costs, then 25 percent of the next $2,405, but then they must pay the next $3,454—the so-called donut hole in the plan. After the individual has paid that total of $4,350.25, the program will again provide benefits. The individual pays approximately $20 to $40 per month for this coverage, depending on the plan. This complex program provides not only some assistance to Medicare recipients, but also it imposes real costs.

Medicare is a better program than would be available to most of the elderly under private insurance programs—it requires no physical examination for coverage, covers preexisting health conditions, is uniformly available throughout the country, and provides some services that might not be available in private plans. The program presents some problems, however, perhaps the greatest of which is that it requires the insured to pay a significant amount out of their own pockets for coverage, even when they are hospitalized. As of 2009, purchasing Part B of the plan requires an annual outlay of over $1,200, which, although not much money for health insurance, may be a relatively large share of a pensioner's income. In addition, the costs of deductibles and coinsurance in both parts of Medicare may place a burden on less affluent beneficiaries.

In addition to the costs to the recipient for services that are covered, Medicare does not cover all the medical expenses that most beneficiaries will incur. For example, it does not pay for eye or dental examinations, eyeglasses or dentures, many preventive examinations, or immunizations; nor does the program cover long-term care. In short, Medicare does not wholly meet the needs of the elderly poor, who are most in need of services. In fact, at least one study shows that the gap between the health status of rich and poor elderly people widened initially after the introduction of Medicare.[62] The more affluent can use the program as a supplement to their own assets or private health insurance programs, while the less affluent still cannot provide adequately for their medical needs, even with Medicare.

One attempt to solve the "medigap" problem has been the introduction of private health insurance programs to fill in the lacunae of Medicare coverage. Unfortunately, most policies of this type do not cover the most glaring deficiencies of Medicare—for example, the absence of coverage for extended nursing home care. In addition, the policies do not cover preexisting health problems, and they frequently have long waiting periods for eligibility.

On the government's side of the Medicare program, the costs of funding medical insurance for the elderly impose a burden on the working-age population and on government resources. Basic hospitalization coverage under Medicare is financed as a part of the Social Security tax, taking 1.45 percent of each worker's salary. Since 1991, the health insurance portion of the Social Security tax has been levied on all earned income, unlike the pension and disability portion, which is levied on only the first $106,800 of earnings per year (as of 2009). With increasing opposition to Social Security taxes have come suggestions to shift the financing of Medicare to general tax revenues, such as the income tax, leaving the entire payroll tax to fund Social Security pensions.[63]

The increasing costs of medical care and the growing number of Americans eligible for Medicare mean that difficulties are likely to arise in financing the program for some years to come. Congress attempted to address the difficulties as a part of the balanced budget bill in summer 1997, creating a number of service plans for Medicare recipients. These include traditional fee-for-service medicine, managed care, preferred provider plans, and medical savings accounts.[64] Any of the shifts from fee-for-service medicine will provide some cost savings, but some, such as the medical savings account, involve the recipient's taking a chance that he or she will remain relatively healthy during a particular time period, a risky gamble for most elderly people.[65]

Finally, problems of quality and fair pricing for Medicare patients are also likely to persist. Medicare regulations allow the Centers for Medicare and Medicaid Services (CMS) to pay "reasonable" costs to physicians and hospitals for services rendered to beneficiaries, and of course, they also require that providers give adequate and "standard" treatment to those patients. In some instances, physicians charge more than the amount designated as reasonable, thereby imposing additional costs on the patient. In other instances, physicians have employed generally unnecessary tests and procedures, knowing that the costs would be largely covered by Medicare.

One move to control costs for public medical programs, called diagnosis related groups (DRGs), is a form of prospective reimbursement. Under this program, adopted in 1983, hospitals are reimbursed for services to Medicare and Medicaid patients according to one of over 400 specific diagnostic groups.[66] The hospital is guaranteed a fixed amount for each patient according to the DRG to which the patient's complaint is assigned. A hospital that is able to treat a patient for less can retain the difference as profit, but if the hospital stay costs more than is allowed under the DRG, the hospital must absorb the loss.

Despite some experience with DRGs, a number of questions remain about how they affect medical care. For example, the doctor determines the course of treatment more than the hospital does, and there has been increased conflict between hospital administrators and physicians about patient care. The program may reduce the quality of care provided to Medicaid and Medicare patients or cause too-early dismissals of patients, shifting costs onto home medical care programs and community medicine; patients are discharged quicker and sicker, and too often, they are readmitted soon after discharge. DRGs also do not easily accommodate the multiple diseases and infirmities characteristic of so many Medicare patients. Nevertheless, the DRG program is an interesting attempt to impose greater cost consciousness on hospitals and physicians without rationing, and it has been copied by some private health insurers.

Medicaid

The Medicaid program was created at the same time as Medicare to provide federal matching funds to state and local governments for medical care of welfare recipients and the "medically indigent," a category intended to include those who do not qualify for public assistance but whose income is not sufficient to cover necessary medical expenses. Because Medicaid is run by the states, the benefits, eligibility requirements, and administration vary considerably. If a state chooses to have a Medicaid program, it must provide medical care benefits for all welfare recipients and for those who receive Supplemental Security Income because of categorical problems—age, blindness, and disability.

Medicaid regulations require states to provide a range of services to program recipients: hospitalization, laboratory and other diagnostic services, X-rays, nursing home care, screening for a range of diseases, and physicians' services. A state may extend benefits to cover prescription drugs and other services. For each service, states may set limits on the amount of care covered and on the rate of reimbursement, and because of increasing costs, they have tended to provide little more than the minimum required under federal law. Federal laws, however, are becoming increasingly stringent, imposing additional costs on the states that are difficult to fund.[67] Most states have been reacting by using alternative service systems, such as HMOs, for their Medicaid clients, and by 2006, almost two-thirds of Medicaid recipients were in managed care.[68]

In addition to the variations in coverage and benefits across the country, other policy problems beset Medicaid. The ones most commonly cited are fraud and abuse. It is sometimes estimated that up to 7 percent of total federal outlays for Medicaid are accounted for by abuse.[69] Almost all such abuse is perpetrated by service providers, rather than by patients, in part because of the complex eligibility requirements and procedures for reimbursement. Still, this pattern of fraud presents a negative image of the program to the public.[70] With the continuing squeeze on public resources, any program that has a reputation for fraud is likely to encounter funding difficulties—regardless of who commits the fraud.

States have had to cut back on optional services and reduce coverage of primary (physician) care, so as to be able to finance hospital care for Medicaid recipients. Some have also limited the amount they will reimburse physicians for each service. These reimbursements are significantly lower than what doctors would receive from private or even Medicare patients; the result is that an increasing number of physicians refuse to accept Medicaid patients. In part because of these trends, Medicaid has increasingly become a program of institutional medical care—which is, paradoxically, the most expensive method of delivering medical services. As with Medicare, however, institutional care through hospitals, emergency rooms, and nursing homes is the one kind of medical care almost sure to be covered under the program. Less than 7 percent of all Medicaid spending goes to home health services, whereas over 35 percent goes to extended care facilities, many of which do not meet federal standards.

Although funded rather differently than Medicaid, the State Children's Health Insurance Program (SCHIP) represents a special drive, in addition to Medicaid, to provide medical insurance for children. Somewhat like Medicaid, SCHIP is provided by the states with federal support. The states set their own rules for eligibility, and some have extended the program's benefits to parents, pregnant women, and other adults. Although the number of uninsured children has continued to rise as the program has experienced financial shortfalls, Congress reauthorized SCHIP in 2009, allowing coverage of four million more children.

Like Medicare, the Medicaid program has done a great deal of good in making medical care available to people who might not otherwise receive it. Nevertheless, some significant Medicaid problems—notably costs and coverage—will remain political issues for years. Proposals for solving those problems range from the abolition of both programs to the establishment of national health insurance, with a number of proposals for amending the programs or using private health insurance between those more radical alternatives.

Health Maintenance Organizations: Managing Managed Care

A fundamental and frequent criticism of U.S. medical care is that it is, or at least has been, fee-for-service medicine. Medical practitioners were paid for each service they performed. As a consequence, they had incentives to use their skills; surgeons made money by wielding their scalpels, and internists made money by ordering diagnostic procedures. Critics have also charged that American medical care has been primarily acute care. The system is oriented toward treating the ill (to make money) rather than toward preventing illness. This point is to some degree substantiated by the relatively low immunization levels among American children, especially given that most of these immunizations can be obtained not only without cost but also are required by law in most states.

The health maintenance organization (HMO) was developed at least partially in response to those failings of the health care system.[71] An HMO provides prepaid medical care—members pay an annual fee, in return for which they receive virtually all their medical care. They may have to pay ancillary costs (e.g., a small set fee for each prescription), but the vast majority of medical expenses are covered through the HMO. Doctors working for the HMO have no incentive to prescribe additional treatments. If anything, given that the doctors commonly share in the profits of the organization or own the HMO themselves, they have an incentive not to prescribe treatments, inasmuch as any surgery or treatment that would cost the organization without providing additional income reduces profits. By the same reasoning, since a healthy member is all profit, while a sick member is all loss, doctors in an HMO have an incentive to keep the members healthy and to practice preventive medicine. By thus reversing the incentives usually presented to physicians, it is argued, HMOs can significantly improve the quality of health care and slow the rapid escalation of medical costs. As noted above, many aspects of the accountable care organizations now being developed in the United States are analogous to the HMOs.

The formation of HMOs was supported by the federal government. In 1973, President Richard Nixon signed into law a bill directed at improving choice in the health care marketplace.[72] The legislation provided for planning and development grants for prospective HMOs, but at the same time it placed a number of restrictions on any HMO using federal funding. Most important, all HMOs had to offer an extensive array of services, including psychiatric care. An employer offering group insurance to employees had to make an equal contribution for any employee who wanted to join an HMO. The HMO movement has also been assisted by federal efforts to restrict the activities of physicians and private insurers who have sought to reduce the competition offered by HMOs, and it continues to be supported by government.

HMOs were the first step in creating managed care, whose basic idea is that doctors cannot make all decisions about what sorts of care to provide, and patients (or their primary care physicians) cannot make their own decisions about what specialists to consult. Physicians, hospitals, and other providers are connected in "networks" or "organizations," and referrals for specialized care are made within those networks. Health care managers make decisions about what sort of care is appropriate and can even prevent a patient's receiving the type of care that he or she, or the physician, wants. The patient may still go to an emergency room or other facility outside the network, but the services received there generally are not covered by insurance.

The managed care system has been successful in reducing the rate of increase in health care costs, but now pressures are building that are beginning to accelerate the price rise again—most important among them, that the system of insurance is becoming so general that many poorer and sicker people are being brought into managed care.[73] There are also some political pressures (in some cases successful) to require managed care plans to permit greater clinical freedom for physicians and to ensure that patients can make their own decisions about some aspects of care, especially visits to the emergency room.[74] The "patient's bill of rights," for example, ensured that patients would have much greater control over their own medical care, despite the probability of higher costs.

Although cost containment is one of the attractions of HMOs, their costs have been moving upward, along with other medical costs. A number of factors are responsible, including the aging of the population, the development of numerous expensive new treatments that can no longer be excluded by HMOs (or other managed care systems) as being experimental, and the increased willingness of the medical profession to resist the controls that the plans attempt to impose.[75] The increasing costs are adding to the incentives for businesses to drop health coverage for their employees or to increase employees' contribution to the cost. In effect, the presumed remedy for the problem of health care costs has itself turned out to be expensive.

Health Care Regulation

Perhaps the most pervasive impact of government on the delivery of health care services in the United States has come from regulation, of which there are many kinds. The adoption of the Employee Retirement Income Security Act (ERISA) in 1974 put the federal government squarely in the center of health care regulation, often superseding state-level regulation.[76] Among the many targets of health care regulation, I will briefly discuss three types: costs, quality, and pharmaceuticals.[77]

Hospital and Physician Costs

As we have said, cost increases have been a major consideration in health care for some time, and hospital costs have increased most rapidly. As hospitals constitute a major component of the total health care bill (approaching one-half of the total) and are readily identifiable institutions with better record keeping than the average physician, it seems sensible to concentrate on them to control medical care costs. Approaches to controlling hospital costs have been varied. One of the more important public programs has been prospective reimbursement; the federal version of this approach for Medicare patients is the diagnosis-related groups described earlier. In essence, DRGs constitute a market approach to cost containment, for they allow hospitals that are efficient to make a profit, while those that are not well run can sustain losses.

Other fundamental causes of price escalation include the principle of fee-for-service medicine, which gives hospitals and doctors incentive to provide more services. Another problem is the related tendency of the medical profession to offer high-cost hospital treatment when lower-cost options would be as effective. This choice is made both for the convenience of the physician and because many health insurance policies will pay for hospital treatments but not for the same treatments performed on an outpatient basis. DRGs and preferred provider plans to limit costs to private insurance companies have helped to rein in this tendency somewhat, but American medical care remains more hospital centered than that of many other countries. Finally, it is important to remember that hospitals do not have patients—doctors do—and hospitals must compete for doctors to fill their available beds. This competition takes place largely through the acquisition of costly technology, such as CAT scanners, MRI systems, and so forth, which must be amortized through the higher price of hospital care.

The federal government also controls the fees it pays physicians providing services to Medicare and Medicaid patients. Physicians are paid according to "relative value units" (RVUs) for each procedure, determined by the Centers for Medicare and Medicaid Services. These RVUs are reviewed every five years and are the product of extensive negotiation between medical associations and government.[78] This is another aspect of the prospective reimbursement logic that has been used to place limits on spending and make it more predictable.

Health Care Quality

The regulation of quality is one of the most controversial areas of government intervention in the health care field. Regulation operates directly against long-established canons of clinical freedom and the right of members of the medical profession to regulate their own conduct. Medical professionals, as well as most of the public, assume that the only person qualified to judge the professional conduct of a physician is another physician. The specter of bureaucrats intervening in medical care is not comforting to the average American.

In addition, private mechanisms for rectifying harm done by a physician in the conduct of his or her profession are well established. They include legal proceedings, such as tort and malpractice lawsuits, which generate their own health care problems and have been cited as one factor causing rapid increases in medical care costs. Some effects of malpractice litigation are direct, as physicians pass their doubled or tripled malpractice insurance costs on to patients in higher fees. In his campaigns for presidency, George W. Bush advocated reducing the awards in malpractice suits to help maintain or reduce health care costs. Although the direct impact of malpractice insurance fees on medical costs appears minimal, the indirect effects—the practice of "defensive medicine"—appear more substantial. A doctor fearing a malpractice suit may prescribe additional diagnostic procedures, extra days in the hospital, or extra treatments to lessen his or her chances of being found legally negligent, and the costs of these extra procedures also are passed on to consumers. Other effects of malpractice suits as a quality control are more systemic, as doctors in specialties such as obstetrics and neurosurgery, which are subject to frequent lawsuits, simply change to other fields. This phenomenon can leave small towns and even small cities without certain types of medical care.

Managed care and the tendency to deny patients some treatments as a means of reducing costs have become a major concern. Several surveys have found that significant majorities of the population want some protection from the economic power of managed care,[79] and even some conservative Republican members of Congress have advocated a stronger governmental role in the regulation of the managed care industry.[80] Some states have acted to enhance the rights of patients to obtain services from their managed care programs and banned the so-called "gag rule" on physicians, but numerous quality problems remain.[81] The federal government also has become involved, as exemplified by the "patient's bill of rights."

Quality improvement programs are an important public instrument for regulating the quality of medical care. These organizations are designed in part to monitor costs of services provided to Medicare patients, but they necessarily become involved in the issue of appropriate and effective treatment as well, for treatments that are ineffective or dangerous can also be costly. Some quality organizations have gone so far as to establish standard profiles of treatment for common conditions and then question physicians whose practice differs significantly from those patterns. Physicians who offer more extensive treatments may be imposing additional costs on the program, while those who are providing unusual or less extensive treatments may be threatening the health of the patient. Medicare and Medicaid have added a number of other quality assurance programs, including monitoring of home care and nursing homes.

The growth of managed care is placing more pressure on government to regulate health care. Patients often believe that they are being denied adequate care by their HMOs or other forms of managed care, and their complaints have generated a number of regulatory interventions or proposals for regulations. For example, at least one state has enabled patients to sue HMOs for malpractice when care is inadequate, rather than placing all the onus on the individual physician.[82]

The attempts to regulate the managed care industry have been impeded to some extent by the early protection given to HMOs and similar organizations. When these forms of providing care were first being considered, they were regarded as a way of combating the dominance of fee-for-service medicine and were promoted both to limit costs and to place greater emphasis on preventive medicine.[83] The organizations were, in fact, made immune from lawsuits for their actions in restricting access to types of care. One of the subsequent proposals for boosting their quality of service, however, is to use the legal system as the mechanism for quality control, as is done in most other aspects of the medical system, extending it to insurers as well as practitioners.[84]

Drug Regulation

The federal government regulates the pharmaceutical industry and controls substances in food and water that are potentially harmful to health. Government regulation of food and drugs began in 1902, with extensive increases in its powers in 1938 and again in 1962. The issues surrounding drug regulation have become substantially more heated since the early 1980s. The Food and Drug Administration (FDA), which is responsible for most drug regulation, has been attacked for being excessively stringent and preventing useful drugs from coming to the market. The AIDS epidemic brought this complaint to the fore and has actually produced some changes in the procedures for licensing new drugs.[85]

The FDA has begun to fast-track some drugs that address deadly conditions, requiring fewer guarantees of safety, and using the argument that risks are certainly worth it if the patient might die otherwise.[86]

Other critics of the FDA believe that its regulations have been too lax and excessively dominated by the pharmaceutical industry and that, as a result, potentially dangerous drugs have been certified for sale.[87] This complaint has become more evident as prescription pharmaceuticals are advertised on television. Critics believe that the FDA does not yet do an adequate job of assessing whether the content of advertisements is fair and accurate, especially after one heavily advertised drug—Vioxx—was shown to have dangerous side effects.[88] The FDA and the drug industry have also been criticized for not paying sufficient attention to the different reactions that women may have to many drugs that were initially tested only on men.[89]

The basic regulatory doctrine applied to pharmaceuticals is that a drug must be shown to be both safe and effective before it can be approved for sale. Several problems arise from that doctrine. For example, almost any drug will have some side effects, so that proving its safety is difficult; some criteria must be established for weighing the benefits of a drug against its side effects. The example commonly cited is common aspirin, which, because of the range of its known side effects, might have considerable difficulty being certified for use under current standards. The safety and effectiveness of a drug must be demonstrated by clinical trials, which are often time consuming and expensive, and potentially important drugs are thereby delayed in coming to the public.

Critics of the drug industry point to other issues in drug regulation and in the pharmaceutical industry as a whole. Examples are the problems of so-called look-alike drugs, which are virtually identical chemically with another drug but have some slight modification to avoid patent restrictions, and the use of brand-name as opposed to generic drugs. It is argued that a great deal of drug research is directed toward finding combinations of drugs that can be marketed under a brand name or in reproducing findings of already proven drugs so that they can be marketed with a different brand name. Because brand-name drugs are invariably more expensive than generic ones, critics charge that the licensing of brand names actually aids the pharmaceutical industry by promoting the sale of higher-priced drugs. They also argue that drugs are sold and prescribed without adequate dissemination of information about their possible side effects. Some states have intervened to reduce the problem of inflated drug costs by allowing pharmacists to substitute a generic drug for a brand-name drug unless the physician specifically forbids such substitution. Many drugstores attempt to make their customers aware of this cost-saving option, so unless the physician believes that a generic drug would not be effective (or opposes its use for some other, allegedly less noble reason), patients are able to choose a cheaper alternative.[90] American consumers have also found ways to purchase cheaper drugs from Canada, either taking trips north of the border or using mail order. Ironically, most of those cheaper drugs were manufactured in the United States.

The domination of drug industries in research is also raising other issues in contemporary medical care. One of the most acute is the lack of research on new antibiotics to combat bacteria that have become resistant to existing medicines. While crucial for saving lives, these medicines are not as profitable as those used for chronic conditions, such as diabetes, arthritis, and various circulatory diseases, and hence, there is little investment in them.[91] Similarly, research on "orphan drugs," or those that might address rare diseases, is minimal because of the absence of profitability.

The FDA regulates food as well as drugs, with special attention to possibly carcinogenic substances in food. The Delaney Amendment (passed in 1958) requires the FDA to remove from the market foods containing any substance that "induces" cancer in human beings or animals. An issue developed over this amendment during the late 1970s when studies in Canada showed that large amounts of the artificial sweetener saccharin tended to produce bladder cancer. Under the Delaney Amendment, the FDA was required to propose a ban on saccharin. Subsequent reports by the National Academy of Sciences then recommended that, instead of prohibiting all such substances, the government establish categories of risk, with attached regulations ranging from complete prohibition to warning labels to no action at all. The academy reports suggested also that such decisions take into consideration possible benefits from the continued sale of the substance. Because many believed that saccharin was highly beneficial for some people and produced only a low risk, they wanted it to remain on sale. Such risk-benefit or cost-benefit considerations are a common aid to decision making in the public sector (see chapter 17), although they are perhaps of questionable validity when applied to risks of the occurrence of a disease such as cancer. Nevertheless, for whatever reasons, Congress reauthorized the continuing sale of saccharin.

Another issue related to the regulation of pharmaceuticals is the regulation of tobacco, especially cigarette smoking. The surgeon general determined many years ago that smoking cigarettes is harmful, required warning labels on packages, and forbade advertising by electronic media. More recently, state and local governments have imposed bans on smoking in public places. The surgeon general and the FDA also have developed evidence on the thousands of deaths caused by smoking. Moreover, several of the plans for national health insurance depend on an increased tax on cigarettes for at least a part of the financing. Such a tax would function like a regulation if its purpose was to encourage people to stop smoking, but that too would pay a benefit by reducing the estimated $65 billion spent annually on diseases caused by smoking. The fundamental question of the capacity of government to control use of cigarettes continues to be pursued in the courts and in legislatures. The states have won major suits against the tobacco companies, and some have used the funds to enhance the availability of medical care for their citizens, especially the less affluent. In 2009, the FDA received power to regulate tobacco, but not to prevent its sale, and this may constitute a significant contribution to improving public health.

The Pursuit of National Health Insurance

The Affordable Care Act represents an attempt to provide national health insurance or direct health service delivery by the public sector for the United States, just as there is in all other advanced industrial democracies. Although approximately 14 percent of the American people now depend directly on the federal government for their health care, another group of the same size receives Medicaid funded jointly by the states and the federal government, and still others receive most or all of their care from emergency rooms in municipal hospitals, there is still resistance to a comprehensive program.

The idea of a national health insurance program for the United States goes back at least to the Truman administration. (Indeed, Theodore Roosevelt, aware of health care programs then beginning in European nations, proposed something like a national health program at the beginning of the twentieth century.) When President Harry Truman proposed a comprehensive national health insurance program in 1945 as a part of the Social Security program, the proposal met with relentless opposition from the American Medical Association (AMA) and conservative business organizations, who called the plan "socialized medicine." The AMA spent millions of dollars on its successful campaign against national health insurance, and most Americans appeared to want to retain the private medical system. The adoption of Medicare in 1965 represented a first partial success for advocates of a national health insurance program.

One major difficulty in the drive for some sort of national health insurance over the past couple of decades has been that several alternative plans are available. Some of the plans have had the backing of powerful interests in the medical establishment (one was even proposed by the AMA), some have had the backing of Republicans and others of Democrats, while still others were proposed by health care advocacy groups. The Clinton administration began the active discussion of national health insurance, but its plan was only one among many. The political problem that has led to the failure of a national health insurance plan, therefore, has been getting enough support to coalesce around any one plan to have it adopted and then implemented successfully (see chapter 5).

We will now look at several broad alternative approaches to national health insurance and then more specifically at several of the plans that have been under active consideration at one time or another. If the Obama health care legislation is declared unconstitutional, then we may in the future be considering one or more of these alternatives to attempt to address continuing health care issues in the United States.

"Play or Pay"

One approach to national health insurance has been called *play or pay*. Under such a program, all employers would have to provide at least minimal health insurance for their employees ("play") or contribute to a public insurance program ("pay") that would cover their employees and everyone else not covered by private health insurance. Most such plans call for a payroll tax of 7 percent or 8 percent for companies not providing health benefits. These plans depend to a great extent on the actions of the private sector, but they do include a public insurance program (usually an expanded Medicare program) to provide a safety net for the unemployed. A program like this has been tried in Hawaii; a more extensive program was tried in Massachusetts but encountered substantial financial difficulties when the economy in that state sustained a number of serious reverses.[92]

The play or pay system largely would preserve the existing insurance system, although probably with more extensive regulation, as well as the existing fee-for-service medical care system, again perhaps with greater regulation of costs. In addition, it would allow companies to provide better benefits to their employees than the minimum mandated under the law, although those benefits might be treated as taxable income for the recipients. The principal difficulty with the plan is the claim by many small employers that health insurance costs would force them out of business, much as many were forced in the 1990s to drop medical coverage of their employees because of the cost.

The health plan enacted in the Obama administration contains some of the elements of the play or pay program.[93] In particular, larger employers who do not provide significant health coverage for their employees would be required to contribute a percentage of their payroll for health care. Unlike some earlier proposals, that plan would not require smaller businesses to participate, so it would not be as much of a burden on business as other programs might. This provision was to be combined with a number of other provisions (see below) designed to reduce the costs of health care and promote more equal access.

Canadian-Style Comprehensive Coverage

The most extreme proposals for public medical care would adopt something like the plan currently in operation in Canada, generally referred to as the *single-payer* system. Although it is referred to as "Canadian" in American debates over health care, this type of plan is actually found in most developed democracies. Such a system would change the medical industry in the United States fundamentally, placing the public sector, not the private providers (doctors and hospitals), in the driver's seat in medicine. The simplest plan of this type would extend Medicare, with its deductibles and copayments, to cover the entire population. Other plans involve issuing all legal residents a card to present to providers, who would then receive reimbursement from the government. Fees would be set, or maximum reimbursements established, and doctors and hospitals would be able to charge more if the patient were willing (and able) to pay.

Critics argue that this program would require large tax increases and would put existing health insurance providers out of business in favor of large public bureaucracies. Critics further claim that in Canada, health care innovation has been slower, and there is some waiting for elective procedures. Advocates of the Canadian system argue that such charges are exaggerated and that the problems have had little real impact on the quality of care. Indeed, they assert that Americans are receiving too many needless tests and treatments because that is the only way for doctors to earn money in a fee-for-service environment. Advocates of the single-payer system argue that those who are better served under the current system will have to pay some costs if a more equitable system of medical care is to be introduced.

Although many experts in the field argue that this would be the most efficient and effective plan for providing health coverage, politically the single-payer plan does not appear feasible. It appears to many people on the political right to be "socialist." Vested interests in the insurance industry do not want to lose their businesses and hence advocate using their companies to provide medical insurance for the entire population.[94] The insurance companies have offered some suggestions on how to control costs within the current system, such as creating a common reimbursement system, but critics argue that that would not really aid in extending coverage to more citizens.[95]

As the economic consequences of the complex and inefficient health insurance system in place have become more apparent, the potential virtues of a comprehensive health care plan have also emerged. Sen. Edward Kennedy, D-MA, drafted a plan for a publicly provided health insurance program that would cover any citizen up to 500 percent of the federal poverty rate ($110,000 for a family of four).[96] This program has some elements of play or pay in that employers would have to pay for part of the plan, but the other aspects of financing this potentially extremely expensive legislation were vague as hearings began in the Senate. Likewise, the level of political support for such a plan was not clear. Still, it represents an important move in the continuing saga of health care reform.[97]

Past Attempts at National Health Care Reform

Since Harry Truman's proposal for a comprehensive national health care system, several administrations have placed the issue on their agendas, but success has eluded every one of them. The administration of George H. W. Bush offered a plan for national health care reform toward the end of its time in office, partly to prevent the Democrats from capturing the issue entirely.[98] Whereas most of its proposals were quite basic—such as a simple, refundable tax credit to assist individuals who purchase private insurance—some in the administration favored a more complete plan of "managed competition." Under such an arrangement, large companies that provided insurance coverage for their employees would receive tax write-offs amounting to only 80 percent of the average current cost of providing similar medical care and would therefore be expected to pressure medical providers to give them preferential rates in exchange for the large volume of business they could offer. The remainder of the population, whether employed or not, would be offered several options for health insurance, and the assumption was that most people would choose to be covered through HMOs, which could bargain with providers for lower rates. This plan would have provided medical care to all citizens and might have stabilized or lowered medical care costs, assuming that the market worked as expected.

The John McCain presidential campaign in 2008 floated a proposal similar to this one, relying on competition to reduce the costs of medical care and to help to make health insurance more affordable. That aspect of the program was to be linked with modest tax credits to enable citizens not covered by employer-provided programs to obtain some form of health coverage. Critics argued that the market had already proved ineffective in reducing costs, citing the managed care programs currently in operation. Furthermore, the tax credits envisioned would be too limited to buy adequate coverage.

The Clinton administration placed health care reform at the top of its domestic agenda when it took office in January 1993. After a series of meetings with "stakeholders" and ordinary citizens, Hillary Rodham Clinton proposed a complex plan that depended on "alliances" of health care providers. Very much as HMOs have done for years, these alliances would supply all the health care needs of their members for a set annual fee, which would be below existing private insurance rates for much of the population. Individuals would also have been required to pay deductibles and copayments for services if they chose the fee-for-service plan. Businesses would have had to pay for their employees (up to 7.9 percent of their payrolls), with subsidies available for small businesses. Employers could provide insurance better than the national minimum, but those extra benefits could be treated as taxable income for the employee or made not deductible by the employer as a business expense.

Universality was the central tenet of the Clinton proposals, and it was the issue over which the president said he would never compromise. It would have tended to create much greater equality of access to medical care than is currently the case in the United States. The program also provided for cost containment, initially through competitive incentives but later through regulated prices, if necessary to reduce medical inflation to the general rate of inflation.[99] Still, many critics, even those who favored universality and employer mandates, regarded the plan as excessively complex and too reliant on the alliances both to provide care and to minimize costs. Many advocated a single-payer plan, such as the Canadian system, instead. Other critics disagreed with the concept of universality, believing that it was too costly, especially for employers. They sought alternatives more like that proposed by the previous Bush administration, relying more on voluntary efforts and the private sector. They also saw the Clinton plan creating a huge and costly federal bureaucracy.

Several alternatives to the Clinton plan, all of which were complex and expensive, emerged in Congress. Sen. Robert Dole, R-KS, devised one that relied heavily on voluntary compliance and private insurance and did not seek universal coverage—the target was 91 percent or 92 percent of the population. Rep. Richard Gephardt, D-MO, presented a plan that had many of the features of the Clinton proposal, most notably universal coverage and employer mandates to cover 80 percent of the cost of the average individual policy, but it provided subsidies to people with much higher incomes. In the Senate, Majority Leader George Mitchell, D-ME, developed a plan that dropped the goal of immediate universality and replaced it with a goal of 95 percent coverage by 2000. If that goal was not reached by voluntary means, a system of mandates might be imposed by 2002. Most of the other features of the Mitchell plan were somewhat simplified versions of the Clinton plan.

In the end, none of the proposals for reforming health care could be passed by the 1994 Congress. Politicians worried about what effect voting for one or another proposal might have on their political careers, especially just before midterm elections. The fear was exacerbated by the vast amounts of lobbying, especially by the insurance and health care industries.[100] It was impossible for liberals and conservatives to put aside their ideological differences to find a compromise that all could accept. For all sides, the pursuit of a perfect plan was the enemy of selecting an acceptable plan.

Although health care did not figure prominently in the George W. Bush administration, one alternative to comprehensive health insurance that Bush offered was the medical savings account, which would have allowed citizens who wanted to avoid the high costs of conventional health insurance to invest money in tax-sheltered medical savings accounts. If they did so, however, they would have very high deductibles and copayments. Primarily appealing to the affluent, this plan was also to some extent a revival of the catastrophic health insurance programs attempted during the late 1980s, providing a safety net only in the cases of severe problems.[101]

Although the federal government has failed so far to generate meaningful reforms, attempts at changing the health care system persist. Indeed, President Obama named health care reform one of his top priorities, pledging to improve quality and coverage and linking good health care with economic benefit and recovery. The Obama administration has expressed support for a government-sponsored health plan that would compete with private coverage to lower costs. Republicans, however, have argued that that amounts to "socialized medicine" and that the government lacks the funds to set such a plan in motion.

Summary

Changing and reforming policies is always difficult, and health care is perhaps a particularly difficult policy field in which to produce change. A number of powerful interests—doctors, hospitals, pharmaceutical companies, and the like—have a direct interest in the area. As issues of universal coverage arise, business interests become concerned about the costs that may be imposed on them. Citizens also worry that by attempting to provide better medical care for the entire population, government may undermine the high quality of care that is currently available to the most fortunate segments of the society.

Although competition is appealing to many Americans as a solution to the problems we have identified in the health care industry, there may be difficulties in implementing the concept. The health care industry differs from other industries in important ways that reduce the utility of competition as a remedy for its problems. In particular, the dominance of professionals in determining the amount and type of care that patients consume makes the usual competitive mechanisms less applicable. Those characteristics of the industry may require a stronger role for the public sector if effective control over costs, quality, and access is to be attained.

Very little information on the price or quality of medical care is available to the consumer. Prices for health care services are rarely advertised; frequently, the consumer does not even consider them when making decisions about care. In fact, in a somewhat perverse way, consumers often choose a higher-priced rather than a lower-priced service in the belief (often correct) that the more expensive service will be superior. And beyond hearsay, little information is available to patients about the quality of services provided by individual physicians or hospitals. The public sector has begun to intervene to make more information about health care quality available, and increasing competition among health insurers and health care providers has provided another source of information—if a biased one—but it is still difficult for the average consumer to make choices.

In addition, the provision of health care is in many ways a monopoly or cartel. Entry into the marketplace by potential suppliers is limited by licensing requirements and further controlled by the professions themselves, which limit the number of places available in medical schools. Thus, unlike some industries, the health care field makes it difficult for competition to develop among suppliers. One possible means of promoting competition would be to break down the

medical profession's monopoly by giving nurse practitioners and other parapro-
fessionals greater opportunity to practice, but the medical profession resists such
changes. Hospitals increasingly compete for patients, however, and with that
competition has come some greater attention to the quality of care.

Bringing about any significant reforms in the delivery of health services in
the United States will be difficult. Powerful interests such as insurance companies oppose changes that might undermine their profits. In the case of the
Affordable Care Act, there is more support from the medical care providers than
for most previous programs, but there is more popular opposition. There are
strong pressures to preserve the status quo, although physicians are becoming
increasingly concerned about the control that insurers exert over their practices
in the name of cost containment. It may well be that only introduction of a
large-scale reform, such as national health insurance, will be sufficient to break
the existing system of finance and delivery to provide better and more equitable
medical care for most Americans.

CHAPTER 12

Income Maintenance: Social Security and Welfare

THE EXISTENCE OF POVERTY in the midst of affluence has been a pressing issue throughout the past century in the United States. Although economic progress had, until the beginning of the twenty-first century, been slowly reducing the level of poverty, a slowed economy and policy changes have caused a recent surge in poverty levels. Inequality has been increasing markedly, with the very affluent benefiting more from economic growth and the vast majority of Americans lagging behind. With these trends in poverty, the full effects of the economic crisis may take some years to be felt in all sectors of the economy. Whether the means of change will come through better jobs in the private sector or through public programs, at least 460 million Americans—a large proportion of them children—were living below the official poverty line at the end of 2011, still waiting to enter the economic mainstream of American life.

The United States has frequently been described as a welfare state "laggard" because its expenditures on social policies are low compared with those of other industrialized nations and because it has not adopted certain public programs, such as child benefits and sickness insurance, that are common in other countries.[1] There is a gap between the United States and other Western democracies, but it has narrowed as U.S. expenditures for social programs continue to increase, while services and expenditures in many other countries have declined or stabilized since the 1980s. Increased spending in the United States reflects some new programs but mostly the rising cost of established programs, particularly Social Security. U.S. social programs, broadly defined, cost almost $2 trillion in 2010 and provided services to millions of clients.[2] They now account for approximately one-third of all federal spending and approximately 40 percent of total public spending.

The debate over social programs in the United States has shifted rather dramatically since the early 1990s. Throughout most of the existence of what has been called "the American welfare state," aid to individuals who could, in principle, work but did not has been controversial. In 1996, the existing "welfare" program—Aid to Families with Dependent Children (AFDC)—was replaced by Temporary Assistance to Needy Families (TANF), a program that is referred to colloquially as "workfare." The new program eliminated many of the complaints that conservatives—and many ordinary citizens—had expressed about aid for the poor, and the issue was effectively defused by that Clinton-era reform.

With controversy over welfare minimized, the Social Security program instead became the center of political conflict. Social Security has been a great success since its inception in the 1930s and has had wide public support. Threats to its solvency, however, and fears about the continuation of benefits made Social Security a central issue in the 2000 and 2004 presidential campaigns. The Democratic candidates (Al Gore in 2000 and John Kerry in 2004) advocated incremental change in the Social Security program, and the Republican candidate, George W. Bush, pressed for permitting younger workers to put at least part of their contributions to the program into private savings accounts, which presumably would provide higher benefits and also help address the problem of low savings levels. That proposal was not implemented, and indeed the attempt to reform Social Security generated a great deal of negative reaction against the Bush administration.[3]

What are these social programs that cost so much and touch the lives of so many citizens? Leaving aside programs such as public housing, education, and health care, all of which have obvious social importance, we are left with an array of programs that provide a broad range of services and benefits. The largest in terms of cost and number of beneficiaries are *social insurance* programs, such as Social Security (old age and disability pensions), unemployment insurance, and workers' compensation (see Table 12.1). These social insurance programs and their costs have continued to grow rapidly, despite the common assumption that there is no American welfare state. Means-tested benefits, such as workfare, food stamps, and Supplemental Security Income—which are available only to individuals willing to demonstrate that their earnings fall below the level of need designated by each program—also are significant expenditures. These *social assistance* programs involve significant state and local as well as federal expenditures; the federal government actually spends relatively little on means-tested social programs. Finally, there are *personal social services* directed toward improving the quality of life for individuals through services such as counseling, adoption, foster care, and rehabilitation.

These three kinds of social programs address different needs and usually benefit different clients. Each has its own programmatic and political problems, which we address in this chapter. Despite their apparent vulnerability to political pressures in a society that has emphasized the virtues of self-reliance, some

TABLE 12.1 Costs of Federal Income Maintenance Programs, 1980–2007
(in millions of dollars)

	1980	1990	2000	2007	Percentage increase
Social Security	117,118	248,600	409,400	586,500	500
Unemployment	18,327	18,900	23,000	39,000	213
Food stamps	9,100	24,000	32,500	55,900	614
Public housing	7,200	15,900	28,900	38,300	532
Public assistance	19,398	34,900	88,300	126,300	651
Other	73,200	57,100	82,400	102,900	140
Total	298,200	399,400	664,500	948,900	318
Percentage of public expenditures	28.2	31.9	37.1	34.0	39.1

Source: Statistical Abstract of the United States (Washington, DC: U.S. Government Printing Office, annual).

characteristics of social programs, especially social insurance programs such as Social Security, make it difficult to reduce them and also produce some demands for increases. Too many people (and/or their aging parents) depend on social insurance programs for their livelihood for politicians to be anxious to cut spending for them, despite rhetoric about the need for fundamental change.

The pressures to preserve and enhance the programs will be insistent as the population continues to age and the full effects of potential reforms become evident. Thus, although President Barack Obama has promised to find ways of reducing entitlement expenditures, social programs are likely to remain a major political battleground in the United States. The pressures for reforming some aspects of entitlement expenditures have been increased by the large federal deficit, but at the same time, the economic crisis has made more people dependent upon unemployment insurance and other social programs.

Social Insurance

The largest single federal expenditure program of any type is Social Security. Although generally thought of as providing pensions for retired workers, Social Security also offers other protections to those who have contributed to it. It provides cash benefits for the survivors of workers who die before retirement, including benefits for a deceased worker's children until they reach the age of eighteen, if they are not employed. It provides disability benefits for workers who become incapable of earning a living and any dependents. Finally, Medicare is

TABLE 12.2   Social Insurance Recipients, 2012

Program	Number
Social Security	
Retired workers and families	38,520,000
Disabled workers and families	10,342,000
Survivors	6,464,000
Unemployment insurance	12,488,000
Workers' compensation	2,234,000

Source: U.S. Bureau of the Census, *Sources of Income* (Washington, DC: U.S. Bureau of the Census, 2012).

linked with Social Security for financing purposes. The two other significant social insurance programs in the United States are unemployment insurance, managed by the states with a federal subsidy, and workers' compensation, managed by the states with employers bearing most of the cost. Workers' compensation is the American equivalent of the industrial accidents insurance common in other industrialized countries.

Table 12.2 provides information about the recipients of social insurance benefits. By far, the largest number is retired workers, although a significant number of citizens also receive benefits under other social insurance programs. Likewise, the largest share of social insurance spending goes to retired persons, although the highest average benefit paid in 2006 was to the unemployed, followed closely by the benefit for disabled workers. Many social changes are responsible for the growing number of social insurance recipients. The most important is that the average age of Americans is increasing, making more people eligible for retirement benefits. Also, the passage of the Americans with Disabilities Act in 1991 made people more conscious of their right to disability benefits, and more attorneys now advertise their availability to pursue disability claims. Social insurance programs are all entitlement programs, meaning that citizens who have paid into them cannot be denied benefits once they meet the criteria for eligibility.

We must understand several important characteristics of social insurance programs, especially Social Security, if we are to comprehend the programs and the political debates that sometimes surround them. First, social insurance programs do relatively little, considering the sums spent on them, to redistribute income across economic classes.[4] Instead, they tend to redistribute income across time and across generations. Unlike a private annuity, in which an individual pays in money that accumulates in a personal account, Social Security is a direct transfer program that taxes working people and their employers and pays out that money to the beneficiaries. Workers and their employers pay taxes into the fund while they are employed, reducing their income at that time, and they receive benefits when they retire or if they become disabled.

Second, although they are not actuarially sound, these programs are conceptualized as insurance. Many citizens continue to believe that they are purchasing an insurance policy through payroll taxes. For example, in one poll almost one-quarter of respondents believed that their contributions were being retained for their own retirement rather than paying for current recipients.[5] Defining the programs as social insurance has been crucial in legitimating them, as many citizens would not have been willing to accept a public pension to which they had not contributed; they would regard it as charity. Furthermore, most members of Congress in 1935 (when the programs were enacted) would not have been willing to vote for the programs if they had not been defined as insurance. This insurance element is also important because of the implicit contract between the citizen and the government. More than any other public program, Social Security is an entitlement program—citizens believe they have a legal and moral claim to receive benefits, in large part because they have contributed throughout their working lives.

The insurance nature of Social Security programs also helps explain their financing, which, as we have said, is accomplished through payroll contributions, paid equally by employers and employees. Social Security taxes are not paid on all earnings, but on only the first $110,100 (in 2012) each year, at a nominal rate of 6.2 percent, although this was reduced in 2012 to 4.2 percent to stimulate the economy. The health insurance component is now paid on all earnings at a rate of 1.45 percent. Rates of tax and the ceiling at which individuals stop paying social insurance taxes have increased over time to cover rising costs. Because it was envisioned as an insurance program and not as a vehicle for redistributive social policy, the Social Security tax has been a flat rate rather than a progressive tax—all income earners pay the same rate on their income up to the annual limit. Most respondents to surveys on Social Security would, however, like to see the upper limit removed, so that the system receives more income from higher-income earners.[6]

All the money collected by this payroll tax is earmarked for Social Security benefits, and only Social Security taxes are available for financing benefits.[7] This system makes the tax, and the program in general, more palatable to many citizens, but it also severely constrains its financial base. In recent years, the specter of the Social Security system "going bankrupt" has been a part of the political debate. Although it was not a dominant issue in the 2008 election, discussion of Social Security bankruptcy continues. Despite some optimistic forecasts about economic growth and associated higher tax revenues, spending for Social Security is expected to begin to outstrip revenues by around 2017, according to the latest estimate.[8]

The second aspect of financing that is crucial for understanding the contemporary debate is the Social Security Trust Fund. During the past several decades—while the large baby boom generation, born in the years immediately after World War II, has been employed and the economy has enjoyed reasonably high rates of growth—the Social Security system has been receiving more income from taxes than it has been spending on benefits. As this generation begins to retire in large numbers around 2010, however, more money will flow out than flows in, and the money that has been accumulating in the trust fund will begin to run out. Conservatives have argued that this is the case especially because the funds have been invested in relatively low yield (but extremely safe) government securities rather than in the stock market. Their preference for a larger private sector element in Social Security has produced proposals to permit citizens to invest at least a part of their Social Security taxes in the market (see below).

Social Security now includes almost all working people—in 2012, well over 90 percent of employed Americans were covered. That includes a large number of self-employed individuals, who pay a self-employment tax equal to the employee's and employer's contributions. The principal groups now excluded from the program are federal government employees hired before 1984, employees of many state and local governments, and some farm workers. These exclusions are made for administrative convenience or because of constitutional inhibitions on the federal government's ability to tax state or local governments, but many employers who could avoid the system opt into it to provide protections for their employees.

Finally, the benefits of the program are only partially related to earnings.[9] Those who pay more into the program during their working lives receive larger benefits when they retire, but those at the bottom of the income ladder receive a higher rate of return on their contributions, and a greater proportion of their earnings is replaced when they retire (see Table 12.3). Social Security is slightly redistributive in that it attempts to ensure that those at the bottom of the earnings ladder have something approximating an adequate retirement income. Still, it is difficult to argue that anyone living entirely on Social Security, even at the full benefit level, receives enough money to live comfortably. The average worker or family receives about 40 percent of preretirement income under Social Security; upper-level earners about 25 percent.

The redistributive element of Social Security has been increased by raising taxes on benefits paid to more affluent recipients. For most of the program's history, the pensions paid to retired Americans have not been taxable, regardless of income. Beginning in 1984, however, Social Security benefits became taxable. In 2012, recipients with taxable incomes $25,000 for an individual or $32,000 for a couple pay tax on 50 percent of their Social Security benefits. At above $34,000 for individuals and $44,000 for couples, tax is levied on 85 percent of benefits.[10]

TABLE 12.3   Current and Projected Earnings Replacement Ratios of Social Security
Benefits (in percentages)

Year	Low earnings[a]	Medium earnings[b]	High earnings[c]	Contributing at the maximum level
2007	54.2	40.2	27.9	24.6
2010	56.3	41.9	34.6	26.9

Source: Social Security Administration, *Annual Report* (Washington, DC: Social Security
Administration, 2007).

a. 65 percent of average Social Security wage rate.

b. 100 percent of average Social Security wage rate.

c. 140 percent of average Social Security wage rate.

Problems in Social Security

Although Social Security is widely accepted and generally very popular with the
public, several problems in the program should be considered. The problems
arise when legislation to amend Social Security is considered, and they were central to the work of the 1996 and 2001 commissions that reviewed it. These policy problems have political ramifications that affect Social Security's treatment in
Congress and by the president. They also reflect the difficulty of making adjustments to a successful program that is threatened by social and demographic
change.[11] Social Security has been maintained with incremental adjustments for
almost eighty years but now may need fundamental reform.

The retirement test.   One problem that is being eliminated gradually is the
retirement test—the penalty imposed on recipients of Social Security who wish
to supplement their benefits by working. As the program is currently managed,
if a recipient earns a certain amount of money (excluding income from private
retirement funds or investments), a penalty is imposed on the benefits paid to
him or her. In 2012, Social Security recipients below their full retirement age
could earn $14,640 a year without penalty but would lose $1 in benefits for every
$2 earned over that amount. In the year an individual reaches his or her full
retirement age, an individual earning over $38,800 a year loses $1 for every $3
earned; after the full retirement age, earnings are unlimited with no penalty on
benefits.[12] For the person younger than sixty-five, there is, in effect, a 50 percent
tax on earnings over the income allowed, a tax rate higher than that imposed on
any individual paying the federal income tax.

There are several good reasons for continuing to remove the retirement test.
First, if the program is conceived as social insurance rather than as a means-tested
benefit, recipients should receive benefits as a matter of right, much as the

recipients of private annuities do. The retirement test thus gives the lie to the idea of Social Security as an insurance program. Because retirees are to some extent punished if they work, attempting to move out of the labor force gradually, they may stop working and cease paying Social Security taxes, whereas if they continued to work more, they could pay some of their own benefits through taxes. The higher tax cost for the program borne by the working-age population becomes especially troubling as the population ages and there are fewer active workers to pay for the benefits of retirees.

There are also humane reasons for eliminating or modifying the retirement test. As the life expectancy of American citizens has increased, many individuals are capable of continuing to work after the usual retirement age. In a society that frequently defines an individual's worth on the basis of his or her work, the inability to work without paying a penalty for it may impose severe psychological as well as economic burdens on the retiree. More flexible or unlimited earnings would allow Social Security recipients to participate in the labor market, although perhaps not to the extent they did previously, and would permit phasing out employment rather than a sudden and often traumatic retirement.

On the other side of the argument, allowing retirees to continue working could have a significant effect on the job prospects of other potential employees, especially those just entering the labor market: Every retiree who continued to work would mean one less job for a young person. Youth unemployment (especially for minority groups) is a significant problem, and the needs of the elderly must be balanced against the needs of younger people. Additionally, allowing retirees to continue working and still receive benefits would amount to a direct transfer of income from the young to the old, based simply on age rather than on participation in the labor market. The strong economy in the late 1990s created a continuing need for the skills and abilities of workers who might otherwise have retired under the Social Security system, but as the economy slowed, it became apparent that opening opportunities for younger workers might be more beneficial.

Fixed retirement age.   Establishing a fixed retirement age is related to the problem of a retirement test. The standard retirement age was sixty-five for a number of years and then increased gradually to sixty-seven. Under the Social Security system, individuals receive some additional benefits for working after this age, although they must continue to pay Social Security taxes on their earnings. In addition, if individuals choose to retire before reaching the official retirement age, their benefits are reduced even if they have been paying into the system for years.

Good justifications can be found both for raising and for lowering the retirement age. If the retirement age were raised, total program costs would be reduced, for people would not depend on the program as long. When Social

Security was adopted in 1935, only about half the male population could expect to live to age sixty-five, and those who reached sixty-five could expect to live about twelve years longer. By 2010, however, 78 percent of males are expected to live to sixty-five and to receive program benefits for over sixteen years thereafter.[13] In addition, the nature of work and the educational level and health status of workers have all been improving. Thus, there are more retirees, and each retiree costs more today, so total program costs are increasing. When the baby boom generation begins retiring in 2010, an additional 77 million recipients will come onto the Social Security rolls; delaying their retirement could help maintain the solvency of Social Security. One preliminary recommendation of the 1998 National Commission on Retirement Policy was to raise the retirement age to seventy.[14] Some workers would not be able to maintain their lifestyles if forced to retire, especially after so many individual retirement plans lost value during the 2008–2009 economic crisis.

On the other side of the argument are some good reasons to lower the retirement age. Many people who have retirement income in addition to Social Security may want to retire while they are still in good health and capable of enjoying more years of leisure. There has been a tendency for people to retire earlier, especially the more affluent. Lowering the retirement age might create additional job openings for unemployed youth. A flexible retirement age could make it easier to modernize the nation's workforce, as workers with obsolete skills might move to Social Security more readily and thus reduce some of the human costs of modernization and economic change.

The treatment of women and families.   When the Social Security system was designed, the vast majority of women were housewives who did not work outside the home and who remained married to the same men for their entire lives. Those characteristics would hardly describe the average woman in the United States today, and therefore, some aspects of the treatment of women under Social Security now appear outdated and even blatantly discriminatory. For example, if a woman is married to a covered employee for fewer than ten years, a divorce cancels her access to the former husband's benefits, and for Social Security purposes it is as if they had never been married. And because the benefits an individual receives are roughly based on contributions, a woman who has not been working but returns to work or begins to work after such a divorce will find it difficult to accumulate enough credits for a significant retirement benefit. Given that marriages that end in divorce last, on average, seven years, a significant number of women (and increasingly some men) lose the Social Security benefits of having been married.

If both husband and wife work, as is now true for many if not most married couples in the United States, the pair receive little additional pension if they remain married. This is true even though they may pay twice as much in Social Security contributions as a couple with only one worker. Benefits are based on each partner's individual work record, and there is no spousal benefit unless one worker would receive more from a spousal benefit than from her or his own work. Therefore, on average, the replacement rate for a one-worker couple with average earnings is 61 percent; for two-earner couples, the replacement rate is 44 percent. At higher rates of income, this "marriage penalty" is even more severe.[15]

An even broader question is whether a woman, or a man, who chooses not to work outside the home should receive some Social Security protection based on her or his contributions to the household and to society through work in the home. A "homemaker's credit" has been proposed to give these individuals their own protection within Social Security. This kind of protection may be especially important in case of disability. If the homemaker becomes disabled, especially with children still in the home, it would impose additional personal or financial burdens on the family, as other family members would have to do the work that the homemaker had performed or pay to have it done. With the current financial pressures on Social Security, however, there is little likelihood of homemakers' benefits being expanded, and if anything, the treatment of women under Social Security may become even less generous.

The disability test.   In addition to providing benefits in retirement or if a family breadwinner dies, Social Security protects families whose breadwinner is unable to work because of sickness or injury. The "substantial gainful employment" test for people seeking to qualify for those benefits is rather harsh, requiring that a person be totally disabled before he or she can receive benefits.[16] The individual must be disqualified from any substantial gainful employment that is available within the area of the potential beneficiary and for which he or she has the requisite skills.[17] These standards are much more stringent than those applied in private disability programs, which require only that the person be unable to engage in his or her customary occupation or in other public programs, such as the black lung program or veterans programs.[18] At present, less than 50 percent of applicants for disability receive benefits. In addition, the Social Security Amendments of 1980 mandated frequent reexaminations of the eligibility of program claimants, with the result that significant numbers of people have been removed from the program.[19] There has been a movement to tighten eligibility for people with substance abuse problems.[20]

The stringency of the disability test requires workers who have any disability to leave the workforce almost entirely if they are to receive disability benefits. A situation can arise, however, in which an individual is too unhealthy to earn an adequate income and yet not unhealthy enough to receive benefits. For both social and financial reasons, it would be beneficial to have a graduated disability test to assist those who have a partial disability but who wish to continue to be as productive as they can. A person could be assigned a percentage disability and compensated accordingly. Such a test is already used by the Veterans Administration.

The disability tests employed in the workers' compensation program (another accident and disability program) vary markedly from state to state, but generally they are less stringent than the Social Security test.[21] There are provisions for permanent partial disability payments that enable a person to continue doing some work other than his or her original occupation. Although the option of granting limited disability is in many ways beneficial, it is also the source of a great deal of litigation. Workers' compensation programs now cover almost 90 percent of the American workforce, but states provide different levels of benefits.[22]

Social Security disability has a number of links with other federal programs. One compilation found ninety-five federal programs directly targeted to the disabled and another ninety-seven programs with some benefits for the disabled.[23] This complex and sometimes contradictory array of programs makes administering the Social Security program in a fair and effective manner all the more difficult.

Social Security and the Economy

Social Security has a significant effect on the American economy. The most commonly cited effect is the reduction of individual savings and the consequent reduction in the amount of capital available for investment. Because individuals know that their retirement will be at least partly financed by Social Security, they do not save as much during their working lives as they might otherwise. Because Social Security does not accumulate as large an amount of reserves to pay future benefits as it might if it were a private annuity program, there is less capital accumulation in the U.S. economy than there might otherwise be.[24] Estimates of the magnitude of savings lost as a result of the Social Security program vary widely. Most experts believe that there is some loss but that the disincentive to save is less than many conservative critics of the program have argued.[25]

The second major effect is reduced labor market participation by older workers. As with the economic effect of reduced savings, estimating the magnitude of this effect on total growth and productivity is difficult, but several empirical studies have documented that there is some effect. Also, as the number of young workers entering the labor market decreases, the skills of older workers become increasingly valuable to the economy. Matching the desire of some workers—but far from all—to continue working and the needs of the economy will require building even greater flexibility into a program that is already substantially more flexible than when initiated.

Financing Social Security

We now come to the most frequently discussed question concerning Social Security: How can the program be financed in a way that will maintain the benefits expected by the people who have paid into it? Periodically since the 1960s, there have been reports that Social Security was going bankrupt, raising the specter that many elderly people would be left with no income for their old age. In 1984, President Reagan said that he did not believe that citizens currently making contributions to the system would ever receive much back in benefits.[26] Many citizens came to believe that negative prognosis, and in the mid-1980s, less than half of all Americans expressed confidence in Social Security. The lack of confidence has been rather stable since that time, with 38 percent of the population in 2009 reporting that they were "not at all confident" that the Social Security system would be able to pay them full benefits throughout their retirement.[27]

The concern about the crisis in Social Security may appear foolish, given that the system is still running a surplus and has accumulated a significant trust fund (see Table 12.4). However, within the next two decades, the retirement of the huge age cohort born between 1945 and 1952 threatens to send the system into deficit and to exhaust reserves. The exact date varies according to the assumptions used, but under most assumptions, funds would be exhausted by around 2020. If the current economic slowdown continues, it would be sooner.

Such dire outcomes, however, are extremely unlikely. Indeed, at other times, the Social Security system has run large surpluses that politicians have used to balance an otherwise unbalanced federal budget.[28] The debate during the 2000 presidential campaign stressed the need to separate Social Security from other parts of the budget, putting the fund in a "lockbox," and the 107th Congress passed legislation to protect the surplus at least partially. But the Social Security system as a program financed entirely by payroll taxes may be in long-term difficulty.[29] Current projections suggest that younger workers may be called on to finance it with ever-higher payroll taxes, but they may be reluctant to do so if they fear that they will not later receive the benefits themselves.[30]

TABLE 12.4   Changes in Social Security Trust Fund, 1980–2010 (in billions of dollars)

	1980	*1985*	*1990*	*1995*	*2000*	*2005*	*2010*
Income	105.3	182.1	288.8	332.9	490.5	604.3	677.1
Benefits paid	105.1	167.2	223.0	291.6	352.7	441.9	584.9
Assets	22.8	35.8	214.2	458.5	931.0	1,663.0	2,429.0

Source: Social Security Administration, *Annual Report of the Board of Trustees* (Washington, DC: Social Security Administration, annual).

As we have said, the most obvious reason for the financial difficulties of Social Security is the increasing number of aging Americans. In 1960, only 9 percent of the U.S. population was over sixty-five; by 1990, that figure had increased to almost 13 percent, and it is expected to increase to almost 20 percent by 2025. In 1984, each Social Security beneficiary was supported by the taxes of approximately 3.3 active workers. In 2001, there were actually 3.4 workers for each beneficiary, but the ratio then began to fall rapidly. By 2030, it is estimated that each beneficiary will be supported by only 2.1 workers, and by 2050, by less than 2.0 active workers.[31]

Another factor increasing the difficulty of financing Social Security has been the indexing of benefits to increases in prices and wages. Under existing arrangements, the initial benefit paid retirees is adjusted annually to reflect changes in the average wages paid in the economy. In addition, in every twelve-month period during which prices increase by more than 3 percent, benefits are adjusted to retain approximately constant purchasing power. Indexing benefits (a cost-of-living adjustment, or COLA) is an obvious target for those seeking to control social program costs. As Social Security faced a crisis in 1983, legislation was passed that imposed a one-time delay of six months in the COLA, a move that saved $40 billion from fiscal 1983 through fiscal 1988. Another suggestion, by a group of economists at the usually moderate-to-liberal Brookings Institution, was to eliminate the COLA in any year in which inflation is less than 5 percent; if inflation is greater than 5 percent, the correction would be the rate of inflation less 5 percent. Another suggestion would have the COLA pegged several percentage points lower than the inflation rate.[32] All these suggestions encountered opposition from the active and expanding lobbying organizations for the elderly because they could produce serious hardships. One study has estimated that a COLA three percentage points below inflation would put more than a million elderly below the official poverty line within several years.

Considering the financial pressures on Social Security, it is reasonable to question whether the system can afford to continue financing itself entirely through payroll taxes. And there are questions about the payroll tax itself, perhaps the most important being that the tax is regressive, exacting a higher percentage of tax from low-paid workers than from the more affluent, as discussed above. The payroll tax is also regressive in that workers actually bear the burden of the employer's contribution (the same 7.65 percent of salaries and wages, up to the cap) because employers count their contribution as a part of the cost of employing a worker and then reduce wages, or the number of employees, accordingly.[33] In addition, the Social Security tax is applied only to salaries and wages, not to earnings from dividends or interest. These disparities are justified because the system is conceptualized as providing insurance and not as providing benefits directly proportional to earnings; once you have paid your annual "premium" on the insurance policy, there is no need to pay more.

The payroll tax has the further disadvantage of being relatively visible to employees.[34] They see the money deducted for Social Security from each paycheck, and they have some idea of how much money they pay into the system. This visibility means that the level of payroll taxation may be limited by real or potential taxpayer resistance. Using this relatively visible tax in conjunction with the personal income tax, however, would make the total tax bite on wages less obvious.

The earmarked payroll tax does have one advantage that some people believe is worth retaining: Because the receipts from this tax are relatively limited, politicians are prevented from using the Social Security system for political gain. That is, because general tax revenue (primarily from the income tax) is not used to finance the system, it would be difficult for a president or Congress to increase benefits just before an election to attempt to win votes from the elderly (although the present cost-of-living adjustments may have some of that potential because they tend to go into effect shortly before election time in November).

Reforming Social Security

Despite its problems, Social Security remains a very popular program, and most citizens would prefer to keep or increase benefits rather than reduce taxes (see Table 12.5). Various proposals have been made to alleviate some of the financial problems. Among the simple, incremental changes proposed is to remove the financing of Medicare from the payroll tax—currently 1.45 percent of the 7.65 percent payroll deduction—and finance it through general revenues. That would leave Social Security with more money, while retaining the existing payroll tax rate. Another possibility is to change the COLA adjustment and timing, as described above, although in a period of high inflation such a change might work a considerable hardship on the elderly. Raising the retirement age, or at least making it more flexible, is another possible solution, as is reduction of some welfare-like benefits attached to the program, such as spouses' benefits. One minor such benefit—the burial allowance—has in some cases already been eliminated.

Another way of tinkering with the program would be to make it truly comprehensive, including all workers. New federal government employees are now in the system, but state and local government employees can still opt out. Bringing these workers under Social Security would expand the base of white-collar workers who earn better-than-average incomes and could help to shore up the system for some time. There might also be psychological benefits to pointing out that all citizens share in the same Social Security system. A large majority of Americans support making the system totally inclusive, but legal barriers exist that may

TABLE 12.5 Opinions on Coping with Problems in Social Security (in percentages)

*"If it were necessary to keep the Social Security program
paying benefits as it does now, would you favor or oppose . . . ?"*

	Favor	Oppose
Increasing the amount of income subject to Social Security tax	53	43
Reducing future benefits for wealthy retirees	46	52
Raising the Social Security tax rate	31	64
Raising the retirement age	33	66

Source: ABC News/*Washington Post* poll, March 10–13, 2011, www.washington post.com/wp-srv/politics/polls/postpoll_03142011.html.

prevent that from happening. Furthermore, given the financial difficulties facing the system, that change might only add claimants while adding little revenue.

A rather more significant change would be to convert the entire basis of Social Security financing from payroll contributions to general revenue, either through the income tax or through a value-added tax (VAT) like that used in Europe.[35] The VAT is a tax levied on businesses at each stage of production, based on the value that each business adds to the raw materials used to create the product it sells. The VAT has the advantages of being virtually invisible, its cost reflected only in the price of a product, and of being somewhat less regressive than the payroll tax, especially if commodities such as food and prescription drugs are untaxed. The invisibility of the VAT would be an advantage for those managing Social Security, although many citizens might not regard it as such; using VAT funds would allow Social Security income to expand with less restraint than the present system of financing. It has also been suggested that all Social Security benefits should be counted as taxable income.

In contrast to the "tinkering" reforms described above, some reformers have proposed an almost complete overhaul of the system.[36] At the extreme, libertarian and conservative critics of Social Security have suggested a move toward complete privatization. Beginning with younger workers, the funds that now go to Social Security would be invested privately, much as 401(k) plan contributions are.[37] These reformers used to argue that current participants in the program are much worse off than they would be if they had been investing in the stock market, or even in safer money market funds. George W. Bush and a panel he commissioned to study Social Security reform made recommendations along these lines, proposing to allow workers to contribute 2 percent of their taxable wages, or 4 percent of their Social Security contributions, to a personal account, with traditional benefits offset by the returns from those accounts.

Privatizing Social Security, or even creating a mixed system as advocated by the president's commission, presents a number of problems. One is transition. The ability of Social Security to pay benefits to current beneficiaries is in part dependent on the inflow of funds from current workers; if they were no longer paying into the system, the feared bankruptcy of the system might become a reality, even if benefits and taxes were phased out over an extended period. The privatization of Social Security also would place a great burden on the individual participant. Participants would have to be willing to take the risk of investing in the stock market and would have to understand that the certainty of Social Security was being sacrificed for the possibility of higher gains, or high losses, in the market (see Figure 12.1). Many such proposals for reforming public retirement looked extremely promising when the stock market was experiencing unprecedented growth in the late 1990s, but recent economic uncertainties and falling stock prices have caused most Americans to breathe a sigh of relief that Social Security had not been changed radically. After the negative possibilities of personal investment accounts as a part of Social Security became more visible, support for the proposal has largely disappeared.

In addition to plans for complete privatization of Social Security, there have been more moderate proposals for involving the private sector. One such proposal is to begin to move the population away from social insurance as we have

Question: "As you may know, a proposal has been made that would allow workers to invest part of their Social Security taxes in the stock market or in bonds, while the rest of those taxes would remain in the Social Security system. Do you favor or oppose this proposal?"

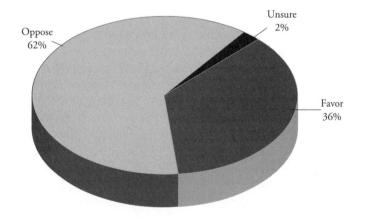

FIGURE 12.1   Opinion on Social Security Privatization (percentages of poll respondents)
Source: CNN/Opinion Research Corporation Poll, October 3–5, 2008.

known it, toward something resembling a private annuity program. The late senator Daniel Patrick Moynihan, D-NY, once proposed a "2 percent solution": reducing Social Security taxes by 2 percent and permitting participants to invest that money in private retirement accounts.[38] Other members of Congress and some economists have favored diverting even more money into private accounts. Benefits for recipients with private accounts would be scaled back, saving public money and ensuring the long-term solvency of the program for the people who depend on it.

The assumption of partial privatization proposals is that greater use of the private sector would give the average retiree more money for retirement, while relieving the public sector of a major potential financial burden. Moving some people into such a new system, however, would not eliminate questions about the solvency of the system or calls for raising the retirement age and making all income taxable. Indeed, there should be some concern whether a privatized system would be able to provide the level of pensions the reformers expect or even the return available under the existing social insurance scheme.

Overall, although it seems clear that the Social Security program will continue, some way must be found to finance a program of public retirement that will provide an adequate, or at least minimal, income for pensioners without bankrupting the working-age population. Some response must also be made to increasing demands for removal of some of the rigidities and discrimination from the system, making it more humane and responsive to changing social and economic conditions. The Social Security system, in all probability, will continue to be a major success story in public policy but one that will remain prominent on the policymaking agenda.

Means-Tested Programs

The second major category of social programs comprises means-tested programs. To qualify for benefits, an individual must satisfy a means test—or more accurately, an absence-of-means test. Applicants cannot earn more than a specified amount nor have any significant assets if they are to qualify for most means-tested programs. Rather obviously, then, these programs benefit groups of people, defined by economic criteria, who are generally neither the most influential in society nor the easiest to mobilize politically. The means testing itself tends to stigmatize and degrade individuals who must apply for the benefits. These programs are not entitlements in the strict sense of the term, although political and judicial actions have tended to make them more matters of right than in the past.[39]

Means-tested programs have been the focus of a good deal of ideological debate, even in a country that tends toward more pragmatic than ideological politics.[40] Some citizens who regard means-tested benefits as "handouts" or "giveaways" describe the recipients as "lazy welfare cheaters" and sing songs about "welfare Cadillacs." President Reagan once referred to recipients of the Aid to Families with Dependent Children (AFDC) program as "welfare queens."[41] More intellectual critics of the programs have blamed them for social disintegration, family breakups, and rising rates of urban crime. Racial issues are also involved in attitudes toward means-tested benefits, for although the majority of welfare recipients are white, a disproportionate share of blacks and Hispanics are aid recipients. Means-tested benefits, including the former AFDC program and its successor, the Personal Responsibility and Work Opportunity Reconciliation Act, as well as food stamps (now SNAP—the Supplemental Nutrition Assistance Program), Supplemental Security Income, and a variety of other programs, provide the only livelihood for many citizens, and they are criticized by some as both inadequate and demeaning.[42] The programs are also criticized as being excessively bureaucratic and difficult to administer, prompting radical proposals such as simple cash grants to the needy. What is clear is that the programs raise several important social, political, and economic issues.

AFDC and the Origins of Welfare

The largest means-tested program, and the one that generated the most political controversy, was AFDC, or welfare. In 1994, this program benefited more than 14 million Americans, including approximately 8 million children. It cost the federal government over $14 billion, or less than 1 percent of its overall expenditures, and was responsible for less than 5 percent of the federal deficit that year. AFDC took a larger share of state government expenditures, especially as the welfare rolls increased substantially during the early 1990s.[43] AFDC was expensive—if perhaps not so expensive as some believed—and because the program provided benefits on the basis of need rather than contributions, it was controversial in a market-oriented society. AFDC was growing in number of recipients and expense, and that produced heavy pressure for reform. Although the program was replaced during the Clinton administration, it is important to understand the nature of the reforms and the ways in which U.S. social policy has been changing in recent years.

It is especially interesting that the controversy over AFDC arose during the 1960s and 1970s, rather than in the 1930s when it was adopted. The program originated as a part of the package that produced Social Security, but at that time, the major controversy was over Social Security rather than AFDC; it was assumed that AFDC would be used by a relatively small number of widows with children.[44] By 1988, however, fewer than 15 percent of the recipients were widows, wives of disabled men, or unemployed—those for whom the program was intended. Changing family patterns also played a part in the low status of AFDC recipients; as many more women went to work in the economy, women generally began to be regarded as perfectly capable of earning their own way. These societal changes contributed to the push for reform of the program.

AFDC, although a national program, was administered by states and localities. The federal government provided a small subsidy to the states for the program; the remainder of the benefits came from state and local funds. The benefits varied widely across states, ranging from $924 a month for a family of three in Alaska (which has a very high cost of living) to $120 a month in Mississippi. In 1992, the average across the nation was $395 per month. None of the benefit levels was munificent, and the substantial disparities were only partly due to differences in the cost of living in the various localities.

The states also used AFDC payments to regulate the behavior of recipients. The image of the "welfare mother" having illegitimate children to qualify for benefits made it difficult for program supporters to improve benefits, and as a result, several states refused to increase payments for mothers who had additional children while receiving AFDC.[45] Some states gave lower AFDC benefits to recipients who had just moved in from out of state. Among other regulations, several states reduced benefits for AFDC recipients whose children did not attend school regularly, others cut off payments to teenage mothers who did not live with a parent or legal guardian, and some even required all welfare recipients to be fingerprinted to help reduce fraud.[46]

The AFDC program was not without major problems, but the problems were often exaggerated in the popular mind. First, AFDC actually cost the federal government relatively little. Most people did not remain on the program for life. In 1994, more than one-third of recipients had been on the program one year or less, and over 78 percent had been on it for five years or less. The median time on the program was twenty-two months. Also, almost as many whites as African Americans were receiving AFDC. Finally, divorce and separation, rather than childbearing without benefit of marriage, were the major reasons for accepting AFDC.

Stigmatization.   Programs that require recipients to prove that they are indigent stigmatize the recipients, especially in a society that places a high value on success and income as symbols of personal worth. Most recipients of welfare benefits are relatively powerless, and the stigma attached to AFDC lessened their feelings of self-worth. That stigmatization may have helped to perpetuate the problems that caused their indigence in the first place. Unfortunately, the AFDC program as designed tended to perpetuate indigence rather than allow people to work their way out of poverty.

Punishment for working.   The aspect of AFDC that appeared to make the least sense was that a recipient could work no more than 100 hours per month, no matter what the rate of pay, and after a certain amount was earned each year (the sum varied by state), the recipient was required to return $2 in benefits for every $3 earned—in effect, a higher rate of tax than any current income tax.[47] Obviously, such a high rate of "tax" on earnings undercut the incentive for individuals to work. In addition, because other benefits, such as food stamps and Medicaid, might be tied to receiving AFDC, going out to take a job meant the loss of a great deal more than the AFDC check.[48]

Family structure.   AFDC also had negative effects on family structure. Under most circumstances, a woman with children could not receive benefits if an able-bodied male resided in the home. This meant that traditional families, whose virtues were stressed by politicians such as Bill Clinton and Dan Quayle, usually were not eligible for AFDC. The requirement also made it more difficult for a woman on AFDC to work, since she must either care for the children herself or find suitable day care facilities. It also had deleterious effects on children, who grew up in fatherless households. The latter became less unusual, however, as single-parent families became more common in the United States.[49]

Costs and benefits.   Depending on whom you asked, the benefits of AFDC were either too high or too low. Critics concerned about the costs of the program argued that "generous" benefits encouraged people to stay on welfare rather than find a job. On the other side of the argument, most recipients of AFDC benefits would point out that even the highest monthly state benefit was hardly sufficient for a life of leisure and that many benefits were too low to provide a decent living for the recipients and their children. Consequently, children inherited a life of poverty along with the substandard housing, low-quality education, family disruption, and poor diet commonly associated with AFDC households.

The Family Support Act

The problems inherent in the AFDC program did not go unnoticed by lawmakers, and one reaction was passage of the Family Support Act of 1988.[50] This act, which was associated especially with Senator Moynihan, attempted to break the "cycle of poverty" that had led to several generations of family members following one another as recipients of AFDC.

First, the act required the states to amend their AFDC programs to provide at least six months' benefits per year to families with both parents unemployed. It also improved child support enforcement and mandated states to provide enhanced job training and child care services, so AFDC recipients would be better able to get and keep jobs.[51] The act also guaranteed temporary Medicaid benefits for people who left welfare to work a job without health benefits.[52]

The Family Support Act certainly was not a cure-all for the problems of the AFDC program. The requirement for implementation by the states produced substantial variations in the benefits and the speed of their adoption.[53] Still, the act was recognition of the types of changes that were needed to provide a basic system of financial support for the indigent.

The 1996 Reforms and PRWORA

In 1996, an agreement between the Clinton administration and the Republican Congress produced a major reform of the welfare system that placed much greater emphasis on work and severely limited the time that any individual could receive social assistance. Building on reforms that were already under way in several states, notably Wisconsin, it fundamentally altered welfare in the United States.[54] There are six basic provisions of workfare, or more formally, the Personal Responsibility and Work Opportunity Reconciliation Act of 1996 (PRWORA):[55]

1. *Repeal of AFDC.* This act terminated AFDC and substituted a work-oriented program with temporary benefits. It also brought the funding for a number of other means-tested benefits, such as Supplemental Security Income, food stamps, and child support enforcement, into a single block grant to the states.

2. *Restriction of eligibility.* A standard critique of the AFDC system was that people never left the program once they were on it. Although that was actually not the case,[56] the notion was an important stimulus to reform. PRWORA limited benefits to two years at any one time and to five years over a lifetime. Food stamp benefits were limited to three months in any three years.

3. *Demands for work.* The reform's rationale was that limiting recipients' time in the program would force them to find some other way of gaining sufficient income to survive. PRWORA required that they either get a job or prepare themselves for a job to receive benefits. This requirement means that state and local governments must develop new job opportunities, and businesses that provide job opportunities for former welfare recipients and the long-term unemployed are given tax breaks. The program uses a relatively lenient definition of work, permitting education and training as a substitute for actual employment.

4. *Treatment of immigrants.* PRWORA limited welfare benefits available to immigrants, even legal immigrants, who were made ineligible for food stamps. Despite the conviction that the act's provisions should save money, especially for states such as California, with large numbers of immigrants,[57] there was some rethinking of this provision in the course of its implementation, and in 2002, President Bush revoked it, a move that was thought to be motivated by both

humane and political concerns.[58] Eligibility for social services became another element of the debate over immigration policy that became prominent in 2006.

5. *Vigorous enforcement of child support.* One means of saving the government money was to have fathers (or, in a few cases, mothers) provide for their children. The Family Support Act of 1988 had stressed enforcement, but the 1996 reform placed even greater pressure on the states to find "deadbeat dads" and extract child support money from those who could provide it. As of 2006, this program was able to track millions of parents (male and female) and recover billions of dollars for custodial parents, over a quarter of whom lived below the poverty line.

Donald Higgs/Getty Images

A woman receives her Social Security check. The Social Security program provides support for millions of retired and disabled Americans. Despite the success of the program over the decades, it faces continuing needs for reform to be able to meet the gradual aging of the American population.

6. *Implementation by the states.* Like AFDC, the new welfare program is implemented by the states, but unlike AFDC, PRWORA was designed to give the states a good deal of latitude in how they interpret and implement policy.[59] Indeed, some states have chosen to work with private firms as implementation agents[60] or to decentralize implementation even further to local governments.[61] The legislation also funds the program through a limited block grant, rather than an open-ended subsidy, so that besides having greater flexibility the states are relieved of the requirement to match federal funding as in the previous regimen. Program benefits, or Temporary Assistance to Needy Families (TANF), are variable across states just as they were under AFDC. As of 2002, the states began to lose part of their block grant if they did not meet work participation targets for their program recipients (see Table 12.6).

The provisions of PRWORA appear extremely punitive, and in some ways they are. However, the final legislation is not as severe as some proposals that were offered in the Republican Congress, where one zealous reformer proposed to deny benefits to teenage mothers and to encourage them to put their children up for adoption. Interestingly, the very politicians who generally talk most about individual autonomy were central in placing many controls on personal behavior in this bill.[62] There remains some question whether the program is really the best thing for welfare recipients, especially children. There is some evidence that children do better—in school, socially, and, ultimately, economically—when they have at least one parent at home regularly to care for and nurture them.[63] The emphasis on work is appealing to most Americans for ideological and financial reasons, but in the long run, it may actually exacerbate a cycle of dependency and have negative consequences for children. President George W. Bush and his administration pushed this argument further, trying to use welfare money to promote marriage and to reduce divorce rates among recipients of public assistance.[64]

TABLE 12.6   Percentages of TANF Recipients Involved in Work, 2009

High		*Low*	
Tennessee	77	Oklahoma	6
Washington	68	Missouri	10
Virginia	53	Wisconsin	10
California	44	Delaware	11
Montana	37	Georgia	12
	National average = 33		

Source: Administration for Children and Families (ACF), Department of Health and Human Services (Washington, DC: ACF, monthly), www.acf.hhs.gov/.

There have been a number of evaluations of the new TANF program, largely on a state-by-state basis, with somewhat mixed findings. As administrators gain more experience with the program, there are pressures for change, including proposals for supporting even more educational opportunities as a means of improving the long-term economic prospects of recipients.[65] What is certain is that the new law has changed the nature of American social policy in a rather fundamental way and that further policy interventions will be required to provide child care, as well as programs for chemical dependency, job placement, and a number of other needs that arise out of the changes.[66] The success of the new program, and of the overall substitution of work for welfare, depends very much on the ability of the economy to provide the needed jobs.[67] Otherwise, the program may simply push the poor into short-term public sector jobs rather than meaningful work in the private sector. Getting people off welfare may prove much easier than keeping them off some of the alternatives.[68]

Implementing Workfare

As noted, PRWORA was designed to provide state governments with substantial latitude in deciding how to make the program work, and the states have availed themselves of that opportunity. There are marked differences in the severity with which the regulations are enforced and hence the proportion of recipients who are being denied benefits or being allowed to engage in training rather than actually take a job.

One important intended consequence of the 1996 reforms of AFDC was to reduce the number of people receiving benefits. That goal was largely achieved, although at different rates in different states. On average, more than 50 percent of public assistance recipients were removed from the rolls by late 2001.[69] Rhode Island, however, had only 21 percent fewer welfare recipients, whereas Idaho had cut off 94 percent and Wyoming 90 percent. There were some apparent political considerations involved in these changes, as states controlled primarily by Republicans eliminated on average 56 percent of their recipients, while those under Democratic control had reduced their welfare rolls by 46 percent. Also, in general, the southern and western states have reduced their welfare rolls much more than the Northeast and Midwest. To some extent the reduction in TANF recipients has been greater in states with higher levels of economic growth in addition to being influenced by the ideology of the state governments.

The implementation of PRWORA was fortunately timed. The late 1990s was a period of extremely high employment and rapid economic growth, which meant that a person who wanted to find a job had a better chance of doing so than at almost any other time in recent history. Furthermore, the salaries that could be earned by workers with even minimal qualifications had increased substantially. Despite the propitious timing, however, numerous studies have found that the creation of jobs that pay enough to support a family adequately and yet are suitable for people without considerable education and skills has lagged behind the need created by the workfare reforms. Dependence on a job that paid only the minimum wage, for example, would put a family below the federal poverty line.

As the American economy went into recession in late 2001, the capacity of this and other means-tested programs to meet demand caused by increased unemployment and underemployment became seriously threatened.[70] Those problems have become even worse toward the end of the first decade of the twenty-first century. Not only are there more people who have lost incomes and need support, but there are also more people who have exhausted their limited time on benefits in the program.

Although the time limits adopted as a part of the program produced no major impact in the early years after its adoption, as more and more recipients began to exhaust their eligibility, the consequences of this provision became clearer.[71] Early evidence showed that people were moving off welfare and getting jobs, but the jobs often were not very good and were threatened by the slowdown of the economy. Besides the need to find adequate employment, recipients face the need for child care and other support for workers, such as adequate public transportation. Child care is expensive, but it is crucial for women with small children who are now expected to enter the labor force. Maintaining employment is to some extent a function of the availability of other government programs such as child care support and public health insurance. Most of the jobs available to former welfare recipients have few benefits, as well as low wages, so they do not provide the same standard of living as is possible from a combination of public programs.

Alternatives for Further Reform of Income Support

With this one major reform implemented, various other programs—some of which are common in western Europe—have been seriously proposed in the United States. The general characteristic of these alternative programs is that they benefit less affluent citizens without the stigma or the administrative complexity of existing means-tested programs. Most such alternatives, however, would require a significant change in contemporary attitudes about the poor and about social policy in the United States.

Family allowances. A system that is employed in virtually all other democratic, industrialized societies is the family allowance, by which families receive a monthly benefit check from the government, usually based on the number of children.[72] For the more affluent, it simply becomes additional taxable income, whereas for the poor, it may be a major source of support. The most important aspect of the program is that it includes everyone, or at least all households with children. The stigma of receiving government benefits is therefore removed, and the program is substantially easier to administer than PRWORA. If adopted in the United States, the program would need to provide a benefit for each child sufficient to match the current level of benefits under TANF. That would require that a great deal of money pass through the public sector as taxes and expenditures, but the effects might justify accepting that difficulty, given the negative consequences of means-tested programs.

The negative income tax. A second alternative to the existing income support program is the negative income tax, under which a minimal level of income would be determined, based on family size.[73] Each family would then file its tax statement, and those earning below the established minimum would receive a rebate or subsidy, while those above that level would pay taxes much as usual. Such a program would provide a guaranteed annual income for all citizens and would be administratively simpler than PRWORA. The recipients themselves would provide a good deal of the information necessary to calculate benefits, instead of having to rely on state and local welfare offices. In addition, this program would establish equal benefits across the United States, with perhaps some adjustment for different costs of living in different parts of the country. The negative income tax, as it is usually conceptualized, would also make it easier to work one's way out of poverty because it imposes only a one-third or one-half reduction of benefits for any money earned.

The negative income tax, or something like it, was seriously proposed in a family assistance plan offered by President Richard Nixon.[74] If that program had been enacted, it would have been the most sweeping reform ever of the welfare system in this country, guaranteeing an annual income for all citizens. The proposal was defeated in Congress by a coalition of liberals who thought its benefits too meager and conservatives who were ideologically opposed to the concept of a guaranteed minimum income. Social workers and other professionals also believed that their jobs were threatened by a program that placed the major burden of proving eligibility on the individual citizen.

Although that program was not adopted, there have been some movements toward a negative income tax in the United States. Most important, the earned income tax credit operates through the tax system to benefit low-income taxpayers with at least one child. The ideas behind this program, introduced in 1975, were to offset the effects of the Social Security tax on low-income individuals and to encourage people to work rather than take AFDC. The program now provides benefits (reduced taxes, or in some cases direct cash transfers) to more than

56 million Americans, making it by far the most widely used means-tested benefit in the country. Because it is administered through the tax system, the earned income tax credit is also inexpensive to manage and less intrusive than many other social programs.

Faith-based initiatives in social policy. During his presidency, George W. Bush emphasized the possibilities of involving faith-based organizations more directly in addressing social problems in the United States. This approach was linked to his interest in reducing the intrusiveness of government and government expenditures, as well as to his commitment to establishing a more prominent place for religion in American life. Bush created an Office of Faith-Based Programs in the White House, but despite the general involvement of Americans in volunteerism and the relative strength of religious organizations in the United States in comparison to other industrial democracies, the program did not get off to the expected strong start. There was some resistance from the religious community itself, as some feared government intrusion in the groups' freedom to serve their clienteles as they would prefer. Despite the apparent failures of the faith-based programs in the Bush administration, President Obama has also launched a program for supporting faith-based social service programs, although this program has not been as central to his social programs as it was during the Bush administration.

Child support. Almost half of those served by the income assistance program find themselves in need of aid because of divorce or separation. They are women with children to support, and they often lack significant job skills and work experience. Several studies have found that a large percentage of the children whose families receive welfare have fathers who are not paying child support, even in cases in which a legal divorce or separation decree has awarded it.

The Family Support Act of 1988 required the states to establish child support enforcement plans, and in 1994, employers were required to deduct support payments from the wages of fathers who were not in compliance with legal mandates to support their children. These efforts have been somewhat successful, recovering over $23 billion from over eight million absent parents in 2006.[75] This approach to the problem of poor children is not without its difficulties, however.[76] First, the delinquent fathers (or mothers) must be identified and located. These irresponsible parents tend to be relatively poor themselves, with 29 percent living below the poverty line, and therefore have little income to extract for support of the children.[77] In spite of those barriers, the states have adopted increasingly vigorous programs of enforcement and now are able to collect 80 percent of in-state support.[78] Some states go so far as to confiscate the property as well as to garnish the wages of fathers who violate support orders.[79] Other states have begun to impose other penalties, such as loss of driver's licenses, on fathers who fail to provide support.[80]

Full employment. Perhaps the simplest means of eliminating many of the problems of means-tested programs is to guarantee jobs rather than social benefits to those who need them. The federal government has been involved in a number of programs for job training and subsidized employment, the most prominent being the Comprehensive Employment and Training Act (CETA), in the 1970s and early 1980s, and then JOBS in the later 1980s.[81] The purpose of these programs was to enable people to acquire job skills by working with local private contractors and then to subsidize their employment for several years until they could be expected to have improved their productivity sufficiently to be able to earn a decent wage. CETA continued in operation until 1981, but it was severely criticized for inefficiency and corruption and for training people to do nonexistent jobs.

The emphasis on job training as a means for addressing social problems continued throughout the following decades. The combination of an economy in recession and continuing pressures to solve the problems of poverty and welfare led the George H. W. Bush administration to announce a "Job Training 2000" initiative, but the shortage of good jobs even for workers with well-developed skills and ample experience hampered the program's success. The welfare reforms implemented during the Clinton administration emphasized work as a solution to the problem of welfare, but they did not rely entirely on the private sector to develop the jobs. Stressing education and training, especially for young people, the initiative built on a number of job programs that the federal government already had in place but whose multiple, often competing goals had limited their effects.[82] The administration of George W. Bush added employment programs that tended to depend on the private sector and the individual participants. For example, the High Growth Job Training Initiative aimed to identify areas that will produce the most jobs in the foreseeable future, ranging from biotechnology to hospitality, and to establish partnerships to train workers for them. These Bush-era programs, however, are not as committed to training the less advantaged and therefore are less effective in combating poverty.

Job-training programs have not had a positive image in the United States, but they are gaining importance under workfare programs. Although they are argued to be beneficial in the long run, in the short run, these programs do not appear to be addressing the immediate needs of many poor citizens. As they have been developing under PRWORA, the resources available for job training have been put to different uses by different groups. Many white recipients have been using the money for college, while many minority recipients have opted for trade schools or vocational programs.

In the midst of the recession beginning in 2008, the Obama administration has been addressing job creation largely through fiscal policy (see chapter 9). The major program was to reduce the payroll tax for Social Security and to provide other business tax credits. The stimulus program also contained some public works support for state and local governments, but these were relatively short-lived and the effects largely expired when the program did.

The War on Poverty

Another attempt at a comprehensive solution to the problems of poverty and means-tested benefits was the Johnson administration's War on Poverty. The War on Poverty differed from other social programs of the time in that it was directed less toward the short-term amelioration of deprivation than toward changing long-standing patterns and conditions of the very poor.[83] War on Poverty programs did more than just hand out money—although they certainly did a good deal of that—by attempting to attack the cultural and social conditions associated with poverty. They also sought to involve the poor in the design and implementation of the programs more directly than had the more paternalistic efforts common at the time.

One aim of the War on Poverty was to educate the children of the poor so that they could compete successfully in school and in the economy, and one of its most popular programs was Head Start, which attempted to prepare poor children to enter school. The program sought to provide the skills that middle-class children generally have when they enter kindergarten but that children from economically deprived households frequently lack. It was found, however, that the "head start" effects rapidly vanished, and without continuing extra assistance, after several years, the Head Start children were not significantly different from others.[84] Depending on one's point of view, this could be an argument either that the program had failed or that it needed more follow-up once the children reached elementary school. A college work-study program was also initiated to try to make it more possible for students from low-income families to attend college. That program has been expanded and continues after the demise of the War on Poverty.

For adults, the War on Poverty initiated a variety of programs concentrating on employment. These programs commonly involved cooperation between the federal government and either state and local governments or private businesses. Many smaller programs provided counseling, loans for small businesses, family planning, and a whole range of other social services. In general, the War on Poverty provided something for almost everyone who needed and wanted work or help.

By the early 1980s most of the programs of the War on Poverty had been dismantled, reduced, or modified. The retreat reflected changes in political ideologies as well as the diminishing availability of tax money as economic growth became less certain.[85] The major programs that have survived are Head Start and college work-study. Were the programs of the War on Poverty, and perhaps the whole war itself, a massive failure or at best a noble experiment in social change? Did they fail, or were they never really tried? The programs represented a major departure from the traditional means of attempting to ameliorate poverty in the United States, and their impact may actually be more enduring than short-term evaluations indicate.

Other Means-Tested Programs

Although cash assistance programs have been the most common topic of discussion when the issue of means-tested benefits arises, there are also a number of other benefits available to less privileged citizens. For example, food stamps are generally available to people on welfare as well as to other people who are working but whose incomes fall below prescribed limits. Participants purchase the stamps at a discount and then use them to buy food and other necessities. Food stamps cannot be used legally other than for these strictly defined necessities, so that some of the common complaints against welfare—misuse of the funds for alcohol, gambling, and the like—can be controlled. The food stamp program helps to increase demand for U.S. agricultural products, so it gains support from those interests as well as from the interests that support social assistance. A similar program—Women, Infants, and Children, called WIC—provides specified nutritional benefits to women and children. Both these programs have been affected by the general moves to reform welfare and now are much less available than in the past.

Supplemental Security Income (SSI) is another important means-tested program, which as of 2010 provided benefits to more than 7.5 million people. The largest number of recipients qualify by falling into the categories of aged, blind, or disabled. The programs were federalized in 1974, removing them from the weaker financial provisions then available at the state level. The benefits are indexed, and so they are probably substantially superior to what would have been available if the programs had remained at the state level.

The Persistence of Poverty in the United States

We began our discussion of agenda setting with the impact of Michael Harrington's book *The Other America* on the development of a poverty program in the United States.[86] Despite the attention that analysts such as Harrington

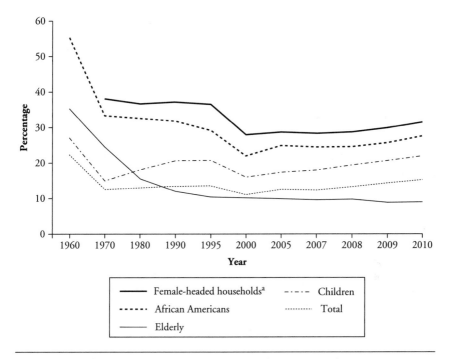

FIGURE 12.2   Changes in Poverty Rates, 1960–2010 (in percentages)

Source: U.S. Bureau of the Census, *Current Population Reports,* Series P-60, annual, www .census.gov/main/www/cprs.html.

a. No available data for 1960.

brought to the problem and programs such as the War on Poverty, in the early twenty-first century, poverty is nearly as great a problem as it was in the mid-1960s when President Johnson declared war on it. Poverty began declining during the 1960s and 1970s, but it increased again for a short period in the early 1990s and has increased significantly since 2000 (see Figure 12.2). The poverty rate is not uniform across the population but is concentrated among female-headed households, blacks and Native Americans, and children. Twenty-two percent of all children under the age of eighteen now live below the official poverty line; well over one-third of all black children and over one-quarter of Hispanic children lived in poverty in 2010. The proportion of the country's children in poverty had been decreasing since the early 1990s but began to increase again in 2001, and unofficial figures show the poverty rate for children increasing rapidly. In contrast, the poverty rate for the elderly has improved substantially and is now less than half of what it was in 1970, despite a growing elderly population.

In general, the social policies of the Reagan and George H. W. Bush administrations seem to have forced more people into poverty than would have been the case if earlier social policies had been continued. A number of other factors such as the recession and slower economic growth for the past decade and changing demographics may have helped increase the poverty rate, but public policy has been an important element.[87] The Clinton administration returned to some of the social activism of previous Democratic administrations, although in a somewhat more restrained manner; for the most part it emphasized developing more jobs and preparing people for jobs. Poverty was hardly discussed by the George W. Bush administration.

More than just jobs may be needed, however, if poverty is to be eliminated. As we pointed out earlier, a minimum-wage job will not pull a family of three or four above the poverty line, and in most areas, it will not do so even for an individual.[88] The minimum wage is lower than in 1995 when inflation is considered, and an increasing proportion of jobs in the United States are at the minimum-wage level. It may be necessary to link social benefits—food stamps, energy assistance, Medicaid—with work more closely than in the past. Such links have been part of welfare reform efforts, and such assistance may need to be extended to working families as well.[89]

Poverty is a symbolic issue, but it is also a matter of careful counting.[90] How do we know who is living in poverty and who is not? The official definition of poverty for 2011 was a family of four living on an annual income of $22,050 or less. "Income" includes government cash benefits, and adjustments are made for family size, urban versus rural areas, and so on. The definition does not include as income noncash public benefits, such as food stamps, Medicare or Medicaid, and housing subsidies. In addition, no allowance is made for taxes that could reduce income below poverty levels.

Because of the availability of numerous public benefits and the relationship of poverty status to eligibility for other public programs, conservative economists during the Reagan–Bush years argued for a change in the definition of poverty such that many fewer people would be counted as poor.[91] That would have benefited administrations that consistently argued that their policies had not harmed the poor. In addition, such a change in definition might have had the effect of a "reverse Harrington"—if the problem could be defined out of existence, it could be eliminated from the public agenda. The Clinton administration and Congress reasserted concern about the definition of poverty and its extent, although they chose to address the problem indirectly—through employment programs and welfare reform—rather than directly.

More recently, the National Academy of Sciences developed its own conception of a more appropriate measure of poverty.[92] This measure would take into account the range of needs of families in different circumstances, along with the effects of all types of available benefits. The measure would therefore be less a simple number applied to all families and more tailored to the real conditions of the less affluent in the United States. Although this measure may make good scientific sense, the older measures tend to persist for political reasons.

The Homeless

In addition to the large number of people living in poverty in the United States is an increasing number of homeless people, who often are not included in the official poverty figures because they are not caught in the statistical nets used to calculate them. The homeless live on the margins of society, often without government benefits of any sort, sleeping in shelters or on the streets and eating in soup kitchens.[93] Were it not for their visibility in many urban areas, the homeless might not be counted as part of the society at all.

The reasons for homelessness are numerous. Government policies have reduced the number of subsidized housing units for low-income people and so have forced many—including families—onto the streets.[94] Changes in mental health laws requiring the minimum possible restraint led during the 1970s to the release of many patients from institutions to poorly prepared community mental health programs, and some of those patients have found their way to the streets.[95] Increases in chemical dependency have also contributed to homelessness, as has the declining number of jobs at which a person with little education can earn a living wage. The latter problem was ameliorated by the economic boom of the 1990s, but it made a comeback as economic growth slowed in the first years of the twenty-first century. The huge increase in the number of home mortgage foreclosures beginning in 2008 has added thousands to the homeless population.[96]

Homelessness is now a significant social policy problem that is not being addressed effectively. The federal government has little or no policy for coping with homelessness. The only federal program of any consequence is the McKinney Act, which authorizes several types of emergency assistance for the homeless, including housing, food, health care, and drug and alcohol treatment. For this purpose, the federal government appropriated over $8 billion from 1987 to 2004, with most being spent through state and local governments. Although this appears to be a significant amount of money, it is rather meager compared with the magnitude of the need, and the program does not address the fundamental causes of the social problem.[97] More homeless persons now are being assisted by private organizations than by governments at any level, and private sector support has done little to solve the underlying problems. Because people are homeless for a variety of reasons, addressing the problem would require a broad and probably expensive strategy. Many of the reasons, such as addiction and mental illness, might be difficult to "solve" through conventional public policy instruments.

Private Social Programs

Finally, we should point out that although most Americans tend to think about social programs as benefits provided directly by government, a huge number of social benefits are actually conferred by the private sector, usually with the indirect support of government. Pensions are a good example. More than 92 million workers had pension rights through their employers or unions in the late 1990s, and millions of others have purchased private annuities or have contributed to individual retirement accounts—almost 31 million participate in 401(k) plans as means of tax-sheltering investments for retirement. The tax system has also assisted millions of people in creating Individual Retirement Accounts (IRAs) that are designed generally to supplement other forms of retirement income.

The federal government supports these private social benefits in at least two ways. First, an employee can deduct most contributions to these programs from his or her taxable income. The contributions by the employer are not taxable until the employee begins to receive the pension. In addition, the federal government now supervises and guarantees pensions through the Pension Benefit Guaranty Corporation, much as it does bank deposits through the Federal Deposit Insurance Corporation. Pension schemes also are regulated through the Employee Retirement Income Security Act (ERISA). Given that most participants in private pension plans are members of the middle class, these supports amount to a major (disguised) social benefit for that segment of the population. Much the same preferential economic distribution holds true for federal support for private medical insurance, disability insurance, and owner-occupied housing through the tax system.[98]

The collapse of the Enron Corporation in 2002 brought to light the weakness of regulations on private pension schemes, and it produced a call for more stringent regulation.[99] Under the legislation of the time, a corporation was allowed to put all the funds its employees paid into their retirement plan into its own stock, thus making the employees totally dependent on the success of that one company, although most financial advisers would urge any investor to diversify and spread risk. Companies could restrict the timing of withdrawals of those funds and thereby force employees to lose their savings if the firm collapsed, as happened at Enron. Congress passed a law during summer 2002 requiring greater corporate integrity, but the protections applied more to investors than to employees hoping for a company pension at the end of their working lives. What had long been a major benefit of working for a large corporation had become major worry instead.

Private pensions have eroded in a number of ways during the past several years. Most important, the courts have been permitting companies facing bankruptcy to reduce or eliminate their pension obligations.[100] Companies that still provide pension plans are shifting from defined benefit plans, providing a guaranteed percentage of previous income, to defined contribution plans, whose benefits depend upon the performance of the stock market or other investments. The number of defined benefit plans decreased by almost 60 percent from 1990 to 2000 and has continued to drop.[101]

Summary

The gap between the poor and the not poor is not evident in Social Security, but it is apparent in almost all other elements of social policy in the United States and in most other countries as well. Especially in the United States, that dual pattern makes the politics of social policy very difficult for reformers, as the political struggle quickly translates into a conflict between the haves and the have-nots. The struggle is exacerbated when the economy is not growing, so benefits for the poor are perceived as directly reducing the standard of living of the middle classes. Even during periods of affluence, there are always alternative uses for money that might be spent on social programs.

A large number of rather diverse social service programs are held together by an overriding concern with individual needs and conditions, some economic and some personal. The programs that have been tried and remain in operation represent attempts by government to improve the conditions of its citizens, although they are by no means entirely satisfactory solutions for those conditions. Several have been as unpopular with their clients as with the taxpayers who fund them. This chapter has described some approaches to modifying existing programs, as well as some more sweeping proposals that might benefit both government finances and program clients. Social problems will not go away; if anything, the first years of the twenty-first century have brought increasing demand for services, especially for the elderly and the homeless. What must be found is a means of providing adequate benefits through a humane mechanism that will not bankrupt the taxpayers. This is no easy task, but it is one that policymakers must address.

CHAPTER 13
Education Policy

EDUCATION TRADITIONALLY HAS HAD a central position in American public policy. Although the United States as a nation has been slow to adopt other social programs—pensions, unemployment insurance, national health insurance, and the like—it has always been among the world leaders in public education. Some 15 percent of all public spending and more than 36 percent of all public employment in the United States are devoted to education. Most public involvement in education has been at the state and local levels; the federal government has become directly involved in elementary and secondary education only relatively recently. Still, by the early twenty-first century, the federal government had become a major actor in education policy at all levels, exerting its influence through direct expenditures as well as through a variety of indirect instruments.

The public role in education began very early in the United States, with the state of New York adopting free public education in 1834. Education later became compulsory in all states until a student reached a designated age. (This provision was temporarily revoked in some southern states as a means of avoiding racial integration.) Even in the early years of the Republic, the federal government had a part in education. The Northwest Ordinance of 1787, in planning the organization of the Northwest Territories of the United States, divided the land into townships and the townships into sections. One of the sixteen sections in every township was to be set aside for supporting free, common education. In 1862, Congress passed the Morrill Act, granting land and a continuing appropriation of federal funds to establish and maintain in each state a college dedicated to teaching "agriculture and mechanical arts." From this act grew the system of land grant colleges that includes such major educational institutions as Cornell, Texas A&M, and the Universities of Wisconsin, Illinois, and Minnesota. In addition to their broader educational activities, the research and extension activities of these institutions have been important for the expansion of American agricultural productivity.

By the end of the twentieth century, the federal government had a large-scale involvement in education. In 2011, the federal government spent approximately $127 billion on education. That may seem a huge amount of money, but it actually represents a smaller percentage (2.8 percent) of total federal spending than was devoted to education in 1980 (5.8 percent). A wide variety of federal organizations provide assistance for education. Most cabinet departments have some involvement in education, as do a variety of other federal agencies, such as the National Science Foundation, the National Aeronautics and Space Administration, the Agency for International Development, and the National Endowments for the Arts and the Humanities.

American education and education policy have several distinctive characteristics. First, the emphasis on education is indicative of the general attitude Americans have taken toward social mobility and social change, the belief that education is important because it gives people "chances, not checks."[1] The prevailing American ethos is that government should attempt to create equal opportunity through education rather than equal outcomes through social expenditure programs. Individuals who have the ability are presumed to be able to better their circumstances through education and to succeed no matter what their social or economic background may have been. It is perhaps important to note that despite the evils of segregation, blacks in the South prior to *Brown v. Board of Education* (1954) were given access to public schools and public educational opportunities through the level of the doctoral degree. One cannot realistically argue that the opportunities were equal, but education was more easily available to African Americans than might be expected, given their social status in those states. The norm of educational opportunity appeared to cover even social groups that were systematically discriminated against.

Related to the role of education in social mobility is the importance of American public schools for social integration and assimilation. The United States has absorbed a huge number of immigrants, eight million in the first decade of the twentieth century alone. The institution that was most important in bringing those new arrivals into the mainstream of American life was the public school system. That was certainly true for adults, who learned English and civics in "Americanism" classes in the evenings. Also important is that the public schools in the United States traditionally taught all the children living in a community. Only a very few wealthy families sent their children to private schools; everyone else in the community went to the same school, often all the way through their elementary and secondary years.[2] The tradition of comprehensive schools that provided a variety of educational opportunities, from college preparatory through vocational, was important in reinforcing the ideology of a classless society and at least in promoting social homogeneity, if not achieving it.

The 1980s and the 1990s were also a period of large-scale immigration to the United States, and the public schools continued to play a role in the assimilation of the children of those millions of new Americans. But the social and economic realities of the early twenty-first century appear to have broken down some of the homogenizing influence of the public schools, as education became increasingly segregated ethnically and economically.[3] To some degree, the decline of homogenization has come by choice, as "multiculturalism" became a rallying cry for those who want a more diverse society and a more diverse educational system to support it.[4] Deciding how to manage increasing social diversity, while still meeting the education needs of all youths, is a major question now facing American education. Bilingual education is another part of the battle, especially in such states as California and Florida, which have large immigrant populations. The role of education is threatened even more fundamentally by laws denying access to the thousands of children in the United States whose parents are in the country illegally.[5]

Despite the centrality of public education at the elementary and secondary levels, there has never been a state monopoly on education. Existing alongside the public schools are religious schools—almost 29 percent of the elementary students in the United States in 2010 attended religious schools—and other private schools. This diversity is especially evident in postsecondary education, with more than 25 percent of college students attending private institutions.[6] Almost anyone can open a school, provided it meets the standards set by government or other accrediting bodies. If anything, the diversity of options for students has been increasing. The sense that the public schools are not doing an adequate job has spawned a variety of new educational providers, ranging from very strict schools concentrating on the three Rs to unstructured attempts to promote greater creativity and free exploration of ideas.

American education has always emphasized local and parental control. Of all the major activities of government, education is the one clearly retaining the greatest degree of local control and local funding. In fact, the largest category of public employment in the United States comprises the public school teachers employed by local governments. And the control that government exercises over education is generally also local. There are almost 14,000 local school boards in the United States and more than 22,000 counties and cities that frequently play a substantial role in providing public education. Despite all those opportunities for local political action, there are pressures for even greater local control and parental involvement—from white suburbanites, from inner-city minority parents, and from ideologues, all of whom believe that the public schools should be doing things differently.

Although the local school has traditionally been a positive symbol of local government and the community, there are now a number of doubts about

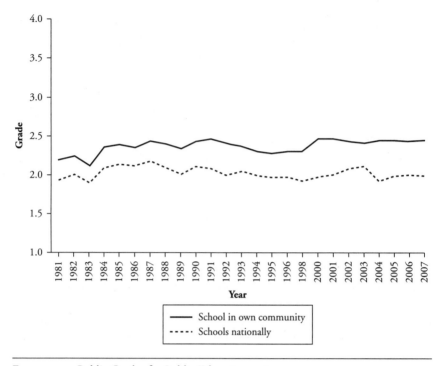

FIGURE 13.1   Public Grades for Public Education, 1981–2007

Source: Phi Delta Kappan, annual.

Note: 4.0 = A; 3.0 = B; 2.0 = C; 1.0 = D; < 1.0 = F.

education and increasing pressures for change. The problems are to some degree reflected in the evaluations Americans give their schools. When asked to grade schools, respondents to national polls have tended to give their own community schools a grade of C and schools nationally a very low C—barely passing (see Figure 13.1). The grades that people give their local schools have been creeping up gradually, but grades for schools nationally have remained rather low—better among parents who have children in public schools. In another poll, less than half of the respondents said they were satisfied with the quality of education in the United States.[7] It should be noted, however, that parents with children in public schools offer substantially higher evaluations of public schools than do people with no children in school or with children in private schools. The assessment of education is another aspect of public life affected adversely by publicity and negative media coverage.

The negative image of public schools is reinforced by numerous findings that American students do not do as well on standardized tests as students in western

Europe, Taiwan, Korea, or Japan. Even here, however, the evidence is not as bleak as it sometimes appears. Students in some states, especially those in the upper Midwest, do as well as or better than students overseas, and removing the effects of socially deprived students on the average puts the United States among the highest performers.[8] Furthermore, American students have been improving their performance on these tests, and they tend to do better on other types of testing. A major research project recently found that students from public schools do as well as, or better than, those from private schools on most tests.[9] I will return later in this chapter to the perceived problems and the reforms proposed to deal with them.

The Federal Government's Role in Education

The involvement of the federal government in education has been controversial. After President Ronald Reagan's first secretary of education, Terrel Bell, pledged to dismantle the recently created Department of Education, his successor, William Bennett, revitalized federal efforts to improve what he considered the deplorable state of American education. His campaign was based on his personal view of good education—a highly structured curriculum stressing basic skills and the canon of Western civilization.[10] Although Bennett's campaign highlighted the importance of a national education policy in a highly competitive, postindustrial world, most evidence indicated little improvement as a result.

George H. W. Bush campaigned in 1988 on a pledge to be the "education president," but it was not until 1991 that President Bush and his new secretary of education, Lamar Alexander, announced an ambitious blueprint titled "America 2000: An Education Strategy." The plan had four major elements. First, it proposed national tests that were to be diagnostic and open to the public, so communities could judge how well their local schools were doing and exert political pressure for better education. The scores on the tests could also be used by prospective employers, thereby pressing both students and schools to do better. Second, the federal government, with supplementary support from business, would fund a new school in each representative and senator's district to show how schools could break the mold of existing educational programs. Third, the plan offered several recommendations for improving the quality of America's teachers, including merit pay and alternative means of certifying competency for teaching (especially in mathematics and science), rather than depending on state certification. Finally, President Bush proposed creation of a market model in education, giving parents more opportunity to choose and placing schools under more pressure to perform. Despite the ambitious goals of "America 2000," in practice, almost nothing actually happened in education at the federal level during the four years of the first President Bush's administration.

Rep. Peter Welch, D-VT, talks to students at the University of Vermont about student debt on April 30, 2012. Although student loans enable many students to attend universities who would not otherwise be able to, many finish their education with thousands of dollars of debt that presents problems for them as they begin their new careers.

The Clinton administration sought to make the federal government role more prominent and emphasized expanded funding and regulation of all areas of education. The adequacy of the educational system continued to be questioned, as American students performed at or near the bottom on some international standardized tests, and poor education was identified as an impediment to economic competitiveness.[11] President Clinton argued for the federal government to do more in addressing the deficiencies, creating programs that emphasized teacher qualification, college preparation, and reducing class sizes, among other targets.[12] The administration also advocated reauthorization of the 1965 Elementary and Secondary Education Act (ESEA), the major source ($10 billion) of federal support for education. Republicans in Congress argued that education was a local issue and that the federal government should not expand its activities in the area. The Republican-controlled Congress of the late 1990s chose not to challenge the existence of the Department of Education directly, but it opposed efforts to impose more federal controls on teacher competence and to provide more money for educational facilities. Given the electoral appeal of education, Republican leaders in Congress advanced some programs of their own, mostly involving vouchers or tax credits supporting private schools.

Education was a central theme of the presidential campaign of George W. Bush, as it had been for his father. Although he tended to favor a smaller role for government in general—and especially for the federal government—the second President Bush advocated a stronger role for the federal government in education. This involvement was to be primarily regulatory, monitoring the quality of education offered by local schools and providing resources, in the form of vouchers, to enable students to leave schools that were failing. These approaches appealed to the president's conservative supporters, who saw them as a means of providing additional funding for private schools. During President Bush's two terms, the federal government set the agenda for education policy in the United States and attempted to use its regulatory powers to impose a quality and accountability regimen on state and local governments.

In particular, George W. Bush's No Child Left Behind program mandated national testing at several grade levels.[13] Schools that did not improve their test scores on an annual basis were termed "failing schools," and their students could move to other schools in the district. If a school did not improve in two consecutive years, then the school district had to offer tutoring to economically disadvantaged students. Although the program was well intentioned and was supported by major Democratic legislators, such as Sen. Edward Kennedy, critics have argued that it has a number of inherent problems. First, many teachers argued that they were forced to "teach to the test" rather than teach in a more constructive and creative manner. Furthermore, the federal government mandated a great deal of teaching, tutoring, and issuing of vouchers but did not provide any funding to the school districts to fulfill those requirements. They thus had to divert funds from other educational purposes.

The Obama administration has increased flexibility in the No Child Left Behind program.[14] While still putting pressure on the states to improve education, the administration has been allowing them to find their own ways to make those improvements.[15] Through the Race to the Top challenge to the states, the Obama administration has also attempted to improve education by providing substantial grants to states that were making major innovations in education. In higher education, the administration has attempted to reduce the burden of student loans on lower-income families by increasing the amount of grant money available but has been blocked by Congress.

Local Financing and the Federal Role

We should discuss one aspect of local control in education because it conditions the need for federal involvement: that is, the traditional funding of public education through the local property tax, which has engendered two significant problems in recent years. First, property tax revenues generally have

TABLE 13.1 Sources of Education Funding (in percentages)

	1980	1990	1995	2000	2006
All education					
Federal government	11.4	8.2	8.8	8.7	8.6
State government	38.8	37.2	34.4	34.8	36.4
Local government	26.1	27.1	26.0	25.6	24.3
All other	23.6	27.4	30.8	31.8	30.7
Elementary and secondary education					
Federal government	9.1	5.6	6.7	6.4	8.0
State government	43.3	43.6	41.4	41.9	45.2
Local government	40.3	40.7	41.8	42.1	39.1
All other	7.3	10.1	10 .1	9.6	7.7

Source: National Center for Education Statistics, *Digest of Education Statistics* (Washington, DC: U.S. Department of Education, annual).

not kept pace with inflation. The administration of the property tax involves assessing property values and applying a rate of tax to the assessed value. In an inflationary period, assessments may not reflect real property values, and they certainly will not reflect the actual costs of goods and services, unless revaluation is done frequently. Many local school boards therefore find that their funding is not adequate for their needs. Second, even if there were no inflation, the tax base available to some school districts is markedly different from that available to others. To provide the same quality of education, parents living in poorer districts must tax themselves at higher rates than those in more affluent areas. This is an extremely regressive way to finance a basic public service, as the poor have to pay a higher rate of tax to obtain the same level of education as the better off.

The usual result of this pattern of funding is that the education that poorer children receive is not as good as that provided to wealthier children.[16] It is thus argued that the local property tax is an inequitable means of financing and that some alternative, such as federal or state general revenues, should be used to equalize access to education. Both federal and state contributions to education funding had been declining for some time but have begun to increase slightly (see Table 13.1). Localities are still left to bear a great portion of the responsibility for funding education. As we shall discuss later, the courts have begun to bring about some changes in school finance in the direction of greater equality and greater state funding, but the inadequacy of local taxation remains an important reason for federal involvement in education.

Higher Education

It has traditionally been more acceptable for the federal government to be involved in higher education than in elementary and secondary education, perhaps because the students are almost adults and are assumed to have formed their basic value systems before the central government could influence them, or perhaps because of the higher per student expense. In addition to supporting the land grant college system, the federal government also runs or supports the military service academies, Gallaudet University (for the deaf), and Howard University. In addition to directly funding almost eighty colleges and universities, at least in part, the federal government provides substantial indirect support for almost every college and university.

The primary form of indirect federal subsidy is aid to individual students. These programs obviously benefit students directly, but they also support many colleges that might have to close if they lost the many students who could not attend without federal assistance. The largest federal program to aid college students has been the so-called GI Bill, which enabled veterans of World War II and Korea, and to a lesser extent Vietnam, the Gulf War, and Iraq and Afghanistan to attend college with the government paying virtually all the costs. Another of the large programs of student aid was also justified as a defense program: The National Defense Education Act, passed in 1958 just after the Soviet Union launched *Sputnik I,* was intended to help the United States catch up in science, although students in the social sciences and foreign languages benefited as well.

Federal assistance began to reach beyond defense-related concerns during the 1960s and 1970s. The College Work-Study program was adopted as part of the War on Poverty but was moved from the Office of Economic Opportunity to the Office of Education, where it began to benefit a wider range of students. Likewise, the Education Amendments of 1972 instituted something approaching a minimum income for college students. The Basic Educational Opportunity Grant (often referred to as a "Pell grant"), the centerpiece of the program, gave a student $1,800 (a figure later increased slightly to account for inflation), minus what the student's family could be expected to contribute. Although not much help if the student wanted to attend Harvard or Yale, it provides the means to attend some institution of higher education. Pell grants are subject to considerably stricter eligibility requirements and lower levels of funding per student than other sources of aid, such as loans.

The federal government also assists students by guaranteeing student loans (Stafford loans) and providing some direct loans for very low-income students (Perkins loans). The guaranteed loans are particularly important because they permit government to leverage a great deal of private money with minimal direct federal outlays. The federal government guarantees a private lending institution that the money the institution lends a student will be repaid, even if the student reneges—as many have done. In turn, the money is offered to the student at a lower interest rate than would otherwise be available, and repayment does not have to begin until after the student leaves higher education. The failure of many students to repay their loans and the fraudulent use of the loans by some trade schools (whose students are also eligible) have brought this program into question, but it remains important. In 2007, the guaranteed loan program benefited over 6.4 million students, accounting for 78 percent of all new federal loans in education.

Largely as a result of the 2008 credit crisis, however, President Obama made efforts to move toward more direct student loans. In 2010, Congress passed the Federal Direct Loan Plan with the Department of Education becoming the primary lender. This plan appears easier to administer and ultimately less expensive, inasmuch as the federal government had subsidized both the administrative costs and interest payments for guaranteed loans. This change, however, brings the federal government even more directly into higher education. This plan was later modified in the "Pay as You Earn" program to link the amount that students must repay to their earnings.[17]

All the above-mentioned programs primarily benefit students entering college just out of high school, but there is one federal program designed to benefit more mature students. Income tax deductions available to students who go to school to maintain or improve their job skills support a variety of trade and technical schools as well as academic institutions. The tax program stimulates attendance at colleges and universities, especially among a segment of the population that might not otherwise attend college, although the university never sees the money. A 1997 tax measure permits parents to develop education–savings accounts for future expenses and provides limited tax deductions for tuition payments made by lower- and middle-income parents. The benefits are rather small in comparison to rising tuition costs, but they offer some relief.[18]

Since 1980, federal funding for students in higher education has not fared well. The Reagan administration cut back on federal support, reducing the base level of the Pell grant by $80 and tightening the income restrictions; that resulted in approximately 100,000 fewer Pell grant recipients in 1983 than in 1981. There was also a drop of some 460,000 in the number of new guaranteed student loans, and there were reductions in federal funding of social science and humanities research through the National Science Foundation and the National Endowment for the Humanities. The George H. W. Bush administration proclaimed that education was a central priority but only slightly increased federal funding for programs such as the National Science Foundation.[19] The Clinton administration sought to increase direct federal support for higher education and to provide more money for students, but it faced severe budget restraints while attempting also to fund a variety of other policy priorities. One of the more creative of its efforts was the AmeriCorps program, which provides scholarship money for students who spend several years in service positions. They receive small salaries while in those positions, but a good deal of the reward for participation comes when they go on to pursue educational opportunities. There were substantial reductions in federal financial support for higher education in the George W. Bush administration, including reductions of direct student loans and changes in tax laws that had privileged students' savings for college.[20] There is no evidence, however, that costs and the possibility of incurring debt are slowing the rate at which young Americans attend colleges and universities, and enrollments continue to increase slightly. The economic downturn of 2008 onward has placed pressure on colleges and universities, and especially on parents, to maintain enrollments, although the lack of job opportunities has encouraged many students to pursue further education.

Other indirect federal supports for higher education include aid for building instructional facilities, through the Higher Education Facilities Act of 1963, and dormitories, through the Department of Housing and Urban Development. Federal research money (more than $25 billion in 2006) helps institutions of higher education meet both direct and indirect costs, and special federal grant programs also exist for such fields as public service and urban studies. In short, the federal government has become central to American higher education in the twenty-first century.

The large amounts it invests in higher education give the federal government substantial control over the policies of the universities, as has been manifested primarily through efforts to promote the hiring of women and members of minority groups as faculty members. In *Grove City College v. Bell* (465 U.S. 555 [1984]), however, the Supreme Court diminished the influence of the federal government in ensuring greater equality in higher-education programs. Previously, a college found to be discriminating might lose all its federal money, but in that ruling, the Court found that only the funds directly supporting the activity in which the discrimination occurred could be withdrawn. So, for example, if discrimination was found in the programs covered by Title IX (athletics and student activities), the government could not withdraw money from student support or from federal research grants. The Clinton administration favored a vigorous program of affirmative action and attempts to improve the status of minority populations. Its efforts were set back in 1999 when the Supreme Court overturned admission and scholarship awards based on race. In June 2003, however, in two cases involving the University of Michigan, the Supreme Court ruled that race could be taken into consideration in university admissions, and it established rough guidelines on how it should and should not be used.[21]

Elementary and Secondary Education

The role of the federal government in elementary and secondary education has historically been less significant than its involvement in higher education. Other than the planning provisions of the Northwest Ordinance, the first federal government initiative in elementary and secondary education resulted from passage of the Smith-Hughes Act (1917), which made funds available for vocational education. In the 1930s, surplus commodities and money were provided to school districts for hot lunch programs, and those programs were expanded during the War on Poverty to include breakfasts for children from poor families. The Lanham Act of 1940 made federal funds available to schools in "federally impacted areas," which was understood to mean areas with large numbers of government employees and especially areas in which tax-exempt government properties reduced the tax base. In 1958, the National Defense Education Act authorized funds to improve science, mathematics, and foreign language teaching in the elementary and secondary schools, as well as at the college level.

The Elementary and Secondary Education Act.   The federal government's major involvement in elementary and secondary education currently is through the Elementary and Secondary Education Act of 1965, which was the culmination of efforts by numerous education and labor groups to secure more federal aid for education.[22] The measure was passed, along with a number of other social and educational programs, during the Johnson administration, but before it could become law, legislators had to address the barriers that had blocked previous attempts.

One of the barriers was the general belief that education should be controlled locally. The Elementary and Secondary Education Act (ESEA) involved direct, general subsidies for education, and some interests initially feared that the federal presence would influence what was taught. However, as the federal government was already becoming increasingly involved in many aspects of education and social life through other mechanisms, such as the courts, the fear of federal control diminished. The matter of funding for religious schools also presented constitutional issues for federal aid to education. Most mainstream Protestant groups opposed aid to parochial schools as a violation of the separation principle, while Catholic groups and some fundamentalist Protestants opposed any federal aid to education that did not provide assistance to parochial schools. ESEA funds eventually went to parochial as well as public schools, with the provision that the money could not be spent for teaching religious subjects. The legislation specified that the federal money was to go to the students, not to the schools directly, which helped defuse some criticism based on separation of church and state.

The 1965 ESEA was part of the War on Poverty, but as implemented, it provided assistance to almost all school districts in the United States—only 5 percent of districts (now roughly 8 percent) received no ESEA money. The law provided funds for hiring teachers' aides, stocking libraries, purchasing audiovisual materials, and developing remedial programs. Its intent was to enable students from poor families to perform better in school and to learn to compete more effectively in the labor market. As with a number of federal programs, ESEA funds were allocated to the states according to a formula. The original formula granted to each state shows federal funds equal to one-half of its annual per pupil expenditure, multiplied by the number of low-income children—a plan that aided high-income states more than low-income states because it was based on the amount of money already being spent. The formula quickly came under attack and was amended in 1967 so that each state received half of its own per pupil expenditures, or half of the national mean per pupil expenditure, whichever was higher. Also, the definition of low-income students was eased so that school districts could claim more students and receive more federal funding. The 1967 amendments to the act equalized funding between richer and poorer states and produced rapid increases in ESEA expenditures.

During the Nixon administration, the categorical nature of the funds allocated through ESEA came under severe attack as a part of the "new federalism."[23] Efforts to convert ESEA funding into another of the block grants that characterized that administration's approach to federal assistance did not succeed, however, and the federal government retained nominal control over the ways in which the money was to be spent. What did change was the formula for computing aid. In 1974, a new formula was adopted that narrowed the range of per pupil grant funds—the very wealthy states could claim only 120 percent of the national average expenditure per low-income pupil when computing aid, and the very poor states could claim only 80 percent of the national average (not the national average). Instead of receiving 50 percent of its per pupil figure, each state could receive only 40 percent. These changes put both rich and poor states at a disadvantage.

In many ways, ESEA is a classic example of a program that was modified through implementation. The U.S. Office of Education, charged with implementing ESEA, was quite passive in ensuring the attainment of the stated goal of the program—equalization of educational opportunity for economically deprived children. The tendency of those who implemented the program at the state and local levels was to "pork barrel" the funds—to spread them around among all school districts regardless of the concentration of low-income students. As a result, wealthier, suburban school districts used ESEA funds to purchase expensive frills, while many inner-city and rural school districts still lacked basic materials and programs that might compensate for the poorer backgrounds of their pupils.[24]

That initial failure in implementation of ESEA resulted in part from the close ties between the U.S. Office of Education and local school districts and in part from misinterpretation of the intention of Congress, which had established the program not as general assistance to education but strictly as a compensatory program. After some changes in the Office of Education and greater attention to the use of the funds, implementation improved, although a number of questions remained about the use of ESEA money. Title I money—that portion of the program that is most directly compensatory (now part of the Compensatory Education Program)—is now targeted more clearly toward the poorer districts, but money available under other provisions of the act is still widely distributed and used by wealthier schools and school districts to supplement their programs.

In addition to its impact on education through its spending programs, the federal government also has a substantial impact through numerous regulations and mandates. Among the most important of these is the Education for All Handicapped Children Act of 1975, which mandated that all handicapped or "exceptional" students be educated in a manner suitable to their special needs. This legislation was intended primarily to help children with physical and learning disabilities to receive education in the public schools. The meaning of the act has been extended to include educationally gifted children, so school districts are now required to provide special programs for a variety of different groups of students. Bilingual education has also been mandated for minority students in some circumstances. All of these programs add to the costs of providing public education but impose most of those costs on state and local governments.

Has all this federal aid and regulation improved the quality of American education? There is some evidence that the ESEA Title I reading programs have been successful in raising the reading levels of low-income students.[25] To the extent that more money can aid education in any number of ways, some of which are difficult to quantify, the programs have certainly produced benefits. It is ironic, however, that in spite of all the federal money directed at it, the quality of American education remains as prominent an issue in the twenty-first century as at any time since the launch of *Sputnik I* in 1957. As was true then, much of the concern centers on education in science, mathematics, and engineering. The difference is that in recent years the perceived need has been to improve competitiveness against the Chinese and Europeans rather than to protect the country against a Soviet military threat. In that competition, there is a strong sense that American education is failing and that the American workforce is decreasingly capable of competing. Some of the blame is placed on families that do not nurture students sufficiently, and some on the students themselves, but a great deal of the blame is directed at the public schools.

No Child Left Behind.   The No Child Left Behind program of the George W. Bush administration was another big federal move into elementary and secondary education.[26] Central to the program is the use of standardized tests to determine the quality of education being provided. All students in grades three through eight are to be tested every year, and if a school's results fall below state standards or fail to show adequate progress toward those standards, it is deemed a *failing school*. Students at failing schools are allowed to move to another public school, and schools that fail three out of four years must provide tutoring assistance for students. Continued failure can result in the closing of the school. "Passing" grades for schools were to increase annually, so education would continue to improve. Teacher competence is also to be tested and certified, so parents can be sure that their children are being taught by well-qualified personnel. The program also has provisions for flexibility in the use of federal funds. It tries to require public schools to provide quality education and to justify their actions to the community.

No Child Left Behind (NCLB) has received intense criticism, partly for its reliance on testing. The critics argue that repetitive testing wastes time and resources that might be better spent on other educational activities and is not the best measure of the learning taking place. Teachers may "teach to the test," rather than teaching the substance of what is important for the future of the students.[27] It is also argued that the program gives the states a strong incentive to weaken their education standards to ensure that the needed percentage of students will pass the tests. Because some of the focus is on failing teachers, as well as failing schools, it gives individual teachers an incentive to avoid difficult teaching situations.[28]

Whatever its merits, the NCLB program has produced major political battles in Washington and in the states. As noted, it is a major federal intervention into what had been primarily a state and local concern. Critics of NCLB raised the issue of its impact on federalism and its status as an "unfunded mandate," a type of federal regulation that reforms of the Republican-led Congress ostensibly had controlled in 1994.[29] Teachers unions also say that NCLB undermines teacher autonomy and professionalism and that it is a thinly veiled attack on public education. Those who hold this negative view also contend that the provisions of the act are an indirect way of introducing a national voucher plan that could not only undermine public education but also threaten the separation of church and state (see chapter 16).

President Barack Obama early in his administration proposed improving the program's assessments and accountability. The administration, among other things, attempted to broaden the interpretation of quality in education to include more than just success on standardized testing. The openness to alternative interpretations then allowed the states to define more of their own criteria for failing schools and also to make more decisions about the remedies. Education Secretary Arne Duncan also sought to broaden the goals of NCLB toward readiness for employment or higher education rather than simply passing standardized tests.[30] The administration also pointed out that there had been relatively little positive change in performance on the tests since the program was implemented, so revising the program seemed appropriate.[31]

Issues of Education Policy

Even with the victory of advocates of federal aid to elementary and secondary education, a number of problems remain in public education, and some new ones are arising. In general, the public schools and their teachers have lost some of the respect with which they were traditionally regarded, and education policy has been the subject of more heated discussion than had been the case during most of U.S. history. In fact, it is not uncommon for politicians or analysts nowadays to charge that the public schools have failed and to call for significant change. President George W. Bush's program for improving the schools, like that of his father, is a statement of that sentiment. Some would counter that it is perhaps not so much that the schools have failed as that too much has been demanded of them—that the schools cannot be expected to solve all of the society's problems. These defenders would argue that the resources and the tasks given the schools have not been equal and that too much has been expected for too little money. Several specific issues illustrate both sides of this argument, but what may be most important is that the U.S. education system, which was long regarded as one of the great success stories of American public policy, is no longer considered quite so successful.

Quality of Education

A common complaint against schools, which has persisted since the 1950s, is that "Johnny can't read"—that is, that the schools are failing in their fundamental task of teaching basic skills. Substantial evidence to support this point includes the decline in Scholastic Aptitude Test (SAT) scores since the late 1960s (see Figure 13.2). It should be noted, however, that an increasing proportion of high school students began taking the SATs in the early 1980s. Lower scores may to some degree reflect the averaging in of the scores of students not intending to go to college but who are required to take the test to judge the quality of their education. Beginning in the early 1980s, the test scores registered a series of small changes up and down, but by the late 1990s, an upward turn gave rise to some sense that perhaps investments in education and some school reforms were beginning to have an impact.

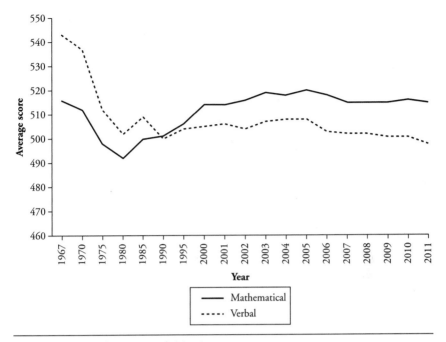

FIGURE 13.2   Scholastic Aptitude Test Scores, 1967–2011

Source: College Entrance Examination Board, *National College-Bound Seniors* (Princeton, NJ: College Entrance Examination Board, annual).

Whereas some charge that the schools are not teaching basic skills, other critics regard the existing education system as excessively rigid and stultifying. Some believe that public schools destroy the innate creativity of children; they would prefer more "open" education with fewer rigid requirements and greater emphasis on creativity and expression. Others feel that the schools are excessively narrow, teaching a single class or racial perception of the world instead of providing a broad perspective on the human experience; they demand a broader curriculum or perhaps different schools for minority children. Quality in education, therefore, is not a self-evident attribute but may have definite class and racial components, and it may include creativity as well as the ability to solve math problems.[32]

Even if schools were serving the needs of the majority, they still might not be doing a good job for disadvantaged students, whose special needs are not met in many conventional classrooms. As we have seen, Title I of the Elementary and Secondary Education Act sought to address that problem, but its success has been limited.[33] When ESEA was reauthorized in 1994, a number of suggestions were made for making it more effective. Unfortunately, the tendency of Congress to convert any legislation possible into pork barrel programs meant that it would remain difficult to keep ESEA from distributing its funds widely.

The No Child Left Behind program is a large-scale attempt to address education quality. Again, the program is not without critics, and several states have chosen to challenge the law in court rather than change their education policies. The political debates have highlighted the importance of education in state and local politics and its importance for the future of the United States. Concerns about quality in education have also led to the search for alternatives, especially to the public school system, through enhanced educational choice.[34]

The Obama administration also sought to encourage innovation in education as a means of enhancing educational quality via, for example, the Race to the Top Challenge Fund.[35] This fund supplies substantial funding to states that develop programs to improve educational quality, especially in terms of the broader educational goals that the administration has for the country. This plan attempts to find ways of making major shifts in performance rather than the more incremental goals of earlier administrations.

Vouchers and Choice

Although the various complaints about education sometimes appear worlds apart, they have in common the desire to change the type of education the public schools provide. One possible response would be to decentralize the school system, which would be in the tradition of local control over education but would merely alter the definition of what the appropriate local area is. In New York City in the 1980s, the conflict between parents in Ocean Hill–Brownsville and the city's public schools was one of the most explosive events of the decentralization movement. Later, Chicago and then Milwaukee largely decentralized their school systems to the individual school level, giving parents significant direct managerial authority over teachers and curriculum. Many judge these experiments in local control to be successes, but for the most pressing problems in public education, decentralization may not always be the answer. If a local school does not have the right leadership, professional and parental, decentralization could prove disastrous.[36]

Related to the idea of decentralization is the possibility of choice among schools within a school system. In almost any school system, some schools are considered better than others. These schools are often in middle-class neighborhoods, with parents who place pressure on the school board, principals, and teachers for high-quality education. Some school systems also use specialized or selective "magnet" schools to promote educational quality and achieve racial integration. One proposed solution to the general problem of quality in education is to allow any student in the public schools to attend any school in the system, thus creating something approaching the market system implied in voucher plans but keeping all the funds in the public school system.

Another proposal is the use of education vouchers—giving each student's parents a "check" for a specified amount of money that would be applicable only for education.[37] The parents could spend that voucher either in the public schools, where it would pay the entire cost of the child's education, or at some other school, where it might not cover the entire cost and the parents would have to make up the difference. Under a voucher plan, parents would have significantly greater control over the kind of education their children would receive, choosing among open schools, schools stressing basic skills and discipline, religiously oriented schools, and any other schools that meet state standards. A voucher or choice program in Milwaukee was specifically created for low-income students and did not require additional parental funds.[38]

The idea of education vouchers has been around for several decades, but it received a large boost from a 1990 book by John Chubb and Terry Moe.[39] These scholars argued that the fundamental problem with public education was organizational—schools and school systems were too bureaucratic to provide good education. They argued that the only way to remedy that problem was to create competition and offer choice to parents and students. Although Chubb and Moe argued that vouchers would not be necessary, vouchers came to be considered a part of their proposed reforms. The George H. W. Bush administration's advocacy of choice in education placed voucher plans at the center of the debate over improving American education. In 1998, Republicans in Congress proposed giving 2,000 students in the District of Columbia vouchers to attend private or suburban schools, the logic being that the city's children should be given the opportunity to escape its financially strapped, poorly performing schools. After President Clinton vetoed the plan, arguing that it would only divert needed money from the public schools,[40] the George W. Bush administration came to office emphasizing the need for vouchers and succeeded in establishing a Washington, D.C., voucher program in 2004. With the Democrats taking charge of Congress and the White House in 2009, however, the program looked to be in jeopardy.[41]

Although voucher plans are appealing as a means of improving education by offering choice, a number of questions have been raised about their potential effects on the education system, and vouchers have been highly contentious politically.[42] Perhaps the most fundamental question is whether vouchers would increase stratification in education. One of the fundamental virtues and goals of American education, after all, has been its attempt to promote social homogeneity and integration. If a voucher plan did not cover the full price of a child's education, many low-income parents would not be able to make up the difference between the value of the voucher and the tuition at a private school, especially one of the better private schools. The plan might simply end up subsidizing middle-class parents without improving the quality of education for the poor, who need that improvement the most (plans like the one in Milwaukee are an obvious exception). A voucher plan might well undo the racial integration that resulted from years of effort and policymaking. All these questions were reinforced by the 1966 Coleman report and numerous other studies of education, which have pointed out that a child's home background is crucial to success in school.[43] A voucher plan would tend to benefit children who would probably succeed anyway, and it might divert funds from schools and children who need the most help.

Although education vouchers could be used only for schools that meet established state standards, questions remain about the propriety of spending public money for education over which the state has no control and about the possibility that a voucher system might actually lower the quality of education. It is not entirely clear where the capital—both human and physical—required to implement such a system would come from. A full-scale voucher plan might result in the formation of a number of small and inadequate schools, none of them providing the quality of education that could be offered by large, comprehensive public schools. It may be that education is a service that is not amenable to market logic and competition. Even so, nearly half the American public now say that they believe vouchers are an acceptable policy instrument in education, although three-quarters also want to ensure high levels of accountability for the use of funds.[44]

Some analysts think that the introduction of competition into the education marketplace will improve the quality of education by increasing the choices available to consumers and placing competitive pressures for improvement on the public schools. For such an education marketplace to function effectively, however, consumers must have access to information about the "product" being produced. That might be difficult if a number of new schools were started in response to a voucher plan. Even in established systems of public and private education, it is difficult to assess quality, especially because much of the difference in the success of students is accounted for by family backgrounds, and much of the effect of education may not be evident until far in the future.

Charter schools are a means of providing choice on a collective rather than an individual basis. These schools are organized by parents or providers as a way to opt out of the local schools but with public financial support.[45] Many states have passed legislation providing funding for charter schools, provided they meet accreditation standards. These schools may be a way of expanding the educational opportunities available in a society rather than simply subsidizing the existing array of educational institutions. Charter schools may also drain some resources away from the mainstream of public education. For that reason, education unions and local school boards have tended to give this innovation in education little political support.[46] Furthermore, the available evidence is that many charter schools are no better, and often worse, than the public schools.[47]

Proposed tuition tax credits for parents sending their children to private schools are similar to vouchers. This option has been actively supported by Republicans as a means of providing education that would be better and more in line with the "cultural and moral values" of the parents. The political and educational arguments for tuition tax credits are similar to those for vouchers: They promote greater pluralism and allow parents greater choice. In addition, as many minority students have performed better in private (especially Roman Catholic) schools, this program could be of substantial benefit to them. Those opposed to tuition tax credits, such as the National Education Association, the Parent-Teacher Association, and the American Federation of Teachers, argue that they would undermine public education by creating a two-class education system. Parents of minority students would still have to have the means of paying anything over the amount of the tax credit, and so the beneficiaries again would be middle-class students who may not need the benefit. Programs such as this, which would tend to benefit parochial and other religion-based schools, also raise the continuing question of the separation of church and state.

Thus, while few educators or policy analysts would claim that the U.S. educational system is currently what most citizens want it to be, it is not entirely clear that a voucher plan or other plans promoting choice would improve it all that much. The benefits of a voucher plan might be as much psychological as real—it would appear to offer parents more choices and to allow them greater control over their children's education. The effects on the general quality of education might be difficult to measure, especially if one effect of the program was to siphon significant amounts of money away from public education for the benefit of private schools. For most students, the effect of "choice" would be less money for their public schools and most likely, therefore, a poorer-quality education.

Competency Testing

Another response to concerns about education quality is competency testing.[48] It would address the claim that students who have not mastered the material required at each grade level are being promoted simply to get them through the school system, with the result that students who cannot read and write are graduating from high school. Competency testing would require a student to pass a test on basic skills—reading, writing, and computation—before being awarded a high school diploma. Advocates of competency testing also argue that it would provide more incentives for students to learn and for teachers to teach. The idea of testing for competency has been extended from just certification for graduation to testing at several grade levels to judge how well schools and teachers are doing.

Although many leaders of minority communities have argued that the public schools do not adequately prepare minority students, they have not been supporters of competency testing. The program has been attacked as racist because a disproportionate share of the students who failed the tests in states where they were first used extensively (most notably Florida) were nonwhite. These competency tests, which continue to be challenged in the courts, are claimed to be biased against nonwhites because they employ standard English and are based on values and concepts that derive from white middle-class culture. Such tests are, at best, a minimal demonstration of educational quality, but the poor scores nevertheless indicate the poor quality of the education being offered to some students.

Even without national testing or standardized tests to determine whether a student can graduate, testing has become an issue in education. On the one hand, parents and state legislatures want some way to hold teachers and education officials accountable for their activities, and they see standardized testing as a means of determining if schools are doing a good job. No Child Left Behind was clearly designed to give parents the opportunity to move their children out of schools that continue to fail to meet standards. On the other hand, critics argue that students were already spending too much time on such tests, to the detriment of other types of learning, before federal intervention. Critics charged that teachers were teaching students to pass standardized tests, not teaching the material that they really need to learn.

Competency testing may also be associated with the continuing rise of school dropout rates. Approximately one-third of all students in the United States do not finish high school, and that number has been increasing.[49] In an economy that is increasingly based on education and knowledge, this is a huge waste of potential talent for both the individuals and the nation. Furthermore, the dropouts are more likely to be members of minority groups; thus, the failure to address this issue effectively is exacerbating the general levels of inequality within the American economy and society.

The Obama administration has entered the debate on dropout levels by putting pressure on the states to increase the mandatory educational age to 18.[50] The argument is that the knowledge base needed in the contemporary economy is much greater than when age limits of 16 or even 15 were written. This pressure has been resisted for several reasons. One is that students who do not want to be in school will be disruptive and inhibit learning for students who do. The other argument is a simple financial point that in a period of declining state and local budgets raising the mandatory age of students will require more teachers and more classrooms, for perhaps limited educational benefits.

Testing Teacher Competence

In addition to testing the quality of the product of the schools—the students—a number of reformers have argued that the producers—the teachers—should also be tested. Traditionally, once a teacher graduated from a school of education, he or she would receive a certificate, usually renewable after additional course-work, and would soon receive tenure to teach for life. Numerous parents and education experts, who thought that the traditional system was insufficient to guarantee that teachers could indeed educate students effectively, proposed that all teachers should be tested. This policy was widely supported by the public (85 percent in one poll), and some form of competency testing for teachers has been adopted in almost every state.

Initial scores on the teacher tests appeared to support the critics of the existing system. In several southern states, only about half the teachers who took a test in the early 1990s passed the first time. As testing became more general across the United States, the failure rate dropped significantly, and testing has become a standard part of the certification process for new teachers. Even though testing is now widespread, there are still a number of complaints. First, just as with pupil competency testing, it is argued that the tests are discriminatory; indeed, a much higher proportion of nonwhites than whites fail the tests. Also, teachers unions argue that the test—especially if given to established classroom teachers—does not adequately measure all the things a teacher must do to be effective. And again, testing is seen as yet another hurdle that can keep teachers out of the classrooms where they are needed.

Competency testing itself certainly cannot guarantee a supply of good teachers. Other problems include low teacher salaries, declining interest in teaching among young women (who were once the major source of talent in elementary and secondary education), and the poor working conditions in many schools, especially problems of discipline and personal safety.[51] Finally, teachers no longer command the respect that they traditionally enjoyed in American society, and many of the psychic rewards of teaching have disappeared. Unless the public schools can attract enough qualified and dedicated teachers, all the other reforms in education policy may be to little avail.[52]

School Facilities

Americans are fond of saying that they will do anything for their children, but if an impartial observer were to walk into many of America's schools, he or she would doubt the sincerity of those statements. Many American schools are dilapidated, and they appear to be unlikely places to find excellence in education. In 1996, the General Accounting Office conducted a survey that concluded that one school building in three in the country was inadequate and almost six in ten had at least one inadequate feature, such as a leaking roof.[53] There were, however, marked differences across the country in the condition of school buildings. Half of the schools in the District of Columbia were labeled inadequate, but less than 19 percent of those in Iowa were found to be so. In the District of Columbia, 91.1 percent of schools had at least one inadequate feature, compared with only 37 percent of schools in Georgia. In addition to the differences by state, there are differences within states, with inner cities generally having worse school facilities.

In 1998, the Clinton administration began to push a national campaign to improve the quality of school facilities.[54] The federal government already had begun to be involved with school building issues through a number of mandates, especially access for the disabled. President Clinton argued that there was a pressing need for improving facilities, in some cases to guarantee basic safety and in many others to ensure that students had a positive learning environment. Schools also needed a range of electronic equipment and access to be adequate to the task of educating for the emerging economy and society. The campaign produced a number of positive public relations events for the administration and in the end some real improvements in facilities. Additionally, some provisions of the No Child Left Behind Act were directed at improving facilities, but no recent survey of facilities has been completed.[55]

The Separation of Church and State

The First Amendment both forbids the establishment of a religion and ensures the free exercise of religion in the United States. These two clauses have caused a number of controversies about education and government's role in it. The two guarantees may, in fact, be interpreted as being in conflict. For example, if schools require a prayer, that is deemed an establishment of religion (*Engel v. Vitale*, 370 U.S. 421 [1962]). Conversely, some see prohibiting prayer as a limitation on the free exercise of religion.

The use of vouchers has also become entangled with the role of government in supporting denominational schools. In a 2006 case, Florida courts ruled that the state's voucher plan violated the state constitution's provisions on separation of church and state and voided it.[56] That case will likely be appealed. Other cases are entering the judicial system that will provide continuing tests of the meaning of "separation." We return to the issue of church and state in chapter 16.

Unionization and Management

The image of the American "schoolmarm" is ingrained in the popular mind. Leaving aside any sexist stereotypes of all elementary and secondary schoolteachers being female, the point is that the image of the schoolteacher has been the positive one of a person dedicated to education and to students. The teacher and the school were considered integral parts of the American community.

The image of the teacher is now changing, however, in part because of increasing unionization and a growing number of teacher strikes.[57] No longer the representatives of culture and learning in small towns, teachers are now more likely to be employed by large school districts and be members of organizations that bargain collectively for improved wages and benefits. One of the two major teachers' organizations is the American Federation of Teachers, a union affiliated with the American Federation of Labor and Congress of Industrial Organizations (AFL-CIO). It has been quite willing to employ the strike weapon in its dealings with school districts. The second, the National Education Association (NEA), is a professional organization, but its local chapters operate as collective bargaining units. The NEA has been more reluctant to use the strike to gain its ends, although a number of its local chapters have struck. As of 2006, more than half of U.S. teachers were members of these organizations, and others were involved in local teachers unions. In almost any year, there are several hundred strikes by public schoolteachers. The sight of teachers picketing and of children out of school until October and even November has changed the once-positive image of the teacher. As local government budgets continue to be squeezed, there will be demands for more students in each classroom and less money for raises, and the teachers strike may become an even more common phenomenon.

In addition to forcing parents to make arrangements for their children's care during strikes, labor unrest in education has other, more important consequences. The sight of educators on strike tends to further erode the public image of education. Of course, those who favor the more militant actions by teachers quite rightly point out that good teachers will not work for the salaries they are sometimes offered and that fewer good students will be attracted to careers in teaching. There are, however, important problems of symbolism and public image when teachers take to the picket line.

The impact of education unions extends beyond the possibility of strikes. The high level of unionization in education also poses significant problems for administrators in their day-to-day management of schools. For example, as we have already noted, school principals and superintendents are under increasing pressure to demonstrate the adequate or superior performance of their schools. They must do that with less control over personnel than they would have in private industry or even in other areas of the public sector.

The economic crisis has placed educators' salaries and benefits under even greater pressure, as have moves in some states such as Wisconsin to limit unionization of public employees.[58] Faced with declining revenues, the states have sought to reduce the number of teachers and other school employees, as well as many other public employees.[59] Furthermore, the longer-term expectations of teachers may be diminished given that public employee benefits and especially generous public pension programs are also being put under stress despite the attempts of unions to maintain them.

Equalization of Resources

As we have already discussed, most public education is financed by local property taxes, and this basis of finance can produce substantial inequities. Local school districts with poor resource bases must either tax their poorer constituents more heavily or, more commonly, provide inferior education to the district's children.[60] Given that poorer school districts frequently have concentrations of minority group families, this way of financing schools affects racial and cultural integration and the perceived fairness of government. The resulting inequalities in educational opportunity may, in turn, perpetuate racial differences in economic and social opportunities.

Reliance on the local property tax to finance public schools has been challenged successfully in the courts, but definite answers to the questions involved have not emerged. In *Serrano v. Priest* (1971), the California Supreme Court ruled that the great disparity in educational funding between richer and poorer school districts in the Los Angeles area violated provisions of both the state constitution and the U.S. Constitution, constituting a denial of equal protection for the residents of the poorer districts. The Court did not, however, make any direct recommendations on how the disparity could be ameliorated to meet constitutional standards. In a similar case in 1973, *San Antonio School District v. Rodriguez*, the Supreme Court ruled that the differences between two Texas school districts were not so great as to violate the Equal Protection Clause; the Court did not say how much of a difference would constitute a violation. That decision left open the constitutionality of continued disparities among school districts, but the problems that local districts face in attempting to provide for decent education from a low property tax base remain quite tangible.[61]

By the 1990s, various state courts had decided that the existing system of school financing violated their state constitutional requirements for "an efficient system for the general diffusion of knowledge." In 1991, the Texas Supreme Court ordered the state of Texas to find some means of redressing the differences among its 1,044 school districts (*Edgewood v. Kirby*, 804, S.W.2D 491 [Tex. 1991]). Those districts exhibited massive disparities: The richest 5 percent of school districts spent $11,801 per pupil, while the poorest 5 percent spent $3,190 per pupil.[62] The state legislature first opted for regional tax sharing, but the voters rejected an amendment to the state constitution allowing it.[63] The final plan called for wealthier school districts to transfer some of their taxable property to poorer districts so that the poorer districts could provide a better education for their pupils.[64]

Lawsuits challenging systems for funding public schools have been brought in forty-five states, and equitable financing for education remains a national problem.[65] Of the states that have addressed equality of funding directly, the most important example is Michigan, which acted following several embarrassing events that included the closing of a school district in northern Michigan several months before the scheduled end of the term because of lack of funds. State leaders decided on a 2 percent sales tax and a tripling of the cigarette tax, instead of the property tax, to fund education. Voters chose those options over increasing the state income tax.[66] These consumption taxes were statewide, and the revenue was to be divided according to the relative needs of the school districts. As this example shows, the states have a variety of options for equalizing funding; ESEA money can also be used for the purpose.[67] One state, Kentucky, which historically had one of the most unequal and least effective school systems in the country, attacked the problem directly by centralizing the funding of schools, with a great deal of apparent success.[68]

Indeed, the state in which a student lives, as well as the school district, may affect the quality of his or her education. There is pronounced variation in funding for public education by state (see Table 13.2), as well as substantial variation in teacher salaries. In 2007, the highest average salary, California's, was 75 percent higher than that in South Dakota. The relatively poor states of the South and upper Midwest perform the worst in support for public education, while the industrial states of the Northeast tend to do the best.

These data illustrate that there is as yet no national education policy or standard, and a child's life chances may depend on geography. The differences in actual educational outcomes, however, may not be as great as the differences in money being spent. Some states with very low per pupil expenditures, such as Iowa, South Dakota, and Utah, have very good results on standardized tests, such as the SAT.[69] In fact, there is actually a slight negative statistical relationship between the amount of money spent per pupil and scores on the SAT.[70] Some of the success of the lower-spending states may be attributed to their relatively homogenous populations, and some may be a function of the smaller schools in rural America and the closer personal attention the pupils receive in those settings. Students in small, rural schools also do not have to cope with as much crime and social disruption as occurs in urban areas, where more money is spent.

Desegregation and Busing

The issues of desegregation and busing have created long-standing controversies in U.S. education. The important question is whether school systems can be

TABLE 13.2   Inequalities in Education Funding

Average teacher salaries, 2007

National average = $50,800

Five highest		Five lowest	
California	$63,600	South Dakota	$35,400
Connecticut	60,800	North Dakota	38,800
New Jersey	59,900	Mississippi	40,200
District of Columbia	59,000	West Virginia	40,500
Massachusetts	58,600	Utah	40,600

Per pupil expenditures, 2007

National average = $10,615

Five highest		Five lowest	
New Jersey	$16,587	Utah	$6,629
New York	15,837	Idaho	7,343
District of Columbia	15,626	Oklahoma	7,623
Connecticut	15,219	Tennessee	7,742
Massachusetts	14,094	Arizona	7,749

Source: U.S. Department of Education, *Digest of Educational Statistics* (Washington, DC: U.S. Government Printing Office, 2010).

expected to solve all of society's problems or whether they should concentrate more narrowly on education. The argument is that little is being done elsewhere in society to change the underlying causes of segregation, especially segregated housing, and that the only institution that has been subjected to such stringent requirements for desegregation is the public school system. Frequently, busing affects popular support for public education, and the decline of public education after desegregation becomes a self-fulfilling prophecy when white parents either remove their children from the integrated schools and send them to private schools or move their families out of the affected areas. The latter is probably more destructive, since it erodes the financial base of the schools.

On the other side of the argument is the central importance of education in the formation of values and attitudes. Desegregation appears to benefit minority children by improving not only the quality of their education but also their self-image. It may also be important in reducing the social isolation of white children from minority children. Social integration has traditionally been one purpose of American public education, and it may be important to continue to pursue that goal through desegregation. After years of fighting for an end to segregation, however, some minority groups have somewhat paradoxically come to favor a resegregation of students. They argue that the curriculums of most public schools do not reflect the interests or needs of their community and that students can learn better without racial tensions and when taught by teachers of their own race. Such resegregation may be occurring de facto, especially in northern cities, as residential patterns continue to be segregated.[71]

Many of the same issues that had arisen over racial desegregation have arisen in the past decade over the inclusion of the children of immigrants, especially illegal immigrants, in the public schools. Discussions contrast the need for these children to receive a good education with the cost of their education and the possible negative impact on quality of the presence of numerous children whose first language is not English. The debate has also been cast in terms of No Child Left Behind requirements, given that the immigrant children may not be expected to score as well on standardized tests, everything else being equal, as children who had no language barrier to overcome.[72]

The new and old issues surrounding desegregation and social inclusion can be, and have been, debated at length, but the issue of busing has been so emotionally charged that rational discourse is frequently impossible. The connection between educational quality and racial equality is an important one for the society that must be pursued within both policy domains.[73] Some argue that education is too central to the formation of the social fabric of the United States to be allowed to become isolated from other social concerns. However, education also may be too important in a highly technological society to be compromised in any way in an attempt to solve other social problems; it may be that too many social responsibilities are being placed on schools and their teachers. How this debate is resolved may say a great deal about the future of American society and the American economy.

If busing has been the most divisive issue in desegregating elementary and secondary schools, affirmative action in admissions and scholarships has been its analogue in higher education. Under pressure from the federal Department of Education and the Department of Justice, as well as from their own state legislatures, a number of state university systems were providing preferences for minority students. In 1997, California and Texas courts found that the states were unlawfully discriminating on the basis of race by providing these preferences and enjoined the state universities from doing so in the future. In 2003, the Supreme Court ruled that race could be used as one of several factors in determining admissions.[74] This may be just one more event in the ongoing struggle to reconcile different interpretations of the word *equality* as it applies to education and other public policies.

Race permeates other aspects of American education as well. For example, discipline in schools appears to be meted out differently by race, and nonwhite students may be encouraged to pursue nonacademic programs at a higher rate than white students.[75] Now issues of language and immigrant status also divide school populations and appear to many citizens to place the focus of education less on learning and more on pursuit of social justice.

Higher Education Costs

We have already pointed out that the federal government provides a good deal of support for students attending institutions of higher education, as well as a variety of supports for the institutions themselves. There is a great deal of money available for student support, but the country still encounters problems in making higher education available for every student who might want to pursue it. This long-standing problem has been exacerbated by continuing increases in the cost of attending a college or university. As shown in Table 13.3, the costs of college have been increasing more rapidly than overall costs in the economy. Costs for public four-year institutions, which enroll approximately 75 percent of all college students, have been increasing more rapidly than costs at other types of institutions. The economic barriers to public higher education also vary by state: Average tuition at public universities in Vermont was $9,333 in 2007 but only $2,844 in Nevada.

The rising costs of higher education derive from a variety of factors. One is that, as labor-intensive organizations, universities are less able than other industries to reduce their costs by investing in capital. Emphasis on quality has an influence in higher education, as well as at lower levels of the educational system, producing demands for smaller classes and more personal attention, which increase staffing requirements and costs. The emphasis on quality also calls for

TABLE 13.3   Increases in the Cost of Higher Education, 1976–2008 (average tuition)

Year	Current	Real
1976	$924	$1,584
1980	1,163	1,479
1985	1,985	1,734
1990	2,839	1,926
1995	4,044	2,236
2000	5,244	2,538
2002	5,646	2,732
2004	6,608	3,548
2006	7,601	4,234
2008	8,505	4,825

Source: U.S. Department of Education, *Digest of Educational Statistics* (Washington, DC: U.S. Government Printing Office, annual).

investment in more technology in laboratories, computer centers, and the like—
which is necessary (and expensive) but may not really improve the productivity
of the institution. Somewhat paradoxically from an economic perspective, the
competition for students among institutions of higher education has also led to
major expenditures on amenities for them, as well as on the means for actually
improving the quality of research and teaching.

The increasing costs of higher education are a growing problem for many
middle-class and less affluent families. Despite the many sources of assistance,
the high cost of many colleges tends to deter many potential students or to force
them to make hard decisions about where they apply. However, public and private assistance has been increasing at approximately the same rate as costs.[76] One
of the growing problems is that increasing numbers of students are graduating
with large debts that impose a heavy burden on them as they begin careers and
start to raise families. The average student graduating from a four-year institution in 2007–2008 had a debt of almost $13,000, and a new medical doctor on
average owes $127,000 when he or she begins practice.

Summary

Education has been and remains a central concern of American public policy.
Traditionally the concern of state and local government, it is increasingly influenced by federal policy, in part because of education's close connection to other
goals such as economic growth. But although education has been an important
and highly respected public function, it is currently under attack. The quality of
education, the competence of school personnel, and the place of education in
social change are all topics of vital concern to many Americans. Several policy
instruments have been proposed to rectify the perceived difficulties in these
areas, the most commonly discussed being the voucher plan, but few statements
on educational policy have gained wide public acceptance.

The debate over educational policy is in part a result of the absence of a
widely accepted theory of causation in education. Unlike science policy, educational policy is a subject about which reasonable people often disagree radically.
Voucher plans are intended in part to allow people to make individual choices
concerning education without having to pay too great an economic price. The
role of government as the funding agent for these programs, however, requires
greater attention to the real benefits of certain forms of education and a decision
about just how far the use of vouchers can be allowed to extend. This is a task
for rational policy analysts who recognize that such proposals must be subjected
to serious political and social scrutiny, especially because education is an issue
about which almost everyone has an opinion. Because the students involved are
the children of those opinionated people, there will be controversy.

CHAPTER 14

Energy and the Environment

A DECADE INTO THE twenty-first century the United States continues to face two significant problems that affect the relationship between its economy and the physical world. One is a virtually insatiable demand for energy that is much higher per capita than in other industrialized economies. The other is the need to manage the effluents of an industrialized society and to preserve as much of the natural environment as possible. These two policy areas will be discussed together here, in part because they are interconnected in several crucial ways.

These policy issues are perhaps most closely linked in the issue of climate change, with the widespread burning of fossil fuels almost certainly linked to continued warming of Earth's atmosphere and, with that, serious challenges to existing ecological patterns. Although this link has been accepted for over a decade by most of the world, the United States under President George W. Bush denied the problem or was not willing to respond to it.[1] The Obama administration has advocated a sweeping energy program based on the premise of climate change, but it will produce rather slow responses to what some scientists see as an immediate problem for global society.[2]

There are two general goals for energy policy. One is to find the means to achieve energy independence for the United States. The very high level of imports of oil from other parts of the world affects not only the American economy, but also the foreign policy of the United States. The other goal, not unrelated to the first, is to reduce or at least control the level of energy consumption, and especially fossil fuel consumption, in the United States. This will not only help with energy independence but also may make the economic system more sustainable.[3]

Background

The high consumption of energy, especially fossil fuels, produces huge quantities of pollution, and the periodic shortages and high prices of petroleum and natural gas place pressure on industries to burn coal instead, which is cheaper but creates even greater pollution. Even the transportation of fossil fuels, especially oil, presents several well-known and politically visible threats to the environment—the *Exxon Valdez* spill in Alaska being one of the more infamous examples. The massive oil pollution in the Gulf of Mexico demonstrated rather dramatically the potential costs of exploiting fossil fuel resources in the United States. Failure to address the energy problem by exploring nontraditional sources of energy or by engaging in extensive conservation efforts will almost certainly exacerbate the environmental problem.

Some regulations issued by the Environmental Protection Agency to reduce pollution, such as emission controls on automobiles, have required using more energy than would otherwise be used. Both energy and environmental issues have a large technical and scientific element, and governments have at times required the development of new technologies to meet environmental strictures.[4] Ultimately, changes in human behavior—including things as simple as energy conservation and recycling used paper, plastic, and metal—may be more important than technological change in producing improvements in the environment.

Both energy policy and environmental policy are closely linked with the economy. Uncertainties about energy supplies, including those arising from political instability in the Persian Gulf region, and rising energy prices make investment decisions more difficult for businesses and contribute to inflation. In an industrial economy, the price of almost every product is influenced by the cost of energy, so increases in energy prices have a pervasive impact. Critics charge that strict environmental controls make economic development projects more expensive or in some cases impossible. When the economy picks up, more pollution is produced.

Energy is an international concern, not only because the United States imports so much of its energy but also because the immense demand of the United States and other industrialized countries tends to increase the price and reduce availability for the developing countries. As China, India, and other mid-level economies have developed, the demand for oil on the international market has increased. Because energy is one of the most widely traded international commodities, excessive demand in one part of the world tends to distort the market. With increasing uncertainties about politics in the Middle East, the question of energy security has become even more pressing.[5] In this chapter, we examine energy and environmental problems, the responses of governments to them, and some possible alternative policies.

Energy is a crucial component of the U.S. way of life. Americans are accustomed to using, and squandering, energy to a degree unimaginable even in other affluent, industrialized societies. The typically large American automobile and more recently massive sports utility vehicles have been symbols of that attitude toward energy use, as is the single person driving an automobile to work each day. Car size tended to decrease when energy was expensive in the 1980s and early 1990s, but by the late 1990s, Americans had reverted to even larger and heavier vans and SUVs. The same cycle was repeated with interest in smaller cars and hybrids when gasoline became increasingly expensive in 2006 and 2007 and with declining interest in efficiency when prices eased. And as gasoline approached $4.00 per gallon, electric and hybrid cars began to get more attention. The United States consumes more than 20 percent of all the energy used in the world—90 percent more energy per person than Sweden or Canada.[6] Although high energy use is related to industrialization and a higher standard of living, the United States appears to use much more than is required to maintain the comfortable living standard to which most of its citizens are accustomed.

That high level of energy use was not perceived to be a problem until the 1973 Organization of the Petroleum Exporting Countries (OPEC) embargo on oil shipments to the United States demonstrated the extent of the country's dependence on imported oil. Thereafter, the rapidly escalating oil prices that resulted from OPEC price fixing restricted production; then, a second embargo emphasized that dependence, even with relatively large quantities of domestic oil, natural gas, and coal. The experiences of the 1970s made it clear that U.S. energy policies needed to be reexamined and probably altered. That policy lesson does not appear to have been learned, as cheaper oil in the 1980s and 1990s restored more relaxed attitudes toward energy use, which persisted despite further alarms during the Iran–Iraq War, the Persian Gulf War, and most recently the invasion of Iraq and tensions with Iran.

Growing energy demand from China and other developing economies, problems of refining, and global economic jitters around the conflict in Iraq drove the price of gasoline and other energy products to all-time highs in 2007–2008, and although prices subsided slightly in late 2008, they are likely to remain quite high. U.S. gas prices have appeared extreme, but not compared with prices in Europe (over $8.00 per gallon in some European countries in May 2008); or if the effects of inflation are discounted, the prices are not far out of line. Price is forcing the United States to reconsider its relaxed attitudes toward energy use and energy policy, but the existing stock of automobiles, inadequate public transport, and commuting patterns will make any significant changes painful.

Energy Sources

Oil

In spite of the importance of foreign petroleum and the American love affair with the automobile, petroleum is not the only U.S. energy source, and other sources could be more highly developed. Oil is, however, the major energy source for the country, accounting for 37 percent of all energy consumed, a

TABLE 14.1   Sources of Energy, 1970–2010 (in percentages)

	Petroleum	Natural gas	Coal	Nuclear	Renewable sources
1970	43.4	34.7	16.5	0.3	5.2
1980	43.6	25.9	18.7	5.4	7.1
1990	42.3	23.4	22.9	6.1	6.3
1995	36.7	24.2	22.1	7.2	7.7
2000	38.8	24.2	22.9	7.9	6.2
2005	40.2	22.5	22.7	8.1	6.4
2008	37.4	24.0	22.6	8.5	7.4
2009	36.8	24.2	22.4	8.6	7.9
2010	36.9	24.6	22.1	8.5	8.2

Source: U.S. Energy Information Agency, *Annual Energy Review* (Washington, DC: Department of Energy, annual).

percentage that has fluctuated little in the past several decades (see Table 14.1). President George W. Bush said in one State of the Union address that the United States was "addicted to oil" and began to lay the groundwork for a reduction in dependency on foreign oil. Approximately 50 percent of the oil consumed in the United States is imported, so a little simple arithmetic reveals that roughly 18 percent of the total U.S. energy supply is imported oil.[7] Imports have been increasing as domestic oil has become more difficult (and expensive) to extract and as demand has continued to grow. This has produced political pressures to permit exploration in environmentally fragile areas, such as the Arctic National Wildlife Refuge, some areas of the Rockies, and off the Florida coast. The George W. Bush administration began lobbying soon after taking office to open the Arctic refuge, but the proposal met strong legal and political opposition and was eventually defeated in a Democratic-led Senate.[8] Very quickly, the administration began to look for exploration options in other parts of the United States.[9] The issue of drilling in the Arctic refuge continued to arise, and legislation to permit it often passed the House of Representatives but was defeated in the Senate, even with its Republican majority.[10] With a Democratic Congress and president elected in 2008, this source of energy seems off the table, although the Obama administration has encouraged greater offshore drilling for oil.[11]

Reliance on imported oil makes U.S. energy supplies uncertain and makes the American economy a hostage to foreign powers. Continuing instability in the Middle East makes the problem worse.[12] Moreover, the money paid for foreign oil goes outside the United States and is difficult to match with exports, aggravating the country's negative balance of payments, with serious consequences for the economy (see chapter 9). Energy accounts for more than 23 percent of U.S.

imports, and without that import bill, the balance of payments deficit would be approximately half of what it is.[13] Oil is a finite resource, and proven world reserves are sufficient only for a limited number of years at current rates of consumption. Eventually, the U.S. economy will have to convert to some other form of energy, and continued reliance on foreign oil will only delay the hard economic, social, and technological choices that will have to be made when this particular energy resource is depleted. Finally, although other energy sources pose environmental risks as well, on average, almost a million gallons of oil are spilled into U.S. waters each year. Most oil spills are not nearly as destructive as the *Exxon Valdez* spill in Alaska, but all have some environmental consequences.

Natural Gas

The United States has been more blessed with reserves of natural gas than with petroleum. Currently, almost all natural gas the country uses comes from domestic sources. Natural gas is also a limited resource, however; somewhere between thirty-five and sixty years' worth of proven reserves are available at current and predicted rates of consumption. That estimate has been increased somewhat over the past several years by the exploitation of the Marcellus Shale deposits in the eastern United States.[14] Even then, however, natural gas thus does not constitute a long-term alternative for the United States. In addition, natural gas is so valuable for industrial uses—in the fabrication of plastics and synthetic fibers, for example—that it may be inefficient to use it to heat buildings and cook meals.

Alternatives to domestically produced natural gas include importing gas in liquid form from Algeria, Qatar, or countries of the former Soviet Union. Those sources would extend natural gas supplies but would present the same political and economic problems as imported oil. In addition, the technology for transporting liquid natural gas has not yet been fully developed, so massive explosions can occur if great care is not exercised. Given the environmental damage already encountered with oil spills, the difficult task of developing a new technology for transporting natural gas, simply to preserve another relatively short-lived energy supply, may not be politically acceptable.

Coal

America's most abundant energy resource is coal. The United States has enough coal to last approximately two hundred years, and it exports substantial quantities of coal to Japan and Europe. In addition to supplying relatively cheap energy, coal can be used as a raw material for industrial purposes, as can natural gas. If coal use were developed more fully, the demand for natural gas and petroleum might be reduced. However, coal has several disadvantages as an energy resource. First, there is the environmental problem: Coal does not burn as cleanly as oil or natural gas, and a good deal of American coal is rather high in sulfur. When burned, it forms sulfur dioxide, which then combines with water to form sulfuric acid—a major source of the "acid rain" that threatens forests and wildlife in the northern United States and Canada. Soot from coal-fired plants allegedly claims 12,000 lives per year, a toll that prompted the George W. Bush administration's plan for gradually cleaning up coal-fired plants beginning in 2008.[15] The pressure on coal-fired plants has been extended and strengthened in the Obama administration.[16]

The extraction of coal presents further environmental difficulties, since much of the available coal is most efficiently extracted by strip mining, a method that deeply scars the landscape and can render the land unusable for years. Improved methods for reclaiming strip-mined land have been developed, but recovery still takes time and money, and the original natural landscape is lost forever.[17] Mining coal by building tunnels presents huge health and safety problems for the miners. Several highly visible mining accidents occurred in Pennsylvania and West Virginia in the early twenty-first century. Some forty or more coal miners still die in accidents each year, and many others die slowly from lung diseases, such as black lung and silicosis.

In addition to the environmental problems, no technology yet exists for using coal to power automobiles or trucks. The "synfuels" project that was one component of President Jimmy Carter's energy plan was intended to find a way to extract a liquid fuel from coal ("gasification"), but at present, there is no process to do so at an acceptable price.[18] Thus, coal can be used to generate electricity and heat but not for transportation, which accounts for almost 30 percent of energy use in the United States. The continuing development of other technologies, such as improved storage batteries and better electric cars, may help expand its utility.

There are also great logistical problems in using coal. Coal is more difficult to transport than petroleum or natural gas, which can be readily moved through pipelines. A good deal of the available coal is located at substantial distances from the points of principal energy demand, and American railroads do not now have sufficient rolling stock or suitable roadbeds to manage big increases in coal shipments. Water transportation might be a better option, but even that possibility would require investment in boats or barges to make greater use of coal more practical than it is at present.

Nuclear Power

In 1998, the United States had 110 nuclear power plants that produced approximately 8 percent of the total energy used in the country and almost 22 percent of the electricity. By 2008, the numbers had dropped to 104 plants and less than 20 percent of electricity. At one time, it was believed that nuclear power would meet future energy needs; particularly with fast-breeder reactors, the supply of energy appeared almost endless. But after the near disaster at the Three Mile Island nuclear plant in 1979; the very real 1986 disaster at Chernobyl, in Ukraine, in the former Soviet Union; and then the Fukushima disaster in Japan in 2011, a nuclear future appears less likely. One reason is that without the breeder reactor and its potential dangers, producers must deal with a limited supply of fissionable uranium. More important, safety and environmental problems and the very real dilemma of how to dispose of nuclear waste have called the feasibility of nuclear power into question for the public as well as for many experts.[19] Because of concern about terrorism, nuclear material is also perceived as a more important threat than in the past.[20]

The Three Mile Island, Chernobyl, and Fukushima incidents pointed to the possibility that nuclear power plants might present health and safety hazards for citizens living near them and possibly even for people living hundreds of miles away. Had the "China syndrome" occurred—melting of the reactor core—the likely extent of damage to the health of citizens is difficult to estimate. If a nuclear power plant has no incidents of this sort, then the additional radioactivity in its vicinity is negligible, but there remains the possibility—although advocates of the technology argue that it is remote—of a serious accident. The accident at Chernobyl caused at least 330 deaths during the first four years after it occurred, and there are estimates of up to a half-million additional deaths as a result of that one nuclear accident.[21] There were few if any deaths attributable to the nuclear plant in Japan, but the danger remains real. The U.S. nuclear industry emphasizes the contrast between the inadequate design of the Soviet-built reactor at Chernobyl and the ever-safer designs available in the United States, but many Americans remember only the atomic horrors produced in the Ukraine and in Japan.

Even if there were no danger of accidents, the environmental and health problems associated with nuclear waste disposal would present difficulties. Some nuclear wastes lose their radioactivity very slowly—the half-life, or time required for half the nuclear activity to be exhausted, of plutonium-239 (one by-product of nuclear reactors) is 24,000 years. This means that the nuclear industry (and ultimately government) must find a means of disposing of these wastes so as to prevent contamination of the environment into the indefinite future. There are proposals for burying the wastes, but almost no one wants the facilities near his or her home—the not in my backyard, or "NIMBY," phenomenon is very strong in this field.[22] Government must also prevent terrorists from gaining control of radioactive material, which would constitute a powerful instrument for blackmail. The disposal of nuclear wastes therefore presents both environmental problems and serious problems that have to do with guarding large areas against possible terrorist attacks and theft. In 2002, the Bush administration settled on Yucca Mountain, Nevada, as the repository for nuclear wastes, but challenges to that decision in the courts prevented any movement to the site, and the Obama administration terminated its development in 2009.[23]

The construction of nuclear power plants has been so slow and so expensive that many electrical utilities have become frustrated and abandoned the projects. The requirements for extensive inspection and reinspection of the plants as they are built, because of the dangers of accidents and contamination, have slowed the construction significantly, as have lawsuits filed by opponents of nuclear power. Operating costs of nuclear power plants will certainly be less than those of fossil fuel plants, but the initial capital investment and the relatively short operating life of a nuclear plant (often thirty years or less) have caused many private utilities to cancel plans to build such facilities. No new ones have been initiated in almost two decades. These problems put much of the burden for energy production back onto fossil fuels, with their associated pollution and finite global supply.

The regulatory difficulties of nuclear power in the United States are indicated by the long controversy over the Seabrook nuclear plant in New Hampshire.[24] The Public Service Company of New Hampshire originally announced plans to build twin reactors at Seabrook in 1972. A series of legal disputes and demonstrations, as well as rising costs, caused the cancellation of one of the reactors in 1984, after $800 million had been spent on it. Construction of Unit 1 was completed in July 1986, but the Chernobyl accident had occurred a few months earlier, and it led the surrounding states and their utility companies to withdraw their cooperation in further work on the plant. Having invested $2.1 billion in Seabrook without generating a single kilowatt, Public Service Company of New Hampshire filed for bankruptcy protection in 1988. After the Reagan administration intervened, the Nuclear Regulatory Commission (NRC) permitted testing of the plant beginning in June 1989, and on March 1, 1990, the NRC granted an operating license to the new owner, Northeast Utilities.[25] While this history represents an extreme case, it is little wonder that all nuclear power plants ordered since 1974 have now been canceled. One nuclear plant owned by the Tennessee Valley Authority has been restarted, and several utility companies are considering returning to nuclear power with new "Generation III" reactor designs.[26] After George W. Bush pushed for nuclear power during his administration, the industry slowly began to respond, and the NRC saw an increase in applications to build nuclear reactors. President Obama's hesitance to support nuclear energy, despite Secretary of Energy Steven Chu's intentions to encourage the industry, rendered the future of nuclear power unclear.

Alternative and Renewable Energy Sources

Several other energy sources are currently being used in the United States, although none accounts for a significant percentage of the total. These sources include hydroelectric power, wood, and some solar, wind, and geothermal power.

David Chiang, project manager at Southern California Edison, performs a visual inspection of solar modules in Porterville, California. Solar energy is one several alternative energy sources that is being supported by government subsidies. Critics argue, however, that the subsidies are as yet insufficient to make alternative energy viable in the United States.

Ken James/Bloomberg via Getty Images

To date, with the exception of hydroelectric power, none has offered much hope for rapid development, although a great deal is promised for solar power, and geothermal power (produced with the heat from natural sources in the Earth) is apparently successful in Iceland and parts of Europe. Wood, perhaps our oldest power source, is renewable, but limited availability, cost, and the pollution it produces limit its usefulness, in spite of a growing number of Franklin stoves and wood-burning furnaces in the northern United States.

As of 2010, only about 8 percent of total energy consumption came from renewable sources, and that figure has been climbing very slowly for some time. At present, there appears to be at least six major alternative energy sources, two of which—extraction of oil from the shale found in Colorado and Wyoming and nuclear fusion (rather than fission)—are variations on existing power sources. The oil shale technology, if developed, would have an immense environmental impact, much like that of strip-mined coal. Furthermore, extracting oil from shale would require huge amounts of water in an area already short of water and would produce a number of undesirable effluents in areas that are both beautiful and environmentally fragile.[27] And all of these environmental costs would yield a relatively small amount of oil, when compared to current levels of consumption and other modes of production.

The technology of nuclear fusion is still in the beginning stages, despite significant research and development expenditures. The idea of this power source is to approximate, in a laboratory or power station, the processes that produce the energy of the sun. That will require temperatures of tens of millions of degrees and the technology to create and then contain a superheated "plasma" of charged particles.[28] Fusion will require great technological advancements, but it may someday produce cheap and virtually limitless energy, with much less radioactivity than is caused by nuclear fission. European researchers have been able actually to produce some limited amounts of power using a fusion technique, and American researchers also have produced a brief sustained fusion.[29]

Limited amounts of solar power are also in use in the United States, heating some houses and businesses and water for home use. But the use of solar power to produce electricity for mass distribution ("big solar") will require technological breakthroughs as well as answers to some environmental questions. Although theoretically solar power is a limitless resource, many areas of the United States may not receive sufficient sunlight when they need it most. For example, northern cities need energy most during the winter, for heating, but they receive little sunlight then. However, solar energy might provide supplementary power during peak-use periods for summer air-conditioning.

The photovoltaic cell—the means of converting sunlight into electrical energy—is at present underdeveloped and inefficient. Thus, to make quantities of electricity sufficient for big solar projects would require devoting large land areas to solar panels, which some environmentalists may regard as just another form of pollution. Solar power is, however, also being harnessed for use in automobiles. There are engineering contests for solar-powered vehicles, although none of the winners so far—most of them extremely small and slow, as were the first gasoline-powered automobiles—appears likely to be available in automobile showrooms anytime soon.

The Obama administration has emphasized solar energy more than previous administrations, spurred on in part by its greater acceptance of the reality of climate change.[30] In addition to general advocacy of this energy source, the administration has also supported manufacturing of solar panels, to overcome the large lead that China and Germany have in this area. That involvement in industry policy, however, came to a poor end as the firm being backed by government declared bankruptcy, losing hundreds of millions of dollars of federal support.

The Bush administration advocated use of hydrogen in fuel cells as part of the solution to the energy problem. This technology would depend on burning hydrogen, found in water among other sources, which would produce little or no greenhouse gases or other pollution.[31] Critics argue that making enough hydrogen to be usable for automobiles would use more energy than would be saved and, further, that the technology is years away from practical use.[32] If this technology is developed, however, Americans will be able to maintain their love affair with automobiles and also create a highly decentralized capacity to generate electricity.[33]

The windmill, once common in rural landscapes, is to many people also the symbol of the energy future. Like solar power, wind power has already been put to use in small and decentralized ways, but the unreliability of the source and the prospect of thousands of very large windmills dotting the American plains and coasts have reduced the attractiveness of this alternative.[34] Possibly, with better means of storing electricity, wind power will become in the future a more practical means of meeting at least some of America's energy requirements.

There also exists the possibility of using U.S. agricultural productivity to address energy needs. Gasohol, a combination of gasoline and ethanol produced from plants, is already sold in many areas of the United States as a fuel for automobiles. The "summer blend" gasoline sold in much of the eastern United States also contains ethanol as a means of reducing ozone pollution. The same plant material used for gasohol could be converted into methane gas and used in the same way as natural gas to heat homes. There are also a number of options for using the substantial forest reserves of the United States and the by-products of timber production as alternative energy resources. Although gasahol may appeal to agricultural interests, it also has put energy supply and food production in competition and has raised important questions about how to use scarce land resources. These concerns have been exacerbated by rising food costs around the world and threats of mass starvation in many countries.

The production of energy from biomass has several advantages. One is that it is renewable. Use of rapidly growing plants—or agricultural by-products, such as cornstalks—would have less impact on the environment than some other energy sources. The methane gas that is one usable product of the biomass process, however, has been demonstrated to be at least as much a culprit in the greenhouse effect as carbon dioxide. In addition, huge amounts of land would have to be cultivated to produce the necessary quantities of organic material. The ethanol produced from biomass has the decided advantage for Americans that— unlike solar, wind, or fusion power—it can be burned in automobiles. More efficient electric automobiles and storage batteries may be developed someday, but gasohol or even pure ethanol already can be burned in a modified internal combustion engine, hybrid electric automobiles are in production, and the technology for burning methane gas in automobiles is also being developed. Biomass production thus may serve the American lifestyle better than other alternative forms of energy. At present, cost is a major barrier to the production of significant quantities of ethanol, for the price of alcohol has been higher than the price of gasoline. As petroleum prices rise and fluctuate while ethanol production increases, however, methanol may yet become a more competitive energy source.

The Formation of Energy Policy

Broadly speaking, there are two ways of addressing the energy problems of the United States (and the world). One strategy is conservation, or discouraging energy consumption by citizens and industry, and the other is producing more energy. The conflict between these two approaches can be seen easily in the history of American energy policy following the oil supply crises in the 1970s. That history also reflects some fundamental ideological differences in approaches to energy policy, with liberals tending to favor conservation, and conservatives more likely to support increased production.

Federal Energy Policy

Conservation was the Carter administration's principal approach to the energy problem. For example, there were specifications for the temperature range in public buildings, as well as tax incentives for insulation and other energy-saving modifications for homes. The Reagan administration, on the other hand, sought to use markets and to increase production. In particular, the administration sought, largely unsuccessfully, to exploit energy resources on public lands, such as Alaska lands locked up under the Carter administration. There was some leasing of federal lands for coal mining, but the favorable prices offered to private coal companies were condemned as poor resource management, especially because the leased areas were environmentally sensitive. Not surprisingly, George H. W. Bush favored a similar approach to energy policy, in general pursuing exploitation of new fossil fuel resources. The National Energy Strategy announced in early 1991 also called for a research and development program on alternative energy sources, such as biomass and solar power.[35] Many critics—even some in business—argued that the president did not place adequate emphasis on energy conservation. Coming to office at a time of relatively plentiful energy and bringing a host of other agenda items with him, President Clinton invested little political capital in energy issues.

The George W. Bush administration came to office in 2001 with a clear preference for producing more energy rather than limiting use—as was to be expected, given the backgrounds of both the president and the vice president in the energy industry and the large contributions to the Bush campaign by energy companies.[36] Formulating a more or less comprehensive energy plan became a major political problem, however, because the consultations organized by Vice President Richard Cheney to seek advice on the plan were held in secret. Public interest groups sued successfully to find out at least who participated in the consultations, and when the list was eventually published, it consisted only of representatives of producer groups.[37] Not surprisingly, given the interests of that advisory faction and the predispositions of the administration itself, the plan's main elements were increasing production and expanding exploration for and exploitation of domestic resources. The principal instruments were to be subsidies (direct and through the tax system) for energy producers, with some little incentive for conservation.[38] The emphasis on increased production was heightened by the terrorist attacks of September 2001 and the perceived need to make the United States less dependent on foreign energy sources.

During the 1970s, it was popular to talk about the energy "crisis" in the United States, as prices soared and supplies dwindled, but by 2001, polls showed that although the public still regarded energy as a problem, it had little sense of crisis.[39] Fears of energy shortages appeared exaggerated, and Americans continued to favor provision of low-cost and plentiful energy even for potentially wasteful uses. Even when gasoline reached an average of $1.60 per gallon in summer 2001—very high by previous standards—the price was still less than half that in most countries in Europe.

That halcyon period may have been only a brief respite from an ongoing energy problem. As rising prices and continuing dependence on foreign oil made the economy and society seem vulnerable to forces over which the United States has no control, yet another energy crisis emerged in 2005 and 2006, and again citizens and government appeared willing to return to active consideration of alternative energy futures for the country.[40] In 2006, there were a variety of proposals for different energy paths for the United States. Some Republicans advocated opening up for oil production in a number of areas that had been closed, the Arctic National Wildlife Refuge and the Florida coast in particular.[41] President Bush advocated alternative energy sources, such as fuel cells and then nuclear power.[42] As short-term responses, he also advocated reducing some tax breaks for energy companies and a halt to adding to the Strategic Petroleum Reserve, perhaps even releasing some of that reserve.[43]

The price of gasoline and other energy has become a major issue and a source of popular discontent with government. One option for encouraging energy conservation has been to increase prices through higher energy taxes, with the revenues used to develop alternative energy. Americans tend to favor conservation in the abstract but to resist higher taxes in almost all circumstances. Still, if the taxes are linked to reducing dependence on foreign oil, one poll found, a majority would accept them.[44] Citizens also tend to support a range of energy conservation measures in the abstract but often do not support them in actual implementation.[45]

The Obama administration took stances on energy and environmental issues early in its tenure and pushed through a massive energy bill in the summer of 2009. At the center of this legislation was a *cap-and-trade* system, which allocated a limited amount of permits to industries for the use of fossil fuels and the emission of carbon dioxide.[46] These permits can be traded, so that more energy-efficient industries are able to obtain more permits. This central part of the plan is supplemented by a range of other programs to increase efficiency in automobiles, homes, and industry, as well as to develop alternative energy sources, such as wind, solar, and geothermal power. The plan has been hailed as a major step by many, but there are also numerous criticisms. First, the plan provides special treatment to a number of industries, lessening its total impact.[47] Furthermore, business has argued that the bill will cost jobs, although many analysts see it creating jobs in alternative energy. Finally, the measure will make energy more expensive for all consumers, with the Congressional Budget Office estimating that it will add $175 to the bills of the average family. Even if imperfect, however, the plan represented the first major response to the problem of climate change.

Although widely applauded by environmentalists, this approach to energy and environmental policy proved to be impossible, especially after the midterm elections in 2010. Somewhat paradoxically, although this method for coping with fossil fuel pollution is based on a market model, it has become anathema to the Republican right and has largely dropped from view. It has been replaced by more piecemeal responses to energy and climate issues, including the solar program mentioned above and attempts at increasing dramatically the energy efficiency of automobiles.[48]

The States and Energy Policy

The preceding discussion has been about the role of the federal government in energy policy, but a good deal of the regulation of energy distribution is done at the state level. The traditional model for this regulation has been to create virtual monopolies in electricity and gas and then regulate rates to allow the privately owned utilities a set return on capital investment (profit), while attempting to offer energy to consumers as inexpensively as possible.[49] In some cities, the local government purchases energy in bulk and distributes it at cost to citizens, resulting in even lower consumer costs.

The spread of neoliberal ideas has led to the deregulation of energy supplies in many states. On the assumption that competition in the market could produce even better outcomes for consumers and also remove the "heavy hand" of government regulation, about half the states had undertaken some form of deregulation as of 2001. In some cases, the policy has been very successful—energy costs in Pennsylvania dropped by over one-third.[50] But deregulation was at least partially responsible for a major energy crisis that hit the state of California in 2000 and 2001.[51] It seems unlikely that energy will ever be as tightly controlled as it once was, but there appears to be a need to monitor the markets if not exert some control over energy distribution.

The states also play a role in regulating and taxing energy that is extracted from their lands. Unlike industrial policies that involve states chasing mobile industries, the coal, oil, and gas (and even large quantities of sunshine) are not movable. Therefore, the states can charge significant severance taxes on these industries and also attempt to mitigate some of the social and environmental costs of extraction. That said, different states have responded differently, with Pennsylvania, for example, charging about 10 percent of what its neighbor Ohio charges for taxes on shale gas.

Environmental Policies

Just as Harriet Beecher Stowe's *Uncle Tom's Cabin* is supposed to have helped initiate the Civil War and as Michael Harrington's *The Other America* is believed to have helped initiate the War on Poverty, it is sometimes said that Rachel Carson's *The Silent Spring* (1964) helped to launch the environmental movement in the United States. Carson's description of the horrors of a spring without the usual sounds of life associated with that time of year made citizens and policymakers understand the possible effects of pollutants—especially insecticides—being poured into the air and water of the United States.

Even after several decades of increased environmental awareness, tons of pollutants are still being dumped into the air and water or stored in rusting barrels with the potential to poison the land for years. It is difficult to determine the amount of disease and the number of deaths that result from such pollution or to estimate the amount of property damage it causes, but the damage produced in each of these categories is clearly substantial. The economic damage may be minimal compared to the human and aesthetic damage that is produced by uncontrolled pollution. Against the images of natural beauty in the country can be set scenes of wastelands made by unthinking human activities.

The United States obviously has a pollution problem, one that is not confined to its own air and water but is global. Scientific research published during the 1980s identified a gradual warming trend in Earth's atmosphere—the "greenhouse effect"—that could alter climates and even produce massive coastal flooding if the polar ice caps melt. The warming appears to be largely the product of putting carbon dioxide into the atmosphere by burning fossil fuels.[52] Other scientists have pointed to the destruction of ozone in Earth's atmosphere, which permits more ultraviolet radiation to reach the surface and thus increases the risk of skin cancers. Much of this atmospheric change is a result of the release of chlorinated fluorocarbons (CFCs) into the atmosphere from aerosol cans, refrigeration units, and numerous industrial applications. Still other scientists have warned of the destruction of the tropical rain forests that supply not only much of the world's oxygen but also a large number of as-yet-undiscovered useful plants.[53] Even outside the tropics, a gradual erosion of biodiversity has been observed in the United States and in the rest of the world. The United States both exports acid rain to Canada and imports some water and air pollution from Mexico, Canada, and also now from China.[54] It no longer appears sufficient to address environmental problems within the context of a single country; concerted international action and policies are needed.

In the United States, environmental problems have been addressed through a variety of statutes now enforced largely by the Environmental Protection Agency.[55] Few people now question the desirability of a clean environment, but some would like to see that value balanced more carefully with other important values, such as economic growth, jobs, and controlling inflation. The slowdowns of the American economy during the late 1980s and early 1990s, and again in recent years, have led many citizens to question whether the nation can afford stringent controls on pollution, especially when many U.S. jobs are perceived to be going to countries that place less stringent environmental controls on manufacturers. It is also argued that environmental controls could contribute to inflation by making some commodities, such as automobiles, more expensive than they would otherwise be. Great progress has been made in environmental policy, but the challenges have changed to some extent, and the connections between energy policy and economic policy are now even clearer.

The Politics of Pollution

It would be difficult to find a group that actively favors environmental degradation. Instead, the politics of pollution is generally phrased in terms of what are acceptable trade-offs between environmental values and other values. There is sufficient public concern about the environment that it would be almost impossible to make wholesale retreats from existing environmental programs. For example, by 1997, over two-thirds of Americans considered themselves environmentalists.[56] In a March 2006 Gallup Poll, almost 80 percent of respondents favored stronger enforcement of environmental regulations, and two-thirds believed that government was not doing enough to protect the environment. At the same time, individuals who want to preserve their own jobs and firms that want to preserve their industries are willing to sacrifice at least part of the environment for those ends, although most respondents in polls tend to favor environmental protection over economic growth. By 2012, however, Americans were more concerned with economic growth than with protecting the environment, an obvious response to the economic crisis.[57]

There are numerous examples of the conflict between environmental and economic interests. For example, in the late 1980s, loggers and environmentalists in the Pacific Northwest fought over the preservation of the habitat of the spotted owl and then continued to dispute over more general concerns about the forests. Environmentalists wanted to save old-growth forests to protect that endangered species, while loggers saw primarily the loss of their livelihoods if the owl were to be saved.[58] Both sides had powerful reasons to support their positions, and the resolution of this and similar controversies will affect the long-term trade-off between the values of the environment and the economy.[59] The more recent and continuing conflict over the preservation of caribou herds that might be threatened by drilling in the Arctic areas of Alaska will certainly not be the last battle of this type, no more than has been the conflict in 2011 and 2012 over building an oil pipeline from Canada to the U.S. gulf.[60]

When the U.S. economy slowed during the 1980s, some of the blame for the slowdown was placed on the more stringent environmental controls in the United States than in other countries. Some argued that the country had to protect American jobs by loosening environmental laws and imposing protections such as tariffs. Similarly, a portion of the inflation problem of that era was blamed on regulations of all kinds, including environmental regulations; the cost of the average American automobile increased by several hundred dollars because of environmental controls.[61] The same environmental controls made the automobile somewhat less energy efficient, so in this case, energy conservation and environmental concerns constituted another trade-off. A similar energy-versus-environment conflict can be seen in coal mining; the cheapest means of mining coal, strip-mining, is extremely destructive of the environment. Even if all Americans are to some degree in favor of a clean environment, it is difficult to agree on how such trade-offs among values should be made in individual cases.

The stakeholders in the environmental arena are obvious. Industry is a major actor, for many environmental regulations restrict the activities of businesses. Local governments are also the objects of environmental controls, for much water pollution is produced by poorly treated sewage coming from local government sources. Federal and state governments have imposed expensive mandates on local governments requiring them to clean up their water supplies. More recently, mandates have been imposed to control runoff from storm drains or, in the language of environmental policy, *nonpoint sources,* such as the runoff from farms that has become an increasing problem.[62] Again, most of the interests affected by pollution legislation have not opposed the legislation so much on ideological grounds as on technical grounds, arguing that many of the regulations are technologically infeasible or are so expensive that enforcing them would make the cost of doing business prohibitive.[63] Local governments have argued that they do not have the money to comply with all the rules being imposed on them, and the unfunded mandates in environmental policy are among the most costly for local governments.

On the other side of the debate are environmental interest groups, such as the Sierra Club, the National Wildlife Federation, and the Friends of the Earth. A few of these organizations—most notably the Sierra Club—have been in existence for years, but the majority are products of the environmental mobilization of the late 1960s and 1970s. By the early part of the twenty-first century, national environmental groups claimed approximately 9.5 million members, and more were members of local organizations.[64] Yet there are disagreements among the groups about both policies and tactics. Some environmental groups have been highly confrontational, employing tactics such as placing large spikes in trees to make them dangerous to cut with power saws and harassing hunters and the wearers of fur coats. Environmentalists no longer all fit the image of the mild-mannered birdwatcher; some are militant advocates of their political and moral positions.

Government itself is an active participant in environmental politics. The major actor in government is the Environmental Protection Agency (EPA), organized in 1970 to take the lead in federal environmental regulation. Given its mission and the time at which it was formed, many employees of the EPA were, and are, committed environmentalists. This commitment put them in conflict with political appointees of the Reagan administration, who did not share those values. With the commitment to environmental politics by Vice President Al Gore,[65] among others, the Clinton administration was somewhat more active in environmental protection in the 1990s, although by no means as active as environmentalists would have liked.[66] In 2000, former governor of New Jersey (the most polluted state in the United States by many counts) Christine Todd Whitman, was appointed administrator of the EPA by President George W. Bush, and she proved more active in pressing the usual agenda of her agency than many critics had predicted. She resigned in 2003, allegedly under pressure from those in the administration opposed to an active environmental policy. The EPA thereafter during the Bush administration was not as active in promoting environmental values as it had been, although more so than many critics might have anticipated.[67]

The EPA is not the only federal agency with environmental concerns; one enumeration found almost thirty federal organizations with some environmental regulatory responsibilities. Some such as the Department of the Interior, which manages federal lands, have a substantial impact on federal policies but may have their own ideologies that are not purely environmental. The Fish and Wildlife Service, in the Department of the Interior, also administers the Endangered Species Act, putting it at the center of many conflicts over environmental policy. The Forest Service, in the Department of Agriculture, manages national forests and tends to consider forests as crops rather than as natural assets. It seeks to make a profit by harvesting them. This preference accorded well with the George W. Bush administration's emphasis on the use of federal lands managed by the Department of the Interior and the Forest Service for economic rather than environmental purposes.[68] The Department of Defense has many environmental responsibilities, including the requirement that it clean up large-scale pollution on military bases.[69] This widespread administrative involvement in the environment has meant some lack of coordination. Attempts to coordinate and to produce greater uniformity in regulation have enjoyed little success because of the diverse interests in this policy community.[70]

Although most attention in environmental policy is focused on the federal government, the states are also important; the major laws in the field depend in part on the states for implementation.[71] Some states, notably California, have been well ahead of the federal government in passing strict environmental laws.[72] Although the states have responsibility for protecting the environment, they often have counterincentives to be relatively permissive in their enforcement to attract industry.[73] During the Clinton administration, there was often conflict between state and local governments and the EPA, even though both the president and his leading EPA administrators had experience as state officials.[74] The states became increasingly aggressive in using the courts to oppose the interventions of the EPA. In a reversal, during the Bush administration, the states often acted to try to prevent the weakening of environmental controls.[75]

Making environmental policy is in part a technical exercise. There are a huge number of complex technical questions about the nature of environmental problems and the feasibility of solutions offered for them. Making environmental policy is also an ideological exercise on the part of many participants, especially environmental groups. The technical dimensions can be used to mask the economic interests and ideologies involved in this debate, but making environmental policy fundamentally means finding trade-offs among environmental values, technical feasibility, and economic growth that can satisfy multiple constituencies.

Because of that complexity, there has been increased interest in *risk-based decision making*. The logic of this approach is that rather than focusing on absolute prohibitions against all hazards, government policymakers should focus on the most dangerous pollutants and seek to reduce those to levels that are deemed "safe."[76] Such an approach calls for balancing the costs and benefits in the production of potentially dangerous substances. Of course, it offends committed defenders of the environment, who would prefer to retain the traditional "command and control" regulatory regimens.[77] The Environmental Protection Agency has attempted to tailor its regulatory interventions to the characteristics of particular industries and to be cooperative in its approach to regulation.[78] For example, the Performance Track program was intended to recognize and reward the cleanest companies with the best environmental records, but it may be enabling those companies to escape controls.[79]

As in so many other areas of federal policy, the courts are also important decision makers. Their role has been manifested on some substantive issues, such as implementation of the Endangered Species Act, but they have been particularly important in defining the procedural rules under which the EPA must function. In particular, the Supreme Court has tended to minimize some of the procedural requirements in environmental laws, including environmental impact statements, and to permit somewhat more rapid decisions on implementing other types of environmental policy actions. The courts also have been important in defining the standing to sue of environmental groups, and the Rehnquist Court tended to diminish the capacity of those groups to bring suits in federal courts.[80]

Environmental Legislation

Except for some older regulatory initiatives, such as the Refuse Act of 1899, the principal environmental protection laws were passed during the 1960s and 1970s. Most contained provisions for their expiration after a certain number of years. The reauthorizations of these acts, each with some variations on the original, brought major political and ideological battles in the mid-1990s.[81] Those battles revealed that even among those committed to environmental protection there is some interest in alternatives to direct regulation as the means of reducing pollution.[82] The need to build policy regimens that produce greater compliance, less impact on economic performance, and smaller administrative costs is recognized by many people in the field. We now discuss each area of legislation and the enforcement of environmental policy, as well as the alternatives proposed to the existing system of regulation.

Water pollution. Federal interest in water pollution goes back to the Refuse Act of 1899, which was intended to prevent the dumping of refuse in navigable waters and was enforced by the Army Corps of Engineers. That legislation provided the principal federal means of attacking water pollution until more stringent laws were passed in the 1970s. Another relatively early federal law was the Water Pollution Control Act of 1956, which allowed interested parties around a polluted body of water to call a conference and make recommendations to state enforcement officials. If the states did not act within six months, then the federal government (through the Department of the Interior) could intervene and seek an injunction to stop the polluting, although only one injunction was issued during the fifteen years the 1956 law was in effect.

The federal government took a major step forward in 1965 with the Water Quality Act, which required each state to submit measurable standards for water quality to the Department of Health, Education, and Welfare (HEW; after 1970, to the Environmental Protection Agency) for approval. These standards were to be translated into specific effluent standards, meaning, for example, that an industry would release only so many tons of pollutants per month. It was anticipated that the states would enforce the standards. Because states were competing with one another to attract industries, however, those that adopted more stringent water quality standards were at a disadvantage. Thus, standards tended to converge on the lowest common denominator, and states rarely if ever enforced them. The federal government, in turn, did little to encourage more vigorous enforcement by the states and nothing at the federal level to enforce them. It became clear that the states had little incentive to enforce pollution standards to clean up their own water and that more effective national standards would be required.

Those national standards were developed through the 1972 Clean Water Act (CWA). Technically amendments to the Water Pollution Control Act, this legislation established national deadlines for all streams to be fishable and swimmable, but those dates had to be abandoned after a flood of lawsuits and an enumeration of the costs persuaded government that they were too optimistic. Still, the legislation required that all private concerns were to adopt the "best practicable technology" by 1977 and the "best available technology" by 1983. Standards for public sewage treatment were less demanding, with all wastes to receive some treatment by 1977 and with the "best practicable technology" standard applied by 1983.[83] As the regulatory regime for water quality has developed, risk assessment became an important tool for analysis. The CWA also established a nationwide discharge permit system, enabling the EPA to specify the amount of effluents that could be released and to monitor compliance with the technology requirements. Although the measure established nationwide standards, a good deal of the implementation was done at the state level. The states now could not use low water quality standards to compete for industry, but their enforcement of the standards continued to vary substantially.

President Reagan vetoed the reauthorization of the Clean Water Act in 1986, arguing that compliance was too expensive for industry and local governments, but Congress overrode the veto, with the perhaps unexpected support of many industrial organizations. Industry appeared to accept the existing standards as a reasonable compromise between what it might want and what more militant environmentalists might want.[84] As part of a general pattern of devolution of authority in the federal system, the Reagan administration also placed greater reliance on the states.[85] Amendments and rewriting during the Clinton administration strengthened some aspects of the law but also weakened some important regulations, including those on control of chlorine and the various compounds formed from chlorine in water.[86] In 1986, the Safe Drinking Water Act was amended to add eighty-six contaminants to the list of substances prohibited from public drinking water. That act was originally passed in 1974, but implementation had been slow because of lawsuits and because of its reliance on state and local governments.

Although water pollution issues have been somewhat less visible than air pollution issues, including global warming, in recent years there have been some important shifts in this policy area. One has been the increased emphasis on nonpoint sources of water pollution, especially from agriculture. These sources are more difficult to monitor than individual plants that may pollute, but they add significantly to overall levels of pollution. A second important change in water pollution control has been that at least some of the states are becoming more active enforcers of federal law as well as their own laws. State governments are discovering that weak environmental regulation may not be good business or good politics.[87]

Air pollution.   Air pollution did not become a matter of federal concern as early as water pollution, perhaps because of the lack of a clear constitutional peg on which to hang enforcement. (Federal control over navigable streams provided such a legal peg for water pollution legislation.) The first federal legislation against air pollution was the Clean Air Act of 1963. It was similar to the 1956 Water Pollution Act in that it relied on conferences, voluntary compliance, and possible HEW enforcement. Only once during the seven years the act was in effect did HEW attempt to force a firm to cease polluting. The act was amended in 1965 to authorize the secretary of HEW to set standards for automobile emissions, using measurable standards as with the Clean Water Act of 1972.

The Clean Air Act was significantly amended in 1970, directing the EPA to establish ambient ("surrounding") air quality standards. There were to be two sets of standards, primary and secondary. Primary standards, those necessary to protect public health, were to be attained by 1975, and secondary standards, those necessary to protect vegetation, paint, buildings, and so forth, were to be attained within "a reasonable time." The EPA also received authority to establish emissions standards for certain new manufacturing plants, such as cement and sulfuric acid factories, and electrical generating stations fired by *point sources* (fossil fuels), which had greater-than-average potential for significant air pollution. The 1977 amendments to the Clean Air Act required development of state plans for controlling new point sources of pollution, as well as higher standards of protection for certain types of areas in a state such as parks.

The Clean Air Act amendments also addressed emissions from automobiles, which still constitute the principal air pollution problem in most American cities. The 1970 standards superseded the weak standards of the 1965 Motor Vehicle Air Pollution Control Act, mandating a 90 percent reduction in hydrocarbons and carbon monoxide emissions by 1975, with similar reductions in oxides of nitrogen to be achieved by 1976. Although the amendments set tough standards, a variety of factors slowed their implementation. Primarily, the technology for achieving the reductions was difficult and expensive to develop, and some of it such as the catalytic converter had side effects that are perhaps as dangerous as the emissions they were designed to eliminate. Many pollution controls reduced gasoline mileage, and increasing energy shortages placed a great deal of unwelcome pressure on automobile manufacturers to create more fuel-efficient and cleaner-running automobiles; after some delay, those standards were largely met. The success of this first round of "technology forcing" standards, however, produced demands for even greater reductions in automobile emissions, which then ran up against countervailing resistance from industry that stalled further changes in air pollution legislation from 1977 to 1990. (Interestingly, the George W. Bush administration in 2002 began advocating technology-forcing legislation to require that more automobiles be powered by electricity rather than gasoline, despite higher cost than more conventional alternatives.)[88] Despite the stagnant legislative scene, the quality of air in the United States continued to improve, in large part because of the old legislation.

The legislative impasse over air pollution legislation was broken in 1990 with a major set of amendments to the Clean Air Act, which not only dealt with some of the traditional concerns over air quality within the United States but also began to address larger, global issues, such as the greenhouse effect and acid rain. The amendments included the following provisions:

1. A ban on use of CFCs in aerosol sprays and regulation of their use as refrigerants, to protect the atmosphere's ozone layer
2. Plans to reduce acid rain by halving emissions of sulfur dioxide and nitrogen oxides and considerably strengthening environmental requirements for fossil fuel power plants
3. New emission regulations for cars and requirements that oil companies create cleaner-burning fuels[89]
4. Authority for the EPA to restrict emissions of over two hundred "toxic air pollutants" from a variety of sources, ranging from coke and steel mills to dry cleaners, and to demand installation of new technologies to limit or eliminate emissions

The 1990 amendments to the Clean Air Act depended largely on traditional command and control regulation. They were not well received in the George H. W. Bush administration that, despite being led by the "environmental president," sought to maximize use of market mechanisms to solve social and economic problems.[90] The Environmental Protection Agency, however, received something of a new lease on life from this measure and the 1990 Pollution Control Act, which gave it more power to clean up America's air.

In line with the general movement of environmental controls away from strict regulatory regimes, there was increasing emphasis on negotiation and accommodation in air pollution policy. For example, in late 1994, the EPA negotiated an agreement with ten northeastern states to reduce air pollution from factories (especially electrical power plants).[91] This followed a similar agreement among twelve states to significantly reduce air pollution from automobiles. The outcomes of these negotiations were not all that either industry or environmentalists wanted, but the bargaining produced agreements that all affected interests, including the states that would implement the agreements, could live with. Citizens complain because provisions such as the use of reformulated gasoline during summer months impose additional costs on them, but there has been a substantial social benefit from reduced pollution.

While President George W. Bush initially chose to maintain some of the strict air quality standards adopted during the Clinton years, the later part of his administration saw some erosion, or at least change, of those standards through regulation rather than legislation. For example, the so-called Clear Skies Initiative was an attempt to use a variety of market-based mechanisms to control air pollution. Its content and effects have been debated extensively, but the net effect is as yet not clear.[92] Some of the restrictions on new plants and other sources of pollution also were relaxed.[93] Shortly before leaving office, Bush attempted to push through rules that gave greater leeway to industrial polluters and eased regulation of greenhouse gas emissions from oil refineries, but President Barack Obama blocked these measures in the days after his inauguration in 2009.

Although the federal government has been making few innovations in air pollution legislation, there have been attempts to enhance enforcement. One of the more important has been the increasing role of individuals and the states in forcing the EPA to enforce the legislation more stringently. For example, in 2011, eleven states sued the EPA over failure to enforce standards on soot, thought to be a major contributor to the increasing levels of asthma among children.[94]

Environmental impact statements.   In addition to the legislation addressing specific kinds of pollution, the National Environmental Policy Act (NEPA) of 1970 established guidelines for environmental controls for projects involving the federal government. The principal component of this legislation was the *environmental impact statement*, which was required for any federally funded project that might affect environmental quality. Before a project can be approved, an environmental impact statement must be filed, detailing the environmental impact of the project, its potential negative consequences, and possible alternatives. The statement must be prepared well in advance of the proposed starting date of the project to allow citizen participation and review; the statements are then filed with the Council on Environmental Quality in the Executive Office of the President. During the George W. Bush administration, there were several proposals to weaken or eliminate requirements for environmental assessment of programs, especially in defense and energy, as a result of pressures from those industries.

NEPA rules also allow citizens to challenge a project on environmental grounds, and over four hundred court challenges were filed during the first five years after the act went into effect. The law requires that environmental considerations be taken into account when a project is planned, but it does not indicate the weight that is to be attached to them compared with other costs and benefits of the project. This ambiguity has been the source of many court cases and many difficult decisions for judges. In the case of the Alaska pipeline, special legislation was required to allow the project to continue in the face of determined opposition and court challenges by conservation groups. That case illustrated the conflict between energy needs and environmental protection, and similar conflicts emerged over proposals to open the Arctic National Wildlife Refuge to oil exploration.

Toxic waste.   Toxic wastes are a by-product of a society that has become dependent on synthetic products for its way of life. The usual EPA estimate of the volume of hazardous waste in the United States is around 250 million tons created each year.[95] Only about 10 percent is disposed of safely.[96] In addition to the hazard itself, the problem with hazardous wastes is that they tend to be persistent chemicals that have to be kept away from people and their water and food supplies for years or even centuries. Such storage is expensive, and before there was a full understanding of the dangers, or proper regulation, industries disposed of these wastes in a very haphazard manner, endangering many citizens.

The issue of hazardous wastes first came to widespread attention in 1977 when the Love Canal dump near Buffalo, New York, spilled wastes into a nearby residential neighborhood. Eventually several hundred residents had to be moved out of their homes, and most never returned. Hazardous wastes again made headlines in 1982 when it was found that the town of Times Beach, Missouri, had been contaminated with the extremely toxic chemical dioxin. It also had to be evacuated. Although these have been the most obvious manifestations of the toxic waste problem, there are approximately 30,000 toxic waste dumps across the United States, and several thousand of them pose serious threats to health. It has been estimated that over $50 billion would be required to clean up existing waste dumps and dispose of all the chemicals stored in them in an environmentally safe manner.

Congress passed two major pieces of legislation to address the problem of toxic wastes. The first was the Resource Conservation and Recovery Act (RCRA) of 1976, which required the EPA to determine what chemicals were hazardous and the appropriate means of disposing of them and to establish a system of permits to ensure that hazardous chemicals were indeed disposed of properly. Because of the technical complexity of the task and the low priority attached to the exercise during the Carter administration, the necessary regulations were not promulgated until 1980.[97] When the Reagan administration came into office in 1981, it attempted to attack the perceived "regulatory excess" of the RCRA by dismantling some of its reporting and permit regulations and cutting funding for the act.[98] These moves met strong opposition from environmental groups and some members of Congress, however, and they failed to achieve the degree of deregulation desired. Under the George H. W. Bush administration, the Quayle Commission, established to review and eliminate regulations, again tended toward weakening the provisions of the RCRA.

The second major effort to deal with toxic wastes is the Comprehensive Environmental Response, Compensation, and Liability Act (CERCLA), or "Superfund" program, which applies funds from a tax on oil and chemical companies to cleaning up hazardous waste sites. As first proposed by the Carter administration, the program would have required industry to clean up its own sites and provided funds to clean up particularly hazardous ones. As finally adopted just before the Reagan administration came into office, the measure imposed substantially weaker penalties for industry violations of the act than had been proposed, but it provided a means of addressing some of the worst hazardous waste sites in the United States.

The Reagan administration quickly moved away from the regulatory strategy and rapid timetable of the Carter administration and toward "negotiated settlements" between industries and the Office of Waste Programs Enforcement in the EPA. There was a great deal of emphasis during this time on having industries clean up their own sites and on avoiding conflict with industries. But as members of Congress grew increasingly impatient with what they regarded as a slowing of the planned cleanup schedule and changes in the law's intent, they investigated the Superfund for mismanagement and removed its head from office. They also passed the Superfund amendments of 1986 (SARA), requiring the manufacturers of toxic chemicals to monitor the types and release of those chemicals.[99]

Under Reagan's second EPA head, William Ruckelshaus, the EPA soon began to pursue cleaning up dumps more actively, but only about a third of the 1,600 hazardous sites on the National Priority List had been cleaned up by 1998.[100] The slowness was in part a function of cost. In the late 1980s, it cost on average over $21 million to clean up one site, and by the early 1990s, that figure had increased to over $30 million.[101] Against that level of need, Congress had appropriated in the vicinity of $9 billion over five years. Despite the magnitude of the problem, the George W. Bush administration made some efforts to cut money for the Superfund.[102] The level of resources available also has been reduced because many firms responsible for the pollution have declared bankruptcy and are no longer providing support. More than 1,200 sites still need cleanup.[103]

Both the RCRA and the Superfund are potentially important for addressing the problem of a massive amount of toxic waste threatening the environment. Their implementation was slowed by difficulties in writing the necessary regulations and by partisan and ideological opposition. Somewhat paradoxically, the "strict liability" provisions of the legislation, which make the producers of toxic wastes responsible for them over their entire lifetime, have also deterred enforcement. It is often cheaper for producers to take the risk of criminal prosecution and dispose of wastes illegally than to identify the wastes to the EPA and then bear the costs of their safe disposal.[104]

There is need for a large-scale effort to identify existing waste sites and clean them, as well as to devise regulatory mechanisms for the safe disposal of such wastes in the future. The government has a number of policy tools at its disposal for addressing these tasks, including prosecution, accommodation, and negotiation, as well as direct federal action to remove the toxic materials.[105] All of these approaches have both advantages and disadvantages. The problem is confounded by the large volume of toxic wastes that the federal government itself generates, especially the Department of Defense (whose own Army Corps of Engineers can determine whether a cleanup is required).[106] Emissions of toxic wastes have been slowed, but they will remain a serious environmental problem for the United States for decades.

The Superfund has benefited from the 2009 Economic Recovery Act. It received $500 million in additional support to address 51 sites across the country. The logic of this additional support was that these activities created significant levels of local employment as well as addressed health and economic development issues in the communities. The sites were selected for their readiness for immediate intervention and for their ability to be returned to productive use rapidly.[107]

Endangered Species Act.   One of the more controversial environmental laws is the Endangered Species Act, originally passed in 1973. This act, which depends more on the Department of the Interior than the EPA for enforcement, enables the U.S. Fish and Wildlife Service (FWS) to designate species as endangered or threatened (as over three hundred have been since the act was passed) and protect their crucial habitats. In a number of famous (and infamous) instances, a seemingly insignificant species (such as the snail darter) has blocked a major public or private project. As noted, the most famous case was that of the spotted owl in the Pacific Northwest and its impact on the logging industry.[108] As of 2009, there were over 1,200 endangered and threatened species on the FWS list, up from 422 two decades ago. The issue of protecting wilderness areas has also been associated with endangered species, and early in his administration, President Obama locked up millions of wilderness acres in nine states from further development.

The Endangered Species Act has produced some significant results, including bringing back the bald eagle population from its formerly depleted state, but it remains controversial in spite of those accomplishments.[109] The legal and philosophical concept of "takings" has been applied particularly against enforcement of this law, meaning that such acts deprive landowners of the use of their property without just compensation.[110] There is little doubt that there has been procedural due process, given that the takings result from an act of Congress, but there is some question whether the substance of the acts is indeed legitimate. The courts have begun to examine environmental legislation from this perspective and sometimes have found in favor of landowners.[111] Conservative political groups have brought dozens of cases challenging the inclusion of species on the endangered list in attempts to allow development of land, especially in the West.[112]

The endangered species law is one of many instances in which government must balance a range of interests and a range of principles. In a society founded on ideals of free enterprise, property rights are important, but they must be weighed against other desirable policy goals such as preservation of the environment. Economic development goals are likewise being weighed against environmental goals. Politicians and citizens groups make highly varying judgments about the relative merits of these goals, and the political process must find ways to accommodate this range of perspectives on good policy. The Bush administration had attempted to make removing species from the list easier, but this has been reversed under the Obama administration.[113]

Global warming and greenhouse gases. The United States has not legislated in any significant way to attempt to control the emission of greenhouse gases or to limit global warming. Clean air legislation controlled emissions of CFCs that attack the ozone layer, but there have been only limited attempts to control emissions of carbon dioxide or methane. Most other industrialized countries have signed the Kyoto Protocol, pledging to reduce significantly the emission of carbon dioxide and other greenhouse gases, but George W. Bush refused to sign the international treaty in 2005, citing economic concerns. The evidence is that emission of these gases has been reduced hardly at all in the United States.

The Obama administration is taking the problem of global warming much more seriously and has agreed to participate more actively in international negotiations on climate control than previous administrations. As already noted, energy legislation in 2009 was built around the need to control the emission of greenhouse gases and to shift the United States toward alternative energy sources. At least at the outset of the Obama administration, this appeared to be the major approach to improving the environment. The move is perhaps especially important politically; some perceived threats to jobs as a result of the legislation, whereas President Obama advocated it at a time of high unemployment in the United States.

Implementation of Environmental Controls

The Environmental Protection Agency is the principal body enforcing the environmental protection laws. In implementing a variety of air, water, and toxic waste programs, the EPA has broad responsibilities and a wide field of action that have inevitably brought it into conflict with other federal and state agencies. When the EPA sought to flex its environmental muscles, it ran into conflicts with agencies that wanted to build dams, roadways, or waterways, or with private industries that believed that the standards the EPA imposed on them were too stringent and impeded their ability to compete, especially on the world market. The EPA received an unenviable task, but because it was made up mostly of people committed to the environmental movement, it set out to accomplish that task with some zeal. The difficulties it encountered were intensified because many of the projects it sought to stop were pet projects of some representative or senator, and the agency's reputation on Capitol Hill was not the best.

The EPA was also given a difficult administrative task. Congress was relatively specific about the dates by which certain levels of pollution reduction were to be achieved, giving the agency little latitude and little opportunity to bargain with polluting industries. In attempting to specify so precisely the conditions for alleviating pollution, Congress often wrote into legislation contradictory paragraphs that created more implementation difficulties for the EPA. Finally, the strategy adopted for a good deal of the program—technology-forcing regulations—created substantial difficulties for implementers and for industries seeking to comply.[114] When standards were adopted to reduce air pollution by 1975 to 10 percent of what it was in 1970, the technology to produce that improvement in air quality simply did not exist. It was believed that passage of the legislation would spur development of the technology, but the actual result was a delay in implementation rather than any technological breakthroughs. Certainly, a number of improvements have been made, especially in the internal combustion engine, as a result of environmental protection legislation, but the major innovations anticipated have not materialized.

One major implementation problem associated with environmental policies has been standard setting. We noted that such phrases as "primary and secondary standards of air quality" and "best available technology" were not clearly defined in the law. Even if they had been defined, it would still have been necessary to convert the standards into permissible levels of emissions from individual sources of pollution (e.g., for each factory and municipal waste treatment facility). Overall goals for pollution reduction are relatively easy to establish, but great difficulty is encountered in translating those goals into workable and enforceable criteria. And the criteria developed must be applicable to polluters, not just to pollution, if significant improvements in environmental quality are to be achieved. At times, the difficulty of setting standards has forced the EPA to adopt a "best practice" doctrine: If a plant is doing things in the same way as every other plant, then it must be doing things right. Also, the standard setters have been under pressure to accept more risk and to be less strict about environmental controls so as to promote economic growth and competitiveness.[115]

The enforcement of established criteria has presented several interesting questions. First, should a mechanism exist for making trade-offs between environmental protection and economic growth? For example, the Sierra Club succeeded in obtaining a court ruling that the air pollution laws did not allow any degradation of existing air quality, an interpretation that had been resisted by the EPA. This ruling meant that people living in an area with very clean air— probably an area with little or no industry—might be forbidden to bring in any industry. A related question is how to allocate any proposed reductions in effluents among industries or other polluters. For example, should there be across-the-board percentage reductions, requiring each polluter to reduce pollution by, say, 20 percent, or should attention be paid both to the level of emissions and the technological feasibility of reducing pollution at each source? For some industries, even minor reductions in effluents might be very difficult to attain, whereas others might be able virtually to eliminate their effluents with only a limited investment. How should these considerations be taken into account?

Second, although environmental protection legislation is replete with legal weapons to force compliance by polluters, including authority to close down an offending industry, in reality, enforcement has been much less draconian. Politically, the EPA cannot afford to close an industry that is a major source of employment, either nationally or in a single community. Thus, the agency's hands frequently are tied, and the level of compliance desired or mandated has not been achieved. This element of political vulnerability may be functional in some ways, given the evidence that cooperation is more effective than adversarial relationships in generating compliance.[116]

Although the Environmental Protection Agency has a number of legal and administrative mechanisms for improving air and water quality, its efforts are frequently hampered by the complex systems for standard setting and implementation. State governments, for example, are essential in devising plans for reducing pollution, and local communities have to become involved in building new waste treatment facilities. The EPA itself is not responsible for distributing federal matching funds for treatment facilities, so instead of being distributed based on the severity of the pollution problem, the funds are allocated on a first-come, first-served basis. Consequently, instead of developing definitive standards and practices, the enforcement of environmental legislation is frequently only a by-product of compromise, negotiation, and bargaining.[117] This characteristic does not, of course, distinguish environmental policy from most other policy, but it does run counter to some of the rhetoric about the EPA "running roughshod" over the interests of industries and local communities.

Alternatives to Regulation

As we have been demonstrating, the principal means of addressing environmental problems has been through direct regulation—mandating certain actions or the attainment of certain standards—enforced through legal penalties or possible closings. It has been argued that a more efficient means of producing improvements in the environment would be to impose effluent charges or taxes.[118] That is, instead of telling an industry that it may emit only a certain number of tons of effluents each year, government would allow it to emit as much as it desired. The polluter would, however, have to pay a tax based on the amount of pollution discharged; therefore, the greater the quantity, the higher would be the cost.

The presumed advantage of effluent charges is that they would allow more efficient industries to pollute, while less efficient industries would either have to close down or improve their environmental standards. The more efficient industries could afford to pay the effluent tax and still make a profit, whereas less efficient industries could not. This market-oriented solution to the pollution problem would be compatible with economic growth and efficiency.[119] It is argued that it would be an improvement over direct regulation as a means of forcing the trade-off between those competing values, and it would give most industries a real incentive to improve their environmental performance as well as their economic efficiency. Some of these ideas for market reform were implemented during the Clinton administration as components of the Reinventing EPA program and, adopting the Common Sense Initiative, were very successful, whereas others demonstrated the difficulties of making markets perform as wished by politicians.[120] This pattern continued into the George W. Bush administration, with increasing use of market-based mechanisms.

Another component of the market-oriented approach to environmental regulation is to issue tradable permits to pollute. The 1990 amendments to the Clean Air Act permit utility firms to trade rights to pollute, particularly emissions of sulfur dioxide and later chlorinated fluorocarbons. The initial allocation of these allowances was related roughly to the amount of pollution the firms emitted in 1987. The amendments required the firms to begin to reduce their total emissions by 1995, with each firm given the choice either to invest in pollution control devices or to buy pollution rights from others that are reducing their emissions.[121] Again, advocates assume that this mechanism will produce efficient allocation of resources as well as reduced pollution.[122] As noted, the climate change legislation passed in 2009 contained tradable permits as the central instrument for reducing, or at least stabilizing, carbon emissions, but the full "cap and trade" legislation has not been adopted.

Effluent taxation and tradable permits have been criticized especially by environmentalists, some of whom regard them as mechanisms for buying the right to pollute and even to kill. To those critics, the value of a clean environment is greater than the value of economic growth in almost any circumstance, and they cannot accept the idea of balancing the two. Another problem is that enforcing a pollution tax might be even more difficult than enforcing existing regulatory standards. Effluents would have to be monitored almost continuously to determine the total amount of discharge, whereas under the present regulatory system, less frequent monitoring often is sufficient, as is less exact measurement.

The air and water of the United States are much cleaner in the early twenty-first century than they were before the passage of the environmental laws. Fish have returned to streams that were once biologically dead, and cities such as Pittsburgh, which was once constantly shrouded in smoke and grit, now can be seen from a distance. Despite these successes, the EPA and the laws it enforces have been attacked from both sides—for being insensitive to the needs of industry and for being too soft on polluters. Questions about the role of the EPA are likely to become even more important as scarce resources and slow economic growth raise the average citizen's concern about national priorities.

Summary

Decisions in one policy area often impinge on many other areas. Environmental policy cannot be discussed apart from energy policy or from policies concerning economic growth. The institutions of government, however, frequently do not provide mechanisms for rectifying these conflicts of values. Each policy area is treated separately, according to its own constellation of interests and professional standards and with an eye on the political returns to each set of constituents. As both national resources and government resources dwindle, however, decisions by such "subgovernments" may be a luxury the United States can no longer afford. There is a need for enhanced policy coordination across several areas, but Washington works better *within* policy areas than across them, and conflict rather than cooperation is the common outcome.

The coming years may be the time when some important questions are decided about the relationship between Americans and their physical environment. The country must decide how much value to attach to a clean and relatively unspoiled environment, compared with the value attached to the mastery of that environment through energy exploration and economic growth. Although renewable energy resources and some shifting of attitudes about the desirability of economic growth may soften these hard choices, the choices must still be made. The choices will arise with respect to specific questions such as whether to open more Alaskan lands to energy exploration or how to manage the oil shale of the western states. They may also arise over issues such as the disposal of increasing quantities of toxic industrial wastes and the need to develop cleaner means of producing the goods to which Americans have become accustomed. In the process, Americans will be asked what they are willing to give up for a cleaner environment. Are styrofoam cups worth the emission of CFCs into the environment and the swelling of solid waste dumps? Are people willing to spend an hour or so every week recycling materials to prevent pollution and conserve energy? The sum of these individual choices, along with the regulatory choices that government makes, will say a good deal about the quality of life in the United States for years to come.

CHAPTER 15

Protective Policies: Defense and Law Enforcement

Background

The U.S. Constitution lists "to provide for the common defense" as a primary purpose of the government of the United States. Going back to Lexington and Concord and the Minutemen, military defense has been a visible and sometimes extremely expensive function in a country favoring small government and few government employees.[1] Not all threats to peace and order are foreign, and from the beginning, law enforcement has also been a major public function. In the United States, policing has been largely a state and local function, but as with education, the federal government has become increasingly involved. Some of that involvement has been purely financial, but more and more, the federal government is directly concerned with enforcing the law. Following the terrorist attacks of September 11, 2001, it became even more active in directing and coordinating law enforcement at all levels.

Both of these two government functions are, in general, salient to the public, but they have varied in their relevance. Until September 11, defense had been declining in relevance to the average citizen, while law enforcement had been a growing concern for some years. In many surveys during the 1990s, respondents considered crime and personal safety the most pressing problems of government (see Table 15.1). The terrorist attacks of 2001 placed both defense and law enforcement at the very center of public concern. The two policy areas have obvious similarities, including the use of force in the name of the public, but there are also some more subtle similarities, such as their potential threats to civil liberties. There are some obvious and important differences between them as well.

TABLE 15.1   Most Important Issues for Americans (in percentages; up to three mentions recorded)

Issue	Nov. 1991	Jan. 1994	Jan. 1997	Jun. 2000	Feb. 2004	Aug. 2006	Mar. 2008
Unemployment	23	18					5
Economy (general)	32	14	21	20	20	11	35
Drugs	10	9	17	16	—	—	—
Health care	6	20	7	12	19	—	8
Crime	6	37	23	20	12	—	1
Terrorism	—	—	—	—	21	7	2
War in Iraq					18	23	21

Sources: Gallup Poll Monthly, September 1992, 11; January 1994, 43; January 1997, 20; March 2008, online; *Polling Report,* August 15, 2006.

Defense Policy

Making defense policy is exceedingly difficult. It involves planning for an uncertain future and dealing with adversaries whose strength and strategies are not readily predictable, as well as with allies whose commitment to a common purpose and a common set of policies may be uncertain. Defense policy also involves making prospective decisions about weapons that may take years or even decades to develop and that may not perform as intended. Finally, defense involves huge costs that may be politically unpopular even when the public strongly supports a strong U.S. military posture. Defense policymaking is a series of gigantic gambles about the future and about events that most of those involved hope never actually occur.

Providing for the common defense is now a much more complex and expensive task than it was when an effective military force could be raised by calling for each man in the community to take down the rifle from over the fireplace. Military spending accounted for 16.5 percent of federal spending in 2000, down from 35 percent in 1980. In 2009, military spending was 3.9 percent of gross national product (GNP) (see Table 15.2)—$4.00 out of every $100 in the economy went for military defense, down from 6.5 percent of GNP in 1985. In some parts of the United States such as Norfolk, Virginia, and Southern California, defense (whether the military itself or civilian defense contractors) is a dominant component of the local economy. U.S. spending on defense is substantially higher than that in most other democracies, especially when the substantially higher level of total GDP is considered.

Defense policy became even more controversial after the end of the Cold War and the short Gulf War. The demands on the defense establishment now

TABLE 15.2   Military Expenditures as Percentage of Gross Domestic Product, 2009

Oman	10.6
Saudi Arabia	9.4
Israel	8.6
Syria	4.8
United States	3.9
Russia	3.4
Greece	3.3
Pakistan	3.3
India	2.5
United Kingdom	2.2
France	2.1
China	2.0
Iraq	2.0
Sweden	1.4
Germany	1.3
Canada	1.2
Japan	0.9

Sources: Stockholm International Peace Research Institute, Military Expenditure Database; U.S. Central Intelligence Agency, *The CIA World Factbook* (New York: Skyhorse, annual).

involve even greater complexity and uncertainty than when the adversary was clear and the types of weapons needed, at least for deterrence, were largely agreed on.[2] Moreover, although many Americans expected a "peace dividend" at the end of the Cold War, most government leaders were not anxious to dismantle the military establishment. Military leaders had accepted the necessity of reducing defense spending in a less supportive political and financial climate, but the 2003 budget of the George W. Bush administration proposed a significant increase in defense spending, for both new technology and manpower. That increase reversed some years of decline, and further increases were implicitly promised in recognition that the world had again become a dangerous place. The higher levels of spending have been maintained because of the conflicts in Iraq and Afghanistan.

Some Americans had also expected a downsizing in the military during the Obama administration, but although the conflict in Iraq was largely terminated, the war in Afghanistan has persisted and become even more problematic in many ways, with the burning of Korans and the massacre of civilians straining relationships with the Afghan government. President Obama has projected large defense cuts in coming years but has yet to get those reductions in force through a seemingly skeptical Congress.[3]

Even before the increases of the Bush budget, however, there were pressures for an increase in defense spending within a very few years, as a number of weapons systems under contract would begin to be delivered and existing systems modernized, posing the obvious question of whether those weapons were still necessary.[4] The shift from nuclear deterrence to conventional warfare and an increased emphasis on peacekeeping also seemed likely to make defense more expensive. A missile can sit in a silo for some time with minimal maintenance costs, but soldiers and sailors have to be paid every month and fed every day. They may cost even more when the economy is good and recruits are difficult to attract.

The wars in Iraq and Afghanistan have further complicated U.S. defense policy decisions. Although it is customary for Americans to rally around the troops and to support the president and his policies in times of war, first Vietnam and now Iraq have provoked significant debate over the use of military force. By the middle of 2006, a majority of Americans disapproved of U.S. involvement in Iraq, although there was less support for immediate withdrawal of the troops. Although the commitment to Iraq began winding down in 2008 and 2009, there was increased commitment to Afghanistan, with President Obama (who had actively opposed the war in Iraq) increasing U.S. troop levels significantly. By March 2012, the American public opposed the war in Afghanistan by a margin of 3 to 1.

Deciding on defense policy has never been easy, but it is likely to become even more difficult because most of the former certainties about strategy have changed in a very short time and there is little certainty about the future. The shift from an identifiable enemy in the Soviet Union to a more complex world with many states that are potential enemies—Iran and North Korea the clearest possibilities—as well as terrorist organizations with no definite national basis, has made defense policy more challenging and complex.[5] Defense and protective policies become further complicated with the change of focus from actions far from America's shores to potential threats in our cities and our own neighborhoods. These domestic issues raise additional questions about maintaining civil liberties and traditional freedoms in light of the need to protect citizens.

The Environment of Defense Policy

A number of factors condition the manner in which defense policy is made and the likely outcomes of the process. Unlike many other policy areas, defense policy is influenced by forces that are, to a great extent, beyond the control of the government officials making the decisions. In part because of the uncertainty involved in making defense policy, there may be greater perceptual differences among the participants than is true for other policy areas.[6] For example, the degree of threat that any decision maker perceives in the international environment will affect his or her willingness to allocate resources to defense. Perceptual differences have been exacerbated since the clear threat of the Soviet Union has been largely ended, leaving the United States to contend with the possibility of smaller-scale, but still dangerous, conflicts around the world. Terrorism and unconventional threats to U.S. security now loom much larger, and they require a different type of military posture.[7]

The prospect of smaller-scale conflicts also raises the question of whether the United States should be the global police officer or merely one more nation in the international community, albeit the only remaining superpower.[8] If the United States is to act as an international police officer, should it do so alone or in concert with international organizations, such as the United Nations, NATO, and the Organization of American States?[9] The actions in Iraq gave a very unilateralist answer to that question. The so-called Bush doctrine, that unilateral and preemptive intervention is justified if the interests of the United States are threatened, provided a similar answer to the question of intervention, but the question remains of how willing even allies are to accept this idea of unilateral action.[10]

An even more basic question is whether the national interests of the United States are really served by using its military forces for peacekeeping and relief functions around the world, no matter how desirable the actions may be on humanitarian grounds.[11] Critics argue that this use of U.S. forces only confuses their mission and their training and may reduce their utility in case of overt conflict. The wars in Iraq and Afghanistan have reduced dramatically the availability of personnel for other purposes, although the humanitarian use of forces in situations such as the tsunami in Asia in late 2004 will certainly continue.

Adversaries and potential adversaries.   For most of the past sixty years, the fundamental factor shaping defense policy was the relationship between the United States and the Soviet Union. Almost as soon as the two superpowers ceased being allies after World War II, they became adversaries on a global scale. Early stages of that adversarial relationship included the Berlin blockade and the Korean War, followed by the U-2 incident, the Cuban missile crisis, Vietnam, and Afghanistan, not to mention hundreds of more minor incidents.[12] None of these involved direct conflict between troops of the two superpowers, although confrontations between the troops of one superpower and those of allies or surrogates of the other occurred several times. The degree of hostility expressed between the United States and the Soviet Union varied, however; periods of détente ameliorated the tensions of the Cold War and some important negotiated agreements (e.g., the nuclear test ban treaty and the Strategic Arms Limitation Talks [SALT] agreements) that lessened tensions, at least for a while.

In addition to conventional conflicts, the nuclear arms race drove each country to develop massive stockpiles of nuclear weapons capable of destroying the world several times over. Nuclear weapons have not been used since World War II, and there were several successful attempts to reduce their numbers (or at least reduce their rate of growth) even during peak Cold War years. As more historical materials from the Cold War period become available to scholars and analysts, it is not only even clearer that the nuclear threat was a major deterrent to conflictual behavior but also that a number of near-disastrous accidents made the world a very dangerous place indeed.[13]

The remaining stockpiles of these weapons represent a crucial factor that defense policymakers must always take into account, especially since the former Soviet Union has disintegrated into a number of smaller states. Several of the new states retain large quantities of weapons and have national ambitions that may lead them to rattle the nuclear saber, if not actually use nuclear weapons.[14] In 2002, Russian president Vladimir Putin and U.S. president George W. Bush reached agreement on major reduction of the two countries' nuclear stockpiles, further limiting the possibility of a nuclear confrontation.[15] Nevertheless, both countries retain hundreds of warheads, quite enough to destroy each other and much of the rest of humanity as well. As earlier treaties began to expire, President Obama visited Russia in summer 2009 to attempt to negotiate new reductions in nuclear arsenals, and meetings at the nuclear summit in 2012 continued these negotiations.

The world was dangerous during the Cold War, but it may be even more dangerous since "peace" has broken out. Instead of one Soviet Union with nuclear weapons, a number of the former Soviet republics now have them. The Gulf War highlighted the presence of nuclear, chemical, and biological weapons in a number of other countries and the apparent willingness of those countries to use force to attain their political and economic goals. Some potential adversaries, such as North Korea,[16] still appear to be fighting the Cold War and persist in the rhetoric of fighting against global capitalism. Others such as Iran and Syria are pursuing more nationalistic or economic goals. There is also evidence that the new nuclear powers are not nearly as cautious as the Soviet Union was in how they develop and deploy weapons.[17] Both India and Pakistan have developed and exploded nuclear weapons, and although their primary target is not the United States, the existence of more nuclear powers adds another variable to an already difficult set of strategic calculations. Finally, there is the fear, if little tangible evidence, that terrorist groups may also possess weapons of mass destruction.

Although many potential adversaries are small and relatively weak militarily, they are widely dispersed around the globe, and the U.S. defense establishment must decide how quickly, and in how many simultaneous situations, it must be prepared to respond.[18] Planners must decide how much force both the United

States and potential adversaries can, and should, bring to bear in those potential conflicts. There is a danger that the United States military has been so attuned to large-scale international conflicts that it will not be capable of coping effectively with the seemingly mundane, low-level conflicts that appear more probable in the post–Cold War era. The "bottom-up review" of defense policy undertaken in 1994 was an attempt to develop a new strategic doctrine, premised on the possibility of several smaller conflicts, such as the Gulf War.[19] The question then became how many such "major regional conflicts" the American military should be able to cope with simultaneously. The basic answer was two, with one being contained while the other was being won.

The war in Iraq has increased the stakes in the debate over the force structure of the United States and prompted another rethinking of military doctrine.[20] The *Quadrennial Review* published by the Department of Defense in 2006 emphasized "the long war." Much of the previous doctrine about "small wars," such as Afghanistan and Iraq, was that they would be quick. Experience now indicates that they will not be, so the armed forces need to learn how to carry out protracted engagements and perhaps how to be occupying forces, rather than quickly vanquishing an enemy and returning to base. The need to be able to fight effectively against insurgents and guerrillas also became evident as a result of the two conflicts still going on in 2009.[21]

Allies.   The United States also has friends in the world, although they do not always agree on defense and foreign policy issues. The country has important defense agreements with Japan, South Korea, Israel, and Australia, but its most important alliance has been the North Atlantic Treaty Organization (NATO), which has linked nations in Europe and North America for their mutual defense since the late 1940s. NATO has been responsible for the defense of western Europe and the North Atlantic, and the United States has committed by far the largest share of men and material to the alliance.[22] The collapse of the Soviet threat in the late 1980s, however, made many people—defense analysts and ordinary citizens alike—question the continuation of NATO, at least in its traditional form. Already NATO has added a number of former members of the Warsaw Pact, and with the European Union considering a more independent security policy, NATO already means something very different from what it formerly did. In fact, many former Warsaw Pact countries, such as Poland and Romania, have been more supportive of American foreign policy in the early twenty-first century than the traditional allies.[23] Economic problems at home and the continuing economic and political integration of western Europe mean that there is less need for a large American military presence in Europe, and almost all of the U.S. divisions stationed in Germany since the end of World War II have returned home. Similarly, the United States was willing to give up major military bases in the Philippines and to consider eliminating bases in Okinawa in the belief that they would be much less valuable in a world without direct East–West confrontations. The increasing importance of China, however, has led to the United States opening a new military base in northern Australia, in cooperation with the Australian government.

Although these alliances are apparently now less valuable, the experience of the Gulf War showed that Western nations, and even some former adversaries from the Warsaw Pact, could band together to confront a common threat. The United Nations' stamp of approval on their actions in the Persian Gulf made the alliance more viable, but there had been a sense that the United States had friends around the world that could be counted on in many military situations. A few old friends, notably Britain, joined the conflict in Iraq. The alliances may be ad hoc arrangements rather than continuing treaty commitments, but they can still generate collective action to maintain international security. Economic and social issues (including human rights) may become more important in defining security arrangements in the near future, and so the United States needs to adjust its thinking about how to make and maintain international alliances.[24]

The importance of U.S. membership in NATO was evident in the attempts to maintain peace in the former Yugoslavia in the 1990s. Several European members of NATO had attempted to control the violence in Croatia and Bosnia, but they had little success until U.S. troops became involved.[25] Their deployment as a NATO activity helped to legitimate the operations of the peacekeeping forces, but the presence of the Americans remained crucial. The initial commitment of troops for one year had to be extended indefinitely to maintain the uneasy peace. The George W. Bush administration was extremely skeptical of this involvement when it first came to office, but after learning more of the situation there, the administration maintained a U.S. role in the Balkans. Again, these activities indicate the extent to which the traditional role of the U.S. military has changed.

The American attack on Afghanistan in late 2001 also involved the creation of a small alliance against the Taliban government accused of harboring al Qaeda terrorists. Most important was creating a working agreement with Pakistan, which served as a staging ground for the campaign. A few other long-standing allies such as Britain joined, but the operation was primarily American. The split within NATO became more pronounced in the Iraq conflict, but in the end, NATO did become involved in the conflict in Afghanistan. This military initiative demonstrated not only the capacity of the U.S. government to project power across the globe but also the fact that alliances in the future may be temporary ones for particular purposes rather than stable and enduring.

The long war in Afghanistan is forcing some more extensive reviews of American strategy and force structure, a review also driven by budget deficits. The basic plan is to reduce more conventional weapons systems in favor of high-technology systems, special operations, and cyberwarfare. These reflect in part the success of special operations such as the killing of Osama bin Laden, as well as the success of technological weapons, such as drones. These plans would mean approximately 100,000 fewer foot soldiers which, it has been argued, will increase overall effectiveness of the military.[26]

Technology

The technology of modern warfare has advanced far beyond that available during the Vietnam conflict or the Gulf War of 1991.[27] Nuclear armaments are a major part of the technological change, but systems for delivering weapons have improved even more rapidly. In the 1950s, it took hours for a plane to fly from the former Soviet Union to the United States; a missile can now make a comparable journey in fifteen minutes, and a missile launched from a submarine off-shore could also arrive in a few minutes. There even are plans for war in space, with "killer satellites" and orbiting weapons as part of an antimissile system ("Star Wars").[28] The technology of conventional warfare now includes the advanced laser-guided weapons, infrared night-vision scopes, stealth airplanes, computers, and antimissile defenses that figured prominently in the Gulf War. The wars in Afghanistan and Iraq demonstrated even more technological capacity to increase the effectiveness and safety of the armed forces—for example, through the use of drone planes—although some rather old-fashioned ideas such as armoring vehicles more thoroughly seemingly have not been implemented fully.[29] There is also discussion of a whole new generation of weapons, including laser weapons, such as would have only been found in science fiction a few years ago.

Advancing weapons technology has several implications for defense policy. One is that defense is a constant activity; there is no longer time to raise an army and then go to war. A standing army historically has been anathema to many Americans, but in the first decade of the twenty-first century, the U.S. military numbered approximately 2.3 million uniformed personnel, plus almost 700,000 civilian employees of the Department of Defense. Another feature of the technology of modern warfare is great cost, beyond maintaining a large military establishment. One new B-1 or B-2 bomber costs almost $1 billion; one army tank now costs approximately $10 million; and a new aircraft carrier proposed for the navy could cost several billion dollars.[30] Any discussion of improving the technical quality of American military forces must be conducted in the context of very high costs.[31]

Public Opinion

U.S. defense policy is made in a relatively open political arena where it is definitely influenced by public opinion, and public opinion about defense is ambiguous. There are few committed advocates of unilateral disarmament in the United States, especially after September 11, and virtually all U.S. politicians advocate a strong defense. Nevertheless, a number of questions remain about program costs, about whether many of the high-technology weapons purchased actually contribute significantly to national security, and about how the military power of the United States should be used (for example, in the Caribbean, Central America, or other parts of the Third World). These questions involve political calculations as well as technical military issues, and they will continue to be fought out in Congress and the media as well as in the Pentagon.

Nuclear weapons constitute an even greater public opinion problem. A significant portion of the American populace, although favoring a strong defense, opposed the nuclear arms race between the United States and the Soviet Union. The public has generally applauded the negotiated freezes on nuclear weapons and reductions in the numbers of such weapons stockpiled by both sides. There is virtual unanimity on one point: The United States should never be the first country to use nuclear weapons in a conflict,[32] whether the conflict is among superpowers or a more limited one, such as the Iraq War. The spread of nuclear weapons to other countries, such as India and Pakistan, and their potential spread to Iran and North Korea make the issue of the safety and control of nuclear weapons all the more relevant. There were a number of reports of plutonium from Russia being available for sale, potentially to terrorists.

The unilateralist strategies of the George W. Bush administration also affected public opinion on the military and the use of force in foreign policy. A number of polls showed that members of the public were less unilateralist than the Bush administration and that they were concerned about the ability of the United States to work with allies in solving international problems.[33] Public opinion tends to be less supportive of military spending than the Bush administration was and to question more intensely the role of the military in American life. Although President Obama has charted a foreign policy course that strays from Bush's unilateralist strategy, high levels of military spending have continued during his administration, largely as a result of the wars in Iraq and Afghanistan.

U.S. Force Configurations

Table 15.3 lists the strategic weapons holdings of the United States, Russia, China, and North Korea. With the end of the Cold War, much of this vast arsenal appears to consist of dinosaurs left from an earlier age. Early pledges from Boris Yeltsin, leader of the Russian federation, and from President George H. W. Bush to dismantle much of the strategic forces meant that these weapons were to follow the path of intermediate-range weapons in Europe and be destroyed.[34]

TABLE 15.3 Nuclear Warheads Possessed by the United States and Major Potential Adversaries

Deliverable by	United States	Russia	China	North Korea
Bombers	1,900	624	150	?
Intercontinental ballistic missiles (ICBMs)	1,700	2,600	120	?
Submarine-launched missiles	3,168	1,700	12	?
Personnel	677,000	360,000	1,600,000	950,000
Main battle tanks	8,200	22,800	7,850	3,500
Artillery	6,500	18,400	15,200	10,400
Submarines	72	51	69	26
Carriers	12	1	0	0
Other major surface combatants	106	26	63[a]	3 vessels

Source: International Institute of Strategic Studies, *The Military Balance, 2004–05* (London: Oxford University Press, 2005).

a. Excludes numerous patrol craft.

More than a decade later, each country retained a nuclear arsenal, but neither was as great as at the height of the Cold War. In particular, most of the missiles are being fitted with a single warhead rather than the multiple warheads formerly on many missiles. In downsizing, the United States has held onto its submarine-launched weapons most dearly, being more willing to trade away other parts of its "triad."[35] As promising as these developments are, the uncertainty about whose "finger is on the button," and indeed how many buttons there are, in the former Soviet Union adds to the world's danger and makes maintaining some nuclear deterrent an important feature of U.S. defense policy.

The balance in nonstrategic forces in the world is less easy to define. The table details the balance of conventional land forces between the United States and potential adversaries. The countries formed out of the former Soviet Union have very large military forces, but the fragmentation among and within them may make those forces less dangerous than they might otherwise be. Still, the actual force levels of the United States are smaller than those of some other countries. In any conflict with those countries, the superior technical capabilities of some American weapons, as well as superiority in the number of attack aircraft, would be needed to level the field.

Although the United States has slightly more surface ships and submarines than its potential adversaries, as shown in the table, that slight numerical difference may underestimate the real advantage, given the striking force of one carrier battle group. In addition, the superior detection equipment and satellite tracking devices on U.S. vessels make the submarines of other countries relatively less effective. Thus, despite reduction in naval construction, and the far-flung missions that its navy must serve, the edge seems to go to the naval forces of the United States. That said, the development of more sophisticated antiship missiles is tending to lessen that advantage.[36]

If nothing else, toting up personnel and weapons systems demonstrates the huge destructive potential that can be unleashed in a few moments by a number of countries in the world. Such great power carries with it great responsibility and the need for effective strategic doctrines to prevent the use of nuclear weapons—or, if possible, any weapons. The doctrines of a bipolar world, such as "mutually assured destruction," are no longer valid, and because of that, there is perhaps less security than even during the height of the Cold War.

Problems of Defense Policy

Maintaining the defenses of the United States presents several significant policy problems, none of which can be solved readily. One is how to manage nuclear strategy in a multipolar world. Other problems are more narrowly focused, such as the interaction of specific defense issues (such as the acquisition of weapons and manpower) with fundamental features of the economic system or with fundamental American values. These problems have grown more complex as uncertainty about the military future of the United States makes the choices more difficult and more risky.

Military Procurement

The first major defense problem is acquiring new weapons systems.[37] In a modern, high-technology military force, new weapons are not bought off the shelf but represent years or even decades of research and development. This presents several problems for the military managers who seek to acquire the weapons. One is attempting to predict years in advance just what sort of weapons will be required to ensure national security. For example, during the Reagan years, a great deal of money was funneled into the Strategic Defense Initiative (SDI, or Star Wars). The program and its sequels have cost approximately $5 billion per year since the mid-1980s. Given changes in the strategic environment, that program now appears to be of limited utility, as there is less chance of strategic missiles being launched at the United States and much greater chance of terrorism or small, limited wars. Despite that, the George W. Bush administration pushed ahead with a missile defense program, renouncing the Anti-Ballistic Missile Treaty with Russia at the same time. The Obama administration has continued with the program, albeit attempting to assuage Russian concerns.[38]

Another problem for procurement officials is deciding what form of competition to demand among potential suppliers of weapons. One option is to have possible competitors develop full-scale operating systems and then to test those prototypes against one another. The other option is to settle on one or a limited number of vendors very early in the development process and then work with them to develop the weapon. Although the former option corresponds to the standard procedures for bidding out contracts, it may ultimately produce more expensive and less effective weapons. If a manufacturer must develop fully operational weapons to compete for a program, it may choose simply not to compete; hence, many potentially useful ideas (especially from smaller firms) might be lost. Second, if such full-scale competition were carried out, any firm competing for government contracts might have to amortize its failures across winning contracts to make a profit, and consequently the costs of weapons systems as a group would increase. Another option would be to sell the weapons to other countries, a strategy that came back to haunt several countries, including the United States, during the Gulf War and thus may not be the best strategy for reducing the level of military tension in the world.

On the other hand, awarding contracts for major weapons systems on the basis of only prototypes and engineering projections may produce numerous disappointments and cost overruns. Despite screening by skilled military and civilian personnel in the Department of Defense, ideas that look good on the drawing board may not work when they are brought to full-scale production and deployment. There are numerous examples among recent weapons systems: The Sergeant York (DIVAD) antiaircraft cannon, the Bradley fighting vehicle, the C-17 aircraft, and several missile systems have not performed as expected.[39] Even if a manufacturer is capable of making a system work as promised, there may be large cost overruns; the delivered price of the C-5A military transport plane was several times the projected price.[40]

Given that most weapons procurement contracts are "cost-plus," virtually guaranteeing the manufacturer a profit, contractors have a strong incentive to bid low on projects and allow costs to escalate. The Department of Defense has instituted controls to try to prevent the most flagrant violations of this contracting system, but it is difficult to control genuine cases of cost underestimation when a project is well into production. If a workable product can be attained, it will almost certainly be better to go ahead with the project despite cost overruns than to begin again.

Another problem arising from the procurement process is that a manufacturer that is awarded a contract for a particular weapons system becomes the sole source for that system and for the parts that go along with it. That allows firms to charge exorbitant prices for spare parts and tools—simple wrenches worth a dollar or less have been billed to the Department of Defense for several thousand dollars. Some revelations about apparent excesses have been more media events than real cost problems, and curbs have been instituted to stop some of the greatest abuses, but the underlying problem in weapons procurement remains. These problems became more apparent during the war in Iraq when a number of noncompetitive contracts with the Halliburton Corporation, long associated with Vice President Cheney, were revealed.[41]

The division among the armed services may also produce problems in procuring weapons or at least may make weapons cost more than they should. Again, there are two options: to attempt to force the services to use the same weapons whenever possible or to allow each service to acquire the systems most suited to its particular needs. For example, since the air force and the navy fly airplanes that perform similar missions, why can they not use the same planes? In addition to coordination problems caused by the long-standing rivalries between the services, however, there could be a danger that weapons resulting from an integrated procurement process would be neither fish nor fowl. For example, the characteristics that suit a plane for carrier landings for the navy might make it less suitable as an air superiority interceptor for the air force.

On the other hand, procurement of a number of different weapons may be more expensive, for the research and development costs of each can be amortized across fewer units produced. The U.S. budget process also presents problems for weapons procurement. Unlike most other countries, the United States has an annual defense budget, creating the possibility (and some real examples) that an ongoing weapons system may not be funded. That possibility, of course, presents problems for both contractors and the military. To date, proposals for a multi-year procurement process have been adopted only in part, for Congress wishes to maintain its control over the public purse.

Continuing fiscal constraints on the federal government after the end of the Cold War have introduced other budget problems into the procurement process. Some procurement plans continue to develop and test prototypes of new weapons but not produce them in any quantity.[42] The idea is that the armed forces can remain technologically modern at limited expense: If there were an outbreak of hostilities, then the weapons could go into production. On the one hand, this approach to procurement appears to violate some of the assumptions about contemporary military preparedness mentioned earlier, in which speed of response is an essential element. On the other hand, it may be the only way to maintain the technological edge demonstrated during the war in Afghanistan and the killing of Osama bin Laden while also reducing the amount of money spent on the military. The stop-go problem in budgeting is reflected even in weapons systems that are developed, with uncertainty and changing levels of funding slowing development and increasing costs.[43]

U.S. Marine Gen. John R. Allen, the supreme allied commander in Afghanistan (center), talks to U.S. Army Capt. Michael Stewart in the town of Andar on April 23, 2012. The continuing war in Afghanistan has raised questions about both the capacity of the armed forces to fight several regional wars at one time, and about U.S. foreign policy in the Middle East and Southwest Asia.

The process of equipping a modern army is made even more difficult by the close ties between the Department of Defense and its defense contractors—the military-industrial complex, or "fifth branch" of the armed forces—which can make independent evaluation of some proposed weapons systems more difficult. Such problems are harder to solve because Congress wants to preserve its budget power, whereas the defense establishment needs the cooperation and capabilities of contractors. Given the importance of hardware and technology for the modern military, significant attention must continue to be given to solving these problems.

But Congress is itself implicated in some of the problems of defense budgeting and procurement. Defense contracts represent jobs in congressional districts, so Congress may want to preserve some contracts when the Department of Defense does not see the need, or sees a reduced need. For example, Secretary of Defense Robert Gates won one battle with Congress over cutting the number of F-22 aircraft in 2009 but may well lose others over the C-17 and F-18.[44]

Updating the Strategic Deterrent

Much of the strategic deterrent force of the United States is aging; in some cases, it may already be obsolete. The B-52 bomber, which entered service in the 1950s, is, despite updates and modifications, a very old weapon. The Minuteman missile is by no means obsolete, but it was vulnerable to a Soviet first strike. These problems with existing weapons led to the development of three new weapons systems—the B-1 and B-2 bombers and the MX missile—all of which have been at the center of controversy.

The B-1 bomber was designed as a supersonic, penetrating, intercontinental bomber that could fly to a target and return, depending on speed and electronic countermeasures for its survival. After several prototypes were built and tested, the Carter administration canceled the project in 1977, arguing that bombers might not be as efficient as Cruise missiles and that the development of "stealth" technology, which would make an airplane less visible to radar, would quickly make the B-1 obsolete. That decision caused a great deal of negative reaction in the military—especially in the air force—and was reversed by the Reagan administration, which called for a force of one hundred B-1 bombers. Eventually, continuing problems with the prototypes of the B-1, and the rapid development of stealth technology incorporated into the B-2, led to the end of the B-1. Then B-2 production was stopped after production of only twenty planes, as a result of the end of the Cold War and tight Pentagon budgets.

Updating the U.S. missile fleet has been even more difficult. The MX was designed to reduce the vulnerability of the current Minuteman missiles, as well as to upgrade the accuracy and number of warheads in the U.S. nuclear arsenal. Whereas the existing Minuteman III missiles had three multiple independently targetable reentry vehicle (MIRVed) warheads, the MX could carry ten. The Reagan administration decided to produce one hundred MX missiles and appointed a bipartisan Commission on Strategic Alternatives (the Scowcroft commission), which recommended developing a new, small missile—known as the "Midgetman"—that could be fired from a mobile launcher and therefore moved almost anywhere, much as Cruise missiles can be. The Midgetman would have only a single, rather small warhead, but given its relatively low cost and relative invulnerability, it could present a serious deterrent, especially given the destructive capacity of even a small warhead. Nevertheless, this missile was not purchased, despite plans for up to six hundred, and only fifty MXs were purchased. Instead, defense planners opted for a rapid development and deployment of less expensive Cruise missiles.

All these advances in weapons technology were once of tremendous importance for the defense of the United States, but their importance now is not clear. Are they really necessary or useful to meet the threats that smaller nuclear powers may pose, or will these and many other strategic weapons become merely rather quaint relics of the past? Already the long journeys of Trident submarines have an element of the Flying Dutchman about them,[45] and in late 1991, the B-52s that had been on constant alert since the 1950s stood down. Again, there is an apparent need for a thorough and careful examination of just what the military purchases of the future should be.

The All-Volunteer Military

During the Vietnam War, the use of conscription to provide manpower for the armed forces became increasingly unpopular in the United States. In 1975, the draft was phased out and replaced by an all-volunteer force. Although this step was politically desirable at the time, and almost certainly is still so today, that policy decision presents several problems for the armed forces.[46] The problems had been reduced, but by no means eliminated, by the "build-down" of forces before the wars in Afghanistan and the Gulf.[47]

The most obvious problem is that the military must now compete directly with civilian employers for the same pool of young people, instead of being able to train young people in the military for a short time and then perhaps induce some of them to remain in the service. Given the risks associated with serving in the military, it is not surprising that filling enlistment quotas has at times been difficult. There are special difficulties in attracting educated and skilled personnel, for these are the people whose services are most in demand in the civilian labor market. Thus, for much of its history, the all-volunteer force has been plagued by stories of low-quality recruits. In the Gulf War, Afghanistan, and then in Iraq, much of the burden has fallen on reservists called up from civilian occupations, often with substantial disruption for them and for their employers. Long and sometimes repeated tours of duty in Iraq have placed an especially large burden on some reservists and their communities.

Recruitment problems diminished during recessions in the early 1980s and the 1990s, when any job seemed attractive, and there were long queues of potential enlistees waiting to enter the armed forces. When the economy was booming in the late 1990s, military enlistment was not nearly as attractive an opportunity. The military has reduced its demand for young men somewhat by placing women in jobs formerly filled by males (although still not in all combat positions) and by using civilians in jobs once filled by uniformed personnel. Problems persist, however, in attracting enough highly skilled people. There seems to be increasing disparity between the skills needed by a military increasingly dominated by technical weapons systems and those of the recruits generally available, although the performance of the all-volunteer forces and the reserves in the Gulf War and then Iraq allayed those fears somewhat. The return to economic hard times after 2008 has made recruitment more attractive.

Associated with the problem of attracting personnel is the problem of compensating them. An obvious means of attracting and retaining people in any job is to pay them adequately, and that is especially true for the military, given the dangers and hardships of serving in the armed forces. Unfortunately, however, military pay is generally not competitive with private sector pay, even when the value of allowances and benefits is included in the comparison. Additionally, the private sector offers those with military training much greater economic rewards than does continuing in the military; for example, an individual who trains as a pilot in the air force is frequently able to command at least twice his military pay working for a private airline. Military pay is much better than it was before the introduction of the all-volunteer military—and accounts for a larger percentage of the defense budget than it did before—but it is not yet capable of attracting and retaining as many of the best people as the armed forces require. The military services have attempted to compensate with inducements such as support for college tuition, but during the Iraq War, recruitment has been down.[48] The retirement option available to military personnel (full retirement benefits after twenty years) may make staying in the service more desirable, but the loss of crucial skilled personnel continues, and there are some pressures to make military retirement less generous.

Finally, there are philosophical and constitutional questions about the development of an all-volunteer military. Given historical patterns and some continuing discrimination in the labor market, an all-volunteer force may be composed increasingly of members of minority groups, and this effect may be seen as imposing an excessive national defense burden on those groups. More generally, the traditional ideal of the U.S. military has been the citizen-soldier, rejecting the idea of a professional standing army. The all-volunteer force makes a professional military more likely and implies that large numbers of young Americans will no longer be serving for a time in the armed forces.

This pattern of recruitment may also make the military more of a group apart from the rest of society and perhaps may make it less amenable to civilian control. Paradoxically, although the country may need a professional military to be able to handle the highly sophisticated weapons in the contemporary arsenal, or to deploy the skills needed for covert actions such as hostage rescue and counterterrorist activities, it may thereby lose some control over those weapons and their potential for massive destruction. The issue of the distinction between civilian and military is even more important as terrorism brings war into the homeland because the military may be called on to serve what might normally be civilian functions. There is little evidence to support a claim that a "warrior caste" has developed in the United States, but the current personnel system of the armed forces may make that development more likely than it would be with conscription.

Other Personnel Issues

The military of the United States cannot be isolated from the social issues that influence life in the country as a whole. In particular, how to integrate women into the armed forces and how to deal with homosexuality have become important concerns for the military. Women have been involved unofficially in the military for the entire history of the United States,[49] but they have been a part of the military officially only since 1942. Most of their involvement has been in support, including clerical duties, nursing, and a variety of other activities removed from actual fighting. Women were traditionally not allowed to serve on ships in the navy.

During the late 1980s and early 1990s, however, the military began to allow women into more positions. Women were already serving on some ships, and the navy extended that to include all ships except submarines. The air force began to train women for combat, and some participated in combat missions during the Gulf War and the wars in Afghanistan and Iraq. The army now permits women to serve in all except frontline combat positions. If the United States should engage in armed conflicts in the future, it is clear that women will be involved more directly than in the past and that there will almost certainly be more women casualties than ever before. A number of women have been killed in the Iraq War, while in nominally noncombatant positions. Despite these changes, many women believe that they are still being denied full equality within the military.[50]

A number of highly publicized sexual harassment and "fraternization" cases have focused attention on the interaction of the two sexes in the military, and some critics claim that harassment of women is endemic.[51] Others argue that the issue has been blown out of proportion. Whatever the reality, it is a public relations problem for the military. One solution has been to return to training in single-sex units, something the marines alone had retained in the 1990s. Training and constant monitoring are also offered as remedies, but there appear to be no quick and easy answers.[52] Fraternization between men and women, especially between officers and enlisted personnel, is hardly new, but again, there are concerns about how to maintain discipline and enforce military codes of conduct. To some critics, especially women's groups, those rules are being implemented unfairly. They cite the case of a female air force pilot forced out of the service for a relationship with an enlisted man, while a male general was not punished nearly as severely for a similar offense.[53]

The right of homosexuals to serve in the armed forces has been even more controversial than the integration of women into combat. During his first presidential campaign Bill Clinton promised to give homosexuals full rights to serve, but once in office, he faced strong pressures from within the military to modify that stance. The suggested compromise was referred to as "Don't ask, don't tell," meaning that recruiters should not inquire about sexual preference and recruits should not volunteer that information. Sexual orientation would not in itself be a cause for dismissal from the armed forces, but dismissal would result from involvement in homosexual acts or causing disruptive incidents.[54]

This compromise position satisfied neither side in the dispute.[55] Members of the homosexual community believed that the president had reneged on his promise and that the compromise policy still did not accord homosexuals the same right as heterosexuals to serve in the military. Opponents in the military services and in Congress believed that the compromise would undermine military discipline and reduce the effectiveness of the armed forces. Not surprisingly, the courts became involved in the controversy and issued a number of rulings, most tending to reinforce the right of homosexuals to serve. Other cases have been settled in favor of the military and its need to maintain discipline.[56] In 2008, the courts refused to hear another challenge to the law, allowing the Obama administration to avoid a confrontation over the rights of its gay supporters.[57]

Conventional Forces and Strategies

Despite all the concern about nuclear weapons and nuclear disarmament, the most likely use of force by the United States would involve conventional forces. Such forces have been used around the world to deal with problems and respond to terrorism. In addition, the navy has been used frequently to "show the flag" in the Caribbean, the Mediterranean, and the Persian Gulf. While these activities were taking place, American troops remained on duty in western Europe, South Korea, Okinawa, Guantánamo Bay in Cuba, and several other places around the globe. The ability of the United States to respond with conventional forces to threats to its interests around the world remains an important element in defense planning.

One of the important elements in the ability of the United States to project its presence around the world is the Rapid Deployment Force. These are troops that are ready to be deployed by air on very short notice. Materials have been positioned in places around the world to supply these troops until seaborne supplies can be delivered to them. Under a program called Prepositioning of Material Configured in Unit Sets, or POMCUS, the Carter and Reagan administrations positioned supplies for up to six divisions in western Europe and the Persian Gulf region; in the event of a confrontation, troops could be flown in without the need to airlift heavy equipment and munitions. These programs are designed to make the U.S. armed forces more flexible and mobile.

Technology is highly important in flexibility and mobility. For example, the deployment of the M-1 tank during the Gulf War indicates that it is an extremely reliable, fast, and effective weapon despite its technological sophistication. The problem becomes acquiring enough of these weapons to meet the needs of the armed forces. But what are those needs? What should the armed forces be preparing for? Current doctrine holds that the armed forces should be preparing for one-and-a-half wars; that is, the armed forces should be preparing for one major and one minor conflict to occur at any one time.[58] Even that level of conflict might strain the available resources, especially if the conflicts involved the logistical problems of the Gulf War and did not include a convenient friendly power, such as Saudi Arabia, as the Iraq War has shown.

Planning to meet contingencies with conventional forces is important not only for the ability to use U.S. forces to implement national policy but also because strong conventional forces make the use of weapons of mass destruction, meaning primarily theater nuclear weapons, less likely. Plans exist for using such weapons in the event of apparent defeat of conventional forces, but once those weapons are used, it would be difficult to contain their escalation. The problem of nuclear escalation has largely been eliminated in Europe, but it would definitely be possible in dealing with smaller powers and might also escalate to include chemical and biological weapons. Thus, the availability of nuclear weapons makes conventional forces that much more important.

An effective conventional deterrent also depends on the readiness of those forces to fight when needed. There is some fear among military leaders, as well as military analysts, that reductions in spending will reduce the military's capacity to meet the demands that may be placed on it. Some fear has been expressed that American defense forces have become "hollow"—that they do not have sufficient readiness to meet another crisis on the order of the Gulf War.[59] Furthermore, the extended missions in Iraq and Afghanistan have worn out both people and equipment, so the forces are not as capable as they would like to be. The demand now is to create forces that are even lighter and more mobile.

Defense and/or Jobs

As the Cold War ended and many Americans, if not most, were ready for a significant cut in the defense budget, it turned out that cutting back was not as simple as it seemed. The economic prosperity of the United States rests in part on its military-industrial complex, so that reducing defense expenditures means reducing employment both for the men and women in the armed services and for employees in defense industries. By 2009, there were somewhat more than 2 million personnel in the armed forces (including reservists), another 800,000 civilian employees in the Department of Defense, and an additional one million people employed in defense industries.[60] There were some job losses in the 1990s in defense industries, but concerns about terror and potential conflicts in the Gulf ratcheted defense employment back up by 2004.

Even when the economy is good, defense cuts have a major impact on the politics of the defense budget. Most members of Congress are in favor of reducing the budget in principle but are much less interested when it directly affects their districts. In an interesting Freudian slip, Sen. Dianne Feinstein, D-CA, once argued that the B-2 bomber did not deliver a "big enough payroll." To a great extent, defense spending has been reconceptualized as a means of providing jobs and as a (thinly) disguised industrial policy.[61] Also, the United States is a successful exporter of arms when it wants to be, so promoting defense industries may be one way to address the balance of payments problem.

In addition to general economic problems, downsizing the military has other costs as well. For the military, it means the loss of a great deal of talent, especially in the officer corps and in career enlisted personnel that could be important for any future military activities. For the individuals who joined the all-volunteer military in the hope of a career, it may mean a huge adjustment of life plans and career prospects. Even for military personnel who remain in the service, reductions can mean very slow promotions and probably some career frustration.[62]

Before Iraq and Afghanistan increased their combat activity, the armed forces had developed some means of ensuring continued employment for their personnel and continued funding from Congress. The most obvious opportunity for the use of the military has been in the "war" on drugs, but there are questions about the desirability of military involvement in that policy area. For example, should American military might be used to attack the drug problem in other countries, especially countries in Latin America, which have unpleasant memories of previous U.S. military expeditions? Is the military really capable of doing the police work necessary to be effective in drug control? As right as such involvement may seem for supporting the military budget, it may be wrong for a variety of other reasons.

As noted, another occasional use of the military has been in peacekeeping. This is in some ways thinly disguised military action, with the hope that weapons do not actually have to be used. In other ways, peacekeeping is police work, involving detection of violations of cease-fires or of agreed borders or perhaps arresting accused war criminals. This is difficult work. It is often dangerous and generally places the troops between two adversaries, neither of which may particularly want them to be there. Still, it is a crucial role in a dangerous world that is divided by numerous ethnic and national conflicts.

Military defense gained renewed importance after September 11, 2001, and promulgation of the Bush doctrine of a more proactive American role in defending its interests. With the "war on terror" and threats from a number of smaller potential adversaries, downsizing the military does not appear to be viable in the first decades of the twenty-first century. Indeed, the demands on personnel, rather than technology, are likely to persist or even expand. But how can those demands be squared with the fiscal restraints now faced by the United States?

Law Enforcement

Defense involves the use of force, or the threat of the use of force, outside the borders of the United States. Law enforcement involves the legitimate use of coercion within the borders of the country. Policing traditionally has been a concern of state and local governments in the United States, but as with most other policy areas, the federal government has begun to play a larger role. This is true in terms of financial support for the subnational governments, as well as in the direct provision of police protection to the public.

Crime has been a salient issue in the United States for the past several decades.[63] Politicians have competed with one another over who could be the toughest on crime. Public concern about crime remained high even after crime rates declined significantly during the 1990s and early 2000s (see Table 15.4). Declines due to very good economic conditions, more effective policing (including "zero tolerance" in cities such as New York),[64] and demographic change[65] brought crime in the United States to levels not much greater than in western Europe and indeed lower than in some European countries. The major exception to that generalization was murder, especially murder involving firearms.

TABLE 15.4   U.S. Crime Rates (crimes per 100,000 population), 1980–2010

	Violent crimes			Property crimes		
	Total	Murder	Assault	Total	Burglary	Car theft
1980	596.6	10.2	298.5	5,353.3	1,684.1	502.2
1985	556.6	7.9	302.9	4,650.5	1,287.3	462.0
1990	731.8	9.4	424.1	5,088.5	1,235.9	657.8
1995	684.6	8.2	418.3	4,591.3	987.1	560.4
1998	567.5	6.3	361.3	4,051.8	863.0	459.8
2000	506.5	5.5	324.0	3,618.3	728.8	412.2
2002	494.6	5.6	310.1	3,624.1	746.2	432.1
2004	465.5	5.5	291.1	3,517.1	729.9	421.3
2006	473.6	5.7	287.5	3,334.5	729.4	398.4
2007	466.9	5.6	283.8	3,263.5	722.5	363.3
2010	403.6	4.8	252.3	2,941.9	696.6	238.8

Source: Federal Bureau of Investigation, *Crime in the United States* (Washington, DC: FBI, annual).

Still, several factors have presented threats to this declining crime rate. One was the release from prison of large numbers of criminals who had been incarcerated in the crackdowns of the early 1990s, few of whom had been rehabilitated by their time in prison. In addition, as the economy was cooling off, more people turned to crime to make a living. And although crime is substantially lower now than in the 1980s or early 1990s, the media and many members of the public do not seem to believe that it is. And in election years, presumably high rates of crime are good campaign claims for outsiders running for office.

Federal Law Enforcement

The role of the federal government in police protection is not entirely new. Indeed, the first organization formed at the federal level—the U.S. Coast Guard—was established primarily to catch smugglers. Countless western movies and television programs have portrayed the U.S. marshal as the principal peace officer in the territories of the American West before they gained statehood. In less dramatic settings, federal marshals have been responsible for implementing the orders of federal courts. The military has also served a law enforcement function in the past, especially when there was a threat of widespread violence or civil disorder. A notable example was President Dwight Eisenhower's use of federal troops to prevent violence when Central High School in Little Rock, Arkansas, was integrated in 1957.

Terrorism has strengthened the federal role in law enforcement, with the USA PATRIOT Act of 2001 giving the federal government new powers of search into previously privileged personal records and activities. Likewise, the federal government has become more central in coordination of state and local law enforcement efforts. The search activities of federal agencies have become a more intense political issue as the immediate threat of terrorism seems to wane and apparent abuses, such as wiretaps without warrants, become more widely known to the public.[66]

Perhaps the most familiar law enforcement organization in the federal government is the Federal Bureau of Investigation (FBI). A component of the Department of Justice, the FBI is responsible for enforcing a number of federal laws, especially the laws against kidnapping and bank robbery. During the Cold War, the FBI also had major responsibility for finding and apprehending foreign agents. That activity continues, now directed against the agents of different countries. The agency's role in protecting against terrorism has expanded, as evidenced, for example, by a massive counterterrorism database with more than 650 million records that the FBI unveiled in 2006. The FBI gained its reputation for efficiency and incorruptibility during the many years that J. Edgar Hoover was its director, and although its reputation has declined somewhat, it remains a very effective law enforcement organization.[67]

In addition to the FBI, the Coast Guard, and the federal marshals, a number of other law enforcement bodies exist within the federal government. The Secret Service, based in the Department of Homeland Security, is responsible both for protecting the safety of the president and the vice president and for catching counterfeiters of U.S. currency. Within the Justice Department, the Bureau of Alcohol, Tobacco, Firearms, and Explosives (ATF) is responsible for enforcing a variety of federal taxes and other laws having to do with the commodities in its title.[68] The Drug Enforcement Administration (DEA) enforces federal laws concerning the sale and possession of illegal drugs. Postal inspectors are responsible for enforcing laws concerning the use of the mail for fraud and other illegal purposes. The Customs Bureau is responsible for enforcing laws about imports into the United States, including some aspects of drug laws and the protection of endangered species. Finally, the Bureau of Citizenship and Immigration Services and the Border Patrol are responsible for enforcing immigration laws. This is a rather long list of organizations for a government presumably having a minimal role in law enforcement.[69]

The federal government's law enforcement activities are predicated on several powers given to it in the Constitution. One is the power to tax; the activities of the ATF and Customs stem largely from that very basic power. Many of the FBI's concerns derive from the power of the federal government to deal with issues that transcend state borders. For example, kidnapping became a federal concern after the kidnapping of the Lindbergh baby and the interstate flight of the criminal in the 1920s. The federal government also exercises its authority over interstate commerce to regulate the sale and distribution of certain drugs, with the DEA obviously deriving most of its powers from that source. Finally, the federal government's duty to protect its own officials and the value of its currency gives the Secret Service its constitutional justification.

Federal Support to State and Local Governments

In addition to providing police protection directly, the federal government supplies some support to the state and local governments that bear the major burden of policing. The type and amount have varied over time, but support from Washington for this important activity is ongoing. Fighting crime is not usually controversial, so politicians usually can feel safe in spending for this function, even when there are pressures to reduce the size of the federal budget.

John DiIulio Jr. has argued that there were two federal "wars on crime," with a third being initiated in the 1990s.[70] Echoing the founders of the programs, he claimed that the first was the War on Poverty, whose programs were an attack on the root causes of crime as well as poverty. This war was also fought with a number of more direct weapons, such as the Omnibus Crime Control and Safe

Streets Act of 1968, which provided substantial federal funding for local governments through the Law Enforcement Assistance Administration (LEAA)—more, in fact, than the entire Department of Justice budget in 1968.

The second federal war on crime opened a more direct attack on crime and criminals. That initiative, during the Reagan administration, was spearheaded by the Comprehensive Crime Control Act of 1984 and the Anti–Drug Abuse Act of 1988. The LEAA was phased out and with it much of federal support for local law enforcement (other than for antidrug programs). This war focused instead on providing stiffer sentences for perpetrators of federal crimes and especially on the links between illegal drugs and other crimes.

The third war on crime contained some elements of the strategies of each of the two previous ones. Like DiIulio's first war, it provided a good deal of money for local law enforcement—presumably 100,000 more police officers were to be on the streets because of the 1994 Crime Control Bill. That bill also contained a strong element of crime prevention and social policy.[71] Like the second war, the 1990s effort focused attention on federal crimes and federal law enforcement, specifying new death penalties for sixty federal crimes. Given public fears of crime in the mid-1990s, there was little question that the federal government should be taking an active role in fighting crime; the policy question was what form that assault should take. Federal support for local policing, other than that directly related to homeland security, has declined over the past decade, so that this third war may now be winding down.

Issues in Law Enforcement Policy

As in most policy areas, there are a number of enduring issues that help illustrate the complexity of law enforcement policy. It is sometimes easy to think that because the government has long been in the business of enforcing laws and policing, the issues and approaches to solving them would be well established. That is not the case, however. In part, the reason is that law enforcement involves the intersection of a variety of issues—whose complexity is becoming more apparent all the time—and a number of other policy areas.

The Causes of Crime

The most fundamental issue is identifying the root causes of crime. On one side is the belief that crime results from the failure of society to enforce its values on people who do not share those values. The advocates of this position argue that the best and perhaps the only way to address problems of crime is to ensure that convicted criminals receive swift, sure, and even harsh punishment.[72] Supporters of this view complain that current programs of parole and pardon put criminals back onto the streets too quickly. For example, in the 1990s, there was a move in several states and at the federal level toward "three strikes and you're out" sentencing, meaning that an individual convicted of three felonies must be imprisoned for life without the possibility of parole.[73] This problem has, in the mind of the critics, been exacerbated by overcrowding in jails that forces release of some prisoners before completing their sentences.

The contrary position is that crime results from social and economic problems, including problems in family structure. From this perspective, the best and most efficient means of dealing with crime is to address those socioeconomic issues.[74] It is argued that instead of punishing the criminal after he or she has already decided to commit a criminal act, an emphasis on the social roots of crime instead would help to prevent it. In addition to general programs for improving socioeconomic conditions, advocates have stressed the need for efforts to help parents learn how to raise their children without the violence that appears to breed additional violence.[75] Even some police forces have begun to think of their role as dealing with "problems" rather than clearing up crime "incidents." Part of the Clinton administration's crime control program, for example, was to emphasize "community-oriented policing," which attempts to develop a more positive social fabric as well as enforcing the law. This approach has been controversial, but it appears to have produced some benefits.[76]

The selection of one model of causation or another for crime in turn initiates a series of choices about how to spend public funds. If the punishment route is selected, government must spend a great deal of money for police protection and for prisons—it costs approximately $30,000 per year to keep an inmate in state prison.[77] Focusing on the social roots of crime requires a good deal of expenditure on education, social services, family support, and other similar programs, as well as on rehabilitative services for prisoners already in jail.

Neither policy choice is without costs and benefits, and the choice itself involves fundamental value decisions. Some of those values will be expressed by professional policy analysts and policymakers. Like education, crime and punishment are subjects about which the average American is likely to have an opinion, as can be seen in the responses to polls about the purpose of prisons. The American public had tended to agree that criminals can be rehabilitated and deserve a second chance, but a spate of violent crime in the 1990s reversed that opinion dramatically, and now most Americans seem to be seeking retribution rather than rehabilitation from the prison system. States are passing legislation removing educational and recreational facilities from prisons, simply as a means of punishing prisoners as harshly as possible.[78]

Gun Control

Many citizens now identify violent crime as the most important problem in their lives. Probably the major instrument of that violence is the firearm.

There are an estimated sixty million handguns in the United States, and millions of other firearms, including semiautomatic assault weapons, are in the hands of private citizens as well. The Second Amendment to the Constitution gives citizens the "right to bear arms," although that right is phrased in the context of the need for a militia.[79] The advocates of gun control point to the number of murders by handguns each year (approximately 7,400 in 2007—over half the total) to argue for their control, especially the cheap "Saturday night specials" that are bought and used in the heat of the moment.[80] Opponents of gun control counter that criminals will always find a way to get guns and that law-abiding citizens need some means of protecting themselves, their families, and their property.

Nearly all large local governments require that handguns be registered. Some also require a waiting period between application for purchase of a handgun and the delivery of the weapon, to give the police time to check on the reliability of the purchaser. The federal government has regulated automatic weapons and other especially dangerous guns since the days of Prohibition and the fight against gangsters. More recently, it began to regulate sales of weapons through the mail, and in 1993, Congress passed the "Brady bill," which imposed a federal requirement for a five-day waiting period between application for a handgun and its delivery.[81] The states have their own laws on gun sales, making firearms more available in some states than in others, although guns are often purchased in one state and then used in another.

It is clear that there is no absolute right for a citizen to own any type of gun he or she wants, or to get it anytime he or she wants. The question is what sort of restrictions are permissible under the Constitution—and politically possible. The National Rifle Association (NRA) has developed into an active, well-financed, and usually successful lobbying organization that is dedicated to opposing gun control. Some thought that the passage of the Brady law was a signal of declining NRA influence.[82] Its power appeared to wane further when its lobbyists failed to remove the ban on assault weapons from the 1994 Clinton crime bill. However, the Republican Congress during the George W. Bush administration was less interested in gun control and in 2004 allowed the ban on assault weapons to lapse. Congress also failed to renew strict gun control laws in the District of Columbia.[83]

Despite lobbying by the NRA, gun control tends to be popular among the American populace. For example, in a poll taken just before Congress allowed the assault weapons ban to lapse, over two-thirds of respondents favored the ban.[84] In a 2009 poll, 60 percent of respondents favored stricter gun laws.[85] The only measure for which there is no majority support is an absolute ban on guns; according to a 2008 poll, only 13 percent of Americans favor a measure of that sort.[86] Tragic events such as the shooting of Trayvon Martin have highlighted the number of guns on the streets of the United States, but state legislatures continue to pass legislation favoring carrying concealed weapons even in church.

The Death Penalty

Related to the question of punishment of criminals is whether government should impose the ultimate sanction, the death penalty. In general, Americans answer yes to that question, which leads to the subsidiary question of the circumstances in which it should be imposed. Thirty-eight states now have prisoners under a sentence of death. Some such as Florida and Texas apply the death penalty vigorously, whereas in other states, it is rarely imposed. The federal government also enforces the death penalty for certain federal crimes, the list of which was increased dramatically by the 1994 crime bill. The increase in the use of the death penalty appears to suit most Americans: 72 percent of respondents favored the death penalty in a 1993 survey, and almost two-thirds continued to support it in 2008.[87]

The arguments over this issue are practical, constitutional, and moral.[88] The practical questions concern whether the death penalty is really an effective deterrent to violent crime. Advocates believe that it is, although some of the states with the highest murder rates are also among those that impose the penalty most readily. Proponents also contend that it is a certain deterrent in preventing the criminal in question from committing any more crimes. Opponents of the death penalty argue that it is not really a deterrent and that most of the acts for which it is now imposed are more products of the passion of the moment than calculated choices by the perpetrators. Opponents also point out that the legal work now required to implement the death penalty is monumental and often costs a government more than might be spent in keeping the convicted criminal in jail for life.

The number of errors in convictions uncovered in 2001 and 2002, using DNA evidence in particular, has led some states such as Illinois to suspend the death penalty and to review all cases. Since the original findings in Illinois, a large number of incorrect convictions have been detected.[89] Those findings have produced dramatic results, even in normally conservative states, but have left the underlying system of capital punishment in place.[90]

The constitutional questions revolve around whether the Eighth Amendment to the Constitution, which outlaws "cruel and unusual punishment," prohibits the death penalty. Supporters of the penalty argue that when that amendment was written, the death penalty was used widely, so it could not be considered *unusual;* that term, they claim, referred instead to practices such as torture. Opponents of the death penalty, on the other hand, argue that it is indeed *cruel* under contemporary interpretations of that word. For several decades, the Supreme Court tended to side with the opponents and in effect outlawed the execution of prisoners.[91] But the Court reversed its stand in 1976 and began to permit the death penalty in certain defined situations. In 2002, the Court ruled, in *Atkins v. Virginia,* that executing criminals with mental retardation constituted "cruel and unusual" punishment. Battles to determine the limits of action in that area have continued.[92]

A second constitutional question is whether the death penalty, as currently administered, violates the Equal Protection Clause of the Fourteenth Amendment. Opponents of capital punishment argue that African Americans and other minorities are much more likely to be put to death than are whites, even when the crimes they have committed are roughly comparable.[93] They also point to a pronounced economic bias in the imposition of the penalty, for poor defendants often have difficulty in securing adequate legal counsel to avoid being sentenced to death.[94] Supporters of the death penalty argue that more violent crimes per capita are committed by members of minority groups and that the differential rate of executions merely reflects an unfortunate social reality.

There is also a moral question about the use of the power of the state to put people to death.[95] Critics of the death penalty argue that it makes government and society little better than the criminals they are punishing and that the finality of the sentence runs the risk of executing innocent people who then have no recourse. As with decision theory, the probability (even if small) that the decision to execute is incorrect will produce social costs that may be greater than any benefits created. Supporters of the death penalty recognize the severity of the punishment, and few if any take the imposition of the death penalty lightly. They argue that individuals who commit extremely brutal crimes and crimes against certain types of victims (children, for example) have forfeited their right to live in a civilized society.

The debate over the death penalty continues. Supporters hailed the inclusion of a large number of new death penalties in the Clinton crime bill and the Supreme Court decision that reduced the capacity of convicts on death row to receive stays of their sentences.[96] Opponents of capital punishment were buoyed when Justice Harry Blackmun, near retirement, wrote a dissenting opinion saying that he would no longer take part in any decisions to execute prisoners, despite the fact that he had voted a number of times previously to permit states to impose the death penalty.[97] That statement by a respected justice caused some reassessment, but there have been no shifts in the legality or use of the death penalty. The more conservative turn in the Supreme Court after two appointments by President George W. Bush is likely to mean its continued and perhaps expanded use.

A number of states have now suspended the use of the death penalty until there can be greater certainty about the validity of the convictions. A number of convictions have been overturned by new DNA evidence, and governors and state legislatures have decided that the risk of wrongful executions is too great.[98] A nongovernmental organization (NGO), the Innocence Project, has been especially active in having possibly suspect cases reviewed and in having a number of convictions overturned.

The Rights of the Accused

In addition to protections against cruel and unusual punishment, the Bill of Rights affirms a number of protections for a person accused of a crime. For example, the accused are protected against self-incrimination (Fifth Amendment) and against unlawful searches and seizures of their persons and properties (Fourth Amendment). They are ensured a trial by an impartial jury, and they are guaranteed that the writ of habeas corpus is available to them so that they will know why they are being arrested and so that they cannot be held for long periods without formal charge (Article I, section 9). Finally, accused citizens have a right to legal counsel when they go to court (and now as soon as they are arrested).

This is an impressive list of protections. In fact, some critics believe that the list is too long and that the police are being handcuffed in their attempts to arrest and convict criminals. That feeling has become more pronounced over the past several decades as the courts have tended to interpret the rights of the accused more broadly and to require the police to be more careful in how they treat the accused. For example, when arrested, a suspect must be advised of his or her legal rights, including the right to counsel.[99] The courts have also tended to interpret the protections against unreasonable search strictly, so the police must have sound reasons to obtain a search warrant and even stronger justification if they search without first receiving a warrant. (Still, in the media event that was the O. J. Simpson trial, the judge admitted some crucial evidence gathered before a search warrant had been issued because it was discovered incidental to other, proper police activities.[100]) All these protections have produced cries that too many criminals are able to escape conviction on mere technicalities.

The defenders of the current restrictions on police behavior contend that civil liberties are more than technicalities; they are fundamental to the nature of the American political system and the judicial process. They argue that if police and prosecutors cannot make sustainable cases against defendants within these restrictions, they are not doing their jobs properly. They further point out that the police now have a number of powerful scientific tools, such as DNA testing, that should enable them to gain convictions without having to resort to dubious means of investigation. These defenders, in fact, would be willing to sacrifice a few convictions to ensure that the fundamental civil liberties of all Americans are protected. Concerns about terrorism have placed civil liberties under greater strain in the United States, with some prisoners being detained without even being identified and domestic surveillance increased. Such actions by the federal government have provoked some public outcry but little change in the direction of government policy in the pursuit of terrorists. Civil libertarians fear that these patterns will become more entrenched for nonterrorist offenses.

Associated with the perceived difficulty of prosecuting accused criminals is the issue of pardon and parole. Newspapers often feature accounts of paroled convicts committing major crimes, sometimes within days of having been released from prison. On the other hand, the possibility of parole is often a motivating factor for cooperation by prisoners in what could otherwise be extremely dangerous settings.[101] In addition, prisons in most states are filled to capacity—the United States has the highest rate of incarceration per capita of any industrial democracy. Without the option for early release, even more prisons would have to be built, imposing further demands on state and local resources. As with most policy problems, there is no quick and easy answer.

Youth Crime

An issue in law enforcement that became prominent in the late 1990s is the problem of violent crimes committed by children. A number of cases in 1997 and 1998 of children taking guns to school and attacking their classmates and teachers produced real shock and made the public highly aware of this issue (although the evidence is that there has always been more such crime than is usually realized).[102] The continuing spate of violent crimes by children and teenagers has kept this issue at the center of the debate on criminal justice. This controversy has been heightened when some states treat children as adults in the criminal justice process and put even preteens into jail for the remainder of their lives.[103]

In light of the earlier discussion of gun control, it is important to observe that all of these notorious incidents of juvenile violence involved guns. That has led to calls for requirements that all guns be locked so that they cannot be accessed by children or others who may want to use them unwisely. Not surprisingly, this proposal has been opposed by the National Rifle Association and other pro-gun groups. Another question raised by these killings is how to treat the young perpetrators. Should they be prosecuted in the same manner as any other crime, or should they, as occurs in almost all instances, be subject to separate legal standards? Two boys who killed four people in Arkansas, for example, can only be kept in jail (or other institutions) until they reach the age of twenty-one.

Summary

We have been discussing the ways in which governments in the United States attempt to protect their citizens from "enemies, domestic and foreign." This is one of the defining duties of any government,[104] and it is one in which governments have been engaged since their inception. The issues involved in this policy area, however, have become more complex in recent years. First, in defense there is no longer a clearly identifiable enemy against which to plot strategy. Instead, the task is to prepare for a wide range of threats to national security, including some for which the military is not particularly well adapted. There are demands for use of the military for a range of purposes that go well beyond conventional national defense and require it to fulfill virtually a social mission on the international scene. Finally, domestic social and political concerns have invaded the world of the armed forces, requiring some rethinking of the values and mores of that world.

Crime is an equally complex policy and political problem. It is perhaps even more complex than defense because the United States attempts to combat crime while maintaining an open and free society. Some police measures that might curtail the growth of crime are simply not possible if an open society is to be maintained. Even without the complications of civil liberties, there would be other difficulties for a government attempting to solve a serious crime problem, not least of which is understanding the root causes of this social pathology and therefore the best means of addressing it.

CHAPTER 16

Culture Wars in American Politics: Regulating Social Life

THE AMERICAN REPUBLIC was founded with the separation of church and state enshrined in the First Amendment to the Constitution. Despite the attempt to create a secular republic, issues having strong moral or religious dimensions—slavery, civil rights, peace in Vietnam—have become defining ones for the country. During the past several decades, politics has again injected intense moral and religious conflicts into the heart of the policy process.[1] Issues such as abortion, school prayer, stem cell research, human cloning, the right to die, and equal treatment of same-sex partnerships have become prominent on the political agenda. And even when U.S. government is not actively engaged in making decisions on these matters, they nevertheless figure as litmus tests for candidates for office at all levels of government. These conflicts have been described as "culture wars" because they tend to divide citizens sharply on the basis of religious, social, and cultural conceptions of right and wrong.

Background

Before proceeding to discuss some of these conflicts in more detail, we should recognize some of their common characteristics that have often profound political consequences. Unfortunately, it is those shared characteristics that make the issues difficult for the political process to handle effectively, in ways that will satisfy the participants in the process. All political problems divide people, but the fissures that these moral issues create are deeper and more difficult to contain within the civil and constrained discourse of the conventional political process. The term *culture wars* is apt, given the intensity with which those involved are likely to approach conflicts among fundamentally different notions of what is acceptable or appropriate in society.[2]

The most obvious point about these issues is that they tend to be nonbargainable for the participants. Most issues that arise in government are resolved through bargaining and compromise, with each side gaining something and each side having to accept some losses. These moral issues, however, are nonbargainable for at least two reasons. The first is simply that they are conceived of as fundamental questions of right and wrong: Abortion is either an appropriate means of limiting fertility, or it is a sin, and there is little ground for compromise. The claims of right and wrong in the cases of abortion and other issues are based on different moral foundations. For opponents of abortion, it is primarily a religious matter, but for advocates of choice it is about a woman's human right to choose how her own body is to be used. The opposing groups have a great deal to scream about but little to talk about.

The difficulty of finding a middle ground on such a subject was well illustrated by President George W. Bush's decision to permit limited federal funding for research on embryonic stem cells in 2001.[3] The decision was an attempt to compromise by allowing federal support for research on existing "lines" of stem cells, while prohibiting funding for creating or doing research on any new lines.[4] The president's decision angered religious conservatives, who regard any stem cell research as using human beings for research purposes and as encouraging abortions as the means of obtaining those cells. On the other side, many scientists believed that the decision did not provide enough freedom for them to pursue the research they believed could lead to cures for Alzheimer's, Parkinson's, and other diseases. These scientists also implied that the decision demonstrated, at least to their minds, a greater commitment to religious than to scientific values, and at least a few top medical researchers then went to Europe, where they felt the climate for research on stem cells was less restrictive.[5] The president's attempt to create a Solomonic compromise was not acceptable to the strong advocates on either side of the issue, and perhaps the only factor preventing an even greater political uproar was the difficulty that the average citizen encountered in attempting to understand the scientific and moral issues involved.[6]

The second reason for the inutility of bargaining over such moral issues is that most of them are not amenable to solution through the application of money. No amount of funding for sex education, adoption, or any other alternative to abortion will make its continuation acceptable in the eyes of opponents. No amount of money spent on benefits for same-sex partners—no matter how desirable that may otherwise be—will make up for the absence of legal recognition for same-sex marriages in the eyes of proponents.[7] In short, although money is the standard lubricant in the political process, it is not likely to be effective in ameliorating conflicts based on fundamental moral and ethical disagreements. Indeed, even the suggestion of a monetary response may be considered insulting or demeaning by activists.

The futility of monetary solutions to these policy problems underscores their nonutilitarian nature. Most policy disputes are framed primarily on pragmatic, utilitarian principles—will the program in question work, and will society be better off (usually as measured in economic terms) if it does work?[8] The moral issues we are discussing here, however, are more often framed in terms of absolute values. It is not likely to matter to the parties involved whether the society would be better off economically if fundamental moral precepts were violated to achieve that utilitarian benefit. In this corner of the policy world, the ends most definitely do not justify the means.

Another common characteristic of these moral policies is that their politics is often carried on as energetically outside formal institutions as within them, and that increases the potential for extremists to become activated by the intensity of the arguments. This characteristic has been most evident in the continuing abortion controversy, but it has also figured in debates over the rights of homosexuals and was clearly manifested during early civil rights struggles. Despite the abundant legislation—and even more attempted legislation—on abortion, the majority of the debate appears to have taken place in the streets. Indeed, some extremists have gone so far as to use guns and bombs in attempts to enforce what they believe to be the correct moral choice and to punish their enemies. Somewhat ironically, a Kansas abortion provider was murdered in church in 2009. For a country in which politics has been largely nonideological and in general rather tame, this militant style of political behavior is both unexpected and more difficult to accept than it might be in other countries.

The politics that these moral issues generate often involves constitutional disputes that must be decided in the courts rather than through legislation. That has been true for abortion (*Roe v. Wade*), for school prayer (*Engel v. Vitale*), and for the use of "under God" in the Pledge of Allegiance (*Newdow v. Elk Grove Unified School District*), on which the principal contemporary debates have been sparked by court cases rather than by acts of Congress or state legislatures.[9] Ever since the Supreme Court ruled that school prayer violated the separation of church and state, proponents of the practice have been attempting to find a formulation—silent prayer, a moment of silence, voluntary prayer—that could permit religious activity while still passing constitutional muster. Even if one or more of these watered-down options is eventually found acceptable by the courts (see below), such compromise is unlikely to please committed advocates of prayer, who will still want to make conventional religious observance a part of the school day. Similarly, there have been any number of legislative attempts to restrict access to abortion services, but the courts have been the final arbiters of what is constitutional and what is not, sanctioning some of the legislative efforts but rejecting others.[10]

Three public policy areas, which I will discuss in this chapter, vividly illustrate the common characteristics of moral issues in politics. Among the most contentious issues in American politics, they have been fought over by activists some of whom are willing to go to jail and even to kill those with whom they disagree because of their strong commitment to the principles involved. The issues vary in the intensity with which they have been contested in the streets, in the courts, and in legislative bodies, but all provoke reactions that surpass those typically expressed on matters of policy. Government and court decisions about these issues have served merely as temporary truces in the continuing battles over values, as the losers in every decision are unwilling to accept it as final and so continue to soldier on in the culture war.

Abortion and Reproductive Rights

If any issue best illustrates our points about moral and cultural politics, it is abortion. In 1972, a woman, who was referred to as "Jane Roe" in legal documents to preserve her privacy and anonymity, sought to have an abortion that did not meet the current legal criteria for the procedure in Texas. At that time in Texas, abortion was only legal to preserve the life of the mother. Other states permitted termination of a pregnancy (a) if it endangered the life or health (including mental health) of the woman, (b) if it was likely to result in a severely deformed infant, or (c) if it was the consequence of rape or incest. When the *Roe* case finally reached the Supreme Court in 1973, the Court ruled that based on the right of privacy, a woman had a constitutionally protected right to terminate a pregnancy within the first trimester, regardless of the reason or possible consequences of the pregnancy.[11]

Abortion had been illegal in most of the United States for some years, although it was not criminalized until the mid-nineteenth century. Therapeutic abortions, albeit often extremely unsafe, were common in the early days of the United States, as they were in Europe at that time.[12] During the American equivalent of the Victorian period in Britain, individual states began to enact legislation limiting abortion and making anyone performing the procedure, and sometimes the woman herself, subject to severe criminal penalties. As a consequence of those laws, although an unknown number of abortions apparently occurred, almost all were done by untrained individuals in settings less than ideal for the health of the pregnant woman. The result was often severe illness or death, although because the procedure was illegal, no accurate enumeration of cases was available.

In part because abortion had been illegal almost universally until the decision in 1973, the religious basis of the laws adopted by the states was not manifest. Indeed, religious groups do not appear to have been directly involved in the criminalization of abortion in the nineteenth century. However, following the familiar political dictum that major policy decisions motivate the losers, the Supreme Court decisions in *Roe v. Wade* and *Doe v. Bolton* activated the Roman

Catholic Church and elements of the religious right, injecting them into American politics to a degree that had rarely been seen previously.[13] Likewise, prior to the time the two women in question brought their cases, there had been relatively little political mobilization around the abortion issue, even among feminists and other elements of the women's movement. Once the Supreme Court acted, however, activist groups on both sides of the issue, but particularly on the antiabortion side, sprang to battle on all political fronts.

It is important to note that the decisions rendered by the Court in *Roe* and *Doe* had little or no basis in the Establishment Clause of the First Amendment, as might have been expected. Instead, the decisions were based directly on the (implied) constitutional right of a woman not to have government intervene in her personal reproductive life. The privacy argument, which is essentially individualistic in its import, might have been thought to please conservatives, but the result was the opposite. Abortion politics brought together a wide range of activists on the political right to defend what they considered traditional moral and religious values. The coalition of religious groups cut across conventional political and denominational lines, bringing together Roman Catholics, Orthodox Jews, fundamentalist Protestants, and Mormons, among others. Abortion was not only (in the view of most of these groups) murder, but also it was a threat to "family values" as they defined them.

As well as being a rallying point for the religious (and less religious) right, abortion rights have been, and continue to be, a touchstone issue for women's political organizations and their supporters, as well as for civil libertarians. In *Roe,* the Supreme Court created what was in essence a new right for women, and many (if not most—see Table 16.1) are loath to relinquish that right. As more time passes, fewer and fewer women who are active politically can remember a time when they did not have the right to a legal, safe abortion should they desire one. The argument of most abortion rights groups is that although abortion is far from the preferred option for controlling fertility, it is one that they want and demand to have available if required.

The Rhetoric of Abortion Politics

The nature of the rhetoric surrounding this issue, as should be evident from the discussion above, serves to illustrate some of the points made earlier about issues of this type. Each side in the controversy tends to employ arguments and terminology that are dear to the hearts of their supporters but that tend to demonize and alienate the opposition. At times, the extremist rhetoric and graphic symbols used may alienate even some moderates, but ideological purity tends to be more important than coalition building in this policy area. As one analyst of the contemporary political scene has observed, this debate over abortion rights has no neutral ground.[14]

TABLE 16.1 Public Attitudes about Abortion, 1996–2012 (in percentages)

	Abortion should be:				
	Always legal	*Legal in most cases*	*Illegal in most cases*	*Never legal*	*Not sure*
June 1996	24	34	25	14	2
July 1998	19	35	29	13	4
July 2000	20	33	26	17	4
August 2001	22	27	28	20	3
January 2003	23	34	25	17	3
December 2005	17	40	27	13	3
July 2007	23	34	28	14	2
June 2009	20	35	26	17	2
March, 2012	21	33	26	17	2

Source: ABC News/*Washington Post* polls, www.washingtonpost.com.

Even the naming of the opposing sides in the debate is calculated to create political advantage and to emphasize the values that the advocates are attempting to promote. On one side, the opponents of abortion use the term *pro-life* to describe their movement. It is difficult to be against life, although the term invites the question of when life begins, but the activists claim that they are favoring life while their opponents are sending thousands of innocent children to their deaths. This rhetorical frame has created a powerful argument for the opponents of abortion, but the attempt to illustrate it by the use of graphic pictures of fetuses has lessened its appeal to the less committed.

On the other side of the debate, the defenders of a woman's right to a legal abortion define their position as being *pro-choice*. Although this term does not carry the emotional appeal of supporting life, in a democratic society, the notion that individuals should have the ability to make their own choices is a powerful political argument. Again, activists on this side of the debate do not advocate abortion as a positive or desirable action but as an option that should be available if a woman deems it necessary. The principle at the center of this side's arguments is that the choice should be made by the woman herself rather than by a doctor or by a public authority of any sort.

Political and Policy Reactions to Roe and Doe

Almost as soon as the Supreme Court announced its decisions legalizing abortion, governments, as well as the foes of abortion, began to find ways to circumvent what appeared to be a sweeping acceptance of abortion rights. Religious and political foes of the rulings engaged in a variety of direct political and social actions, including blockading clinics and even hospitals providing abortion services. In reaction, leaders of the pro-choice movement developed programs to escort women wanting to go to those facilities through the gauntlets of pro-testers, and in some cases, they also were able to get police protection for the clients of the clinics.

Not only was there direct political mobilization around the abortion issue, but interest groups also began to mobilize to support, and especially to oppose, freely available abortion services. The early supporters of abortion rights were women's organizations, such as the National Organization for Women (NOW), but after the increased politicizing of the issue, more narrowly focused organizations such as the National Abortion and Reproductive Rights Action League, or NARAL (now NARAL Pro-Choice America), were formed to protect the rights that had been secured through the Court decisions. On the other side of the political conflict, interest groups and religious organizations have mobilized to attempt to reverse *Roe,* and they have focused on an annual event at the National Mall and the Supreme Court building that has brought out thousands of abortion opponents.

Abortion politics demonstrates the capacity of intense political mobilization to shape policies. When asked in public opinion polls, the majority of Americans (and a large majority of women) favor preserving a woman's right to seek an abortion in some or all cases. In 2008, only 17 percent of Americans said they would ban abortions entirely, and another 26 percent said they would permit them only in cases of threat to the mother's life.[15] These figures appear to have remained relatively stable over time. Thus, the majority of Americans would permit abortions in a relatively wide range of cases, yet the majority of state legislatures have passed laws that would severely restrict access. The Christian Coalition, the Roman Catholic Church, and their allies have been able to influence legislatures to make policies that do not correspond closely to public opinion on the issue.

Abortion law has been made primarily at the state level in the United States. The major Court decisions brought the federal government more into the policy area by striking down state laws that were deemed unconstitutional, but they did not by any means end the dominant state role. Since the time of *Roe* and *Doe,* state legislatures have generated a large number of policy responses, most being attempts to prevent abortions through means other than direct prohibition, such as restricting availability of the procedure, without directly confronting the rulings of the Court. A common strategy has been to require women below a certain age to obtain the consent of one or both parents or guardians before having an abortion.[16] The courts, however, have tended to disallow such blanket requirements, again in the interest of privacy, and have required the states to provide alternative mechanisms for approval, usually through the judicial system (*Bellotti v. Baird,* 1976; *Hodgson v. Minnesota,* 1990). Likewise, a number of states have adopted provisions requiring the woman's male partner to consent to an abortion, but those restrictions generally have also been disallowed by the courts.

Another regulatory strategy has been to impose waiting periods ("cooling-off periods") and detailed reporting requirements on hospitals and doctors. The logic of this approach seems to be that the trouble of having to come to a hospital or center twice may persuade a woman to abandon the attempt or may offer abortion opponents the chance to identify women seeking the procedure so as to attempt to dissuade them. The courts, however, have tended to throw out restrictions without clear medical reasons to justify them and to negate specific medical requirements imposed by legislation. One exception has been that most states now ban late-term abortions, and this legislation has largely been successful.

The control of public spending has been a major means by which governments have attempted to discourage abortion. In general, this policy instrument has been more successful than have the regulatory instruments described above (see chapter 5). At the federal level, the Hyde Amendment to the 1976 appropriations bill for the Labor and Health, Education, and Welfare Departments (named after Rep. Henry Hyde, R-IL) prohibited the use of federal funds for abortions. At the state level, many public hospitals have been barred from performing abortions except in the most extreme cases. In 2003, Congress passed the Partial Birth Abortion Act, outlawing a certain abortion procedure except in extreme cases of threat to the mother's health. Several states had already enacted such laws, and most of those, and the federal law, have been found to be unconstitutional for much the same reasons as in *Roe v. Wade.*

On the other side of the controversy, there have been some legislative and administrative attempts to defend women's access to abortion services. For example, the courts have upheld the use of antiracketeering laws to punish conspiracies to use violence against abortion providers. Congress also has passed legislation—the Freedom of Access to Clinic Entrances Act (FACE)—that attempts to protect women from harassment when they go to an abortion clinic and also provides some protection to the abortion providers. This legislation was designed to deter physical intimidation by abortion opponents, and it has been deemed constitutional by the Supreme Court, in part because it protects individuals and organizations engaged in interstate commerce.[17]

Both antiabortion groups and abortion rights groups have been active in scrutinizing judicial appointees and in placing pressure on the president and governors to appoint judges who will conform to the groups' preferred policies. Antiabortion groups, which want abortion views to be the litmus test for appointees to public office, were very active in the early days of the George W. Bush administration, hoping to ensure that another "stealth" pro–abortion rights justice would not be appointed to the Supreme Court, as had occurred during the administration of George H. W. Bush.[18] The abortion rights groups also have been active in scrutinizing candidates, but they have not been so vociferous in promoting views on abortion as the single criterion for judging prospective judicial appointees. These issues were argued strongly in the confirmation hearings of Supreme Court justices John Roberts and Samuel Alito in 2006.[19] Likewise, in summer 2009, abortion rights advocates expressed uneasiness about the centrist views of Sonia Sotomayor, President Obama's nominee to the Supreme Court, on the issue.

The controversy over abortion and contraception came to the political agenda again in 2012 when the Obama administration required all insurance programs, even those offered by Catholic institutions, to provide contraception and abortion services to their female participants. The Catholic Church argued that this was an infringement of their religious freedom, while women's organizations argued for the reproductive health of women (especially those working in Catholic institutions but who were not themselves Catholic).[20]

Although abortion remains constitutional, the net effect of the various political actions during the past several decades has been to limit access to abortion in much of the country. Physical intimidation, legal restrictions, and high insurance premiums have driven out potential providers. After an initial increase when *Roe v. Wade* was decided, the number of legal abortions performed in the United States has been declining because of both behavioral changes and legal constraints.[21]

Gay Rights: Politics Comes Out of the Closet

Abortion policy has been conceptualized by abortion rights groups as an issue that affects all women, even if only a very small number of women actually have the need or the desire to resort to it. The issue of the rights of gay and lesbian citizens affects, directly or indirectly, all members of those groups, although they are a relatively small segment of the American population. Political mobilization around rights and protections for homosexuals grew most rapidly during the 1980s and 1990s, although the event usually cited as the movement's beginning point was the Stonewall riots in New York in 1969, directed against police harassment of a gay bar by that name. By 1993, the movement could muster 300,000 supporters for a march in Washington.[22]

Perhaps even more than abortion, homosexuality has historically and traditionally been suppressed by law and custom in most societies. Western societies had, and continue to have in some cases, laws that punish homosexual activities rather severely. The social stigma has been at least as powerful, with gay people bearing the brunt of jokes, exclusion, and violence. Most members of the homosexual community thus opted to stay "in the closet," publicly denying their sexual preference. For much of history, keeping that sexual preference secret was a wise strategy, given that openly admitting it might cause loss of employment, social ostracism, and even personal violence.

The politics of gay and lesbian issues is about identity as well as rights. An important motivation for political mobilization has been to claim the right of individuals with sexual preferences different from those of the majority to be treated as the equals of the majority. Slogans such as "Gay Pride" have been used to rally supporters and to create a greater sense of belonging within the homosexual community. The idea of such political rhetoric is that not only is it acceptable to be gay, but also it has become a source of pride and activism for many. In response, the opposition has attempted to deny the appropriateness of that pride, and even that identity, and to drive the gay movement and its members back into the closet.

The coalition that has opposed gay rights is rather similar to that which has opposed abortion rights for women. In this case, however, the Roman Catholic Church is not so prominent, leaving conservative, fundamentalist Protestants to lead the fight instead. Although the Catholic Church has hardly been supportive of gay and lesbian rights, its condemnation of homosexuality has not been so overt, despite denying admitted homosexuals the opportunity to be priests.[23] The political opposition to gay rights has argued that the groups are seeking special rights and special protections for which there is no constitutional basis. At the extreme, opponents also insist that gay rights groups' demands for recognition and acceptance are undermining the moral standards of the country and are opposed to "family values"—a term that has to some extent become a code name for conservative, fundamentalist conceptions of morality.[24]

Members of gay and lesbian groups regard their political activity as simply demanding the right to equal treatment. For example, when claiming employee benefits for same-sex partners, gays and lesbians argue that they want only to have their relationships treated like other stable partnerships, qualifying them for the same legal and financial benefits that are routinely extended to heterosexual married couples. The opposition forces, again often basing their arguments on traditional religious values, characterize these claims as something more.[25] They argue, for example, that employee benefit packages are intended for married couples only and that in many cases, unmarried heterosexual couples are not eligible, even if they are in stable relationships. More recently, the right for gays to marry legally has been a central issue, with numerous states passing legislation recognizing such a right. This in turn has forced conflicts between the Federal Protection of Marriage Act and the rights of states to regulate such matters.

The conflict over the status and rights of the gay population has not been extended as broadly throughout the political community as has the conflict over abortion rights. Some interest groups have been formed, and some lobbying and other attempts to influence policy have been initiated. Rather than a collection of interest groups, however, mobilization of the gay community initially assumed the form of a social movement, whose approach was less one of direct contact with government and bargaining over specific policies than it was attempting to raise the issues of concern to the group through broad public appeals and to create solidarity among the members.

Again, the battle over gay rights is often joined not so much in the legislative arena as in the courts. In particular, legal cases have been filed to prevent landlords from discriminating in housing and employers from dismissing workers because of their sexual orientation. Although not as visible as *Roe v. Wade,* these cases are as important to the members of the gay community, as well as to their opponents. For example, the courts have been central in defining rights to gay marriage at the state level. Also, state and federal courts have been involved in ruling on a variety of state laws and constitutional amendments, with the cases usually brought on the grounds of equal protection.[26]

Gay Rights and Public Policy

Gay rights is itself an important public policy issue, with strong elements of civil rights and equality. However, the political mobilization of the gay community has also raised a number of more immediate policy issues. Some of those have affected only the homosexual community, but others have had wider relevance such as AIDS research and treatment. As we noted earlier, the style of political activism invoked on gay rights issues has been less that of interest groups and more that of a movement. Still, as that movement has become institutionalized, so too have the forms of interaction between it and government.

One of the most important political milestones in that interaction occurred during the Clinton administration with respect to military service. During his first presidential campaign, Bill Clinton had advocated greater rights for the gay community and had received overwhelming support from those voters. One issue that his gay supporters wanted addressed was elimination of the prohibition against homosexuals' serving in the military. Once elected, President Clinton encountered substantial resistance from the military to any change in the existing policy. Military leaders defended their traditional stance of excluding homosexuals by arguing that permitting homosexuals to serve alongside heterosexual soldiers would be detrimental to morale.

The solution that the Clinton administration developed was labeled "Don't ask, don't tell," meaning that there would be no efforts on the part of the military to seek out gays within its ranks so long as those individuals did nothing that was indeed detrimental to the morale or good conduct of their unit. Again,

Alex Wong/Getty Images

Sandra Fluke, a law student at Georgetown University, meets with House Minority Leader. Nancy Pelosi, D-CA, on February 23, 2012, as Rep. Elijah Cummings , D-MD, looks on, following her testimony before the House Democratic Steering and Policy Committee on contraception. Social issues such as abortion and same-sex marriage divide the American population and continue to motivate political actions to oppose and support the various proposals being debated in Congress and in the states.

compromises are rarely entirely satisfying on issues of this sort, and this was no exception. The gay community thought that President Clinton had reneged on his commitments once elected and faced with opposition. On the other hand, many leaders in the military believed that this policy did indeed undermine discipline and morale and that a president with no military experience had intervened in an unacceptable manner. In 2011, this policy was repealed so that more openly homosexual recruits would be accepted into the military.

In addition to issues of identity, the gay community's political involvement has focused on how to combat HIV/AIDS. When the nature and epidemiology of the disease became known during the 1980s, it sparked widespread recognition within the gay community that rather than being a question of lifestyle, politics in the gay community had become a question of life. This produced high levels of mobilization and political organization in cities such as San Francisco, and the gay community became active in public health and safe-sex campaigns. At the national level, this mobilization also produced campaigns to increase funding for research on a cure for HIV/AIDS. A massive increase in such research has since led to drug regimens that can at least hold the disease in check, if not cure it.

One interesting consequence of this campaign for new treatments for HIV/ AIDS is that it put pressure on the Food and Drug Administration to fast-track drugs that might be beneficial for treating the disease. That is, rather than accepting the usual lengthy approval process required before drugs are allowed to go on the market, interest groups such as Human Rights Campaign, Lambda Legal, and National Gay and Lesbian Task Force exerted pressure to speed up approval for drugs that might help. Pointing out that individuals with AIDS were in imminent danger of death, activists argued that trying something was better than just letting them die. This successful campaign opened the door for more rapid approval of drugs for other extremely deadly diseases. There have been some cases of drugs reaching the market that have extreme side effects or relatively little efficacy, but most people with such diseases appear willing to opt for a chance while they are living rather than a certainty after they are dead.

Another unusual aspect of the political conflict over the rights of homosexuals is that referendums to guarantee the right to equal treatment in employment and housing have been contested in a number of localities. In some cases, these elections were promoted by advocates of equal rights for gay and lesbian citizens and in other cases by opponents, generally in response to actions by state or local governments that extended such rights. The arguments advanced in these elections are rather predictable. Advocates of the rights of gays and lesbians contend that they should not be discriminated against because of their sexual preference and that they are entitled to the same protections as other minority groups. Some opponents base their objections on religious grounds, asserting that government should not protect a lifestyle that they believe contradicts biblical teachings. Others more simply maintain that there is no constitutional basis for this kind of protection, and therefore it is not appropriate. That is in many cases simply a more polite and legalistic version of the first argument.

Referendums on gay rights have achieved highly variable outcomes, winning in some unlikely places and failing in others where success seemed more likely. As is often the case in the referendum process, the precise wording of the proposition on the ballot plays a role in determining the outcome. So, for example, referendums expressed in terms of granting rights to groups appear to be less successful than ones phrased in terms of preventing negative discrimination against gay and lesbian people. In general, however, the concept of defending the rights of all segments of society, rather than specific segments, appears to have substantial appeal to the public.

Legislation by Congress and state legislatures to create greater rights for members of the gay and lesbian communities has been relatively infrequent, given that much of the voting population is conservative on issues of sexual preference and the opposition tends to be well organized and vocal. Nevertheless, some states have passed legislation that supports the policy goals of gay activists.

For example, Vermont has passed legislation permitting same-sex civil unions, and a number of states have prohibited discrimination on the basis of sexual preference, on the same principle as is used to ban discrimination based on race or gender. That legislation has not gone unchallenged, however, and in a number of instances, it has led to further legal and political conflicts over allegations of special treatment for these groups.

State courts, more than the federal courts, have been active in advancing some of the interests of the gay and lesbian communities. For example, the Supreme Court of Massachusetts decided in 2005 that the state constitution did not permit discrimination against gay couples who wanted to marry. State legislatures have responded by attempting to overturn such court decisions by law or amendments to state constitutions, but in some instances, the rights of gay couples to marry have been maintained.

On the other hand, some measures have been introduced to limit the use of public funds for any programs that advance the goals of the gay and lesbian community. For example, the Defense of Marriage Act, passed by Congress in 1996, stated that for the purposes of any federal program, marriage was to be defined as between two people of the opposite sex and, further, that no state would be required to recognize same-sex marriages performed in another state. Couples coming from those few states that have sanctioned same-sex marriages thus may find themselves in a legal limbo if they move, or even travel, to another state.[27]

The passage of the federal act, however, has not prevented further action by state governments and courts. In 2006, President George W. Bush and the Republican majority in Congress pushed for an amendment to the Constitution that would define marriage in heterosexual terms and thus preempt state actions to permit other definitions, but the measure failed to pass the House.[28] A number of states have adopted legislation that would limit the right of gay and lesbian couples to marry or in some cases have any sort of legally defined partnerships. Critics have argued that these legislative actions are politically motivated and are attempts to extend further the culture wars that have become central to many aspects of American life. Several religious denominations are also confronting questions such as the ordination of homosexual clergy and the blessing of gay unions.

The Separation of Church and State: School Prayer and Other Issues

The First Amendment to the U.S. Constitution forbids the establishment of a national religion and also ensures the free exercise of religion. That is, the framers attempted to prevent government from endorsing or supporting any particular religion and also forbade it to interfere with individuals' practicing their own version of religion, whatever that might be. Although the framers may have thought those two provisions were compatible, many contemporary citizens do not. They contend that rulings designed to prohibit the establishment of religion instead prevent them from free exercise of their religious beliefs. This conflict between the two dimensions of religious liberty arises in part because the courts have decided against permitting any religious observance at publicly funded events. Citizens committed to the free exercise of religion regard any restrictions on public observance—even when other people involved are of different religions or profess no religion at all—as an infringement of their rights. This attitude is more likely to arise when there is a dominant religious community that sees no reason why it should not have religious observances at public events.

Public education has been one of the principal battlegrounds in this continuing conflict. For much of American history, it was quite common, and indeed expected, that the school day began with a prayer, which was almost invariably a Christian one and often was prescribed by the school board or some other public body. The clear and direct role of government in prescribing these prayers led the Supreme Court to deem them an establishment of religion.[29] That decision began an ongoing political and legal fight over the limits of government-mandated prayer and other religious observance in the public schools, in which the judiciary has struggled to find some way to balance the Establishment and Free Exercise Clauses. These controversies themselves are, somewhat ironically, often resolved by a Supreme Court that opens its own sessions with a prayer.

Issues of separation of church and state in education arise in several areas. The first is school prayer, specifically the attempts of local school boards to permit some form of prayer at school. Since 1962, when the Supreme Court outlawed official school prayer, various religious groups have attempted to reintroduce it, either through a constitutional amendment permitting prayer in schools or through mechanisms such as silent meditation and voluntary attendance at prayer sessions. The issue resurfaced in 1984, when the Reagan administration proposed allowing local school boards to permit a moment of silent meditation at the beginning of the school day; this practice was presumed to promote discipline as well as moral education. Individual states' attempts to impose such plans have been struck down by the Supreme Court,[30] but in 1990, the Court did permit religious groups formed by students to use school facilities after school hours; that seemed likely to be an entering wedge for greater use of the public schools for religious exercises. Indeed, in 2000, the Court allowed even more general use of school buildings for religious functions, further narrowing the separation of public sector facilities and religious observance.

Other questions have been raised about religious expression in public education; for example, the Supreme Court has in most instances maintained that religious rituals at events held outside normal school hours—at football games and graduations—violate the Establishment Clause. The Court's general direction has been to maintain the principle of separation between the system of public education and the church, even where there appears to be strong public support for breaching the wall.

If the Supreme Court were to follow the election returns, the justices would have sided with President Reagan, both Presidents Bush, and their fundamentalist supporters on school prayer. Large majorities of the U.S. population have expressed opinions in favor of permitting prayer in schools. As in many other issues, however, political elites tend to be more sensitive to the issues of minority rights involved in school prayer, and so attempts in Congress to pass a school prayer amendment to the Constitution have been unsuccessful. The usual tactic of opponents has been to block consideration of the issue through procedural mechanisms in the legislature, rather than calling for formal votes that would make it clear to constituents how their Congress members dealt with school prayer.

Another area of controversy concerning the separation of church and state is public support for religious schools. In deciding these cases, the Supreme Court has been forced to make a number of difficult decisions. Over the years, however, the Court has been tending to allow greater public support for religious education. For example, in 1930, it upheld the right of states to provide textbooks for students in parochial schools on the same basis that they provide them to students in public schools,[31] and in 1947, the Court ruled in favor of providing bus transportation for parochial school students at public expense.[32] Both policies were upheld on the grounds that these expenditures benefited the students involved, not the church.

In contrast, in 1971, the Supreme Court struck down a Pennsylvania law that had the state pay part of parochial school teachers' salaries, arguing that this was of direct benefit to the church (essentially subsidizing church employees) and created excessive entanglement between church and state.[33] The Court has also permitted states to provide teachers for exceptional students in parochial schools, but not on the premises of the schools. In somewhat contradictory fashion, in 1976, the Court upheld general grants of public money to church-affiliated colleges.[34] It later restricted the ability of those institutions to use the funds for religious purposes.[35] Then, in 1994, the Court ruled that the state of New York had violated the separation principle by creating a school district that served only the disabled children of a Hasidic Jewish sect that did not want its children to attend public schools.[36]

The issue of government support of religious education continues to be pressed on both sides, in part because of the importance of vouchers and charter schools in the contemporary debate over education, as we noted when discussing education policy (see chapter 13). Parochial schools and other religion-based schools would likely be the principal beneficiaries of any greater use of vouchers. As in the case of abortion, public support for religious schools brings together a rather unlikely coalition of the Roman Catholic Church and fundamentalist

Protestant sects that have been forming their own schools so as to incorporate school prayer and religious instruction into the educational program. The opposition has been based in a coalition of secular proponents of public education, along with mainstream Protestant churches and some liberal Jewish leaders. In 2002, the Supreme Court ruled in a landmark case that the use of vouchers supporting religious schools did not violate separation of church and state.[37]

All these court decisions on funding religion-based education feature reasoning that may appear tortuous, but principles stand out. The first is that aid to students and their families is more acceptable than is aid to institutions that are connected to churches. If parents and children have made their own choice to seek a religious education, they should be able to do so. These citizens are, in principle, as much entitled to public support for education as their fellow citizens who choose public schools for their children—as one aspect of free exercise of religion. Second, institutions of higher education are permitted more entanglement between church and state than are elementary and secondary schools. The assumption is that more mature students are less vulnerable to the influence of any overt religious teachings. Third, the public sector should not have to spend additional money on education because of the special religious demands of a group, but neither should it impose additional financial burdens on religious groups.

Finally, the conflict between church and state has also been manifested in conflicts over control of the curriculum being taught in the public schools—particularly over the teaching of evolution. Religious conservatives prefer that evolution be replaced or at least supplemented by so-called creationism, or "creation science," which accepts literally the biblical story of divine creation of all species on Earth at once, as written in Genesis. At a minimum, these conservatives want evolution taught as a speculative theory rather than as settled scientific fact. They argue, for example, that gaps in the fossil record make it impossible to demonstrate that evolution did in fact occur as its proponents argue.[38]

Whereas most of the battle over the relation between church and state has been fought in the courts, the battle over curriculum has been overtly political, being joined in states and local communities with elected school boards. The most extreme case of this type occurred in Kansas, where the elected state board of education was captured for a short time by creationists who attempted to remove evolution from the science curriculum. A subsequent election returned control of the board to a more moderate group, but the power of well-organized activist groups in education-politics had been demonstrated rather clearly. The religious right has been extremely successful in organizing politically to take control of local boards, which have been able in some cases to shift the curriculum to reflect their views about evolution, as well as to take on other curricular issues such as sex education. Several local school boards have imposed a creationist agenda, sometimes called "intelligent design," on their schools, although in one significant case (*Kitzmiller v. Dover Area School District*, 106LRP 262 M.D. Pa.) the federal court declared that the curriculum was a clear attempt to establish religion in public education.[39] Political polling indicates that these groups generally do not hold majorities in the communities in which they are successful, but the religious right's ability to get out the vote of citizens who feel intensely about the issues enables it to win elections.

The issue of the public school curriculum also arises with respect to the growth in home schooling and the spread of charter schools (see chapter 13). Parents who do not want their children exposed to ideas opposed to their own creationist perspectives either remove their children from schools and educate them at home or band together to create charter schools, which are supported at least in part by public funds but allow greater control by the parents. Even then, parents may not be able to escape completely the curriculum of public education, given that state departments of education regulate what must be offered at home or in the charter schools. Education is central in shaping culture, and in the culture wars that are becoming increasingly important in American political life, it occupies a pivotal position.

Summary

Moral and cultural issues have become central to contemporary policy debates in the United States. The Puritan tradition has been strong and influential in American social and political life, and it has tended to shape much of national policy. However, the spate of moral issues arising in politics in recent decades has created intense political divisions. The issues are important, but they are extremely difficult for the political system to process effectively. While most of the other policy issues we have discussed to this point can be addressed through bargaining and compromise, moral issues generally are not open to compromise, for participants in the process usually are unwilling to compromise their values in these debates.

The problem for government is that these issues are unlikely to go away and indeed may intensify. Scientific progress in the area of reproductive technology and the increasing social, cultural, and religious diversity of American society all but guarantee that there will continue to be conflicts of this type. Furthermore, the political parties have become somewhat aligned along cultural lines, as well as along a left–right continuum, ensuring that the issues will continue to be carried directly into political debates. Moral and political issues tend to create rather unusual political and even religious coalitions that make political calculations all the more difficult for policymakers, and so they may contribute to additional conflict and instability within the policymaking system.

PART FOUR

Analyzing Public Policy

CHAPTER 17

Policy Analysis: Cost-Benefit Analysis and Ethical Analysis

MUCH OF THIS BOOK has been concerned with the characteristics of policies in the United States and with the process through which policies are adopted. This chapter shows a change in approach somewhat by the discussion of two ways of analyzing policy choices. One of these, *cost-benefit analysis,* is based on a utilitarian, economic logic that assumes that the best policies are those that create the greatest net benefit for society. The other, *ethical analysis,* looks at nonutilitarian bases for justifying policy choices and contrasts them with the economic methods. Both of these methods have something to say about what a good policy choice is, but the answers are likely to be quite different. In this chapter, I will discuss the two forms of analysis separately and then provide some comparison.

Cost-Benefit Analysis

Because governments operate with limited resources and limited ability to predict the future, they must employ techniques to help them decide how to use those scarce resources. Cost-benefit analysis is the most commonly employed technique, other than the informal promptings of intuition and experience. The fundamental principle of cost-benefit analysis is that any project undertaken should produce a benefit for society greater than its cost.[1] A second principle is that when several projects promise to yield benefits and all cannot be undertaken because of limited resources, the project that creates the greatest net benefit to the society should be selected. The technique is perhaps most applicable to capital projects, such as building highways or dams, but it can also be applied to other types of public activities. In fact, cost-benefit analysis was adopted during the Reagan administration as a way to assess proposed regulations, in an attempt to curb government involvement in the economy. Formally or informally, it remains a central approach to policy analysis to this day.

Obviously, a decided utilitarian bias underlies cost-benefit analysis.[2] All of the costs and benefits of a project are compared along the single measuring rod of money, and the projects that create the greatest net benefit are deemed superior. This implies that the dominant value in society is economic wealth and, further, that more is always better. Total wealth is presumed to be of paramount importance, even if accompanied by rather perverse distributional consequences. I will discuss the philosophical and practical implications that arise with cost-benefit analysis later in the chapter; they may be sufficiently troubling, especially in a democratic system, for some critics to argue for alternative means of evaluating policies. Cost-benefit analysis does have the advantage of reducing all the costs and benefits of public programs to that single economic dimension, whereas other forms of analysis may produce confusion because of the lack of a common standard of comparison. On that single dimension, cost-benefit analysis can give an answer as to whether a project is desirable or not, whereas other methods tend to produce more ambiguous results.

Principles of Cost-Benefit Analysis

In the world of cost-benefit analysis, more is always better. Although it has serious intellectual foundations, the method is in many ways no more than a systematic framework within which to collect data concerning the merits and demerits of a public program. And it is not a new idea: The Army Corps of Engineers used the technique as early as 1900 to evaluate the merits of proposed improvements to rivers and harbors. The basic procedure is to enumerate, and attach a monetary value to, the positive features of a program and then do the same for the negative features. The net balance of costs and benefits will then determine whether a program is economically feasible, although many other questions about its desirability may remain.

A principal concept underlying cost-benefit analysis comes from the tradition in welfare economics that has sought to develop an acceptable social welfare function, or a socially desirable means for making collective policy decisions.[3] That is, how can societies take the numerous and often conflicting views of citizens and generate the policy choices that are the most acceptable to the society? One of the first welfare criteria of this sort was the *Pareto principle,* which argued that a policy move was optimal if no move away from it could be made to benefit someone without hurting someone else.[4] Stated another way, a Pareto optimal policy would be one that benefits at least one person without hurting anyone. In the real world of political decision making, policies of this kind are rare indeed, and politics is frequently about who gets what at whose expense. Therefore, using the Pareto principle would be extremely conservative, supporting very few public interventions.

Nicholas Kaldor and John Hicks advanced a different welfare criterion. They argued that a policy change is socially justified if the winners gain a sufficient amount to compensate the losers and still have something left for themselves.[5] That does not imply that the winners necessarily *will* compensate the losers or that government can even identify the losers, but it presumes that the society as a whole is better off because of the overall increase in benefits.[6] This welfare criterion obviously is a justification of the reliance by cost-benefit analysis on the production of the greatest possible net benefit. It can be hoped that at least part of the benefits created will somehow find their way to the individuals who may have been harmed by the policy choice, but at least those benefits have been created. Intellectually, this approach also contains another problem in that it requires aggregating utilities across a range of individuals, and that requires doing the practically impossible—making interpersonal comparisons of utility.[7]

A second fundamental idea underlying cost-benefit analysis is the *consumer's surplus*.[8] Stated simply, this is the amount of money a consumer would be willing to pay for a given product, minus the amount he or she must actually pay. Consumers tend to value the first unit of a product or service they receive more highly than the second and the second more highly than the third: The first quart of milk where there has been none is more valuable than the second. But the units of a product are not priced marginally but sold at an average price, which means increased production will give consumers surplus value. Thus, any investment that reduces the cost of the product or service produces a benefit in savings that increases the consumer surplus. The government's investment in a new superhighway that reduces the cost to consumers of driving the same number of miles—in time, in gasoline, and in potential loss of life and property—creates a consumer surplus. And as the time, gasoline, and lives saved by the new highway may be used for other increased production, the actual savings represent a minimum definition of the improvement to society resulting from the construction of the new highway.

Also important in understanding cost-benefit analysis is the concept of *opportunity costs,* meaning that any resource used in one project cannot be used in another. For example, the concrete, steel, and labor used to build a superhighway cannot be used to build a new dam. Consequently, all projects must be evaluated against other possible projects to determine the most appropriate way to use resources, especially financial resources. Projects are also compared, implicitly if not explicitly, with taking no action and allowing the money to remain in the hands of individual citizens. Again, the basic idea of getting the most "bang for the buck" is fundamental to understanding cost-benefit analysis. When identifying and assessing costs and benefits, the analyst must also be concerned with the range of effects of the proposed program and the point at which the analysis disregards effects as being too remote for consideration.[9] For example, building a municipal waste incinerator in Detroit, Michigan, will have pronounced effects in Windsor, Ontario, Canada, that must be considered—even though that city is outside the United States. The prevailing air currents may mean that some ash and acid from the incinerator also reach Norway and Sweden, but those effects may be so minimal and so remote that they can safely be disregarded. This form of analysis requires making judgments about what effects are sufficiently proximate and important to be included in the calculations.

Finally, time is important in evaluating costs and benefits. The costs and benefits of most projects do not occur at once but accrue over a number of years. If our superhighway is built, it will be serviceable for fifty years and will be financed over twenty years through government bonds. Policymakers must be certain that the long-term costs and benefits, as well as the short-term consequences, are positive. This, of course, requires some estimation of what the future will be like. We may estimate that our new superhighway will be useful for fifty years, but oil shortages may so reduce driving during that period that the real benefits will be much less. Or, conversely, the price of gasoline may increase so much that the savings produced are more valuable than assumed at present. These kinds of assumptions about the future must be built into the model of valuation if it is to aid a decision maker.

In part because of the uncertainty over future costs and benefits and in part because of the general principle that people prefer a dollar today to a dollar next year, the costs and benefits of projects must be converted to present values before useful cost-benefit calculations can be made. That is to say, the benefits that accrue to the society in the future have their value discounted and are consequently worth less than benefits produced in the first year of the project. Costs that occur in future years are likewise valued less than costs that occur in the first few years. Cost-benefit analysis thus appears to favor projects that offer quick payoffs rather than greater long-term benefits but perhaps also higher maintenance and operation costs. Although there may be good logical justification for these biases, they influence the kinds of programs that will be selected, and that has definite social implications, not least for future generations. Other analytic aids for government decision makers, such as "decision trees," include probabilities of outcomes to cope with the uncertainties of the future, but cost-benefit analysis tends to rely on discounting future costs and benefits.

Doing Cost-Benefit Analysis

To better understand the application of cost-benefit analysis, we now work through the steps required to justify the construction of a new dam on the Nowhere River. The Army Corps of Engineers is proposing this project, and we have to determine whether or not it should be undertaken. We must first decide

Building a dam, or making any other large public investment, usually involves careful assessment of the project's costs and benefits. Attaching a price to some of those costs and benefits, such as natural beauty, is a difficult process.

if the project is feasible and acceptable on its own and then decide whether it is preferable to other projects that could be funded with the same resources. Again, this decision is being made first on economic grounds, although we may have to bring other forms of analysis (politics) and other criteria (the environment may be trumps) into the decision process at a later time.

Determining costs and benefits.   One important factor to consider when performing a cost-benefit analysis, especially of a public project, is that all costs and benefits should be enumerated. Unlike projects that might be undertaken in the private sector, public projects require identification of the social, or external, costs and benefits. In the public sector, projects whose strictly economic potential outweighs their costs may be rejected because of the possibility of pollution or the loss of external benefits such as natural beauty. In fact, one of the principal logical justifications for the existence of the public sector is that it should take into account those external factors and attempt to correct them in ways not possible in the private sector.[10] Even with that social justification, however, the values of the costs and benefits are usually computed in economic terms, just as if they were to accrue in the private market. This reliance on market logic for nonmarket decisions in the public sector is a fundamental irony in cost-benefit analysis.[11]

TABLE 17.1   Costs and Benefits of a Dam Project

Costs	Benefits
Construction costs	Hydroelectric power
Flooded land	Flood control
Relocation of families	Irrigation
Loss of recreation	New recreational opportunities

For our dam project, we can think of two lists of attributes (see Table 17.1). On one side are the costs of the project, the main one being the money cost of constructing the dam, which should reflect the market valuation of the opportunity costs of using the same resources for other purposes. The dam will also impose an economic cost by flooding the houses and farmland of present inhabitants of the area, and there are social, or human, costs involved as well, for these farms have been in the same families for generations, and the farmers have resisted the project from the beginning. There are additional social costs in that the proposed dam will impound a river that currently has some recreational value for canoeists and is essentially an unspoiled natural area.

On the other side of the ledger are benefits of the program. First, the dam will provide hydroelectric power for the region, and it would be a source of electric power that does not consume scarce fossil fuels or create the air pollution that would result from producing the same amount of power with fossil fuels. The dam would also help control the raging Nowhere River, which every spring floods a number of towns, cities, and farms downstream. The impounded water behind the dam will provide irrigation water for the farmers who remain, enabling them to grow crops more reliably than if they had to rely on rainfall alone. And although canoeists will lose some recreational benefits as a result of the dam, citizens who enjoy power boating and waterskiing will benefit from the large lake formed behind the dam. Thus, although this proposed dam imposes a number of costs on society, it also provides a number of benefits in return. To proceed with the analysis, we must now begin to attach some quantitative values to these costs and benefits.

Assigning value.   Assigning a real monetary value to all costs and benefits of this mythical project would be difficult. The market directly provides a value for some aspects: We know, or can estimate accurately, the cost of building the dam and the market value of the hydroelectric power it will produce. Although such costs are generally measurable through the market, the market may not reflect the costs and benefits fully. For example, if our dam is built in a remote area with little more than subsistence agriculture, bringing in a large number of highly skilled and highly paid workers may distort prices and increase the cost of building the dam. Similarly, not only is the hydroelectric power salable, but it may also produce substantial secondary benefits (or perhaps costs) by stimulating industrialization in this remote rural area. The experience of the Tennessee Valley Authority and the impact on the Tennessee Valley of the development of cheap electric power illustrate this point rather nicely.[12] We cannot fully predict these secondary benefits, nor can we rely on them to make the project feasible, but they frequently occur.

Some other costs and benefits of the project, although not directly measurable through the market, can be estimated in other ways. For example, we have to estimate the dam's recreational value to the people who will use the lake for waterskiing and the cost to those who will no longer be able to use the river for canoeing. We can do this by estimating the people's willingness to pay for their recreation[13]—just how much time and money are they willing to invest to enjoy these recreational activities? Evidence for this calculation can be gathered from surveys of recreation participants or from their actual behavior in renting equipment and travel to recreation sites. The calculations will offer some measure of the economic value of the lake and of the free-flowing stream to the population.

The creation of the dam and the lake behind it helps to illustrate another point about valuing costs and benefits. The lake will produce lakefront property, which tends to have higher market value than other, nearby property, so something of the aesthetic value of the impoundment can be calculated. This method of valuation is analogous to estimating the value of clean air by comparing prices of similar housing in polluted and less polluted areas of a city.[14]

This method of valuation returns to the concept of the consumer's surplus. The first unit of a particular commodity is valued more highly than any subsequent units, so as production is increased, each unit is marginally less valuable. In our dam example, if there already have been a number of impoundments in the area—as there have been in the Tennessee Valley—a new lake will have less value to recreation consumers, and they will be less willing to pay than if this were the first lake in an area with numerous free-flowing streams. Likewise, one more hydroelectric power station in an area that already has cheap electrical power is less valuable than it would be in an economically backward area, and consequently, citizens will be less willing to pay for that new power plant.

On some aspects of the project, the market provides little or no guidance about valuation. For the farmers who are displaced by the project, we can calculate the economic value of their land, their houses, and their moving costs, but we cannot readily assign an economic value to the houses that are the ancestral homes of families and are therefore more valuable psychologically than ordinary houses.[15] Similarly, there is some value in not disturbing a natural setting, simply because it is natural, and that is a difficult thing to assign an economic value. Because of such considerations, absolute prohibitions are sometimes written into legislation to prevent certain actions, so planners cannot depend entirely on net benefit ratios. The Environmental Protection Agency's (EPA's) guideline for preserving the habitats of endangered species, which resulted in the now-notorious case of the snail darter in the Little Tennessee River and the more recent case of the delta smelt in California, is an example of the application of regulations to prevent some actions regardless of the relative economic costs and benefits.[16]

The willingness-to-pay approach to valuation questions the people directly involved with the project about their own valuation of costs and benefits. For some of those costs and benefits, the population at large may be equally important as judges of value. Federal regulators are now under congressional mandate to find ways to assess the value that the public assigns to the costs of environmental problems, such as oil spills. These *contingent value* measurements by passive users are now being undertaken using survey methods. The National Oceanic and Atmospheric Administration conducted the first of these and gained broad support from environmental groups.[17] On the other hand, this method of valuation has met general opposition from business and has been contested in the courts.[18]

It is fortunate that the dam we are building does not require direct decisions about loss of life or injury to human beings. Projects that do—for example, building the superhighway as a means of saving lives—raise perhaps the most difficult problem of valuation: estimating the value of human life.[19] Although it is convenient to say that life is priceless, in practice, decisions are made that deprive some people of their lives even when that loss of life is preventable. When that is the case, some subjective, if not objective, evaluation is made of the worth of lives. A standard method of making such judgments involves *discounted future earnings,* meaning that the life of the individual is worth whatever the individual could have earned in the course of his or her working life, discounted to present value. By that method, a corporate executive's life is valued more highly than a housewife's or a college professor's. This mechanism for evaluating lives clearly conforms to the basic market valuation but can be contested on humane grounds— its use in distributing compensation payments to the families of victims in the terrorist attacks of September 11 generated a great deal of political controversy.[20]

Another method of assigning value to lives for the purpose of cost-benefit analysis uses the size of awards to plaintiffs in legal cases involving negligence or malpractice that resulted in loss of life. In other words, what do panels of citizens or judges consider a human life to be worth? This is yet another version of the market criterion, albeit one in which considerations of human suffering and "loss of companionship" have a greater—some would say too great because of the emotionalism involved—impact on the economic valuation than does earning power. This valuation is affected, particularly in the minds of the insurance companies responsible for most of the payments, by emotional appeals by attorneys.

One can also use a method somewhat similar to the willingness-to-pay criterion. In theory, individuals would be willing to pay almost anything to preserve their own lives and the lives of their loved ones. However, individuals engage in risky behavior and risky occupations all the time, and when they do, they make a subjective statement about the value of their lives.[21] Because we know how much more likely it is for a coal miner to be killed at work—either in the mines or as a result of black lung disease—than for a construction worker, we can estimate from any differences in wages how much these individuals appear to value their lives. This method implies a certain level of knowledge that individuals may not have, and it assumes that the collective bargaining process, through which the wages of coal miners and construction workers are determined, accurately reflects both individual preferences and the market values of lives. It offers another feasible means of estimating the value of life, one that uses assessments by individual citizens rather than the market or the courts.

Discounting. We now return to the problem of time. The costs and benefits of a project do not all magically appear as soon as it is completed but typically are stretched over a number of years. Table 17.2 shows the stream of benefits coming from the dam on the Nowhere River over a twenty-year period. That is the projected feasible lifetime of the project because the Nowhere River carries a great deal of silt, which is expected to have filled the lake behind the dam by the end of that period. How do we assess these benefits and come up with a single number to compare with costs to determine the economic feasibility of the project?

To calculate such a figure, we must compute the present value of the future benefits. We have already decided on the time span of the project; the only task that remains is to determine the discount rate that should be applied to the public investment. And as with the valuation of costs and benefits, disagreements may arise about what that rate should be.[22] One method is to use the opportunity costs of the use of the funds. Presumably, any money used in a public project will be extracted from the private sector by taxation or borrowing; consequently, the rate of return that that money could earn if it were invested in private sector projects is the appropriate discount rate for public projects. This is not always a

TABLE 17.2   Hypothetical Costs and Benefits of the Dam Project for Twenty Years

	Year																			
	1	*2*	*3*	*4*	*5*	*6*	*7*	*8*	*9*	*10*	*11*	*12*	*13*	*14*	*15*	*16*	*17*	*18*	*19*	*20*
Costs	5	8	7	2	1	1	1	1	1	1	1	1	1	1	1	1	1	1	1	1
Benefits	0	0	0	3	4	5	5	5	5	5	5	5	5	5	5	4	4	4	3	2

practical solution, however, as rates of return differ for different kinds of investments, and investors apparently choose to put some money into each kind. Is building a dam more like speculative mining investments, building a steel mill, or investing in an insured savings account? Which of the many possible rates of return should be selected?

Several other issues arise with respect to the selection of a discount rate. First, in discussing projects most of whose benefits are to accrue in the future, there is an element of uncertainty. In our example, we have assumed that the probable life span of the dam will be twenty years, but in reality the lake may fill up with silt in fifteen years. Consequently, it may be more prudent to select a discount rate higher than that found in the market because we cannot be sure of the real occurrence or real value of the benefits. And because the benefits are expected to be more distant in time, they are less certain; therefore, even higher rates of discount should be applied. Consideration of the effects of inflation and the uncertainties that exist about the development of new energy sources may also influence us to be more conservative about discount rates.

Second, some analysts argue that there should be a "social rate of discount" lower than that established by the market.[23] Such an arbitrarily set discount rate would be justified on the basis of the need for greater public investment to provide a capital infrastructure for future generations. And as the size of the public sector is to some degree determined by the rate of discount, that rate should be set not by the market but by conscious political choices concerning the appropriate level of public activity. The economic counterargument is that, in the long term, the society will be better off if resources are allocated on the basis of their opportunity costs. If a public project is deemed infeasible because of a market-determined discount rate, then the resources that would have been used in that project would, it is argued, produce greater social benefit in a project that is feasible under that rate of discount; this would be true regardless of whether the project is in the public or the private sector. If no such project is available, then the money would be better saved until such a project materializes.

Finally, a question arises about intergenerational equity: What do we owe to posterity, or to put it the other way around, what has posterity ever done for us? If the discount rate is set lower than that determined by the market, we will tend to undertake more projects that have an extended time value and that will benefit future generations. But we will also deprive the present generation of opportunities for consumption by using those resources as investment capital. This is as much a philosophical as a practical issue, but it is important for our understanding of alternative consequences arising from alternative choices of a rate of discount for public projects.

Using several discount rates, we now work through the example of benefits from the dam. Let us assume that the prime interest rate in the United States is approximately 8 percent. If we use that market-determined interest rate, the $100 in benefits produced after one year would be worth

$$V = \$100/1.08 = \$92.59.$$

And $100 in benefits produced after two years would be worth

$$V = \$100/(1.08)2 = \$85.73.$$

And $100 in benefits produced in the twentieth year of the project would be worth only $21.45 in present value. Thus, if we use this market rate of discount in evaluating our proposed project, the net benefit of the project at present value is positive. This project has a rather high cost during its early years, with the benefits occurring gradually over the twenty years. At a higher discount rate, such a project is not feasible. If we used a discount rate of 18 percent, which would have seemed very reasonable in the late 1970s (but absurd in the 1990s), the net benefit of the dam at present value would be negative, and the project would be economically infeasible.

Discounting is a means of reducing all costs and benefits of a project to present value, based on the assumption that benefits created in the future are worth less than those created immediately. Philosophically or ideologically, one might desire a low discount rate to encourage public investment but object to the entire process of discounting. Should we not simply look to see if the stream of benefits created is greater than the total costs, no matter how or when they occur? That would, of course, be equivalent to a discount rate of zero. This point may be valid philosophically, but until the argument is accepted by economists, financiers, and government decision makers, public investment decisions will be made on the basis of present value and on the basis of interest rates that approximate the real rate of return in the private sector.

Choosing among projects. We have determined that our dam on the Nowhere River is feasible, given that a benevolent deity has provided us a discount rate of 8 percent for this project. But it is not yet time to break ground. We must first compare our project with alternative projects for funding. Thus, the opportunity cost question arises not only with respect to the single project being considered and the option of allowing the money to remain in private hands, but also it is with regard to choices among other possible projects in the public sector.

We have argued that the fundamental rule is to select the project that will produce the greatest total benefit to society. If we apply the Kaldor-Hicks criterion, we see that this project is justified simply because it will create more benefits to spread around in the society and presumably will compensate those who have lost something because the project was built. Thus, in the simplest case, if we were to choose to undertake only a single project this year—perhaps because of limited manpower for supervision—we would choose Project D from Table 17.3 simply because it creates the highest level of net benefit. By investing less money in Projects A and B, we could have produced slightly more net benefit for society, but we are administratively constrained from making that decision and must choose only the one most productive investment.

More commonly, however, a particular resource—usually money—is limited, and with that limitation in mind, we must choose one or more projects that will produce maximum benefits. Let us say that the ten projects listed in Table 17.4 are all economically feasible and that we have been given a budget of $50 million for capital projects. Which projects should we select for funding? In such a situation, we should rank the projects according to the ratio of net benefits to initial costs (the costs that will be reflected in our capital budget), and then we should begin with the best projects, in terms of that ratio, until the budget is exhausted. In this way, we will get the greatest benefit for the expenditure of our limited funds. Projects that we might have selected if we were choosing only a single project would not be selected under these conditions of resource constraint.

TABLE 17.3   Costs and Benefits of Alternative Projects (in millions of dollars)

Projects	Costs	Benefits	Net benefit
A.	70	130	60
B.	75	120	45
C.	200	270	70
D.	150	250	100

TABLE 17.4   Choosing a Package of Projects by Net Benefit Ratio (in millions of dollars)

Project	Costs	Cumulative costs	Benefits	Net benefits	Net benefit ratio
A.	2	2	12	10	5.0
B.	4	6	20	16	4.0
C.	10	16	40	30	3.0
D.	10	26	35	25	2.5
E.	8	34	28	20	2.5
F.	16	50	51	35	2.2
G.	2	52	6	4	2.0
H.	15	67	42	27	1.8
I.	10	77	26	16	1.6
J.	18	95	45	27	1.5

The problem of selecting among projects arises from the application of the basic rule of cost-benefit analysis. Given the budgetary process and the allocation of funds among agencies, we may produce "multiorganizational suboptimization." This is a fancy way of saying that if our agency has been given $50 million, we will spend it, even if other agencies have projects that would produce greater benefits for society but do not have the money in their budgets to fund them. Thus, if I had the money, I would continue to fund the projects listed in Table 17.4, even though several have relatively low net benefit ratios and even though there might be better projects that other government bureaus want to fund. Of course, I will have been asked what benefits my proposed projects would produce when the capital budget was being considered, but because of political considerations arising in the process, my budget is excessive in light of the benefits that could be produced from alternative uses of the money. This is not, of course, a flaw in the method; it is a flaw in the application of the method in complex and competitive government settings.

A related problem is that cost-benefit analysis places relatively little importance on efficiency or cost effectiveness. It looks primarily at total benefits produced rather than at the ratio of benefits to costs. It could be argued that the method tends to favor the axe over the scalpel as a cutting tool; in other words, it tends to favor large projects over small projects. That may be an inefficient use of resources, and it may lock government into costly projects, whereas smaller projects might provide greater flexibility and greater future opportunities for innovation. Capital projects are inherently lumpy, so only projects of a certain size are feasible, but the concentration on total net benefits in cost-benefit analysis may exaggerate the problems of size and inflexibility.

We have now worked our way from the initial step of deciding what costs and benefits our project provides to deciding if it is the best project to undertake, given a limited budget and the competing uses of the money. At each stage of the process, we have had to adopt a number of assumptions and approximations to reach a decision. Thus, although cost-benefit analysis provides a "hard" answer as to whether or not we should undertake a project, that answer should not remain unquestioned. We now discuss some criticisms of cost-benefit analysis and some possible ways of building greater political and economic sophistication into its application.

Extensions

We have so far been discussing a very basic approach to cost-benefit analysis. There are, however, a number of extensions and modifications of the method that are important for thinking about its utility. First, other techniques, such as cost-effectiveness analysis, have many things in common with cost-benefit analysis but offer their own particular perspectives. For example, cost-effectiveness analysis does not require assessment of the value of various outcomes to the extent required in cost-benefit analysis but rather assumes that an outcome is desirable.[24] Unlike cost-benefit analysis, this technique cannot tell the analyst whether an outcome is beneficial, only what it will cost to achieve a specified quantity of the outcome. Cost-effectiveness analysis tends to be used frequently in health policy and medicine, where curing a disease is a *prima facie* good and the question is how much it will cost.[25] Even then, however, some physicians do not like the concept of attaching a price to a cure and thinking about efficiency in medical care.[26]

Another extension of the logic of cost-benefit analysis is to attempt to bring in the concept of risk when assessing costs and benefits. Increasingly, governments are concerned with the risks of certain outcomes and need to be able to link the probability of their occurring with their relative costs and benefits. This approach has been especially relevant for regulatory decision making and is also applicable to a range of other public decisions.[27]

Criticism and Modification

Such things as the difficulty of assigning monetary values to nonmonetary outcomes, the choice of time ranges and discount rates, and the reliance on total net benefit as the criterion introduce uncertainties about the usefulness of cost-benefit analysis. We now discuss more fundamental problems concerning the method itself and its relationship to the political process. Perhaps the most important is that some naive politicians and analysts might let the method make decisions for them, instead of using the information derived from the analysis as one among many elements in their decision-making process. If the method is used naively and uncritically, the result can be decisions that many people would deem socially undesirable. For example, all costs and benefits are counted as equal in the model, and even if they could be calculated accurately, some critics argue that the cost of death might be more important than other costs. Thus, we might wish first to reduce deaths to the lowest possible level and then perhaps apply a cost-benefit analysis. We might use this "lexicographic preference" as a means of initially sorting projects when a single dominant value, such as life or the preservation of an endangered species, is involved. That is, we would take only projects that pass the one crucial test and then subject those to cost-benefit analysis.

Perhaps the most socially questionable aspect of cost-benefit analysis is that it gives little attention to the distributive questions involved in all policies.[28] All benefits and costs are counted equally, regardless of who receives or bears them. A project that increased the wealth of a wealthy individual by several million dollars and was financed by regressive taxation of $100,000 would be preferred in cost-benefit calculations to a project that produced a benefit of $900,000 for unemployed workers and was financed by progressive taxation of $200,000. This is an extreme example, but it shows the distributional blindness of cost-benefit analysis. Advocates of the method justify it by saying that the society as a whole will be better off with the greatest increase in benefits, and presumably winners can later compensate losers. In reality, however, winners rarely, if ever, do so, and usually losers cannot be directly identified anyway. Redistributional goals can be included directly in the analysis by attaching some weight greater than one to positive changes in the salaries of low-income or unemployed persons, or they may be imposed on the analysis after the fact. Because government exists in part to attempt to redress some of the inequities produced in the marketplace, some attention must be given to redistributional goals when evaluating public projects.

Furthermore, the utilitarian and "econocratic" foundations of cost-benefit analysis may not be entirely suitable for a functioning political democracy.[29] Money alone is the measure of all things in cost-benefit analysis, and decisions made using this method can be expected to be based on economic rather than political values. In the next section, I discuss some possible ethical alternatives that may be more suitable in a democracy. The difficulty is that the alternatives lack the apparent precision of cost-benefit analysis and its ability to provide clear-cut answers to questions about the desirability of a policy intervention.

Cost-benefit analysis has been referred to as "nonsense on stilts."[30] This rather rude description implies that there are so many assumptions involved in the calculations, and so many imponderables about the future effects of projects, that cost-benefit analysis is the functional equivalent of witchcraft in the public sector. Although phrased in exaggerated language, this criticism is to some degree well taken. It is difficult, if not impossible, to know the value of eliminating an externality, just as it is difficult to know just how much life, health, and snail darters are worth economically. Cost-benefit analysis can be used to avoid difficult political decisions and to yield responsibility to experts who can supply the "correct" answer. Such fundamental abdication of political responsibility is indeed an "insidious poison in the body politick." Only when the results of analysis are integrated with other forms of analysis, including ethical analysis, and combined with sound political judgment can the "correct decision" be made.

Ethical Analysis of Public Policy

There are numerous alternatives to the utilitarian logic that undergirds cost-benefit analysis. These alternatives do not provide answers as neat as the ones cost-benefit analysis provides, but they do raise crucial questions. Most important policy decisions involve an assessment of what government should do, as much as they involve the feasibility question of what government can do. The range of technical possibilities before policymakers is frequently broader than the range of ethically justifiable possibilities for acting "in the public interest." But, unfortunately, many values that should affect policy decisions in the public sector conflict with one another and with the utilitarianism of cost-benefit analysis. Analysts frequently confront choices among competing positive values rather than clear-cut decisions about options that are either completely right or completely wrong.

In making almost all decisions about allocating resources among the programs of government, policymakers must choose among worthy ends. They do not have the luxury of picking the only acceptable policy. Which is more important, the jobs of five hundred loggers or an endangered species of owl? Policymakers must also choose among alternative means to reach desired goals, and those means themselves may have substantial ethical implications. For example, we may want to ensure that all children are vaccinated, for their own good and for the good of other people, but to make sure would require very draconian means that would not be acceptable in an individualistic society. And some religious groups do not approve of vaccination; should their rights be sacrificed in the name of public health? Such ethical issues about control and privacy also have constitutional and institutional implications, as debates over the instruments to be used in the "war on terror" have shown.[31] These debates have become more intense, as the Obama administration has claimed the right to kill American citizens suspected of terrorism without the usual legal proceedings.[32]

Finally, in attempting to make decisions on ethical grounds, decision makers are confronted with an overwhelmingly utilitarian bias in the discussion and implementation of public policy.[33] The prevailing conception is that government should do what creates the greatest economic value for the society rather than worry too much about the "softer" values that we discuss in this chapter.

The concept behind *utilitarianism*—producing the greatest net benefit to society—is in the main admirable, but it can be used to justify actions that violate both procedural norms and the usual conceptions of fair distribution of the benefits of society. The utilitarian approach tends to reduce all dimensions of policy to a common economic one, even though a variety of other values may be equally important for determining the proper course of government action. In this section, I present several important ethical premises that pose alternatives to the dominant utilitarianism and that can guide policy decisions. We will also discuss some of the difficulties of implementing these alternative ethical and moral values in real public sector decisions.

Fundamental Value Premises

Any number of premises have been used to justify policy decisions, including such concepts as "Americanism," "Aryan purity," "the principles of Marxism-Leninism," and that old standby, "the public interest," as well as philosophical or religious principles.[34] The main difficulty in ethical analysis of policy is finding principles that can consistently produce acceptable decisions for a number of different situations.[35] Words such as *justice, equity,* and *good* are tossed about in rather cavalier fashion in debates over public policies. The analyst must attempt to systematize his or her values and learn to apply them consistently. The policy analyst therefore must be a moral actor as well as a technician or else remain what Arnold Meltsner refers to as a "baby analyst" throughout his or her career.[36] As I pointed out when discussing the application of cost-benefit analysis to public policy, values are in action throughout the policy process, embedded in policy options and in commonly used analytic methods. To understand what one wants, one must explicate and examine those values.

In this section, I discuss five important nonutilitarian value premises for making policy decisions: preservation of life, preservation of individual autonomy, and concepts of truthfulness, fairness, and desert. These values would probably be widely accepted by the public as important standards for assessing policies, and they are applicable across a wide range of policy issues. As I will show, however, these values cannot be applied unambiguously, and the conflicts they encounter are embedded in each issue as well as ranging across several issues. In many cases, there are even conflicts among the values themselves, so the analyst must decide how to weight different values.

The preservation of life.   The preservation of human life is one of the most fundamental values that we might expect to see manifested in the policy process. The sanctity of life is, after all, a fundamental value of Judeo-Christian ethics and is embodied in all professional codes of ethics.[37] Despite the universal acceptance of this value as an ethical criterion, a number of conflicts arise over its application in real-world decision-making situations. These often are "tragic choices" because the resources available do not permit everyone to be aided, and those not aided are condemned to die earlier than they might otherwise.[38] The ethical question then becomes which lives to preserve.

One obvious conflict in the use of resources to save lives exists between identifiable lives and statistical lives. Here we are faced with the tendency of individuals to allocate resources differently when known lives of specific individuals are at stake than they would in cases where some unspecified persons would be saved at some time in the future. If we know that particular individuals will die in the near future, we tend to provide them the resources they need to save themselves, even though the same resources could save many more unidentified lives in the future if allocated differently.

In medical care, this problem is manifested in the conflict between acute and preventive medicine. Preventive medicine is almost certainly the most cost-effective means of saving lives from being lost to cancer, circulatory diseases, or accidents, but it is difficult to identify the direct beneficiaries. The victims of the disease are clearly identifiable, however. They have identifiable families; consequently, it is more difficult to refuse care to them than to the unknown statistical beneficiaries of preventive medicine. This pattern of decision making has been described as the "mountain climber syndrome," in which we feel compelled to spend thousands of dollars to save a stranded mountain climber, even though many more lives could be saved if the same amount of money were spent on highway accident prevention. It is virtually impossible to say no to stranded mountain climbers and their families, although if the appropriate ethical criterion is to save as many lives as possible, that is perhaps what we should do.

But even if all the lives at stake in a decision are identifiable, allocative decisions must be made in some instances. Table 17.5, although it concentrates on a relatively small number of individuals who are potential recipients of a liver transplant, illustrates the broader problem of being forced to choose among lives. Each individual described in the table is worthy of receiving the lifesaving treatment simply because he or she is a human being, but because organs for transplants are scarce and the demand for them far exceeds the supply, decisions must be made that will allow some people to live and force others to die. What criteria can be applied in making such a choice? One might be the conventional utilitarian criterion: The individuals who will contribute the most to the community (especially economically) should be allowed to live. Another criterion might be longevity: The youngest persons should be allowed to receive the treatment, thus saving the greatest number of person-years of life. Another criterion might be autonomy: The individuals who have the greatest probability of returning to active and useful lives after treatment should receive the treatment.[39] Another criterion might be whether or not the disease requiring the treatment is self-inflicted. For example, should chronic alcoholics be given the same preference for receiving a new liver as other patients? At least one state in the United States has ruled that Medicaid should not pay for such treatments for active alcoholics and drug abusers.[40]

A variety of other criteria could be used to justify the choice of one transplant candidate over another, but a choice must still be made among real lives. In addition, some even broader allocative questions arise from this example: How many transplant centers should be developed in U.S. hospitals? Should there be sufficient capacity to help all the patients who might need this treatment, regardless of the cost and the underutilization of the facilities most of the time? Or should only enough centers be developed to meet average demand? Should individuals who can afford to pay be allowed to jump ahead of others in line to receive new organs if their payments can fund future surgeries for the less fortunate?

These questions have arisen in a very real way in the debate over allocation of the limited supply of donor organs among transplant centers around the

TABLE 17.5 "Who Shall Live, and Who Shall Die?" Liver Transplant Candidates

Patient	Sex and age	Occupation	Home life	Medical stability	Civic activities and other considerations
A.	M 55	Cardiac surgeon on the verge of a major new technique	Married; two adult children	Bad long-term prognosis, maybe two years	Philanthropist with very high net worth; rumors of unfaithfulness
B.	F 38	Owner of successful designer shop	Widow; three children, ages 4, 8, and 13	Good	From out of state; excellent violinist in community orchestra
C.	M 46	Medical technician	Married; six children, ages 8 to 14	Good	Union boss
D.	M 29	Assembly-line worker	Single	Good	Retarded—mental age, 10 years; ward of the state
E.	F 36	Well-known historian, college professor; PhD	Divorced; custodian of one son, age 5; ex-husband alive	Fair prognosis, but odd case that would allow perfection of new surgical technique	Excessive eater, drinker, and smoker; very popular professor; other medical conditions
F.	M 60	Ex-state senator, now retired	Widower	Good	Criminal record (extortion)
G.	M 45	Vice president of local bank	Happily married; three sons, ages 15 to 25	Good	Deacon of local church; member of Rotary Club

Source: "Who Shall Live," Washington Post, March 22, 1981.

country. One model of allocation would keep the organ in the area where it was procured and permit the local transplant center to use it, whereas another would have a centralized system of allocation, providing the organ to the patient who is most in need—that is, the nearest to death.[41] Since the sicker patients tend to cluster at a few major transplant centers, that alternative might put smaller centers out of business. That in turn raises several ethical questions: Why should an individual's chance of survival depend on where he or she lives rather than on medical criteria? Should there not be some attempt to keep more centers open and promote the technology for longer-term benefits?

Even though the preservation of life may be an important or even dominant value in public policymaking, in many situations, the definition of life itself is subject to debate, legally as well as morally. The use of therapeutic abortion as a means of birth control presents one problem of this sort: determining when human life begins.[42] This issue has been fought in the court system and in the streets of many American cities and towns, but no resolution has been found that both sides can accept. Even here, the question is not always clear-cut, for many abortion opponents would accept abortions in the case of rape or incest, and many abortion supporters would reject the procedure as a means of selecting gender.

Issues concerning artificial means of prolonging life, even when a person would be considered dead by many clinical criteria, illustrate the problem of defining life at the other end of the life cycle.[43] This issue moved to center stage in American politics in 2004 and 2005 in the case of Terri Schiavo, a Florida woman who had been in a "persistent vegetative state" since 1990. Her husband appealed to the Florida courts to permit her feeding tube to be withdrawn so that she could die a natural death. Her parents fought the petition, and they were joined by a number of politicians, including Gov. Jeb Bush of Florida and Senator Bill Frist, R-TN, as well as a number of Roman Catholic and evangelical religious leaders. The courts ultimately permitted the tube to be withdrawn, and Terri Schiavo died in March 2005.[44] Leaving aside the politics involved, the ethical issue was the definition of life and whether someone should be kept alive by artificial means when she had said (by most accounts), while she was still able, that she would not want such treatment.[45]

The possibility of assisted suicide for the terminally ill has raised conflicts between the values of preserving life and preserving autonomy (a concept discussed later in this chapter).[46] If an adult wants to end his or her life—because of a terminal and painful disease, for example—should government have the obligation, or even the right, to prevent that adult from doing so? Should the individual have access to assisted suicide if he or she is simply depressed or despondent? Thus, although all policymakers and all citizens may agree on the importance of preserving human life, serious disagreements arise over just what constitutes a human life and who can dispense with it.

In some situations, of course, the government sanctions and actively encourages the taking of human lives. The most obvious example is war; others are capital punishment and, in some instances, the management of police officers' response to threats to their own lives and safety. The question that arises here is what criteria governments can use to justify the taking of some lives, while the society deplores and prohibits the taking of others.[47] Obvious criteria that we might apply are self-preservation and the protection of society against elements that could undermine it or take other lives. But there is a degree of inconsistency in the arguments here, and government must justify placing higher value on some lives than on others. Again, the fundamental point is that although there may be broad agreement in society on the importance of preserving human lives as a goal of all public policies, this criterion is not obviously and unambiguously enforceable in all policy situations. We require detailed analysis of all such situations and some understanding of the particular application of the criterion in each.

The preservation of individual autonomy.   Another important value for public policy, especially in a democracy, is maximization of the autonomy of each citizen to make decisions about his or her own life. This principle underlies a considerable body of conservative political thought, which assumes that the interests of the individual are, everything else being equal, more important than those of the society as a whole.[48] It also assumes that individuals may at times select alternatives that many other people, and society as a whole acting through government, might deem unacceptable. Thus, child labor, sweatshops, and extremely long working hours at low wages were all justified at one time because they preserved the right of the individual to "choose" his or her own working conditions.[49]

If it adhered to an extreme definition of individual autonomy, which includes the right to choose conditions or products that are inherently harmful, the public sector would be excluded from almost all forms of social and economic activity. Even by this extreme version of autonomy, however, the state has been able to intervene to protect individuals against fraud and breach of contract, and it has to some degree protected children and other less competent individuals more than it does adults, who presumably are able to make their own decisions. In contrast, advocates of an enhanced role for the public sector have argued that the welfare state, by increasing the options available to citizens, especially less advantaged citizens, actually enhances individual freedom and autonomy.[50]

Several interesting questions arise in the public sector in regard to individual autonomy. One involves the legitimacy of state intervention: What groups in society should the state attempt to protect, either against themselves or against those who would defraud them or otherwise infringe on their rights?

Children have traditionally been protected—even against their own parents—because they have been assumed to be incapable of exercising full, autonomous choice, and the state has been empowered to operate *in loco parentis* to attempt to preserve the rights of children.[51] Likewise, the state has protected mentally incompetent adults who cannot make rational, autonomous choices. Less justifiably by most criteria, the state has operated to limit the choices of welfare recipients, unwed mothers, and individuals who, although they may have full mental capabilities, are stigmatized in some fashion by society and punished for making questionable choices in the past. As Desmond King points out, liberal societies, such as the United States, have at times adopted extremely illiberal policies, policies that limit exercise of free choice by the individual, when they believe there is some compelling state interest involved.[52] Again, the question is, What criteria should be used to decide which groups the state should treat as its children?

The state may also intervene to protect the life of an individual who has made an autonomous decision to end his or her life. Legislation that makes suicide a crime and attempts to prevent individuals from purposely ending their lives reflects a judgment that the value of preserving life supersedes the value of preserving individual autonomy. In this hierarchy of values, the decision to end one's own life by definition indicates that the individual needs the protection of the state. The same principle is apparently applied to individuals who have made it clear that they do not wish to be kept "alive" by artificial means when all hope of recovery to a fully conscious and autonomous life is lost. Such instances raise several conflicting values and return us to the question of what actually constitutes a human life. Does it matter that an individual may have declared while in good health that he or she does not want to be kept alive by artificial means?[53] The potentially conflicting principles of preserving life and preserving autonomy become even more confused here because an individual who once made an autonomous choice about how he or she would like to be treated may, at the crucial time, no longer be able to decide anything autonomously and may, in fact, never be able to do so again.

In less extreme instances, the state may also restrain the autonomy of an individual for the sake of protecting him or her from the adverse consequences of a personal choice. Consumer protection is an obvious example—government may disregard the traditional principle of *caveat emptor* and simply prohibit the sale of potentially harmful products to protect the citizen. On the one hand, the conservative who is interested in preserving individual choice would argue that such protections are harmful, inasmuch as the paternalistic actions of government prevent citizens from being truly free actors. On the other hand, the complexity of the marketplace, the number of products offered for sale, and the absence of full information may prevent individuals from making meaningful judgments.[54] As a consequence, government is justified in intervening, especially because many of the products banned would affect persons incapable of making their own informed choices—for example, children. A less extreme example is government's requirement for labeling and full disclosure of information so that citizens are able to make more rational and informed autonomous decisions about the products they purchase.

At times, government also forces citizens to consume certain goods and services because they are presumably for the citizens' own good. Two examples of these "merit goods" concern the requirements that people riding in automobiles should have to wear seat belts and that people riding motorcycles should have to wear helmets.[55] A number of safety organizations and many citizens support measures of this kind, but other citizens argue that they should be "free to be foolish," to make their own choices, and to assume certain risks.[56] As appealing as that argument sounds in a free society, risky decisions also have potential costs that extend beyond the individuals who are willing to take the chance. Their families are potentially harmed, both emotionally and economically, by such risky behavior. The society as a whole may have a stake in the individual decision because public money may well have to pay for a long and expensive hospitalization from a preventable injury. Thus, as with all of the ethical principles that can be applied to public decisions, there are few absolutes, and there is a great deal of balancing of ideas and ethical criteria when government must act to make policy. As noted already, some of the debate over the Obama health care plan concerns the right of the federal government to force individuals to purchase health insurance, even though it may benefit them to do so.[57]

Professional licensing and laws that control the licensing of drugs have also been criticized as unduly restricting the free choice of individuals. It is argued that individuals should have the right to select the form of treatment they would like, even if the medical establishment deems it quackery. So, for example, activists for people with AIDS have criticized the U.S. Food and Drug Administration for delaying approval of some drugs that may have potential for ameliorating the symptoms of AIDS and slowing the progress of the disease.[58] The criticisms have been particularly pointed because the drugs are already licensed and available in other industrialized countries. Of course, the counterargument from the Food and Drug Administration is that this restriction is justified because it increases the probability that the individual will receive treatments that are known to have some beneficial effects. If there were no licensing, the individual might rely on a treatment without any real therapeutic value until it was too late to use other treatments. The question from the perspective of ethics is, Who should be able to make the choice about the best treatment—the individual affected or a government organization?

Truthfulness.   Most systems of ethics and morality prohibit lying.[59] People generally regard lying as wrong simply "because it is wrong," but it also allows one individual to deprive another of his or her autonomy. When one person lies to another, the liar deprives the other person of the ability to make rational and informed decisions. In some instances, telling "little white lies" may prevent awkward social situations, but perhaps more stringent criteria should be applied to justify lies told by government, especially in a democracy.

Lying to the public by public officials has been justified primarily as being for the public's own good. Political leaders who accept this paternalistic argument assume that public officials have more information and are unwilling to divulge it either for security reasons or because they believe that the information will only "confuse" citizens. They may therefore lie to the public to get average citizens to behave in ways that they—the public officials—prefer. They also seem to believe that the citizens would behave in that same way if they had all the information available to the political leader, but even if citizens would not behave as public officials want them to, officials think that they *should* behave in that manner, and the lie is therefore justified as a means of protecting the public from its own irresponsibility or ignorance.

Such lying obviously limits the autonomy of the average citizen when making policy choices or evaluating the performance of those in office. Even white lies are questionable—the importance of autonomy in democratic political systems may require much closer attention to honesty, even though the short-term consequences of telling the truth may not benefit incumbents. In times of war, officials may need to lie, or at a minimum withhold information, for security reasons or to maintain morale, but even that largely justifiable behavior will tend to undermine the legitimacy of a democratic system. In part, citizens may find it difficult to know when the lying has stopped; that problem became very evident during the Cold War, and it has resurfaced to some extent in regard to terrorism and the war in Iraq.[60]

Other white lies told to the public involve withholding information that might cause panic or other responses that are potentially very dangerous. For example, a public official may learn that a nuclear power plant has had a minor and apparently controllable accident that is not believed to endanger anyone. The official may withhold that information from the public in the belief that doing so will prevent a panic; a mass flight from the scene could cause more harm than the accident. But as with other ethical situations, decisions to lie about one thing and not about others make it difficult for the official (and government as a whole) to behave consistently. Perhaps the only standard that can be applied with any consistency in this case is the utilitarian criterion: The harm prevented by the lie must outweigh the ill effects caused by the lie. Determining this utilitarian ratio is relatively easy when we are balancing the possible few deaths and limited property damage from a minor nuclear accident against probable widespread and violent panic. Continued lying, however, will eventually generate a public loss of trust in government and its officials, and the cost of such skepticism is difficult to calculate.[61]

A special category of lying is the withholding of information by public officials to protect their own careers. This is a problem for the *whistle-blowers* who would expose deceit, as well as for the liars, and it occurs in the private sector as well as the public sector.[62] Attempting to act ethically and responsibly has placed many individuals in difficult situations. For example, the man who blew the whistle on government cost overruns on the Lockheed C-5A airplane lost his job, as did the EPA official who exposed the agency's shortcomings under Rita Lavelle, as well as many other conscientious officials in less dramatic circumstances.[63] The problem caused when someone blows the whistle is especially difficult to analyze when the individual at fault does not lie directly but simply does nothing to expose errors government has made.

The whistle-blower must go to some lengths to make the information about official lying known to the public and must accept substantial career risks. Because of these difficulties, policymakers may want to devise means to encourage whistle-blowers and to protect them against reprisals. The federal government and many state and local governments in the United States have devised programs to protect whistle-blowers, but there are still substantial risks for the individual who chooses to act in what he or she considers the responsible manner. In conjunction with, or in the absence of, programs encouraging officials to divulge information, laws such as the Freedom of Information Act can at least make it more difficult for government to suppress information.

Thus, in addition to the general moral prohibition, lying carries a particular onus in the public sector because it can destroy an individual citizen's ability to make appropriate and informed choices about government. Although a lie may be told for good reasons (at least in the mind of the liar), it must be questioned unless it has extremely positive benefits and is not told just for the convenience of the individual official. The long-term consequences for government of even "justifiable" lying may be negative. Citizens who learn that government lies to them for good reasons may soon wonder if it will not also lie to them for less noble reasons, and they may find it difficult to believe the official interpretation of anything. In the United States, for example, the Vietnam War, Watergate, and claims about weapons of mass destruction in Iraq created distrust and disaffection toward government.[64]

If strictures against lying are to some degree dependent on a desire to preserve the political community and the sense of trust within it, somewhat different rules may apply in international politics. Although there is a concept of an international community of nations, the moral bonds within that community tend to be weaker than those within a single nation. Moreover, a national political leader's paramount responsibilities are to his or her own citizens. Lying in international politics may therefore be more acceptable; political leaders regularly face the problem of "dirty hands," which seems to be part of the job of being a political leader in an imperfect world.[65] That is to say, leaders may be forced to engage in activities that they know to be wrong in most circumstances, such as lying, to serve the (largely utilitarian) goals of protecting and preserving the interests of their own country.

Fairness.   Fairness is a value to which citizens expect government to assign maximum importance. One standard justification for the existence of government, even for conservatives, is that it protects and enforces the civil and political rights of all individuals, with as much equality as possible. It is further argued (at least by liberals) that government has the legal and economic capacity to redress inequities in the distribution of goods and services that result from the operations of the marketplace.[66] Government, then, is charged with ensuring that citizens are treated fairly in the political system and perhaps in the economy and society.

But just what is "fair treatment of citizens"? As employed by different schools of social and political thought, the word *fair* has had different meanings. To a conservative, for example, fairness means allowing individuals maximum opportunity to exercise their own abilities and to keep what they earn in the marketplace through those abilities. Some conservatives consider it fair that people who cannot provide for themselves should suffer, along with their families, although they disagree about how much suffering is acceptable.[67] Many conservatives do not consider it fair for government to take property from some citizens to benefit others; in that view, property has rights, just as people do.[68]

The familiar Marxist doctrine "From each according to his abilities, to each according to his needs" suggests a very different standard of fairness, implying that all members of the society, provided they are willing to contribute their own abilities (however limited), are entitled to have their material needs satisfied.[69] According to this standard, those with lower earning capacity need not suffer, although the doctrine does not guarantee absolute equality. There is, however, no uncontested definition of "needs," so this standard could be an open-ended entitlement for citizens were it to be accepted.

The standard of fairness applied in most contemporary welfare states is something of a mixture of the conservative and Marxist standards, although it generally lacks the intellectual underpinnings of either extreme.[70] The mixed-economy welfare state that operates in industrialized societies usually allows productive citizens to retain most of their earnings and at the same time requires them to help build a floor of benefits so that the less fortunate can maintain at least a minimal standard of living. Unlike the situation in the Marxist state, this redistribution of goods and services to the less fortunate from the more success-ful is conducted in the context of free and open politics.

Besides being concerned with fairness across classes and among individuals, governments increasingly must be concerned about fairness across generations. The current generation is custodian of the natural resources of the society and must make decisions about the use of those resources. Is it *fair* for the current generation to consume such a large share of the proven reserves of resources, such as oil, copper, chromium, and the like? Is it *fair* for this generation to incur a massive public (and private) debt that will impose burdens on, and restrain the opportunities of, future generations? What principles can be used to justify choices that have intergenerational consequences?[71] How can those principles be included in the analytic techniques used to reach policy decisions?[72]

Can these operating principles of the contemporary welfare state—principles that arise largely from political accidents and a pragmatic evolution process—be systematized and developed on a more intellectual plane? One promising approach to such a systematic justification of the welfare state can be found in philosopher John Rawls's concept of social justice. In his essay "Justice as Fairness,"[73] Rawls develops two principles of justice for a society. The first is that "Each person participating in a practice, or affected by it, has an equal right to the most extensive liberty compatible with like liberty of all." This is a restate-ment of the basic right of individuals to be involved in governmental decisions that affect them, a principle not incompatible with the cry "No taxation without representation!" This first principle of justice would place the burden of proof on anyone who would seek to limit another's participation in political life; it can therefore be seen as a safeguard for procedural democracy in contemporary societies. Rawls thus places pronounced emphasis on the decision-making pro-cedures employed when evaluating the fairness of decisions and societal institu-tions. This principle may present great difficulties for the citizen and the analyst, however, if the decisions reached by participatory means conflict with more substantive conceptions of fairness.

Rawls's second principle of fairness is more substantive and also more prob-lematic. Referred to as the "difference principle," it states that "Social and eco-nomic inequalities are to be arranged so that they are both: (a) to the greatest benefit of the least advantaged; and (b) attached to offices and positions open to all under conditions of fair equality of opportunity."[74] This principle places the burden of proof on those who attempt to justify a system of inequalities, which can be seen as just only if all other possible arrangements would produce lowered expectations for the least well-off group in society. To help a society that is striv-ing for equality, citizens are asked to think of their own place in society as shrouded behind a "veil of ignorance," so that it cannot be known to them in advance.[75] Would they be willing to gamble on being in the lowest segment of the society when they decide on a set of inequalities for the society? If they would not, then they have good reason to understand the society's need to equalize the distribution of goods and services. Of course, it is impossible to apply the logic of the veil of ignorance within existing societies, but it is a useful concept for understanding the rational acceptance of redistributive government policies and in justifying such policies politically.

Several interesting questions arise with respect to Rawls's difference principle. One is the place of natural endowments and individual differences in producing and justifying inequalities. Should individuals who have special natural abilities be allowed to benefit from them? This borders on the basic ethical principle of *desert*, or the degree to which any individual deserves what he or she receives in the world (discussed in the next section). The question is reminiscent of a Kurt Vonnegut story in *Player Piano*, in which individuals' particular talents are balanced by the "great handicapper."[76] Individuals who can run particularly fast, for instance, are required to wear heavy weights to slow them down, and those who have creative gifts are required to wear earphones through which come loud and discordant noises to distract them from thinking and using that creativity. Does Rawls regard such a homogeneous and ultimately dull society as desirable or fair? One would think not, but he does point out that natural endowments are desirable primarily because they can be used to assist those in the lowest segment of society. Thus, *noblesse oblige* is expected of those who possess natural talents.

Does the same expectation hold true for those whose endowments are economic rather than physical or intellectual? Rawls's view seems to be that equality is a natural principle that can be justified by decision making that occurs behind the veil of ignorance, as well as by the cooperative instincts that Rawls believes are inherent in humans. Again, in his view, economic endowments should exist only to the extent they can be used for the betterment of the lowest segments in society.

In contrast, critics point to what they consider the natural rights of individuals to retain their holdings and to the incentives for work and investment that are inherent in a system of economic inequality.[77] Inequalities are argued to be functional for a society because they supply a spur to ambition and an incentive to produce more—both artistically and economically—which in turn can be considered to benefit the entire society. This is obviously related to the utilitarian logic that undergirds cost-benefit analysis. Thus, to critics of Rawls's philosophy, the tendency toward equality may be inappropriate on ethical grounds because it would deny individuals benefits that they have received through either genetics or education, and it may be wrong on utilitarian grounds because it reduces the total production of the society along several dimensions.

Finally, the Rawlsian framework is discussed primarily within the context of a single society, or a single institution, in which cooperative principles would at least be considered, if not always followed. Could these principles be applied to a broader context? In particular, should they be applied to a global community? In other words, should the riches accumulated in industrialized countries be used to benefit the citizens of the most impoverished countries of the world?[78] Such a policy would, of course, be politically difficult to implement, even if it could be shown to be morally desirable. Nevertheless, the ethical underpinnings of foreign aid must be considered, especially as the world moves into an era of increased scarcity as well as increased interdependence.

Although we have been discussing issues of fairness primarily in economic terms, increasingly these issues are conceptualized in terms of race, ethnicity, and gender. The same logic of analysis may well be applicable, however, for fairness could be maximized by assuming the same veil of ignorance for making decisions about these social differences as for decisions about economic differences. The social categories, however, also raise issues of compensation for past injustices, along with a perceived need to create structures and programs that will encourage future achievement by the previously disadvantaged groups. Such remedies for past unfairness, in turn, create resentment on the part of those who feel that their natural endowments of skills and abilities are being devalued. This kind of resentment arises in response to scholarships granted on the basis of race or gender, hiring quotas, and a variety of other "affirmative action" policies intended to change existing social and economic patterns.[79] Furthermore, although economic inequalities may be justified as providing incentives for individuals to do more for themselves and to change their own condition, it is generally not feasible for individuals to change gender or race. No question of equality and fairness is easy to resolve, but the issues of race and gender have proved to be among the most difficult for the political system to cope with.

Although opinions may differ about the applicability of Rawls's ideas in the real world of policymaking, and even about the desirability of such application, his work raises interesting and important ethical questions for those attempting to design public policies. Many industrialized democracies have been making redistributive economic policy decisions for years, often justifying them on pragmatic or political grounds rather than on ethical principles.[80] The work of Rawls provides intellectual underpinnings for those policies, even though no government has gone as far in redistributing income and wealth as Rawls's difference principle would demand. Those governments are now facing more decisions about race and gender inequalities, and there, too, some guidance beyond simple political expediency may be required.

The concept of desert.   Discussion of the values of the welfare state raises the question of *desert*. What does a citizen deserve as a member of the society, and what does the individual deserve as a human being with particular needs and virtues? As we have said, the American people enjoy some rights by virtue of the Constitution and the Bill of Rights. The existence of those rights is largely incontestable, although there certainly are multiple interpretations of their meaning. The more interesting cases involve benefits coming from government that have come to be considered rights but are much less clearly grounded in the basic law of the land.

The concept of "entitlement" is the most important instance of desert being constructed by policy and then accepted by the population.[81] Social insurance programs are the clearest example of entitlements, for the citizen has paid for the program over his or her working life and has received a commitment from government to provide the benefits when the citizen needs them—because of retirement, unemployment, or disability. These programs were designed to be regarded not as charity or a government handout but rather as a right. Moreover, entitlement programs were designed to make it difficult for subsequent generations of politicians to dismantle them.

When we move away from social insurance and other contributory programs, however, the concept of desert becomes more difficult to sustain within the public sector in the United States. It is clear that young people do have a right to a free public education, but only through high school. Why does the right not extend through college or even through graduate school?[82] The debate over health care reform in 1994 raised the question of whether citizens have a right to health care, and if they do, to what level of health care. If there is a right to basic health care, is there also a right to the most advanced and expensive treatments available? If the right is restricted to basic services, where does the entitlement stop and why? Certain public goods, such as clean air and water, also are often conceptualized as the entitlements of citizens. Why?

Can there be "negative desert"? Do some citizens deserve certain punishments and sanctions? It is sometimes argued that the perpetrators of certain crimes "deserve" the death penalty.[83] It is also argued that those responsible for economic or environmental crimes deserve certain severe penalties (but not death). On what basis can it be said that people deserve a specified form of punishment, particularly one as severe and final as the death penalty? At a less extreme level, do people who have other perceived failings such as having to accept public assistance deserve to be punished or controlled in other ways?[84] In chapter 12, we noted the increasing number of restrictions and regulations being imposed on welfare recipients; do those people deserve that treatment, and if so, why?

A final point about desert is that it is often defined in terms of particular communities, with those outside the community being excluded. In a search to find alternatives to big government and utilitarian values, one strand of communitarian thinking in the United States has argued for greater devolution of decision making to communities.[85] Empowering communities to make decisions for themselves, however, could easily lead to an us-versus-them conception of governing, with (paradoxically) a great deal of mutuality within the community and substantial exclusion of outsiders. For example, would equalization of school funding be an appropriate policy under communitarian governance? The concept of community has a powerful appeal to many Americans, but its restrictive concept of desert raises a number of questions about membership in the community.

Summary

The ethical system most often applied to public policy analysis is utilitarianism, by which actions are justified as producing the greatest net benefit for the society as a whole. As noted earlier in the chapter, this principle undergirds the dominant analytic approaches in the field, such as cost-benefit analysis. In this chapter, we have discussed several ethical questions that arise in making and implementing public policies, as well as some possible answers to those questions, mostly reflecting a nonutilitarian perspective. Ultimately, however, just as no one can provide definitive answers to these ethical questions in public policy, public officials may face policy questions that have no readily acceptable answers, economically, politically, or ethically. Values and ethical principles are frequently in conflict, and sometimes the policymaker must violate one firmly held ethical position to protect another.

Despite these practical difficulties, it is important for citizens and policymakers to think about policy in ethical terms. Perhaps too much policymaking has been conducted without attention to anything but the political and economic consequences. Of course, such utilitarian values are important bases for evaluating a program, but they may not be the only relevant criteria. Both the policymaker and the citizen must be concerned also with matters of justice and trust in government. Indeed, it may be that justice and social trust ultimately make the best policies—and even the best politics.

Notes

Chapter 1

1. U.S. Census Bureau, *Census of Governments*, Vol. 1 (Washington, DC: Department of Commerce, 2007).
2. See Lester Salamon, ed., *Handbook of Policy Instruments* (New York: Oxford University Press, 2001), Introduction.
3. Richard Nelson, *The Moon and the Ghetto* (New York: Norton, 1977).
4. Richard Rose, "The Programme Approach to the Growth of Government," *British Journal of Political Science* 15 (1985): 1–28.
5. Jacob Torfing, B. Guy Peters, Jon Pierre, and Eva Sørensen, *Interactive Governance: Advancing the Paradigm* (Oxford: Oxford University Press, 2012).
6. For example, the Department of Defense now has several programs for cleaning up environmental damage from military bases and for creating more environmentally sustainable programs in the military.
7. Brian W. Hogwood and B. Guy Peters, *The Pathology of Public Policy* (Oxford: Oxford University Press, 1985); and Craig W. Thomas, "Public Management as Interagency Cooperation," *Journal of Public Administration Research and Theory* 7 (1997): 221–246.
8. Peter J. May, "Policy Design and Implementation," in *Handbook of Public Administration*, ed. B. G. Peters and Jon Pierre, 2nd ed. (London: Sage); Helen Ingram and Anne Schneider, "Improving Implementation through Framing Smarter Statutes," *Journal of Public Policy* 10 (1990): 67–88.
9. Private actors do, of course, have recourse to law as a means of influencing policy and forcing government action. This is especially true in the United States, where the courts are so important for determining policy. For example, in addition to the enforcement activities of the Federal Trade Commission and the Antitrust Division of the Department of Justice, private individuals also bring suit to enforce antitrust laws.
10. *Bragdon v. Abbott*, 524 U.S. 624 (1998).
11. B. Guy Peters and Martin O. Heisler, "Thinking about Public Sector Growth," in *Why Governments Grow: Measuring Public Sector Size*, ed. C. L. Taylor (Beverly Hills, CA: Sage, 1983). See also Giandomenico Majone, *Regulating Europe* (London: Routledge, 1996).

12. The costs of these regulatory interventions was made popular by Murray Wiedenbaum. See his original article, "The High Costs of Government Regulation," *Challenge,* November 1979, 32–39. More recently the Small Business Administration (2011) estimated the costs of compliance with regulations as $1.7 trillion. These costs were not without their political motivations—for example, to demonstrate the high costs of government—and they usually failed to include the offsetting value of the benefits of regulation.

13. William T. Gormley, *Privatization and Its Alternatives* (Madison: University of Wisconsin Press, 1991).

14. Penelope Lemov, "Jailhouse, INC," *Governing* 6 (May 1993): 44–48; Mildred Warner and Amir Hefetz, "Applying Market Solutions to Public Services," *Urban Affairs Review* 38 (2002): 70–89.

15. Donald F. Kettl, *Government by Proxy: (Mis)Managing Federal Programs?* (Washington, DC: CQ Press, 1988); and Patricia W. Ingraham, "Quality in the Public Services," in *Governance in a Changing Environment,* ed. B. Guy Peters and Donald J. Savoie (Montreal: McGill/Queens University Press, 1995).

16. Charles H. Levine and Paul L. Posner, "The Centralizing Effects of Fiscal Austerity on the Intergovernmental System," *Political Science Quarterly* 96 (1981): 67–85.

17. James D. Chesney, "Intergovernmental Politics in the Allocation of Block Grant Funds for Substance Abuse in Michigan," *Publius* 24 (1994): 39–46; and Doug Peterson, "Block Grant 'Turn-Backs' Revived in Bush Budget," *Nation's Cities Weekly* 15 (February 3, 1992): 6.

18. Brian K. Collins and Brian J. Gerber, "Redistributive Policy and Devolution: Is State Administration a Road Block (Grant) to Equitable Access to Federal Funds," *Journal of Public Administration Research and Theory* 16 (2006): 613–632.

19. Stanley S. Surrey and Paul R. McDaniel, *Tax Expenditures* (Cambridge, MA: Harvard University Press, 1985).

20. Aaron Wildavsky, "Keeping Kosher: The Epistemology of Tax Expenditures," *Journal of Public Policy* 5 (1985): 413–431; Edward D. Kleinbard, "The Congress Within Congress: How Tax Expenditures Distort Our Budget and Political Processes," *University of Southern California Law Review* (2010), Paper 61.

21. Charles L. Schultze, *The Public Use of Private Interest* (Washington, DC: Brookings Institution Press, 1977).

22. Richard Hula, *Market-Based Public Policy* (New York: St. Martin's, 1988).

23. Ibid.; more generally, see Salamon, *Handbook of Policy Instruments.*

24. Douglas F. Elliott, *Uncle Sam in Pinstripes: Evaluating Federal Credit Programs* (Washington, DC: Brookings Institution Press, 2010).

25. Thomas Anton, *Moving Money* (Cambridge, MA: Oelgeschlager, Hain and Gunn, 1980).

26. Johan Fritzell, "Income Inequality Trends in the 1980s: A Five-Country Comparison," *Acta Sociologica* 36 (1993): 47–62; and Daniel Rigney, *The Matthew Effect: How Advantage Begets Further Advantage* (New York: Columbia University Press, 2010).

27. On taxation, see B. Guy Peters, *The Politics of Taxation: A Comparative Perspective* (Oxford: Blackwell, 1991). On conscription, see Margaret Levi, *Consent, Dissent, Patriotism* (Cambridge: Cambridge University Press, 1997).

28. Anthony King, "Ideas, Institutions and Policies of Government: A Comparative Analysis," *British Journal of Political Science* 5 (1975): 418.

29. See Linda M. Bennett and Stephen Earl Bennett, *Living with Leviathan: Americans Coming to Terms with Big Government* (Lawrence: University Press of Kansas, 1990).

30. Lloyd A. Free and Hadley Cantril, *The Political Beliefs of Americans* (New York: Simon and Schuster, 1968).

31. David O. Sears and Jack Citrin, *Tax Revolt: Something for Nothing in California,* rev. ed. (Berkeley: University of California Press, 1991).

32. See chapter 10; ABC News Polls for a number of years have found that Americans think government wastes about half of the money it collects in taxes.

33. Peter Bachrach and Aryeh Botwinick, *Power and Empowerment: A Radical Theory of Participatory Democracy* (Philadelphia: Temple University Press, 1992).

34. Michael Cooper and Megan Thee-Brenan, "Disapproval Rate for Congress at Record 82% After Debt Talks," *The New York Times,* August 4, 2011.

35. Michael T. Hayes, *Incrementalism* (New York: Longman, 1992).

36. See, for example, Charles O. Jones, *The Reagan Legacy* (Chatham, NJ: Chatham House, 1989).

37. Shaan K. Hathiramani, "The Politics of Pensions: Trouble for Both Parties Looms in Social Security Debate," *Harvard Political Review* 32, no. 2 (2005): 24–25.

38. Robin Toner, "House Democrats Support Abortion in Health Plans," *New York Times,* July 14, 1994.

39. See William Schneider, "What Else Do They Want?" *National Journal,* May 16, 1998, 1150; Susan B. Hansen.

40. Morris P. Fiorina, "Parties and Partisanship: A 40-Year Retrospective," *Political Behavior* 24 (2002): 93–115.

41. Jackie Calmes, "House Passes Stimulus Plan with No GOP Votes," *New York Times,* January 28, 2009.

42. See Robert Reich, *The Work of Nations* (New York: Norton, 1991); and Ann O. Kreuger, *The Political Economy of American Trade Policy* (Chicago: University of Chicago Press, 1995).

43. "Race, Class and Hurricane Katrina," *Political Affairs* 84, no. 10 (2005): 36–39.

44. Andrew Hacker, *Two Nations: Black and White, Separate, Hostile, Unequal* (New York: Scribner, 1992).

Chapter 2

1. Charles H. Levine, "Human Resource Erosion and the Uncertain Future of the U.S. Civil Service: From Policy Gridlock to Structural Fragmentation," *Governance* 1 (1988): 115–143.

2. See Terry Sanford, *Storm over the States* (New York: McGraw-Hill, 1967), 80.

3. Deil S. Wright, *Understanding Intergovernmental Relations,* 3rd ed. (Belmont, CA: Brooks/Cole, 1988), 83–86; the term *multilevel governance* is increasingly used to describe these relationships. See B. Guy Peters, "Developments in Intergovernmental Relations: Towards Multi-level Governance," *Policy and Politics* 29 (2001): 131–135.

4. Ibid.

5. Joseph A. Zimmerman, *Contemporary American Federalism: The Growth of National Power,* 2nd ed. (Albany: State University of New York Press, 2008).

6. John Kincaid, "From Cooperative to Coercive Federalism," *Annals* 509 (1990): 139–152.

7. Angela Antonelli, "Promises Unfilled: Unfunded Mandates Reform Act of 1995," *Regulation* 19, no. 2 (1996): 44–52.

8. U.S. Bureau of the Census, *Census of Governments, 1997* (Washington, DC: U.S. Government Printing Office, 1998).

9. Jerry Mitchell, *Public Authorities and Public Policy: The Business of Government* (New York: Greenwood, 1992); and Kathryn A. Foster, *The Political Economy of Special Purpose Government* (Washington, DC: Georgetown University Press, 1998).

10. During the mid-1980s, the states averaged over 11 percent surpluses in their total budgets. See the Tax Foundation, *Facts and Figures on Government Finance,* vol. 38, 1991 (Baltimore: Johns Hopkins University Press, 2004), Table E2.

11. Linda Greenhouse, "Supreme Court Agrees to Hear Gun Control Case," *New York Times,* November 20, 2007.

12. On the concept of "veto points," see George Tsebelis, *Veto Players: How Institutions Work* (Princeton, NJ: Princeton University Press, 2002).

13. Mark Peterson, *Legislating Together* (Cambridge, MA: Harvard University Press, 1992).

14. See, for example, James Q. Wilson, *Bureaucracy* (New York: Basic Books, 1989); Charles T. Goodsell, *Mission Mystique: Belief Systems in Public Agencies* (Washington, DC: CQ Press, 2011).

15. See Cornelius Kerwin, *Rulemaking,* 4th ed. (Washington, DC: CQ Press, 2011).

16. Daniel Carpenter, *Forging Bureaucratic Autonomy* (Princeton, NJ: Princeton University Press, 2001).

17. George Krause, *A Two-Way Street: The Institutional Dynamics of the Modern Administrative State* (Pittsburgh: University of Pittsburgh Press, 2000).

18. Morris P. Fiorina, "An Era of Divided Government," *Political Science Quarterly* 107 (1992): 387–410; and James L. Sundquist, *Constitutional Reform and Effective Government,* rev. ed. (Washington, DC: Brookings Institution Press, 1992).

19. David Mayhew, *Divided We Govern* (New Haven, CT: Yale University Press, 1991); Charles O. Jones, *The Presidency in a Separated System* (Washington, DC: Brookings Institution Press, 1994); Nelson Polsby, *Policy Innovation in America* (New Haven, CT: Yale University Press, 1984); and John E. Schwartz, *America's Hidden Success,* rev. ed. (New York: Norton, 1988). For a critique, see Alberto Alesina and Howard Rosenthal, *Partisan Politics, Divided Government and the Economy* (Cambridge: Cambridge University Press, 1996).

20. Michael T. Hayes, *Incrementalism* (New York: Longman, 1992); Carter A. Wilson, "Policy Regimes and Policy Change," *Journal of Public Policy* 20, 247–274.

21. Charles E. Lindblom, *The Intelligence of Democracy: Decision Making through Mutual Adjustment* (New York: Free Press, 1965).

22. For example, a poll in late 2003 found that 79 percent of the American populace supported health care for all Americans even if it meant higher taxes; see "Poll," *Washington Post,* October 13, 2003. When faced with the reality of the Obama health care reforms, however, less than half supported the changes in early 2012 (see chapter 11).

23. Brian W. Hogwood and B. Guy Peters, *Policy Dynamics* (Brighton, UK: Wheatsheaf, 1982); and Robert E. Goodin, *Political Theory and Public Policy* (Chicago: University of Chicago Press, 1986).

24. The classic statement is in J. Leiper Freeman, *The Political Process: Executive Bureau–Legislative Committee Relations* (New York: Random House, 1965).

25. The classic statement of this point is in Theodore J. Lowi, *The End of Liberalism,* 2nd ed. (New York: Norton, 1979).

26. Peter L. Hall and C. Lawrence Evans, "The Power of Subcommittees," *Journal of Politics* 52 (1990): 335–355.

27. See D. Roderick Kiewiet and Mathew D. McCubbins, *The Logic of Delegation* (Chicago: University of Chicago Press, 1991).

28. Gregory J. Wawro, *Legislative Entrepreneurship in the U.S. House of Representatives* (Ann Arbor: University of Michigan Press, 2000).

29. D. McCool, "Subgovernments as Determinants of Political Viability," *Political Science Quarterly* 105 (1990): 269–293.

30. André Blais and Stéphane Dion, *The Budget-Maximizing Bureaucrat* (Pittsburgh: University of Pittsburgh Press, 1992).

31. Peter B. Natchez and Irvin C. Bupp, "Policy and Priority in the Budgetary Process," *American Political Science Review* 67 (1973): 951–963.

32. See Robert H. Salisbury, J. P. Heinz, R. L. Nelson, and Edward O. Laumann, "Triangles, Networks and Hollow Cores: The Complex Geometry of Washington Interest Representation," in *The Politics of Interests,* ed. Mark P. Petracca (Boulder, CO: Westview Press, 1992), 141–166.

33. Rufus E. Miles, "A Cabinet Department of Education: An Unwise Campaign Promise or a Sound Idea?" *Public Administration Review* 39 (1979): 103–110.

34. For example, the Cooperative Extension Service in the Department of Agriculture eliminated hundreds of county offices.

35. See D. F. Kettl, *The Department of Homeland Security's First Year: A Report Card* (New York: Century Foundation Press, 2004).

36. Robert Brodsky, "Administration Hopes to Leave Performance Management Legacy," *Government Executive,* April 21, 2008.

37. See Jack L. Walker, *Mobilizing Interest Groups in America* (Ann Arbor: University of Michigan Press, 1991).

38. Charles O. Jones, *The United States Congress* (Homewood, IL: Dorsey, 1982).

39. Try it!

40. Some scholars make a great deal over the differences between these concepts, with a community being a more unified and tightly knit set of groups than a network. See Martin J. Smith, *Pressure, Power and Policy* (Pittsburgh: University of Pittsburgh Press, 1994).

41. James Kuhnhenn, "Congress Proves Unable to Cut Back on Pork," *Knight-Ridder Washington Bureau,* October 2, 2005.

42. See Martin Jaffe, "Earmark Hypocrisy," http://abcnews.go.com/Politics/hypocrisy-alert-abc-news-grills-gop-leaders-earmarks/story?id=12403958.

43. See Richard Rose and B. Guy Peters, *Can Government Go Bankrupt?* (New York: Basic Books, 1976).

44. Richard A. McGowan, *Privatize This? Assessing the Opportunities and Costs of Privatization* (Santa Barbara, CA: Praeger, 2011).

45. See Linda L. M. Bennett and Stephen Earl Bennett, *Living with Leviathan: Americans Come to Terms with Big Government* (Lawrence: University Press of Kansas, 1990); Jeff Madrick, *The Case for Big Government* (Princeton, NJ: Princeton University Press).

46. Jonas Prager, "Contracting Out Government Services: Lessons from the Private Sector," *Public Administration Review* 54 (1994): 176–184; and Steven Rathgeb Smith and Michael Lipsky, *Nonprofits for Hire: The Welfare State in the Age of Contracting* (Cambridge, MA: Harvard University Press, 1993).

47. B. Guy Peters, "Public and Private Provision of Services," in *The Private Provision of Public Services,* ed. Dennis Thompson (Beverly Hills, CA: Sage, 1986).

48. This form of organization has not been typical in the United States. See Robert H. Salisbury, "Why No Corporatism in America?" in *Trends toward Corporatist Intermediation,* ed. Philippe C. Schmitter and Gerhard Lehmbruch (Beverly Hills, CA: Sage, 1979); and Susan B. Hansen, "Industrial Policy and Corporatism in the American States," *Governance* 2 (1989): 172–197.

49. U.S. Government Accountability Office, *Core Principles and a Strategic Approach Would Enhance Stakeholder Participation in Developing Quota-Based Programs* (Washington, DC: USGAO), GAO-06-289, February 24, 2005.

50. Federal Advisory Committee Act Database (General Services Administration, 2011), www. fido.gov/facadatabse.

51. For a more complete treatment of public employment, see Hans-Ulrich Derlien and B. Guy Peters, *Who Works for Government and What Do They Do?* (Bamberg, Germany: University of Bamberg, Administrative Sciences, 1998).

52. See Jonathan R. T. Hughes, *The Governmental Habit Redux: Economic Controls from Colonial Times to the Present* (Princeton, NJ: Princeton University Press, 1993).

53. The figures for later years would be somewhat lower but with a significant number of jobs still being created by defense purchases.

54. Tax Foundation, *Facts and Figures on Government Finance,* 37th ed. (Baltimore: Johns Hopkins University Press, 2004).

55. Thomas D. Hopkins, *Regulatory Costs in Profile* (St. Louis: Weidenbaum Center, Washington University, 2001).

56. See Thomas D. Hopkins, "OMB's Regulatory Accounting Report Falls Short of the Mark," *Policy Study* 142 (St. Louis: Washington University Center for the Study of American Business, November 1997).

Chapter 3

1. Robert A. Dahl, "The Concept of Power," *Behavioral Science* 2 (1957): 201–215.

2. E. E. Schattschneider, *The Semi-Sovereign People* (New York: Holt, Rinehart, 1960).

3. Peter Bachrach and Morton S. Baratz, "The Two Faces of Power," *American Political Science Review* 56 (1962): 947–952; Steven Lukes, *Power: A Radical View* (Basingstoke, UK: Palgrave, 2005).

4. Charles O. Jones, *An Introduction to the Study of Public Policy* (Monterey, CA: Brooks/Cole, 1984); and Michael J. Hill, *The Public Policy Process* (London: Longman, 2005).

5. John W. Kingdon, *Agendas, Alternatives and Public Policies,* 2nd ed. (New York: HarperCollins, 1995).

6. George Tsebelis, *Veto Players: How Real Institutions Work* (Princeton, NJ: Princeton University Press, 2000).

7. Brian W. Hogwood and B. Guy Peters, *Policy Dynamics* (Brighton, UK: Wheatsheaf, 1983).

8. R. Kent Weaver and Bert A. Rockman, *Do Institutions Matter?* (Washington, DC: Brookings Institution Press, 1994).
9. James G. March and J. P. Olsen, "The New Institutionalism: Organizational Factors in Political Life," *American Political Science Review* 78 (1984): 734–749; and B. Guy Peters, *Institutional Theory in Political Science*, 3rd ed. (London: Continuum, 2011).
10. See Charles T. Goodsell, *Mission Mystique: Belief Systems in Public Agencies* (Armonk, NY: M. A. Sharpe, 2010).
11. Paul Pierson, "Increasing Returns, Path Dependence and the Study of Politics," *American Political Science Review* 94 (2000): 251–267.
12. Wolfgang Streek and Kathleen Thelen, *Beyond Continuity: Institutional Change in Advanced Political Economies* (Oxford: Oxford University Press, 2005).
13. Elinor Ostrom, "Institutional Rational Choice," in *Theories of the Policy Process,* ed. P. A. Sabatier (Boulder, CO: Westview Press, 2007), 21.
14. Kenneth Shepsle, "Institutional Equilibrium and Equilibrium Institutions," in *Political Science: The Science of Politics,* ed. H. F. Weisberg (New York: Agathon Press, 1986), 51.
15. George Tsebelis, *Veto Points: How Institutions Work* (Princeton, NJ: Princeton University Press, 2000).
16. See Vivien Schmidt, "Taking Ideas and Discourse Seriously: Explaining Change through Discursive Institutionalism," *European Political Science Review* 2, 1–25.
17. Paul A. Sabatier and Hank Jenkins-Smith, *Policy Change and Learning: An Advocacy-Coalition Framework* (Boulder, CO: Westview Press, 1993).
18. On wicked problems, see Robert Hoppe, *Puzzling, Power in and Participation* (Cambridge: Policy Press, 2011).
19. B. Guy Peters, Jon Pierre, and Desmond S. King, "The Politics of Path Dependency: Political Conflict and Historical Institutionalism," *Journal of Politics* 67 (2005): 1275–1300.
20. Theodore J. Lowi, "Four Systems of Policy, Politics, Choice," *Public Administration Review* 32 (1972): 298–310.
21. Robert Salisbury and John Heinz, "A Theory of Policy Analysis and Some Preliminary Applications," in *Policy Analysis in Political Science,* ed. Ira Sharkansky (Chicago: Markham, 1970), 59.
22. K. B. Smith, "Typologies, Taxonomies and the Benefits of Policy Classification," *Policy Studies Journal* 30 (2002): 379–395.
23. Claudio Radaelli, "The Europeanization of Public Policy," in *The Politics of Europeanization,* ed. Kenneth Featherstone (Oxford: Oxford University Press, 2004), 27.
24. Jeremy J. Richardson, *Policy Styles in Western Europe* (Boston: Allen and Unwin, 1982).
25. Frans van Waarden, "Persistence of National Policy Styles: A Study of Their Institutional Foundations," in *Convergence of Diversity?* ed. B. Under and F. van Waarden (Aldershot, UK: Avebury, 1995), 333–372.
26. Gary Freeman, "National Styles and Policy Sectors: Explaining Structured Variation," *Journal of Public Policy* 5 (1985): 467–496.
27. The freedom from interest groups would be easy to overstate. Interest groups have become more active in international policy issues as globalization reduces some of the barriers between domestic and international politics.

28. Christopher Hood, *The Tools of Government* (Chatham, NJ: Chatham House, 1978); B. Guy Peters and F. Van Nispen, *Public Policy Instruments: Evaluating the Tools of Public Administration* (Cheltenham, UK: Edward Elgar, 1998); and Lester M. Salamon, Introduction, in *The Handbook of Policy Instruments*, ed. Salamon (New York: Oxford University Press, 2001).

29. Ulrika Morth, *Soft Law in Governance and Regulation* (Cheltenham, UK: Edward Elgar, 2004).

30. Stephen H. Linder and B. G. Peters, "The Analysis of Design or the Design of Analysis," *Policy Studies Review* 7 (1988): 738–750; and Pearl Eliadis, Margaret Hill, and Michael Howlett, eds., *Designing Government: From Instruments to Governance* (Montreal: McGill/Queens University Press, 2005).

31. B. Guy Peters and John A. Hoornbeek, "The Problem of Policy Problems," in *Designing Government: From Instruments to Governance*, ed. Eliadis, Hill, and Howlett (Montreal: McGill/Queens University Press, 2005), 77.

32. Michael Laver, *Private Desires, Public Action* (London: Sage, 1997).

33. William Niskanen, *Bureaucracy and Representative Government* (Chicago: Aldine/Atherton, 1971).

34. E. Patashnik, "After the Public Interest Prevails: The Political Sustainability of Political Reform," *Governance* 16 (2003): 203–234.

35. Michael D. Cohen, James. G. March, and J. P. Olsen, "A Garbage Can Model of Organizational Decision-Making," *Administrative Science Quarterly* 17 (1972): 1–25.

36. Kingdon, *Agendas, Alternatives and Public Policy.*

37. N. Zahariadis, "Multiple Streams Framework: Structure, Limitations, Prospects," in *Theories of the Policy Process*, ed. P. A. Sabatier (Boulder, CO: Westview Press, 2007), 71–108.

38. Jennifer LaFleur, "Infrastructure Spending in Stimulus Bill and Unemployment Rate," *Pro Publica*, January 26, 2009.

39. Davis, M. A. H. Dempster, and Aaron Wildavsky, "A Theory of the Budgetary Process," *American Political Science Review* 60 (1966): 529–547.

40. Charles E. Lindblom, *The Intelligence of Democracy: Policy-Making through Mutual Adjustment* (New York: Free Press, 1965).

41. Leiper Freeman, *The Political Process* (New York: Random House, 1965).

42. H. Brinton Milward and Kevin Provan, "Managing the Hollow State," *Journal of Public Administration Research and Theory* 10 (2000): 359–380.

43. Eva Sorenson and Jacob Torfing, *Theories of Democratic Network Governance* (Basingstoke, UK: Palgrave, 2007).

44. Charles Wolfe, "Market and Non-Market Failures: Comparison and Assessment," *Journal of Public Policy* 7 (1987): 43–70.

45. The standard definition of *public goods* is a good or service from which individuals cannot be excluded—for example, clean air, that and therefore cannot be priced.

46. Even laws against murder may disadvantage psychopaths while making most citizens better off.

47. Helen Ingram, Anne B. Schneider, and Peter DeLeon, "Social Constructivism and Policy Design," in *Theories of the Policy Process*, ed. Paul A. Sabatier (Boulder, CO: Westview Press, 2007), 93.

48. Peters and Hoornbeek, "The Problem of Policy Problems."

49. T. Payan, *Cops, Soldiers and Diplomats: Explaining Agency Behavior in the War on Drugs* (Lanham, MD: Lexington Books, 2006).

50. John S. Dryzek, *Deliberative Democracy and Beyond* (Oxford: Oxford University Press, 2000).

51. Frank Fischer, *Reframing Public Policy: Discursive Politics and Deliberative Practices* (Oxford: Oxford University Press, 2003); and M. Hajer and H. Wagenaar, *Understanding Governance in a Network Society* (Cambridge: Cambridge University Press, 2003).

52. Herbert Gottweiss, "Argumentative Policy Analysis," in *The Handbook of Public Policy,* ed. B. G. Peters and J. Pierre (London: Sage, 2006), 461.

53. Harold D. Lasswell, *Politics: Who Gets What, When, How* (London: Whittlesey House, 1936).

54. See Graham T. Allison and P. Zelikow, *Essence of Decision: Explaining the Cuban Missile Crisis,* 2nd ed. (New York: Longman, 1999).

Chapter 4

1. See Michael Harrington, *The Other America: Poverty in America* (New York: Macmillan, 1963). The huge number of more recent books explicitly on the topic of poverty includes Loretta Schwartz-Nobel, *Growing Up Empty: The Hunger Epidemic in America* (New York: HarperCollins, 2002); Robert Asen, *Visions of Poverty: Welfare Policy and Political Imagination* (East Lansing: Michigan State University Press, 2002); Judith A. Chafel, *Child Poverty and Public Policy* (Washington, DC: Urban Institute Press, 1993); Marisa Chappell, *The War on Welfare: Family, Poverty and Policy in the United States* (Philadelphia: University of Pennsylvania Press, 2010).

2. But see Barbara J. Nelson, *Making an Issue of Child Abuse* (Chicago: University of Chicago Press, 1984).

3. James Agee, *Let Us Now Praise Famous Men* (Boston: Houghton Mifflin, 1941). This is a book of photographs and text about the plight of rural America during the Great Depression, funded by the Farm Security Administration. The book clearly had some impact, but that impact was more limited than a comprehensive attack on poverty.

4. Anthony Downs, "Up and Down with Ecology: 'The Issue Attention Cycle,'" *Public Interest* 28 (1972): 28–50; and B. Guy Peters and Brian W. Hogwood, "In Search of the Issue-Attention Cycle," *Journal of Politics* 47 (1985): 238–253.

5. Peter Hennessey, Susan Morrison, and Richard Townsend, "Routines Punctuated by Orgies: The Central Policy Review Staff," *Strathclyde Papers on Government and Politics,* no. 30 (1985).

6. Frank Baumgartner and Bryan D. Jones, *Agendas and Instability in American Politics* (Chicago: University of Chicago Press, 1993). The same description that is being applied to the system as a whole could be applied to individual policy areas.

7. See also Bryan D. Jones, *Reconceiving Decision-Making in Democratic Politics* (Chicago: University of Chicago Press, 1994).

8. Michael D. Cohen, James G. March, and Johan P. Olsen, "The Garbage Can Model of Organizational Choice," *Administrative Science Quarterly* 17 (1972): 1–25; and John Kingdon, *Agendas, Alternatives, and Public Policy,* 2nd ed. (Boston: Little, Brown, 2003).

9. Joel Best, *Images of Issues* (New York: Aldine DeGruyter, 1989).

10. T. Payan, *Cops, Soldiers and Diplomats: Explaining Agency Behavior in the War on Drugs* (Lanham, MD: Lexington Books, 2006).

11. Roger W. Cobb and Charles D. Elder, *Participation in American Politics* (Baltimore: Johns Hopkins University Press, 1983), 85.

12. This is what Peter Bachrach and Morton S. Baratz referred to as the "second face of power." See their "Decisions and Nondecisions: An Analytic Framework," *American Political Science Review* 57 (1964): 632–642; and Steven Lukes, *Power: A Radical View* (London: Macmillan, 1974).

13. Cobb and Elder, *Participation in American Politics,* 86.

14. Ibid., 96.

15. U.S. Department of Defense, *Quadrennial Defense Review Report* (Washington, DC: Department of Defense, September 30, 2001). The quadrennial review published September 30, 2001, had relatively little on terrorism, but the one published in early 2006 was dominated by terrorism.

16. This has often been the case for social policy programs, given that in the United States these programs generally have low status, and so politicians may be able to score political points by reducing expenditures and benefits dispensed by them.

17. Jack L. Walker, "Setting the Agenda in the U.S. Senate: A Theory of Problem Selection," *British Journal of Political Science* 7 (1977): 423–445.

18. Glenn Kessler, "Explaining the Debt Ceiling Debate," *Washington Post,* June 29, 2011.

19. See David Dery, "Rethinking Agenda Setting" (unpublished paper, Department of Political Science, Hebrew University of Jerusalem, June 2002).

20. See A. Grant Jordan, "The Pluralism of Pluralism: An Anti-Theory," *Political Studies* 38 (1990): 286–301.

21. For agenda setting in another, similarly disaggregated setting, see B. Guy Peters, "Agenda-Setting in the European Community," *Journal of European Public Policy* 1 (1994): 9–26.

22. C. Wright Mills, *The Power Elite* (New York: Oxford University Press, 1961); and Charles E. Lindblom, *Democracy and the Market System* (New York: Oxford University Press, 1988).

23. Carter A. Wilson, "Policy Regimes and Policy Change," *Journal of Public Policy* 20 (2000): 247–274.

24. E. E. Schattschneider, *The Semi-Sovereign People* (New York: Holt, Rinehart and Winston, 1969).

25. Dave Gibson and Carolyn Perot, "It's the Inequality, Stupid," *Mother Jones* (March 2011).

26. Lance deHaven Smith, *Philosophical Critiques of Policy Analysis: Lindblom, Habermas and the Great Society* (Gainesville: University of Florida Press, 1988). Habermas proposes the development of a more participatory "dialogical democracy" as a means of effectively including all interests. See also Jon Elster, ed., *Deliberative Democracy* (New York: Cambridge University Press, 1998).

27. Bachrach and Baratz, "Decisions and Nondecisions."

28. Martin J. Smith, *Pressure, Power and Policy* (Pittsburgh: University of Pittsburgh Press, 1993).

29. K. Beckett, "Media Depictions of Drug Abuse: The Impact of Official Sources," *Research in Political Sociology* 7 (1995): 161–182.

30. J. Leiper Freeman, *The Political Process: Executive Bureau–Legislative Committee Relations* (New York: Random House, 1965).

31. Advisory Commission in Intergovernmental Relations, *The Federal Role in the Federal System* (Washington, DC: ACIR, 1980).

32. Many of these programs, as noted in chapter 2, confer particular benefits on one constituency or another, but many are also more general.

33. Nelson Polsby, *Policy Innovation in America* (New Haven, CT: Yale University Press, 1984); and John E. Schwartz, *America's Hidden Successes*, rev. ed. (New York: Norton, 1988). More recent is Paul C. Light, *Government's Greatest Achievements* (Washington, DC: Brookings Institution Press, 2002).

34. Samuel Kernell, *Going Public: New Strategies of Presidential Leadership*, 3rd ed. (Washington, DC: CQ Press, 1997); Charles O. Jones, *Separate but Equal Branches: Congress and the Presidency* (Chatham, NJ: Chatham House, 1994).

35. See Robert S. Gilmour and Alexis A. Halley, eds., *Who Makes Public Policy? The Struggle for Control between Congress and the Executive* (Chatham, NJ: Chatham House, 1994).

36. Sarah Cliff, "The Romneycare-Obamacare Connection," *Washington Post*, October 11, 2011.

37. See, for example, Baumgartner and Jones, *Agendas and Instability.*

38. Best, *Images of Issues*; and Anne Schneider and Helen Ingram, "Social Construction of Target Populations: Implications for Policy and Politics," *American Political Science Review* 87 (1993): 34–47.

39. John W. Kingdon, *Agendas, Alternatives and Public Policy* (Boston: Little, Brown, 1984); and Nancy C. Roberts, "Public Entrepreneurship and Innovation," *Policy Studies Review* 11 (1992): 55–73.

40. See Newt Gingrich and Robert Egge, "To Fight the Flu, Change How Government Works," *New York Times,* November 6, 2005.

41. See James Q. Wilson, *The Politics of Regulation* (New York: Basic Books, 1980).

42. Robert H. Salisbury, "The Paradox of Interest Groups in Washington—More Groups, Less Clout," in *The New American Political System*, ed. Anthony King (Washington, DC: American Enterprise Institute, 1990), 203–230; "Three Decades of Lobbying Scandal and Repercussion," *CQ Weekly,* January 20, 2006, 239.

43. Theodore R. Marmor, *The Politics of Medicare* (Chicago: Aldine, 1973).

44. In part because of those choices, the plan appears unnecessarily complex and has been difficult for senior citizens to manage. See Milt Freudenheim, "The Drug Decision," *New York Times,* November 24, 2005.

45. Brian W. Hogwood and B. Guy Peters, *Policy Dynamics* (Brighton, UK: Wheatsheaf, 1983).

46. See Joel Slemrod and Jon Bakija, *Taxing Ourselves: A Citizen's Guide to the Debate over Taxes,* 3rd ed. (Cambridge, MA: MIT Press, 2004).

47. Aaron Wildavsky, "Policy as Its Own Cause," *Speaking Truth to Power* (Boston: Little, Brown, 1979), 62–85.

48. Advocates for the victims of the disease argue that there were significant delays in responding to the issue, in part because of "homophobia." See Gregory M. Herek and Beverly Greene, *AIDS, Identity and Community* (Beverly Hills, CA: Sage, 1995). On the other hand, the National Institutes of Health at one point was spending $33,513 in research for every AIDS death in the country, compared with $1,162 for

each heart disease death. "Panel Criticizes NIH Spending," *USA Today,* July 9, 1998.

49. Jonathan Weisman, "Linking Tax to Death May Have Brought Its Doom," *USA Today,* May 21, 2001.

50. But see Peter Self, *Government by the Market? The Politics of Public Choice* (Boulder, CO: Westview Press, 1991).

51. James M. Buchanan, *The Demands and Supply of Public Goods* (Chicago: Rand McNally, 1958), 3–7.

52. A classic statement of the issue is R. H. Coase, "The Problem of Social Cost," *Journal of Law and Economics* 3 (1960): 1–44.

53. Market approaches to redressing externalities have become increasingly common. See Joseph J. Cordes, "Corrective Taxes, Charges and Tradeable Permits," in *The Tools of Government,* ed. Lester M. Salamon (New York: Oxford University Press, 2002), 255–281.

54. Charles Wolf Jr., *Markets or Governments?* (Cambridge, MA: MIT Press, 1987).

55. Cohen, March, and Olsen, "The Garbage Can Model."

56. Abraham Kaplan, *The Conduct of Inquiry* (San Francisco: Chandler, 1964).

57. See Frank Fischer and Herbert Gottweiss, *The Argumentative Turn Revisited* (Durham, NC: Duke University Press, 2012).

58. On instruments, see Christopher Hood, *Tools of Government* (Chatham, NJ: Chatham House, 1986); Stephen H. Linder and B. Guy Peters, "Instruments of Government: Perceptions and Contexts," *Journal of Public Policy* 9 (1989): 35–58; and Salamon, *The Tools of Government.*

59. See Pearl Eliadas, Margaret Hill, and Michael Howlett, eds., *Designing Government* (Montreal: McGill/Queens University Press, 2004).

60. For example, organizational resistance within government to privatizing Social Security, as well as political pressure from outside, helped save the program when it was under threat. See chapter 12.

61. They are argued to be so by, among others, William Niskanen, *Bureaucracy and Representative Government* (Chicago: Aldine/Atherton, 1971); but see André Blais and Stéphane Dion, *The Budget-Maximizing Bureaucrat* (Pittsburgh: University of Pittsburgh Press, 1991).

62. Kenneth J. Meier, *Politics and the Bureaucracy,* 3rd ed. (Pacific Grove, CA: Brooks/Cole, 1993).

63. Mark A. Eisner, "Bureaucratic Professionalism and the Limits of Political Control Thesis: The Case of the Federal Trade Commission," *Governance* 6 (1992): 127–153.

64. John DiIulio, ed., *Deregulating the Public Service* (Washington, DC: Brookings Institution Press, 1994); and B. Guy Peters, *The Future of Governing,* 2nd ed. (Lawrence: University Press of Kansas, 2002).

65. See Andrew Rich, *Think Tanks, Public Policy and the Politics of Expertise* (Cambridge: Cambridge University Press, 2000).

66. See Charles L. Heatherly, ed., *Mandate for Change: Policy Management in a Conservative Administration* (Washington, DC: Heritage Foundation, 1981).

67. See, for example, *The Work of Nations: Preparing Ourselves for Twenty-First Century Capitalism* (New York: Knopf, 1991); and *Education and the Next Economy* (Washington, DC: National Education Association, 1988).

68. For example, the website of the *National Journal* listed several dozen responses to the 2006 State of the Union address.

69. M. Eshbaugh-Sona, "The Politics of Presidential Agendas," *Political Research Quarterly* 58: 257–268.

70. Michael Malbin, *Our Unelected Representatives* (New York: Basic Books, 1980). For a conservative critique, see Eric Felten, "Little Princes," *Policy Review* 63 (1993): 51–57.

71. David H. Rosenbloom, *Building a Legislative-Centered Public Administration: Congress and the Administrative State* (Tuscaloosa: University of Alabama Press).

72. See W. Kip Viscusi, "The Value of Risks to Life and Health," *Journal of Economic Literature* 31 (1993): 1912–1946; Richard Zeckhauser and W. Kip Viscusi, "Risk within Reason," *Science* 248 (May 4, 1990): 559–564; and R. Hahn, *Risks, Costs and Lives Saved* (Oxford: Oxford University Press, 1996).

73. Robert Eisner, *The Misunderstood Economy* (Cambridge, MA: Harvard Business School, 1994).

74. There have been a number of books and articles about "crises" in Social Security, but the pattern of decision making tends to be more incremental. See Theodore R. Marmor, *Social Security: Beyond the Rhetoric of Crisis* (Princeton: Princeton University Press, 1988); and Martha Derthick, *Agency under Stress, NJ Social Security Administration in American Government* (Washington, DC: Brookings Institution Press, 1990).

75. See Richard Topf, "Science, Public Policy, and the Authoritativeness of the Governmental Process," in *The Politics of Expert Advice,* ed. Anthony Barker and B. Guy Peters (Pittsburgh: University of Pittsburgh Press, 1993).

76. R. Kent Weaver, "Setting and Firing Policy Triggers," *Journal of Public Policy* 9 (1989): 307–336.

77. Paulette Kurzer, "The Politics of Central Banks: Austerity and Unemployment in Europe," *Journal of Public Policy* 8 (1988): 21–48.

78. Indeed, reducing values such as clean air, natural beauty, and social equality to dollars and cents (as is necessary to make cost-benefit analysis work) represents an extreme form of utilitarianism.

79. See Henry J. Aaron, Thomas E. Mann, and Timothy Taylor, *Values and Public Policy* (Washington, DC: Brookings Institution Press, 1994).

80. Moshe F. Rubenstein, *Patterns of Problem Solving* (Englewood Cliffs, NJ: Prentice-Hall, 1975).

81. The political risks for the mayor may be different than the actual risks to the city and its people. The mayor does not want to be seen as panicking in the face of a crisis, but the unnecessary loss of life may be the most damaging possibility of all for a political leader.

82. Stephen H. Linder and B. Guy Peters, "From Social Theory to Policy Design," *Journal of Public Policy* 4 (1984): 237–259; and Davis Bobrow and John S. Dryzek, *Policy Analysis by Design* (Pittsburgh: University of Pittsburgh Press, 1987).

83. Anne L. Schneider and Helen M. Ingram, for example, argue that policy design runs directly opposite to the pluralistic politics that dominates policymaking in the United States. See their *Policy Design for Democracy* (Lawrence: University Press of Kansas, 1997).

Chapter 5

1. Peter G. Brown, *Restoring the Public Trust* (Boston: Beacon Press, 1994); and Rodney Barker, *Political Legitimacy and the State* (Oxford: Clarendon Press, 1990).

2. The government of the United Kingdom suspended civil liberties in Northern Ireland in response to the sectarian violence there. For at least a portion of the population, this action reduced its legitimacy. For other citizens, the extreme crisis of sectarian violence and terrorism justified the action.

3. Donald L. Westerfield, *War Powers: The President, the Congress, and the Question of War* (Westport, CT: Praeger, 1996).

4. Kathy Kiely, "Some Lawmakers Balk at Proposed Boost in Salaries," *USA Today,* June 26, 2006.

5. Christopher F. Karpowitz, J. Quin Monson, Kelly D. Patterson, and Jeremy C. Pope, "Tea Time in America?: The Impact of the Tea Party Movement in the 2010 Midterm Elections," *PS: Political Science and Politics* 44, 303–309.

6. See, for example, Alan Brinkley, "What's Wrong with American Political Leadership?" *Wilson Quarterly* 18, no. 2 (1994): 46–54; and Paul Krugman, "A Can't Do Government," *New York Times,* September 2, 2005.

7. The very high figure in 1991 appears to be at least in part a function of the Gulf War (see also the figure for the military in that year)—presidents often get a popularity boost from wars. George W. Bush enjoyed the same high levels after September 11, 2001.

8. His approval rating was 22 percent as he left office in the CBS/*Washington Post* poll.

9. Bruce Gilley, *Right to Rule: How Nations Win and Lose Legitimacy* (Cambridge: Cambridge University Press, 2009).

10. In addition to the rational economic dimension of housing, there is the emotional attachment to the "American Dream" of owning a home.

11. This is to some degree what Aaron Wildavsky meant when he argued that policy analysts must "speak truth to power" in his book *Speaking Truth to Power* (Boston: Little, Brown, 1979).

12. Arnold J. Meltsner, "Political Feasibility and Policy Analysis," *Public Administration Review* 32 (1972): 859–867; and Giandomenico Majone, "The Feasibility of Social Policies," *Policy Sciences* 6 (1975): 49–69.

13. For nonmajoritarian legitimation see G. Majone, "Nonmajoritarian Institutions and the Limits of Democratic Governance," *Journal of Institutional and Theoretical Economics* 157: 57–78.

14. Joel D. Aberbach, *Keeping a Watchful Eye: The Politics of Congressional Oversight* (Washington, DC: Brookings Institution Press, 1991).

15. *Immigration and Naturalization Service v. Chadha,* 462 U.S. 919 (1983); and John D. Huber and Charles R. Shipan, "The Costs of Control: Legislators, Agencies and Transaction Costs," *Legislative Studies Quarterly* 25 (2000): 25–52.

16. Jessica Korn, *The Power of Separation: American Constitutionalism and the Myth of the Legislative Veto* (Princeton, NJ: Princeton University Press, 1997); and J. Mitchell Pickerill, *Constitutional Deliberation in Congress* (Durham, NC: Duke University Press, 2005).

17. Walter J. Oleszek, *Congressional Procedures and the Policy Process* (Washington, DC: CQ Press, 1988); and Sarah A. Binder and Steven S. Smith, *Filibustering: Politics or Principle* (Washington, DC: Brookings Institution Press, 1997).

18. There are, therefore, a number of "veto points," a concept similar to "clearance points" in implementation theory. See Ellen Immergut, *Health Care Politics* (Cambridge: Cambridge University Press, 1992).

19. Jeff Flake, "Earmarked Men," *New York Times,* February 9, 2006.

20. There have been majorities in favor of reforming medical care for some time, but there is as yet no major change. Likewise, there has been a majority for stronger handgun control for some time but little policy change.

21. Lori Montgomery and Paul Kane, "Debt-Limit Debate: 43 Republicans Say They Will Reject Reid's Plan?," *Washington Post,* July 29, 2011.

22. Charles E. Lindblom and Edward J. Woodhouse, *The Policy-Making Process,* 3rd ed. (Englewood Cliffs, NJ: Prentice-Hall, 1993).

23. James Buchanan and Gordon Tullock, *The Calculus of Consent* (Ann Arbor: University of Michigan Press, 1962), 120–144.

24. See John A. Hamman, "Universalism, Program Development, and the Distribution of Federal Assistance," *Legislative Studies Quarterly* 18 (1993): 553–568.

25. Morris P. Fiorina, *Congress: Keystone of the Washington Establishment* (New Haven, CT: Yale University Press, 1981).

26. Douglas R. Arnold, *Congress and the Bureaucracy* (New Haven, CT: Yale University Press, 1979).

27. Diana Evans, *Greasing the Wheels: Using the Pork Barrel to Build Majority Coalitions in Congress* (Cambridge: Cambridge University Press, 2005).

28. Many programs will do that; the question is whether there is also a broader public interest involved.

29. James Kitfield, "The Battle of the Depots," *National Journal,* April 4, 1998.

30. Jane Gordon, "In a Hurry to Diversify beyond Submarines and Luck," *New York Times,* December 18, 2005.

31. William R. Riker and Peter Ordeshook, *Positive Political Theory* (Englewood Cliffs, NJ: Prentice-Hall, 1973), 97–114.

32. Kenneth Arrow, *Social Choice and Individual Values,* 2nd ed. (New York: Wiley, 1963).

33. Aberbach, *Keeping a Watchful Eye.*

34. These terms come from Mathew McCubbins and Thomas Schwartz, "Congressional Oversight Overlooked: Police Patrols versus Fire Alarms," *American Journal of Political Science* 28 (1984): 165–179.

35. Cornelius M. Kerwin and Scott Furlong, *Rulemaking: How Government Agencies Write Law and Make Policy,* 4th ed. (Washington, DC: CQ Press, 2011).

36. Marc Allen Eisner, *Regulatory Politics in Transition* (Baltimore: Johns Hopkins University Press, 2000).

37. OMB Watch, "Turning Back the Clock: The Obama Administration and the Legacy of Bush Era Midnight Regulations," February 5, 2009, www.ombwatch.org/node/10497?page=0%2C10.

38. Margaret T. Kriz, "Kibitzer with Clout," *National Journal,* May 30, 1987, 1404–1408.

39. Thomas O. McGarity, *Reinventing Rationality: The Role of Regulatory Analysis in the Federal Bureaucracy* (Cambridge: Cambridge University Press, 1991).

40. Viveca Novak, "The New Regulators," *National Journal,* July 17, 1993, 1801–1804.
41. Reuters, "Six Areas of Obama Regulatory Reform," August 24, 2011.
42. Martin Shapiro, "APA: Past, Present and Future," *Virginia Law Review* 72 (1986): 447–492.
43. Jerry L. Mashaw, "Prodelegation: Why Administrators Should Make Political Decisions," *Journal of Law, Economics and Organization* 5 (1985): 141–164.
44. Even then, there was a concentration of participation, with only a few interest groups taking advantage of this opportunity. See Barry Boyer, "Funding Public Participation in Agency Proceedings: The Federal Trade Commission Experience," *Georgetown Law Journal* 70 (1981): 51–172.
45. See Glen O. Robinson, *American Bureaucracy: Public Choice and Public Law* (Ann Arbor: University of Michigan Press, 1991), 139–147.
46. Stephen Williams, "Hybrid Rulemaking under the Administrative Procedures Act: A Legal and Empirical Analysis," *University of Chicago Law Review* 42 (1975): 401–456.
47. *International Harvester Co. v. Ruckelshaus*, 478 F. 2nd 615 (1973).
48. William Gormley Jr., *Taming the Bureaucracy* (Princeton, NJ: Princeton University Press, 1989), 94–97.
49. Philip Harter, "Negotiated Rulemaking: A Cure for the Malaise," *Georgetown Law Review* 71 (1982): 1–28; "Assessing the Assessors: The Actual Performance of Negotiated Rulemaking," *New York University Environmental Law Journal* 9 (2001), 32–64; and Thomas McGarrity, "Some Thoughts on Deossifying the Rulemaking Process," *Duke Law Journal* 41 (1992): 1385–1462.
50. David Pritzker and Deborah Dalton, *Negotiated Rulemaking Sourcebook* (Washington, DC: Administrative Conference of the United States, 1990).
51. Philippe C. Schmitter, "Still the Century of Corporatism?" *Review of Politics* 36 (1974): 85–131.
52. See Robert Kvavik, *Interest Groups in Norwegian Politics* (Oslo, Norway: Universitetsforlaget, 1980).
53. Mike Mills, "President to Stage Timber Summit," *Congressional Quarterly Weekly Report* 51 (March 13, 1993): 593.
54. This could hardly be corporatist, however, since it involved only the one side of a complex policy debate. See William Schneider, "It's Cheney vs. Carter in the New Energy War," *National Journal,* May 12, 2001, 649.
55. See Colin S. Diver, "A Theory of Regulatory Enforcement," *Public Policy* 29 (1980): 295–296.
56. Theodore J. Lowi, *The End of Liberalism,* 2nd ed. (New York: Norton, 1979).
57. Richard A. Harris and Sidney M. Milkis, *The Politics of Regulatory Change* (New York: Oxford University Press, 1989).
58. David Schoenbrod, *Power without Responsibility* (New Haven, CT: Yale University Press, 1993).
59. Martha Derthick and Paul J. Quirk, *The Politics of Deregulation* (Washington, DC: Brookings Institution Press, 1985).
60. Robert A. Kagan, "Adversarial Legalism and American Government," *Journal of Policy Analysis and Management* 10 (1991): 369–406; and Robert J. Samuelson, "Whitewater: The Law as Bludgeon," *International Herald Tribune,* March 8, 1994.

61. Federal Judge Frank Johnson, in Alabama, literally took over the prisons and mental hospitals of that state. See *Wyatt v. Stickney*, 344 F. Supp. 373 (M.D. Ala. 1972), and *Pugh v. Locke*, 406 F. Supp. 318 (M.D. Ala. 1976).

62. Thomas J. Cronin, *Direct Democracy* (Cambridge, MA: Harvard University Press, 1989). See also Ian Budge, *The New Challenge of Direct Democracy* (Cambridge, MA: Polity Press, 1996).

63. National Council of State Legislatures, "What the Voters Have Decided So Far: The Thicket," (NCSL blog), November 6, 2008, www.ncsl.org/magazine/the-thicket-a -legislative-blog.aspx.

64. Benjamin R. Barber, *Strong Democracy: Participatory Politics in a New Age* (Berkeley: University of California Press, 1984); and James Bohman and William Rehig, *Deliberative Democracy: Essays on Reason and Politics* (Cambridge, MA: MIT Press). For a less philosophical discussion, see Phil Duncan, "American Democracy in Search of Debate," *Congressional Quarterly Weekly Report* 51 (October 16, 1993): 2850.

Chapter 6

1. Michael Lipsky, *Street Level Bureaucracy* (New York: Russell Sage, 1980).

2. Cass Sunstein, *After the Rights Revolution: Reconceiving the Regulatory State* (Cambridge, MA: Harvard University Press, 1990); John D. Huber and Charles R. Shipan, *Deliberate Discretion: The Institutional Foundations of Bureaucratic Autonomy* (Cambridge: Cambridge University Press, 2002).

3. See U.S. Senate, Committee on Governmental Affairs, *The Federal Executive Establishment: Evolution and Trends* (Washington, DC: U.S. Government Printing Office, 1980), 23–63.

4. Harold Seidman and Robert S. Gilmour, *Politics, Position and Power*, 4th ed. (New York: Oxford University Press, 1986).

5. The degree of central control in the Defense Department can be exaggerated. See C. Kenneth Allard, *Command, Control, and the Common Defense* (New Haven, CT: Yale University Press, 1990); Joseph Metcalf III, "Decision-Making and the Grenada Rescue Operation," in *Ambiguity and Control*, ed. J. G. March and R. Wessinger-Baylon (Boston: Pirman, 1987).

6. John Hart, *The Presidential Branch*, 2nd ed. (Chatham, NJ: Chatham House, 1994).

7. B. Guy Peters, R. A. W. Rhodes, and Vincent Wright, eds., *Administering the Summit* (London: Macmillan, 1998).

8. Frederick C. Mosher, *The GAO* (Boulder, CO: Westview Press, 1979); and Ray C. Rist, *Program Evaluation and Management of Government* (New Brunswick, NJ: Transaction, 1990).

9. Daily reports from the Government Accountability Office can be found at www .gao.gov.

10. Marc Alan Eisner, *Regulatory Politics in Transition* (Baltimore: Johns Hopkins University Press, 1993).

11. The classic statement is Samuel P. Huntington, "The Marasmus of the ICC," *Yale Law Review* 61 (April 1952): 467–509. For a very different perspective, see Jonathan R. Mezey, "Organizational Design and Political Control of Administrative Agencies," *Journal of Law, Economics and Organization* 8 (1992): 93–110.

12. The growth of the consumer movement has placed additional pressures on regulatory agencies to escape capture. See Michael D. Reagan, *Regulation: The Politics of Policy* (Boston: Little, Brown, 1987).

13. Michael Dorf, "Artifactions: The Battle over the National Endowment for the Arts," *Brookings Review* 26 (Winter 1993): 32–35.

14. On June 25, 1998, the Court argued that there is no right to a grant, so artists could not argue that this denied them any fundamental rights. *National Endowment for the Arts v. Finley,* 524 U.S. 569 (1998).

15. Annemarie Hauck Walsh, *Managing the Public's Business* (Cambridge, MA: MIT Press, 1980), 41–44.

16. See Peter Passell, "The Sticky Side of Privatization: Sale of U.S. Nuclear Fuel Plants Raises Host of Conflicts," *New York Times*, August 30, 1997.

17. The level of autonomy of the Federal Reserve has decreased substantially in the economic crisis, as it became more closely linked to the Obama administration's efforts to revive the economy. See "The Fed," Times Topics, *New York Times,* January 29, 2012.

18. Seidman and Gilmour, *Politics, Position and Power*, 274.

19. Charles Duhigg, "Two Mortgage Giants Are Unlikely to Be Restored," *New York Times,* March 3, 2009.

20. Marc Alan Eisner, *Antitrust and the Triumph of Economics* (Chapel Hill: University of North Carolina Press, 1992).

21. Martin Landau, "The Rationality of Redundancy," *Public Administration Review* 29 (1969): 346–358; Jonathan R. Bendor, *Parallel Politics* (Berkeley: University of California Press, 1985).

22. James L. Sundquist, "Needed: A Political Theory for a New Era of Coalition Government in the United States," *Political Science Quarterly* 108 (1988): 613–635.

23. U.S. Federal Reserve Board, "The Role of the Federal Reserve in Preserving Monetary and Financial Stability," joint press release, March 23, 2009, www.federalreserve .gov/newsevents/press/monetary/20090323b.htm.

24. U.S. Senate, Committee on Governmental Affairs, *The Federal Executive Establishment,* 27–30.

25. "In God We Trust," *Harvard Political Review* 28 (2001): 15–27.

26. Woodrow Wilson, "The Study of Administration," *Political Science Quarterly* 1 (1887): 197–222.

27. This is perhaps especially true of American government given the number of "veto points" that exist within the system. See Ellen Immergut, *Health Care Politics: Ideas and Institutions in Western Europe* (Cambridge: Cambridge University Press, 1992).

28. See Else Oyen, S. M. Miller, and S. A. Samad, *Poverty: A Global Review* (Oslo, Norway: Scandinavian University Press, 1996).

29. Daniel Patrick Moynihan, *The Politics of Guaranteed Income* (New York: Vintage, 1973), 240.

30. The importance of laser technologies is demonstrated in William Broad, *Teller's War: The Top-Secret Story behind the Star Wars Initiative* (New York: Simon and Schuster, 1992).

31. David Runk, "Bush Highlights Alternative Energy Plans in Michigan," *USA Today,* February 8, 2006.

32. Bill Vladic, "Obama Reveals Details of Gas Mileage Rules," *New York Times,* July 20, 2011.

33. That difference is discussed well in Richard R. Nelson, *The Moon and the Ghetto* (New York: Norton, 1977).

34. That decision eventually was rescinded after a public outcry. However, in 1998 another decision by the Department of Agriculture made salsa a vegetable for school lunches, provided it was made from fresh vegetables (there's that word again).

35. Tax legislation is sufficiently complex that it is possible to hide benefits for particular groups even in legislation that ostensibly is general tax relief. See Paul Krugman, *Fuzzy Math: The Essential Guide to the Bush Tax Plan* (New York: Norton, 2001).

36. Theodore J. Lowi, *The End of Liberalism,* 2nd ed. (New York: Norton, 1979), 42–63.

37. Christopher Hood, *The Limits of Administration* (New York: Wiley, 1976).

38. Burt Solomon, "Twixt Cup and Lip," *National Journal,* October 24, 1992, 2410–2415; and Paul C. Light, *Thickening Government: Federal Hierarchy and the Diffusion of Accountability* (Washington, DC: Brookings Institution Press, 1995).

39. A classic description of the dangers of this occurring is found in Herbert Kaufman, *The Forest Ranger* (Baltimore: Johns Hopkins University Press, 1960); M. K. Meyers and S. Vorsanger, "Street-Level Bureaucrats and Policy Implementation," in *Handbook of Public Administration,* ed. G. Peters and J. Pierre (London: Sage, 2004).

40. Janet Schrader, "Lost on the Road to Reform: Some of My Clients Can't Do the Jobs Out There," *Washington Post,* May 11, 1997.

41. Peter M. Blau, *The Dynamics of Bureaucracy* (Chicago: University of Chicago Press, 1955), 184–193.

42. Eugene Bardach and Robert A. Kagan, *Going by the Book: The Problem of Regulatory Unreasonableness* (Philadelphia: Temple University Press, 1982).

43. This is now often phrased in terms of a "principal" controlling its agents. See Dan Wood and Richard Waterman, *Bureaucratic Dynamics: The Role of Bureaucracy in a Democracy* (Boulder, CO: Westview Press, 1994).

44. Martha A. Derthick, *Agency under Stress: The Social Security Administration in American Government* (Washington, DC: Brookings Institution Press, 1990).

45. Arthur Stinchcombe, *Information and Organizations* (Berkeley: University of California Press, 1990).

46. James G. March and Herbert A. Simon, *Organizations* (New York: Wiley, 1958).

47. On the other hand, too much similarity in backgrounds and training enhances the possibilities of "groupthink" and an absence of error correction within the organization. See Paul T. Hart, Eric K. Stern, and Bengt Sundelius, *Beyond Groupthink: Political Group Dynamics and Foreign Policy-Making* (Ann Arbor: University of Michigan Press, 1997).

48. The Gore commission (National Performance Review) reforms have had the effect of reducing drastically the number of levels in organizations, with the presumed effect of empowering employees at lower levels and improving internal communications.

49. James McGregor Burns, *Roosevelt: The Lion and the Fox* (New York: Harcourt, Brace, 1956).

50. Harold Wilensky, *Organizational Intelligence* (New York: Basic Books, 1967), 130–145.

51. Hood, *The Limits of Administration,* 85–87.

52. Ibid., 192–197.
53. For a good compilation, see Peter Hall, *Great Planning Disasters* (London: Weiden-field and Nicolson, 1980). We should remember, however, that these failings are as common in large private organizations as in the public sector, but there they tend to be less publicized. See Charles T. Goodsell, *The Case for Bureaucracy: A Public Administration Polemic*, 4th ed. (Chatham, NJ: Chatham House, 2003).
54. Paul R. Schulman, *Large-Scale Policy Analysis* (New York: Elsevier, 1980).
55. Richard A. Rettig, *Cancer Crusade* (Princeton, NJ: Princeton University Press, 1977).
56. This assumes that this disease is similar to cancer in requiring a more decentralized research format.
57. Benny Hjern and David O. Porter, "Implementation Structures: A New Unit of Organisational Analysis," *Organisational Studies* 2 (1981): 211–228.
58. Eugene Bardach, "Turf Barriers to Interagency Collaboration," in *The State of Public Management*, ed. D. F. Kettl and H. B. Milward (Baltimore: Johns Hopkins University Press, 1996), 168.
59. See Kevin P. Kearns, *Private Sector Strategies for Public Sector Success* (San Francisco: Jossey-Bass, 2000).
60. Jeffrey L. Pressman and Aaron Wildavsky, *Implementation* (Berkeley: University of California Press, 1979).
61. Ibid., 145–168.
62. Judith Bowen, "The Pressman-Wildavsky Paradox," *Journal of Public Policy* 2 (1982): 1–22; and Ernst Alexander, "Improbable Implementation: The Pressman-Wildavsky Paradox Revisited," *Journal of Public Policy* 9 (1989): 451–465.
63. See David Osborne and Ted Gaebler, *Reinventing Government* (Reading, MA: Addison-Wesley, 1992); and B. Guy Peters, "Can't Row, Shouldn't Steer: What's a Government to Do?" *Public Policy and Administration* 12, no. 2 (1997): 51–61.
64. Rochelle L. Stanfield, "Between the Cracks," *National Journal*, October 11, 1997, 314–318.
65. William T. Gormley, "Regulating Mr. Rogers's Neighborhood: The Dilemmas of Day Care Regulation," *Brookings Review* 8 (1990): 21–28.
66. Barry Meier, "Fight in Congress Looms on Fishing," *New York Times*, September 19, 1994.
67. R. Lewis Bowman, Eleanor C. Main, and B. Guy Peters, "Coordination in the Atlanta Model Cities Program" (mimeo, Department of Political Science, Emory University, Atlanta, GA, 1971).
68. Jon Pierre, "The Marketization of the State: Citizens, Consumers and the Emergence of Public Markets," in *Governance in a Changing Environment*, ed. Donald Savoie and B. Guy Peters (Montreal: McGill/Queens University Press, 1995), 55.
69. Richard F. Elmore, "Backward Mapping and Implementation Research and Policy Decisions," in *Studying Implementation*, ed. Walter Williams (Chatham, NJ: Chatham House, 1984).
70. M. Kiviniemi, "Public Policies and Their Targets: A Typology of the Concept of Implementation," *International Social Science Quarterly* 108 (1986): 251–265.
71. Elmore, "Backward Mapping"; Paul A. Sabatier, "Top-down and Bottom-up Models of Policy Implementation: A Critical Analysis and Suggested Synthesis," *Journal of Public Policy* 6 (1986): 21–48; and Stephen H. Linder and B. Guy Peters,

"Implementation as a Guide to Policy Formulation: A Question of 'When' Rather Than 'Whether,'" *International Review of Administrative Sciences* 55 (1989): 631–652.

72. Linder and Peters, "Implementation as a Guide."

73. Giandomenico Majone, "The Feasibility of Social Policies," *Policy Sciences* 6 (1975): 49–69.

74. Malcolm L. Goggin, Ann O'M. Bowman, James P. Lester, and Laurence J. O'Toole, *Implementation Theory and Practice: Toward a Third Generation* (New York: Harper-Collins, 1990); and Soren Winter, "The Implementation Perspective," in *Handbook of Public Administration,* ed. G. Peters and J. Pierre (London: Sage, 2004), 212.

75. Laurence O'Toole, "Interorganizational Relations in Implementation," in *Handbook of Public Administration,* ed. G. Peters and J. Pierre (London: Sage, 2004), 234.

Chapter 7

1. But see David Jackson and John Fritze, "Obama Vows to Cut Pork, Later," *USA Today,* March 11, 2009.

2. Jan-Erik Lane, *The Public Sector: Concepts, Models, and Approaches* (London: Sage, 1994).

3. Rather than a question of the efficient division of resources between the public and private sectors, this is an intergenerational equity question. The huge deficit that the federal government has incurred will impose costs on American citizens for generations to come. See David Rosnick and Dean Parker, *Taming the Deficit: Saving Our Children from Themselves* (Washington, DC: Center for Economic and Policy Research, 2009).

4. In the budget debates after 2009, entitlements are now more subject to careful scrutiny and cuts than in the past. See Helene Cooper, "Obama Offers Plan to Cut Deficit by Over $3 Trillion," *New York Times,* September 11, 2011.

5. Charles Stewart III, *Budget Reform Politics* (New York: Cambridge University Press, 1989).

6. Louis Fisher, *Presidential Spending Power* (Princeton, NJ: Princeton University Press, 1975).

7. "After Years of Wrangling, Accord Is Reached on Plan to Balance Budget by 2002," *New York Times,* May 3, 1997.

8. Nancy Roberts, "The Synoptic Model of Strategic Planning and GPRA," *Public Productivity and Management Review* 23 (2000): 297–311.

9. General Accounting Office, *Biennial Budgeting for the Federal Government* (Washington, DC: U.S. General Accounting Office, October 7, 1993), GAO/T-AIMED-94-4; and Louis Fisher, "Biennial Budgeting in the Federal Government," *Public Budgeting and Finance* 17, no. 3 (1997): 87–97.

10. "Federal Capital Budgeting," *Intergovernmental Perspective* 20 (1994): 8–16; Beverly S. Bunch, "Current Practices and Issues in Capital Budgeting and Reporting," *Public Budgeting and Finance* 16, no. 2 (1996): 7–25. The *Special Analyses of the Budget* also contains information about the investment features of federal spending.

11. See *Washington Post,* "The Long Path to the Federal Budget," February 4, 2002; "The Federal Budget Process," January 31, 2010.

12. Charles L. Schultze, "Paying the Bills," in *Setting Domestic Priorities,* ed. Henry J. Aaron and Charles L. Schultze (Washington, DC: Brookings Institution Press, 1992), 295–317.

13. Paul E. Peterson and Mark Rom, "Macroeconomic Policymaking: Who Is in Control," in *Can the Government Govern?* eds. John E. Chubb and Paul E. Peterson (Washington, DC: Brookings Institution Press, 1989), 167–198.

14. This official was Murray Weidenbaum. See David Stockman, *The Triumph of Politics* (New York: Harper and Row, 1986), 104.

15. See Roy T. Meyers, *Strategic Budgeting* (Ann Arbor: University of Michigan Press, 1994), 52–60.

16. Aaron Wildavsky and Naomi Caiden, *The New Politics of the Budgetary Process,* 5th ed. (New York: Longman, 2004), 50–54.

17. Ibid., 81–82.

18. Office of Management and Budget, *Preparation and Submission of "Current Services" Budget Estimates,* Bulletin 76–4 (Washington, DC: U.S. Office of Management and Budget, August 13, 1975), 2–4.

19. See Thomas W. Wander, F. Ted Hebert, and Gary W. Copeland, *Congressional Budgeting* (Baltimore: Johns Hopkins University Press, 1984); and Robin Toner, "Putting Prices on Congress's Ideas," *New York Times,* August 21, 1994.

20. John W. Ellwood and James A. Thurber, "The Politics of the Congressional Budget Process Re-considered," in *Congress Reconsidered,* ed. Lawrence C. Dodd and Bruce Oppenheimer, 2nd ed. (Washington, DC: CQ Press, 1981), 124–141. There has been some tendency to disperse this power, with appropriations committees now handling only about two-thirds of the total budget. See John F. Cogan, "Congress Has Dispersed the Power of the Purse," *Public Affairs Report* 35 (September 1994): 7–8.

21. Paul Starobin, "Bringing It Home," *National Journal,* June 26, 1993, 1642–1645.

22. D. Roderick Kiewiet and Mathew D. McCubbins, *The Logic of Delegation* (Chicago: University of Chicago Press, 1991).

23. See Irene Rubin, *The Politics of Public Budgeting,* 4th ed. (Chatham, NJ: Chatham House, 2002), 75–76; and James Thurber, "Congressional Budget Reform: Impact on Congressional Appropriations Committees," *Public Budgeting and Finance* 17, no. 3 (1997): 62–73.

24. Carl Hulse, "Whistle-Stops and War Whoops Bury Budget Woes," *New York Times,* October 1, 2002.

25. David Baumann, "Congress—Does a Budget Really Matter?" *National Journal,* April 15, 2006.

26. The dispute concerning the FAA has been over minute points of agency management rather than over fundamental issues concerning the utility of the agency.

27. Fisher, *Presidential Spending Power.*

28. David Baumann, "Line-Item Lite," *National Journal,* April 8, 2006.

29. Gary Therkildsen, "Obama Requests Enhanced Rescission Authority," *OMB Watch,* May 11, 2010.

30. Frederick C. Mosher, *The GAO: The Quest for Accountability in American Government* (Boulder, CO: Westview Press, 1979), 169–200; and Ray C. Rist, "Management Accountability: The Signals Sent by Auditing and Evaluation," *Journal of Public Policy* 9 (1989): 355–369.

31. James D. Savae, *Balanced Budgets and American Politics* (Ithaca, NY: Cornell University Press, 1988); Barry C. Burden and Joseph Neal Rice Sanderg, "Budget Rhetoric in Presidential Campaigns from 1952 to 2000," *Political Behavior* 25 (2003): 97–118.

32. Technically, the general fund is borrowing the money from the Social Security Trust Fund, although the presentation of deficit figures does not make that distinction clear. See General Accounting Office, *Retirement Income: Implications of Demographic Trends for Social Security and Pension Reform* (Washington, DC: U.S. General Accounting Office, July 1997), GAO/HEHS-97-81.

33. Glenn Kessler, "Use of Retirement Funds to Widen Debt Limit Fight," *Washington Post,* April 3, 2002.

34. These changes have been in part in response to accounting fiascos in the private sector, for example, in Enron and WorldCom.

35. See Bruce Bartlett, "The 81 Percent Tax Increase," *Forbes,* May 15, 2009.

36. Jim Cooper, "A Truer Measure of America's Ballooning Deficit," *Financial Times,* May 1, 2006.

37. Stephen Taub, "Accrual Accounting Raises Federal Deficit," *Today in Finance,* March 2, 2004.

38. Else Foley, "House GOP Votes Down Clean Debt Ceiling Limit Increase, Eyes Medicare in Deal," *Huffington Post,* May 31, 2011.

39. See Robert D. Reischauer, "The Unfulfillable Promise: Cutting Nondefense Discretionary Spending," in *Setting National Priorities: Budget Choices for the Next Century,* ed. Robert D. Reischauer (Washington, DC: Brookings Institution Press, 1997), 123–126.

40. Rob Norton, "Every Budget Tells a Story, and This Is No Exception," *Washington Post,* March 10, 2002.

41. Michael D. Shear, "Obama Pledges Entitlement Reform," *Washington Post,* January 16, 2009.

42. Glenn Kessler, "Obama and the Defense Budget," *Washington Post,* February 14, 2012.

43. Jeff Shear, "The Untouchables," *National Journal,* July 16, 1994; "America's Budget: The Elephant in the Room," *Economist,* May 7, 2011.

44. A variety of federal loan programs account for over $200 billion in outstanding direct loans and over $700 billion in guaranteed loans. The Tax Foundation, *Facts and Figures on Government Finance,* 1993 (Washington, DC: Tax Foundation, 1994).

45. Office of Management and Budget, *Analytical Perspectives on the Budget,* 2006 (Washington, DC: U.S. Office of Management and Budget, 2005).

46. Ben Wildavsky, "After the Deficit," *National Journal,* November 29, 1997, 2408–2410.

47. General Accounting Office, *Budgeting for Federal Insurance Programs* (Washington, DC: U.S. General Accounting Office, September 1997), GAO/AIMD-97-16.

48. The federal government has been fortunate that during a period of high deficits the interest rates it has had to pay have been exceptionally low.

49. Office of Management and Budget, *Budget of the United States, FY 2007, Analytical Perspectives* (Washington, DC: U.S. Government Printing Office, 2007).

50. For Germany, see Russell J. Dalton, *Politics in Germany,* 2nd ed. (New York: Harper Collins, 1993), 372–377; More generally, see Wallace Oates, "Toward a Second

Generation Theory of Fiscal Federalism," *International Tax and Public Finance* 12 (2005): 197–215.

51. These surpluses tended to be, on average, 11 percent of total state revenues, although some 15 percent of total state revenues comes from grants from the federal government.

52. Philip J. Candreva and L. R. Jones, "Congressional Delegation of Spending Power to the Defense Department in the Post 9-11 Period," *Public Budgeting and Finance* 25 (2005): 1–19.

53. ABC News, "Classified Spending Still High, Report Says," August 1, 2007, http://blogs.abcnews.com/theblotter/2007/08/classified-spen.html.

54. James McCaffrey and Paul Godek, "Defense Supplementals and the Budget Process," *Public Budgeting and Finance* 23 (2003): 53–72.

55. Marcia Clemmitt, "Pork Barrel Politics," *CQ Researcher,* June 16, 2006, entire issue.

56. Steve Ellis, "Earmark Reform: Understanding the Obligations of Funds Transparency Act," testimony before House Homeland Security and Governmental Affairs Committee, U.S. Congress, March 16, 2006.

57. Citizens against Government Waste, *2010 Congressional Pig Book* (Washington, DC: Citizens against Government Waste, 2011).

58. See Clemmitt, "Pork Barrel Politics."

59. Diana Evans, *Greasing the Wheels: Using Pork Barrel Projects to Build Majority Coalitions in Congress* (Cambridge: Cambridge University Press, 2004).

60. Brian Riedl, "How Pork Corrupts," *Washington Post,* January 29, 2006.

61. Paul Kane and Scott Wilson, "Obama Signs Spending Bill, Promises Earmark Reform," *Washington Post,* March 12, 2009.

62. William D. Berry, "The Confusing Case of Budgetary Incrementalism: Too Many Meanings for a Single Concept," *Journal of Politics* 52 (1990): 167–196.

63. M. A. H. Dempster and Aaron Wildavsky, "On Change: Or, There Is No Magic Size for an Increment," *Political Studies* 28 (1980): 371–389.

64. See David Braybrooke and Charles E. Lindblom, *A Strategy for Decision* (New York: Free Press, 1963).

65. Otto A. Davis, M. A. H. Dempster, and Aaron Wildavsky, "A Theory of the Budgetary Process," *American Political Science Review* 60 (1969): 529–547. These findings are now quite old, but there is little evidence that the process or the outcomes have changed significantly.

66. Aaron Wildavsky, *Budgeting: A Comparative Theory of the Budgetary Process,* rev. ed. (New Brunswick, NJ: Transaction, 1986): 7–27.

67. Michael T. Hayes, *Incrementalism and Public Policy* (New York: Longman, 1992), 131–144; see also Meyers, *Strategic Budgeting.*

68. Peter B. Natchez and Irvin C. Bupp, "Policy and Priority in the Budgetary Process," *American Political Science Review* 64 (1973): 951–963.

69. Dempster and Wildavsky, "On Change."

70. John R. Gist, "'Increment' and 'Base' in the Congressional Appropriation Process," *American Journal of Political Science* 21 (1977): 341–352.

71. Robert E. Goodin, *Political Theory and Public Policy* (Chicago: University of Chicago Press, 1983), 22–38.

72. Brian W. Hogwood and B. Guy Peters, *The Pathology of Public Policy* (New York: Oxford University Press, 1985), 124–126.

73. David Novick, *Program Budgeting: Program Analysis and the Federal Budget* (Cambridge, MA: Harvard University Press, 1967).
74. Robert H. Haveman and Burton A. Weisbrod, "Defining Benefits from Public Programs: Some Guidance from Policy Analysts," in *Public Expenditure and Policy Analysis,* ed. Robert H. Haveman and Julius Margolis, 3rd ed. (Boston: Houghton-Mifflin, 1983), 135; and Philip G. Joyce, "Using Performance Measures for Federal Budgeting: Proposals and Prospects," *Public Budgeting and Finance* 13 (1993): 3–17.
75. Aaron Wildavsky, "Political Implications of Budgetary Reform," *Public Administration Review* 21 (1961): 183–190.
76. Lenneal J. Henderson, "GPRA: Mission, Metrics, and Marketing," *Public Manager* 24, no. 1 (1995): 7–10; and Beryl A. Radin, "The Government Performance and Results Act (GPRA): Hydra-Headed Monster or Flexible Management Tool?" *Public Administration Review* 58 (1998): 307–316.
77. General Accounting Office, *Managing for Results: Agency Progress in Linking Performance Plans with Budgets and Financial Statements* (Washington, DC: U.S. General Accounting Office, January 2002), GAO-02-236. See also Roy T. Meyers and Philip G. Joyce, "Congressional Budgeting at Age 30: Is It Worth Saving?" *Public Budgeting and Finance* 25 (2005): 68–82.
78. See Jon Blondal, Dirk-Jan Kraan, and Michael Ruffner, "Budgeting in the United States," *OECD Journal of Budgeting* 3 (2003): 1–45.
79. These solutions are examples of "formula budgeting," which substitutes formulas for political judgment and political will. See Eric A. Hanushek, "Formula Budgeting: The Economics and Politics of Fiscal Policy under Rules," *Journal of Public Analysis and Management* 6 (1986): 3–19.
80. James D. Savage, *Balanced Budgets and American Politics* (Ithaca, NY: Cornell University Press, 1988).
81. *Bowsher v. Synar,* 478 U.S. 714 (1986); see also Lance T. LeLoup, Barbara Luck Graham, and Stacey Barwick, "Deficit Politics and Constitutional Government: The Impact of Gramm-Rudman-Hollings," *Public Budgeting and Finance* 7 (1987): 83–103.
82. Congressional Budget Office, *The Economic and Budget Outlook, 1992–96* (Washington, DC: U.S. Government Printing Office, 1991).
83. Philip G. Joyce, "Congressional Budget Reform: The Unanticipated Implications of Federal Policy Making," *Public Administration Review* 56 (1996): 317–324.
84. Allen Schick, *The Federal Budget: Politics, Policy and Process* (Washington, DC: Brookings Institution Press, 1995), 40–41.
85. Karl O'Lessker, "The Clinton Budget for FY 1994: Taking Aim at the Deficit," *Public Budgeting and Finance* 13 (1993): 7–19.
86. "The Supercommittee Collapses" *New York Times,* November 21, 2011.
87. Alvin Rabushka, "Fiscal Responsibility: Will Anything Less than a Constitutional Amendment Do?" in *The Federal Budget,* ed. Michael J. Boskin and Aaron Wildavsky (San Francisco: Institute for Contemporary Studies, 1982), 333–350. See also Henry J. Aaron, "The Balanced Budget Blunder," *Brookings Review,* (1994): 41; and James V. Saturno and Richard G. Forgette, "The Balanced Budget Spring Amendment: How Would It Be Enforced?" *Public Budgeting and Finance* 18, no. 1 (1998): 33–53.

88. Rudolph G. Penner and Alan J. Abramson, *Broken Purse Strings: Congressional Budgeting 1974–1988* (Washington, DC: Urban Institute Press, 1989), 95–100. For more recent figures, see Bill Montague, "New Budget Forecasts 'Solid,'" *USA Today*, December 13, 1995.

89. Updated by the author from Rudolph G. Penner, "Forecasting Budget Totals: Why We Can't Get It Right," in *The Federal Budget*, ed. Boskin and Wildavsky, 89–110. See also Donald F. Kettl, *Deficit Politics* (New York: Macmillan, 1992), 109–117.

90. U.S. House of Representatives, Committee on the Budget, *The Line-Item Veto: An Appraisal* (Washington, DC: U.S. Government Printing Office, 1984).

91. See Norman Ornstein, "Why GOP Will Rue Line-Item Veto," *USA Today*, November 18, 1997.

92. Jeff Flake, "Earmarked Men," *New York Times*, February 9, 2006.

93. Eric Lichtblau, "New Earmark Rules Have Lobbyists Scrambling," *New York Times*, March 11, 2010.

94. Viveca Novak, "Defective Remedy," *National Journal*, March 27, 1993.

95. These included one provision that would have provided $84 million to one sugar beet processor in Texas and another that benefited certain potato growers in Idaho. See Robert Pear, "Justice Department Belatedly Finds New Defense of Line-Item Veto," *New York Times*, March 26, 1998.

96. See *Getting Back in the Black: Pew-Peterson Committee on Budget Reform* (Philadelphia: Pew Charitable Trust, November, 2010).

97. Daniel Tarschys, "Rational Decremental Budgeting: Elements of an Expenditure Policy for the 1980s," *Policy Sciences* 14 (1982): 49–58.

98. For some members of Congress, there is also a strong desire to reduce the level of services and to return the federal government to some sort of Acadian past. See Paul Kane, "House GOP Revs Up for a Repeal, Reduce and Rein-in Agenda for the Fall," *Washington Post*, August 28, 2011.

99. President's Private Sector Survey on Cost Containment (Grace Commission), *Report to the President* (Washington, DC: PPSSCC, 1984).

100. Sar A. Levitan and Alexandra B. Noden, *Working for the Sovereign* (Baltimore: Johns Hopkins University Press, 1983), 85.

101. National Performance Review, *Making Government Work Better and Cost Less* (The Gore Report) (Washington, DC: U.S. Government Printing Office, 1993).

102. Robert Pear, "As Deadline Nears, Deficit Panel Still at Deep Impasse," *New York Times*, November 19, 2011.

103. Aaron Wildavsky, "A Budget for All Seasons: Why the Traditional Budget Lasts," *Public Administration Review* 38 (1978): 501–509. See also Dirk-Jan Kraan, *Budgetary Decisions: A Public Choice Approach* (Cambridge: Cambridge University Press, 1996); and Christopher G. Reddick, "Testing Rival Decision-Making Theories on Budget Outputs," *Public Budgeting and Finance* 22 (2002): 1–25.

Chapter 8

1. For a good summary of the issues involved in evaluating public sector programs, see Evert Vedung, *Public Policy and Program Evaluation* (New Brunswick, NJ: Transaction, 1997).

2. Martin Painter and Jon Pierre, eds., *Challenges to State Policy Capacity* (London: Routledge, 2005).

3. Elaine Morley, Scott P. Bryant, and Harry P. Hatry, *Comparative Performance Measurement* (Washington, DC: Urban Institute, 2001).

4. J. N. Noy, "If You Don't Care Where You Get To, Then It Doesn't Matter Which Way You Go," in *The Evolution of Social Policy,* ed. C. C. Abt (Beverly Hills, CA: Sage, 1976), 97–120.

5. David L. Sills, *The Volunteers* (Glencoe, IL: Free Press, 1956), 253–268.

6. To get some idea of the current orientation of the organization, take a look at the Bureau of Indian Affairs website, www.doi.gov/bureau-indian-affairs.html.

7. Daniel A. Mazmanian and Jeanne Nienaber, *Can Organizations Change?* (Washington, DC: Brookings Institution Press, 1979).

8. There is a growing literature on the means of minimizing and controlling changes in the missions of regulatory agencies. Jonathan R. Mezey, "Organizational Design and the Political Control of Regulatory Agencies," *Journal of Law, Economics and Organization* 8 (1992): 93–110; Patrick D. Schmidt, *Lawyers and Regulation: The Politics of the Administrative Process* (New York: Cambridge University Press, 2005).

9. Robert K. Merton, "Bureaucratic Structure and Personality," *Social Forces* 18 (1940): 560–568.

10. Anthony Downs, *Inside Bureaucracy* (Boston: Little, Brown, 1967), 92–111.

11. See Paul Light, *Tides of Reform* (New Haven, CT: Yale University Press, 1998).

12. Morley, Bryant, and Hatry, *Comparative Performance Measurement.*

13. See Christopher Hood, B. Guy Peters, and Helmutt Wollmann, "Sixteen Ways to Consumerise the Public Sector," *Public Money and Management* 16, no. 4 (1996): 43–50.

14. William Alonzo and Paul Starr, *The Politics of Numbers* (New York: Russell Sage, 1987).

15. Geert Bouckaert, Derry Ormond, and B. Guy Peters, *A Potential Governance Agenda for Finland* (Helsinki: Ministry of Finance, 2000).

16. Richard N. Haass, *The Reluctant Sheriff: The United States after the Cold War* (Washington, DC: Brookings Institution Press, 1997).

17. I. C. R. Byatt, "Theoretical Issues in Expenditure Decisions," in *Public Expenditure: Allocation among Competing Ends,* ed. Michael V. Posner (Cambridge: Cambridge University Press, 1977), 22–27.

18. Michael Woolcock, "The Importance of Time and Trajectories in Understanding Program Effectiveness," *World Bank Blog,* May 5, 2011.

19. Lester M. Salamon, "The Time Dimension in Policy Evaluation: The Case of New Deal Land Reform," *Public Policy, (Spring 1979):* 129–183.

20. See Robert E. Goodin, *Political Theory and Public Policy* (Chicago: University of Chicago Press, 1983), 26–29.

21. Debra Viadero, "'Fade-Out' in Head Start Gains Linked to Later Schooling," *Education Week,* (April 20, 1994): 9.

22. For a discussion of this point, see Henry J. Aaron, *Politics and the Professors* (Washington, DC: Brookings Institution Press, 1978), 84–85. More recent research indicates that there may be some more durable effects; see Edward Zigler and Susan Muenchow, *Head Start: The Inside Story of America's Most Successful Educational Experiment* (New York: Basic Books, 1992).

23. Gerald Schneider, *Time, Planning and Policymaking* (Bern, Switzerland: Peter Lang, 1991); Christopher Pollitt, *Time, Policy, Management: Governing with the Past* (Oxford: Oxford University Press).

24. On social experiments, see William Dunn, *The Experimenting Society* (New Brunswick, NJ: Transaction, 1998); and Norma R. A. Romm, *Accountability in Social Research: Issues and Debates* (New York: Kluwer, 2001).

25. Donald T. Campbell and Julian C. Stanley, *Experimental and Quasi-Experimental Design for Research* (Chicago: Rand-McNally, 1966); and Richard E. Neustadt and Ernest R. May, *Thinking in Time: The Uses of History for Decision-Makers* (New York: Free Press, 1986).

26. In the economic downturn of 2008–2009, the large majority of home mortgage foreclosures were in suburban areas, perhaps accelerating the downward turn of these areas.

27. Campbell and Stanley, *Experimental and Quasi-Experimental Design for Research*, 44–53.

28. For a discussion of the role of experimentation in assessing social policy, see R. A. Berk et al., "Social Policy Experimentation: A Position Paper," *Education Research* 94 (1985): 387–429.

29. Peter Passell, "Like a New Drug, Social Programs Are Put to the Test," *New York Times,* March 9, 1993. Also, the reforms of Medicare after the Balanced Budget Act involve an experiment of 300,000 using Medical Savings Plans.

30. Helen Ingram and Anne Schneider, "The Choice of Target Populations," *Administration and Society* 23 (1991): 149–167; and Anne Schneider and Helen Ingram, "Social Construction of Target Populations: Implications for Politics and Policy," *American Political Science Review* 87 (1993): 334–347.

31. Government Accountability Office, *Prekindergarten: Four States Expanded Access* (Washington, DC: U.S. Government Accountability Office, September 9, 2004), GAO-04-852.

32. Peter Townsend, ed., *Inequalities in Health* ("The Black Report") (London: Penguin, 1988).

33. Brian W. Hogwood and B. Guy Peters, *The Pathology of Public Policy* (Oxford: Oxford University Press, 1985).

34. Welfare had already tended to be short-term for many of the recipients, so the fact that many people could move on should have been no surprise.

35. Barbara J. Holt, "Targeting in Federal Grant Programs: The Case of the Older Americans Act," *Public Administration Review* 54 (1994): 444–449. Michael Hill and Peter Hupe, *Implementing Public Policy*, 2nd ed. (London: Sage, 2009).

36. P. H. Rossi, M. W. Lipsey, and H. E. Freeman, *Evaluation: A Systematic Analysis* (London: Sage, 2004).

37. Sam D. Sieber, *Fatal Remedies* (New York: Plenum, 1980).

38. Arnold Meltsner, *Policy Analysts in the Bureaucracy* (Berkeley: University of California Press, 1976).

39. See B. Guy Peters, *The Future of Governing: Two Decades of Administrative Reform*, 2nd ed. (Lawrence: University Press of Kansas, 2001).

40. General Accounting Office, *Managing for Results: Critical Issues for Improving Federal Agencies' Strategic Plans* (Washington, DC: U.S. General Accounting Office,

September 16, 1997), GAO/GGD-97-180. A full range of information on GPRA can be obtained from the GAO's website, www.gao.gov/sp/.

41. Donald F. Kettl and John J. DiIulio, eds., *Inside the Reinvention Machine: Appraising Governmental Reform* (Washington, DC: Brookings Institution Press, 1995).

42. Rochelle L. Stanfield, "Education Wars," *National Journal,* March 7, 1998, 506–509.

43. Michael Nelson, "What's Wrong with Policy Analysis," *Washington Monthly,* September 1979, 53–60. See also Dan Durning, "Participatory Policy Analysis in a Social Service Agency: A Case Study," *Journal of Policy Analysis and Management* 12 (1993): 297–322.

44. Brian W. Hogwood and B. Guy Peters, *Policy Dynamics* (Brighton, UK: Wheatsheaf, 1983).

45. Ibid.

46. Janet E. Franz, "Reviving and Revising a Termination Model," *Policy Sciences* 25 (1992): 175–189; Joseph Stewart., D. M. Hedge, and J. P. Lester, *Public Policy: An Evolutional Approach,* 3rd ed. (Boston: Thompson Wadsworth, 2008).

47. Laurence E. Lynn Jr. and David deF. Whitman, *The President as Policymaker: Jimmy Carter and Welfare Reform* (Philadelphia: Temple University Press, 1981).

48. Downs, *Inside Bureaucracy.*

49. Rufus E. Miles, "Considerations for a President Bent on Reorganization," *Public Administration Review* 37 (1977): 157.

50. Jean-Claude Thoenig and Eduard Friedberg, "The Power of the Field Staff," in *The Management of Change in Government,* ed. Arne F. Leemans (The Hague, Netherlands: Martinus Nijhoff, 1976), 176–188.

51. On networks, see Edward O. Laumann and David Knoke, *The Organizational State: Social Change in National Policy Domains* (Madison: University of Wisconsin Press, 1987); E. Klijn, J. Koopenjaan, and W. J. M. Kickert, *Policy Networks* (London: Routledge, 2004); Jacob Torfing and Eva Sørensen, *Theories of Democratic Network Governance* (Basingstoke, UK: Macmillan, 2007).

52. See Jan Kooiman, "Societal Governance," in *Debating Governance,* ed. Jon Pierre (Oxford: Oxford University Press, 1998), 138.

53. R. Kent Weaver, "Setting and Firing Policy Triggers," *Journal of Public Policy* 9 (1989): 307–336.

54. William T. Gormley Jr., *Taming the Bureaucracy: Muscles, Prayers and Other Strategies* (Princeton, NJ: Princeton University Press, 1989), 205–207.

55. Karen Kaplan and Nbah H. Levey, "Barack Obama to Reverse Bush Policy on Federal Funding for Stem Cell Research," *Chicago Tribune,* March 7, 2009.

Chapter 9

1. See Michael Stewart, *Keynes and After* (Harmondsworth, UK: Penguin, 1972); and Peter A. Hall, *The Political Power of Economic Ideas: Keynesianism across Nations* (Princeton, NJ: Princeton University Press, 1989).

2. Robert Skidelsky, *Politicians and the Slump* (London: Macmillan, 1967).

3. Walter Heller, *New Dimensions of Political Economy* (Cambridge, MA: Harvard University Press, 1966).

4. This problem has been especially evident with the Bush tax cuts, given that the majority of the benefits have gone to the more affluent who tend to spend a smaller proportion of their income. See Paul Krugman, "Now That's Rich," *New York Times*, August 22, 2010.

5. This trade-off is referred to as the "Phillips Curve." See "A Cruise around the Phillips Curve," *Economist*, February 19, 1994, 82–83; and M. G. Hayes, *The Economics of Keynes: A New Guide to the General Theory* (Cheltenham, UK: Edward Elgar, 2008).

6. In fairness, they often have been promised more of everything by politicians and often without any associated costs. See Isabel V. Sawhill, "Reaganomics in Retrospect," in *Perspectives on the Reagan Years,* ed. John L. Palmer (Washington, DC: Urban Institute Press, 1986), 91.

7. We will point out, however, that although the average has been getting higher, the degree of inequality of distribution of the benefits of growth has also been increasing.

8. For a discussion of this "treble affluence," see Richard Rose and B. Guy Peters, *Can Government Go Bankrupt?* (New York: Basic Books, 1978).

9. Lester Thurow, *The Zero-Sum Society* (New York: Basic Books, 1979).

10. Martin Crutsinger, "Savings Rate at Lowest Level Since 1933," Associated Press, January 30, 2006.

11. U.S. Census Bureau, *Income, Poverty and Health Insurance Coverage in the United States, 2010* (Washington, DC: Census Bureau, September 2011).

12. Organization for Economic Cooperation and Development, *Divided We Stand: Why Inequality Keeps Rising* (Paris: OECD, May 2011).

13. David Leonhardt, "Income Inequality," *New York Times*, January 16, 2011.

14. "The Occupy Movement," *New York Times*, February 12, 2012.

15. Although employment in manufacturing has been declining, value added has been relatively stable. Industries are finding ways to produce with less labor or are shifting toward high-value-added products such as computers and other information technologies. Also, the resurgence of the automobile industry after the intervention of the federal government has returned a significant amount of employment in manufacturing. Jeremy W. Peters, "Bailout Stand Trails Romney in Car Country," *New York Times,* February 16, 2012.

16. Service industries include a wide range of activities such as insurance, medical care, computer services, and banking, in addition to dry cleaners, restaurants, and so forth. For some, wages and benefits are excellent, but many also are minimum-wage jobs with no benefits.

17. Emily Kaiser, "Economists See Longest Recession Since World War II," Reuters News Service, January 10, 2009.

18. Frank Ahrens, "Actual U.S. Unemployment 15.8%," *Washington Post,* May 8, 2009.

19. Fred Hirsch and John H. Goldthorpe, *The Political Economy of Inflation* (Cambridge, MA: Harvard University Press, 1978).

20. R. Kent Weaver, *The Politics of Indexation* (Washington, DC: Brookings Institution Press, 1987).

21. This is the so-called Baumol's disease, named after the economist William J. Baumol; see his "The Macroeconomics of Unbalanced Growth: The Anatomy of Urban Crisis," in *Is Economics Relevant?* eds. Robert L. Heilbroner and A. M. Ford (Pacific Palisades, CA: Goodyear, 1971), 32–45.

22. John T. Woolley, *Monetary Politics: The Federal Reserve and the Politics of Monetary Policy* (Cambridge: Cambridge University Press, 1987).

23. Gøsta Esping-Anderson, *The Three Worlds of Welfare Capitalism* (Princeton, NJ: Princeton University Press, 1990).

24. Simon Johnson, "A Second Great Depression, or Worse?" *New York Times,* August 11, 2011.

25. Yuka Hayashi, "Japan Braces for Protracted Stretch of Deflation," *Wall Street Journal,* May 1, 2009.

26. Nitsan Chorey, *Remaking U.S. Trade Policy: From Protectionism to Globalization* (Ithaca, NY: Cornell University Press, 2006).

27. William S. Harat and Thomas D. Willett, eds., *Monetary Policy for a Volatile Global Economy* (Washington, DC: AEI Press, 1991).

28. Martin Tolchin and Susan Tolchin, *Buying into America: How Foreign Money Is Changing the Face of Our Nation* (New York: Times Books, 1988).

29. David Barboza, "China Urges New Money Reserve to Replace Dollar," *New York Times,* March 24, 2009.

30. See Susan Strange, *The Retreat of the State: The Diffusion of Power in the World Economy* (Cambridge: Cambridge University Press, 1996).

31. Michael M. Weinstein, "Twisting Controls on Currency and Capital," *New York Times,* September 10, 1998; and Martin Wolf, *Why Globalization Works* (New Haven, CT: Yale University Press, 2004).

32. M. Hallerberg and S. Basinger, "Internationalization and Changes in Tax Policy in OECD Countries: The Importance of Domestic Veto Players," *Comparative Political Studies* 31 (1998): 321–352; and David Vogel, *Trading Up: Consumer and Environmental Regulation in a Global Economy* (Cambridge, MA: Harvard University Press, 1995).

33. At least some of this relative success is the result of the Troubled Asset Relief Program (TARP). See Yalman Oranan and Alexis Leondis, "Bank Bailout Yields 8.2%, Beating Treasury Yields," *Bloomberg Financial Reporter,* October 20, 2010.

34. Henry Kaufman, "European Debt Crisis Can Prompt U.S. Credit Squeeze," *Huffington Post,* December 18, 2011.

35. Terry F. Buss, "The Effects of State Tax Incentives on Economic Growth and Firm Location Decisions," *Economic Development Quarterly* 15 (2001): 90–105.

36. Fred R. Bleakley, "Infrastructure Dollars Pay Big Dividends," *Wall Street Journal,* August 12, 1997.

37. Robert J. Reinshuttle, *Economic Development: A Survey of State Activities* (Lexington, KY: Council of State Governments, 1984).

38. N. Edward Coulson, "Sectoral Sources of the Massachusetts Miracle," *Journal of Regional Science* 41 (2002): 617–637; Scott Shane, *Academic Entrepreneurship: Academic Spinoffs and Wealth Creation* (Cheltenham, UK: Edward Elgar, 2006).

39. Federal Reserve Bank of San Francisco, "What Is the Difference between Monetary and Fiscal Policy," September, 2002).

40. See Strange, *The Retreat of the State*; and K. Ohmae, *The End of the Nation State* (New York: Free Press, 1995). For a contrary view, see Linda Weiss, *The Myth of the Powerless State* (Cambridge: Cambridge University Press, 1998).

41. Andrew P. Cortell, *Mediating Globalization: Domestic Institutions and Industrial Policies in the United States and Britain* (Albany, NY: SUNY Press, 2006).

42. For one view, see Robert B. Reich, "Trade Accords That Spread the Wealth," *New York Times,* September 2, 1997.

43. John Maggs, "Back from the Dead," *National Journal,* February 2, 2002, 304–307.

44. See Robert E. Litan, "Trade Policy: What Next?" *Brookings Review* 18 (Fall 2000): 41–44.

45. Paul Magnusson, "Bush Trade Policy: Crazy Quilt Like a Fox," *Business Week,* April 15, 2002.

46. "Jobs and Protectionism in the Stimulus Package," *Business Week,* February 16, 2009.

47. James D. Savage, *Balanced Budgets and American Democracy* (Ithaca, NY: Cornell University Press, 1988).

48. Rose and Peters, *Can Government Go Bankrupt?* 135–141; and James M. Buchanan and Richard Wagner, *Democracy in Deficit: The Political Legacy of Lord Keynes* (New York: Academic Press, 1978), 38–48.

49. When one listens to the debates about the impact of budgets in most parliaments or central agencies, it is clear that the ideas of Keynesianism are far from dead.

50. "The Undeniable Shift to Keynes," *Financial Times,* January 23, 2009.

51. Henry Aaron et al., *Setting National Priorities: The 1980 Budget* (Washington, DC: Brookings Institution Press, 1979). For a critique, see William H. Buiter, "A Guide to Public Sector Deficits," *Economic Policy* 1 (1985): 3–15.

52. Richard W. Stevenson, "House Republicans to Seek Big Tax Cuts," *New York Times,* September 10, 1998.

53. G. Calvin Mackenzie and Saranna Thornton, *Bucking the Deficit: Economic Policymaking in America* (Boulder, CO: Westview Press, 1996).

54. "Budget Resolution Embraces Clinton Plan," *CQ Almanac 1993* (Washington, DC: CQ Press, 1994), 102–121.

55. "Pact Aims to Erase Deficit by 2002," *CQ Almanac 1997* (Washington, DC: CQ Press, 1998), February 18–February 23.

56. Jackie Calmes, "House Passes Stimulus Package with No Republican Votes," *New York Times,* January 28, 2009.

57. Douglas A. Hibbs, *The American Political Economy: Macroeconomics and Electoral Choice* (Cambridge, MA: Harvard University Press, 1987).

58. Paul Craig Roberts, *The Supply-Side Revolution: An Insider's Account of Policymaking in Washington* (Cambridge, MA: Harvard University Press, 1984), esp. 27–33.

59. Yannis Gabriel and Tim Lang, *The Unmanageable Consumer* (Thousand Oaks, CA: Sage, 2006).

60. B. Douglas Bernheim, *The Vanishing Nest Egg: Reflections on Saving in America* (New York: Twentieth Century Fund, 1991).

61. Bruce Bartlett and Timothy P. Roth, eds., *The Supply-Side Solution* (Chatham, NJ: Chatham House, 1983). George H. W. Bush once referred to this assumption as "voodoo economics."

62. For an extended critique see Alice M. Rivlin and Isabel Sawhill, eds., *Restoring Fiscal Sanity 2005* (Washington, DC: Brookings Institution Press, 2005).

63. *New York Times,* "Job Losses in the Public Sector," February 18, 2012.

64. Donald F. Kettl, *Leadership at the Fed* (New Haven, CT: Yale University Press, 1986). For a more muckraking account, see William Greider, *Secrets of the Temple: How the Federal Reserve Runs the Country* (New York: Simon and Schuster, 1987).

65. Sen. Harry Reid, D-NV, called Greenspan "one of the biggest political hacks in Washington," in a CNN interview with Judy Woodruff on March 6, 2005.

66. See topics.nytimes.com/topics/reference/timestopics/organizations/federalreserve-system.

67. Ben Bernanke, "The Crisis and the Policy Response," *Federal Reserve*, January 13, 2009.

68. Robert Shiller, "A Failure of Control of Animal Spirits," *Financial Times,* May 12, 2009.

69. See B. Guy Peters, "Institutionalization and Deinstitutionalization: Regulatory Institutions in American Government," in *Comparative Regulatory Institutions,* ed. G. Bruce Doern and Stephen Wilks (Toronto: University of Toronto Press, 1998), 212–239.

70. Marc Alan Eisner, *Antitrust and the Triumph of Economics* (Chapel Hill: University of North Carolina Press, 1991).

71. The Department of Justice had been the only enforcement agency. It retained its powers after the passage of the Clayton Act, and both it and the Federal Trade Commission enforce antitrust legislation.

72. Joel Brinkley, "Strategies Set in Microsoft Antitrust Case," *New York Times,* September 14, 1998.

73. Some of this argument appears specious given that all firms will face the same wage increases.

74. See Herbert Stein, *Presidential Economics: Making Economic Policy from Roosevelt to Clinton,* 3rd ed. (Washington, DC: AEI Press, 1994).

75. William Pfaff, "Deregulation Is a False God," *Los Angeles Times,* June 27, 2002.

76. June Fletcher, "Is the Party Really Over for the Housing Bubble?" *Wall Street Journal,* February 10, 2007.

77. Viral V. Achyra et al., *Regulating Wall Street: The Dodd-Frank Act and the New Architecture of Global Finance* (New York: Wiley Finance, 2012).

78. Author's calculation based on the federal budget documents.

79. J. C. Gray and D. A. Spina, "State and Local Government Industrial Location Incentives: A Well-Stocked Candy Store," *Journal of Corporation Law* 5 (1980): 517–687; and Andrew Ward, "U.S. States Become Addicted to Use of Economic Sweeteners," *Financial Times,* March 23, 2006.

80. William S. Dietrich, *In the Shadow of the Rising Sun: The Political Roots of American Economic Decline* (University Park: Pennsylvania State University Press, 1991).

81. The most famous was Ross Perot, who characterized the predicted large loss of jobs to Mexico under NAFTA as a "large sucking sound." See also G. Bruce Doern and Brian W. Tomlin, *Faith and Fear: The Free Trade Story* (Toronto: Stoddard, 1991).

82. Edmund L. Andrews and David E. Sanger, "U.S. Finds its Role in Business Hard to Unwind," *New York Times,* September 15, 2009.

83. Nick Bunkley, "GM Still Hopeful of Fully Paying Back the Government," *New York Times,* June 7, 2011.

84. Jonathan T. R. Hughes, *The Governmental Habit Redux: Economic Controls from Colonial Times to the Present,* 2nd ed. (Princeton, NJ: Princeton University Press, 1991).

85. That support may come through direct subsidies or through protection from foreign competition. See David B. Yoffie, "American Trade Policy: An Obsolete Bargain," in *Can the Government Govern?* eds J. Chubb and P. Peterson (Washington, DC: Brookings Institution Press, 1989), 100–138.

86. Jim Rutenberg and Bill Vlasic, "Chrysler Files to Seek Bankruptcy Protection," *New York Times,* May 1, 2009.

87. Bureau of Labor Statistics, *Productivity Statistics*, monthly, www.bls.gov/lpc/.

88. *Business Week*, "Behind America's Jobless Recovery," July 15, 2011.

89. Steven Greenhouse, "The Wageless, Profitable Recovery," *New York Times,* June 30, 2011.

90. See Marie-Louise Bermelmans-Videc, Ray C. Rist, and Evert Vedung, eds., *Carrots, Sticks and Sermons: Policy Instruments and Their Evaluation* (New Brunswick, NJ: Transaction Books, 1998).

Chapter 10

1. Henry J. Aaron and William G. Gale, eds., *Economic Effects of Fundamental Tax Reform* (Washington, DC: Brookings Institution Press, 1996).

2. Charles E. McLure, *The Value-Added Tax: Key to Deficit Reduction?* (Washington, DC: American Enterprise Institute, 1987); and R. E. Hall, "The Simple, Progressive Value-Added Consumption Tax," in *Toward Fundamental Tax Reform,* ed. K. A. Haslett and A. J. Auerbach (Washington, DC: American Enterprise Institute, 2005), 203–228.

3. B. Guy Peters, *Taxation: A Comparative Perspective* (Oxford: Blackwell, 1991).

4. For example, John Dougherty, "Property Tax Conflict Enters Nevada Governor's Race," *Nevada Journal,* January 28, 2010, http://nevadajournal.com/2010/01/28/property-tax-conflict-enters-nevada-governors-race/.

5. See Cathie Jo Martin, "Business Influence and State Power: The Case of U.S. Corporate Tax Policy," *Politics and Society* 17 (1989): 189–223. For a somewhat polemical account of recent developments, see Christopher Lasch, *The Revolt of the Elites and the Betrayal of Democracy* (New York: Norton, 1995); William F. Holmes, *American Populism* (New York: D. C. Heath, 1994), provides a more *balanced* treatment of populism.

6. David Brunori, *State Tax Policy: A Political Perspective* (Washington, DC: Urban Institute, 2005).

7. Stanley S. Surrey and Paul R. McDaniel, *Tax Expenditures* (Cambridge: Cambridge University Press, 1985).

8. Richard W. Stevenson, "The Secret Language of Social Engineering," *New York Times,* July 6, 1997.

9. Robert Pear, "Now, Special Tax Breaks Get Hidden in Plain Sight," *New York Times,* August 1, 1997.

10. Janet Novack, "The Dirty Little Secret of Tax Reform," *Forbes,* July 29, 2011.

11. Christopher Howard, *The Hidden Welfare State: Tax Expenditures and Social Policy in the United States* (Princeton, NJ: Princeton University Press, 1997); Marie Gottschalk, *The Shadow Welfare State: Labor, Business and the Politics of Health Care* (Ithaca, NY: Cornell University Press).

12. For a useful review of public opinion on tax reform, see "Public Opinion on Taxes," *American Enterprise Institute (AEI) Studies in Public Opinion,* April 10, 2009, www .aei.org/search/Studies+in+Public+Opinion%2C+April+10%2C+2009.

13. ABC News Polls, "Flat Tax Outpaces 9-9-9, Notably among Conservatives," October 25, 2011, http://abcnews.go.com/blogs/politics/2011/10/in-poll-flat-tax-outpaces-9-9-9-notably-among-conservatives/. Less than half the respondents favored a flat tax.

14. The two standard ideas are ability to pay, justifying a progressive system of taxation, and benefits received, which can justify more of a flat-rate system of taxation.

15. See O. Listhaug and Arthur H. Miller, "Public Support for Tax Evasion: Self-Interest or Symbolic Politics?" *European Journal of Political Research* 13 (1985): 265–282. See also John T. Scholz and Mark Lubell, "Adaptive Political Attitudes: Duty, Trust and Fear as Monitors of Tax Policy," *American Journal of Political Science* 42 (1998): 903–920.

16. Gallup Poll, March 24–26, 1997; March 25–27, 2001, available at www.pollingreport .com, a comprehensive listing of U.S. polling results.

17. Robert Greenstein, *How Would Families at Different Income Levels Benefit from the Bush Tax Cut?* (Washington, DC: Center for Budget and Policy Priorities, April 2001). The effects of those tax cuts have been exacerbated since that time. One estimate by the Center for Budget and Policy Priorities (December 2005) is that the average taxpayer in the top 1 percent of income earners has saved $34,900 as a result, while the average saved by the lower 20 percent was $18.

18. See Citizens for Tax Justice, *Overall Tax Rates Have Flattened Sharply under Bush* (Washington, DC: Citizens for Tax Justice, April 2004).

19. Glenn Kessler, "Revisiting the Cost of the Bush Tax Cuts," *Washington Post,* May 10, 2011.

20. It does, of course. Leaving aside how one counts the protective services delivered by the military, there are the Veterans Administration and its hospitals, the Postal Service, the National Park Service, agricultural extension agents, and a host of others.

21. National Center on Alcohol and Drug Dependency, *Washington Report,* December 2005, entire issue.

22. This is, however, bad news for health advocates who are attempting to use the cigarette tax as a means of deterring smoking. It may be more of a deterrent for the main target group—teen smokers—who have less disposable income.

23. See William F. Shugart, ed., *Taxing Choices: The Predatory Politics of Fiscal Discrimination* (New Brunswick, NJ: Transaction, 1997).

24. CBS News poll, April 2001, www.pollingreport.com.

25. ABC News poll, March 2001, www.pollingreport.com.

26. In addition to conventional polling, deliberative polling shows the preference for services and fiscal responsibility as opposed to tax cuts. See Edmund Andrews, "Public's Deficit Fix May Stun Politicians," *New York Times,* July 30, 2006.

27. David O. Sears and Jack Citrin, *Tax Revolt: Something for Nothing in California,* enl. ed. (Cambridge, MA: Harvard University Press, 1985).

28. J. Owens, "Fundamental Tax Reform: An International Perspective," *National Tax Journal* (March 1, 2006): 131–164.

29. Joel Slemrod, "Which Is the Simplest Tax System of Them All?" in *Economic Effects of Fundamental Tax Reform,* ed. Henry J. Aaron and William G. Gale (Washington, DC: Brookings Institution Press, 1996), 355.

30. Scott A. Hodge, J. Scott Moody, and Wendy P. Warcholik, "The Rising Cost of Complying with Federal Income Tax," *Special Report* (Washington, DC: The National Tax Foundation, January 10, 2006).

31. Even at the minimum wage of $7.25 per hour, this would amount to over $7 billion in free work by citizens.

32. Tami Luhby, "Reeling States Hit by April Tax Shortfalls," *CNN Money,* May 7, 2009, http://money.cnn.com/2009/05/07/news/economy/state_budget_gaps/index.htm.

33. Richard A. Musgrave, *Fiscal Systems* (New Haven, CT: Yale University Press, 1969).

34. Laura Sanders, "The Campeau Coup and the May Maneuver," *Forbes,* October 31, 1988, 98–99.

35. L. E. Burman, W. G. Gale, Jeffrey Rohaly, and M. Hall, *Key Points on the Alternative Minimum Tax* (Washington, DC: Urban Institute–Brookings Tax Policy Center, January 21, 2004).

36. Joseph A. Pechman, *Who Paid the Taxes, 1966–85?* (Washington, DC: Brookings Institution Press, 1986).

37. Cathy Dodge and Kate Anderson Brower, "Obama Calls on Wealthy Americans to Pay More Tax to Restore Fairness," *Bloomberg News,* January 2, 2012.

38. Paul E. Peterson and Mark Rom, "Lower Taxes, More Spending and Budget Deficits," in *The Reagan Legacy,* ed. Charles O. Jones (Chatham, NJ: Chatham House, 1988), 213.

39. Calculated from Internal Revenue Service, *Statistics of Income Bulletin* (quarterly), various issues.

40. Harold Wilensky, *The "New Corporatism," Centralization, and the Welfare State* (Beverly Hills, CA: Sage, 1976).

41. The author, for example, pays four separate income taxes, three property taxes, sales and excise taxes, etc. Some of these taxes are small, but they do add up.

42. W. W. Pommerehne and F. Schneider, "Fiscal Illusion, Political Institutions and Local Public Spending," *Kyklos* 31 (1978): 381–408.

43. William H, Gale, *The Value-Added Tax in the United States: Part of the Solution* (Washington, DC: Brookings Institution Press, July 22, 2010).

44. Guy Peters, *The Politics of Taxation: A Comparative Perspective* (Oxford: Blackwell's, 1991), 165–167.

45. Sven Steinmo, *Taxation and Democracy* (New Haven, CT: Yale University Press, 1992).

46. J. M. Verdier, "The President, Congress and Tax Reform: Patterns over Three Decades," *Annals* 499 (1988): 114–123.

47. Even after reform, the federal income tax was considered the least fair tax by a plurality of respondents in surveys. See Advisory Commission on Intergovernmental Relations, *Changing Public Attitudes on Government and Taxes* (Washington, DC: ACIR, 1992).

48. Timothy J. Conlan, Margaret T. Wrightson, and David R. Beam, *Taxing Choices: The Politics of Tax Reform* (Washington, DC: CQ Press, 1989); and J. H. Birnbaum and A. S. Murray, *Showdown at Gucci Gulch* (New York: Random House, 1987).

49. Gary Mucciaroni, "Public Choice and the Politics of Comprehensive Tax Reform," *Governance* 3 (1990): 1–32.

50. Conlan, Wrightson, and Beam, *Taxing Choices.*

51. John W. Kingdon, *Agendas, Alternatives, and Public Policies,* 2nd ed. (Boston: Little, Brown, 2003).

52. For example, if I had invested in a piece of land in 1970 for $100 and then sold it in 1998 for $500, there would be an apparent profit of $400. If, however, inflation were taken into account, the "real" profit would be less than $200 (in 1998 dollars). On what basis should I be taxed?

53. In 1995, 82 percent of all returns reporting capital gains cited incomes less than $100,000, although 76 percent of all capital gains income does go to people earning over $100,000.

54. Henry J. Aaron and William A. Gale, "Truth in Taxes," *Brookings Review* 18 (Spring 2000): 12–15.

55. William Gale and Joel B. Slemrod, *Rethinking the Estate and Gift Tax* (Ann Arbor: University of Michigan Business School, January 2001).

56. Carl Hulse, "Battle on Estate Tax: How Two Well-Organized Lobbies Sprang into Action," *New York Times,* June 14, 2001.

57. Suzanne Malvaux, "Obama to Introduce Tax Reforms That Target Overseas Loopholes," CNN Politics.com, May 4, 2009, http://edition.cnn.com/2009/POLITICS/05/04/obama.tax.code/index.html.

58. Lori Montgomery, "Once Considered Unthinkable, U.S. Sales Tax Gets Fresh Look," *Washington Post,* May 27, 2009.

59. This resentment came to a head in 1997 and 1998 with a series of congressional hearings about the Internal Revenue Service and its treatment of citizens. See Daniel J. Murphy, "IRS: An Agency Out of Control?" *Investor's Business Daily,* October 1, 1997. More recently, it became evident that the IRS was focusing much of its attention on less affluent taxpayers, who were easier targets, not being protected by a phalanx of accountants and lawyers like the more affluent. See David Cay Johnston, "IRS Will Cut Tax Lawyers Who Audit the Richest," *New York Times,* July 23, 2006.

60. In 2002, the effective tax rate for earners with incomes of $100,000 was less than this 17 percent, but the marginal rate was 28 percent. Thus, the flat tax would be a real boon for the very affluent but would produce higher taxes for the middle classes.

61. But see Aaron Wildavsky, "Keeping Kosher: The Epistemology of Tax Expenditures," *Journal of Public Policy* 5 (1985): 413–431.

62. See Robert S. McIntyre, "The 23 Percent Solution," *New York Times,* January 23, 1998.

63. Psychologically that may create demands for increases in wages, even though people should have a great deal more take-home pay with the elimination of the income tax.

64. See David F. Bradford, *Untangling the Income Tax* (Cambridge, MA: Harvard University Press, 1986); and General Accounting Office, *Tax Administration: Potential Impact of Alternate Taxes on Taxpayers and Administrators* (Washington, DC: U.S. General Accounting Office, January 1998), GAO/GGD-98-37, appendix VIII.

65. See Thomas J. DiLorenzo and James T. Bennett, "National Nannies Seek Taxes on All We Consume," *USA Today,* December 23, 1997.

66. That is, 24 million business returns plus 115 million personal returns.

67. Ben Wildavsky, "A Taxing Question," *National Journal,* February 8, 1998: 440–444.

Chapter 11

1. U.S. Centers for Medicare and Medicaid Services, Office of the Actuary, *Health Accounts* (Washington, DC: Department of Health and Human Services, 2005).
2. Victor R. Fuchs and Ezekiel J. Emmanuel, "Health Care Reform: Why? What? When?" *Health Affairs* 24 (2005): 1399–1414.
3. CBS News/*New York Times* poll, March 1, 2007.
4. "Federal, State, Local, or Private Action," *American Enterprise,* November/December 1997, 94; and Gina Kolata, "An Economist's View of Health Care Reform," *New York Times,* May 2, 2000.
5. Pam Belluck, "Massachusetts Sets Health Plan for Nearly All," *New York Times,* April 5, 2006.
6. Julie Appleby, "States Take Health Care Problems into Their Own Hands," *USA Today,* November 9, 2005.
7. With the loss of welfare also came a loss of Medicaid coverage, but another federal law funded care for children in states that adopted a suitable program. See Peter T. Kilborn, "States to Provide Health Insurance to More Children," *New York Times,* September 21, 1997; and Thomas M. Selden, Jessica S. Bathin, and Joel W. Cohen, "Trends: Medicaid's Problem Children: Eligible but Not Enrolled," *Health Affairs* 17, no. 3 (1998): 192–200.
8. Jonathan Gruber, "Incremental Universalism in the United States: The States Move Fast," *Journal of Economic Perspectives* 22 (2008): 51–68.
9. World Health Organization, *World Health Statistics Annual* (Geneva: World Health Organization, 2011).
10. J. Banks, M. Marmot, Z. Oldfield, and J. P. Smith, "Disease and Disadvantage in the United States and in England," *Journal of the American Medical Association* 295 (May 3, 2006): 2037–2047.
11. "The Public Decides on Health Care Reform," *Public Perspective* 5 (September/October 1994): 23–28. See also note 4.
12. U.S. Census Bureau, *Current Population Reports,* census data series P60-226 (Washington, DC: U.S. Census Bureau, 2010).
13. Ibid.
14. Ibid.; see also Robert Pear, "Tough Decision on Health Care if Employers Won't Pay the Bill," *New York Times,* July 9, 1994.
15. Despite its good intentions, the indications are that Kennedy-Kassebaum is not as effective as it might be because the rates at which the portable insurance can be charged are not adequately controlled. See Robert Pear, "High Rates Hobble Law to Guarantee Health Insurance," *New York Times,* March 17, 1998.
16. Peter Townsend, ed., *Inequalities in Health: The Black Report* (London: Penguin, 1988).
17. Lisette Alvarez, "A Conservative Battles Corporate Health Care," *New York Times,* February 12, 1998; Alina Tugend, "Hands to Hold When Health Care Becomes a Maze," *New York Times,* October 13, 2007.
18. Peter T. Kilborn, "Black Americans Trailing Whites in Health, Studies Say," *New York Times,* January 26, 1998; see also U.S. Center for Health Statistics, *Health 2006* (Washington, DC: Department of Health and Human Services, 2007).
19. Sheryl Gay Stolberg, "Race Gap Seen in Health Care of Equally Insured Patients," *New York Times,* March 21, 2002.

20. U.S. Centers for Disease Control and Prevention, *Vital Statistics of the United States* (Atlanta, GA: Centers for Disease Control and Prevention, 2006).

21. Rural areas tend to have a number of hospital beds but very low occupancy rates, and that drives up costs.

22. Dan Verango, "The Operation You Get Often Depends on Where You Live," *USA Today,* September 19, 2000; see www.dartmouth.edu/~atlas.

23. Peter T. Kilborn, "Roving Doctors Paying House Calls to Towns," *New York Times,* April 16, 2000.

24. *Rural Health Clinics: Rising Program Expenditures Not Focused on Improving Care in Isolated Areas,* testimony of Bernice Steinhardt (Washington, DC: U.S. General Accounting Office, February 13, 1997), GAO/T-HEHS-97-65.

25. Nicholas Eberstadt, "Why Are So Many American Babies Dying?" *American Enterprise* 2 (September 1991): 37–45. This finding, of course, supports conservative arguments for individual responsibility and minimizes the need for government intervention in the medical marketplace.

26. See Henry J. Aaron, *The Problem That Won't Go Away: Reforming U.S. Health Care Financing* (Washington, DC: Brookings Institution Press, 1995).

27. These constraints on access to referrals were challenged successfully in the courts. Mark Carriden, "High Court Hears Suit on HMO Referrals," *Dallas Morning News,* January 15, 2002.

28. Cathy Cowan, Aaron Catlin, Cynthia Smith, and Arthur Sensening, "National Health Expenditures, 2002," *Health Care Financing Review* 25 (2004): 143–166.

29. Catherine Rampell, "Medicare Care Prices Fell for First Time in 35 Years," *New York Times,* August 13, 2010.

30. Milt Freudenheim, "Many HMOs Easing the Rules on Specialists' Care," *New York Times,* February 2, 1997; Cowan et al., "National Health Expenditures, 2002."

31. See Robert Pear, "Bush Seeks Surplus via Medicare Cuts," *New York Times,* January 31, 2008.

32. Henry J. Aaron and Bruce K. McLaury, *Serious and Unstable Condition: Financing America's Health Care* (Washington, DC: Brookings Institution Press, 1991), 8–37.

33. Service employees, including health services, in both the public and private sectors are the only segment of the labor force with increasing levels of unionization.

34. *Health USA, 2007* (Washington, DC: Department of Health and Human Services, 2008).

35. Spencer Rich, "Hospital Administration Costs Put at 25%," *Washington Post,* August 6, 1993.

36. U.S. Government Accountability Office, *VA Health Care: Status of Inspector General Recommendations for Health Care Services Contracting* (Washington, DC: Government Accountability Office, October 31, 2007).

37. Joshua M. Wiener and Laura Hixon Illston, "Health Care Reform: Six Questions for President Clinton," *Brookings Review* 11 (Spring 1993): 22–25.

38. Aaron and McLaury, *Serious and Unstable Condition,* 45–47.

39. M. M. Mello, D. M. Studdert, and T. A. Brennen, "The New Medical Malpractice Crisis," *New England Journal of Medicine* 348 (2002): 2281–2286.

40. Julie Kosterlitz, "Wanted: GPs," *National Journal,* September 5, 1992.

41. Susan Hosek et al., *The Study of Preferred Provider Organizations* (Santa Monica, CA: RAND, 1990). Doctors are beginning to fight back against managed care. See Reed Abelson, "A Medical Resistance Movement," *New York Times,* March 25, 1998.

42. Health Care Financing Administration, *Health Care Financing Review* (annual) (Washington, DC: Health Care Financing Administration, 2004); figures are for 1995.

43. Garrett Hardin and John Baden, *Managing the Commons* (San Francisco: W. H. Freeman, 1977).

44. Bob Herbert, "Curing Health Costs: Let the Sick Suffer," *New York Times,* September 1, 2005.

45. T. Bodenheimer, "The Oregon Health Plan: Lessons for the Nation," *New England Journal of Medicine* 337 (1997): 651–659.

46. Susan Feigenbaum, "Denying Access to Life-Saving Technologies: Budgetary Implications of a Moral Dilemma," *Regulation* 16, no. 4 (1994): 74–79.

47. On the latter point, see Ivan Illich, *Medical Nemesis* (New York: Pantheon, 1976).

48. Abelson, "A Medical Resistance Movement"; and R. Pear, "The Tricky Business of Keeping Doctors Quiet," *New York Times,* September 22, 1996.

49. As of spring 1997, eight states had comprehensive laws providing managed care rights to citizens, two others had regulations and were writing legislation, and nineteen others had legislation under active consideration.

50. These efforts to regain control often have been less than successful. See Nancy Wolff and Mark Schlesinger, "Clinicians as Advocates: An Exploratory Study of Responses to Managed Care by Mental Health Professionals," *Journal of Behavioral Health Services and Research* 29 (2004): 274–288.

51. The same questions arise concerning developments in medical technology, such as artificial hearts. See "One Miracle, Many Doubts," *Time,* December 10, 1984, 10.

52. Henry R. Glick, *The Right to Die* (New York: Columbia University Press, 1994); Gunther Lewy, *Assisted Death in Europe and America: Four Regimes and Their Lessons* (Oxford: Oxford University Press, 2011).

53. See G. Magill, "Resolving the Case of Terry Schiavo," *Health Care Ethics USA* 11, no. 2 (2005), www.slu.edu/centers/chce/hceusa/.

54. Robert Pear, "Obama Returns to End-of-Life Plan That Caused Stir," *The New York Times,* December 25, 2010.

55. Gregg Bloche. *The Hippocratic Myth: Why Doctors Are Under Pressure to Ration Care, Practice Politics and Compromise Their Oath as They Heal* (New York: Palgrave, 2011).

56. Adam Liptak, "On Day 3, Justices Weigh What-ifs of Health Ruling," *New York Times,* March 28, 2012.

57. Bruce Japsen, "Small Picture Approach Flips Medical Economics," *New York Times,* March 12, 2012.

58. Robert Pear, "House Votes to Kill a Medicare Cost Panel," *New York Times,* March 22, 2012.

59. Elizabeth A. McGlynn et al., "The Quality of Health Care Delivered to Adults in the United States," *New England Journal of Medicine,* 348 (2003): 2635–2645.

60. Amy Goldstein and N. C. Aizenman, "House Votes to Repeal Health Care Law," *Washington Post,* January 20, 2011.

61. Higher-income Medicare enrollees now must pay higher deductibles.

62. Karen Davis, "Equal Treatment and Unequal Benefits," *Milbank Memorial Fund Quarterly* (Fall 1975): 449–488; and Robert Ball, "What Medicare's Architects Had in Mind," *Health Affairs* 14, no. 4 (1995): 62–72.
63. Advisory Council on Social Security, *Report on Medicare Projections by the Health Technical Panel* (Washington, DC: U.S. Government Printing Office, 1991).
64. Marilyn Werber Serafini, "Brave New World," *National Journal*, August 16, 1997.
65. In a medical savings account, Medicare buys the patient a catastrophic care policy and covers part of the deductible payments for care under the policy. If there are any savings over the year—if, for example, the recipient is healthy and actually spends less than under the standard program—then he or she gets to keep the difference.
66. Louise B. Russell and Carrie Lynn Manning, "The Effect of Prospective Payment on Medicare Expenditures," *New England Journal of Medicine* 330 (1989): 439–444.
67. Jeffrey A. Buck and Mark S. Kamlet, "Problems with Expanding Medicaid for the Uninsured," *Journal of Health Politics, Policy and Law* 18 (1993): 1–25. In 1999, Medicaid spending accounted for approximately one dollar in five of state expenditures.
68. Health Care Financing Administration, *Health Care Financing Review*, annual (Washington, DC: Health Care Financing Administration, 2009).
69. Paul Jesilow, Gilbert Geis, and Henry Pontell, "Fraud by Physicians against Medicaid," *Journal of the American Medical Association* 266 (1991): 3318–3322; see also M. K. Wynia, D. S. Cummins, J. B. VanGeest, and I. B. Wilson, "Physician Manipulation of Reimbursement Rules for Patients," *Journal of the American Medical Association* 283 (2000): 1858–1865; Katie Thomas, "Seven Charged in Health Care Fraud," *New York Times*, February 25, 2012.
70. U.S. Government Accountability Office (GAO), *Medicare and Medicaid Fraud Waste and Abuse*, March 9, 2011 (USGAO-11-409T), Washington, DC: Government Printing Office.
71. Karen Davis et al., *Health Care Cost Containment* (Baltimore: Johns Hopkins University Press, 1990), 222ff.
72. Patricia Baumann, "The Formulation and Evolution of Health Maintenance Organization Policy, 1970–73," *Social Science and Medicine* 10 (1976): 129–142.
73. See Lester C. Thurow, "As HMOs Lose Control, Patient Costs Head Skyward," *USA Today*, December 16, 1997.
74. Milt Freudenheim, "Big HMO to Give Decisions on Care Back to Doctors," *New York Times*, November 9, 1999.
75. Julie Appleby, "HMOs: What Happens When the Band Aids Run Out?" *USA Today*, December 8, 2000.
76. Stephen Linder and Pauline Vaillancourt Rousseau, "Health Care Policy," in *Developments in American Politics* 4, ed. Gillian Peele et al. (Basingstoke, England: Palgrave, 2002), 222–233.
77. One of the older forms of health care regulation, the control of facilities through certificates of need, has ceased to be of great relevance, given the emphasis on cost containment in managed care.
78. MedPac, *Report to Congress: Medicare Payment Process* (Washington, DC: Center for Medicare Statistics, March 2006).

79. Peter H. Stone, "Ready for Round Two," *National Journal,* January 3, 1998; and "Health Care Reform," *Public Perspective,* February/March 1998, 39.
80. In particular, Rep. Charles Norwood, R-GA, led a campaign for more extensive regulation of HMOs. This had him making common cause with Sen. Edward Kennedy, D-MA, one of the more liberal members of the Senate.
81. Mark A. Hall, "Managed Care: Patient Protection or Provider Protection?" *American Journal of Medicine* 117 (2004): 932–937.
82. Sam Howe Verhovek, "Texas Is Lowering HMO Legal Shield," *New York Times,* June 5, 1997.
83. There is some evidence that managed care systems do invest more in preventive care. Steven Findlay, "Survey Shows HMO Care Varies Widely," *USA Today,* October 2, 1997.
84. Tort actions may not be as effective as ex ante controls, but they do at least force the industry to consider the long-run costs of any decisions it may make.
85. Peter S. Arno and Karyn L. Feiden, *Against the Odds: The Story of AIDS Drug Development, Politics and Profits* (New York: HarperCollins, 1992).
86. Carol Rados, "The FDA Speeds Medical Treatments for Serious Conditions," *FDA Consumer* 40, no. 2 (2006): 9–12.
87. Susan Okie, "Medical Journals Try to Curb Drug Companies' Influence on Research," *Washington Post,* August 5, 2001; and Dennis Cauchon, "FDA Advisers Tied to Industry," *USA Today,* September 25, 2000.
88. Anna Wilde Mathews, "FDA to Review Drug Marketing to Consumers," *Wall Street Journal,* August 2, 2005.
89. General Accounting Office, *Drug Safety: Most Drugs Withdrawn in Recent Years Have Greater Health Risks for Women* (Washington, DC: U.S. General Accounting Office, January 10, 2001), GAO-01-286R.
90. See Sheryl Gay Stolberg and Jeff Gerth, "How Companies Stall Generics and Keep Themselves Healthy," *New York Times,* July 23, 2000.
91. Andrew Pollack, "Antibiotics Research Subsidies Weighed by U.S.," *New York Times,* November 5, 2010.
92. Howard Leichter, *Health Policy Reform in America: Innovations from the States,* 2nd ed. (Armonk, NY: M. E. Sharpe, 1997).
93. See www.barackobama/issues/healthcare.
94. See Paul Krugman, "Keeping Them Honest," *New York Times,* June 5, 2009.
95. Rebecca Vesely, "AHIP: Surely 30% Possible," *Modern Healthcare,* December 8, 2008.
96. Robert Pear, "Sweeping Health Care Plan Is Drafted by Kennedy," *New York Times,* June 6, 2009.
97. Helene Cooper, "Obama Urges Effort for Health Care," *New York Times,* June 6, 2009.
98. Some aspects of the plan have been implemented in various states under the same name. See, for example, A. C. Enthoven and S. J. Singer, "Managed Competition and California's Health Care Economy," *Health Affairs* 15, no. 1 (1996): 39–57.
99. Robert Pear, "Bill Passed by Panel Would Open Medicare to Millions of Uninsured People," *New York Times,* July 1, 1994.

100. The degree of choice actually existing in the current medical care system appeared to have been exaggerated by the opponents of reform. See Robin Toner, "Ills of Health System Outlive Debate on Care," *New York Times,* October 2, 1994.

101. Victor R. Fuchs, "What's Ahead for Health Insurance in the United States," *New England Journal of Medicine* 346 (2002): 1822–1824.

Chapter 12

1. See Theodore R. Marmor, Jerry L. Mashaw, and Philip L. Harvey, *America's Misunderstood Welfare State* (New York: Basic Books, 1990).

2. Indeed, in 2011, almost half of American households received some form of government benefit. See Sara Murray, "Nearly Half of U.S. Lives in Households Receiving Government Benefits," *Wall Street Journal,* January 17, 2012.

3. See Allan Sloan, "Bush's Social Security Sleight of Hand," *Washington Post,* February 8, 2006.

4. Donald O. Parsons and Douglas R. Munro, "Intergenerational Transfers in Social Security," in *The Crisis in Social Security,* ed. Michael J. Boskin (San Francisco: Institute for Contemporary Studies, 1977), 65–86.

5. Kaiser Family Foundation, *Survey on Social Security,* February 2005, www.kff.org/newsmedia/washpost/7280.cfm.

6. Ibid.; 81 percent of respondents in 2005 wanted to eliminate the top limit. In a poll in 2011, only 53 percent supported this change.

7. The separation of pensions and other social insurance benefits from general taxation is unusual in the rest of the world. See Margaret S. Gordon, *Social Security Policies in Industrial Countries: A Comparative Analysis* (Cambridge: Cambridge University Press, 1990). The separation also contributes to the somewhat artificial sense that Social Security can go bankrupt, since if general taxation were provided for the system there is no reason for bankruptcy.

8. Social Security Administration, *The Future of Social Security* (Baltimore: Social Security Administration, 2009).

9. Michael D. Hurd and John B. Shoven, "The Distributional Impact of Social Security," in *Pensions, Labor and Individual Choice,* ed. David Wise (Chicago: University of Chicago Press, 1985); Jeffrey Liebman, "Does Social Security Distribute to Low Income Groups?" (NBER Working Paper 8625) (Cambridge, MA: National Bureau of Economic Research, 2002).

10. The actual determination of taxability is somewhat more complicated. See David Pattison and David E. Harrington, "Proposals to Modify the Taxation of Social Security Benefits: Options and Distributional Effects," *Social Security Bulletin* 56 (Summer 1993): 3–13.

11. This program has been, like so many, "path dependent," and its initial formulation has largely determined its development. See B. Guy Peters, *Institutional Theory in Political Science,* 3rd ed. (London: Continuum, 2011), chap. 4.

12. Joseph Bondar, "Beneficiaries Affected by the Annual Earnings Test, 1989," *Social Security Bulletin* 56 (Spring 1993): 20–34.

13. Social Security Administration, Office of the Actuary, *Life Tables for the United States Social Security Area, 1900–2080* (Baltimore: Social Security Administration, 1992).

14. "Commission: Raise Retirement Age to 70," *USA Today,* May 19, 1998.

15. C. Eugene Steuerle and Jon M. Bakija, *Retooling Social Security for the Twenty-first Century* (Washington, DC: Urban Institute Press, 1994), 97.

16. Deborah Stone, *The Disabled State* (Philadelphia: Temple University Press, 1985).

17. General Accounting Office, *SSA Disability Programs: Fully Updating Disability Criteria Has Implications for Program Design* (Washington, DC: U.S. General Accounting Office, July 11, 2002), GAO-02-919T.

18. General Accounting Office, *SSA and VA Disability Programs: Reexamination of Disability Criteria Needed to Help Ensure Program Integrity* (Washington, DC: U.S. General Accounting Office, August 9, 2002), GAO-02-597.

19. Bernadine Weatherford, "The Disability Insurance Program: An Administrative Attack on the Welfare State," in *The Attack on the Welfare State,* ed. Anthony Champagne and Edward J. Harpham (Prospect Heights, IL: Waveland Press, 1984), 37.

20. General Accounting Office, *Social Security Disability: SSA Needs to Improve Continuing Disability Review Program* (Washington, DC: U.S. General Accounting Office, July 1993), GAO/HRD-93-109.

21. "Workers' Compensation," *Social Security Bulletin* 56 (Winter 1993): 28–31.

22. The maximum payment in Iowa is $1,134 per week, while that in Mississippi is $351 per week.

23. Government Accountability Office, *Federal Disability Assistance: Wide Array of Programs Needs to Be Reexamined in Light of 21st Century Challenges* (Washington, DC: U.S. Government Accountability Office, June 2005), GAO-05-626.

24. As noted, Social Security does accumulate funds in its trust fund but not at a rate sufficient to finance future benefits—which continue to be paid largely from current revenues from Social Security taxation.

25. For a detailed analysis, see Henry J. Aaron, Barry P. Bosworth, and Gary Burtless, *Can America Afford to Grow Old? Paying for Social Security* (Washington, DC: Brookings Institution Press, 1989), 55–75.

26. Practical politics, however, prevented President Reagan from doing anything to reduce Social Security benefits. See Paul E. Peterson and Mark Rom, "Lower Taxes, More Spending, and Budget Deficits," in *The Reagan Legacy,* ed. Charles O. Jones (Chatham, NJ: Chatham House, 1988), 224–225.

27. ABC News/*Washington Post* poll, February 19–22, 2009, www.washingtonpost.com/wp-srv/politics/postpoll_022309.html.

28. Jonathan Rauch, "False Security," *National Journal,* February 14, 1987, 362–365, www.nationaljournal.com.

29. Aaron, Bosworth, and Burtless, *Can America Afford to Grow Old?*

30. Paula Span, "Social Security and Younger Americans," *New York Times,* August 25, 2010.

31. Board of Trustees of the Federal Old-Age, Survivors, and Disability Insurance Trust Funds, *Annual Report, 2010* (Washington, DC: U.S. Government Printing Office, 2010). These figures are based on intermediate assumptions about the future of the system. Under less optimistic assumptions, there would be only 1.7 workers per recipient in 2050.

32. Linda E. Demkovich, "Budget Cutters Think the Unthinkable—Social Security Cuts Would Stem Red Ink," *National Journal,* June 23, 1984.
33. George F. Break, "The Economic Effects of Social Security Financing," in *Social Security Financing,* ed. Felicity Skidmore (Cambridge, MA: MIT Press, 1981), 45–80.
34. See B. Guy Peters, *The Politics of Taxation* (Oxford: Basil Blackwell, 1992).
35. Charles E. McLure, "VAT versus the Payroll Tax," in *Social Security Financing,* ed. Felicity Skidmore (Cambridge, MA: MIT Press, 1981), 129.
36. For a review of the proposals, see Henry J. Aaron and Robert D. Reischauer, "Should We Reform Social Security?" *Brookings Review* 17 (Winter 1999): 6–11.
37. These retirement plans take their name from the section of the U.S. Internal Revenue Code that governs their creation and use.
38. Ben Wildavsky, "The Two Percent Solution," *National Journal,* April 11, 1998, 794–797.
39. R. Shep Melnick, *Between the Lines* (Washington, DC: Brookings Institution Press, 1994).
40. Most of these critics are on the political right, for example, Charles Murray, *Losing Ground* (New York: Basic Books, 1984) and his "Stop Favoring Welfare Mothers," *New York Times,* January 16, 1992; and Lawrence M. Mead, *The New Politics of Poverty* (New York: Basic Books, 1992). There are also critics on the left, for example, David T. Ellwood, *Poor Support: Poverty and the American Family* (New York: Basic Books, 1988); and Frances Fox Piven and Richard Cloward, *Regulating the Poor,* 2nd ed. (New York: Vintage, 1993).
41. M. Gilens, *Why Americans Hate Welfare: Race, Media and the Politics of Anti-Poverty Policy* (Chicago: University of Chicago Press, 2000).
42. See James L. Morrison, *The Healing of America: Welfare Reform in a Cyber Economy* (Brookfield, VT: Ashgate, 1997).
43. Penelope Lemov, "Putting Welfare on the Clock," *Governing,* November 1993, 29–30.
44. Edwin W. Witte, *The Development of the Social Security Act* (Madison: University of Wisconsin Press, 1962), 5–39.
45. Julie Kosterlitz, "Behavior Modification," *National Journal,* February 1, 1992, 271–275. The earlier attempts to control behavior pale in comparison to those of the 1996 reforms.
46. Kevin Sack, "Fingerprinting Allowed in Welfare Fraud Fight," *New York Times,* July 9, 1994.
47. Some evidence appearing just as workfare was being implemented placed some doubt on the efficacy of permitting greater earnings. See Jason DeParle, "More Questions about Incentives to Get Those on Welfare to Work," *New York Times,* August 28, 1997.
48. As noted, despite those disincentives to leave, the majority of people on AFDC did not stay long. The other problems with the program, and the relatively meager benefits, attracted few long-term beneficiaries.
49. Julie Kosterlitz, "Reworking Welfare," *National Journal,* September 26, 1992.
50. Michael Wiseman, "Research and Policy: A Symposium on the Family Support Act of 1988," *Journal of Policy Analysis and Management* 10 (1991): 588–589.
51. Kay E. Sherwood and David A. Long, "JOBS Implementation in an Uncertain Environment," *Public Welfare* 49 (1991): 17–27.

52. This problem would, of course, have been rectified if the Clinton plan, or any other plan, for universal health insurance had been adopted.

53. Sherwood and Long, "JOBS Implementation in an Uncertain Environment."

54. Amy L. Sherman, "The Lessons of W-2," *Public Interest* 140 (Summer 2000): 36–46. Tommy Thompson, the governor of Wisconsin responsible for implementing the program, became secretary of health and human services in the Bush administration.

55. The title of the bill is a masterpiece of symbol manipulation in the process of agenda setting and legitimation.

56. For a discussion of this and other myths, see Steven M. Teles, *Whose Welfare? AFDC and Elite Politics* (Lawrence: University Press of Kansas, 1996).

57. Robert Pear, "Governors Limit Revisions Sought in Welfare Law," *New York Times,* February 3, 1997.

58. The political motivation was to please Hispanic voters, given the number of immigrants from Mexico and other Latin countries who had been denied benefits.

59. See Jonathan Rabinowitz, "Connecticut Welfare Law Cuts Hundreds Off the Rolls," *New York Times,* November 3, 1997; and Richard Wolf, "Some States Still at Welfare Impasse," *USA Today,* July 2, 1997.

60. Nina Bernstein, "Giant Companies Enter Race to Run State Welfare Programs," *New York Times,* September 15, 1996.

61. Judith Havemann, "Welfare Reform Still on a Roll as States Bounce It Down to Counties," *Washington Post,* August 29, 1997.

62. Dilys Hills, "Social Policy," in *Developments in American Politics III,* ed. Gillian Peele et al. (New York: Chatham House, 1998), 214–235.

63. Rochelle L. Stanfield, "Valuing the Family," *National Journal,* July 4, 1992, 1562–1566.

64. Marilyn Werber Serafini, "Get Hitched, Stay Hitched," *National Journal,* March 9, 2002, 694–697.

65. Laura Meckler, "Bush Outlining Welfare Plans," Associated Press, February 26, 2002.

66. See General Accounting Office, *Welfare Reform: States Are Restructuring Programs to Reduce Welfare Dependency* (Washington, DC: U.S. General Accounting Office, June 18, 1998), GAO/HEHS-98-109. Oregon, for example, found that half the welfare caseload would require treatment for chemical dependency before they would be likely to be employable.

67. D. Card and R. M. Blank, *Findings Jobs: Work and Welfare Reform* (New York: Russell Sage, 2000).

68. Rochelle L. Stanfield, "Cautious Optimism," *National Journal,* May 2, 1998.

69. Administration for Children and Families, Department of Health and Human Services, *U.S. Welfare Caseloads Information* (Washington, DC: Administration for Children and Families, monthly).

70. Marilyn Werber Serafini, "As More Jobs Vanish, the Worries Mount," *National Journal,* September 29, 2001.

71. Ibid.

72. Sheila Kammerman and Alfred Kahn, "Universalism and Testing in Family Policy: New Perspectives on an Old Debate," *Social Work* 32 (1987): 277–280.

73. Hermione Parker, *Instead of the Dole: An Enquiry into the Integration of Tax and Benefit Systems* (London: Routledge, 1989).

74. M. Kenneth Bowler, *The Nixon Guaranteed Income Proposal: Substance and Process in Policy Change* (Cambridge, MA: Ballinger, 1974).

75. Office of Child Support Enforcement, *Annual Report to Congress, 2006* (Washington, DC: Office of Child Support Enforcement, Department of Health and Human Services, 2006).

76. Irwin Garfinkel, Sara S. McLanahan, and Philip K. Robins, *Child Support and Child Well-Being* (Washington, DC: Urban Institute Press, 1994).

77. General Accounting Office, *Child Support Assurance: Effects of Applying State Guidelines to Determine Fathers' Payments* (Washington, DC: U.S. General Accounting Office, January 1993), GAO/HRD-93-26.

78. Administration for Children and Families, *Annual Report, 2009* (Washington, DC: ACF, 2010).

79. Mimi Hall, "Child Support: States Pay if Parents Don't," *USA Today*, March 28, 1994.

80. At least one state has already done so; see "In Maine, No Child Support, No Driving," *New York Times*, June 28, 1994.

81. For a general discussion of employment policy, see Margaret Weir, *Politics and Jobs* (Princeton, NJ: Princeton University Press, 1992).

82. General Accounting Office, *Multiple Employment Training Programs: Conflicting Requirements Hamper Delivery of Services* (Washington, DC: U.S. General Accounting Office, January 1994), GAO/HEHS-94-78.

83. Sar A. Levitan, *The Great Society's Poor Law: A New Approach to Poverty* (Baltimore: Johns Hopkins University Press, 1969).

84. Some later research, however, found some latent effects of Head Start, much like the "sleeper effects" described in chapter 7. See William Celis III, "Study Suggests Head Start Helps beyond School," *New York Times*, April 20, 1993; see also Carlotta C. Joyner, "Head Start: Research Insufficient to Assess Program Impact," testimony to the Subcommittee on Early Childhood, Youth and Families, Committee on Labor and Human Resources, U.S. Senate, March 26, 1998.

85. Richard Rose and B. Guy Peters, *Can Government Go Bankrupt?* (New York: Basic Books, 1978).

86. For a more recent view, see Michael Harrington, *The New American Poverty* (New York: Holt, Rinehart, and Winston, 1984).

87. Sabrina Tavernise, "Soaring Poverty Casts Spotlight on 'Lost Decade,'" *New York Times*, September 13, 2011.

88. Sar Levitan, Frank Gallo, and Isaac Shapiro, *Working but Poor: America's Contradiction*, rev. ed. (Baltimore: Johns Hopkins University Press, 1993).

89. Ibid., 99–125.

90. Patricia Ruggles, *Drawing the Line: Alternative Poverty Measures and Their Implications for Public Policy* (Washington, DC: Urban Institute Press, 1990).

91. John L. Palmer, Timothy Smeeding, and Barbara Boyle Torrey, eds., *The Vulnerable* (Washington, DC: Urban Institute Press, 1988); Jacob S Hacker and Paul Pierson, *Winner-Take-All Politics: How Washington Makes the Rich Richer and Turned Its Back on the Middle Class* (New York: Simon and Schuster, 2010).

92. National Academy of Sciences, Panel on Poverty and Family Assistance, *Alternative Poverty Measures* (Washington, DC: National Academy of Sciences, 1995).

93. The current fashionable term for these problems, made popular by the Labour government in Britain, is "social exclusion."

94. Maybeth Shinn and Colleen Gillespie, "The Roles of Housing and Poverty in the Origins of Homelessness," *American Behavioral Scientist* 37 (1994): 505–521.

95. Ann Braden Johnson, *Out of Bedlam: The Truth about Deinstitutionalization* (New York: Basic Books, 1990); and Julian Leff, *Care in the Community: Myth or Reality* (New York: John Wiley, 1997).

96. Manny Fernandez, "Helping to Keep Homelessness at Bay as Foreclosures Increase," *New York Times,* February 4, 2009.

97. General Accounting Office, *Homelessness: McKinney Act Programs Provide Assistance but Are Not Designed to Be the Solution* (Washington, DC: U.S. General Accounting Office, May 1994), GAO/RCED-94-37.

98. Jacob S. Hacker, The Divided Welfare State: The Battle over Public and Private Social Benefits in the United States (Cambridge: Cambridge University Press, 2002).

99. General Accounting Office, *Private Pensions: Key Issues to Consider Following the Enron Collapse,* testimony by David M. Walker (Washington, DC: U.S. General Accounting Office, February 27, 2002), GAO-02-480T.

100. J. Dao, "Miners' Benefits Vanish with Bankruptcy Ruling," *New York Times,* October 24, 2004.

101. F. Norris, "As Baby Boom Ages, Era of Guaranteed Retirement Income Fades," *New York Times,* November 12, 2004.

Chapter 13

1. Richard Hofferbert, "Race, Space and the American Policy Paradox" (paper presented at the conference of the Southern Political Science Association, Atlanta, GA, November 1980).

2. In areas in which parochial schools were important, they also tended to draw from a wide range of social classes, if not religions.

3. Karen De Witt, "Nation's Schools Learn a Fourth R: Resegregation," *New York Times,* January 19, 1992.

4. For diverse views on this topic, see Gerald Graff, *Beyond the Culture Wars: How Teaching the Conflicts Can Revitalize American Education* (New York: Norton, 1992); and Russell Jacoby, *Dogmatic Wisdom: How the Culture Wars Divert Education and Distract America* (New York: Doubleday, 1994).

5. Andrew Rosenthal, "Oppression Is not a State's Right," *New York Times,* November 8, 2011.

6. Bureau of the Census, *Statistical Abstract of the United States, 2009* (Washington, DC: U.S. Government Printing Office, 2009).

7. Gallup Poll, January 5–8, 2012. Ten percent of respondents said they were completely satisfied, and 30 percent were somewhat satisfied.

8. Students in Iowa and North Dakota, on average, scored as well as those in Korea and better than those in any European country on math and science tests.

9. Diana Jean Schemo, "Public School Students Score Well in Math in Large-Scale Government Study," *New York Times,* January 21, 2006.

10. See William Bennett, *Our Country and Our Children: Improving America's Schools and Affirming Our Common Culture* (New York: Touchstone, 1988). There have been a number of books advocating such a traditional curriculum for American schools,

including Allan Bloom, *The Closing of the American Mind* (New York: Touchstone, 1987).

11. Catherine S. Mangold, "Students Make Strides but Fall Short of Goals," *New York Times,* August 18, 1994. U.S. rankings in elementary and secondary education have, however, been slipping. See "U.S. Slipping in Education Ranking," UPI.com, November 19, 2008.

12. "Poll Readings," *National Journal,* February 14, 1998, 368.

13. See Times Topics, "No Child Left Behind," *New York Times,* n.d., accessed June 23, 2009, http://topics.nytimes.com/top/reference/timestopics/subjects/n/no_child_left_behind_act/index.html.

14. "No Child Left Behind: Obama Administration Grants 10 Waivers," *Los Angeles Times,* February 9, 2012.

15. This is rather paradoxical given that the Republicans have been tending to advocate states rights against the presumed centralizing powers of Washington.

16. Jonathan Kozol, *Savage Inequalities: Children in America's Schools* (New York: Crown, 1991).

17. Michelle Singletary, "Obama's Student Plan Isn't So New," *Washington Post,* October 16, 2011.

18. The states also have taken new steps to assist parents, permitting them to invest in tax-free accounts for their children's education or to pay in the current year, at present rates, for future tuition.

19. Rochelle L. Stanfield, "We Have a Tradition of Not Learning," *National Journal,* September 7, 1991, 2156–2157.

20. David Cay Johnston, "Despite Pledge, Taxes Increase for Teenagers," *New York Times,* May 21, 2006.

21. See *Texas et al. v. Lesage,* 528 U.S. 18 (1999); the Michigan cases are *Gratz v. Bollinger,* 539 U.S. 244 (2003) and *Grutter v. Bollinger,* 539 U.S. 306 (2003).

22. Norman C. Thomas, *Educational Policy in National Politics* (New York: David McKay, 1975).

23. Michael D. Reagan, *The New Federalism* (New York: Oxford University Press, 1972).

24. Jerome T. Murphy, "Title I of ESEA: The Politics of Implementing Federal Educational Reform," *Harvard Education Review* 41 (1971): 35–63.

25. *Title I of ESEA: Is It Helping Poor Children?* (Washington, DC: NAACP Legal Defense Fund, 1969).

26. Stephen Phillips, "Union Joins Attack on Bush Flagship Program," *Times Education Supplement,* April 29, 2004, 20; Diana Jean Schemo, "Group Pushes Education Act as 2004 Issue," *New York Times,* August 12, 2004.

27. Lance D. Fusarelli, "Gubernatorial Reactions to No Child Left Behind: Politics, Pressure and Educational Reform," *Peabody Journal of Education* 80 (2005): 120–136.

28. James E. Ryan, "The Perverse Incentives of the No Child Left Behind Act," *New York University Law Review* 79 (2004): 932–989.

29. Kathryn A. McDermott and Laura S. Jensen, "Dubious Sovereignty: Federal Conditions of Aid and No Child Left Behind," *Peabody Journal of Education* 80 (2005): 39–56.

30. Kenneth Jost, "Revising No Child Left Behind," *CQ Researcher,* April 16, 2010, 337–360.

31. Shelley Dietz, "How Many Schools Have Not Met Adequate Yearly Progress Standards," *Center on Education Policy*, March 10, 2011.

32. Some polls show that minority parents, like majority parents, want good basic education instead of a distinctive curriculum. See "Minority Parents Seek Quality over Diversity," *USA Today*, July 29, 1998. The support from minority parents for vouchers and charter schools is further support for this contention.

33. Rochelle L. Stanfield, "Making the Grade?" *National Journal*, April 17, 1993.

34. Neil King, Jr. and Barbara Martinez, "Squaring Off on U.S Schools," *Wall Street Journal*, March 15, 2010.

35. U.S. Department of Education, "The Race to the Top Fund," n.d., www2.ed.gov/programs/racetothetop/index.html.

36. It seems that in Milwaukee there has been a good deal of effective and committed leadership in the schools. Emily Van Dunk and Anneliese Dickman, "School Choice Accountability," *Urban Affairs Review* 37 (2002): 844–856.

37. Myron Lieberman, *Privatization and Educational Choice* (New York: St. Martin's, 1989).

38. John Witte, "The Milwaukee Parental Choice Program Third Year Report," *LaFollette Policy Report* 6 (1994): 6–7.

39. John E. Chubb and Terry M. Moe, *Politics, Markets, and America's Schools* (Washington, DC: Brookings Institution Press, 1990); see also Paul E. Peterson, *Choice and Competition in American Education* (Lanham, MD: Rowman and Littlefield, 2005).

40. Rochelle L. Stanfield, "Education Wars," *National Journal*, March 7, 1998.

41. See Sean Lengell, "House Votes to Restart D.C. Vouchers," *Washington Times*, March 30, 2011.

42. Jeffrey R. Henig, *Rethinking School Choice: Limits of the Market Metaphor* (Princeton, NJ: Princeton University Press, 1994); Clive Belfield and Henry M. Levin, "Vouchers and Public Policy: When Ideology Trumps Evidence," *American Journal of Education* 111 (2005): 548–567.

43. James S. Coleman, *Equality of Educational Opportunity* (Washington, DC: U.S. Government Printing Office, 1966). Since that time, Coleman has modified his view to be substantially less supportive of busing.

44. Gallup Poll, "Public Attitudes to Education" (Princeton, NJ: Gallup Organization, 2005).

45. For a positive view, see James N. Goenner, "Charter Schools: The Revitalization of Public Education," *Phi Delta Kappan* 78 (September 1996): 32, 34–36.

46. "States Ignore Traps Tripping Up Charter Schools," *USA Today*, April 2, 2002.

47. See U.S. Department of Education, *The Evaluation of the Public Charter School Program* (Washington, DC: U.S. Department of Education, 2004); Institute of Educational Sciences, *The Evaluation of Charter School Impacts: Final Report* (Washington, DC: U.S. Department of Education, June, 2010).

48. D. M. Lewis, "Certifying Functional Literacy: Competency and the Implications for Due Process and Equal Educational Opportunity," *Journal of Law and Education* 8 (1979): 145–183; and Chubb and Moe, *Politics, Markets, and America's Schools*, 197–198.

49. Educational Testing Service, *One-Third of a Nation: Rising Dropout Rates and Declining Opportunities* (Princeton, NJ: Educational Testing Service, 2005).

50. Tamar Lewin, "Obama Wades into Issue of Raising Dropout Rate," *New York Times,* January 29, 2012.

51. Jessica Portner, "Educators Keeping Eye on Measures Designed to Combat Youth Violence," *Education Week,* February 9, 1994, 21.

52. For some discussion of the lengths to which school systems may go to recruit teachers, see Jacques Steinberg, "As Demand for Teachers Exceeds Supply, Schools Sweeten Their Offers," *New York Times,* September 7, 1998.

53. General Accounting Office, *School Facilities: America's Schools Report Differing Conditions* (Washington, DC: U.S. General Accounting Office, June 1996), GAO/HEHS-96-103.

54. Richard W. Stevenson, "Clinton Proposes Spending $25 Billion on Education," *New York Times,* January 27, 1998.

55. David Branham, "The Wise Man Builds His House upon the Rock: The Effects of Inadequate School Building Infrastructure on School Attendance," *Social Science Quarterly* 85 (2004): 1112–1128.

56. Michael D. Simpson, "Voucher Victory," *NEA Today,* March 2006, 19.

57. See, for example, Lonnie Harp, "Michigan Bill Penalizes Teachers for Job Actions," *Education Week,* April 27, 1994, 9.

58. Monica Davey, "Wisconsin Court Reinstates Law on Union Rights," *New York Times,* June 14, 2011.

59. Morgan Smith, "Texas Schools Face Bigger Classes and Smaller Staffs," *New York Times,* March 16, 2012.

60. Stephen M. Barro, "Countering Inequity in School Finance," in *Federal Policy Options for Improving the Education of Low-Income Students,* vol. 3 (Santa Monica, CA: Rand, 1994).

61. Another equity funding case was contested in Alabama—*Alabama Coalition for Equity, Inc. v. Guy Hunt,* 1992.

62. Sam Howe Verhovek, "Texas to Hold Referendum on School-Aid Shift to Poor," *New York Times,* February 16, 1993.

63. Lonnie Harp, "Texas Voters Reject Finance Plan: Consolidation Called Last Resort," *Education Week,* May 12, 1993, 1, 16.

64. Lonnie Harp, "Texas Finance Ruling Angers Both Rich, Poor Districts," *Education Week,* January 12, 1994, 18.

65. Tamar Lewin, "Patchwork of School Financing Schemes Offers Few Answers and Much Conflict," *New York Times,* April 8, 1998.

66. William Schneider, "Voters Get an Offer They Can't Refuse," *National Journal,* March 26, 1994, 754.

67. Rochelle L. Stanfield, "Equity and Excellence," *National Journal,* November 23, 1991, 3860–3864.

68. Reagan Walker, "Blueprint for State's New School System Advances in Kentucky," *Education Week,* March 7, 1990, 1, 21.

69. Dirk Johnson, "Study Says Small Schools Are Key to Learning," *New York Times,* September 21, 1994.

70. The Spearman rank-order correlation is −0.26. This finding is to some degree confounded by the different percentages of students taking the SAT in different states. Many of the high-scoring states had a small percentage of students taking the SAT.

71. De Witt, "Nation's Schools Learn a Fourth R."

72. Tom Loveless, *Test-Based Accountability: The Promise and the Perils* (Washington, DC: Brown Center on Educational Policy, Brookings Institution, 2005).

73. Rochelle L. Stanfield, "Reform by the Book," *National Journal,* December 4, 1994, 2885–2887.

74. Peter Schmidt, Jeffrey Selingo, Sara Hebel, and Jeffrey R. Young, "The Michigan Cases: The Repercussions," *Chronicle of Higher Education* 49 (July 2003): 3.

75. For example, in 1998, blacks constituted 17 percent of the school population but had 31 percent of all expulsions (U.S. Department of Education, Office of Civil Rights, unpublished data). In 2010, black students were three and a half times more likely to be severely disciplined than whites (U.S. Department of Education, Office of Civil Rights).

76. College Board, *Trends in Student Aid, 2005* (Washington, DC: College Board, 2006).

Chapter 14

1. Timothy Wirth, "Hot Air over Kyoto: The United States and the Politics of Global Warming," *Harvard International Review* 23 (2002): 72–77.

2. John M. Broder, "Obama Affirms Climate Change Goals," *New York Times,* November 18, 2008.

3. Clifford Krauss and Eric Lipton," U.S. Inches Toward Goal of Energy Independence," *New York Times,* March 23, 2012.

4. See, for example, Glennda Chui, "Scientific American Gives California High Marks for Technology," *San Jose Mercury News,* November 12, 2002.

5. *America's Energy Needs and Our National Security Policy,* hearing before the Subcommittee on Energy and Resources, Committee on Government Reform, U.S. House of Representatives, April 6, 2006.

6. U.S. Energy Information Administration, *International Energy Statistics,* 2006 (Washington DC: Department of Energy, 2007).

7. Energy Information Agency, *Annual Energy Review 2010* (Washington, DC: U.S. Dept. of Energy, 2011).

8. Eric Pianin, "A Stinging Repudiation Engineered by Three Democrats," *Washington Post,* April 19, 2002.

9. Dan Morgan and Ellen Nakashima, "Search for Oil Targets Rockies," *Washington Post,* April 19, 2002.

10. See Michael Janofsky, "House Votes to Allow Drilling in Alaska Refuge," *New York Times,* May 26, 2006.

11. John M. Broder, "Obama Shifts to Speed Oil and Gas Drilling," *New York Times,* May 14, 2011.

12. Peter H. Stone, "Mixing Oil and Instability," *National Journal,* November 10, 2001.

13. Bureau of Economic Analysis, *International Economic Accounts,* Table 2a, U.S. Trade in Goods (Washington, DC: Department of Commerce, June 17, 2009).

14. Christime Burmma, "U.S. Cuts Estimate of Marcellus Shale Gas by 66 percent," *Bloomberg News,* January 12, 2012.

15. Traci Watson, "EPA: Power Plant Plan Could Save 12,000 Lives per Year," *USA Today,* July 3, 2002.

16. Brad Plumer, "Get Ready for a Wave of Coal Plant Shutdowns," *Washington Post,* August 19, 2011.

17. James M. McElfish and Ann E. Beier, *Environmental Regulation of Coal Mining* (Washington, DC: Environmental Law Institute, 1990); Robert F. Duffy, "King Coal vs Reclamation: Federal Regulation of Mountaintop Removal in Appalachia," *Administration & Society* 41 (October 2009): 573–592.

18. Processes of this type have existed for some time; Germany used a process like this in World War II. It is not, however, economically feasible at anything like current energy prices.

19. Felicity Barringer, "Four Years Later, Soviets Reveal Wider Scope to Chernobyl Horror," *New York Times,* April 28, 1990; and David Marples, *The Social Impact of the Chernobyl Disaster* (New York: St. Martin's, 1988); "One Year Post Fukushima Americans Are Divided about the Risks of Nuclear Power," *New York Times,* March 14, 2012.

20. See Shankar Vendantum, "Storage of Spent Nuclear Fuel Criticized," *Washington Post,* March 28, 2005.

21. John L. Campbell, *Collapse of an Industry: Nuclear Power and the Contradictions of U.S. Policy* (Ithaca, NY: Cornell University Press, 1988).

22. Richard Balzhiser, "Future Consequences of Nuclear Non-Policy," in *Energy: Production, Consumption, Consequences,* ed. John L. Helm (Washington, DC: National Academy Press, 1990), 184.

23. General Accounting Office, *Nuclear Waste: Uncertainties about the Yucca Mountain Repository Project* (Washington, DC: U.S. General Accounting Office, March 21, 2000), GAO-02-539T; and Alison M. McFarlane and Rodney C. Ewings, *Uncertainty Underground: Yucca Mountain and the Nation's High-Level Energy Waste* (Cambridge, MA: MIT Press, 2006).

24. Henry F. Bedford, *Seabrook Station: Citizen Politics and Nuclear Power* (Amherst: University of Massachusetts Press, 1990).

25. Matthew L. Wald, "License Is Granted to Nuclear Plant in New Hampshire," *New York Times,* March 2, 1990.

26. Testimony of Deputy Energy Secretary Clay Sell before Senate Committee on Energy and Natural Resources, hearing on Department of Energy Nuclear Power Program for 2010, April 26, 2005.

27. The "fracking" technology associated with recovering natural gas from shale involves the use of fluids that, along with the gas itself, may pollute water supplies.

28. Rodman D. Griffin, "Nuclear Fusion," *CQ Researcher* 3 (January 22, 1993): 51–64.

29. Michael Kenward, "Fusion Becomes a Hot Bet for the Future," *New Scientist* 132 (November 1991): 10–11.

30. Scott Wilson, "Obama Touts Solar in Nev. as Part of Four State Energy Tour," *Washington Post,* March 22, 2012.

31. The hydrogen would essentially be converted back into water. See Matthew Wald, "Questions about a Hydrogen Economy," *Scientific American,* May 2004, 64, 73.

32. Greg Schneider, "Automakers Put Hydrogen Power on the Fast Track," *Washington Post,* January 9, 2005.

33. Jeremy Rifkin, *The Hydrogen Economy* (New York: Tarcher Putnam, 2005).

34. Todd Wilkinson, "Gone with the Wind," *Backpacker,* September 1992, 11.

35. "Briefing on Energy Policy," *Weekly Compilation of Presidential Documents* 27 (February 25, 1991): 188–190.

36. *Reliable, Affordable and Environmentally Sound Energy for America's Future: Report of the National Energy Development Group* (Washington, DC: Executive Office of the President, May 2001).

37. Natural Resources Defense Council, "Energy Department Documents Verify Industry Influence over Bush Policies," press release, May 21, 2002.

38. See "Wasteful Handouts Skew Energy Benefit's Plan," *USA Today*, May 30, 2001.

39. An NBC/*Wall Street Journal* poll in April 2001 showed that 25 percent of the respondents thought there was a crisis, but 60 percent did see a distinct problem.

40. Michael Janofsky, "Democrats Offer Alternative to Republican Energy Plan," *New York Times*, May 18, 2006.

41. Ibid.

42. Jim Rutenberg, "Solution to Greenhouse Gases Is New Nuclear Plants, Bush Says," *New York Times*, May 25, 2006.

43. David E. Sanger, "Bush Takes Steps to Stem Increase in Energy Prices," *New York Times*, April 26, 2006.

44. *New York Times*/CBS News poll, February 22–26, 2006, www.nytimes.com/packages/pdf/national/20060228_poll_results.pdf.

45. Judith Mantel, "Energy Efficiency," *CQ Researcher* 16 (May 19, 2006): 19.

46. Deborah Henry, "Republicans Highly Critical of Obama Energy Bill," *New York Times*, June 29, 2009.

47. Many of these provisions were added by members of Congress attempting to protect industries in their home districts.

48. This policy became more attractive in spring 2012, when gasoline reached $4.00 per gallon. This is a huge price for Americans, if only a third or less than what most Europeans pay.

49. Claudia Golden and Gary D. Libecap, *The Regulated Economy* (Chicago: University of Chicago Press, 1994).

50. Center for the Advancement of Energy Markets, www.caem.org, February 1, 2001.

51. T. Munroe and L. Baroody, "California's Flawed Deregulation: Implications for the State and Nation," *Journal of Energy and Development* 26 (2001): 159–179.

52. S. George Philander, *Is the Temperature Rising? The Uncertain Science of Global Warming* (Princeton, NJ: Princeton University Press, 1998); and Marcel Leroux, *Global Warming: Myth or Reality* (Berlin: Springer, 2005).

53. The journal *Diversity* is a good source of information about the resources existing in these settings.

54. Keith Bradsher and David Barboza, "Pollution from Chinese Coal Casts a Global Shadow," *New York Times*, June 11, 2006.

55. One can, however, identify over thirty federal organizations with environmental responsibilities; see Walter A. Rosenbaum, *Environmental Politics and Policy*, 8th ed. (Washington, DC: CQ Press, 2010).

56. Riley E. Dunlap, "Trends in Public Opinion toward Environmental Issues, 1965–1990," *Society and Natural Resources* 4 (1991): 285–312; and Jerry Spangler, "Survey Shows Environmental Values Deeply Rooted," *Deseret News* [Utah], October 9, 1997.

57. Gallup Poll, January 5–8, 2012.

58. Margaret E. Kriz, "Jobs vs. Owls," *National Journal,* November 30, 1993, 2913–2916.

59. Another manifestation of the issue was the congressional use of a rider on an EPA appropriations act in 1996 to permit more lumbering of old-growth forests. For the consequences of these conflicts, see E. Niemi and E. Whitelaw, "Bird of Doom, or Was It?" *Amicus Journal* 22 (1997): 19–25.

60. On the caribou issue, see Paul Feine, "Beware Porcupine Caribou," *Energy Economist* 2 (1995): 2–19; more generally, see Kolson L. Schlosser, "U.S. National Security Discourse and the Political Construction of the Arctic National Wildlife Refuge," *Society and Natural Resources* 19 (2006): 3–18.

61. Murray Weidenbaum, "Return of the 'R' Word: The Regulatory Assault on the Economy," *Policy Review* 59 (1992): 40–43.

62. See John Hoornbeek, "Runaway Bureaucracies or Congressional Control: Water Pollution Policies in the American States" (PhD diss., University of Pittsburgh, PA., 2004).

63. For example, the Safe Drinking Water Act requires monitoring for eighty-three substances, although a number have never been found in any public water supply. See Margaret E. Kriz, "Cleaner than Clean?" *National Journal,* April 23, 1994, 946–949.

64. Christopher J. Bosso, "After the Movement: Environmental Activism in the 1990s," in *Environmental Policy in the 1990s,* 3rd ed., ed. Norman J. Vig and Michael E. Kraft (Washington, DC: CQ Press, 1997), 60. Updated from websites, personal conversations. See also Jacqueline Vaughan, *Environmental Politics: Domestic and Global Dimensions* (New York: Wadsworth, 2011).

65. Vice President Gore's book on environmental politics became a part of the presidential campaign in 1992. See Al Gore, *Earth in the Balance: Ecology and the Human Spirit* (Boston: Houghton Mifflin, 1992).

66. Margaret Kriz, "That Was the Week That Was," *National Journal,* February 2, 1994, 393.

67. Christine Todd Whitman, "This Land Is Our Land," *Environmental Forum* 22 (2005): 24–35.

68. "A Light in the Forest," *New York Times,* September 9, 2005; and Margaret Kriz, "Working the Land: Bush Aggressively Opens Doors to New Drilling and Logging in Federal Lands," *National Journal,* February 23, 2002.

69. Government Accountability Office, *Greater EPA Enforcement and Reporting Are Needed to Enhance Cleanup of DOD Sites* (Washington, DC: U.S. General Accounting Office, March 13, 2009), GAO-09-728.

70. This has been described as "bureaucratic pluralism," with some even within the EPA itself. See Walter A. Rosenbaum, "Into the 1990s at EPA," in *Environmental Policy in the 1990s,* 3rd ed., Norman J. Vig and Michael E. Kraft. (Washington, DC: CQ Press, 1997), 146.

71. Evan Ringquist, Environmental Protection at the State Level (Armonk, NY: M. E. Sharpe, 1994); John A. Hoornbeek, *Water Pollution Policies and the American States: Runaway Bureaucracies or Congressional Control* (Albany: State University of New York Press, 2010).

72. See W. Michael Hanneman, "How California Came to Pass AB 32, the Global Warming Solutions Act of 2006" (unpublished manuscript, University of California, Berkeley, School of Law, January 2007).

73. On the possibilities of a "race to the bottom," see Mary Graham, "Environmental Protection and the States," *Brookings Review* 16 (Winter 1998): 22–25.
74. Margaret Kriz, "Feuding with the Feds," *National Journal,* August 9, 1997, 1598–1601.
75. Michael Janofsky, "Judges Overturn Bush Bid to Ease Pollution Rules," *New York Times,* March 18, 2006.
76. Richard N. L. Andrews, "Risk-Based Decisionmaking," in *Environmental Policy in the 1990s,* ed. Norman J. Vig and Michael E. Kraft, 3rd ed. (Washington, DC: CQ Press, 1997), 208.
77. Donald T. Hornstein, "Reclaiming Environmental Law: A Normative Critique of Comparative Risk Analysis," *Columbia Law Review* 29 (1992): 562–633.
78. Margaret Kriz, "The Greening of Environmental Regulation," *National Journal,* June 18, 1994, 1464–1467.
79. Janet Pelley, "Is EPA's Performance Track Running Off the Rails?" *Environmental Science and Technology* 40 (2006): 2499–2550.
80. *Lujan v. Defenders of Wildlife,* 504 U.S. 555 (1992). The courts tend to limit suits to those who have experienced a direct loss because of an action.
81. See Michael E. Kraft, "Environmental Policy in Congress," in *Environmental Policy,* Norman J. Vig and Michael E. Kraft (Washington, DC: CQ Press, 2010), 124.
82. James R. Kahn, *An Economic Approach to the Environment and Natural Resources* (New York: Dryden Press, 1995).
83. For a review of developments, see Debra S. Knopman and Richard A. Smith, "Twenty Years of the Clean Water Act," *Environment* 35 (1993): 17–20, 34–41.
84. "Oil Officials Fear Stricter Water Act Provisions from New Congress," *Oilgram News* 74, no. 218 (1986): 2.
85. James P. Lester, "New Federalism and Environmental Policy," *Publius* 16 (1986): 149–165.
86. Margaret E. Kriz, "Clashing over Chlorine," *National Journal,* March 19, 1994, 659–661.
87. Tom Arrandale, "The Pollution Puzzle," *Governing,* August 2002, 22–26.
88. Paul Raeburn, "Hybrid Care: Less Fuel but More Costs," *Business Week,* April 15, 2002, 107.
89. Margaret Kriz, "Clean Machines," *National Journal,* November 16, 1991, 2789–2794.
90. Mary H. Cooper, "Air Pollution Conflict," *CQ Researcher* 13 (November 2003): 20–26.
91. James C. McKinley Jr., "Ten States Agree on a Program for Air Quality," *New York Times,* October 2, 1994.
92. Denny A. Ellerman and Paul L. Joskow, "Clearing the Polluted Sky," *New York Times,* May 1, 2002.
93. National Academy of Sciences, *Interim Report on Changes in New Source Programs for Stationary Sources of Air Pollution* (Washington, DC: National Academy of Sciences, 2005).
94. Mireya Navarro, "E.P.A. Is Sued over Delays in Soot Standards," *New York Times* February 10, 2012.

95. Mark Crawford, "Hazardous Waste: Where to Put It?" *Science* 235 (January 9, 1987): 156.

96. Peter A. A. Berle, "Toxic Tornado," *Audubon* 87 (1985): 4.

97. See Charles E. Davis, *The Politics of Hazardous Waste* (Englewood Cliffs, NJ: Prentice Hall, 1993).

98. Steven Cohen, "Federal Hazardous Waste Programs," in *Environmental Policy in the 1990s*, ed. Norman J. Vig and Michael E. Kraft, 3rd ed. (Washington, DC: CQ Press, 1997), 45.

99. Thomas Church and Robert Nakamura, *Cleaning Up the Mess: Implementation Strategies in Superfund* (Washington, DC: Brookings Institution Press, 1993).

100. Environmental Protection Agency, Office of Emergency and Remedial Response, *Superfund Facts* (Washington, DC: EPA, annual).

101. Environmental Protection Agency, *A Preliminary Analysis of the Public Costs of Environmental Protection, 1981–2000* (Washington, DC: U.S. Environmental Protection Agency, May 1990); and Milton E. Russell, William Colglazier, and Bruce E. Tonn, "U.S. Hazardous Waste Legacy," *Environment* 34 (1992): 12–15, 34–39.

102. Katharine Q. Seelye, "Bush Slashing Aid of EPA Cleanup at 33 Toxic Sites," *New York Times,* July 1, 2002.

103. Government Accountability Office, *Environmental Liabilities: EPA Should Do More to Ensure That Liable Parties Meet Their Cleanup Obligations* (Washington, DC: U.S. Government Accountability Office, August 17, 2005), GAO-05-658.

104. Zachary A. Smith, *The Environmental Policy Paradox* (Englewood Cliffs, NJ: Prentice Hall, 1991), 179–186.

105. Church and Nakamura, *Cleaning Up the Mess* (Washington, DC: Brookings Institution Press, 1993).

106. General Accounting Office, *Environmental Contamination: Corps Needs to Reassess Its Determination That Many Former Defense Sites Do Not Need Cleanup* (Washington, DC: U.S. General Accounting Office, August 23, 2002), GAO-02-658.

107. Environmental Protection Agency, "Superfund Program Implements the Recovery Act" (May 15, 2009), www.epa.gov/superfund/eparecovery/index.html.

108. Douglas Bevington, *The Rebirth of Environmentalism: From the Spotted Owl to the Polar Bear* (Washington, DC: Island Press, 2009).

109. Shannon Petersen, *Acting for Endangered Species: The Statutory Ark* (Lawrence: University Press of Kansas, 2002).

110. Richard A. Epstein, *Takings: Private Property and the Power of Eminent Domain* (Cambridge, MA: Harvard University Press, 1985).

111. Nancie G. Marzulla and Roger J. Marzulla, *Property Rights: Understanding Takings and Environmental Regulation* (Rockville, MD: Government Institutes, 1997).

112. Lara Parker, "Species on the Endangered List Challenged," *USA Today,* June 1, 2006.

113. Cornelia Dean, "Bid to Undo Bush Memo on Threat to Species," *New York Times,* March 3, 2009.

114. Charles O. Jones, "Speculative Augmentation in Federal Air Pollution Policymaking," *Journal of Politics* 42 (1975): 438–464.

115. Graeme Browning, "Taking Some Risks," *National Journal,* June 1, 1991, 1279–1282.

116. L. J. Lindquist, *The Hare and the Tortoise* (Ann Arbor: University of Michigan Press, 1986).

117. Some analysts have argued that there may be *insufficient* negotiation in the enforcement of environmental legislation and that better compliance could be achieved through bargaining rather than conventional regulatory enforcement. See Eugene Bardach and Robert Kagan, *Going by the Book* (Philadelphia: Temple University Press, 1983); and David Vogel, *Trading Up: Consumer and Environmental Regulation in a Global Economy* (Cambridge, MA: Harvard University Press, 1995).

118. Robert N. Stavins, "Lessons from the American Experience with Market-Based Environmental Policies," in *Market-Based Governance,* ed. John D. Donahue and Joseph S. Nye (Washington, DC: Brookings Institution Press, 2002), 173.

119. Barnaby J. Feder, "Sold: $21 Million of Air Pollution," *New York Times,* March 30, 1993. For a somewhat skeptical view, see General Accounting Office, *Environmental Protection: Implications for Using Pollution Taxes to Supplement Regulation* (Washington, DC: U.S. General Accounting Office, February 1993), GAO/RCED-93-13; and Peter Berck and Gloria E. Helfland, "The Case for Markets versus Standards for Pollution Policy," *Natural Resources Journal* 45 (2005): 345–368.

120. See Walter A. Rosenbaum, *Environmental Politics and Policy,* 5th ed. (Washington, DC: CQ Press, 2001), 109–110; and Stavins, "Lessons from the American Experiment with Market-Based Environmental Policies."

121. Margaret Kriz, "Emission Control," *National Journal,* July 3, 1993, 1696–1701.

122. See Renee Rico, "The U.S. Allowance Trading System for Sulphur Dioxide: An Update on Market Experience," *Environmental and Resource Economics* 5 (1995): 115–129.

Chapter 15

1. For some sense of the ups and downs of defense employment (civilian and uniformed), see B. Guy Peters, "Public Employment in the United States," in *Public Employment in Western Democracies,* ed. Richard Rose et al. (Cambridge: Cambridge University Press, 1985), 125–145; and H.-U. Derlien and B. Guy Peters, eds., "The United States," in *Who Works for Government and What Do They Do?* (Cheltenham, UK: Edward Elgar, 2009).

2. See "Building Arms for the Wrong War," *New York Times,* May 10, 2002.

3. Elizabeth Bumiller and Thom Shanker, "Obama Puts His Stamp on Strategy for a Leaner Military," *The New York Times,* January 5, 2012.

4. John D. Steinbruner and William W. Kaufmann, "International Security Reconsidered," in *Setting National Priorities: Budget Choices for the Next Century,* ed. Robert D. Reischauer (Washington, DC: Brookings Institution Press, 1997).

5. Graham Allison, "How to Stop Nuclear Terror," *Foreign Affairs* 83, no. 1 (2004): 64–74.

6. See, for example, Robert K. Jervis, *Perception and Misperception in International Politics* (Princeton, NJ: Princeton University Press, 1976).

7. For example, there have been a number of assertions about marked differences in policy preferences among members of the Bush administration following September 11.

8. Joseph S. Nye, *Bound to Lead: The Changing Nature of American Power* (New York: Basic Books, 1992).

9. Gregory L. Schulte, "Bringing Peace to Bosnia and Change to the Alliance," *NATO Review* 45 (March 1997): 22–25.

10. Ivo Daalder and James M. Lindsay, *America Unbound: The Bush Revolution in Foreign Policy* (Washington, DC: Brookings Institution Press, 2003).

11. *Does UN Peacekeeping Serve U.S. Interests?* Hearing before the Committee on International Relations, U.S. House of Representatives, April 9, 1997.

12. See, for example, James A. Nathan and James K. Oliver, *United States Foreign Policy and World Order*, 2nd ed. (Boston: Little, Brown, 1981).

13. Paul Boyer, *Fallout: A Historian Reflects on America's Half-Century Encounter with Nuclear Weapons* (Columbus: Ohio State University Press, 1998).

14. Dunbar Lockwood, "Purchasing Power," *Bulletin of the Atomic Scientists* 50 (March 1994): 10–12; and "Former Soviet Republics Clear Way for Nunn-Lugar Monies," *Arms Control Today* 24 (1994): 28–29.

15. At the same time, this amounted to the end of the Anti-Ballistic Missile Treaty, one of the early attempts to negotiate arms control in the Cold War. See D. E. Sanger and M. Wines, "With a Shrug, a Monument to Cold War Fades Away," *New York Times*, June 14, 2002.

16. Recent evidence points to continuing nuclear weapons development in North Korea, despite agreements with both South Korea and the United States. See Steven Lee Meyers and Choe San-Hun, "North Koreans Agree to Freeze Nuclear Work," *New York Times*, February 26, 2012.

17. Bradley Graham, "Missile Threat to U.S. Greater Than Thought," *International Herald Tribune*, July 17, 1998.

18. Patrick E. Tyler, "As Fear of a Big War Fades, Military Plans for Little Ones," *New York Times*, February 3, 1992.

19. David C. Morrison, "Bottoming Out?" *National Journal*, September 17, 1994, 2126–2130; see also Donald J. Savoie and B. Guy Peters, "Comparing Programme Review," in *Programme Review in Canada*, ed. E. Lundquist and D. J. Savoie (Ottawa: Canadian Centre for Management Development, 1999), 56–75.

20. Mark Sappenfield, "How Iraq, Afghanistan Have Changed War 101," *Christian Science Monitor*, June 28, 2006.

21. As always, generals run the risk of learning the lessons of the last conflict but not anticipating adequately what the next conflict will be. See Brad Knickerbocker, "How Iraq Will Change U.S. Military Doctrine," *Christian Science Monitor*, July 2, 2004.

22. Julian Critchley, *The North Atlantic Alliance and the Soviet Union in the 1980s* (London: Macmillan, 1982).

23. Joshua B. Spero, "Beyond Old and New Europe," *Current History* 103 (2004): 103–105.

24. Robert L. Bernstein and Richard Dicker, "Human Rights First," *Foreign Policy* 94 (1994): 43–47; and William Korey, *The Promises We Keep: Human Rights, the Helsinki Process and American Foreign Policy* (New York: St. Martin's, 1993).

25. See Christoph Bluth, Emil Kirchner, and James Sperling, *The Future of European Security* (Aldershot, England: Dartmouth, 1995).

26. Bumiller and Shanker, "Obama Puts His Stamp on Strategy."

27. For example, the much-heralded accuracy of "smart bombs" during the Gulf War apparently would be crude in comparison to that of contemporary weapons.

28. For an analysis of the famous Reagan Strategic Defense Initiative program, see Congressional Budget Office, *Analysis of the Costs of the Administration's Strategic Defense Initiative, 1985–89* (Washington, DC: Congressional Budget Office, May 1984). This idea was revived in the 1990s.

29. James Dao and Andrew C. Revkin, "Machines Are Filling In for Troops," *New York Times*, April 16, 2000; and Government Accountability Office, *Several Factors Limited the Production and Installation of Army Truck Armor during Current Wartime Operations* (Washington, DC: U.S. Government Accountability Office, March 2006), Report No. GAO-06-160.

30. Michael E. O'Hanlon, "Too Big a Buck for the Bang," *Washington Post*, January 6, 2003.

31. Gordon Adams, *The Politics of Defense Contracting: The Iron Triangle* (New Brunswick, NJ: Transaction, 1981); and "Mission Implausible," *U.S. News & World Report*, October 14, 1991, 24–31.

32. Of course, the United States is the only country that has ever used these weapons in war.

33. See, for example, the Pew Center poll "Defense and International Relations" of July 8–18, 2004 (Washington, DC: Pew Center on the Press and the Public).

34. William Newman, "Causes of Change in National Security Processes: Carter, Reagan, Bush Decision Making on Arms Control," *Presidential Studies Quarterly* 31 (2001): 69–103.

35. Owen Cote, "The Trident and the Triad," *International Security Quarterly* 16 (1991): 117–136.

36. Ria Novosti, "Iran Tests Indigenous Anti-Ship Missile in Gulf Drills," *Defense Talk*, July 7, 2011.

37. Pat Towell, "Pentagon Banking on Plans to Reinvent Procurement," *Congressional Quarterly Weekly Report*, April 16, 1994, 899; and Lauren Holland, "Explaining Weapons Procurement: Matching Operational Performance and National Security Needs," *Armed Forces and Society* 19 (1993): 353–376.

38. Clifford J. Levy and Peter Baker, "Russian Reaction on Missile Plan Leaves Iran Issue Hanging," *New York Times*, September 11, 2009.

39. The Government Accountability Office has done a number of evaluations of these and other poorly performing weapons systems—for example, *Defense Acquisition: Major Weapons Systems Continue to Experience Cost and Schedule Problems* (Washington, DC: U.S. Government Accountability Office, April 2006), Report No. USGAO-06-368. See also Scott Shuger, "The Stealth Bomber Story You Haven't Heard," *Washington Monthly* 23 (January 1991): 1–2, 14–22.

40. Moshe Schwartz, *Defense Acquisition: How DOD Acquires Weapons Systems and Recent Efforts to Reform the Process* (Washington, DC: Congressional Research Service, April 23, 2010).

41. Frank Rich, "The Road from K Street to Yusufiya," *New York Times*, June 5, 2006.

42. Eric Schmitt, "Military Proposes to End Production of Most New Arms," *New York Times*, January 24, 1992.

43. Leslie Wayne, "Runaway Arms Costs: Threat to U.S. Security?" *New York Times,* July 11, 2006.

44. Andrew Taylor, "Obama Defense Contractor Battle Only Just Begun," Associated Press, April 22, 2009.

45. Eric Schmitt, "Run Silent, Run Deep, Beat Foes (Where?)," *New York Times,* January 30, 1992.

46. Beth L. Bailey, *America's Army: Making the All Volunteer Force* (Cambridge, MA: Harvard University Press, 2009).

47. David McCormick, *The Downsized Warrior: America's Army in Transition* (New York: New York University Press, 1998).

48. See Cindy Williams, "Paying Tomorrow's Military," *Regulation* 29 (Summer 2006): 26–31.

49. For example, Molly Pitcher played a partly real, partly mythical part in the Battle of Monmouth during the Revolutionary War.

50. See Andrea Stone, "They're 'Not an Experiment Anymore,'" *USA Today,* January 11, 2002.

51. Linda Bird Francke, *Ground Zero: The Gender Wars in the Military* (New York: Simon and Schuster, 1997).

52. See James Kitfield, "Front and Center," *National Journal,* October 25, 1997, 1097–1111.

53. The Department of Defense argued that the fundamental reason for dismissal of the female pilot was her lying about the existence of a relationship and then continuing once ordered to terminate it.

54. Michael R. Gordon, "Pentagon Spells Out Rules for Ousting Homosexuals; Rights Group Vows a Fight," *New York Times,* December 23, 1993.

55. Tamar Lewin, "At Bases, Debate Rages over Impact of New Gay Policy," *New York Times,* December 24, 1993.

56. Eric Schmitt, "How Is This Strategy Working? Don't Ask," *New York Times,* December 19, 1999.

57. Lara Jakes, "Court Rejects Challenge to Don't Ask Don't Tell," Associated Press, June 8, 2009.

58. Tim Weiner, "Proposal Cuts Back on Some Weapons to Spend More on Personnel," *New York Times,* February 8, 1994. Another version of this is to fight one war while maintaining a holding action in another.

59. William W. Kaufmann, "'Hollow' Forces," *Brookings Review* 12 (1994): 24–29.

60. Other estimates show substantially greater employment generated by defense purchases. These are rather conservative estimates from the Department of Labor.

61. James Kitfeld, "The New Partnership," *National Journal,* August 6, 1994, 8749.

62. David C. Morrison, "Painful Separation," *National Journal,* March 3, 1990, 768–773.

63. John DiIulio Jr., "Federal Crime Policy," *Brookings Review* 19 (Winter 1999): 17–21; and Michael E. Dupre and David A. Mackey, "Crime in the Public Mind," *Journal of Criminal Justice and Popular Culture* 8 (2001): 1–24.

64. V. Beiser, "Why the Big Apple Feels Safer," *Maclean's,* September 11, 1995, 39ff.

65. Generally, young adults are the most prone to commit crimes; this group has been declining rapidly as a percentage of the American population.

66. James Risen and Eric Lichtblau, "Bush Secretly Lifted Limits on Spying in U.S. after 9/11, Officials Say," *New York Times,* December 15, 2005.

67. Hoover himself had a somewhat more complex career. See Anthony Summers, *Official and Confidential* (New York: Putnam, 1993).

68. This organization became very visible during the siege of the Branch Davidian compound in Waco, Texas, in 1993.

69. Actually, it does not exhaust the list of federal enforcement activities, which also include, for example, law enforcement by park rangers (Department of the Interior) in national parks.

70. John DiIulio, "Crime," in *Setting Domestic Priorities: What Can Government Do?* ed. Henry J. Aaron and Charles L Schultze (Washington, DC: Brookings Institution Press, 1992), 101.

71. Included here was the (in)famous "midnight basketball"—keeping recreation centers in poorer areas open long hours to give young people something more constructive to do than commit crimes.

72. For a discussion of this controversy in the context of the Clinton crime bill, see W. John Moore, "Shooting in the Dark," *National Journal,* February 2, 1994, 358–363.

73. See "Crime in California: Three Strikes, You're Out," *Economist,* January 15, 1994, 29–32; and Michael G. Turner, "Three Strikes and You're Out Legislation: A National Assessment," *Federal Probation* 59 (1995): 16–35.

74. Committee on Ways and Means, U.S. House of Representatives, *Children and Families at Risk* (Washington, DC: U.S. Government Printing Office, January 1994).

75. This appears to be especially true for child and spousal abuse. See David J. Kolko, "Characteristics of Child Victims of Physical Abuse," *Journal of Interpersonal Violence* 7 (1992): 244–276; and Cathy Spatz Widom, "Avoidance of Criminality in Abused and Neglected Children," *Psychiatry* 54 (1991): 162–174.

76. Government Accountability Office, *Community Policing Grants: COPS Grants Were a Modest Contributor to Declines in Crime in the 1990s* (Washington, DC: U.S. Government Accountability Office, October 2005), Report No. GAO-05-104.

77. U.S. Bureau of Justice Statistics, *State Prison Expenditures* (Washington, DC: BJS, annual).

78. Most correctional officials oppose these changes, arguing that all this will do is make the prison population more restive and difficult to control.

79. The amendment is worded as follows: "A well regulated Militia, being necessary to the security of a free State, the right of the people to keep and bear Arms, shall not be infringed."

80. Federal Bureau of Investigation, *Crime in the United States* (Washington, DC: U.S. Government Printing Office, annual).

81. The act was named after James Brady, President Reagan's press secretary, who was wounded severely in the attempted assassination of Reagan in 1981. After that experience, his wife, Sarah Brady, became a vigorous advocate of gun control.

82. Peter H. Stone, "Under the Gun," *National Journal,* June 5, 1993, 1334–1338; and Holly Idelson and Paul Nyhan, "Gun Rights and Restrictions: The Territory Reconfigured," *Congressional Quarterly Weekly Report,* April 24, 1993, 1021–1027.

83. Bob Adams, "The Gun Control Debate," *CQ Researcher* 40, no. 14 (November 2004).

84. *2004 National Annenberg Election Survey* (Philadelphia: Annenberg Center), www .srbi.com/election_2004.html.

85. CBS News/*New York Times* poll, April 22–26, 2009, www.nytimes.com.

86. CNN/Opinion Research Corporation poll, June 4–5, 2008, www.pollingreport .com/guns.htm.

87. George Pettinico, "Crime and Punishment: America Changes Its Mind," *Public Perspective* 5 (September/October 1994): 29; Gallup Poll, October 3–5, 2008, www .gallup.com/.

88. Welsh S. White, *The Death Penalty in the Nineties: An Examination of the Modern System of Capital Punishment* (Ann Arbor: University of Michigan Press, 1991).

89. Stanley Cohen, *The Wrong Men: America's Epidemic of Wrongful Death Row Convictions* (New York: Carroll and Graf, 2003); Franklin E. Zimring, *The Contradictions of American Capital Punishment* (New York: Oxford University Press, 2003).

90. James Dao, "Governor Finds New Middle Ground in Capital Punishment Debate," *New York Times,* January 14, 2006.

91. *Furman v. Georgia,* 408 U.S. 238 (1972).

92. Linda Greenhouse, "Justices Bar Death Penalty for Retarded Defendants," *New York Times,* June 21, 2002; and Adam Liptak, "Inmate's Rising IQ Score Could Mean His Death," *New York Times,* February 6, 2005.

93. Gregory D. Russell, *The Death Penalty and Racial Bias: Overturning Supreme Court Assumptions* (Westport, CT: Greenwood, 1994).

94. This may not be strictly a constitutional argument, since the Constitution and its amendments do not mention economics as a forbidden category for differentiating among individuals.

95. Hugo Adam Bedau and Paul G. Casswell, *Debating the Death Penalty: Should America Have Capital Punishment?* (New York: Oxford University Press, 2004).

96. Stephen Reinhardt, "The Supreme Court, the Death Penalty and the Harris Case," *Yale Law Journal* 102 (1992): 205–222.

97. Marcia Coyle, "Blackmun's Turnabout on the Death Penalty," *National Law Journal* 16 (March 7, 1994): 39.

98. Robbie Brown, "Tennessee Exoneration after 22 Years on Death Row," *New York Times,* May 13, 2009.

99. This is called "Mirandizing" an arrestee, after Ernesto Miranda, whose conviction was overturned because he was not told of his right to remain silent (*Miranda v. Arizona,* 384 U.S. 436 [1966]).

100. Kenneth B. Noble, "Ruling Helps Prosecution of Simpson," *New York Times,* September 20, 1994.

101. Prisons are already dangerous enough. See Mark S. Fleisher, *Warehousing Violence* (Newbury Park, CA: Sage, 1989); and George M. Anderson, "Prison Violence: Victims behind Bars," *America,* November 26, 1988, 430–433.

102. W. A. Corbitt, "Violent Crimes among Juveniles," *FBI Law Enforcement Bulletin* 69 (June 2000): 18–21.

103. Center for Disease Control and Prevention, *Youth Violence Facts, 2009* (Atlanta, GA: CDCP, June 29, 2009).

104. See Richard Rose, "On the Priorities of Government," *European Journal of Political Research* 4 (1973): 247–289.

Chapter 16

1. See John Kenneth White, *The Values Divide: American Politics and Culture in Transition* (New York: Chatham House, 2002); and Raymond Tatlovich and Byron W. Daynes, *Moral Controversies in American Politics* (Armonk, NY: M. E. Sharpe, 2004).

2. Jonathan Zimmerman, *Whose America: Culture Wars in the Public Schools* (Cambridge, MA: Harvard University Press, 2002).

3. See Gilbert Meilaender, "The Point of a Ban, or How to Think about Stem Cell Research," *Hastings Center Report* 31 (2001): 9–16; Thomas F. Banchoff, *Embryo Politics: Ethics and Policy in Atlantic Democracies* (Ithaca, NY: Cornell University Press).

4. By *line*, scientists mean a collection of cells derived from a common background. The common genetic background of the cells makes research less subject to possible spurious findings.

5. In 2006, Harvard University decided to go ahead with a large-scale program in stem cell research using private resources rather than wait for more federal funds that may or may not materialize.

6. "The Politics of Genes: America's Next Ethical War," *Economist*, April 14, 2001, 21–24.

7. School prayer may approach being bargainable in this way: If enough vouchers are made available, parents who want their children in schools where prayer is permitted may be able to find those opportunities, while the public schools remain secular. Some advocates, however, believe that the absence of school prayer undermines the fundamental values of the country. Opponents argue that public support for religious schools is fundamentally wrong.

8. On policy framing, see D. A. Schon and M. Rein, *Frame Selection: On Solving Intractable Policy Disputes* (New York: Basic Books, 1994).

9. John E. Thompson, "What's the Big Deal: The Unconstitutionality of God in the Pledge of Allegiance," *Harvard Civil Rights–Civil Liberties Law Review* 38 (2003): 563–574.

10. Julie Preston, "Partial Birth Abortion Act Ruled Unconstitutional by U.S. Courts," *New York Times*, February 1, 2006.

11. The right of privacy is itself implied rather than stated in the Constitution. See Madeleine Mercedes Plascencia, *Privacy and the Constitution* (New York: Garland, 1999).

12. Lawrence Tribe, *Abortion: The Clash of Absolutes* (New York: Norton, 1992), 29.

13. In *Doe v. Bolton* (1973), the Court ruled that not only could abortions not be criminalized but also the states could not make them unreasonably difficult to obtain.

14. Karen O'Connor, *No Neutral Ground: Abortion Politics in an Age of Absolutes* (Boulder, CO: Westview Press, 1996).

15. NBC News/*Wall Street Journal* poll conducted by the polling organizations of Peter Hart (D) and Neil Newhouse (R), September 6–8, 2008, http://topics.wsj.com/subject/W/wall-street-journal/nbc-news-polls/6052. Note: The more recent polls do not ask the questions in precisely the same ways.

16. The logic is that this is a major decision that is irreversible. Moreover, many other medical procedures for males or females may require parental approval. The intended effect, of course, is to prevent the female minor from having the procedure, either

because the parent will not approve it or because there is fear of even discussing the possibility.

17. The Interstate Commerce Clause (Article 1, section 8, clause 3) has been used to provide Congress with the power to regulate in a variety of areas that might not appear to be directly economic—for example, civil rights.

18. Justice David Souter was assumed to oppose abortion when President George H. W. Bush appointed him in 1990, but he tended to side with the pro–abortion rights majority on the Court.

19. "Judge Alito on Abortion," *Washington Post*, November 6, 2005.

20. Robert Pear, "U.S. Clarifies Policy on Birth Control for Religious Groups," *New York Times*, March 16, 2012.

21. See *Health, United States, 2005* (Atlanta, GA: Centers for Disease Control and Prevention, 2005), Table 16.

22. Barry D. Adam, *The Rise of the Gay and Lesbian Movement* (New York: Twayne, 1995).

23. The position, along with that of most mainstream Protestant churches, has been to "hate the sin but love the sinner."

24. One of the more extreme examples occurred after the 2001 terrorist attacks in New York and Washington, D.C. Religious right leaders Jerry Falwell and Pat Robertson argued that the terrorists were facilitated by the undermining of the moral fiber of the country by gay rights advocates, as well as other "secularists." See Gustav Niebuhr, "Falwell Apologizes for Saying an Angry God Allowed Attacks," *New York Times*, September 18, 2001.

25. Mike Allen, "Bush Allows Death Benefits to Gays," *Washington Post*, June 26, 2002.

26. See, for example, John Schwartz, "After New York, New Look at Defense of Marriage Act," *New York Times*, June 27, 2010.

27. The U.S. Constitution (Article IV) mandates that states give "full faith and credit" to the legal actions of the other states, so failure to accept the marital status of a gay couple may violate that provision.

28. Jim Ruttenberg and Carl Hulse, "Conservatives Watching Senate Debate on Gay Marriage," *New York Times*, June 6, 2006.

29. Engel v. Vitale, 370 U.S. 421 (1962).

30. See *Wallace v. Jaffree*, 472 U.S. 38 (1985).

31. *Cochran v. Board of Education*, 281 U.S. 370 (1930).

32. *Everson v. Board of Education*, 330 U.S. 1 (1947).

33. *Lemon v. Kurzman*, 403 U.S. 602 (1971).

34. *Roemer v. Maryland*, 426 U.S. 736 (1976).

35. See *Mitchell v. Helms*, 530 U.S. 793 (2000).

36. *Board of Education of the Kiryas Joel School District v. Grument*, 512 U.S. 708 (1994).

37. Charles Lane, "Court Upholds Ohio School Vouchers," *Washington Post*, June 28, 2002.

38. In fairness, a number of scientists are concerned about those gaps. For a defense, see Stephen Jay Gould, *The Structure of Evolutionary Theory* (Cambridge, MA: Harvard University Press, 2002).

39. Bill Toland, "Intelligent Design Goes on Trial in Pennsylvania," *Pittsburgh Post Gazette*, September 27, 2005.

Chapter 17

1. Edward C. Gramlich, *Benefit-Cost Analysis for Government Programs* (Englewood Cliffs, NJ: Prentice Hall, 1981); R. O. Zerbe, *Benefit Cost Analysis in Theory and Practice* (New York: HarperCollins, 1994).
2. Steven Kelman, "Cost-Benefit Analysis: An Ethical Critique," *Regulation* 4 (1981): 33–40.
3. Kenneth Arrow, *Social Choice and Individual Values* (New York: Wiley, 1963); and Allan Feldman, *Welfare Economics and Social Choice Theory* (Boston: Martinus Nijhoff, 1986).
4. P. Hennipman, "Pareto Optimality: Value Judgment or Analytical Tool?" in *Relevance and Precision,* ed. J. S. Cramer, A. Heertje, and P. Venekamp (New York: North-Holland, 1976), 39; E. J. Mishan and Euston Quah, *Cost Benefit Analysis,* 5th ed. (London: Routledge, 2007), 45–56.
5. Nicholas Kaldor, "Welfare Propositions of Economics and Interpersonal Comparisons of Utility," *Economic Journal* 49 (1939): 549–552; and John R. Hicks, "The Valuation of the Social Income," *Economica* 7 (1940): 105–124.
6. Richard Posner, "Cost-Benefit Analysis: Definition, Justifications and Comments," in *Cost Benefit Analysis,* ed. R. Posner (Cambridge, MA: Harvard University Press, 2001).
7. Richard Posner, *The Economics of Justice* (Cambridge, MA: Harvard University Press, 1983).
8. E. J. Mishan, *Cost-Benefit Analysis,* expanded ed. (New York: Praeger, 1967), 24–54.
9. David Whittington and Duncan MacRae Jr., "The Issue of Standing in Cost-Benefit Analysis," *Journal of Policy Analysis and Management* 5 (1986): 665–682; R. O. Zerbe, "A Place to Stand for Environmental Law and Economic Analysis," (n.d.), www.cserge.ucl.ac.uk/Zerbe.pdf.
10. E. J. Mishan, "The Post-War Literature on Externalities: An Interpretative Essay," *Journal of Economic Literature* 16 (1978): 1–28; and Neva R. Goodwin, *As if the Future Mattered: Translating Social and Economic Theory into Human Behavior* (Ann Arbor: University of Michigan Press, 1996).
11. John Martin Gilroy, "The Ethical Poverty of Cost-Benefit Methods: Autonomy, Efficiency and Public Policy Choice," *Policy Sciences* 25 (1992): 83–102.
12. "The TVA—Hardy Survivor," *Economist,* July 1, 1989, 22–23.
13. Edith Stokey and Richard Zeckhauser, *A Primer for Policy Analysis* (New York: Norton, 1978), 149–152; and J. Frykblom, "Hypothetical Question Modes and Real Willingness to Pay," *Journal of Environmental Economics and Management* 34 (1998), 275–287.
14. This is referred to as a "hedonic price model," in which the contributions of intangibles to price are assessed. See Paul Portney, "Housing Prices, Health Effects and Valuing Reductions in the Risk of Death," *Journal of Environmental Economics and Management* 8 (1981): 72–78.
15. Robin Gregory, Donald McGregor, and Sarah Lichtenstein, "Assessing the Quality of Expressed Preference Measures of Value," *Journal of Economic Behavior and Organization* 17 (1992): 277–292.
16. *The Road Back: Endangered Species Recovery* (Washington, DC: U.S. Department of the Interior, 1998), see chap. 13.

17. Peter Passell, "Polls May Help Government Decide the Worth of Nature," *New York Times,* September 6, 1993. See also J. A. Hausman, *Contingent Valuation: A Critical Assessment* (Amsterdam, Netherlands: North-Holland, 1993).

18. Robert E. Niewijk, "Misleading Quantification: The Contingent Valuation of Environmental Quality," *Regulation* 17, no. 1 (1994): 60–71.

19. Steven E. Rhoads, ed., *Valuing Life: Public Policy Dilemmas* (Boulder, CO: Westview Press, 1980); and W. Kip Viscusi, "Alternative Approaches to Valuing the Health Impact of Accidents: Liability Law and Prospective Evaluations," *Law and Contemporary Problems* 46 (1983): 49–68.

20. "What's a Life Worth? 9/11 Fund Stirs Anger," *USA Today,* January 8, 2002; and David W. Chen, "Hundreds of 9/11 Families File for Right to Sue Port Authority," *New York Times,* July 10, 2002.

21. Jack Hirschleifer and David L. Shapiro, "The Treatment of Risk and Uncertainty," in *Public Expenditure and Policy Analysis,* 3rd ed., ed. Robert H. Haveman and Julius Margolis (Boston: Houghton Mifflin, 1983), 145–166.

22. For a general discussion of the problems of discounting, see Robert E. Goodin, "Discounting Discounting," *Journal of Public Policy* 2 (1982): 53–71; Hal R. Varian, "Recalculating the Costs of Global Climate Change," *New York Times* December 14, 2006.

23. William J. Baumol, "On the Social Rate of Discount," *American Economic Review* 10 (1968): 788–802.

24. Marthe R. Gold et al., *Cost-Effectiveness in Health and Medicine* (New York: Oxford University Press, 1996).

25. Ray Robinson, "Cost-Effectiveness Analysis," *British Medical Journal* 307 (September 25, 1993): 793–795.

26. David M. Eddy, "Cost-Effectiveness Analysis: Will It Be Accepted?" *Journal of the American Medical Association* 268 (1992): 132–136.

27. See Sidney A. Shapiro and Robert L. Glicksman, *Risk Regulation at Risk: Restoring a Pragmatic Approach* (Stanford, CA: Stanford University Press, 2005).

28. Alphonse G. Holtman, "Beyond Efficiency: Economists and Distributional Analysis," in *Policy Analysis and Economics: Developments, Tensions, Prospects,* ed. David L. Weimer (Boston: Kluwer, 1991); and Elio Londero, *Benefits and Beneficiaries: An Introduction to Estimating Distributional Effects in Cost-Benefit Analysis,* 2nd ed. (Washington, DC: Inter-American Development Bank, 1996).

29. Peter Self, *Econocrats and the Policy Process: The Politics and Philosophy of Cost-Benefit Analysis* (London: Macmillan, 1975).

30. Peter Self, "Nonsense on Stilts: Cost-Benefit Analysis and the Roskill Commission," *Political Quarterly* 10 (1970): 30–63; and Kelman, "Cost-Benefit Analysis."

31. See Bruce Ackerman, "The Emergency Constitution," *Yale Law Journal* 113 (2004): 1029–1088.

32. Charlie Savage, "Secret U.S. Memo Made Legal Case to Kill a Citizen," *New York Times,* October 8, 2011.

33. Russell Hardin, *Morality within the Limit of Reason* (Chicago: University of Chicago Press, 1988).

34. See Martin E. Marty, *The One and the Many: America's Struggle for the Common Good* (Cambridge, MA: Harvard University Press, 1997).

35. Victor Grassian, *Moral Reasoning* (Englewood Cliffs, NJ: Prentice Hall, 1981).
36. Arnold Meltsner, *Policy Analysts in the Bureaucracy* (Berkeley: University of California Press, 1976), 3–25.
37. Abraham Kaplan, "Social Ethics and the Sanctity of Life," in *Life or Death: Ethics and Options,* ed. D. H. Labby (London: Macmillan, 1968), 58–71.
38. Guido Calabresi and Phillip Bobbitt, *Tragic Choices* (New York: Norton, 1978), 21. See also B. Guy Peters, "Tragic Choices: Administrative Rulemaking and Policy Choice," in *Ethics in Public Service,* ed. Richard A. Chapman (Edinburgh, UK: University of Edinburgh Press, 1993), 43.
39. Sheryl Gay Stolberg, "Live and Let Die over Transplants," *New York Times,* April 5, 1998; Philip Newton, "Do Alcoholics Deserve Liver Transplants," *Psychology Today,* February 15, 2009.
40. As a part of its rationing program, the state of Oregon made this determination. The justification was primarily utilitarian, based on the assumption that the treatment would be less beneficial for people with substance abuse problems.
41. Dave Davis, Ted Wendling, and Joan Mazzolini, "U.S. Orders Revisions in Rules on Transplants: Current System's Range of Waits Is Called Unfair," *Cleveland Plain Dealer,* March 27, 1998.
42. Bonnie Steinbock, *Life before Birth: The Moral and Legal Status of Embryos and Fetuses* (New York: Oxford University Press, 1992).
43. Ronald Dworkin, *Life's Dominion: An Argument about Abortion, Euthanasia and Individual Freedom* (New York: Knopf, 1993).
44. For a detailed account see Rebecca Dresser, "A Hard Case Makes Questionable Law," *Hastings Center Report* 34 (2004): all; Michael Patrick Allen, "Congress and Terri Schiavo: A Primer on the American Constitutional Order," *West Virginia Law Review* 108 (2006): 309–360.
45. Individuals have the option of making "living wills" specifying their choices about such end-of-life issues; there was not a formal document present in this case.
46. Steven H. Miles, "Doctors and Their Patients' Suicides," *Journal of the American Medical Association* 271 (June 8, 1994): 1786–1788; and Daniel Avila, "Medical Treatment Rights of Older Persons and Persons with Disabilities," *Issues in Law and Medicine* 9 (1994): 345–360.
47. Jonathan Glover, *Causing Deaths and Saving Lives* (Harmondsworth, UK: Penguin, 1977).
48. Robert Nozick, *Anarchy, State, and Utopia* (New York: Basic Books, 1974).
49. This individualistic and conservative interpretation of the law was common during the late nineteenth and early twentieth centuries. See, for example, *Lochner v. New York,* 198 U.S. 45 (1905).
50. Robert E. Goodin, *Reasons for Welfare* (Princeton, NJ: Princeton University Press, 1988), 312–331; and Christian Bay, *The Structure of Freedom* (New York: Athenaeum, 1965).
51. John Kultgen, *Autonomy and Intervention: Paternalism in the Caring Life* (New York: Oxford University Press, 1994).
52. Desmond King, *Illiberal Policies in Liberal States* (Oxford: Oxford University Press, 1999).
53. See Dennis A. Robbins, *Ethical and Legal Issues in Home Health and Long-Term Care: Challenges and Solutions* (Gaithersburg, MD: Aspen, 1996); and Bonnie Steinbock

and Alastair Norcross, *Killing and Letting Die,* 2nd ed. (New York: Fordham University Press, 1994).

54. Some conservatives have argued, for example, that even professional licensure of doctors and lawyers should be abandoned in the name of free choice. In the long run, it is argued, the market would take care of the problem.

55. Jerome S. Legge, *Traffic Safety Reform in the United States and Great Britain* (Pittsburgh: University of Pittsburgh Press, 1991); and Kenneth E. Warner, "Bags, Buckles and Belts: The Debate over Mandatory Passive Restraints in Automobiles," *Journal of Health Politics, Policy and Law* 8 (1983): 44–75.

56. Howard M. Leichter, *Free to be Foolish* (Princeton, NJ: Princeton University Press, 1991).

57. For one perspective, see Mario Loyola, "Challenging Obamacare's Coercive Medicaid Provisions," *National Review,* June 7, 2011.

58. The FDA has to some extent relaxed its usual guidelines for drugs that may help victims of AIDS and a few other extremely deadly diseases—for example, Lou Gehrig's Disease. See Harold Edgar and David J. Rothman, "New Rules for New Drugs: The Challenge of AIDS to the Regulatory Process," in *A Disease of Society,* ed. Dorothy Nelkin, David P. Willis, and Scott V. Parris (Cambridge: Cambridge University Press, 1991), 84; see also Peter Davis, *Contested Ground: Public Purpose and Private Interest in the Regulation of Prescription Drugs* (New York: Oxford University Press, 1996).

59. Sissela Bok, *Lying: Moral Choice in Public and Private Life* (New York: Vintage, 1979).

60. Loch K. Johnson, *Secret Agencies: U.S. Intelligence in a Hostile World* (New Haven, CT: Yale University Press, 1996); James P. Pfiffner, "Did President Bush Mislead the Country in His Arguments for War in Iraq?" *Presidential Studies Quarterly* 34 (2004): 25–46.

61. See Raymond L. Goldstein and John K. Schoor, *Demanding Democracy after Three Mile Island* (Gainesville: University of Florida Press, 1991).

62. James C. Petersen, *Whistleblowing: Ethical and Legal Issues in Expressing Dissent* (Dubuque, IA: Kendall/Hunt, 1986); Daniel P. Westman, *Whistleblowing: The Law of Retaliatory Discharge* (Washington, DC: Bureau of National Affairs, 1991); and U.S. Merit Systems Protection Board, *Whistleblowing in the Federal Government* (Washington, DC: U.S. Merit Systems Protection Board, 1993).

63. See, respectively, Edward Weisband and Thomas M. Franck, *Resignation in Protest* (New York: Penguin, 1975); and David Burnham, "Paper Chase of a Whistleblower," *New York Times,* October 16, 1982.

64. See Joseph S. Nye, Philip D. Zelikow, and David C. King, eds., *Why People Don't Trust Government* (Cambridge, MA: Harvard University Press, 1997).

65. Michael Walzer, "Political Action: The Problem of Dirty Hands," *Philosophy and Public Affairs* 1 (1973): 160–180; and Thomas Nagel, "Ruthlessness in Public Life," in *Public and Private Life,* ed. Stuart Hampshire (Cambridge: Cambridge University Press, 1978), 145–168.

66. Jan-Erik Lane, *The Public Sector: Concepts, Models and Approaches* (Newbury Park, CA: Sage, 1993).

67. See Robert E. Goodin, *Protecting the Vulnerable: A Re-Analysis of Our Social Responsibilities* (Chicago: University of Chicago Press, 1985). Even such a committed conservative as Charles Murray could argue that "There is no such thing as an

undeserving five-year-old"; see his *Losing Ground* (New York: Basic Books, 1984).

68. Richard Allen Epstein, *Takings: Private Property and the Power of Eminent Domain* (Cambridge, MA: Harvard University Press, 1985); and William A. Fischel, *Regulatory Takings: Law, Economics and Politics* (Cambridge, MA: Harvard University Press, 1995).

69. Karl Marx, *Criticism of the Gotha Program* (New York: International Universities Press, 1938), vol. 929, 14.

70. For an important attempt to provide such a justification, see Goodin, *Reasons for Welfare*, 287–305. See also Bo Rothstein, *Just Institutions Matter: The Moral and Political Logic of the Universal Welfare State* (Cambridge: Cambridge University Press, 1998).

71. Edith Brown Weiss, *In Fairness to Future Generations: International Law, Common Patrimony, and Intergenerational Equity* (Tokyo: United Nations University, 1988).

72. Peter S. Burton, "Intertemporal Preferences and Intergenerational Equity Considerations in Optimal Resource Harvesting," *Journal of Environmental Economics and Management* 24 (1993): 119–132; and Laurence J. Kotlikoff, *Generational Accounting* (New York: Free Press, 1992).

73. John Rawls, "Justice as Fairness," *Philosophical Review* 77 (1958): 164–194, esp. 166.

74. John Rawls, *A Theory of Justice* (Cambridge, MA: Harvard University Press, 1971), esp. 57, 65, 72, 93.

75. Ibid., 19.

76. For an earlier literary treatment of this view of fairness, see L. P. Hartley, *Facial Justice* (London: Hamish Hamilton, 1960). On desert, see George Bernard Shaw's *Doctor's Dilemma: A Tragedy* (London: Penguin, 1957).

77. Epstein, *Takings*.

78. Roberto Alejandro, *The Limits of Rawlsian Justice* (Baltimore: Johns Hopkins University Press, 1998).

79. Richard A. Epstein, *Forbidden Grounds: The Case against Employment Discrimination Laws* (Cambridge, MA: Harvard University Press, 1992); and Russell Nieli, ed., *Racial Preference and Racial Justice: The New Affirmative Action Controversy* (Washington, DC: Ethics and Public Policy Center, 1991).

80. Douglas E. Ashford, *The Emergence of the Welfare State* (Oxford: Basil Blackwell, 1986). But see T. H. Marshall, *Class, Citizenship, and Social Development* (New York: Doubleday, 1965).

81. See Gareth Davies, *From Opportunity to Entitlement* (Lawrence: University Press of Kansas, 1996).

82. In a few places—for example, the City University of New York—there was once free higher education as well, but budget constraints have forced the imposition of fees in those institutions.

83. See also Kimberly J. Cook, *Divided Passions: Public Opinions on Abortion and the Death Penalty* (Boston: Northeastern University Press, 1997).

84. Frances Fox Piven and Richard A. Cloward, *Regulating the Poor,* 2nd ed. (New York: Viking, 1993).

85. Amitai Etzioni, ed., *New Communitarian Thinking: Virtues, Institutions, and Communities* (Charlottesville: University Press of Virginia, 1995).

Index

About the Author

B. Guy Peters is Maurice Falk Professor of American Government at the University of Pittsburgh. He is also professor of comparative governance at Zeppelin University in Germany. He is currently coeditor of the *European Political Science Review* and on the editorial boards of a number of other journals. His recent publications include *Institutional Theory in Political Science*, 3rd ed., and *Interactive Governance: Advancing the Paradigm*, with Jacob Torfing, Jon Pierre, and Eva Sørensen.

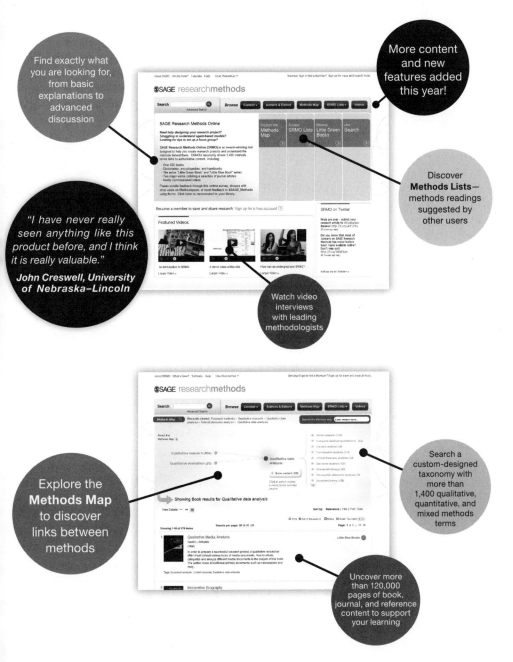

⑤SAGE research**methods**

The essential online tool for researchers from the world's leading methods publisher

Find exactly what you are looking for, from basic explanations to advanced discussion

More content and new features added this year!

Discover **Methods Lists**— methods readings suggested by other users

"I have never really seen anything like this product before, and I think it is really valuable."
John Creswell, University of Nebraska–Lincoln

Watch video interviews with leading methodologists

Explore the **Methods Map** to discover links between methods

Search a custom-designed taxonomy with more than 1,400 qualitative, quantitative, and mixed methods terms

Uncover more than 120,000 pages of book, journal, and reference content to support your learning

Find out more at
www.sageresearchmethods.com